2008

HOWARD J. CURTIS

MIDLAND

An imprint of
Ian Allan Publishing

Contents

Photographs by Howard J Curtis (HJC) unless otherwise credited

This twenty-ninth edition published 2008

ISBN 978 1 85780 290 0

Published by Ian Allan Publishing
an imprint of Ian Allan Publishing Ltd,
Hersham, Surrey KT12 4RG.

Printed in England by Ian Allan Printing Ltd,

Hersham, Surrey KT12 4RG
Code: 0803/4

Visit the Ian Allan Publishing web site at: www.ianallanpublishing.com

Front cover: RAF Panavia Tornado F3 ZE161/GB of No 43 Squadron at RAF Leuchars. *Richard Cooper*

Introduction

This twenty-ninth annual edition of *abc Military Aircraft Markings*, follows the pattern of previous years and lists in alphabetical and numerical order the aircraft that carry a United Kingdom military serial, and which are normally based, or might be seen, in the UK. It also includes airworthy and current RAF/RN/Army aircraft that are based permanently or temporarily overseas. The term 'aircraft' used here covers powered, manned aeroplanes, helicopters, airships and gliders as well as target drones. Included are all the current Royal Air Force, Royal Navy, Army Air Corps, Ministry of Defence, QinetiQ - operated, manufacturers' test aircraft and civilian-owned aircraft with military markings or operated for the Ministry of Defence.

Aircraft withdrawn from operational use but which are retained in the UK for ground training purposes or otherwise preserved by the Services and in the numerous museums and collections are listed. The serials of some incomplete aircraft have been included, such as the cockpit sections of machines displayed by the RAF, aircraft used by airfield fire sections and for service battle damage repair training (BDRT), together with significant parts of aircraft held by preservation groups and societies. Where only part of the aircraft fuselage remains, the abbreviation <ff> for front fuselage/cockpit section or <rf> for rear fuselage, is shown after the type. Many of these aircraft are allocated, and sometimes wear, a secondary identity, such as an RAF 'M' maintenance number. These numbers are listed against those aircraft to which they have been allocated.

A serial 'missing' from a sequence is either because it was never issued as it formed part of a 'black-out block' or because the aircraft has been written off, scrapped, sold abroad or allocated an alternative marking. Aircraft used as targets on MoD ranges to which access is restricted, and UK military aircraft that have been permanently grounded and are based overseas and unlikely to return to Britain have generally been omitted. With the appearance of some military registered UAVs, drones and small target aircraft at public events and ground displays, these have now been included if they are likely to be seen.

In the main, the serials listed are those markings presently displayed on the aircraft. Where an aircraft carries a false serial it is quoted in *italic type*. Very often these serials are carried by replicas, that are denoted by <R> after the type. The manufacturer and aircraft type are given, together with recent alternative, previous, secondary or civil identity shown in round brackets. Complete records of multiple previous identities are only included where space permits. The operating unit and its based location, along with any known unit and base code markings in square brackets, are given as accurately as possible. Where aircraft carry special or commemorative markings, a $ indicates this. The unit markings are normally carried boldly on the sides of the fuselage or on the aircraft's fin. In the case of RAF and AAC machines currently in service, they are usually one or two letters or numbers, while the RN continues to use a well-established system of three-figure codes between 000 and 999 together with a tail letter code denoting the aircraft's operational base. RN squadrons, units and bases are allocated blocks of numbers from which individual aircraft codes are issued. To help identification of RN bases and landing platforms on ships, a list of tail-letter codes with their appropriate name, helicopter code number, ship pennant number and type of vessel, is included; as is a helicopter code number/ships' tail-letter code grid cross-reference.

Code changes, for example when aircraft move between units and therefore the markings currently painted on a particular aircraft, might not be those shown in this edition because of subsequent events. Aircraft still under manufacture or not yet delivered to the Service, such as Eurofighter Typhoons, Hawk T2s and Airbus A400Ms are listed under their allocated serial numbers. Likewise there are a number of newly built aircraft for overseas air arms that carry British serials for their UK test and delivery flights. The airframes which will not appear in the next edition because of sale, accident, etc, have their fates, where known, shown in italic type in the *locations* column.

The Irish Army Air Corps fleet is listed, together with the serials of other overseas air arms whose aircraft might be seen visiting the UK from time to time. The serial numbers are as usually presented on the individual machine or as they are normally identified. Where possible, the aircraft's base and operating unit have been shown.

USAF, US Army and US Navy aircraft based in the UK and in Western Europe, and types that regularly visit the UK from the USA, are each listed in separate sections by aircraft type. The serial number actually displayed on the aircraft is shown in full, with additional Fiscal Year (FY) or full serial information also provided. Where appropriate, details of the operating wing, squadron allocation and base are added. The USAF is, like the RAF, in a continuing period of change, resulting in the adoption of new unit titles, squadron and equipment changes and the closure of bases. Only details that concern changes effected by January 2008 are shown.

Veteran and vintage aircraft which carry overseas military markings but which are based in the UK or regularly visit from mainland Europe, have been separately listed showing their principal means of identification. The growing list of aircraft in government or military service, often under contract to private operating companies, that carry civil registrations has again been included at the end of the respective country.

With the use of the Internet now very well established as a rich source of information, the section listing a selection of military aviation 'world wide web' sites, has again been expanded and updated this year. Although only a few of these provide details of aircraft serials and markings, they do give interesting insights into air arms and their operating units, aircraft, museums and a broad range of associated topics.

Information shown is believed to be correct at 31 January 2008.

Acknowledgements

The compiler wishes to thank the many people who have taken the trouble to send comments, additions, deletions and other useful information since the publication of the previous edition of abc Military Aircraft Markings. In particular the following individuals: Allan Barley, Ian Carroll, Phil Charlton, Glyn Coney, Mick Coombes, Keith Cruttenden, Patrick Dirksen, Herman Goud, Howard Heeley, Geoff Hooper, Tommy Johansson, Phil Jones, Tim Jones, Tom Kaminski, James Lawson, Mike Lawson, Peter R. March, Tony McCarthy, Julian Moody, Tony Osborne, Per Thorup Pedersen, Dave Peel, Mark Ray, Dave Reid, Norman Robertson, Paul Rushton, Jimmi Richmond-Cole, Mark Shepherd, Kev Slade, Kev Storer, John Tearle, Bob Turner, Howard Walker, Richard Ward, David Webb.

The 2008 edition has also relied upon the printed publications and/or associated internet web-sites as follows: Aerodata Quantum+, Air-Britain Information Exchange, 'Air-Britain News', Airfields e-mail group, 'Air Forces Monthly', Airliners.net web site, BAEG e-mail group, 'British Roundel' magazine, CAA G-INFO Web Site, Cottesmore Aviation Group, Graham Gaff/East London Aviation Society, Fighter Control, 'FlyPast', Andy Carney/Harrier List UK, JetPhotos.net web site, Joe Baugher's Home Page, Brian Pickering/'Military Aviation Review', Mil Spotters' Forum, NAMAR e-mail group, P-3 Orion Research Group, Pacific Database, RAF Leeming e-mail group, RAF Shawbury web site, Roger Smith/Lowestoft Aviation Society, Mark Walton/'Scottish Air News', 'Scramble', Tom McGhee/UK Serials Resource Centre, Geoff Goodall/Warbirds Directory 4 and Mick Boulanger/Wolverhampton Aviation Group.

Finally, mention must be made of the sterling efforts of Peter R. March, who began the 'Military Aircraft Markings' series with edition 1 in 1980. This is the first edition for which I have sole charge, after several years of shared authorship with Peter and a personal involvement running back to edition 3 of 1983. Peter's hours of work on setting up and developing this publication are greatly appreciated and, on a personal note, I might add that his support and guidance have been incalculable to me. I hope that I can continue to maintain the high standard that Peter has set as I now 'go solo', albeit with Peter's continued help in the background.

HJC

January 2008

Abbreviations

AAC Army Air Corps
AACS Airborne Air Control Squadron
AACTS Airborne Air Control Training Squadron
ACC Air Combat Command
ACCGS Air Cadets Central Gliding School
ACW Airborne Control Wing
AD&StA Aberdeen, Dundee & St Andrews
AEF Air Experience Flight
AESS Air Engineering & Survival School
AEW Airborne Early Warning
AF Arméflyget (Army Air Battalion)
AFB Air Force Base
AFD Air Fleet Department
AFRC Air Force Reserve Command
AFSC Air Force Systems Command
AFSK Armeflygskolan (Army Flying School)
AFWF Advanced Fixed Wing Flight
AG Airlift Group
AGA Academia General del Aire (General Air Academy)
AkG Aufklärüngsgeschwader (Reconnaissance Wing)
AMC Air Mobility Command
AMD-BA Avions Marcel Dassault-Breguet Aviation
AMF Aircraft Maintenance Flight
AMG Aircraft Maintenance Group
AMIF Aircraft Maintenance Instruction Flight
AMW Air Mobility Wing
ANG Air National Guard
APS Aircraft Preservation Society
ARF Aircraft Repair Flight
ARS Air Refueling Squadron
ARW Air Refueling Wing
ARWS Advanced Rotary Wing Squadron
AS Airlift Squadron/Air Squadron
ASF Aircraft Servicing Flight
AS&RU Aircraft Salvage and Repair Unit
ATC Air Training Corps
ATCC Air Traffic Control Centre
AVDEF Aviation Defence Service
Avn Aviation
AW Airlift Wing/Armstrong Whitworth Aircraft
AWC Air Warfare Centre
BAC British Aircraft Corporation
BAe British Aerospace PLC
BAPC British Aviation Preservation Council
BATSUB British Army Training Support Unit Belize
BATUS British Army Training Unit Suffield
BBMF Battle of Britain Memorial Flight
BDRF Battle Damage Repair Flight
BDRT Battle Damage Repair Training
Be Beech
Bf Bayerische Flugzeugwerke
BG Bomber Group
BGA British Gliding & Soaring Association
bk black (squadron colours and markings)
bl blue (squadron colours and markings)
BNFL British Nuclear Fuels Ltd
BP Boulton & Paul
br brown (squadron colours and markings)
BS Bomber Squadron
B-V Boeing-Vertol
BW Bomber Wing
CAARP Co-operative des Ateliers Air de la Région Parisienne
CAC Commonwealth Aircraft Corporation
CARG Cotswold Aircraft Restoration Group
CASA Construcciones Aeronautics SA
Cav Cavalry
CC County Council
CCF Combined Cadet Force/Canadian Car & Foundry Company
CDE Chemical Defence Establishment
CEAM Centre d'Expérimentation Aériennes Militaires (Military Air Experimental Centre)
CEPA Centre d'Expérimentation Pratique de l'Aéronautique Navale
CEV Centre d'Essais en Vol (Flight Test Centre)
CFS Central Flying School
CGMF Central Glider Maintenance Flight
CHFMU Commando Helicopter Force Maintenance Unit
CIFAS Centre d'Instruction des Forces Aériennes Stratégiques (Air Strategic Training Centre)
CinC Commander in Chief
CinCLANT Commander in Chief Atlantic
CITac Centre d'Instruction Tactique (Tactical Training Centre)
CLV Centrum Leteckeho Vycviku (Air Training Centre)
Co Company
Comp Composite with
CT College of Technology
CTE Central Training Establishment
CV Chance-Vought
D-BA Daimler-Benz Aerospace
D-BD Dassault-Breguet Dornier
D&G Dumfries and Galloway
DARA Defence Aviation Repair Agency
DCAE Defence College of Aeronautical Engineering
DE&S Defence Equipment & Support
DEFTS Defence Elementary Flying Training School
DEODS Defence Explosives Ordnance Disposal School
Det Detachment
DH de Havilland
DHC de Havilland Canada
DHFS Defence Helicopter Flying School
DLMW Dywizjon Lotniczy Marynarki Wojennej
DMS Defence Movements School
DSDA Defence Storage & Distribution Agency
DS&TL Defence Science & Technology Laboratory
DTI Department of Trade and Industry
EA Escadron Aérien (Air Squadron)
EAAT Escadrille Avions de l'Armée de Terre
EAC Ecole de l'Aviation de Chasse (Fighter Aviation School)
EAP European Aircraft Project
EAT Ecole de l'Aviation de Transport (Transport Aviation School)
EC Escadre de Chasse (Fighter Wing)
ECM Electronic Counter Measures
ECS Electronic Countermeasures Squadron
EDA Escadre de Detection Aéroportée (Air Detection Wing)
EdC Escadron de Convoyage
EDCA Escadron de Détection et de Control Aéroportée (Airborne Detection & Control Sqn)
EE English Electric/Escadrille Electronique
EEA Escadron Electronique Aéroporté
EFTS Elementary Flying Training School
EH Escadron d'Helicoptères (Helicopter Flight)
EHI European Helicopter Industries
EKW Eidgenössiches Konstruktionswerkstätte
EL Escadre de Liaison (Liaison Wing)
EL Eskadra Lotnicza (Air Sqn)
ELT Eskadra Lotnictwa Taktycznego (Tactical Air Squadron)
ELTR Eskadra Lotnictwa Transportowego (Air Transport Squadron)
EMA East Midlands Airport
EMVO Elementaire Militaire Vlieg Opleiding (Elementary Flying Training)
ENOSA Ecole des Navigateurs Operationales Systemes d'Armees (Navigation School)
EoN Elliot's of Newbury

EPAA	Ecole de Pilotage Elementaire de l'Armée de l'Air (Air Force Elementary Flying School)
EPE	Ecole de Pilotage Elementaire (Elementary Flying School)
EPNER	Ecole du Personnel Navigant d'Essais et de Reception
ER	Escadre de Reconnaissance (Reconnaissance Wing)
ERS	Escadron de Reconnaissance Stratégique (Strategic Reconnaissance Squadron)
ES	Escadrille de Servitude
Esc	Escuadron (Squadron)
Esk	Eskadrille (Squadron)
Eslla	Escuadrilla (Squadron)
Esq	Esquadra (Squadron)
ET	Escadre de Transport (Transport Squadron)
ETE	Escadron de Transport et Entrainment (Transport Training Squadron)
ETEC	Escadron de Transport d'Entrainement et de Calibration (Transport Training & Calibration Sqn)
ETL	Escadron de Transport Légère (Light Transport Squadron)
ETO	Escadron de Transition Operationnelle
ETOM	Escadron de Transport Outre Mer (Overseas Transport Squadron)
ETPS	Empire Test Pilots' School
ETS	Engineering Training School
FAA	Fleet Air Arm/Federal Aviation Administration
FBS	Flugbereitschaftstaffel
FBW	Fly-by-wire
FC	Forskokcentralen (Flight Centre)
FE	Further Education
FETC	Fire and Emergency Training Centre
ff	Front fuselage
FG	Fighter Group
FH	Fairchild-Hiller
FI	Falkland Islands
FJWOEU	Fast Jet & Guided Weapon Operational Evaluation Unit
FlSt	Flieger Staffel (Flight Squadron)
Flt	Flight
FMA	Fabrica Militar de Aviones
FMT	Flotila Militara de Transport (Transport Regiment)
FMV	Forsvarets Materielwerk
FONA	Flag Officer Naval Aviation
FRADU	Fleet Requirements and Air Direction Unit
FRA	FR Aviation
FS	Fighter Squadron
FSAIU	Flight Safety & Accident Investigation Unit
FSCTE	Fire Services Central Training Establishment
FTS	Flying Training School
FTW	Flying Training Wing
Fw	Focke Wulf
FW	Fighter Wing/Foster Wickner
FWTS	Fixed Wing Test Squadron
FY	Fiscal Year
F3 OCU	Tornado F3 Operational Conversion Unit
GAF	Government Aircraft Factory
GAL	General Aircraft Ltd
GAM	Groupe Aerien Mixte (Composite Air Group)
gd	gold (squadron colours and markings)
GD	General Dynamics
GDSH	Gazelle Depth Support Hub
GHL	Groupe d'Helicopteres Legeres (Light Helicopter Group)
GI	Ground Instruction/Groupement d'Instruction (Instructional Group)
gn	green (squadron colours and markings)
GRD	Gruppe fur Rustunggdienste (Group for Service Preparation)
GRV	Groupe de Ravitaillement en Vol (Air Refuelling Group)
GT	Grupo de Transporte (Transport Wing)
GTT	Grupo de Transporte de Tropos (Troop Carrier Wing)
gy	grey (squadron colours and markings)
H&W	Hereford and Worcester
HAF	Historic Aircraft Flight
HC	Helicopter Combat Support Squadron
HCS	Hunting Contract Services
HF	Historic Flying Ltd
HFUS	Heeresfliegerunterstützungsstaffel
HFVAS	Heeresfliegerverbindungs/ Aufklärungsstaffel
HFVS	Heeresfliegerversuchstaffel
HFWS	Heeresflieger Waffenschule (Army Air Weapons School)
Hkp.Bat	Helikopter Bataljon (Helicopter Battalion)
HMA	Helicopter Maritime Attack
HMF	Harrier Maintenance Flight/Helicopter Maintenance Flight
HMS	Her Majesty's Ship
HOCU	Harrier OCU
HP	Handley-Page
HQ	Headquarters
HRO	Harcàszati Repülö Ezred
HS	Hawker Siddeley
IAF	Israeli Air Force
IAP	International Airport
INTA	Instituto Nacional de Tecnica Aerospacial
IOW	Isle Of Wight
IWM	Imperial War Museum
JATE	Joint Air Transport Establishment
JbG	Jagdbombergeschwader (Fighter Bomber Wing)
JFACTSU	Joint Forward Air Control Training & Standards Unit
JG	Jagdgeschwader (Fighter Wing)
JHF	Joint Helicopter Force
KHR	Kampfhubschrauberregiment
Kridlo	Wing
lbvr	letka Bitevnich Vrtulníkù (Attack Helicopter Squadron)
Letka	Squadron
LTG	Lufttransportgeschwader (Air Transport Wing)
LTO	Transportna en Letalska Transportni Oddelek
LTV	Ling-Temco-Vought
LVG	Luftwaffen Versorgungs Geschwader (Air Force Maintenance Wing)/Luft Verkehrs Gesellschaft
LZO	Letecky Zku ební Odbor (Aviation Test Department)
m	multi-coloured (squadron colours and markings)
MAPK	Mira Anachestisis Pantos Kerou (All Weather Interception Sqn)
MASD	Marine Air Support Detachment
MASU	Mobile Aircraft Support Unit
MBB	Messerschmitt Bolkow-Blohm
MCAS	Marine Corps Air Station
McD	McDonnell Douglas
MDMF	Merlin Depth Maintenance Facilities
Med	Medical
MFG	Marine Flieger Geschwader (Naval Air Wing)
MH	Max Holste
MIB	Military Intelligence Battalion
MiG	Mikoyan — Gurevich
Mod	Modified
MoD	Ministry of Defence
MR	Maritime Reconnaissance
MRH	Multi-role Helikopters
MS	Morane-Saulnier
MTHR	Mittlerer Transporthubschrauber Regiment (Medium Transport Helicopter Regiment)
MTM	Mira Taktikis Metaforon (Tactical Transport Sqn)
NA	North American
NACDS	Naval Air Command Driving School
NAEW&CF	NATO Airborne Early Warning & Control Force

NAF	Naval Air Facility
NAS	Naval Air Station
NASU	Naval Air Support Unit
NATO	North Atlantic Treaty Organisation
NAWC	Naval Air Warfare Center
NAWC-AD	Naval Air Warfare Center Aircraft Division
NBC	Nuclear, Biological and Chemical
NE	North-East
NFATS	Naval Force Aircraft Test Squadron
NI	Northern Ireland
NMSU	Nimrod Major Servicing Unit
NOCU	Nimrod Operational Conversion Unit
NSW	Naval Strike Wing
NTOCU	National Tornado Operational Conversion Unit
NYARC	North Yorks Aircraft Restoration Centre
OCU	Operational Conversion Unit
OEU	Operation Evaluation Unit
OFMC	Old Flying Machine Company
OGMA	Oficinas Gerais de Material Aeronautico
or	orange (squadron colours and markings)
OSAC	Operational Support Airlift Command
OSBL	Oddelek Sholskih Bojni Letal (Training & Combat School)
OVH Kmp	Observations-Helicopter Kompagni
PAT	Priority Air Transport Detachment
PBN	Pilatus Britten-Norman
PLM	Pulk Lotnictwa Mysliwskiego (Fighter Regiment)
pr	purple (squadron colours and markings)
PRU	Photographic Reconnaissance Unit
PVH Kmp	Panservaerns-Helicopter Kompagni
r	red (squadron colours and markings)
R	Replica
RAeS	Royal Aeronautical Society
RAF	Royal Aircraft Factory/Royal Air Force
RAFC	Royal Air Force College
RAFM	Royal Air Force Museum
RAFGSA	Royal Air Force Gliding and Soaring Association
RE	Royal Engineers
Regt	Regiment
REME	Royal Electrical & Mechanical Engineers
rf	Rear fuselage
RFA	Royal Fleet Auxiliary
RJAF	Royal Jordanian Air Force
RM	Royal Marines
RMB	Royal Marines Base
RMC of S	Royal Military College of Science
RN	Royal Navy
RNAS	Royal Naval Air Station
RNGSA	Royal Navy Gliding and Soaring Association
ROF	Royal Ordnance Factory
RQS	Rescue Squadron
R-R	Rolls-Royce
RS	Reid & Sigrist/Reconnaissance Squadron
RSV	Reparto Sperimentale Volo (Experimental Flight School)
RW	Reconnaissance Wing
SA	Scottish Aviation
SAAB	Svenska Aeroplan Aktieboleg
SAH	School of Air Handling
SAL	Scottish Aviation Limited
SAR	Search and Rescue
Saro	Saunders-Roe
SARTU	Search and Rescue Training Unit
SCW	Strategic Communications Wing
SDoLt	Samostatna Dopravniho Letka (Independent Transport Squadron)
SEAE	School of Electrical & Aeronautical Engineering
SEPECAT	Société Européenne de Production de l'avion Ecole de Combat et d'Appui Tactique
SFDO	School of Flight Deck Operations

SHAPE	Supreme Headquarters Allied Forces Europe
SHOPS	Sea Harrier Operational Support Unit
si	silver (squadron colours and markings)
SIET	Section d'Instruction et d'Etude du Tir
SKTU	Sea King Training Unit
Skv	Skvadron (Squadron)
SLK	Stíhacie Letecké Kridlo (Fighter Air Wing)
slt	stíhací letka (Fighter Squadron)
SLV	School Licht Vliegwezen (Flying School)
Sm	Smaldeel (Squadron)
smdl	Smisena Dopravní Letka
SNCAN	Société Nationale de Constructions Aéronautiques du Nord
SOF	Special Operations Flight
SOG	Special Operations Group
SOS	Special Operations Squadron
SoTT	School of Technical Training
SOW	Special Operations Wing
SPAD	Société Pour les Appareils Deperdussin
SPP	Strojirny Prvni Petilesky
Sqn	Squadron
SWWAPS	Second World War Aircraft Preservation Society
TA	Territorial Army
TAP	Transporten Avio Polk (Air Transport Regiment)
TFC	The Fighter Collection
TGp	Test Groep
TIARA	Tornado Integrated Avionics Research Aircraft
TL	Taktická Letka (Tactical Squadron)
tlt	taktická letka (Tactical Squadron)
TMF	Tornado Maintenance Flight
TMTS	Trade Management Training School
TOCU	Typhoon Operational Conversion Unit
tpzlt	taktická a prùzkumná letka (Tactical & Reconnaissance Squadron)
TS	Test Squadron
TsAGI	Tsentral'ny Aerogidrodinamicheski Institut (Central Aero & Hydrodynamics Institute)
TsLw	Technische Schule der Luftwaffe (Luftwaffe Technical School)
TW	Test Wing
UAS	University Air Squadron
UAV	Unmanned Air Vehicle
Uberwg	Uberwachunggeschwader (Surveillance Wing)
UK	United Kingdom
UKAEA	United Kingdom Atomic Energy Authority
UNFICYP	United Nations' Forces in Cyprus
US	United States
USAF	United States Air Force
USAFE	United States Air Forces in Europe
USAREUR	US Army Europe
USCGS	US Coast Guard Station
USEUCOM	United States European Command
USMC	United States Marine Corps
USN	United States Navy
NWTSPM	United States Navy Test Pilots School
VAAC	Vectored thrust Advanced Aircraft flight Control
VFW	Vereinigte Flugtechnische Werke
VGS	Volunteer Gliding Squadron
VLA	Vojenska Letecka Akademia
vlt	vycviková letka (Training Squadron)
VMGR	Marine Aerial Refuelling/Transport Squadron
VMGRT	Marine Aerial Refuelling/Transport Training Squadron
VQ	Fleet Air Reconnaissance Squadron
VR	Fleet Logistic Support Squadron
VrK	Vrtulnikové Letecké Kridlo
VS	Vickers-Supermarine
VSD	Vegyes Szàllitorepülö Dandàr (Aircraft Transport Brigade)
w	white (squadron colours and markings)
Wg	Wing
WHL	Westland Helicopters Ltd
WLT	Weapons Loading Training
WRS	Weather Reconnaissance Squadron
WS	Westland
WSK	Wytwornia Sprzetu Kominikacyjnego
WTD	Wehrtechnische Dienstelle (Technical Support Unit)
WW2	World War II
y	yellow (squadron colours and markings)
zDL	základna Dopravního Letectva (Air Transport Base)
zL	základna Letectva
ZmDK	Zmi aný Dopravný Kridlo (Mixed Transport Wing)
zSL	základna Speciálního Letectva (Training Air Base)
zTL	základna Taktického Letectva (Tactical Air Base)
zVrL	základna Vrtulníkového Letectva (Helicopter Air Base)

Typhoon F2 ZJ920 of 29(R) Squadron, based at RAF Coningsby, blasts off for another air display.

A Guide to the Location of Operational Military Bases in the UK

This section is to assist the reader to locate the places in the United Kingdom where operational military aircraft (including helicopters and gliders) are based.

The alphabetical order listing gives each location in relation to its county and to its nearest classified road(s) (*by* means adjoining; *of* means proximate to), together with its approximate direction and mileage from the centre of a nearby major town or city. Some civil airports are included where active military units are also based, but **excluded** are MoD sites with non-operational aircraft (eg *gate guardians*), the bases of privately-owned civil aircraft that wear military markings and museums.

User	*Base name*	*County/Region*	*Location*	*Distance/direction from (town)*
Army	Abingdon	Oxfordshire	W by B4017, W of A34	5m SSW of Oxford
RAF	Aldergrove/ Belfast Airport	Co Antrim	W by A26	13m W of Belfast
RM	Arbroath	Angus	E of A933	2m NW of Arbroath
RAF/HCS	Barkston Heath	Lincolnshire	W by B6404, S of A153	5m NNE of Grantham
RAF	Benson	Oxfordshire	E by A423	1m NE of Wallingford
QinetiQ/ RAF	Boscombe Down	Wiltshire	S by A303, W of A338	6m N of Salisbury
RAF	Boulmer	Northumberland	E of B1339	4m E of Alnwick
RAF	Brize Norton	Oxfordshire	W of A4095	5m SW of Witney
Marshall	Cambridge Airport/ Teversham	Cambridgeshire	S by A1303	2m E of Cambridge
RM/RAF	Chivenor	Devon	S of A361	4m WNW of Barnstaple
RAF	Church Fenton	Yorkshire North	S of B1223	7m WNW of Selby
Army	Colerne	Wiltshire	S of A420, E of Fosse Way	5m NE of Bath
RAF	Coningsby	Lincolnshire	S of A153, W by B1192	10m NW of Boston
DCAE	Cosford	Shropshire	W of A41, N of A464	9m WNW of Wolverhampton
RAF	Cottesmore	Rutland	W of A1, N of B668	9m NW of Stamford
RAF	Cranwell	Lincolnshire	N by A17, S by B1429	5m WNW of Sleaford
RN	Culdrose	Cornwall	E by A3083	1m SE of Helston
Army	Dishforth	Yorkshire North	E by A1	4m E of Ripon
USAF	Fairford	Gloucestershire	S of A417	9m ESE of Cirencester
RN	Fleetlands	Hampshire	E by A32	2m SE of Fareham
RAF	Halton	Buckinghamshire	N of A4011, S of B4544	4m ESE of Aylesbury
RAF	Henlow	Bedfordshire	E of A600, W of A6001	1m SW of Henlow
RAF	Honington	Suffolk	E of A134, W of A1088	6m S of Thetford
Army	Hullavington	Wiltshire	W of A429	1m N of M4 jn 17
RAF	Kenley	Greater London	W of A22	1m W of Warlingham
RAF	Kinloss	Grampian	E of B9011, N of B9089	3m NE of Forres
RAF	Kirknewton	Lothian	E by B7031, N by A70	8m SW of Edinburgh
USAF	Lakenheath	Suffolk	W by A1065	8m W of Thetford
RAF	Leeming	Yorkshire North	E by A1	5m SW of Northallerton
RAF	Leuchars	Fife	E of A919	7m SE of Dundee
RAF	Linton-on-Ouse	Yorkshire North	E of B6265	10m NW of York
RAF	Lossiemouth	Grampian	W of B9135, S of B9040	4m N of Elgin
RAF	Lyneham	Wiltshire	W of A3102, S of A420	10m WSW of Swindon
RAF	Marham	Norfolk	N by A1122	6m W of Swaffham
Army	Middle Wallop	Hampshire	S by A343	6m SW of Andover
USAF	Mildenhall	Suffolk	S by A1101	9m NNE of Newmarket
RAF	Northolt	Greater London	N by A40	3m E of M40 jn 1
RAF	Odiham	Hampshire	E of A32	2m S of M3 jn 5
RN	Predannack	Cornwall	W by A3083	7m S of Helston
MoD	St Athan	South Glamorgan	N of B4265	13m WSW of Cardiff
RAF	St Mawgan/Newquay	Cornwall	N of A3059	4m ENE of Newquay
RAF	Scampton	Lincolnshire	W by A15	6m N of Lincoln
RAF	Shawbury	Shropshire	W of B5063	7m NNE of Shrewsbury
RAF	Syerston	Nottinghamshire	W by A46	5m SW of Newark
RAF	Ternhill	Shropshire	SW by A41	3m SW of Market Drayton

User	Base name	County/Region	Location	Distance/direction from (town)
RAF/Army	Topcliffe	Yorkshire North	E of A167, W of A168	3m SW of Thirsk
RAF	Valley	Gwynedd	S of A5 on Anglesey	5m SE of Holyhead
RAF	Waddington	Lincolnshire	E by A607, W by A15	5m S of Lincoln
Army/RAF	Wattisham	Suffolk	N of B1078	5m SSW of Stowmarket
RAF	Weston-on-the-Green	Oxfordshire	E by A43	9m N of Oxford
RAF	Wittering	Cambridgeshire	W by A1, N of A47	3m S of Stamford
RAF	Woodvale	Merseyside	W by A565	5m SSW of Southport
RAF	Wyton	Cambridgeshire	E of A141, N of B1090	3m NE of Huntingdon
RN	Yeovilton	Somerset	S by B3151, S of A303	5m N of Yeovil

Harvard IIB KF488 is a composite of several machines, rebuilt at the Bournemouth Aviation Museum. It carries the name 'Billie' on the other side of the nose.

Typhoon F2 ZJ936 wears the markings of 3 Squadron, RAF Coningsby.

British Military Aircraft Serials

The Committee of Imperial Defence through its Air Committee introduced a standardised system of numbering aircraft in November 1912. The Air Department of the Admiralty was allocated the first batch 1-200 and used these to cover aircraft already in use and those on order. The Army was issued with the next block from 201-800, which included the number 304 which was given to the Cody Biplane now preserved in the Science Museum. By the outbreak of World War 1 the Royal Navy was on its second batch of serials 801-1600 and this system continued with alternating allocations between the Army and Navy until 1916 when number 10000, a Royal Flying Corps BE2C, was reached.

It was decided not to continue with five digit numbers but instead to start again from 1, prefixing RFC aircraft with the letter A and RNAS aircraft with the prefix N. The RFC allocations commenced with A1 an FE2D and before the end of the year had reached A9999, an Armstrong Whitworth FK8. The next group commenced with B1 and continued in logical sequence through the C, D, E and F prefixes. G was used on a limited basis to identify captured German aircraft, while H was the last block of wartime-ordered aircraft. To avoid confusion I was not used, so the new postwar machines were allocated serials in the J range. A further minor change was made in the serial numbering system in August 1929 when it was decided to maintain four numerals after the prefix letter, thus omitting numbers 1 to 999. The new K series therefore commenced at K1000, which was allocated to an AW Atlas.

The Naval N prefix was not used in such a logical way. Blocks of numbers were allocated for specific types of aircraft such as seaplanes or flying-boats. By the late 1920s the sequence had largely been used up and a new series using the prefix S was commenced. In 1930 separate naval allocations were stopped and subsequent serials were issued in the 'military' range which had by this time reached the K series. A further change in the pattern of allocations came in the L range. Commencing with L7272 numbers were issued in blocks with smaller blocks of serials between not used. These were known as blackout blocks. As M had already been used as a suffix for Maintenance Command instructional airframes it was not used as a prefix. Although N had previously been used for naval aircraft it was used again for serials allocated from 1937.

With the build-up to World War 2 the rate of allocations quickly accelerated and the prefix R was being used when war was declared. The letters O and Q were not allotted, and nor was S which had been used up to S1865 for naval aircraft before integration into the RAF series. By 1940 the serial Z9999 had been reached, as part of a blackout block, with the letters U and Y not used to avoid confusion. The option to recommence serial allocation at A1000 was not taken up; instead it was decided to use an alphabetical two-letter prefix with three numerals running from 100 to 999. Thus AA100 was allocated to a Blenheim IV.

This two-letter, three-numeral serial system which started in 1940 continues today. The letters C, I, O, Q, U and Y were, with the exception of NC, not used. For various reasons the following letter combinations were not issued: DA, DB, DH, EA, GA to GZ, HA, HT, JE, JH, JJ, KR to KT, MR, NW, NZ, SA to SK, SV, TN, TR and VE. The first postwar serials issued were in the VP range while the end of the WZs had been reached by the Korean War. In January 1952 a civil servant at the then Air Ministry penned a memo to his superiors alerting them to the fact that a new military aircraft serial system would soon have to be devised. With allocations accelerating to accommodate a NATO response to the Korean War and a perceived Soviet threat building, he estimated that the end of the ZZs would quickly be reached. However, over five decades later the allocations are only at the start of the ZKs and at the present rate are unlikely to reach ZZ999 until the end of this century!

Military aircraft serials are allocated by the Defence Procurement Agency, where the Military Aircraft Register is maintained. A change in policy in 2003 has resulted in the use of the first 99 digits in the ZK sequence (ZK001 to ZK099), following on from ZJ999. The first of these, ZK001 to ZK004, were allocated to AgustaWestland Merlins. There is also a growing trend for 'out-of-sequence' serial numbers to be issued. At first this was to a manufacturer's prototype or development aircraft. However, following the Boeing C-17 Globemasters leased and subsequently purchased from Boeing (ZZ171-ZZ174), more allocations have been noted, including ZM400 to ZM424 for the RAF's prospective Airbus A400Ms and ZR321 to ZR323 for a trio of Agusta A.109Es for No 32 (The Royal) Squadron. In a strange twist ZZ190-191 have been allocated to a pair of former Swiss Air Force Hawker Hunter F58s operated under a military contract.

Since 2002 there has also been a new official policy concerning the use of military serial numbers on some types of UAV. 'Where a UAV is of modular construction the nationality and registration mark shall be applied to the fuselage of the vehicle or on the assembly forming the main part of the fuselage. To prevent the high usage of numbers for target drones which are eventually destroyed, a single registration mark (prefix) should be issued relating to the UAV type. The agency or service operating the target drone will be responsible for the identification of each individual UAV covered by that registration mark by adding a suffix.' This has resulted in the use of the same serial on a number of UAVs with a letter following it. Hence the appearance of ZK201A, ZK201B, ZK201C et seq on Army Meggitt Banshee drones. UAVs using this system are denoted in the text by an asterisk (*).

Note: The compiler will be pleased to receive comments, corrections and further information for inclusion in subsequent editions of *Military Aircraft Markings* and the monthly up-date of additions and amendments. Please send your information to Military Aircraft Markings, Ian Allan Publishing Ltd, Riverdene Business Park, Molesey Road, Hersham, Surrey, KT12 4RG or e-mail to HJCurtis@aol.com.

British Military Aircraft Markings

A serial in *italics* denotes that it is not the genuine marking for that airframe.

Serial	*Type (code/other identity)*	*Owner/operator, location or fate*	*Notes*
168	Sopwith Tabloid Scout <R> (G-BFDE)	RAF Museum, Hendon	
304	Cody Biplane (BAPC 62)	Science Museum, South Kensington	
687	RAF BE2b <R> (BAPC 181)	RAF Museum, Hendon	
2345	Vickers FB5 Gunbus <R> (G-ATVP)	RAF Museum, Hendon	
2699	RAF BE2c	Imperial War Museum, Lambeth	
2783	RAF BE2c <R>	Privately owned, Boscombe Down	
3066	Caudron GIII (G-AETA/9203M)	RAF Museum, Hendon	
5964	DH2 <R> (BAPC 112)	Privately owned, Stretton on Dunsmore	
5964	DH2 <R> (G-BFVH)	Privately owned, RAF Lyneham	
6232	RAF BE2c <R> (BAPC 41)	Yorkshire Air Museum, stored Elvington	
8359	Short 184 <ff>	FAA Museum, RNAS Yeovilton	
9917	Sopwith Pup (G-EBKY/N5180)	The Shuttleworth Collection, Old Warden	
A301	Morane BB (frame)	RAF Museum Reserve Collection, Stafford	
A1452	Vickers FB5 Gunbus <R>	Privately owned, Sywell	
A1742	Bristol Scout D <R> (BAPC 38)	Bristol Aero Collection, Kemble	
A7317	Sopwith Pup <R> (BAPC 179)	Midland Air Museum, Coventry	
A8226	Sopwith 1½ Strutter <R> (G-BIDW)	RAF Museum, Hendon	
B595	RAF SE5a <R> (G-BUOD) [W]	Privately owned, Kemble	
B2458	Sopwith 1F.1 Camel <R> (G-BPOB/*F542*) [R]	Privately owned, Compton Abbas	
B5539	Sopwith 1F.1 Camel <R>	Privately owned, Compton Abbas	
B5577	Sopwith 1F.1 Camel <R> (*D3419*/BAPC 59) [W]	Montrose Air Station Heritage Centre	
B6401	Sopwith 1F.1 Camel <R> (G-AWYY/C1701)	FAA Museum, RNAS Yeovilton	
B7270	Sopwith 1F.1 Camel <R> (G-BFCZ)	Brooklands Museum, Weybridge	
C1904	RAF SE5a <R> (G-PFAP) [Z]	Privately owned, Castle Bytham, Leics	
C3009	Currie Wot (G-BFWD)	Privately owned, Dunkeswell	
C3011	Phoenix Currie Super Wot (G-SWOT) [S]	Privately owned, Temple Bruer, Lincs	
C4451	Avro 504J <R> (BAPC 210)	Solent Sky, Southampton	
C4918	Bristol M1C <R> (G-BWJM)	The Shuttleworth Collection, Old Warden	
C4994	Bristol M1C <R> (G-BLWM)	RAF Museum, Hendon	
C5430	RAF SE5a <R> (G-CCXG) [V]	Privately owned, Wrexham	
C9533	RAF SE5a <R> (G-BUWE) [M]	Privately owned, Boscombe Down	
D276	RAF SE5a <R> (BAPC 208) [A]	Prince's Mead Shopping Centre, Farnborough	
D5329	Sopwith 5F.1 Dolphin	RAF Museum Restoration Centre, Cosford	
D5649	Airco DH9	Imperial War Museum, Duxford	
D7560	Avro 504K	Science Museum, South Kensington	
D8084	Bristol F2b Fighter (G-ACAA/F4516) [S]	*Sold to New Zealand, January 2007*	
D8096	Bristol F2b Fighter (G-AEPH) [D]	The Shuttleworth Collection, Old Warden	
E449	Avro 504K (G-EBJE/9205M)	RAF Museum, Hendon	
E2466	Bristol F2b Fighter (BAPC 165) [I]	RAF Museum, Hendon	
E2581	Bristol F2b Fighter [13]	Imperial War Museum, Duxford	
E8894	Airco DH9 (G-CDLI)	Aero Vintage, Westfield, Sussex	
F141	RAF SE5a <R> (G-SEVA) [G]	Privately owned, Boscombe Down	
F235	RAF SE5a <R> (G-BMDB) [B]	Privately owned, Boscombe Down	
F904	RAF SE5a (G-EBIA)	The Shuttleworth Collection, Old Warden	
F938	RAF SE5a (G-EBIC/9208M)	RAF Museum, Hendon	
F943	RAF SE5a <R> (G-BIHF) [S]	Museum of Army Flying, Middle Wallop	
F943	RAF SE5a <R> (G-BKDT)	Yorkshire Air Museum, Elvington	
F1010	Airco DH9A [C]	RAF Museum, Hendon	
F3556	RAF RE8	Imperial War Museum, Duxford	
F5447	RAF SE5a <R> (G-BKER) [N]	Privately owned, Bridge of Weir	
F5459	RAF SE5a <R> (G-INNY) [Y]	Privately owned, North Coates	
F5475	RAF SE5a <R> (BAPC 250)	Brooklands Museum, Weybridge	
F6314	Sopwith 1F.1 Camel (9206M) [B]	RAF Museum Restoration Centre, Cosford	

Notes	*Serial*	*Type (code/other identity)*	*Owner/operator, location or fate*
	F8010	RAF SE5a <R> (G-BDWJ) [Z]	Privately owned, Langport, Somerset
	F8614	Vickers FB27A Vimy IV <R> (G-AWAU)	RAF Museum, Hendon
	H1968	Avro 504K <R> (BAPC 42)	Yorkshire Air Museum, stored Elvington
	H2311	Avro 504K (G-ABAA)	Gr Manchester Mus of Science & Industry
	H3426	Hawker Hurricane <R> (BAPC 68)	NW Aviation Heritage Group, Hooton Park
	H5199	Avro 504K (BK892/3118M/ G-ACNB/G-ADEV)	The Shuttleworth Collection, Old Warden
	J7326	DH53 Humming Bird (G-EBQP)	Mosquito Aircraft Museum, London Colney
	J8067	Westland Pterodactyl 1a	Science Museum, South Kensington
	J9941	Hawker Hart 2 (G-ABMR)	RAF Museum, Hendon
	K1786	Hawker Tomtit (G-AFTA)	The Shuttleworth Collection, Old Warden
	K1930	Hawker Fury <R> (G-BKBB/OO-HFU)	Privately owned, Wevelgem, Belgium
	K2048	Isaacs Fury II (G-BZNW)	Privately owned, Fishburn
	K2050	Isaacs Fury II (G-ASCM)	Privately owned, English Bicknor
	K2059	Isaacs Fury II (G-PFAR)	Privately owned, Netherthorpe
	K2060	Isaacs Fury II (G-BKZM)	Privately owned, Haverfordwest
	K2075	Isaacs Fury II (G-BEER)	Privately owned, Combrook, Warks
	K2227	Bristol 105 Bulldog IIA (G-ABBB)	RAF Museum, Hendon
	K2567	DH82A Tiger Moth (DE306/7035M/G-MOTH)	Privately owned, Tadlow
	K2572	DH82A Tiger Moth (NM129/G-AOZH)	Privately owned, Wanborough, Wilts
	K2585	DH82A Tiger Moth II (T6818/G-ANKT)	The Shuttleworth Collection, Old Warden
	K2587	DH82A Tiger Moth <R> (G-BJAP)	Privately owned, Shobdon
	K3241	Avro 621 Tutor (K3215/G-AHSA)	The Shuttleworth Collection, Old Warden
	K3661	Hawker Nimrod II (G-BURZ) [362]	Aero Vintage, Duxford
	K3731	Isaacs Fury <R> (G-RODI)	Privately owned, Hailsham
	K4232	Avro 671 Rota I (SE-AZB)	RAF Museum, Hendon
	K4259	DH82A Tiger Moth (G-ANMO) [71]	Privately owned, Sywell
	K4672	Hawker Hind (BAPC 82)	RAF Museum, Cosford
	K4972	Hawker Hart Trainer IIA (1764M)	RAF Museum, Hendon
	K5054	Supermarine Spitfire <R> (BAPC 190/*EN398*)	Privately owned, Hawkinge
	K5054	Supermarine Spitfire <R> (BAPC 214)	Tangmere Military Aviation Museum
	K5054	Supermarine Spitfire <R> (G-BRDV)	Solent Sky, stored Romsey
	K5054	Supermarine Spitfire <R>	Kent Battle of Britain Museum, Hawkinge
	K5054	Supermarine Spitfire <R>	Southampton Airport, on display
	K5414	Hawker Hind (G-AENP/BAPC 78) [XV]	The Shuttleworth Collection, Old Warden
	K5600	Hawker Audax I (2015M/G-BVVI)	Aero Vintage, Westfield, Sussex
	K5673	Isaacs Fury II (G-BZAS)	Privately owned, Bournemouth
	K5673	Hawker Fury I <R> (BAPC 249)	Brooklands Museum, Weybridge
	K5674	Hawker Fury I (G-CBZP)	Aero Vintage, Westfield, Sussex
	K6035	Westland Wallace II (2361M)	RAF Museum, Hendon
	K7271	Hawker Fury II <R> (BAPC 148)	Shropshire Wartime Aircraft Recovery Grp Mus, Sleap
	K7271	Isaacs Fury II <R> (G-CCKV)	Privately owned, Lands End
	K7985	Gloster Gladiator I (L8032/G-AMRK)	The Shuttleworth Collection, Old Warden
	K8042	Gloster Gladiator II (8372M)	RAF Museum, Hendon
	K8203	Hawker Demon I (G-BTVE/2292M)	Demon Displays, Hatch
	K8303	Isaacs Fury II (G-BWWN) [D]	Privately owned, Wisbech St Mary
	K9926	VS300 Spitfire I <R> (BAPC 217) [JH-C]	RAF Bentley Priory, on display
	K9942	VS300 Spitfire I (8383M) [SD-D]	RAF Museum, Cosford
	L1070	VS300 Spitfire I <R> (BAPC 227) [XT-A]	Edinburgh airport, on display
	L1592	Hawker Hurricane I [KW-Z]	Science Museum, South Kensington
	L1639	Hawker Hurricane I	Cambridge Fighter & Bomber Society
	L1679	Hawker Hurricane I <R> (BAPC 241) [JX-G]	Tangmere Military Aviation Museum
	L1710	Hawker Hurricane I <R> (BAPC 219) [AL-D]	RAF Biggin Hill, on display
	L2301	VS Walrus I (G-AIZG)	FAA Museum, RNAS Yeovilton

Serial	Type (code/other identity)	Owner/operator, location or fate	Notes
L2940	Blackburn Skua I	FAA Museum, RNAS Yeovilton	
L5343	Fairey Battle I [VO-S]	RAF Museum/Medway Aircraft Pres Society, Rochester	
L6906	Miles M14A Magister I (G-AKKY/T9841/BAPC 44)	Museum of Berkshire Aviation, Woodley	
L7005	Boulton Paul P82 Defiant I <R> [PS-B]	Boulton Paul Association, Wolverhampton	
L7181	Hawker Hind (G-CBLK)	Aero Vintage, Duxford	
L8756	Bristol 149 Bolingbroke IVT (RCAF 10001) [XD-E]	RAF Museum, Hendon	
N248	Supermarine S6A (*S1596*)	Solent Sky, Southampton	
N500	Sopwith LC-1T Triplane <R> (G-PENY/G-BWRA)	Privately owned, Yarcombe, Devon/RNAS Yeovilton	
N546	Wright Quadruplane 1 <R> (BAPC 164)	Solent Sky, Southampton	
N1671	Boulton Paul P82 Defiant I (8370M) [EW-D]	RAF Museum, Hendon	
N1854	Fairey Fulmar II (G-AIBE)	FAA Museum, RNAS Yeovilton	
N2078	Sopwith Baby (8214/8215)	FAA Museum, RNAS Yeovilton	
N2532	Hawker Hurricane I <R> (BAPC 272) [GZ-H]	Kent Battle of Britain Museum, Hawkinge	
N2980	Vickers Wellington IA [R]	Brooklands Museum, Weybridge	
N3194	VS300 Spitfire I <R> (BAPC 220) [GR-Z]	RAF Biggin Hill, on display	
N3200	VS300 Spitfire IA (wreck)	Privately owned, Braintree	
N3289	VS300 Spitfire I <R> (BAPC 65) [DW-K]	Kent Battle of Britain Museum, Hawkinge	
N3310	VS361 Spitfire IX [A] <R>	Privately owned, Wellesbourne Mountford	
N3313	VS300 Spitfire I <R> (*MH314*/BAPC 69) [KL-B]	Kent Battle of Britain Museum, Hawkinge	
N3317	VS361 Spitfire IX <R> (BAPC 268)	Privately owned, St Mawgan	
N3378	Boulton Paul P82 Defiant I	Boulton Paul Association, Wolverhampton	
N3788	Miles M14A Magister I (V1075/G-AKPF)	Privately owned, Old Warden	
N4389	Fairey Albacore (N4172) [4M]	FAA Museum, RNAS Yeovilton	
N4877	Avro 652A Anson I (G-AMDA) [MK-V]	Imperial War Museum, Duxford	
N5177	Sopwith 1½ Strutter <R>	Privately owned, Sedgensworth, Hants	
N5182	Sopwith Pup <R> (G-APUP/9213M)	RAF Museum, Hendon	
N5195	Sopwith Pup (G-ABOX)	Museum of Army Flying, Middle Wallop	
N5199	Sopwith Pup <R> (G-BZND)	Privately owned, Yarcombe, Devon	
N5459	Sopwith Triplane <R> (BAPC 111)	FAA Museum, RNAS Yeovilton	
N5579	Gloster Sea Gladiator	FAA Museum, RNAS Yeovilton	
N5628	Gloster Gladiator II	RAF Museum, Hendon	
N5719	Gloster Gladiator II (G-CBHO)	Privately owned, Dursley, Glos	
N5903	Gloster Gladiator II (*N2276*/G-GLAD) [H]	The Fighter Collection, Duxford	
N5912	Sopwith Triplane (8385M)	RAF Museum, Hendon	
N6290	Sopwith Triplane <R> (G-BOCK)	The Shuttleworth Collection, Old Warden	
N6452	Sopwith Pup <R> (G-BIAU)	FAA Museum, RNAS Yeovilton	
N6466	DH82A Tiger Moth (G-ANKZ)	Privately owned, Winchester	
N6473	DH82A Tiger Moth (G-AOBO)	Privately owned, Orbigny, France	
N6537	DH82A Tiger Moth (G-AOHY)	Privately owned, France	
N6635	DH82A Tiger Moth (comp G-APAO & G-APAP) [25]	Imperial War Museum, Duxford	
N6720	DH82A Tiger Moth (G-BYTN/7014M) [VX]	Privately owned, Henlow	
N6797	DH82A Tiger Moth (G-ANEH)	Privately owned, Swyncombe	
N6812	Sopwith 2F.1 Camel	Imperial War Museum, Lambeth	
N6847	DH82A Tiger Moth (G-APAL)	Privately owned, Leicester	
N6965	DH82A Tiger Moth (G-AJTW) [FL-J] (wreck)	Privately owned, Tibenham	
N7033	Noorduyn AT-16 Harvard IIB (FX442)	Kent Battle of Britain Museum, Hawkinge	
N9191	DH82A Tiger Moth (G-ALND)	Privately owned, Pontypool	
N9192	DH82A Tiger Moth (G-DHZF) [RCO-N]	Privately owned, Sywell	
N9389	DH82A Tiger Moth (G-ANJA)	Privately owned, Seething	

Notes	Serial	Type (code/other identity)	Owner/operator, location or fate
	N9899	Supermarine Southampton I (fuselage)	RAF Museum, Hendon
	P1344	HP52 Hampden I (9175M) [PL-K]	RAF Museum Restoration Centre, Cosford
	P1344	HP52 Hampden I <rf> (parts Hereford L6012)	RAF Museum, Hendon
	P2617	Hawker Hurricane I (8373M) [AF-A]	RAF Museum, Hendon
	P2725	Hawker Hurricane I (wreck)	Imperial War Museum, Lambeth
	P2793	Hawker Hurricane I <R> (BAPC 236) [SD-M]	Eden Camp Theme Park, Malton, North Yorkshire
	P2902	Hawker Hurricane I (G-ROBT)	Privately owned, Milden
	P2921	Hawker Hurricane I <R> (BAPC 273) [GZ-L]	Kent Battle of Britain Museum, Hawkinge
	P2970	Hawker Hurricane I <R> [US-X]	Battle of Britain Memorial, Capel le Ferne, Kent
	P3059	Hawker Hurricane I <R> (BAPC 64) [SD-N]	Kent Battle of Britain Museum, Hawkinge
	P3175	Hawker Hurricane I (wreck)	RAF Museum, Hendon
	P3179	Hawker Hurricane I <ff>	Tangmere Military Aviation Museum
	P3208	Hawker Hurricane I <R> (BAPC 63/*L1592*) [SD-T]	Kent Battle of Britain Museum, Hawkinge
	P3386	Hawker Hurricane I <R> (BAPC 218) [FT-A]	RAF Bentley Priory, on display
	P3395	Hawker Hurricane IV (KX829) [JX-B]	Millennium Discovery Centre, Birmingham
	P3554	Hawker Hurricane I (composite)	The Air Defence Collection, Salisbury
	P3679	Hawker Hurricane I <R> (BAPC 278) [GZ-K]	Kent Battle of Britain Museum, Hawkinge
	P3717	Hawker Hurricane I (composite) (DR348)	Privately owned, Milden
	P3873	Hawker Hurricane I <R> (BAPC 265) [YO-H]	Yorkshire Air Museum, Elvington
	P4139	Fairey Swordfish II (HS618) [5H]	FAA Museum, RNAS Yeovilton
	P6382	Miles M14A Hawk Trainer 3 (G-AJRS) [C]	The Shuttleworth Collection, Old Warden
	P7350	VS329 Spitfire IIA (G-AWIJ) [XT-D]	RAF BBMF, Coningsby
	P7540	VS329 Spitfire IIA [DU-W]	Dumfries & Galloway Avn Mus, Dumfries
	P7966	VS329 Spitfire II <R> [D-B]	Manx Aviation & Military Museum, Ronaldsway
	P8140	VS329 Spitfire II <R> (*P9390*/BAPC 71) [ZF-K]	Norfolk & Suffolk Avn Museum, Flixton
	P8448	VS329 Spitfire II <R> (BAPC 225) [UM-D]	RAF Cranwell, on display
	P9374	VS300 Spitfire IA (G-MKIA)	Privately owned, Braintree
	P9444	VS300 Spitfire IA [RN-D]	Science Museum, South Kensington
	R1914	Miles M14A Magister (G-AHUJ)	Privately owned, Strathallan
	R3821	Bristol 149 Bolingbroke IVT (G-BPIV/*Z5722*) [UX-N]	Blenheim(Duxford) Ltd, Duxford (on rebuild)
	R4115	Hawker Hurricane I <R> (BAPC 267) [LE-X]	Imperial War Museum, Duxford
	R4118	Hawker Hurricane I (G-HUPW) [UP-W]	Privately owned, Didcot, Oxon
	R4922	DH82A Tiger Moth II (G-APAO)	Privately owned, Henlow
	R4959	DH82A Tiger Moth II (G-ARAZ) [59]	Privately owned, Temple Bruer, Lincs
	R5136	DH82A Tiger Moth II (G-APAP)	Privately owned, Henlow
	R5172	DH82A Tiger Moth II (G-AOIS) [FIJ-E]	Privately owned, Breighton
	R5868	Avro 683 Lancaster I (7325M) [PO-S]	RAF Museum, Hendon
	R6690	VS300 Spitfire I <R> (BAPC 254) [PR-A]	Yorkshire Air Museum, Elvington
	R6915	VS300 Spitfire I	Imperial War Museum, Lambeth
	R9125	Westland Lysander III (8377M) [LX-L]	RAF Museum, Hendon
	R9371	HP59 Halifax II <ff>	Privately owned, Charlton Kings
	S1287	Fairey Flycatcher <R> (G-BEYB)	FAA Museum, RNAS Yeovilton
	S1579	Hawker Nimrod I <R> (G-BBVO) [571]	Privately owned, Wreningham
	S1581	Hawker Nimrod I (G-BWWK) [573]	The Fighter Collection, Duxford
	S1595	Supermarine S6B	Science Museum, South Kensington

Serial	*Type (code/other identity)*	*Owner/operator, location or fate*	*Notes*
T5298	Bristol 156 Beaufighter I (4552M) <ff>	Midland Air Museum, Coventry	
T5424	DH82A Tiger Moth II (G-AJOA)	Privately owned, Swindon	
T5672	DH82A Tiger Moth II (G-ALRI)	*Sold to Thailand, 2007*	
T5854	DH82A Tiger Moth II (G-ANKK)	Privately owned, Baxterley	
T5879	DH82A Tiger Moth II (G-AXBW) [RUC-W]	Privately owned, Frensham	
T6296	DH82A Tiger Moth II (8387M)	RAF Museum, Hendon	
T6313	DH82A Tiger Moth II (G-AHVU)	Privately owned, Langham	
T6562	DH82A Tiger Moth II (G-ANTE)	Privately owned, Sywell	
T6953	DH82A Tiger Moth II (G-ANNI)	Privately owned, Goodwood	
T6991	DH82A Tiger Moth II (HB-UPY/DE694)	Privately owned, Lausanne, Switzerland	
T7230	DH82A Tiger Moth II (G-AFVE)	*Sold to Poland, August 2007*	
T7281	DH82A Tiger Moth II (G-ARTL)	Privately owned, Egton, nr Whitby	
T7793	DH82A Tiger Moth II (G-ANKV)	Privately owned, Croydon, on display	
T7842	DH82A Tiger Moth II (G-AMTF)	Privately owned, Headcorn	
T7909	DH82A Tiger Moth II (G-ANON)	Privately owned, Sherburn-in-Elmet	
T7997	DH82A Tiger Moth II (NL750/G-AHUF)	Privately owned, Wickenby	
T8191	DH82A Tiger Moth II (G-BWMK)	Privately owned,	
T9707	Miles M14A Magister I (G-AKKR/8378M/T9708)	Museum of Army Flying, Middle Wallop	
T9738	Miles M14A Magister I (G-AKAT)	Privately owned, Breighton	
V3388	Airspeed AS10 Oxford I (G-AHTW)	Imperial War Museum, Duxford	
V6028	Bristol 149 Bolingbroke IVT (G-MKIV) [GB-D] <rf>	The Aircraft Restoration Co, stored Duxford	
V6799	Hawker Hurricane I <R> (BAPC 72/*V7767*) [SD-X]	Gloucestershire Avn Coll, stored Gloucester	
V7350	Hawker Hurricane I (fuselage)	Brenzett Aeronautical Museum	
V7467	Hawker Hurricane I <R> (BAPC 223) [LE-D]	RAF High Wycombe, on display	
V7467	Hawker Hurricane I <R> [LE-D]	Wonderland Pleasure Park, Farnsfield, Notts	
V7497	Hawker Hurricane I (G-HRLI)	Hawker Restorations, Milden	
V9367	Westland Lysander IIIA (G-AZWT) [MA-B]	The Shuttleworth Collection, Old Warden	
V9673	Westland Lysander IIIA (V9300/G-LIZY) [MA-J]	Imperial War Museum, Duxford	
V9723	Westland Lysander IIIA (V9546/OO-SOT) [MA-D]	SABENA Old Timers, Brussels, Belgium	
V9312	Westland Lysander IIIA (G-CCOM)	The Aircraft Restoration Co, Duxford	
W1048	HP59 Halifax II (8465M) [TL-S]	RAF Museum, Hendon	
W2068	Avro 652A Anson I (9261M/VH-ASM) [68]	RAF Museum, Hendon	
W2718	VS Walrus I (G-RNLI)	Solent Sky, Southampton	
W4041	Gloster E28/39 [G]	Science Museum, South Kensington	
W4050	DH98 Mosquito	Mosquito Aircraft Museum, London Colney	
W5856	Fairey Swordfish II (G-BMGC) [A2A]	RN Historic Flight, Yeovilton	
W9385	DH87B Hornet Moth (G-ADND) [YG-L,3]	Privately owned, Hullavington	
X4276	VS300 Spitfire I (G-CDGU)	Privately owned,	
X4590	VS300 Spitfire I (8384M) [PR-F]	RAF Museum, Hendon	
X7688	Bristol 156 Beaufighter I (3858M/G-DINT)	Privately owned, Hatch	
Z1206	Vickers Wellington IV (fuselage)	Midland Warplane Museum, Baxterley	
Z2033	Fairey Firefly I (G-ASTL) [275]	FAA Museum, stored RNAS Yeovilton	
Z2186	Douglas Boston III	Privately owned, Hinckley, Leics	
Z2315	Hawker Hurricane IIA [JU-E]	Imperial War Museum, Duxford	
Z2389	Hawker Hurricane IIA [XR-T]	Brooklands Museum, Weybridge	
Z5140	Hawker Hurricane XIIA (*Z7381*/G-HURI) [HA-C]	Historic Aircraft Collection, Duxford	
Z5207	Hawker Hurricane IIB (G-BYDL)	Privately owned, Dursley, Glos	
Z5252	Hawker Hurricane IIB (G-BWHA/Z5053) [GO-B]	Privately owned, Milden	

Notes	Serial	Type (code/other identity)	Owner/operator, location or fate
	Z7015	Hawker Sea Hurricane IB (G-BKTH) [7-L]	The Shuttleworth Collection, Old Warden
	Z7197	Percival P30 Proctor III (G-AKZN/8380M)	RAF Museum Reserve Collection, Stafford
	Z7258	DH89A Dragon Rapide (NR786/G-AHGD)	Privately owned, Membury (wreck)
	AB196	Supermarine Aircraft Spitfire 26 (G-CCGH)	Privately owned, Horsham
	AB550	VS349 Spitfire VB <R> (BAPC 230/*AA908*) [GE-P]	Eden Camp Theme Park, Malton, North Yorkshire
	AB910	VS349 Spitfire VB (G-AISU) [RF-D]	RAF BBMF, Coningsby
	AD540	VS349 Spitfire VB (wreck)	Kennet Aviation, North Weald
	AE436	HP52 Hampden I [PL-J] (parts)	Lincolnshire Avn Heritage Centre, E Kirkby
	AL246	Grumman Martlet I	FAA Museum, RNAS Yeovilton
	AP506	Cierva C30A (G-ACWM)	The Helicopter Museum, Weston-super-Mare
	AP507	Cierva C30A (G-ACWP) [KX-P]	Science Museum, South Kensington
	AR213	VS300 Spitfire IA (*K9853*/G-AIST) [PR-D]	Privately owned, Booker
	AR501	VS349 Spitfire LF VC (G-AWII/*AR4474*) [NN-A]	The Shuttleworth Collection, Old Warden
	BB697	DH82A Tiger Moth (G-ADGT)	Privately owned, Andrewsfield
	BB807	DH82A Tiger Moth (G-ADWO)	Solent Sky, Southampton
	BD707	Hawker Hurricane XIIB (G-HURR) [AE-C]	*Crashed Shoreham, 15 September 2007*
	BD713	Hawker Hurricane IIB	Privately owned, Taunton
	BE417	Hawker Hurricane XIIB (G-HURR) [LK-A]	*Repainted as BD707, 2007*
	BE421	Hawker Hurricane IIC <R> (BAPC 205) [XP-G]	RAF Museum, Hendon
	BL614	VS349 Spitfire VB (4354M) [ZD-F]	RAF Museum, Hendon
	BL655	VS349 Spitfire VB (wreck)	Lincolnshire Avn Heritage Centre, East Kirkby
	BL924	VS349 Spitfire VB <R> (BAPC 242) [AZ-G]	Tangmere Military Aviation Museum
	BM361	VS349 Spitfire VB <R> [XR-C]	RAF Lakenheath, on display
	BM481	VS349 Spitfire VB <R> [YO-T] (also wears *PK651*/RAO-B)	Thornaby Aerodrome Memorial
	BM597	VS349 Spitfire LF VB (5718M/G-MKVB) [JH-C]	Historic Aircraft Collection, Duxford
	BN230	Hawker Hurricane IIC (LF751/5466M) [FT-A]	RAF Manston, Memorial Pavilion
	BR600	VS361 Spitfire IX <R> (BAPC 222) [SH-V]	RAF Uxbridge, on display
	DD931	Bristol 152 Beaufort VIII (9131M) [L]	RAF Museum, Hendon
	DE208	DH82A Tiger Moth II (G-AGYU)	Privately owned, Newtownards
	DE470	DH82A Tiger Moth II (G-ANMY) [16]	Privately owned, RAF Cosford
	DE623	DH82A Tiger Moth II (G-ANFI)	Privately owned, Withybush
	DE673	DH82A Tiger Moth II (6948M/G-ADNZ)	Privately owned, Old Buckenham
	DE992	DH82A Tiger Moth II (G-AXXV)	Privately owned, Upavon
	DF112	DH82A Tiger Moth II (G-ANRM)	Privately owned, Clacton/Duxford
	DF128	DH82A Tiger Moth II (G-AOJJ) [RCO-U]	Privately owned, White Waltham
	DF155	DH82A Tiger Moth II (G-ANFV)	Privately owned, Shempston Farm, Lossiemouth
	DF198	DH82A Tiger Moth II (G-BBRB)	Privately owned, Biggin Hill
	DG202	Gloster F9/40 (5758M) [G]	RAF Museum, Cosford
	DG590	Miles M2H Hawk Major (8379M/G-ADMW)	RAF Museum Reserve Collection, Stafford
	DP872	Fairey Barracuda II (fuselage)	FAA Museum, stored RNAS Yeovilton
	DV372	Avro 683 Lancaster I <ff>	Imperial War Museum, Lambeth
	DZ313	DH98 Mosquito B IV <R>	Privately owned, Kemble
	EE416	Gloster Meteor F3 <ff>	Martin Baker Aircraft, Chalgrove, fire section

Serial	Type (code/other identity)	Owner/operator, location or fate	Notes
EE425	Gloster Meteor F3 <ff>	Gloucestershire Avn Coll, stored Gloucester	
EE531	Gloster Meteor F4 (7090M)	Midland Air Museum, Coventry	
EE549	Gloster Meteor F4 (7008M) [A]	Tangmere Military Aviation Museum	
EF545	VS349 Spitfire LF VC (G-CDGY)	Aero Vintage, Rye	
EJ693	Hawker Tempest V (N7027E) [SA-J]	Privately owned, Booker	
EJ922	Hawker Typhoon IB <ff>	Privately owned, Hawkinge	
EM720	DH82A Tiger Moth II (G-AXAN)	Privately owned, Little Gransden	
EN224	VS366 Spitfire F XII (G-FXII)	Privately owned, Newport Pagnell	
EN343	VS365 Spitfire PR XI <R> (BAPC 226)	RAF Benson, on display	
EN398	VS361 Spitfire F IX <R> [JE-J]	Shropshire Wartime Aircraft Recovery Grp Mus, Sleap	
EN398	VS361 Spitfire F IX <R> (BAPC 184)	Rolls-Royce, Derby	
EN526	VS361 Spitfire IX <R> (*MH777*/BAPC 221) [SZ-G]	RAF Northolt, on display	
EP120	VS349 Spitfire LF VB (5377M/8070M/G-LFVB) [AE-A]	The Fighter Collection, Duxford	
EX976	NA AT-6D Harvard III (FAP 1657)	FAA Museum, RNAS Yeovilton	
FB226	Bonsall Mustang <R> (G-BDWM) [MT-A]	Privately owned, Gamston	
FE695	Noorduyn AT-16 Harvard IIB (G-BTXI) [94]	The Fighter Collection, Duxford	
FE788	CCF Harvard IV (MM54137/G-CTKL)	Privately owned, Rochester	
FE905	Noorduyn AT-16 Harvard IIB (LN-BNM)	RAF Museum, Hendon	
FJ992	Boeing-Stearman PT-17 Kaydet (OO-JEH) [44]	Privately owned, Wevelgem, Belgium	
FL586	Douglas C-47B Dakota (OO-SMA) [AI-N] (fuselage)	Privately owned, North Weald	
FR886	Piper L-4J Cub (G-BDMS)	Privately owned, Old Sarum	
FS628	Fairchild Argus 2 (43-14601/G-AIZE)	RAF Museum, Cosford	
FS668	Noorduyn AT-16 Harvard IIB (PH-TBR)	Privately owned, Gilze-Rijen, The Netherlands	
FS728	Noorduyn AT-16 Harvard IIB (D-FRCP)	Privately owned, Gelnhausen, Germany	
FT118	Noorduyn AT-16 Harvard IIB (G-BZHL)	Privately owned, Spanhoe	
FT323	NA AT-6D Harvard III (FAP 1513)	Air Engineering Services, Swansea	
FT391	Noorduyn AT-16 Harvard IIB (G-AZBN)	Privately owned, Shoreham	
FX301	NA AT-6D Harvard III (EX915/G-JUDI) [FD-NQ]	Privately owned, Bryngwyn Bach, Clwyd	
FX322	Noorduyn AT-16 Harvard IIB <ff>	Privately owned, Doncaster	
FX760	Curtiss P-40N Kittyhawk IV (9150M) [GA-?]	RAF Museum, Hendon	
FZ626	Douglas Dakota III (KN566/G-AMPO) [YS-DH]	RAF Lyneham, on display	
HB275	Beech C-45 Expeditor II (G-BKGM)	Privately owned, Exeter	
HB751	Fairchild Argus III (G-BCBL)	Privately owned, Woolsery, Devon	
HG691	DH89A Dragon Rapide (G-AIYR)	Privately owned, Clacton/Duxford	
HH268	GAL48 Hotspur II (HH379/BAPC 261) [H]	Museum of Army Flying, Middle Wallop	
HJ711	DH98 Mosquito NF II [VI-C]	Night-Fighter Preservation Tm, Elvington	
HM503	Miles M12 Mohawk (G-AEKW)	RAF Museum Restoration Centre, Cosford	
HM580	Cierva C-30A (G-ACUU) [KX-K]	Imperial War Museum, Duxford	
HS503	Fairey Swordfish IV (BAPC 108)	RAF Museum Reserve Collection, Stafford	
IR206	Eurofighter Typhoon F2 <R> [IR]	RAF M&RU, Bottesford	
JF343	Supermarine Aircraft Spitfire 26 (G-CCZP) [JW-P]	Privately owned, Panshangar	
JG891	VS349 Spitfire LF VC (A58-178/G-LFVC)[T-B]	Spitfire Ltd, Duxford	
JP843	Hawker Typhoon IB [Y]	Privately owned, Shrewsbury	

Notes	*Serial*	*Type (code/other identity)*	*Owner/operator, location or fate*
	JR505	Hawker Typhoon IB <ff>	Midland Air Museum, Coventry
	JV482	Grumman Wildcat V	Ulster Aviation Society, Langford Lodge
	JV579	Grumman FM-2 Wildcat (N4845V/G-RUMW) [F]	The Fighter Collection, Duxford
	JV928	Consolidated PBY-5A Catalina (N423RS) [Y]	Super Catalina Restoration, Lee-on-Solent
	KB889	Avro 683 Lancaster B X (G-LANC) [NA-I]	Imperial War Museum, Duxford
	KB976	Avro 683 Lancaster B X <ff>	Privately owned, Lee-on-Solent, Hants
	KB976	Avro 683 Lancaster B X (G-BCOH) <rf>	Aeroventure, Doncaster
	KB994	Avro 683 Lancaster BX (G-BVBP) <ff>	Privately owned, Martham, Norfolk
	KD345	Goodyear FG-1D Corsair (88297/G-FGID) [130-A]	The Fighter Collection, Duxford
	KD431	CV Corsair IV [E2-M]	FAA Museum, RNAS Yeovilton
	KE209	Grumman Hellcat II	FAA Museum, RNAS Yeovilton
	KE418	Hawker Tempest <rf>	RAF Museum Restoration Centre, Cosford
	KF183	Noorduyn AT-16 Harvard IIB [3]	MoD/AFD/QinetiQ, Boscombe Down
	KF435	Noorduyn AT-16 Harvard IIB <ff>	Privately owned, Swindon
	KF488	Noorduyn AT-16 Harvard IIB	Bournemouth Aviation Museum
	KF532	Noorduyn AT-16 Harvard IIB <ff>	Newark Air Museum, Winthorpe
	KF584	CCF T-6J Texan (*FT239*/G-BIWX/G-RAIX) [RAI-X]	Privately owned, Lee-on-Solent
	KF729	CCF T-6J Texan (G-BJST)	Privately owned, Thruxton
	KG651	Douglas Dakota III (G-AMHJ)	Assault Glider Trust, Shawbury
	KJ351	Airspeed AS58 Horsa II (TL659/BAPC 80) [23]	Museum of Army Flying, Middle Wallop
	KJ994	Douglas Dakota III (F-AZTE)	Dakota et Cie, La Ferté Alais, France
	KK116	Douglas Dakota IV (G-AMPY)	Air Atlantique Classic Flight, Coventry
	KK995	Sikorsky Hoverfly I [E]	RAF Museum, Hendon
	KL216	Republic P-47D Thunderbolt (45-49295/9212M) [RS-L]	RAF Museum, Hendon
	KN353	Douglas Dakota IV (G-AMYJ)	Yorkshire Air Museum, Elvington
	KN448	Douglas Dakota IV <ff>	Science Museum, South Kensington
	KN645	Douglas Dakota IV (*KG374*/8355M)	RAF Museum, Cosford
	KN751	Consolidated Liberator C VI (IAF HE807) [F]	RAF Museum, Hendon
	KP208	Douglas Dakota IV [YS]	Airborne Forces Museum, Aldershot
	KZ191	Hawker Hurricane IV (frame only)	Privately owned, East Garston, Bucks
	LA198	VS356 Spitfire F21 (7118M) [RAI-G]	Kelvingrove Art Gallery & Museum, Glasgow
	LA226	VS356 Spitfire F21 (7119M)	RAF Museum Reserve Collection, Stafford
	LA255	VS356 Spitfire F21 (6490M) [JX-U]	RAF No 1 Sqn, Cottesmore (preserved)
	LB264	Taylorcraft Plus D (G-AIXA)	RAF Museum, Hendon
	LB294	Taylorcraft Plus D (G-AHWJ)	Museum of Army Flying, Whitchurch, Hants
	LB312	Taylorcraft Plus D (*HH982*/G-AHXE)	Privately owned, Netheravon
	LB323	Taylorcraft Plus D (G-AHSD)	Privately owned, Shipdham
	LB367	Taylorcraft Plus D (G-AHGZ)	Privately owned, Henstridge
	LB375	Taylorcraft Plus D (G-AHGW)	Privately owned, Coventry
	LF363	Hawker Hurricane IIC [YB-W]	RAF BBMF, Coningsby
	LF738	Hawker Hurricane IIC (5405M) [UH-A]	RAF Museum, Cosford
	LF789	DH82 Queen Bee (K3584/BAPC 186) [R2-K]	Mosquito Aircraft Museum, London Colney
	LF858	DH82 Queen Bee (G-BLUZ)	Privately owned, Henlow
	LH291	Airspeed AS51 Horsa I <R> (BAPC 279)	Assault Glider Trust, RAF Shawbury
	LS326	Fairey Swordfish II (G-AJVH) [L2]	RN Historic Flight, Yeovilton
	LV907	HP59 Halifax III (HR792) [NP-F]	Yorkshire Air Museum, Elvington
	LZ551	DH100 Vampire	FAA Museum, RNAS Yeovilton
	LZ766	Percival P34 Proctor III (G-ALCK)	Imperial War Museum, Duxford
	LZ842	VS361 Spitfire F IX [EF-D]	Privately owned, Sandown
	MB293	VS357 Seafire IIC (wreck)	Privately owned, Braintree
	MD338	VS359 Spitfire LF VIII	Privately owned, Sandown
	MF628	Vickers Wellington T10 (9210M)	RAF Museum, Hendon

Serial	*Type (code/other identity)*	*Owner/operator, location or fate*	*Notes*
MH434	VS361 Spitfire LF IXB (G-ASJV) [ZD-B]	The Old Flying Machine Company, Duxford	
MH486	VS361 Spitfire LF IX <R> (BAPC 206) [FF-A]	RAF Museum, Hendon	
MH415	VS361 Spitfire IX <R> (*MJ751*/BAPC 209) [DU-V]	The Aircraft Restoration Co, Duxford	
MJ147	VS361 Spitfire LF IX	Privately owned, Kent	
MJ627	VS509 Spitfire T9 (G-BMSB) [9G-P]	Privately owned, Norwich	
MJ832	VS361 Spitfire IX <R> (*L1096*/BAPC 229) [DN-Y]	RAF Digby, on display	
MK356	VS361 Spitfire LF IXC (5690M) [2I-V]	RAF BBMF, Coningsby	
MK356	VS361 Spitfire LF IXC <R> [2I-V]	Kent Battle of Britain Museum, Hawkinge	
MK356	VS361 Spitfire LF IXC (BAPC 289) <R>	RAF Cosford, on display	
ML407	VS509 Spitfire T9 (G-LFIX) [OU-V]	Privately owned, Duxford	
ML411	VS361 Spitfire LF IXE (G-CBNU)	Privately owned, Ashford, Kent	
ML427	VS361 Spitfire IX (6457M) [HK-A]	Millennium Discovery Centre, Birmingham	
ML796	Short S25 Sunderland V	Imperial War Museum, Duxford	
ML824	Short S25 Sunderland V [NS-Z]	RAF Museum, Hendon	
MN235	Hawker Typhoon IB	RAF Museum, Hendon	
MP425	Airspeed AS10 Oxford I (G-AITB) [G]	RAF Museum, Hendon	
MS902	Miles M25 Martinet TT1 (TF-SHC)	Museum of Berkshire Aviation, Woodley	
MT197	Auster IV (G-ANHS)	Privately owned, Spanhoe	
MT438	Auster III (G-AREI)	Privately owned, Eggesford	
MT818	VS505 Spitfire T8 (G-AIDN)	Privately owned, West Sussex	
MT847	VS379 Spitfire FR XIVE (6960M) [AX-H]	Gr Manchester Mus of Science & Industry	
MT928	VS359 Spitfire HF VIIIC (G-BKMI/ MV154/*AR654*)[ZX-M]	Privately owned, East Garston, Bucks	
MV262	VS379 Spitfire FR XIV (G-CCVV)	Privately owned, Booker	
MV268	VS379 Spitfire FR XIVE (MV293/ G-SPIT) [JE-J]	The Fighter Collection, Duxford	
MW401	Hawker Tempest II (IAF HA604/G-PEST)	Privately owned, Hemswell, Lincs	
MW763	Hawker Tempest II (IAF HA586/G-TEMT) [HF-A]	Privately owned, Wickenby	
NF370	Fairey Swordfish III [NH-L]	Imperial War Museum, Duxford	
NF389	Fairey Swordfish III [D]	RN Historic Flight, Yeovilton	
NJ633	Auster 5D (G-AKXP)	Privately owned, English Bicknor	
NJ673	Auster 5D (G-AOCR)	Privately owned, Shenington, Oxon	
NJ695	Auster 4 (G-AJXV)	Privately owned, Newark	
NJ703	Auster 5 (G-AKPI)	Privately owned, Ellerton	
NJ719	Auster 5 (TW385/G-ANFU)	Newcastle Motor Museum	
NL750	DH82A Tiger Moth II (T7997/G-AOBH)	Privately owned, Eaglescott	
NL985	DH82A Tiger Moth I (7015M/G-BWIK)	Privately owned, Sywell	
NM181	DH82A Tiger Moth I (G-AZGZ)	Privately owned, Rush Green	
NP294	Percival P31 Proctor IV [TB-M]	Lincolnshire Avn Heritage Centre, E Kirkby	
NV778	Hawker Tempest TT5 (8386M)	RAF Museum, Hendon	
NX534	Auster III (G-BUDL)	Privately owned, Netheravon	
NX611	Avro 683 Lancaster B VII (8375M/G-ASXX) [DX-C,LE-C]	Lincolnshire Avn Heritage Centre, E Kirkby	
PA474	Avro 683 Lancaster B I [BQ-B,HW-R]	RAF BBMF, Coningsby	
PD685	Slingsby T7 Cadet TX1	Air Training Heritage Collection, Wolverhampton	
PF179	HS Gnat T1 (XR541/8602M)	Global Aviation, stored Humberside	
PK624	VS356 Spitfire F22 (8072M)	The Fighter Collection, Duxford	
PK664	VS356 Spitfire F22 (7759M) [V6-B]	Science Museum, South Kensington	
PK683	VS356 Spitfire F24 (7150M)	Solent Sky, Southampton	
PK724	VS356 Spitfire F24 (7288M)	RAF Museum, Hendon	
PL256	VS361 Spitfire IX <R> [TM-L]	East Midlands Airport Aeropark	
PL344	VS361 Spitfire LF IXE (G-IXCC/N644TB) [TL-B]	Spitfire Ltd, Duxford	
PL965	VS365 Spitfire PR XI (G-MKXI) [R]	Hangar 11 Collection, North Weald	
PL983	VS365 Spitfire PR XI (G-PRXI)	Privately owned, Duxford (on rebuild)	

Notes	*Serial*	*Type (code/other identity)*	*Owner/operator, location or fate*
	PM631	VS390 Spitfire PR XIX	RAF BBMF, Coningsby
	PM651	VS390 Spitfire PR XIX (7758M) [X]	RAF Museum Reserve Collection, Stafford
	PN323	HP Halifax VII <ff>	Imperial War Museum, Lambeth
	PP566	Fairey Firefly 1 <rf>	Privately owned, Newton Abbott
	PP972	VS358 Seafire LF IIIC (G-BUAR)	Privately owned, stored Greenham Common
	PR536	Hawker Tempest II (IAF HA457) [OQ-H]	RAF Museum, Hendon
	PS853	VS390 Spitfire PR XIX (G-RRGN) [C]	Rolls-Royce, Filton
	PS890	VS390 Spitfire PR XIX (F-AZJS)	Privately owned, Dijon, France
	PS915	VS390 Spitfire PR XIX (7548M/7711M)	RAF BBMF, Coningsby
	PT462	VS509 Spitfire T9 (G-CTIX/N462JC) [SW-A]	Privately owned, Caernarfon/Duxford
	PV303	Supermarine Aircraft Spitfire 26 (G-CCJL) [ON-B]	Privately owned, Perranporth
	PZ865	Hawker Hurricane IIC (G-AMAU) [JX-E]	RAF BBMF, Coningsby
	RA848	Slingsby T7 Cadet TX1	Privately owned, Leeds
	RA854	Slingsby T7 Cadet TX1	Yorkshire Air Museum, Elvington
	RA897	Slingsby T7 Cadet TX1	Newark Air Museum, Winthorpe
	RA905	Slingsby T7 Cadet TX1 (BGA1143)	Trenchard Museum, RAF Halton
	RB142	Supermarine Aircraft Spitfire 26 (G-CEFC) [DW-B]	Privately owned, Basingstoke, Hants
	RD220	Bristol 156 Beaufighter TF X	Royal Scottish Mus'm of Flight, stored E Fortune
	RD253	Bristol 156 Beaufighter TF X (7931M)	RAF Museum, Hendon
	RF398	Avro 694 Lincoln B II (8376M)	RAF Museum, Cosford
	RG333	Miles M38 Messenger IIA (G-AIEK)	Privately owned, Felton, Bristol
	RH746	Bristol 164 Brigand TF1 (fuselage)	Bristol Aero Collection, stored Kemble
	RL962	DH89A Dominie II (G-AHED)	RAF Museum Reserve Collection, Stafford
	RM221	Percival P31 Proctor IV (G-ANXR)	Privately owned, Biggin Hill
	RM689	VS379 Spitfire F XIV (G-ALGT) (remains)	Rolls-Royce, Filton
	RM694	VS379 Spitfire F XIV (6640M)	Privately owned, Booker
	RM927	VS379 Spitfire F XIV	Privately owned, Sandown
	RN201	VS379 Spitfire FR XIV (SG-31/*SG-3*/G-BSKP) [D]	*Sold as N201TB, October 2006*
	RN218	Isaacs Spitfire <R> (G-BBJI) [N]	Privately owned, Builth Wells
	RR232	VS361 Spitfire HF IXC (G-BRSF)	Privately owned, Langford, Devon
	RT486	Auster 5 (G-AJGJ) [PF-A]	Privately owned, Lee-on-Solent
	RT520	Auster 5 (G-ALYB)	Aeroventure, Doncaster
	RT610	Auster 5A-160 (G-AKWS)	Privately owned, Crowfield
	RW382	VS361 Spitfire LF XVIE (7245M/8075M/N382RW) (wreck)	Privately owned, Sandown
	RW386	VS361 Spitfire LF XVIE (6944M/SE-BIR) [NG-D]	Privately owned, Angelholm, Sweden
	RW388	VS361 Spitfire LF XVIE (6946M) [U4-U]	Stoke-on-Trent City Museum, Hanley
	RX168	VS358 Seafire L IIIC (IAC 157/G-BWEM)	Privately owned, Exeter
	SL611	VS361 Spitfire LF XVIE	Supermarine Aero Engineering, Stoke-on-Trent
	SL674	VS361 Spitfire LF IX (8392M) [RAS-H]	RAF Museum Reserve Collection, Stafford
	SM520	VS361 Spitfire LF IX (G-BXHZ/G-ILDA)	Privately owned, Thruxton
	SM845	VS394 Spitfire FR XVIII (G-BUOS) [GZ-J]	Silver Victory Collection, Duxford
	SM969	VS394 Spitfire F XVIIIE (G-BRAF) [D-A]	The Fighter Collection, Duxford
	SX137	VS384 Seafire F XVII	FAA Museum, RNAS Yeovilton
	SX336	VS384 Seafire F XVII (G-KASX) [105/VL]	Kennet Aviation, North Weald
	TA122	DH98 Mosquito FB VI [UP-G]	Mosquito Aircraft Museum, London Colney
	TA634	DH98 Mosquito TT35 (G-AWJV) [8K-K]	Mosquito Aircraft Museum, London Colney

Serial	Type (code/other identity)	Owner/operator, location or fate	Notes
TA639	DH98 Mosquito TT35 (7806M) [AZ-E]	RAF Museum, Cosford	
TA719	DH98 Mosquito TT35 (G-ASKC)	Imperial War Museum, Duxford	
TA805	VS361 Spitfire HF IX (G-PMNF) [FX-M]	Privately owned, Biggin Hill	
TB382	VS361 Spitfire LF XVIE (*X4277/MK673*)	RAF BBMF, stored Coningsby	
TB675	VS361 Spitfire LF XVIE (RW393/7293M) [4D-V]	RAF Museum Reserve Collection, Stafford	
TB752	VS361 Spitfire LF XVIE (8086M) [KH-Z]	RAF Manston, Memorial Pavilion	
TD248	VS361 Spitfire LF XVIE (7246M/G-OXVI) [CR-S]	Spitfire Limited, Duxford	
TD248	VS361 Spitfire LF XVIE [8Q-T] (fuselage)	Norfolk & Suffolk Avn Mus'm, Flixton	
TD314	VS361 Spitfire LF IX (*N601DA*)	Privately owned, Bentwaters	
TE311	VS361 Spitfire LF XVIE (*MK178*/7241M)	RAF BBMF, Coningsby (on rebuild)	
TE462	VS361 Spitfire LF XVIE (7243M)	Royal Scottish Mus'm of Flight, E Fortune	
TE517	VS361 Spitfire LF IXE (G-CCIX) [HL-K]	Privately owned, Sussex	
TG263	Saro SR A1 (G-12-1)	Solent Sky, Southampton	
TG511	HP67 Hastings C1 (8554M)	RAF Museum, Cosford	
TG517	HP67 Hastings T5	Newark Air Museum, Winthorpe	
TG528	HP67 Hastings C1A	Imperial War Museum, Duxford	
TJ118	DH98 Mosquito TT35 <ff>	Mosquito Aircraft Museum, stored London Colney	
TJ138	DH98 Mosquito B35 (7607M) [VO-L]	RAF Museum, Hendon	
TJ343	Auster 5 (G-AJXC)	Privately owned, Hook	
TJ398	Auster AOP6 (BAPC 70)	Privately owned, South Shields	
TJ534	Auster 5 (G-AKSY)	Privately owned, Breighton	
TJ565	Auster 5 (G-AMVD)	Privately owned, Hardwick, Norfolk	
TJ569	Auster 5 (G-AKOW)	Museum of Army Flying, Middle Wallop	
TJ672	Auster 5D (G-ANIJ) [TS-D]	Privately owned, Melksham, Wilts	
TJ704	Beagle A61 Terrier 2 (VW993/G-ASCD) [JA]	Yorkshire Air Museum, Elvington	
TK718	GAL59 Hamilcar I	National Tank Museum, Bovington	
TK777	GAL59 Hamilcar I (fuselage)	Museum of Army Flying, Middle Wallop	
TS291	Slingsby T7 Cadet TX1 (BGA852)	Royal Scottish Mus'm of Flight, stored E Fortune	
TS798	Avro 685 York C1 (G-AGNV)	RAF Museum, Cosford	
TV959	DH98 Mosquito T III [AF-V]	Privately owned, Martham, Norfolk	
TW439	Auster 5 (G-ANRP)	The Real Aeroplane Company, Breighton	
TW467	Auster 5 (G-ANIE)	Privately owned, Spanhoe	
TW511	Auster 5 (G-APAF)	Privately owned, Henstridge	
TW536	Auster AOP6 (7704M/G-BNGE) [TS-V]	Privately owned, Netheravon	
TW591	Auster 6A (G-ARIH) [N]	Privately owned, Spanhoe	
TW641	Beagle A61 Terrier 2 (G-ATDN)	Privately owned, Biggin Hill	
TX213	Avro 652A Anson C19 (G-AWRS)	North-East Aircraft Museum, Usworth	
TX214	Avro 652A Anson C19 (7817M)	RAF Museum, Cosford	
TX226	Avro 652A Anson C19 (7865M)	Air Atlantique Classic Flight, Coventry	
TX235	Avro 652A Anson C19	Air Atlantique Classic Flight, Coventry	
VF301	DH100 Vampire F1 (7060M) [RAL-G]	Midland Air Museum, Coventry	
VF512	Auster 6A (G-ARRX) [PF-M]	Privately owned, Popham	
VF516	Beagle A61 Terrier 2 (G-ASMZ)	Privately owned, Eggesford	
VF519	Auster AOP6 (G-ASYN)	Privately owned, Doncaster	
VF526	Auster 6A (G-ARXU) [T]	Privately owned, Netheravon	
VF560	Auster 6A (frame)	Aeroventure, Doncaster	
VF581	Beagle A61 Terrier 1 (G-ARSL)	Privately owned, Eggesford	
VH127	Fairey Firefly TT4 [200/R]	FAA Museum, RNAS Yeovilton	
VL348	Avro 652A Anson C19 (G-AVVO)	Newark Air Museum, Winthorpe	
VL349	Avro 652A Anson C19 (G-AWSA) [V7-Q]	Norfolk & Suffolk Avn Mus'm, Flixton	
VM325	Avro 652A Anson C19	Privately owned, Carew Cheriton, Pembrokeshire	
VM360	Avro 652A Anson C19 (G-APHV)	Royal Scottish Mus'm of Flight, E Fortune	

Notes	Serial	Type (code/other identity)	Owner/operator, location or fate
	VM684	Slingsby Cadet T2 (BGA791)	NW Aviation Heritage Museum, Hooton Park
	VM687	Slingsby T8 Tutor (BGA794)	Privately owned, Lee-on-Solent
	VM791	Slingsby Cadet TX3 (XA312/8876M)	RAF Manston History Museum
	VN485	VS356 Spitfire F24 (7326M)	Imperial War Museum, Duxford
	VN799	EE Canberra T4 (WJ874/G-CDSX)	Air Atlantique Classic Flight, Coventry
	VP293	Avro 696 Shackleton T4 [X] <ff>	Privately owned, Duxford
	VP519	Avro 652A Anson C19 (G-AVVR) <ff>	Privately owned, Wolverhampton
	VP952	DH104 Devon C2 (8820M)	RAF Museum, Cosford
	VP955	DH104 Devon C2 (G-DVON)	Privately owned, Little Rissington
	VP957	DH104 Devon C2 (8822M) <ff>	No 1137 Sqn ATC, Belfast
	VP967	DH104 Devon C2 (G-KOOL)	Privately owned, Redhill
	VP975	DH104 Devon C2 [M]	Science Museum, Wroughton
	VP981	DH104 Devon C2 (G-DHDV)	Air Atlantique Classic Flight, Coventry
	VR137	Westland Wyvern TF1	FAA Museum, stored RNAS Yeovilton
	VR192	Pervical P40 Prentice T1 (G-APIT)	SWWAPS, Lasham
	VR249	Percival P40 Prentice T1 (G-APIY) [FA-EL]	Newark Air Museum, Winthorpe
	VR259	Percival P40 Prentice T1 (G-APJB) [M]	Air Atlantique Classic Flight, Coventry
	VR930	Hawker Sea Fury FB11 (8382M) [110/Q]	RN Historic Flight, Yeovilton
	VS356	Percival P40 Prentice T1 (G-AOLU)	Privately owned, Montrose
	VS562	Avro 652A Anson T21 (8012M)	Maes Artro Craft Village, Llanbedr
	VS610	Percival P40 Prentice T1 (G-AOKL)[K-L]	The Shuttleworth Collection, Old Warden
	VS623	Percival P40 Prentice T1 (G-AOKZ)[KQ-F]	Midland Air Museum, Coventry
	VT409	Fairey Firefly AS5 <rf>	North-East Aircraft Museum, stored Usworth
	VT812	DH100 Vampire F3 (7200M) [N]	RAF Museum, Hendon
	VT871	DH100 Vampire FB6 (J-1173/*LZ551*/G-DHXX) [G]	Privately owned, Bournemouth
	VT935	Boulton Paul P111A (VT769)	Midland Air Museum, Coventry
	VT987	Auster AOP6 (G-BKXP)	Privately owned, Thruxton
	VV106	Supermarine 510 (7175M)	FAA Museum, stored RNAS Yeovilton
	VV217	DH100 Vampire FB5 (7323M)	North-East Aircraft Museum, stored Usworth
	VV612	DH112 Venom FB50 (J-1523/*WE402*/G-VENI)	Privately owned, Bournemouth
	VV901	Avro 652A Anson T21	Yorkshire Air Museum, Elvington
	VW453	Gloster Meteor T7 (8703M) [Z]	RAF Innsworth, on display
	VW957	DH103 Sea Hornet NF21 <rf>	Privately owned, Chelmsford
	VX113	Auster AOP6 (G-ARNO)	Privately owned, Eggesford
	VX147	Alon A2 Aircoupe (G-AVIL)	Privately owned, Kent
	VX185	EE Canberra B(I)8 (7631M) <ff>	Royal Scottish Mus'm of Flight, E Fortune
	VX250	DH103 Sea Hornet NF21 [48] <rf>	Mosquito Aircraft Museum, London Colney
	VX272	Hawker P.1052 (7174M)	FAA Museum, stored RNAS Yeovilton
	VX275	Slingsby T21B Sedbergh TX1 (8884M/BGA572)	RAF Museum Reserve Collection, Stafford
	VX281	Hawker Sea Fury T20S (G-RNHF)	RN Historic Flight, North Weald
	VX573	Vickers Valetta C2 (8389M)	RAF Museum, stored Cosford
	VX580	Vickers Valetta C2	Norfolk & Suffolk Avn Museum, Flixton
	VX595	WS51 Dragonfly HR1	FAA Museum, stored RNAS Yeovilton
	VX665	Hawker Sea Fury FB11 <rf>	RN Historic Flight, at BAE Systems Brough
	VX926	Auster T7 (G-ASKJ)	Privately owned, Congleton
	VX927	Auster T7 (G-ASYG)	Privately owned, Scampton
	VZ345	Hawker Sea Fury T20S	RN Historic Flight, stored Yeovilton
	VZ477	Gloster Meteor F8 (7741M) <ff>	Midland Air Museum, Coventry
	VZ608	Gloster Meteor FR9	Newark Air Museum, Winthorpe
	VZ634	Gloster Meteor T7 (8657M)	Newark Air Museum, Winthorpe
	VZ638	Gloster Meteor T7 (G-JETM) [HF]	Gatwick Aviation Museum, Charlwood, Surrey
	VZ728	RS4 Desford Trainer (G-AGOS)	Snibston Discovery Park, stored Coalville
	VZ962	WS51 Dragonfly HR1 [904]	The Helicopter Museum, Weston-super-Mare
	WA346	DH100 Vampire FB5	RAF Museum Restoration Centre, Cosford
	WA473	VS Attacker F1 [102/J]	FAA Museum, RNAS Yeovilton

Serial	Type (code/other identity)	Owner/operator, location or fate	Notes
WA576	Bristol 171 Sycamore 3 (7900M/G-ALSS)	Dumfries & Galloway Avn Mus, Dumfries	
WA577	Bristol 171 Sycamore 3 (7718M/G-ALST)	North-East Aircraft Museum, Usworth	
WA591	Gloster Meteor T7 (7917M/G-BWMF) [W]	Air Atlantique Classic Flight, Coventry	
WA630	Gloster Meteor T7 [69] <ff>	Robertsbridge Aviation Society, Newhaven	
WA634	Gloster Meteor T7/8	RAF Museum, Cosford	
WA638	Gloster Meteor T7(mod)	Martin Baker Aircraft, Chalgrove	
WA662	Gloster Meteor T7	Aeroventure, Doncaster	
WA829	Gloster Meteor F8 (WA984) [A]	Tangmere Military Aviation Museum	
WB188	Hawker Hunter F3 (7154M)	Tangmere Military Aviation Museum	
WB188	Hawker Hunter GA11 (WV256/G-BZPB)	Privately owned, Kemble (duck egg green)	
WB188	Hawker Hunter GA11 (XF300/G-BZPC)	Privately owned, Kemble (red)	
WB440	Fairey Firefly AS6 <ff>	Privately owned, Newton Abbott	
WB491	Avro 706 Ashton 2 (TS897/G-AJJW) <ff>	Newark Air Museum, Winthorpe	
WB555	DHC1 Chipmunk T10 <ff>	Privately owned, Ellerton	
WB556	DHC1 Chipmunk T10 (fuselage)	Privately owned, Frome, Somerset	
WB560	DHC1 Chipmunk T10 (comp WG403)	Aeroventure, Doncaster	
WB565	DHC1 Chipmunk T10 (G-PVET) [X]	Privately owned, Kemble	
WB569	DHC1 Chipmunk T10 (G-BYSJ) [R]	Privately owned, Duxford	
WB571	DHC1 Chipmunk T10 (G-AOSF) [34]	Privately owned, Trier, Germany	
WB584	DHC1 Chipmunk T10 (7706M) <ff>	Royal Scottish Mus'm of Flight, stored E Fortune	
WB585	DHC1 Chipmunk T10 (G-AOSY) [M]	Privately owned, Seething	
WB588	DHC1 Chipmunk T10 (G-AOTD) [D]	Privately owned, Old Sarum	
WB615	DHC1 Chipmunk T10 (G-BXIA) [E]	Privately owned, Blackpool	
WB624	DHC1 Chipmunk T10 <ff>	Newark Air Museum, Winthorpe	
WB626	DHC1 Chipmunk T10 <ff>	No 1365 Sqn ATC, Aylesbury	
WB627	DHC1 Chipmunk T10 (9248M) [N]	Dulwich College CCF	
WB652	DHC1 Chipmunk T10 (G-CHPY) [V]	Privately owned, Little Rissington	
WB654	DHC1 Chipmunk T10 (G-BXGO) [U]	Privately owned, Booker	
WB657	DHC1 Chipmunk T10 [908]	RN Historic Flight, Yeovilton	
WB670	DHC1 Chipmunk T10 (comp WG303)(8361M)	Privately owned, East Fortune	
WB671	DHC1 Chipmunk T10 (G-BWTG) [910]	Privately owned, Epse, The Netherlands	
WB685	DHC1 Chipmunk T10 (comp WP969/G-ATHC) [C]	North-East Aircraft Museum, Usworth	
WB685	DHC1 Chipmunk T10 <rf>	North-East Aircraft Museum, stored Usworth	
WB697	DHC1 Chipmunk T10 (G-BXCT) [95]	Privately owned, Wickenby	
WB702	DHC1 Chipmunk T10 (G-AOFE)	Privately owned, Kindford	
WB703	DHC1 Chipmunk T10 (G-ARMC)	Privately owned, White Waltham	
WB711	DHC1 Chipmunk T10 (G-APPM)	Privately owned, Sywell	
WB726	DHC1 Chipmunk T10 (G-AOSK) [E]	Privately owned, Audley End	
WB733	DHC1 Chipmunk T10 (comp WG422)	Aeroventure, Doncaster	
WB763	DHC1 Chipmunk T10 (G-BBMR) [14]	Privately owned, Tollerton	
WB922	Slingsby T21B Sedbergh TX1 (BGA4366)	Privately owned, Hullavington	
WB924	Slingsby T21B Sedbergh TX1 (BGA3901)	Privately owned, Dunstable	
WB943	Slingsby T21B Sedbergh TX1 (BGA2941)	Privately owned, Rufforth	
WB944	Slingsby T21B Sedbergh TX1 (BGA3160)	Privately owned, Bicester	
WB971	Slingsby T21B Sedbergh TX1 (BGA 3324)	Privately owned, Tibenham	
WB975	Slingsby T21B Sedbergh TX1 (BGA 3288)	Privately owned, Drumshade, Fife	

Notes	Serial	Type (code/other identity)	Owner/operator, location or fate
	WB981	Slingsby T21B Sedbergh TX1 (BGA 3238)	Privately owned, Keevil
	WD286	DHC1 Chipmunk T10 (G-BBND)	Privately owned, Little Gransden
	WD292	DHC1 Chipmunk T10 (G-BCRX)	Privately owned, White Waltham
	WD293	DHC1 Chipmunk T10 (7645M) <ff>	No 30F Sqn ATC, Cardiff
	WD305	DHC1 Chipmunk T10 (G-ARGG)	Privately owned, Prestwick
	WD310	DHC1 Chipmunk T10 (G-BWUN) [B]	Privately owned, Deanland
	WD325	DHC1 Chipmunk T10 [N]	AAC Historic Aircraft Flight, Middle Wallop
	WD331	DHC1 Chipmunk T10 (G-BXDH) [J]	Privately owned, Enstone
	WD347	DHC1 Chipmunk T10 (G-BBRV)	Privately owned, Sheffield
	WD355	DHC1 Chipmunk T10 (WD335/G-CBAJ)	Privately owned, Stamford
	WD363	DHC1 Chipmunk T10 (G-BCIH) [5]	Privately owned, Audley End
	WD370	DHC1 Chipmunk T10 <ff>	No 225 Sqn ATC, Brighton
	WD373	DHC1 Chipmunk T10 (G-BXDI) [12]	Privately owned, Duxford
	WD377	DHC1 Chipmunk T10 <ff>	RAF Millom Museum, Haverigg
	WD379	DHC1 Chipmunk T10 (WB696/G-APLO) [K]	Privately owned, Jersey
	WD386	DHC1 Chipmunk T10 (comp WD377)	Dumfries & Galloway Avn Mus, Prestwick
	WD390	DHC1 Chipmunk T10 (G-BWNK) [68]	Privately owned, Breighton
	WD413	Avro 652A Anson T21 (7881M/G-VROE)	Air Atlantique Classic Flight, Coventry
	WD615	Gloster Meteor TT20 (WD646/8189M) [R]	RAF Manston History Museum
	WD686	Gloster Meteor NF11	Muckleburgh Collection, Weybourne
	WD790	Gloster Meteor NF11 (8743M)<ff>	North-East Aircraft Museum, Usworth
	WD889	Fairey Firefly AS5 <ff>	North-East Aircraft Museum, Usworth
	WD931	EE Canberra B2 <ff>	RAF Museum, stored Cosford
	WD935	EE Canberra B2 (8440M) <ff>	Aeroventure, Doncaster
	WD954	EE Canberra B2 <ff>	Privately owned, St Mawgan
	WE113	EE Canberra B2 <ff>	Privately owned, Woodhurst, Cambridgeshire
	WE122	EE Canberra TT18 [845] <ff>	Blyth Valley Aviation Collection, Walpole, Suffolk
	WE139	EE Canberra PR3 (8369M)	RAF Museum, Hendon
	WE168	EE Canberra PR3 (8049M) <ff>	Norfolk & Suffolk Avn Museum, Flixton
	WE173	EE Canberra PR3 (8740M) <ff>	Robertsbridge Aviation Society, Mayfield
	WE188	EE Canberra T4	Solway Aviation Society, Carlisle
	WE192	EE Canberra T4 <ff>	Blyth Valley Aviation Collection, Walpole, Suffolk
	WE275	DH112 Venom FB50 (J-1601/G-VIDI)	BAE Systems Hawarden, Fire Section
	WE569	Auster T7 (G-ASAJ)	Privately owned, Bourn, Lincs
	WE570	Auster T7 (G-ASBU)	Privately owned, Stonehaven
	WE600	Auster T7 Antarctic (7602M)	RAF Museum, Cosford
	WE724	Hawker Sea Fury FB11 (VX653/G-BUCM) [062]	The Fighter Collection, Duxford
	WE982	Slingsby T30B Prefect TX1 (8781M)	RAF Museum, stored Cosford
	WE987	Slingsby T30B Prefect TX1 (BGA2517)	Aeroventure, Doncaster
	WE990	Slingsby T30B Prefect TX1 (BGA2583)	Privately owned, stored Beds
	WE992	Slingsby T30B Prefect TX1 (BGA2692)	Privately owned, Keevil
	WF118	Percival P57 Sea Prince T1 (G-DACA)	Gatwick Aviation Museum, Charlwood, Surrey
	WF122	Percival P57 Sea Prince T1 [575/CU]	Aeroventure, Doncaster
	WF128	Percival P57 Sea Prince T1 (8611M)	Norfolk & Suffolk Avn Museum, Flixton
	WF137	Percival P57 Sea Prince C1	SWWAPS, Lasham
	WF145	Hawker Sea Hawk F1 <ff>	Privately owned, Ingatestone, Essex
	WF219	Hawker Sea Hawk F1 <rf>	FAA Museum, stored RNAS Yeovilton
	WF225	Hawker Sea Hawk F1 [CU]	RNAS Culdrose, at main gate
	WF259	Hawker Sea Hawk F2 [171/A]	Royal Scottish Mus'm of Flight,E Fortune

Serial	*Type (code/other identity)*	*Owner/operator, location or fate*	*Notes*
WF369	Vickers Varsity T1 [F]	Newark Air Museum, Winthorpe	
WF372	Vickers Varsity T1 [A]	Brooklands Museum, Weybridge	
WF376	Vickers Varsity T1	Bristol Airport Fire Section	
WF408	Vickers Varsity T1 (8395M) <ff>	Privately owned, Booker	
WF643	Gloster Meteor F8 [P]	Norfolk & Suffolk Avn Museum, Flixton	
WF714	Gloster Meteor F8 (WK914)	RAF Millom Museum, Haverigg	
WF784	Gloster Meteor T7 (7895M)	Gloucestershire Avn Coll, stored Gloucester	
WF825	Gloster Meteor T7 (8359M) [A]	Meteor Flight, Yatesbury	
WF911	EE Canberra B2 [CO] <ff>	Gloster Avn Club, Gloucester	
WF922	EE Canberra PR3	Midland Air Museum, Coventry	
WG308	DHC1 Chipmunk T10 (G-BYHL) [71]	Privately owned, RAF Cranwell	
WG316	DHC1 Chipmunk T10 (G-BCAH)	Privately owned, Leicester	
WG321	DHC1 Chipmunk T10 (G-DHCC)	Privately owned, Wevelgem, Belgium	
WG348	DHC1 Chipmunk T10 (G-BBMV)	Privately owned, Sywell	
WG350	DHC1 Chipmunk T10 (G-BPAL)	Privately owned, Cascais, Portugal	
WG362	DHC1 Chipmunk T10 (8437M/8630M/*WX643*) <ff>	No 1094 Sqn ATC, Ely	
WG407	DHC1 Chipmunk T10 (G-BWMX) [67]	Privately owned, Croydon, Cambs	
WG418	DHC1 Chipmunk T10 (8209M/G-ATDY) <ff>	No 1940 Sqn ATC, Levenshulme, Gr Manchester	
WG419	DHC1 Chipmunk T10 (8206M) <ff>	Sywell Aviation Museum	
WG422	DHC1 Chipmunk T10 (8394M/G-BFAX) [16]	Privately owned, Eggesford	
WG432	DHC1 Chipmunk T10 [L]	Museum of Army Flying, Middle Wallop	
WG458	DHC1 Chipmunk T10 (N458BG) [2]	Privately owned, Breighton	
WG465	DHC1 Chipmunk T10 (G-BCEY)	Privately owned, White Waltham	
WG469	DHC1 Chipmunk T10 (G-BWJY) [72]	Privately owned, Sligo, Eire	
WG471	DHC1 Chipmunk T10 (8210M) <ff>	Thameside Aviation Museum, East Tilbury	
WG472	DHC1 Chipmunk T10 (G-AOTY)	Privately owned, Bryngwyn Bach, Clwyd	
WG477	DHC1 Chipmunk T10 (8362M/G-ATDP) <ff>	No 281 Sqn ATC, Birkdale, Merseyside	
WG486	DHC1 Chipmunk T10 [G]	RAF BBMF, Coningsby	
WG498	Slingsby T21B Sedbergh TX1 (BGA3245)	Privately owned, Aston Down	
WG511	Avro 696 Shackleton T4 (fuselage)	Flambards Village Theme Park, Helston	
WG719	WS51 Dragonfly HR5 (G-BRMA)	The Helicopter Museum, Weston-super-Mare	
WG724	WS51 Dragonfly HR5 [932]	North-East Aircraft Museum, Usworth	
WG751	WS51 Dragonfly HR5 [710/GJ]	World Naval Base, Chatham	
WG760	EE P1A (7755M)	RAF Museum, Cosford	
WG763	EE P1A (7816M)	Gr Manchester Mus of Science & Industry	
WG768	Short SB5 (8005M)	RAF Museum, Cosford	
WG774	BAC 221	Science Museum, at FAA Museum, RNAS Yeovilton	
WG777	Fairey FD2 (7986M)	RAF Museum, Cosford	
WG789	EE Canberra B2/6 <ff>	Norfolk & Suffolk Avn Museum, Flixton	
WH132	Gloster Meteor T7 (7906M) [J]	No 276 Sqn ATC, Chelmsford	
WH166	Gloster Meteor T7 (8052M) [A]	Privately owned, Birlingham, Worcs	
WH291	Gloster Meteor F8	SWWAPS, Lasham	
WH301	Gloster Meteor F8 (7930M) [T]	RAF Museum, Hendon	
WH364	Gloster Meteor F8 (8169M)	Gloucestershire Avn Coll, stored Gloucester	
WH453	Gloster Meteor D16 [L]	Bentwaters Cold War Air Museum	
WH646	EE Canberra T17A <ff>	Midland Air Museum, Coventry	
WH657	EE Canberra B2	Brenzett Aeronautical Museum	
WH665	EE Canberra T17 (8763M) [J]	*Submerged at Tidenham, Glos, 2006*	
WH725	EE Canberra B2	Imperial War Museum, Duxford	
WH734	EE Canberra B2(mod) <ff>	Privately owned, Pershore	
WH739	EE Canberra B2 <ff>	No 2475 Sqn ATC, Ammanford, Dyfed	
WH740	EE Canberra T17 (8762M) [K]	East Midlands Airport Aeropark	
WH773	EE Canberra PR7 (8696M)	Gatwick Aviation Museum, Charlwood, Surrey	
WH775	EE Canberra PR7 (8128M/8868M) <ff>	Privately owned, Welshpool	
WH779	EE Canberra PR7 <ff>	East Midlands Airport Aeropark	
WH779	EE Canberra PR7 [BP] <rf>	RAF, stored Shawbury	

Notes	Serial	Type (code/other identity)	Owner/operator, location or fate
	WH791	EE Canberra PR7 (8165M/8176M/8187M)	Newark Air Museum, Winthorpe
	WH840	EE Canberra T4 (8350M)	Privately owned, Flixton
	WH846	EE Canberra T4	Yorkshire Air Museum, Elvington
	WH850	EE Canberra T4 <ff>	Privately owned, Narborough
	WH863	EE Canberra T17 (8693M) [CP] <ff>	Newark Air Museum, Winthorpe
	WH876	EE Canberra B2(mod) <ff>	Boscombe Down Aviation Collection
	WH887	EE Canberra TT18 [847] <ff>	Privately owned, Crondall, Hants
	WH903	EE Canberra B2 <ff>	Yorkshire Air Museum, Elvington
	WH904	EE Canberra T19	Newark Air Museum, Winthorpe
	WH953	EE Canberra B6(mod) <ff>	Blyth Valley Aviation Collection, Walpole, Suffolk
	WH957	EE Canberra E15 (8869M) <ff>	Lincolnshire Avn Heritage Centre, East Kirkby
	WH960	EE Canberra B15 (8344M) <ff>	Rolls-Royce Heritage Trust, Derby
	WH964	EE Canberra E15 (8870M) <ff>	Privately owned, Lewes
	WH984	EE Canberra B15 (8101M) <ff>	City of Norwich Aviation Museum
	WH991	WS51 Dragonfly HR3	Yorkshire Helicopter Preservation Group, Elvington
	WJ231	Hawker Sea Fury FB11 (*WE726*) [115/O]	FAA Museum, Yeovilton
	WJ306	Slingsby T21B Sedbergh TX1 (BGA3240) [FGB]	Privately owned, Weston-on-the-Green
	WJ358	Auster AOP6 (G-ARYD)	Museum of Army Flying, Middle Wallop
	WJ368	Auster AOP6 (G-ASZX)	Privately owned, Eggesford
	WJ565	EE Canberra T17 (8871M) <ff>	Aeroventure, Doncaster
	WJ567	EE Canberra B2 <ff>	Privately owned, Houghton, Cambs
	WJ576	EE Canberra T17 <ff>	Boulton Paul Association, Wolverhampton
	WJ581	EE Canberra PR7 <ff>	Privately owned, Canterbury
	WJ633	EE Canberra T17 <ff>	City of Norwich Aviation Museum
	WJ639	EE Canberra TT18 [39]	North-East Aircraft Museum, Usworth
	WJ640	EE Canberra B2 (8722M) <ff>	*Currently not known*
	WJ676	EE Canberra B2 (7796M) <ff>	Privately owned, South Shields
	WJ677	EE Canberra B2 <ff>	Privately owned, Redruth
	WJ717	EE Canberra TT18 (9052M) <ff>	RAF St Athan, Fire Section
	WJ721	EE Canberra TT18 [21] <ff>	No 2405 Det Flt ATC, Gairloch
	WJ731	EE Canberra B2T [BK] <ff>	Privately owned, Golders Green
	WJ821	EE Canberra PR7 (8668M)	Army, Bassingbourn, on display
	WJ865	EE Canberra T4	Boscombe Down Aviation Collection
	WJ866	EE Canberra T4	MoD, Bicester
	WJ880	EE Canberra T4 (8491M) <ff>	Dumfries & Galloway Avn Mus, Dumfries
	WJ903	Vickers Varsity T1 <ff>	Aeroventure, Doncaster
	WJ945	Vickers Varsity T1 (G-BEDV) [21]	Imperial War Museum, Duxford
	WJ975	EE Canberra T19 <ff>	Aeroventure, Doncaster
	WJ992	EE Canberra T4	Bournemouth Airport, Fire Section
	WK001	Thales Watchkeeper UAV	Thales, for Army
	WK002	Thales Watchkeeper UAV	Thales, for Army
	WK003	Thales Watchkeeper UAV	Thales, for Army
	WK004	Thales Watchkeeper UAV	Thales, for Army
	WK005	Thales Watchkeeper UAV	Thales, for Army
	WK006	Thales Watchkeeper UAV	Thales, for Army
	WK007	Thales Watchkeeper UAV	Thales, for Army
	WK008	Thales Watchkeeper UAV	Thales, for Army
	WK009	Thales Watchkeeper UAV	Thales, for Army
	WK010	Thales Watchkeeper UAV	Thales, for Army
	WK011	Thales Watchkeeper UAV	Thales, for Army
	WK012	Thales Watchkeeper UAV	Thales, for Army
	WK013	Thales Watchkeeper UAV	Thales, for Army
	WK014	Thales Watchkeeper UAV	Thales, for Army
	WK015	Thales Watchkeeper UAV	Thales, for Army
	WK016	Thales Watchkeeper UAV	Thales, for Army
	WK017	Thales Watchkeeper UAV	Thales, for Army
	WK018	Thales Watchkeeper UAV	Thales, for Army
	WK019	Thales Watchkeeper UAV	Thales, for Army
	WK020	Thales Watchkeeper UAV	Thales, for Army
	WK021	Thales Watchkeeper UAV	Thales, for Army
	WK022	Thales Watchkeeper UAV	Thales, for Army
	WK023	Thales Watchkeeper UAV	Thales, for Army
	WK024	Thales Watchkeeper UAV	Thales, for Army
	WK025	Thales Watchkeeper UAV	Thales, for Army

Serial	*Type (code/other identity)*	*Owner/operator, location or fate*	*Notes*
WK026	Thales Watchkeeper UAV	Thales, for Army	
WK027	Thales Watchkeeper UAV	Thales, for Army	
WK028	Thales Watchkeeper UAV	Thales, for Army	
WK029	Thales Watchkeeper UAV	Thales, for Army	
WK030	Thales Watchkeeper UAV	Thales, for Army	
WK031	Thales Watchkeeper UAV	Thales, for Army	
WK032	Thales Watchkeeper UAV	Thales, for Army	
WK033	Thales Watchkeeper UAV	Thales, for Army	
WK034	Thales Watchkeeper UAV	Thales, for Army	
WK035	Thales Watchkeeper UAV	Thales, for Army	
WK036	Thales Watchkeeper UAV	Thales, for Army	
WK037	Thales Watchkeeper UAV	Thales, for Army	
WK038	Thales Watchkeeper UAV	Thales, for Army	
WK039	Thales Watchkeeper UAV	Thales, for Army	
WK040	Thales Watchkeeper UAV	Thales, for Army	
WK102	EE Canberra T17 (8780M) <ff>	Privately owned, Welshpool	
WK118	EE Canberra TT18 <ff>	Privately owned, Chipperfield, Herts	
WK122	EE Canberra TT18 <ff>	Hawker Hunter Aviation Ltd, Scampton	
WK124	EE Canberra TT18 (9093M) [CR]	MoD FSCTE, Manston	
WK126	EE Canberra TT18 (N2138J) [843]	Gloucestershire Avn Coll, stored Gloucester	
WK127	EE Canberra TT18 (8985M) <ff>	Privately owned, Peterborough	
WK146	EE Canberra B2 <ff>	Gatwick Aviation Museum, Charlwood, Surrey	
WK163	EE Canberra B2/6 (G-BVWC)	Air Atlantique Classic Flight, Coventry	
WK198	VS Swift F4 (7428M) (fuselage)	North-East Aircraft Museum, Usworth	
WK275	VS Swift F4	Privately owned, Upper Hill, nr Leominster	
WK277	VS Swift FR5 (7719M) [N]	Newark Air Museum, Winthorpe	
WK281	VS Swift FR5 (7712M) [S]	Tangmere Military Aviation Museum	
WK393	DH112 Venom FB1 <ff>	Aeroventure, Doncaster	
WK436	DH112 Venom FB50 (J-1614/G-VENM)	Kennet Aviation, North Weald	
WK512	DHC1 Chipmunk T10 (G-BXIM) [A]	Privately owned, Brize Norton	
WK514	DHC1 Chipmunk T10 (G-BBMO)	Privately owned, Wellesbourne Mountford	
WK517	DHC1 Chipmunk T10 (G-ULAS)	Privately owned, Denham	
WK518	DHC1 Chipmunk T10 [K]	RAF BBMF, Coningsby	
WK522	DHC1 Chipmunk T10 (G-BCOU)	Privately owned, Duxford	
WK549	DHC1 Chipmunk T10 (G-BTWF)	Privately owned, Breighton	
WK570	DHC1 Chipmunk T10 (8211M) <ff>	No 424 Sqn ATC, Solent Sky, Southampton	
WK576	DHC1 Chipmunk T10 (8357M) <ff>	No 1206 Sqn ATC, Lichfield	
WK577	DHC1 Chipmunk T10 (G-BCYM)	Privately owned, Littel Rissington	
WK584	DHC1 Chipmunk T10 (7556M) <ff>	No 2008 Sqn ATC, Bawtry	
WK585	DHC1 Chipmunk T10 (9265M/G-BZGA)	Privately owned, Duxford	
WK586	DHC1 Chipmunk T10 (G-BXGX) [V]	Privately owned, Slinfold	
WK590	DHC1 Chipmunk T10 (G-BWVZ) [69]	Privately owned, Spanhoe	
WK608	DHC1 Chipmunk T10 [906]	RN Historic Flight, Yeovilton	
WK609	DHC1 Chipmunk T10 (G-BXDN) [93]	Privately owned, Booker	
WK611	DHC1 Chipmunk T10 (G-ARWB)	Privately owned, Thruxton	
WK620	DHC1 Chipmunk T10 [T] (fuselage)	Privately owned, Twyford, Bucks	
WK622	DHC1 Chipmunk T10 (G-BCZH)	Privately owned, Horsford	
WK624	DHC1 Chipmunk T10 (G-BWHI)	Privately owned, Woodvale	
WK626	DHC1 Chipmunk T10 (8213M) <ff>	Aeroventure, stored Doncaster	
WK628	DHC1 Chipmunk T10 (G-BBMW)	Privately owned, Goodwood	
WK630	DHC1 Chipmunk T10 (G-BXDG)	Privately owned, Felthorpe	
WK633	DHC1 Chipmunk T10 (G-BXEC) [A]	Privately owned, Redhill	
WK638	DHC1 Chipmunk T10 (G-BWJZ) (fuselage)	Privately owned, Eccleshall, Staffs	
WK640	DHC1 Chipmunk T10 (G-BWUV) [C]	Privately owned, Bagby	
WK642	DHC1 Chipmunk T10 (G-BXDP) [94]	Privately owned, Kilrush, Eire	
WK654	Gloster Meteor F8 (8092M) [B]	City of Norwich Aviation Museum	
WK800	Gloster Meteor D16 [Z]	MoD/QinetiQ, Boscombe Down (wfu)	
WK864	Gloster Meteor F8 (WL168/7750M) [C]	Yorkshire Air Museum, Elvington	
WK935	Gloster Meteor Prone Pilot (7869M)	RAF Museum, Cosford	

Notes	*Serial*	*Type (code/other identity)*	*Owner/operator, location or fate*
	WK991	Gloster Meteor F8 (7825M)	Imperial War Museum, Duxford
	WL131	Gloster Meteor F8 (7751M) <ff>	Aeroventure, Doncaster
	WL181	Gloster Meteor F8 [X]	North-East Aircraft Museum, Usworth
	WL332	Gloster Meteor T7 [888]	Privately owned, Long Marston
	WL345	Gloster Meteor T7	St Leonard's Motors, Hollington, E Sussex
	WL349	Gloster Meteor T7 [Z]	Gloucestershire Airport, Staverton, on display
	WL375	Gloster Meteor T7(mod)	Dumfries & Galloway Avn Mus, Dumfries
	WL405	Gloster Meteor T7	Meteor Flight, Yatesbury
	WL419	Gloster Meteor T7	Martin Baker Aircraft, Chalgrove
	WL505	DH100 Vampire FB9 (7705M/G-FBIX)	Privately owned, Bournemouth
	WL505	DH100 Vampire FB6 (J-1167/*VZ304*/G-MKVI)	Privately owned, Wickenby
	WL626	Vickers Varsity T1 (G-BHDD) [P]	East Midlands Airport Aeropark
	WL627	Vickers Varsity T1 (8488M) [D] <ff>	Privately owned, Preston, E Yorkshire
	WL679	Vickers Varsity T1 (9155M)	RAF Museum, Cosford
	WL732	BP P108 Sea Balliol T21	RAF Museum, Cosford
	WL795	Avro 696 Shackleton MR2C (8753M) [T]	RAF St Mawgan, on display
	WL798	Avro 696 Shackleton MR2C (8114M) <ff>	Privately owned, Elgin
	WM145	AW Meteor NF11 <ff>	Privately owned, Gatenby, Lincs
	WM167	AW Meteor NF11 (G-LOSM)	Air Atlantique Classic Flight, Coventry
	WM267	AW Meteor NF11 <ff>	City of Norwich Aviation Museum
	WM292	AW Meteor TT20 [841]	FAA Museum, stored RNAS Yeovilton
	WM311	AW Meteor TT20 (WM224/8177M)	East Midlands Airport Aeropark
	WM366	AW Meteor NF13 (4X-FNA) (comp VZ462)	SWWAPS, Lasham
	WM367	AW Meteor NF13 <ff>	Jet Avn Preservation Grp, Long Marston
	WM571	DH112 Sea Venom FAW21 [VL]	Solent Sky, stored, Romsey
	WM729	DH113 Vampire NF10 <ff>	Mosquito Aircraft Museum, London Colney
	WM913	Hawker Sea Hawk FB5 (8162M) [456/J]	Newark Air Museum, Winthorpe
	WM961	Hawker Sea Hawk FB5 [J]	Caernarfon Air World
	WM969	Hawker Sea Hawk FB5 [10/Z]	Imperial War Museum, Duxford
	WN105	Hawker Sea Hawk FB3 (WF299/8164M)	Privately owned, Birlingham, Worcs
	WN108	Hawker Sea Hawk FB5 [033]	Ulster Aviation Society, Langford Lodge
	WN149	BP P108 Balliol T2	Boulton Paul Association, Wolverhampton
	WN411	Fairey Gannet AS1 (fuselage)	Privately owned, Sholing, Hants
	WN493	WS51 Dragonfly HR5	FAA Museum, RNAS Yeovilton
	WN499	WS51 Dragonfly HR5	Aeroventure, Doncaster
	WN516	BP P108 Balliol T2 <ff>	North-East Aircraft Museum, Usworth
	WN534	BP P108 Balliol T2 <ff>	Boulton Paul Association, Wolverhampton
	WN890	Hawker Hunter F2 <ff>	Air Defence Collection, Boscombe Down
	WN904	Hawker Hunter F2 (7544M) [3]	RE 39 Regt, Waterbeach, on display
	WN907	Hawker Hunter F2 (7416M) <ff>	Robertsbridge Aviation Society, Newhaven
	WN957	Hawker Hunter F5 <ff>	Privately owned, Stockport
	WP185	Hawker Hunter F5 (7583M)	Privately owned, Great Dunmow, Essex
	WP190	Hawker Hunter F5 (7582M/8473M/*WP180*) [K]	Tangmere Military Aviation Museum
	WP255	DH113 Vampire NF10 <ff>	Aeroventure, Doncaster
	WP270	EoN Eton TX1 (8598M)	RAF Museum Reserve Collection, Stafford
	WP308	Percival P57 Sea Prince T1 (G-GACA) [572/CU]	Gatwick Aviation Museum, Charlwood, Surrey
	WP313	Percival P57 Sea Prince T1 [568/CU]	FAA Museum, stored RNAS Yeovilton
	WP314	Percival P57 Sea Prince T1 (8634M) [573/CU]	Privately owned, Carlisle Airport
	WP321	Percival P57 Sea Prince T1 (G-BRFC) [750/CU]	Privately owned, Bournemouth
	WP772	DHC1 Chipmunk T10 [Q] (wreck)	RAF Manston History Museum
	WP784	DHC1 Chipmunk T10 <ff>	Privately owned, Twyford
	WP788	DHC1 Chipmunk T10 (G-BCHL)	Privately owned, Sleap
	WP790	DHC1 Chipmunk T10 (G-BBNC) [T]	Mosquito Aircraft Museum, London Colney

Serial	*Type (code/other identity)*	*Owner/operator, location or fate*	*Notes*
WP795	DHC1 Chipmunk T10 (G-BVZZ) [901]	Privately owned, Lee-on-Solent	
WP800	DHC1 Chipmunk T10 (G-BCXN) [2]	Privately owned, Halton	
WP803	DHC1 Chipmunk T10 (G-HAPY) [G]	Privately owned, Booker	
WP805	DHC1 Chipmunk T10 (G-MAJR) [D]	Privately owned, Lee-on-Solent	
WP808	DHC1 Chipmunk T10 (G-BDEU)	Privately owned, Hurstbourne Tarrant, Hants	
WP809	DHC1 Chipmunk T10 (G-BVTX) [78]	Privately owned, Husbands Bosworth	
WP833	DHC1 Chipmunk T10 (G-BZDU) [H]	Privately owned, Newcastle	
WP835	DHC1 Chipmunk T10 (D-ERTY)	Privately owned, The Netherlands	
WP839	DHC1 Chipmunk T10 (G-BZXE) [A]	*Sold to Australia, February 2008*	
WP840	DHC1 Chipmunk T10 (G-BXDM) [9]	Privately owned, Halton	
WP844	DHC1 Chipmunk T10 (G-BWOX) [85]	Privately owned, Shobdon	
WP857	DHC1 Chipmunk T10 (G-BDRJ) [24]	Privately owned, Prestwick	
WP859	DHC1 Chipmunk T10 (G-BXCP) [E]	Privately owned, Spanhoe	
WP860	DHC1 Chipmunk T10 (G-BXDA) [6]	Privately owned, Kirknewton	
WP863	DHC1 Chipmunk T10 (8360M/G-ATJI) <ff>	No 1011 Sqn ATC, Boscombe Down	
WP869	DHC1 Chipmunk T10 (8215M) <ff>	Privately owned, Rush Green	
WP870	DHC1 Chipmunk T10 (G-BCOI) [12]	Privately owned, Rayne Hall Farm, Essex	
WP896	DHC1 Chipmunk T10 (G-BWVY)	Privately owned, White Waltham	
WP901	DHC1 Chipmunk T10 (G-BWNT) [B]	Privately owned, East Midlands Airport	
WP903	DHC1 Chipmunk T10 (G-BCGC)	Privately owned, Henlow	
WP912	DHC1 Chipmunk T10 (8467M)	RAF Museum, Cosford	
WP921	DHC1 Chipmunk T10 (G-ATJJ) <ff>	Privately owned, Brooklands	
WP925	DHC1 Chipmunk T10 (G-BXHA) [C]	Privately owned, Seppe, The Netherlands	
WP927	DHC1 Chipmunk T10 (8216M/G-ATJK) <ff>	Privately owned, St Neots, Cambs	
WP928	DHC1 Chipmunk T10 (G-BXGM) [D]	Privately owned, Shoreham	
WP929	DHC1 Chipmunk T10 (G-BXCV) [F]	Privately owned, Duxford	
WP930	DHC1 Chipmunk T10 (G-BXHF) [J]	Privately owned, Redhill	
WP962	DHC1 Chipmunk T10 (9287M) [C]	RAF Museum, Hendon	
WP971	DHC1 Chipmunk T10 (G-ATHD)	Privately owned, Denham	
WP977	DHC1 Chipmunk T10 (G-BHRD) <ff>	Privately owned, Yateley, Hants	
WP983	DHC1 Chipmunk T10 (G-BXNN) [B]	Privately owned, Eggesford	
WP984	DHC1 Chipmunk T10 (G-BWTO) [H]	Privately owned, Little Gransden	
WR360	DH112 Venom FB50 (J-1626/G-DHSS) [K]	Privately owned, Bournemouth	
WR410	DH112 Venom FB50 (J-1539/G-DHUU/*WE410*)	Privately owned, Bournemouth	
WR410	DH112 Venom FB54 (J-1790/G-BLKA) [N]	Mosquito Aircraft Museum, London Colney	
WR421	DH112 Venom FB50 (J-1611/G-DHTT)	Privately owned, Bournemouth	
WR470	DH112 Venom FB50 (J-1542/G-DHVM)	Air Atlantique Classic Flight, Coventry	
WR539	DH112 Venom FB4 (8399M) <ff>	Mosquito Aircraft Museum, London Colney	
WR960	Avro 696 Shackleton AEW2 (8772M)	Gr Manchester Mus of Science & Industry	
WR963	Avro 696 Shackleton AEW2	Air Atlantique Classic Flight, Coventry	
WR971	Avro 696 Shackleton MR3 (8119M) [Q]	Fenland & W Norfolk Aviation Museum, Wisbech	
WR974	Avro 696 Shackleton MR3 (8117M) [K]	Gatwick Aviation Museum, Charlwood, Surrey	
WR977	Avro 696 Shackleton MR3 (8186M) [B]	Newark Air Museum, Winthorpe	
WR982	Avro 696 Shackleton MR3 (8106M) [J]	Gatwick Aviation Museum, Charlwood, Surrey	
WR985	Avro 696 Shackleton MR3 (8103M) [H]	Privately owned, Long Marston	
WS103	Gloster Meteor T7 [709/VL]	FAA Museum, stored RNAS Yeovilton	
WS692	Gloster Meteor NF12 (7605M) [C]	Newark Air Museum, Winthorpe	
WS726	Gloster Meteor NF14 (7960M) [H]	No 1855 Sqn ATC, Royton, Gr Manchester	
WS739	Gloster Meteor NF14 (7961M)	Newark Air Museum, Winthorpe	
WS760	Gloster Meteor NF14 (7964M)	Meteor Flight, stored Yatesbury	
WS776	Gloster Meteor NF14 (7716M) [K]	Privately owned, Bournemouth	

Notes	*Serial*	*Type (code/other identity)*	*Owner/operator, location or fate*
	WS788	Gloster Meteor NF14 (7967M) [Z]	Yorkshire Air Museum, Elvington
	WS792	Gloster Meteor NF14 (7965M) [K]	Brighouse Bay Caravan Park, Borgue, D&G
	WS807	Gloster Meteor NF14 (7973M) [N]	Gloucestershire Avn Coll, stored Gloucester
	WS832	Gloster Meteor NF14	Solway Aviation Society, Carlisle
	WS838	Gloster Meteor NF14	Midland Air Museum, Coventry
	WS843	Gloster Meteor NF14 (7937M) [J]	RAF Museum, Cosford
	WT121	Douglas Skyraider AEW1 [415/CU]	FAA Museum, stored RNAS Yeovilton
	WT205	EE Canberra B15 <ff>	RAF Manston History Museum
	WT308	EE Canberra B(I)6	RN, Predannack Fire School
	WT309	EE Canberra B(I)6 <ff>	Farnborough Air Sciences Trust, Farnborough
	WT319	EE Canberra B(I)6 <ff>	Bentwaters Cold War Air Museum
	WT333	EE Canberra B6(mod) (G-BVXC)	Privately owned, Bruntingthorpe
	WT339	EE Canberra B(I)8 (8198M)	RAF Barkston Heath Fire Section
	WT483	EE Canberra T4 [83]	Privately owned, Long Marston
	WT486	EE Canberra T4 (8102M) <ff>	Privately owned, Newtownards
	WT507	EE Canberra PR7 (8131M/8548M) [44] <ff>	No 384 Sqn ATC, Mansfield
	WT520	EE Canberra PR7 (8094M/8184M) <ff>	No 967 Sqn ATC, Warton
	WT525	EE Canberra T22 <ff>	Privately owned, RAF Wyton
	WT532	EE Canberra PR7 (8728M/8890M) <ff>	Privately owned, Bournemouth
	WT534	EE Canberra PR7 (8549M) [43] <ff>	Aeroventure, Doncaster
	WT536	EE Canberra PR7 (8063M) <ff>	Privately owned, Shirrell Heath, Hants
	WT537	EE Canberra PR7	BAE Systems Samlesbury, at main gate
	WT555	Hawker Hunter F1 (7499M)	Vanguard Haulage, Greenford, London
	WT569	Hawker Hunter F1 (7491M)	No 2117 Sqn ATC, Kenfig Hill, Mid-Glamorgan
	WT612	Hawker Hunter F1 (7496M)	RAF Henlow, on display
	WT619	Hawker Hunter F1 (7525M)	Gr Manchester Mus of Science & Industry
	WT648	Hawker Hunter F1 (7530M) <ff>	Air Defence Collection, Boscombe Down
	WT651	Hawker Hunter F1 (7532M)	Newark Air Museum, Winthorpe
	WT660	Hawker Hunter F1 (7421M) [C]	Privately owned, Beauly, Highland
	WT680	Hawker Hunter F1 (7533M) [J]	Privately owned, Holbeach, Lincs
	WT684	Hawker Hunter F1 (7422M) <ff>	Bentwaters Cold War Air Museum
	WT694	Hawker Hunter F1 (7510M)	Caernarfon Air World
	WT711	Hawker Hunter GA11 [833/DD]	Air Atlantique Classic Flight, Coventry
	WT720	Hawker Hunter F51 (RDAF E-408/8565M) [B]	Privately owned, North Scarle, Lincs
	WT722	Hawker Hunter T8C (G-BWGN) [878/VL]	Air Atlantique Classic Flight, Coventry
	WT723	Hawker Hunter PR11 (G-PRII) [866/VL,3]	Hunter Flying Ltd, Exeter
	WT741	Hawker Hunter GA11 <ff>	*Currently not known*
	WT744	Hawker Hunter GA11 [868/VL]	Privately owned
	WT799	Hawker Hunter T8C [879]	Blue Lagoon Diving Centre, Womersley, Yorks
	WT804	Hawker Hunter GA11 [831/DD]	FETC, Moreton-in-Marsh, Glos
	WT806	Hawker Hunter GA11	Northbrook College, Shoreham Airport
	WT859	Supermarine 544 <ff>	Boscombe Down Aviation Collection
	WT867	Slingsby T31B Cadet TX3	Privately owned, Eaglescott
	WT877	Slingsby T31B Cadet TX3	Air Training Heritage Collection, Wolverhampton
	WT899	Slingsby T31B Cadet TX3	Privately owned, stored Swindon
	WT900	Slingsby T31B Cadet TX3 (BGA33372)	Privately owned, Lee-on-Solent
	WT905	Slingsby T31B Cadet TX3	Privately owned, Keevil
	WT908	Slingsby T31B Cadet TX3 (BGA3487)	Privately owned, Dunstable
	WT910	Slingsby T31B Cadet TX3 (BGA3953)	Privately owned, Llantisilio
	WT914	Slingsby T31B Cadet TX3 (BGA3194) (fuselage)	Privately owned, Tibenham
	WT933	Bristol 171 Sycamore 3 (G-ALSW/7709M)	Newark Air Museum, Winthorpe
	WV106	Douglas Skyraider AEW1 [427/C]	FAA Museum, stored RNAS Yeovilton

Serial	Type (code/other identity)	Owner/operator, location or fate	Notes
WV198	Sikorsky S55 Whirlwind HAR21 (G-BJWY) [K]	Solway Aviation Society, Carlisle	
WV318	Hawker Hunter T7B (9236M/G-FFOX)	Delta Jets, Kemble	
WV322	Hawker Hunter T8C (G-BZSE/9096M) [Y]	Hunter Flying Ltd, Exeter	
WV332	Hawker Hunter F4 (7673M) <ff>	Tangmere Military Aircraft Museum	
WV372	Hawker Hunter T7 (G-BXFI) [R]	Privately owned, Kemble	
WV381	Hawker Hunter GA11 [732/VL] <ff>	Privately owned, Kemble	
WV382	Hawker Hunter GA11 [830/VL]	Jet Avn Preservation Grp, Long Marston	
WV383	Hawker Hunter T7	Farnborough Air Sciences Trust, Farnborough	
WV396	Hawker Hunter T8C (9249M) [91]	RAF Valley, at main gate	
WV486	Percival P56 Provost T1 (7694M) [N-D]	Privately owned, Thatcham, Berks	
WV493	Percival P56 Provost T1 (G-BDYG/7696M) [29]	Royal Scottish Mus'm of Flight, stored E Fortune	
WV499	Percival P56 Provost T1 (G-BZRF/7698M) [P-G]	Privately owned, Westonzoyland, Somerset	
WV562	Percival P56 Provost T1 (7606M) [P-C]	RAF Museum, Cosford	
WV605	Percival P56 Provost T1 [T-B]	Norfolk & Suffolk Avn Museum, Flixton	
WV606	Percival P56 Provost T1 (7622M) [P-B]	Newark Air Museum, Winthorpe	
WV679	Percival P56 Provost T1 (7615M) [O-J]	Wellesbourne Wartime Museum	
WV705	Percival P66 Pembroke C1 <ff>	Privately owned, Awbridge, Hants	
WV740	Percival P66 Pembroke C1 (G-BNPH)	Privately owned, Bournemouth	
WV746	Percival P66 Pembroke C1 (8938M)	RAF Museum, Cosford	
WV781	Bristol 171 Sycamore HR12 (G-ALTD/7839M)	Caernarfon Air World	
WV783	Bristol 171 Sycamore HR12 (G-ALSP/7841M)	RAF Museum, Hendon	
WV787	EE Canberra B2/8 (8799M)	Newark Air Museum, Winthorpe	
WV795	Hawker Sea Hawk FGA6 (8151M)	Privately owned, Dunsfold	
WV797	Hawker Sea Hawk FGA6 (8155M) [491/J]	Midland Air Museum, Coventry	
WV798	Hawker Sea Hawk FGA6 [026/CU]	SWWAPS, Lasham	
WV838	Hawker Sea Hawk FGA4 [182] <ff>	Privately owned, Liverpool	
WV856	Hawker Sea Hawk FGA6 [163]	FAA Museum, RNAS Yeovilton	
WV903	Hawker Sea Hawk FGA4 (8153M) [128/C]	Privately owned, Ilminster, Somerset	
WV908	Hawker Sea Hawk FGA6 (8154M) [188/A]	RN Historic Flight, Yeovilton	
WV910	Hawker Sea Hawk FGA6 <ff>	Boscombe Down Aviation Collection	
WV911	Hawker Sea Hawk FGA4 [115/C]	RN Historic Flight, stored Yeovilton	
WW138	DH112 Sea Venom FAW22 [227/Z]	FAA Museum, stored RNAS Yeovilton	
WW145	DH112 Sea Venom FAW22 [680/LM]	Royal Scottish Mus'm of Flight, E Fortune	
WW217	DH112 Sea Venom FAW22 [351]	Newark Air Museum, Winthorpe	
WW388	Percival P56 Provost T1 (7616M) [O-F]	Shropshire Wartime Aircraft Recovery Grp, Sleap	
WW421	Percival P56 Provost T1 (WW450/G-BZRE/7689M) [P-B]	Privately owned, Bournemouth	
WW442	Percival P56 Provost T1 (7618M) [N]	Gatwick Aviation Museum, Charlwood, Surrey	
WW444	Percival P56 Provost T1 [D]	Privately owned, Brownhills, Staffs	
WW447	Percival P56 Provost T1	Privately owned, Grazeley, Berks	
WW453	Percival P56 Provost T1 (G-TMKI) [W-S]	Privately owned, Westonzoyland, Somerset	
WW654	Hawker Hunter GA11 [834/DD]	Privately owned, Ford, W Sussex	
WW664	Hawker Hunter F4 <ff>	Privately owned, Newark	
WX788	DH112 Venom NF3	Aeroventure, Doncaster	
WX853	DH112 Venom NF3 (7443M)	Mosquito Aircraft Museum, London Colney	
WX905	DH112 Venom NF3 (7458M)	Newark Air Museum, Winthorpe	
WZ425	DH115 Vampire T11	Privately owned, Birlingham, Worcs	
WZ450	DH115 Vampire T11 <ff>	Privately owned, Headcorn	

Notes	Serial	Type (code/other identity)	Owner/operator, location or fate
	WZ507	DH115 Vampire T11 (G-VTII) [74]	Vampire Preservation Group, North Weald
	WZ515	DH115 Vampire T11 [60]	Solway Aviation Society, Carlisle
	WZ518	DH115 Vampire T11	North-East Aircraft Museum, Usworth
	WZ549	DH115 Vampire T11 (8118M) [F]	Ulster Aviation Society, Langford Lodge
	WZ553	DH115 Vampire T11 (G-DHYY) [40]	Air Atlantique Classic Flight, Coventry
	WZ557	DH115 Vampire T11	Highland Aviation Museum, Inverness
	WZ572	DH115 Vampire T11 (8124M) [65] <ff>	Privately owned, Sholing, Hants
	WZ581	DH115 Vampire T11 <ff>	The Vampire Collection, Hemel Hempstead
	WZ584	DH115 Vampire T11 (G-BZRC) [K]	Privately owned, Martham, Norfolk
	WZ589	DH115 Vampire T11 [19]	Privately owned, Rochester
	WZ589	DH115 Vampire T55 (U-1230/LN-DHZ)	Privately owned, Norway
	WZ590	DH115 Vampire T11 [19]	Imperial War Museum, Duxford
	WZ662	Auster AOP9 (G-BKVK)	Privately owned, Eggesford
	WZ706	Auster AOP9 (7851M/G-BURR)	Privately owned, Middle Wallop
	WZ711	Auster AOP9/Beagle E3 (G-AVHT)	Privately owned, Spanhoe
	WZ721	Auster AOP9	Museum of Army Flying, Middle Wallop
	WZ724	Auster AOP9 (7432M)	AAC Middle Wallop, at main gate
	WZ729	Auster AOP9 (G-BXON)	Privately owned, Newark-on-Trent
	WZ736	Avro 707A (7868M)	Gr Manchester Mus of Science & Industry
	WZ744	Avro 707C (7932M)	RAF Museum, Cosford
	WZ753	Slingsby T38 Grasshopper TX1	Solent Sky, Southampton
	WZ755	Slingsby T38 Grasshopper TX1 (BGA3481)	Air Training Heritage Collection, Wolverhampton
	WZ757	Slingsby T38 Grasshopper TX1 (comp XK820)	Privately owned, Kirton-in-Lindsey, Lincs
	WZ767	Slingsby T38 Grasshopper TX1	North-East Aircraft Museum, stored Usworth
	WZ772	Slingsby T38 Grasshopper TX1	Trenchard Museum, RAF Halton
	WZ773	Slingsby T38 Grasshopper TX1	Edinburgh Academy
	WZ784	Slingsby T38 Grasshopper TX1	Privately owned, Dirleton, East Lothian
	WZ791	Slingsby T38 Grasshopper TX1 (8944M)	RAF Museum, Hendon
	WZ792	Slingsby T38 Grasshopper TX1	Privately owned, Sproughton
	WZ793	Slingsby T38 Grasshopper TX1	Privately owned, Keevil
	WZ796	Slingsby T38 Grasshopper TX1	Privately owned, stored Nympsfield
	WZ798	Slingsby T38 Grasshopper TX1	Privately owned, Bournemouth
	WZ816	Slingsby T38 Grasshopper TX1 (BGA3979)	Privately owned, Redhill
	WZ818	Slingsby T38 Grasshopper TX1 (BGA4361)	Privately owned, Nympsfield
	WZ819	Slingsby T38 Grasshopper TX1 (BGA3498)	Privately owned, Halton
	WZ820	Slingsby T38 Grasshopper TX1	Sywell Aviation Museum
	WZ822	Slingsby T38 Grasshopper TX1	Aeroventure, stored Doncaster
	WZ824	Slingsby T38 Grasshopper TX1	Solway Aviation Society, Carlisle
	WZ826	Vickers Valiant B(K)1 (XD826/7872M) <ff>	Privately owned, Rayleigh, Essex
	WZ828	Slingsby T38 Grasshopper TX1 (BGA4421)	Privately owned, Hullavington
	WZ831	Slingsby T38 Grasshopper TX1	Privately owned, stored Nympsfield, Glos
	WZ846	DHC1 Chipmunk T10 (G-BCSC/8439M)	No 2427 Sqn ATC, Biggin Hill
	WZ847	DHC1 Chipmunk T10 (G-CPMK) [F]	Privately owned, Sleap
	WZ869	DHC1 Chipmunk T10 (8019M) <ff>	Privately owned, South Molton, Devon
	WZ872	DHC1 Chipmunk T10 (G-BZGB) [E]	Privately owned, Newcastle
	WZ876	DHC1 Chipmunk T10 (G-BBWN) <ff>	Privately owned, Yateley, Hants
	WZ879	DHC1 Chipmunk T10 (G-BWUT) [X]	Privately owned, Duxford
	WZ882	DHC1 Chipmunk T10 (G-BXGP) [K]	Privately owned, Eaglescott
	XA109	DH115 Sea Vampire T22	Royal Scottish Mus'm of Flight, E Fortune
	XA127	DH115 Sea Vampire T22 <ff>	FAA Museum, RNAS Yeovilton
	XA129	DH115 Sea Vampire T22	FAA Museum, stored RNAS Yeovilton
	XA225	Slingsby T38 Grasshopper TX1	Privately owned, Upavon
	XA226	Slingsby T38 Grasshopper TX1	Norfolk & Suffolk Avn Museum, Flixton
	XA228	Slingsby T38 Grasshopper TX1	Royal Scottish Mus'm of Flight, stored E Fortune
	XA230	Slingsby T38 Grasshopper TX1 (BGA4098)	Privately owned, Henlow

Serial	Type (code/other identity)	Owner/operator, location or fate	Notes
XA231	Slingsby T38 Grasshopper TX1 (8888M)	RAF Manston History Museum	
XA240	Slingsby T38 Grasshopper TX1 (BGA4556)	Privately owned, Keevil	
XA241	Slingsby T38 Grasshopper TX1	Shuttleworth Collection, Old Warden	
XA243	Slingsby T38 Grasshopper TX1 (8886M)	Privately owned, Gransden Lodge, Cambs	
XA244	Slingsby T38 Grasshopper TX1	Privately owned, Keevil	
XA282	Slingsby T31B Cadet TX3	Caernarfon Air World	
XA289	Slingsby T31B Cadet TX3	Privately owned, Eaglescott	
XA290	Slingsby T31B Cadet TX3	Privately owned, stored Rufforth	
XA293	Slingsby T31B Cadet TX3 <ff>	Privately owned, Breighton	
XA295	Slingsby T31B Cadet TX3 (BGA3336)	Privately owned, Aston Down	
XA302	Slingsby T31B Cadet TX3 (BGA3786)	RAF Museum, Hendon	
XA310	Slingsby T31B Cadet TX3 (BGA4963)	Privately owned, Keevil	
XA459	Fairey Gannet ECM6 [E]	Privately owned, White Waltham	
XA460	Fairey Gannet ECM6 [768/BY]	Aeroventure, Doncaster	
XA466	Fairey Gannet COD4 [777/LM]	FAA Museum, stored Yeovilton	
XA508	Fairey Gannet T2 [627/GN]	FAA Museum, at Midland Air Museum, Coventry	
XA564	Gloster Javelin FAW1 (7464M)	RAF Museum, Cosford	
XA634	Gloster Javelin FAW4 (7641M)	RAF Leeming, on display	
XA699	Gloster Javelin FAW5 (7809M)	Midland Air Museum, Coventry	
XA847	EE P1B (8371M)	Privately owned, Stowmarket, Suffolk	
XA862	WS55 Whirlwind HAR1 (G-AMJT) <ff>	Yorkshire Helicopter Preservation Group, Elvington	
XA864	WS55 Whirlwind HAR1	FAA Museum, stored Yeovilton	
XA870	WS55 Whirlwind HAR1 [911]	Aeroventure, Doncaster	
XA880	DH104 Devon C2 (G-BVXR)	Privately owned, Little Rissington	
XA893	Avro 698 Vulcan B1 (8591M) <ff>	RAF Museum, Cosford	
XA903	Avro 698 Vulcan B1 <ff>	Privately owned, Wellesbourne Mountford	
XA917	HP80 Victor B1 (7827M) <ff>	Privately owned, Cupar, Fife	
XB259	Blackburn B101 Beverley C1 (G-AOAI)	Fort Paull Armoury	
XB261	Blackburn B101 Beverley C1 <ff>	Newark Air Museum, Winthorpe	
XB446	Grumman TBM-3 Avenger ECM6B	FAA Museum, Yeovilton	
XB480	Hiller HT1 [537]	FAA Museum, stored Yeovilton	
XB812	Canadair CL-13 Sabre F4 (9227M) [U]	RAF Museum, Cosford	
XD145	Saro SR53	RAF Museum, Cosford	
XD163	WS55 Whirlwind HAR10 (8645M) [X]	The Helicopter Museum, Weston-super-Mare	
XD165	WS55 Whirlwind HAR10 (8673M)	Caernarfon Airfield Fire Section	
XD215	VS Scimitar F1 <ff>	Privately owned, Cheltenham	
XD235	VS Scimitar F1 <ff>	Privately owned, Ingatestone, Essex	
XD317	VS Scimitar F1 [112/R]	FAA Museum, RNAS Yeovilton	
XD332	VS Scimitar F1 [194/C]	Solent Sky, stored Romsey	
XD377	DH115 Vampire T11 (8203M) <ff>	Aeroventure, stored Doncaster	
XD382	DH115 Vampire T11 (8033M)	East Midlands Airport Aeropark	
XD425	DH115 Vampire T11 <ff>	RAF Millom Museum, Haverigg	
XD434	DH115 Vampire T11 [25]	Fenland & W Norfolk Aviation Museum, Wisbech	
XD445	DH115 Vampire T11 [51]	Privately owned, Abbots Bromley	
XD447	DH115 Vampire T11 [50]	Jet Avn Preservation Grp, Long Marston	
XD452	DH115 Vampire T11 (7990M) [66] <ff>	Privately owned, Dursley, Glos	
XD459	DH115 Vampire T11 [63] <ff>	Aeroventure, stored Doncaster	
XD506	DH115 Vampire T11 (7983M)	Gloucestershire Avn Coll, stored Gloucester	
XD515	DH115 Vampire T11 (7998M/*XM515*)	Privately owned, Rugeley, Staffs	
XD525	DH115 Vampire T11 (7882M) <ff>	*Scrapped*	
XD534	DH115 Vampire T11 [41]	East Midlands Airport Aeropark	
XD542	DH115 Vampire T11 (7604M) [N]	Montrose Air Station Heritage Centre	
XD547	DH115 Vampire T11 [Z] (composite)	Dumfries & Galloway Avn Mus, Dumfries	
XD593	DH115 Vampire T11 [50]	Newark Air Museum, Winthorpe	

Notes	*Serial*	*Type (code/other identity)*	*Owner/operator, location or fate*
	XD595	DH115 Vampire T11 <ff>	Privately owned, Glentham, Lincs
	XD596	DH115 Vampire T11 (7939M)	Solent Sky, Southampton
	XD599	DH115 Vampire T11 [A] <ff>	Sywell Aviation Museum
	XD602	DH115 Vampire T11 (7737M) (composite)	Privately owned, South Shields
	XD616	DH115 Vampire T11 [56]	Mosquito Aircraft Museum, stored Gloucester
	XD622	DH115 Vampire T11 (8160M)	No 2214 Sqn ATC, Usworth
	XD624	DH115 Vampire T11 [O]	Manchester Museum of Science & Industry, stored
	XD626	DH115 Vampire T11 [Q]	Midland Air Museum, Coventry
	XD674	Hunting Jet Provost T1 (7570M) [T]	RAF Museum, Cosford
	XD693	Hunting Jet Provost T1 (XM129/G-AOBU) [Z-Q]	Kennet Aviation, North Weald
	XD816	Vickers Valiant B(K)1 <ff>	Brooklands Museum, Weybridge
	XD818	Vickers Valiant B(K)1 (7894M)	RAF Museum, Cosford
	XD857	Vickers Valiant B(K)1 <ff>	Norfolk & Suffolk Aviation Museum, Flixton
	XD875	Vickers Valiant B(K)1 <ff>	Highland Aviation Museum, Inverness
	XE317	Bristol 171 Sycamore HR14 (G-AMWO) [S-N]	Aeroventure, stored Doncaster
	XE339	Hawker Sea Hawk FGA6 (8156M) [149/E]	Privately owned, Ilminster, Somerset
	XE340	Hawker Sea Hawk FGA6 [131/Z]	FAA Museum, at Montrose Air Station Heritage Centre
	XE368	Hawker Sea Hawk FGA6 [200/J]	Privately owned, Barrow-in-Furness
	XE489	Hawker Sea Hawk FGA6 (G-JETH)	Gatwick Aviation Museum, Charlwood, Surrey
	XE521	Fairey Rotodyne Y (parts)	The Helicopter Museum, Weston-super-Mare
	XE584	Hawker Hunter FGA9 <ff>	Privately owned, Stretford, Lancs
	XE597	Hawker Hunter FGA9 (8874M) <ff>	Privately owned, Bromsgrove
	XE601	Hawker Hunter FGA9 (G-ETPS)	Skyblue Aviation Ltd, Exeter
	XE606	Hawker Hunter F6A (*XJ673*/8841M)	RAF Cottesmore, preserved
	XE624	Hawker Hunter FGA9 (8875M) [G]	Privately owned, Sileby, Leics
	XE627	Hawker Hunter F6A [T]	Imperial War Museum, Duxford
	XE643	Hawker Hunter FGA9 (8586M) <ff>	RAF M&RU, Aldergrove
	XE650	Hawker Hunter FGA9 (G-9-449) <ff>	Farnborough Air Sciences Trust, Farnborough
	XE664	Hawker Hunter F4 <ff>	Gloucestershire Avn Coll, stored Gloucester
	XE665	Hawker Hunter T8C (G-BWGM) [876/VL]	Air Atlantique Classic Flight, Kemble
	XE668	Hawker Hunter GA11 [832/DD]	Privately owned, Bristol
	XE670	Hawker Hunter F4 (7762M/8585M) <ff>	RAF Museum, Cosford
	XE683	Hawker Hunter F51 (RDAF E-409) [G]	City of Norwich Aviation Museum
	XE685	Hawker Hunter GA11 (G-GAII) [861/VL]	Privately owned, Sleap
	XE689	Hawker Hunter GA11 (G-BWGK) [864/VL]	Privately owned, Kemble
	XE786	Slingsby T31B Cadet TX3 (BGA4033)	Privately owned, Arbroath
	XE793	Slingsby T31B Cadet TX3 (8666M)	Privately owned, Tamworth
	XE796	Slingsby T31B Cadet TX3	Privately owned, stored North Weald
	XE799	Slingsby T31B Cadet TX3 (8943M) [R]	Privately owned, Abbots Bromley
	XE802	Slingsby T31B Cadet TX3 (BGA5283)	Privately owned, Burton-on-Trent
	XE849	DH115 Vampire T11 (7928M) [V3]	Privately owned, Corby
	XE852	DH115 Vampire T11 [H]	No 2247 Sqn ATC, Hawarden
	XE855	DH115 Vampire T11	Midland Air Museum, Coventry
	XE856	DH115 Vampire T11 (G-DUSK)	Privately owned, Bournemouth
	XE864	DH115 Vampire T11(comp XD435) <ff>	Privately owned, Ingatstone, Essex
	XE872	DH115 Vampire T11 [62]	Midland Air Museum, Coventry
	XE874	DH115 Vampire T11 (8582M)	Privately owned, Leeds
	XE897	DH115 Vampire T11 (XD403)	Privately owned, Errol, Tayside
	XE897	DH115 Vampire T55 (U-1214/G-DHVV)	Privately owned, Bournemouth
	XE921	DH115 Vampire T11 [64] <ff>	Privately owned, Yarmouth, IoW

Serial	Type (code/other identity)	Owner/operator, location or fate	Notes
XE935	DH115 Vampire T11	Aeroventure, Doncaster	
XE946	DH115 Vampire T11 (7473M) <ff>	RAF Cranwell Aviation Heritage Centre	
XE956	DH115 Vampire T11 (G-OBLN)	De Havilland Aviation, stored Rochester	
XE979	DH115 Vampire T11 [54]	Privately owned, Birlingham, Worcs	
XE982	DH115 Vampire T11 (7564M) [01]	Privately owned, Weston, Eire	
XE985	DH115 Vampire T11 (*WZ476*)	Hunter Flying Ltd, Exeter	
XE993	DH115 Vampire T11 (8161M)	Privately owned, Cosford	
XE998	DH115 Vampire T11 (*U-1215*)	Solent Sky, Southampton	
XF113	VS Swift F7 [19] <ff>	Boscombe Down Aviation Collection	
XF114	VS Swift F7 (G-SWIF)	Solent Sky, stored Romsey	
XF303	Hawker Hunter F58A (J-4105/G-BWOU) [105,A]	Privately owned, Exeter	
XF314	Hawker Hunter F51 (RDAF E-412) [N]	Brooklands Museum, Weybridge	
XF321	Hawker Hunter T7 <ff>	*Currently not known*	
XF321	Hawker Hunter T7 <rf>	Phoenix Aviation, Bruntingthorpe	
XF375	Hawker Hunter F6A (8736M/G-BUEZ) [05]	Boscombe Down Aviation Collection	
XF382	Hawker Hunter F6A [15]	Midland Air Museum, Coventry	
XF383	Hawker Hunter F6 (8706M) <ff>	Privately owned, Kidlington	
XF418	Hawker Hunter F51 (RDAF E-430)	Gatwick Aviation Museum, Charlwood, Surrey	
XF506	Hawker Hunter F4 (WT746/7770M) [A]	Dumfries & Galloway Avn Mus, Dumfries	
XF509	Hawker Hunter F6 (8708M)	Humbrol Paints, Marfleet, E Yorkshire	
XF515	Hawker Hunter F6A (8830M/G-KAXF) [R]	Hunter Flying Ltd, Exeter	
XF522	Hawker Hunter F6 <ff>	No 2532 Sqn ATC, Milton Keynes	
XF526	Hawker Hunter F6 (8679M) [78/E]	Privately owned, Birlingham, Worcs	
XF527	Hawker Hunter F6 (8680M)	RAF Halton, on display	
XF545	Percival P56 Provost T1 (7957M) [O-K]	Privately owned, Thatcham	
XF597	Percival P56 Provost T1 (G-BKFW) [AH]	Privately owned, Thatcham	
XF603	Percival P56 Provost T1 (G-KAPW)	Shuttleworth Collection, Old Warden	
XF690	Percival P56 Provost T1 (8041M/G-MOOS)	Kennet Aviation, North Weald	
XF708	Avro 716 Shackleton MR3 [C]	Imperial War Museum, Duxford	
XF785	Bristol 173 (7648M/G-ALBN)	Bristol Aero Collection, Kemble	
XF836	Percival P56 Provost T1 (8043M/G-AWRY) [JG]	Privately owned, Thatcham	
XF877	Percival P56 Provost T1 (G-AWVF) [JX]	Privately owned, Brimpton, Berks	
XF926	Bristol 188 (8368M)	RAF Museum, Cosford	
XF994	Hawker Hunter T8C [873/VL]	Boscombe Down Aviation Collection	
XF995	Hawker Hunter T8B (G-BZSF/9237M) [K]	Hawker Hunter Aviation/ETPS, Boscombe Down	
XG154	Hawker Hunter FGA9 (8863M) [54]	RAF Museum, Hendon	
XG160	Hawker Hunter F6A (8831M/G-BWAF) [U]	Privately owned, Bournemouth	
XG164	Hawker Hunter F6 (8681M)	Privately owned, Wellington, Somerset	
XG168	Hawker Hunter F6A (XG172/8832M) [10]	City of Norwich Aviation Museum	
XG190	Hawker Hunter F51 (RDAF E-425) [C]	Midland Air Museum, Coventry	
XG193	Hawker Hunter FGA9 (XG297) (comp with WT741) <ff>	Aeroventure, Doncaster	
XG195	Hawker Hunter FGA9 <ff>	Privately owned, Lewes	
XG196	Hawker Hunter F6A (8702M) [31]	Army, Mytchett, Surrey, on display	
XG209	Hawker Hunter F6 (8709M) <ff>	Privately owned, Kingston-on-Thames	
XG210	Hawker Hunter F6	Privately owned, Beck Row, Suffolk	
XG225	Hawker Hunter F6A (8713M)	DCAE Cosford, at main gate	
XG226	Hawker Hunter F6A (8800M) <ff>	RAF Manston History Museum	
XG252	Hawker Hunter FGA9 (8840M) [U]	Privately owned, Bosbury, Hereford	
XG254	Hawker Hunter FGA9 (8881M)	Norfolk & Suffolk Avn Museum, Flixton	
XG274	Hawker Hunter F6 (8710M) [71]	Privately owned, Newmarket	
XG290	Hawker Hunter F6 (8711M) <ff>	Air Defence Collection, Boscombe Down	
XG297	Hawker Hunter FGA9 <ff>	Aeroventure, Doncaster	

Notes	Serial	Type (code/other identity)	Owner/operator, location or fate
	XG325	EE Lightning F1 <ff>	No 1476 Sqn ATC, Southend
	XG329	EE Lightning F1 (8050M)	Privately owned, Flixton
	XG331	EE Lightning F1 <ff>	Privately owned, Glos
	XG337	EE Lightning F1 (8056M) [M]	RAF Museum, Cosford
	XG452	Bristol 192 Belvedere HC1 (7997M/G-BRMB)	The Helicopter Museum, Weston-super-Mare
	XG454	Bristol 192 Belvedere HC1 (8366M)	Gr Manchester Mus of Science & Industry
	XG462	Bristol 192 Belvedere HC1 <ff>	The Helicopter Museum, stored Weston-super-Mare
	XG474	Bristol 192 Belvedere HC1 (8367M) [O]	RAF Museum, Hendon
	XG502	Bristol 171 Sycamore HR14	Museum of Army Flying, Middle Wallop
	XG518	Bristol 171 Sycamore HR14 (8009M) [S-E]	Norfolk & Suffolk Avn Museum, Flixton
	XG523	Bristol 171 Sycamore HR14 <ff> [V]	Norfolk & Suffolk Avn Museum, Flixton
	XG547	Bristol 171 Sycamore HR14 (G-HAPR) [S-T]	The Helicopter Museum, Weston-super-Mare
	XG574	WS55 Whirlwind HAR3 [752/PO]	FAA Museum, stored RNAS Yeovilton
	XG588	WS55 Whirlwind HAR3 (G-BAMH/VR-BEP)	East Midlands Airport Aeropark
	XG592	WS55 Whirlwind HAS7	*Task Force* Adventure Park, Cowbridge, S Glam
	XG594	WS55 Whirlwind HAS7 [517/PO]	FAA Museum, stored Yeovilton
	XG596	WS55 Whirlwind HAS7 [66]	The Helicopter Museum, Weston-super-Mare
	XG613	DH112 Sea Venom FAW21	Imperial War Museum, Duxford
	XG629	DH112 Sea Venom FAW22	Privately owned, Stone, Staffs
	XG680	DH112 Sea Venom FAW22 [438]	North-East Aircraft Museum, Usworth
	XG692	DH112 Sea Venom FAW22 [668/LM]	Privately owned, Stone, Staffs
	XG730	DH112 Sea Venom FAW22 [499/A]	Mosquito Aircraft Museum, London Colney
	XG736	DH112 Sea Venom FAW22	Privately owned, East Midlands
	XG737	DH112 Sea Venom FAW22 [220/Z]	Jet Avn Preservation Grp, stored Long Marston
	XG743	DH115 Sea Vampire T22 [597/LM]	Imperial War Museum, Duxford
	XG775	DH115 Vampire T55 (U-1219/G-DHWW) [VL]	Privately owned, Bournemouth
	XG797	Fairey Gannet ECM6 [277]	Imperial War Museum, Duxford
	XG831	Fairey Gannet ECM6 [396]	Flambards Village Theme Park, Helston
	XG882	Fairey Gannet T5 (8754M) [771/LM]	Privately owned, Errol, Tayside
	XG883	Fairey Gannet T5 [773/BY]	FAA Museum, at Museum of Berkshire Aviation, Woodley
	XG900	Short SC1	Science Museum, South Kensington
	XG905	Short SC1	Ulster Folk & Transpt Mus, Holywood, Co Down
	XH131	EE Canberra PR9	Privately owned, Kemble
	XH134	EE Canberra PR9 (G-OMHD)	Privately owned, Kemble
	XH135	EE Canberra PR9	Privately owned, Kemble
	XH136	EE Canberra PR9 (8782M) [W] <ff>	Phoenix Aviation, Bruntingthorpe
	XH165	EE Canberra PR9 <ff>	Blyth Valley Aviation Collection, Walpole
	XH168	EE Canberra PR9	RAF Marham Fire Section
	XH169	EE Canberra PR9	RAF Marham, on display
	XH170	EE Canberra PR9 (8739M)	RAF Wyton, on display
	XH171	EE Canberra PR9 (8746M) [U]	RAF Museum, Cosford
	XH174	EE Canberra PR9 <ff>	Privately owned, Crondall, Hants
	XH175	EE Canberra PR9 <ff>	Privately owned, Bewdley, Worcs
	XH177	EE Canberra PR9 <ff>	Newark Air Museum, Winthorpe
	XH278	DH115 Vampire T11 (8595M/7866M) [42]	Yorkshire Air Museum, Elvington
	XH312	DH115 Vampire T11 [18]	Privately owned, Dodleston, Cheshire
	XH313	DH115 Vampire T11 (G-BZRD) [E]	Privately owned, Godstone, Surrey
	XH318	DH115 Vampire T11 (7761M) [64]	Privately owned, Sholing, Hants
	XH328	DH115 Vampire T11 <ff>	Mosquito Aircraft Museum, London Colney
	XH330	DH115 Vampire T11 [73]	Privately owned, Camberley, Surrey
	XH537	Avro 698 Vulcan B2MRR (8749M) <ff>	Privately owned, Bournemouth
	XH558	Avro 698 Vulcan B2 (G-VLCN)	Vulcan To The Sky Trust, Bruntingthorpe
	XH560	Avro 698 Vulcan K2 <ff>	Privately owned, Foulness
	XH563	Avro 698 Vulcan B2MRR <ff>	Privately owned, Bruntingthorpe

Serial	Type (code/other identity)	Owner/operator, location or fate	Notes
XH584	EE Canberra T4 (G-27-374) <ff>	Aeroventure, Doncaster	
XH592	HP80 Victor K1A (8429M) <ff>	Phoenix Aviation, Bruntingthorpe	
XH648	HP80 Victor K1A	Imperial War Museum, Duxford	
XH669	HP80 Victor K2 (9092M) <ff>	Privately owned, Foulness	
XH670	HP80 Victor SR2 <ff>	Privately owned, Foulness	
XH672	HP80 Victor K2 (9242M)	RAF Museum, Cosford	
XH673	HP80 Victor K2 (8911M)	RAF Marham, on display	
XH767	Gloster Javelin FAW9 (7955M) [L]	Yorkshire Air Museum, Elvington	
XH783	Gloster Javelin FAW7 (7798M) <ff>	Privately owned, Catford	
XH837	Gloster Javelin FAW7 (8032M) <ff>	Caernarfon Air World	
XH892	Gloster Javelin FAW9R (7982M) [J]	Norfolk & Suffolk Avn Museum, Flixton	
XH897	Gloster Javelin FAW9	Imperial War Museum, Duxford	
XH903	Gloster Javelin FAW9 (7938M)	Gloucestershire Avn Coll, stored Gloucester	
XH992	Gloster Javelin FAW8 (7829M) [P]	Newark Air Museum, Winthorpe	
XJ314	RR Thrust Measuring Rig	Science Museum, South Kensington	
XJ380	Bristol 171 Sycamore HR14 (8628M)	Boscombe Down Aviation Collection	
XJ389	Fairey Jet Gyrodyne (XD759/G-AJJP)	Museum of Berkshire Aviation, Woodley	
XJ398	WS55 Whirlwind HAR10 (XD768/G-BDBZ)	Aeroventure, Doncaster	
XJ409	WS55 Whirlwind HAR10 (XD779)	Museum of Memorabilia, Llanbedr	
XJ435	WS55 Whirlwind HAR10 (XD804/8671M) [V]	RAF Manston History Museum, spares use	
XJ476	DH110 Sea Vixen FAW1 <ff>	No 424 Sqn ATC, Solent Sky, Southampton	
XJ481	DH110 Sea Vixen FAW1 [VL]	FAA Museum, stored RNAS Yeovilton	
XJ482	DH110 Sea Vixen FAW1 [713/VL]	Norfolk & Suffolk Avn Museum, Flixton	
XJ488	DH110 Sea Vixen FAW1 <ff>	Robertsbridge Aviation Society, Mayfield	
XJ494	DH110 Sea Vixen FAW2	Privately owned, Bruntingthorpe	
XJ560	DH110 Sea Vixen FAW2 (8142M) [243/H]	Newark Air Museum, Winthorpe	
XJ565	DH110 Sea Vixen FAW2 [127/E]	Mosquito Aircraft Museum, London Colney	
XJ571	DH110 Sea Vixen FAW2 (8140M) [242/R]	Solent Sky, Southampton	
XJ575	DH110 Sea Vixen FAW2 <ff> [SAH-13]	Wellesbourne Wartime Museum	
XJ579	DH110 Sea Vixen FAW2 <ff>	Midland Air Museum, Coventry	
XJ580	DH110 Sea Vixen FAW2 [131/E]	Tangmere Military Aviation Museum	
XJ615	Hawker Hunter T8C(mod) (XF357/G-BWGL)	*Repainted in Dutch marks as N-321, May 2007*	
XJ714	Hawker Hunter FR10 (comp XG226)	Jet Avn Preservation Grp, Long Marston	
XJ723	WS55 Whirlwind HAR10	Privately owned, Newcastle upon Tyne	
XJ726	WS55 Whirlwind HAR10 [F]	Caernarfon Air World	
XJ727	WS55 Whirlwind HAR10 (8661M) [L]	Privately owned, Ramsgate	
XJ758	WS55 Whirlwind HAR10 (8464M) <ff>	Privately owned, Welshpool	
XJ771	DH115 Vampire T55 (U-1215/G-HELV)	Air Atlantique Classic Flight, Coventry	
XJ772	DH115 Vampire T11 [H]	Mosquito Aircraft Museum, London Colney	
XJ823	Avro 698 Vulcan B2A	Solway Aviation Society, Carlisle	
XJ824	Avro 698 Vulcan B2A	Imperial War Museum, Duxford	
XJ917	Bristol 171 Sycamore HR14 [H-S]	Bristol Sycamore Group, stored Kemble	
XJ918	Bristol 171 Sycamore HR14 (8190M)	RAF Museum, Cosford	
XK416	Auster AOP9 (7855M/G-AYUA)	Privately owned, Widmerpool	
XK417	Auster AOP9 (G-AVXY)	Privately owned, Messingham, Lincs	
XK418	Auster AOP9 (7976M)	SWWAPS, Lasham	
XK421	Auster AOP9 (8365M) (frame)	Privately owned, Eggesford	
XK488	Blackburn NA39 Buccaneer S1	FAA Museum, stored RNAS Yeovilton	
XK526	Blackburn NA39 Buccaneer S2 (8648M)	RAF Honington, at main gate	
XK527	Blackburn NA39 Buccaneer S2D (8818M) <ff>	Privately owned, North Wales	
XK532	Blackburn NA39 Buccaneer S1 (8867M) [632/LM]	Highland Aviation Museum, Inverness	

Notes	*Serial*	*Type (code/other identity)*	*Owner/operator, location or fate*
	XK533	Blackburn NA39 Buccaneer S1 <ff>	Royal Scottish Mus'm of Flight, stored E Fortune
	XK590	DH115 Vampire T11 [V]	Wellesbourne Wartime Museum
	XK623	DH115 Vampire T11 (*G-VAMP*) [56]	Caernarfon Air World
	XK624	DH115 Vampire T11 [32]	Norfolk & Suffolk Avn Museum, Flixton
	XK625	DH115 Vampire T11 [14]	Brenzett Aeronautical Museum
	XK627	DH115 Vampire T11	Privately owned, Lavendon, Bucks
	XK637	DH115 Vampire T11 [56]	RAF Millom Museum, Haverigg
	XK695	DH106 Comet C2(RC) (G-AMXH/9164M) <ff>	Mosquito Aircraft Museum, London Colney
	XK699	DH106 Comet C2 (7971M)	RAF Lyneham on display
	XK724	Folland Gnat F1 (7715M)	RAF Museum, Cosford
	XK740	Folland Gnat F1 (8396M)	Solent Sky, Southampton
	XK776	ML Utility 1	Museum of Army Flying, Middle Wallop
	XK788	Slingsby T38 Grasshopper TX1	Privately owned, Sproughton
	XK789	Slingsby T38 Grasshopper TX1	Midland Air Museum, stored Coventry
	XK790	Slingsby T38 Grasshopper TX1	Privately owned, stored Husbands Bosworth
	XK819	Slingsby T38 Grasshopper TX1	Privately owned, Breighton
	XK822	Slingsby T38 Grasshopper TX1	Boulton Paul Association, Wolverhampton
	XK895	DH104 Sea Devon C20 (G-SDEV) [19/CU]	Air Atlantique Classic Flight, Coventry
	XK896	DH104 Sea Devon C20 (G-RNAS)	*Sunk at Chepstow, 2006*
	XK907	WS55 Whirlwind HAS7 [U]	Midland Air Museum, Coventry
	XK911	WS55 Whirlwind HAS7 [519/PO]	Privately owned, Colerne
	XK936	WS55 Whirlwind HAS7 [62]	Imperial War Museum, Duxford
	XK940	WS55 Whirlwind HAS7 (G-AYXT) [911]	The Helicopter Museum, Weston-super-Mare
	XK970	WS55 Whirlwind HAR10 (8789M)	Army, Bramley, Hants
	XL149	Blackburn B101 Beverley C1 (7988M) <ff>	Aeroventure, Doncaster
	XL160	HP80 Victor K2 (8910M) <ff>	Norfolk & Suffolk Avn Museum, Flixton
	XL164	HP80 Victor K2 (9215M) <ff>	Gatwick Aviation Museum, Charlwood, Surrey
	XL190	HP80 Victor K2 (9216M) <ff>	RAF Manston History Museum
	XL231	HP80 Victor K2	Yorkshire Air Museum, Elvington
	XL318	Avro 698 Vulcan B2 (8733M)	RAF Museum, Hendon
	XL319	Avro 698 Vulcan B2	North-East Aircraft Museum, Usworth
	XL360	Avro 698 Vulcan B2A	Midland Air Museum, Coventry
	XL388	Avro 698 Vulcan B2 <ff>	Aeroventure, Doncaster
	XL391	Avro 698 Vulcan B2	Privately owned, Blackpool
	XL426	Avro 698 Vulcan B2 (G-VJET)	Vulcan Restoration Trust, Southend
	XL445	Avro 698 Vulcan K2 (8811M) <ff>	Norfolk & Suffolk Avn Museum, Flixton
	XL449	Fairey Gannet AEW3 <ff>	Privately owned, Camberley, Surrey
	XL472	Fairey Gannet AEW3 [044/R]	Gatwick Aviation Museum, Charlwood, Surrey
	XL497	Fairey Gannet AEW3 [041/R]	Dumfries & Galloway Avn Mus, Dumfries
	XL500	Fairey Gannet AEW3 (G-KAEW) [CU]	Kennet Aviation, North Weald
	XL502	Fairey Gannet AEW3 (8610M/G-BMYP)	Yorkshire Air Museum, Elvington
	XL503	Fairey Gannet AEW3 [070/E]	FAA Museum, RNAS Yeovilton
	XL563	Hawker Hunter T7 (9218M)	Privately owned, Bosbury, Hereford
	XL564	Hawker Hunter T7 (fuselage)	Boscombe Down Aviation Collection
	XL565	Hawker Hunter T7 (parts of WT745)	Privately owned, Bruntingthorpe
	XL568	Hawker Hunter T7A (9224M) [C]	RAF Museum, Cosford
	XL569	Hawker Hunter T7 (8833M)	East Midlands Airport Aeropark
	XL571	Hawker Hunter T7 (XL572/8834M/G-HNTR) [V]	Yorkshire Air Museum, Elvington
	XL573	Hawker Hunter T7 (G-BVGH)	Hunter Flying Ltd, Exeter
	XL577	Hawker Hunter T7 (G-BXKF/8676M)	Delta Jets, Kemble
	XL578	Hawker Hunter T7 (comp XL586)	Kemble Airfield Fire Section
	XL580	Hawker Hunter T8M [723]	FAA Museum, stored RNAS Yeovilton
	XL586	Hawker Hunter T7 (comp XL578)	Delta Jets, Kemble
	XL587	Hawker Hunter T7 (8807M/G-HPUX) [Z]	Hawker Hunter Aviation, stored Scampton
	XL591	Hawker Hunter T7	Gatwick Aviation Museum, Charlwood, Surrey
	XL592	Hawker Hunter T7 (8836M) [Y]	Hunter Flying Club, Kemble

Serial	Type (code/other identity)	Owner/operator, location or fate	Notes
XL601	Hawker Hunter T7 (G-BZSR) [874/VL]	Classic Fighters, Brustem, Belgium	
XL602	Hawker Hunter T8M (G-BWFT)	Hunter Flying Ltd, Exeter	
XL609	Hawker Hunter T7 <ff>	Privately owned, Yarmouth, IoW	
XL612	Hawker Hunter T7 [2]	Hunter Flying Ltd, Exeter	
XL618	Hawker Hunter T7 (8892M) [05]	Caernarfon Air World	
XL621	Hawker Hunter T7 (G-BNCX)	Privately owned, Dunsfold	
XL623	Hawker Hunter T7 (8770M)	The Planets Leisure Centre, Woking	
XL629	EE Lightning T4	MoD/QinetiQ Boscombe Down, at main gate	
XL703	SAL Pioneer CC1 (8034M)	RAF Museum, Cosford	
XL714	DH82A Tiger Moth II (T6099/G-AOGR)	Privately owned, Boughton, Lincs	
XL716	DH82A Tiger Moth II (T7363/G-AOIL)	Privately owned, Compton Abbas	
XL738	Saro Skeeter AOP12 (7860M)	Privately owned, Aeroventure, Doncaster	
XL739	Saro Skeeter AOP12	AAC Wattisham, on display	
XL762	Saro Skeeter AOP12 (8017M)	Royal Scottish Mus'm of Flight, E Fortune	
XL763	Saro Skeeter AOP12	Privately owned, Aeroventure, Doncaster	
XL764	Saro Skeeter AOP12 (7940M) [J]	Newark Air Museum, Winthorpe	
XL765	Saro Skeeter AOP12	cMelksham, Wilts	
XL770	Saro Skeeter AOP12 (8046M)	Solent Sky, Southampton	
XL809	Saro Skeeter AOP12 (G-BLIX)	Privately owned, Wilden, Beds	
XL811	Saro Skeeter AOP12	The Helicopter Museum, Weston-super-Mare	
XL812	Saro Skeeter AOP12 (G-SARO)	Privately owned, Wattisham	
XL813	Saro Skeeter AOP12	Museum of Army Flying, Middle Wallop	
XL814	Saro Skeeter AOP12	AAC Historic Aircraft Flight, Middle Wallop	
XL824	Bristol 171 Sycamore HR14 (8021M)	Gr Manchester Mus of Science & Industry	
XL829	Bristol 171 Sycamore HR14	The Helicopter Museum, Weston-super-Mare	
XL840	WS55 Whirlwind HAS7	Privately owned, Bawtry	
XL853	WS55 Whirlwind HAS7 [PO]	FAA Museum, stored RNAS Yeovilton	
XL875	WS55 Whirlwind HAR9	Perth Technical College	
XL929	Percival P66 Pembroke C1 (G-BNPU)	Air Atlantique Classic Flight, stored Coventry	
XL954	Percival P66 Pembroke C1 (9042M/N4234C/G-BXES)	Air Atlantique Classic Flight, Coventry	
XL993	SAL Twin Pioneer CC1 (8388M)	RAF Museum, Cosford	
XM135	BAC Lightning F1 [B]	Imperial War Museum, Duxford	
XM144	BAC Lightning F1 (8417M) <ff>	Privately owned, Greenodd, Cumbria	
XM169	BAC Lightning F1A (8422M) <ff>	Highland Aviation Museum, Inverness	
XM172	BAC Lightning F1A (8427M)	Privately owned, Greenodd, Cumbria	
XM173	BAC Lightning F1A (8414M) [A]	Privately owned, Preston	
XM191	BAC Lightning F1A (7854M/8590M) <ff>	RAF M&RU, Bottesford	
XM192	BAC Lightning F1A (8413M) [K]	Thorpe Camp Preservation Group, Lincs	
XM223	DH104 Devon C2 (G-BWWC) [J]	Air Atlantique Classic Flight, Coventry	
XM279	EE Canberra B(I)8 <ff>	Privately owned, Flixton	
XM300	WS58 Wessex HAS1	Welsh Industrial & Maritime Mus'm, stored Cardiff	
XM328	WS58 Wessex HAS3 [653/PO]	The Helicopter Museum, Weston-super-Mare	
XM330	WS58 Wessex HAS1	The Helicopter Museum, Weston-super-Mare	
XM349	Hunting Jet Provost T3A (9046M) [T]	Global Aviation, Humberside	
XM350	Hunting Jet Provost T3A (9036M) [89]	Aeroventure, Doncaster	
XM351	Hunting Jet Provost T3 (8078M) [Y]	RAF Museum, Cosford	
XM355	Hunting Jet Provost T3 (8229M) [D]	Privately owned, Newcastle	
XM358	Hunting Jet Provost T3A (8987M) [53]	Privately owned, Newbridge, Powys	
XM362	Hunting Jet Provost T3 (8230M)	DCAE, No 1 SoTT, Cosford	
XM365	Hunting Jet Provost T3A (G-BXBH) [37]	Privately owned, Norwich	
XM369	Hunting Jet Provost T3 (8084M) [C]	Privately owned, Rossendale, Lancs	
XM370	Hunting Jet Provost T3A (G-BVSP) [10]	Privately owned, Long Marston	
XM383	Hunting Jet Provost T3A [90]	Newark Air Museum, Winthorpe	

Notes	Serial	Type (code/other identity)	Owner/operator, location or fate
	XM402	Hunting Jet Provost T3 (8055AM) [J]	Fenland & W Norfolk Aviation Museum, Wisbech
	XM404	Hunting Jet Provost T3 (8055BM)	FETC, Moreton-in-Marsh, Glos
	XM409	Hunting Jet Provost T3 (8082M) <ff>	Air Scouts, Guernsey Airport
	XM410	Hunting Jet Provost T3 (8054AM) [B]	DEODS, Chattenden, Kent
	XM411	Hunting Jet Provost T3 (8434M) <ff>	Aeroventure, Doncaster
	XM412	Hunting Jet Provost T3A (9011M) [41]	Privately owned, Kinross, Scotland
	XM414	Hunting Jet Provost T3A (8996M)	Ulster Aviation Society, Langford Lodge
	XM417	Hunting Jet Provost T3 (8054BM) [D] <ff>	Privately owned, Cannock
	XM419	Hunting Jet Provost T3A (8990M) [102]	Privately owned, Newcastle
	XM425	Hunting Jet Provost T3A (8995M) [88]	Privately owned, Longton, Staffs
	XM463	Hunting Jet Provost T3A [38] (fuselage)	RAF Museum, Hendon
	XM468	Hunting Jet Provost T3 (8081M) <ff>	Privately owned, Terrington St Clement, Norfolk
	XM473	Hunting Jet Provost T3A (8974M/*G-TINY*)	Bedford College, instructional use
	XM474	Hunting Jet Provost T3 (8121M) <ff>	No 2517 Sqn ATC, Levenshulme
	XM478	Hunting Jet Provost T3A (8983M/G-BXDL)	Privately owned, Swansea
	XM479	Hunting Jet Provost T3A (G-BVEZ) [54]	Privately owned, Newcastle
	XM480	Hunting Jet Provost T3 (8080M)	4x4 Car Centre, Chesterfield
	XM496	Bristol 253 Britannia C1 (EL-WXA)	Britannia Preservation Society, Kemble
	XM497	Bristol 175 Britannia 312F (G-AOVF)	RAF Museum, Cosford
	XM529	Saro Skeeter AOP12 (7979M/G-BDNS)	Privately owned, Handforth
	XM553	Saro Skeeter AOP12 (G-AWSV)	Privately owned, Middle Wallop
	XM555	Saro Skeeter AOP12 (8027M)	RAF Museum, Hendon
	XM561	Saro Skeeter AOP12 (7980M)	Aeroventure, Doncaster
	XM564	Saro Skeeter AOP12	National Tank Museum, Bovington
	XM569	Avro 698 Vulcan B2 <ff>	Gloucestershire Avn Coll, stored Gloucester
	XM575	Avro 698 Vulcan B2A (G-BLMC)	East Midlands Airport Aeropark
	XM594	Avro 698 Vulcan B2	Newark Air Museum, Winthorpe
	XM597	Avro 698 Vulcan B2	Royal Scottish Mus'm of Flight, E Fortune
	XM598	Avro 698 Vulcan B2 (8778M)	RAF Museum, Cosford
	XM602	Avro 698 Vulcan B2 (8771M) <ff>	Vulcan To The Sky Trust, Bruntingthorpe
	XM603	Avro 698 Vulcan B2	Avro Aircraft Heritage Society, Woodford
	XM607	Avro 698 Vulcan B2 (8779M)	RAF Waddington, on display
	XM612	Avro 698 Vulcan B2	City of Norwich Aviation Museum
	XM652	Avro 698 Vulcan B2 <ff>	Privately owned, Welshpool
	XM655	Avro 698 Vulcan B2 (G-VULC)	Privately owned, Wellesbourne Mountford
	XM660	WS55 Whirlwind HAS7	RAF Millom Museum, Haverigg
	XM685	WS55 Whirlwind HAS7 (G-AYZJ) [513/PO]	Newark Air Museum, Winthorpe
	XM692	HS Gnat T1 <ff>	Privately owned, South Molton, Devon
	XM693	HS Gnat T1 (7891M)	BAE Systems Hamble, on display
	XM697	HS Gnat T1 (G-NAAT)	Privately owned, Carluke, S Lanarkshire
	XM708	HS Gnat T1 (8573M)	Privately owned, Lytham St Annes
	XM715	HP80 Victor K2	Cold War Jets Collection, Bruntingthorpe
	XM717	HP80 Victor K2 <ff>	RAF Museum, Hendon
	XM819	Lancashire EP9 Prospector (G-APXW)	Museum of Army Flying, Middle Wallop
	XM833	WS58 Wessex HAS3	SWWAPS, Lasham
	XM870	WS58 Wessex HAS3 [PO]	RN, Predannack Fire School
	XN126	WS55 Whirlwind HAR10 (8655M) [S]	Pinewood Studios, Elstree
	XN157	Slingsby T21B Sedbergh TX1 (BGA3255)	Privately owned, stored Long Mynd
	XN185	Slingsby T21B Sedbergh TX1 (8942M/BGA4077)	RAF Museum Reserve Collection, Stafford

Serial	Type (code/other identity)	Owner/operator, location or fate	Notes
XN186	Slingsby T21B Sedbergh TX1 (BGA3905) [HFG]	Privately owned, Watton	
XN187	Slingsby T21B Sedbergh TX1 (BGA3903)	Privately owned, Halton	
XN198	Slingsby T31B Cadet TX3	Privately owned, Bodmin	
XN238	Slingsby T31B Cadet TX3 <ff>	Aeroventure, Doncaster	
XN239	Slingsby T31B Cadet TX3 (8889M) [G]	Imperial War Museum, Duxford	
XN246	Slingsby T31B Cadet TX3	Solent Sky, Southampton	
XN258	WS55 Whirlwind HAR9 [589/CU]	North-East Aircraft Museum, Usworth	
XN297	WS55 Whirlwind HAR9 (XN311) [12]	Privately owned, Hull	
XN298	WS55 Whirlwind HAR9 [810/LS]	International Fire Training Centre, Chorley	
XN299	WS55 Whirlwind HAS7 [758]	Tangmere Military Aviation Museum	
XN304	WS55 Whirlwind HAS7 [WW/B]	Norfolk & Suffolk Avn Museum, Flixton	
XN332	Saro P531 (G-APNV) [759]	FAA Museum, stored RNAS Yeovilton	
XN334	Saro P531	FAA Museum, stored RNAS Yeovilton	
XN341	Saro Skeeter AOP12 (8022M)	Stondon Transport Mus & Garden Centre, Beds	
XN344	Saro Skeeter AOP12 (8018M)	Science Museum, South Kensington	
XN351	Saro Skeeter AOP12 (G-BKSC)	Privately owned, Ipswich	
XN380	WS55 Whirlwind HAS7	RAF Manston History Museum	
XN385	WS55 Whirlwind HAS7	Battleground Paintball, Yarm, Cleveland	
XN386	WS55 Whirlwind HAR9 [435/ED]	Aeroventure, Doncaster	
XN412	Auster AOP9	Auster 9 Group, Melton Mowbray	
XN437	Auster AOP9 (G-AXWA)	Privately owned, North Weald	
XN441	Auster AOP9 (G-BGKT)	Privately owned, Eggesford	
XN458	Hunting Jet Provost T3 (8234M/*XN594*)	Privately owned, Northallerton	
XN459	Hunting Jet Provost T3A (G-BWOT)	Transair(UK) Ltd, North Weald	
XN462	Hunting Jet Provost T3A [17]	FAA Museum, stored RNAS Yeovilton	
XN466	Hunting Jet Provost T3A [29] <ff>	No 1005 Sqn ATC, Radcliffe, Gr Manchester	
XN492	Hunting Jet Provost T3 (8079M) <ff>	Wings Museum, Redhill, Surrey	
XN493	Hunting Jet Provost T3 (XN137) <ff>	Privately owned, Camberley	
XN494	Hunting Jet Provost T3A (9012M) [43]	Crawley Technical College	
XN500	Hunting Jet Provost T3A [48]	Norfolk & Suffolk Avn Museum, Flixton	
XN503	Hunting Jet Provost T3 <ff>	Boscombe Down Aviation Collection	
XN508	Hunting Jet Provost T3A <ff>	MoD/DARA, St Athan	
XN510	Hunting Jet Provost T3A (G-BXBI) [40]	Privately owned, Sproughton	
XN511	Hunting Jet Provost T3 [64] <ff>	Aeroventure, Doncaster	
XN549	Hunting Jet Provost T3 (8235M) <ff>	Privately owned, Warrington	
XN551	Hunting Jet Provost T3A (8984M)	Privately owned, Felton Common, Bristol	
XN554	Hunting Jet Provost T3 (8436M) [K]	Gunsmoke Paintball, Hadleigh, Suffolk	
XN573	Hunting Jet Provost T3 [E] <ff>	Newark Air Museum, Winthorpe	
XN579	Hunting Jet Provost T3A (9137M) [14]	Gunsmoke Paintball, Hadleigh, Suffolk	
XN582	Hunting Jet Provost T3A (8957M) [95,H]	Privately owned, Bruntingthorpe	
XN584	Hunting Jet Provost T3A (9014M) [E]	Phoenix Aviation, Bruntingthorpe	
XN586	Hunting Jet Provost T3A (9039M) [91,S]	Brooklands Technical College	
XN589	Hunting Jet Provost T3A (9143M) [46]	RAF Linton-on-Ouse, on display	
XN597	Hunting Jet Provost T3 (7984M) <ff>	RAF Millom Museum, Haverigg	
XN607	Hunting Jet Provost T3 <ff>	Highland Aviation Museum, Inverness	
XN623	Hunting Jet Provost T3 (XN632/8352M)	Privately owned, Birlingham, Worcs	
XN629	Hunting Jet Provost T3A (G-BVEG/G-KNOT) [49]	Privately owned, North Weald	
XN634	Hunting Jet Provost T3A <ff>	Privately owned, Preston, Lancs	
XN634	Hunting Jet Provost T3A [53] <rf>	BAE Systems Warton Fire Section	
XN637	Hunting Jet Provost T3 (G-BKOU) [03]	Privately owned, North Weald	

Notes	Serial	Type (code/other identity)	Owner/operator, location or fate
	XN647	DH110 Sea Vixen FAW2 <ff>	Privately owned, Bicester
	XN650	DH110 Sea Vixen FAW2 <ff>	Privately owned, Newton Abbot
	XN651	DH110 Sea Vixen FAW2 <ff>	Privately owned, Olney, Bucks
	XN685	DH110 Sea Vixen FAW2 (8173M) [03/VL]	Midland Air Museum, Coventry
	XN714	Hunting H126	RAF Museum, Cosford
	XN726	EE Lightning F2A (8545M) <ff>	Boscombe Down Aviation Collection
	XN728	EE Lightning F2A (8546M) [V]	Privately owned, Balderton, Notts
	XN774	EE Lightning F2A (8551M) <ff>	Privately owned, Boston
	XN776	EE Lightning F2A (8535M) [C]	Royal Scottish Mus'm of Flight, E Fortune
	XN795	EE Lightning F2A <ff>	Privately owned, Foulness
	XN817	AW660 Argosy C1	QinetiQ West Freugh Fire Section
	XN819	AW660 Argosy C1 (8205M) <ff>	Newark Air Museum, Winthorpe
	XN923	HS Buccaneer S1 [13]	Gatwick Aviation Museum, Charlwood, Surrey
	XN928	HS Buccaneer S1 (8179M) <ff>	Privately owned, Gravesend
	XN957	HS Buccaneer S1 [630/LM]	FAA Museum, RNAS Yeovilton
	XN964	HS Buccaneer S1 [118/V]	Newark Air Museum, Winthorpe
	XN967	HS Buccaneer S1 [233] <ff>	City of Norwich Aviation Museum
	XN972	HS Buccaneer S1 (8183M/XN962) <ff>	RAF Museum, Cosford
	XN974	HS Buccaneer S2A	Yorkshire Air Museum, Elvington
	XN979	HS Buccaneer S2 <ff>	Aeroventure, Doncaster
	XN983	HS Buccaneer S2B <ff>	Fenland & W Norfolk Aviation Museum, Wisbech
	XP110	WS58 Wessex HAS3 [55/FL]	DCAE AESS, *HMS Sultan*, Gosport, BDRT
	XP137	WS58 Wessex HAS3 [711/DD]	RN, Predannack Fire School
	XP142	WS58 Wessex HAS3	FAA Museum, stored Yeovilton
	XP150	WS58 Wessex HAS3 [LS]	FETC, Moreton-in-Marsh, Glos
	XP165	WS Scout AH1	The Helicopter Museum, Weston-super-Mare
	XP190	WS Scout AH1	Aeroventure, Doncaster
	XP191	WS Scout AH1	Privately owned, Prenton, The Wirral
	XP226	Fairey Gannet AEW3	Newark Air Museum, Winthorpe
	XP241	Auster AOP9 (G-CEHR)	Privately owned, Eggesford
	XP242	Auster AOP9 (G-BUCI)	AAC Historic Aircraft Flight, Middle Wallop
	XP244	Auster AOP9 (7864M/*M7922*)	Privately owned, Stretton on Dunsmore
	XP248	Auster AOP9 (7863M/WZ679)	Privately owned, Sandy, Beds
	XP254	Auster AOP11 (G-ASCC)	Privately owned, Widmerpool
	XP279	Auster AOP9 (G-BWKK)	Privately owned, Popham
	XP280	Auster AOP9	Snibston Discovery Park, Coalville
	XP281	Auster AOP9	Imperial War Museum, Duxford
	XP286	Auster AOP9	Privately owned, Eggesford
	XP299	WS55 Whirlwind HAR10 (8726M)	RAF Museum, Hendon
	XP330	WS55 Whirlwind HAR10	CAA Fire School, Durham/Tees Valley
	XP344	WS55 Whirlwind HAR10 (8764M) [H723]	RAF North Luffenham Training Area
	XP345	WS55 Whirlwind HAR10 (8792M) [UN]	Yorkshire Helicopter Preservation Group, Doncaster
	XP346	WS55 Whirlwind HAR10 (8793M)	Privately owned, Long Marston
	XP350	WS55 Whirlwind HAR10	Privately owned, Bassetts Pole, Staffs
	XP351	WS55 Whirlwind HAR10 (8672M) [Z]	Gatwick Aviation Museum, Charlwood, Surrey
	XP355	WS55 Whirlwind HAR10 (8463M/G-BEBC)	City of Norwich Aviation Museum
	XP360	WS55 Whirlwind HAR10 [V]	Privately owned, Bicton, nr Leominster
	XP398	WS55 Whirlwind HAR10 (8794M)	Gatwick Aviation Museum, Charlwood, Surrey
	XP404	WS55 Whirlwind HAR10 (8682M)	The Helicopter Museum, Weston-super-Mare
	XP411	AW660 Argosy C1 (8442M) [C]	RAF Museum, Cosford
	XP454	Slingsby T38 Grasshopper TX1	Privately owned, Sywell
	XP463	Slingsby T38 Grasshopper TX1 (BGA4372)	Privately owned, Lasham
	XP488	Slingsby T38 Grasshopper TX1	Fenland & W Norfolk Aviation Museum, stored Wisbech
	XP490	Slingsby T38 Grasshopper TX1 (BGA4552)	Privately owned, stored Watton
	XP492	Slingsby T38 Grasshopper TX1 (BGA3480)	Privately owned, Gallows Hill, Dorset

Serial	Type (code/other identity)	Owner/operator, location or fate	Notes
XP493	Slingsby T38 Grasshopper TX1	Privately owned, stored Aston Down	
XP494	Slingsby T38 Grasshopper TX1	Privately owned, Rattlesden, Suffolk	
XP502	HS Gnat T1 (8576M)	Privately owned, Kemble	
XP505	HS Gnat T1	Science Museum, Wroughton	
XP516	HS Gnat T1 (8580M) [16]	Farnborough Air Sciences Trust, Farnborough	
XP540	HS Gnat T1 (8608M) [62]	Privately owned, North Weald	
XP542	HS Gnat T1 (8575M)	Solent Sky, Southampton	
XP556	Hunting Jet Provost T4 (9027M) [B]	RAF Cranwell Aviation Heritage Centre	
XP557	Hunting Jet Provost T4 (8494M) [72]	Dumfries & Galloway Avn Mus, Dumfries	
XP558	Hunting Jet Provost T4 (8627M) <ff>	Privately owned, Eckington, Derbyshire	
XP558	Hunting Jet Provost T4 (8627M) [20] <rf>	Privately owned, Sproughton	
XP563	Hunting Jet Provost T4 (9028M) [C]	Privately owned, Sproughton	
XP568	Hunting Jet Provost T4	Jet Avn Preservation Grp, Long Marston	
XP573	Hunting Jet Provost T4 (8236M) [19]	Jersey Airport Fire Section	
XP585	Hunting Jet Provost T4 (8407M) [24]	NE Wales Institute, Wrexham	
XP627	Hunting Jet Provost T4	North-East Aircraft Museum, Usworth	
XP629	Hunting Jet Provost T4 (9026M) [P]	Gunsmoke Paintball, Hadleigh, Suffolk	
XP640	Hunting Jet Provost T4 (8501M) [27]	Yorkshire Air Museum, Elvington	
XP642	Hunting Jet Provost T4 <ff>	Privately owned, Lavendon, Bucks	
XP672	Hunting Jet Provost T4 (8458M/G-RAFI) [03]	Privately owned, Sproughton	
XP680	Hunting Jet Provost T4 (8460M)	FETC, Moreton-in-Marsh, Glos	
XP686	Hunting Jet Provost T4 (8401M/8502M) [G]	Gunsmoke Paintball, Hadleigh, Suffolk	
XP701	BAC Lightning F3 (8924M) <ff>	Robertsbridge Aviation Society, Mayfield	
XP703	BAC Lightning F3 <ff>	City of Norwich Aviation Museum	
XP706	BAC Lightning F3 (8925M)	Aeroventure, Doncaster	
XP743	BAC Lightning F3 <ff>	No 351 Sqn ATC, Burton-upon-Trent	
XP745	BAC Lightning F3 (8453M) <ff>	Greenford Haulage, West London	
XP820	DHC2 Beaver AL1	AAC Historic Aircraft Flight, Middle Wallop	
XP821	DHC2 Beaver AL1 [MCO]	Museum of Army Flying, Middle Wallop	
XP822	DHC2 Beaver AL1	Museum of Army Flying, Middle Wallop	
XP831	Hawker P.1127 (8406M)	Science Museum, South Kensington	
XP841	Handley-Page HP115	FAA Museum, RNAS Yeovilton	
XP847	WS Scout AH1	Museum of Army Flying, Middle Wallop	
XP848	WS Scout AH1	DCAE Arborfield, on display	
XP853	WS Scout AH1	Privately owned, Sutton, Surrey	
XP854	WS Scout AH1 (7898M/TAD043)	Privately owned, Sproughton	
XP855	WS Scout AH1	DCAE SEAE, Arborfield	
XP856	WS Scout AH1	Privately owned, Dunkeswell	
XP883	WS Scout AH1	Privately owned, Bruntingthorpe	
XP884	WS Scout AH1	AAC Middle Wallop, instructional use	
XP885	WS Scout AH1	AAC Wattisham, instructional use	
XP886	WS Scout AH1	Yeovil College	
XP888	WS Scout AH1	Privately owned, Sproughton	
XP890	WS Scout AH1 [G] (fuselage)	Privately owned, Ipswich	
XP893	WS Scout AH1	AAC Middle Wallop, BDRT	
XP899	WS Scout AH1 [D]	DCAE SEAE, Arborfield	
XP900	WS Scout AH1	AAC Wattisham, instructional use	
XP902	WS Scout AH1 <ff>	Aeroventure, Doncaster	
XP905	WS Scout AH1	*Currently not known*	
XP907	WS Scout AH1 (G-SROE)	Privately owned, Wattisham	
XP910	WS Scout AH1	Museum of Army Flying, Middle Wallop	
XP924	DH110 Sea Vixen D3 (G-CVIX) [134/E]	De Havilland Aviation, Bournemouth	
XP925	DH110 Sea Vixen FAW2 [752] <ff>	No 1268 Sqn ATC, Haslemere, Surrey	
XP980	Hawker P.1127	FAA Museum, RNAS Yeovilton	
XP984	Hawker P.1127	Brooklands Museum, Weybridge	
XR220	BAC TSR2 (7933M)	RAF Museum, Cosford	
XR222	BAC TSR2	Imperial War Museum, Duxford	
XR232	Sud Alouette AH2 (F-WEIP)	Museum of Army Flying, Middle Wallop	

Notes	Serial	Type (code/other identity)	Owner/operator, location or fate
	XR239	Auster AOP9	Privately owned, Stretton on Dunsmore
	XR240	Auster AOP9 (G-BDFH)	Privately owned, Eggesford
	XR241	Auster AOP9 (G-AXRR)	Privately owned, Eggesford
	XR244	Auster AOP9	AAC Historic Aircraft Flight, Middle Wallop
	XR246	Auster AOP9 (7862M/G-AZBU)	Privately owned, North Coates
	XR267	Auster AOP9 (G-BJXR)	Privately owned, Widmerpool
	XR271	Auster AOP9	Royal Artillery Experience, Woolwich
	XR346	Northrop Shelduck D1 (comp with XW578)	Privately owned, Bournemouth
	XR371	SC5 Belfast C1	RAF Museum, Cosford
	XR379	Sud Alouette AH2	AAC Historic Aircraft Flight, Middle Wallop
	XR453	WS55 Whirlwind HAR10 (8873M) [A]	RAF Odiham, on gate
	XR458	WS55 Whirlwind HAR10 (8662M) [H]	Privately owned, Chipping Sodbury
	XR485	WS55 Whirlwind HAR10 [Q]	Norfolk & Suffolk Avn Museum, Flixton
	XR486	WS55 Whirlwind HCC12 (8727M/G-RWWW)	The Helicopter Museum, Weston-super-Mare
	XR498	WS58 Wessex HC2 (9342M) [X]	DCAE, No 1 SoTT, Cosford
	XR501	WS58 Wessex HC2	Army, Keogh Barracks, Aldershot, instructional use
	XR502	WS58 Wessex HC2 (G-CCUP) [Z]	Privately owned, Redhill
	XR503	WS58 Wessex HC2	MoD FSCTE, Manston
	XR506	WS58 Wessex HC2 (9343M) [V]	DCAE AESS, *HMS Sultan*, Gosport
	XR507	WS58 Wessex HC2	Privately owned, Hixon, Staffs
	XR516	WS58 Wessex HC2 (9319M) [V]	RAF Shawbury, for display
	XR517	WS58 Wessex HC2 [N]	Ulster Aviation Society, Langford Lodge
	XR518	WS58 Wessex HC2 [J]	DCAE AESS, *HMS Sultan*, Gosport
	XR523	WS58 Wessex HC2 [M]	RN *HMS Raleigh*, Torpoint, instructional use
	XR525	WS58 Wessex HC2 [G]	RAF Museum, Cosford
	XR526	WS58 Wessex HC2 (8147M)	The Helicopter Museum, Weston-super-Mare
	XR528	WS58 Wessex HC2	RAF Lyneham, fire section
	XR529	WS58 Wessex HC2 (9268M) [E]	RAF Aldergrove, on display
	XR534	HS Gnat T1 (8578M) [65]	Newark Air Museum, Winthorpe
	XR537	HS Gnat T1 (8642M/G-NATY)	De Havilland Aviation, Bournemouth
	XR538	HS Gnat T1 (8621M/G-RORI) [01]	Privately owned, North Weald
	XR571	HS Gnat T1 (8493M)	RAF *Red Arrows*, Scampton, on display
	XR574	HS Gnat T1 (8631M) [72]	Trenchard Museum, RAF Halton
	XR595	WS Scout AH1 (G-BWHU) [M]	Privately owned, Staddon Heights, Devon
	XR597	WS Scout AH1 (fuselage)	Privately owned, Sproughton
	XR601	WS Scout AH1	DCAE SEAE, Arborfield
	XR627	WS Scout AH1 [X]	Privately owned, Townhill, Fife
	XR628	WS Scout AH1	Privately owned, Ipswich
	XR629	WS Scout AH1 (fuselage)	Privately owned, Ipswich
	XR635	WS Scout AH1	Coventry University, instructional use
	XR650	Hunting Jet Provost T4 (8459M) [28]	Boscombe Down Aviation Collection
	XR654	Hunting Jet Provost T4 <ff>	Privately owned, Chester
	XR658	Hunting Jet Provost T4 (8192M)	Deeside College, Connah's Quay, Clwyd
	XR662	Hunting Jet Provost T4 (8410M) [25]	Air Training Heritage Collection, Wolverhampton
	XR672	Hunting Jet Provost T4 (8495M) [50]	RAF Halton, Fire Section
	XR673	Hunting Jet Provost T4 (G-BXLO/9032M) [L]	Privately owned, Sandtoft
	XR681	Hunting Jet Provost T4 (8588M) <ff>	Robertsbridge Aviation Society, Mayfield
	XR700	Hunting Jet Provost T4 (8589M) <ff>	RAF Aldergrove
	XR713	BAC Lightning F3 (8935M) [C]	RAF Leuchars, on display
	XR718	BAC Lightning F6 (8932M) [DA]	Privately owned, Over Dinsdale, N Yorks
	XR724	BAC Lightning F6 (G-BTSY)	The Lightning Association, Binbrook
	XR725	BAC Lightning F6	Privately owned, Binbrook
	XR726	BAC Lightning F6 <ff>	Privately owned, Harrogate
	XR728	BAC Lightning F6 [JS]	Lightning Preservation Grp, Bruntingthorpe
	XR747	BAC Lightning F6 <ff>	Privately owned, Cubert, Cornwall
	XR749	BAC Lightning F3 (8934M) [DA]	Privately owned, Peterhead
	XR751	BAC Lightning F3	Privately owned, Tremar, Cornwall
	XR753	BAC Lightning F6 (8969M) [XI]	RAF Coningsby on display
	XR753	BAC Lightning F53 (ZF578)	Tangmere Military Aviation Museum

Serial	Type (code/other identity)	Owner/operator, location or fate	Notes
XR754	BAC Lightning F6 (8972M) <ff>	Aeroventure, Doncaster	
XR755	BAC Lightning F6	Privately owned, Callington, Cornwall	
XR757	BAC Lightning F6 <ff>	Privately owned, Grainthorpe, Lincs	
XR759	BAC Lightning F6 <ff>	Privately owned, Haxey, Lincs	
XR770	BAC Lightning F6 [AA]	Privately owned, Grainthorpe, Lincs	
XR771	BAC Lightning F6 [BM]	Midland Air Museum, Coventry	
XR806	BAC VC10 C1K (9285M) <ff>	RAF Brize Norton, BDRT	
XR807	BAC VC10 C1K [Q]	RAF No 101 Sqn, Brize Norton	
XR808	BAC VC10 C1K	RAF No 101 Sqn, Brize Norton	
XR810	BAC VC10 C1K <ff>	MoD/DARA St Athan	
XR944	Wallis WA116 (G-ATTB)	Privately owned, Reymerston Hall, Norfolk	
XR954	HS Gnat T1 (8570M) [30]	Privately owned, Bournemouth	
XR977	HS Gnat T1 (8640M) [3]	RAF Museum, Cosford	
XR991	HS Gnat T1 (8624M/XS102/G-MOUR)	Delta Jets, Kemble	
XR993	HS Gnat T1 (8620M/XP534/G-BVPP)	Kennet Aviation, North Weald	
XS100	HS Gnat T1 (8561M) <ff>	Privately owned, London SW3	
XS104	HS Gnat T1 (8604M/G-FRCE)	Privately owned, North Weald	
XS111	HS Gnat T1 (8618M/XP504/G-TIMM)	Kennet Aviation, North Weald	
XS122	WS58 Wessex HAS3 [655/PO]	*Sunk at Chepstow, December 2007*	
XS149	WS58 Wessex HAS3 [661/GL]	The Helicopter Museum, Weston-super-Mare	
XS165	Hiller UH12E (G-ASAZ) [37]	Privately owned, Sherburn-in-Elmet	
XS176	Hunting Jet Provost T4 (8514M) <ff>	Highland Aviation Museum, Inverness	
XS177	Hunting Jet Provost T4 (9044M) [N]	Privately owned, Metheringham	
XS179	Hunting Jet Provost T4 (8237M) [20]	Gr Manchester Mus of Science & Industry	
XS180	Hunting Jet Provost T4 (8238M) [21]	RAF St Athan, Fire Section	
XS181	Hunting Jet Provost T4 (9033M) <ff>	Privately owned, Bruntingthorpe	
XS183	Hunting Jet Provost T4 <ff>	Privately owned, Plymouth	
XS186	Hunting Jet Provost T4 (8408M) [M]	Metheringham Airfield Visitors Centre	
XS209	Hunting Jet Provost T4 (8409M)	Solway Aviation Society, Carlisle	
XS216	Hunting Jet Provost T4 <ff>	No 2357 Sqn ATC, Goole	
XS218	Hunting Jet Provost T4 (8508M) <ff>	No 447 Sqn ATC, Henley-on-Thames, Berks	
XS231	BAC Jet Provost T5 (G-ATAJ)	Privately owned, Barnstaple	
XS235	DH106 Comet 4C (G-CPDA)	Cold War Jets Collection, Bruntingthorpe	
XS416	BAC Lightning T5	Privately owned, Grainthorpe, Lincs	
XS417	BAC Lightning T5 [DZ]	Newark Air Museum, Winthorpe	
XS420	BAC Lightning T5	Privately owned, Farnborough	
XS421	BAC Lightning T5 <ff>	Privately owned, Foulness	
XS456	BAC Lightning T5 [DX]	Privately owned, Wainfleet	
XS457	BAC Lightning T5 <ff>	Privately owned, Grainthorpe, Lincs	
XS458	BAC Lightning T5 [T]	T5 Projects, Cranfield	
XS459	BAC Lightning T5 [AW]	Privately owned, Emneth, Norfolk	
XS463	WS Wasp HAS1 (comp XT431)	Crawley College, West Sussex	
XS481	WS58 Wessex HU5	Aeroventure, Doncaster	
XS482	WS58 Wessex HU5	RAF Manston History Museum	
XS486	WS58 Wessex HU5 (9272M) [524/CU,F]	The Helicopter Museum, Weston-super-Mare	
XS488	WS58 Wessex HU5 (9056M) [XK]	DCAE AESS, *HMS Sultan*, Gosport	
XS489	WS58 Wessex HU5 [R]	Privately owned, Redhill	
XS493	WS58 Wessex HU5	MoD/DARA, stored Fleetlands	
XS496	WS58 Wessex HU5 [625/PO]	DCAE AESS, *HMS Sultan*, Gosport	
XS498	WS58 Wessex HC5C (comp XS677) [WK]	Privately owned, Hixon, Staffs	
XS507	WS58 Wessex HU5	DCAE AESS, *HMS Sultan*, Gosport	
XS508	WS58 Wessex HU5	FAA Museum, stored RNAS Yeovilton	
XS510	WS58 Wessex HU5 [626/PO]	No 1414 Sqn ATC, Crowborough, Sussex	
XS511	WS58 Wessex HU5 [M]	Tangmere Military Aircraft Museum	
XS513	WS58 Wessex HU5 [419/CU]	RNAS Yeovilton Fire Section	
XS514	WS58 Wessex HU5 [L]	DCAE AESS, *HMS Sultan*, Gosport	
XS515	WS58 Wessex HU5 [N]	Army, Keogh Barracks, Aldershot, instructional use	
XS516	WS58 Wessex HU5 [Q]	RN, Predannack Fire School	
XS520	WS58 Wessex HU5 [F]	RN, Predannack Fire School	

Notes	Serial	Type (code/other identity)	Owner/operator, location or fate
	XS522	WS58 Wessex HU5 [ZL]	RN, Predannack Fire School
	XS527	WS Wasp HAS1	FAA Museum, RNAS Yeovilton
	XS529	WS Wasp HAS1	RN, Predannack Fire School
	XS539	WS Wasp HAS1 [435]	DARA Fleetlands Apprentice School
	XS567	WS Wasp HAS1 [434/E]	Imperial War Museum, Duxford
	XS568	WS Wasp HAS1 [441]	DCAE AESS, *HMS Sultan*, Gosport
	XS569	WS Wasp HAS1	DARA Fleetlands Apprentice School
	XS570	WS Wasp HAS1 [445/P]	Warship Preservation Trust, Birkenhead
	XS574	Northrop Shelduck D1 <R>	FAA Museum, stored RNAS Yeovilton
	XS576	DH110 Sea Vixen FAW2 [125/E]	Imperial War Museum, Duxford
	XS587	DH110 Sea Vixen FAW(TT)2 (8828M/G-VIXN)	Gatwick Aviation Museum, Charlwood, Surrey
	XS590	DH110 Sea Vixen FAW2 [131/E]	FAA Museum, RNAS Yeovilton
	XS596	HS Andover C1(PR)	MoD/AFD/*Open Skies*, Boscombe Down
	XS598	HS Andover C1 (fuselage)	FETC, Moreton-in-Marsh, Glos
	XS606	HS Andover C1	MoD/ETPS, Boscombe Down
	XS639	HS Andover E3A (9241M)	RAF Museum, Cosford
	XS643	HS Andover E3A (9278M) <ff>	Privately owned, Stock, Essex
	XS646	HS Andover C1(mod)	MoD/AFD/QinetiQ, Boscombe Down
	XS652	Slingsby T45 Swallow TX1 (BGA1107)	Privately owned, Rufforth
	XS674	WS58 Wessex HC2 [R]	Privately owned, Hixon, Staffs
	XS695	HS Kestrel FGA1	RAF Museum Restoration Centre, Cosford
	XS709	HS125 Dominie T1 [M]	RAF No 3 FTS/55(R) Sqn, Cranwell
	XS710	HS125 Dominie T1 (9259M) [O]	RAF Cranwell Fire Section
	XS711	HS125 Dominie T1 [L]	RAF No 3 FTS/55(R) Sqn, Cranwell
	XS712	HS125 Dominie T1 [A]	RAF No 3 FTS/55(R) Sqn, Cranwell
	XS713	HS125 Dominie T1 [C]	RAF No 3 FTS/55(R) Sqn, Cranwell
	XS714	HS125 Dominie T1 (9246M) [P]	MoD FSCTE, Manston
	XS726	HS125 Dominie T1 (9273M) [T]	Privately owned, Sproughton
	XS727	HS125 Dominie T1 [D]	RAF No 3 FTS/55(R) Sqn, Cranwell
	XS728	HS125 Dominie T1 [E]	RAF No 3 FTS/55(R) Sqn, Cranwell
	XS729	HS125 Dominie T1 (9275M) [G]	Privately owned, Sproughton
	XS730	HS125 Dominie T1 [H]	RAF No 3 FTS/55(R) Sqn, Cranwell
	XS731	HS125 Dominie T1 [J]	RAF No 3 FTS/55(R) Sqn, Cranwell
	XS733	HS125 Dominie T1 (9276M) [Q]	Privately owned, Sproughton
	XS734	HS125 Dominie T1 (9260M) [N]	Privately owned, Sproughton
	XS735	HS125 Dominie T1 (9264M) [R]	Penwyllt Adventure Training Centre, Powys
	XS736	HS125 Dominie T1 [S]	Privately owned, Sproughton
	XS737	HS125 Dominie T1 [K]	RAF No 3 FTS/55(R) Sqn, Cranwell
	XS738	HS125 Dominie T1 (9274M) [U]	RN, Predannack Fire School
	XS739	HS125 Dominie T1 [F]	RAF No 3 FTS/55(R) Sqn, Cranwell
	XS743	Beagle B206Z Basset CC1	MoD/ETPS, Boscombe Down
	XS765	Beagle B206Z Basset CC1 (G-BSET)	MoD, QinetiQ, Boscombe Down (spares use)
	XS770	Beagle B206Z Basset CC1 (G-HRHI)	Privately owned, Cranfield
	XS790	HS748 Andover CC2 <ff>	Boscombe Down Aviation Collection
	XS791	HS748 Andover CC2 (fuselage)	Privately owned, Stock, Essex
	XS862	WS58 Wessex HAS3	Privately owned, Hixon, Staffs
	XS863	WS58 Wessex HAS1 [304]	Imperial War Museum, Duxford
	XS876	WS58 Wessex HAS1 [523/PO]	East Midlands Airport Aeropark
	XS885	WS58 Wessex HAS1 [512/DD]	RN, Predannack Fire School
	XS886	WS58 Wessex HAS1 [527/CU]	Sea Scouts, Evesham, Worcs
	XS887	WS58 Wessex HAS1 [403/FI]	Aeroventure, Doncaster
	XS888	WS58 Wessex HAS1 [521]	Guernsey Airport Fire Section
	XS897	BAC Lightning F6	Aeroventure, Doncaster
	XS898	BAC Lightning F6 <ff>	Privately owned, Lavendon, Bucks
	XS899	BAC Lightning F6 <ff>	City of Norwich Aviation Museum
	XS903	BAC Lightning F6 [BA]	Yorkshire Air Museum, Elvington
	XS904	BAC Lightning F6 [BQ]	Lightning Preservation Grp, Bruntingthorpe
	XS919	BAC Lightning F6	Wonderland Pleasure Park, Farnsfield, Notts
	XS922	BAC Lightning F6 (8973M) <ff>	Privately owned, Ulverston, Cumbria
	XS923	BAC Lightning F6 <ff>	Privately owned, Welshpool
	XS925	BAC Lightning F6 (8961M) [BA]	RAF Museum, Hendon
	XS928	BAC Lightning F6 [AD]	BAE Systems Warton, on display
	XS932	BAC Lightning F6 <ff>	Privately owned, Ulverston, Cumbria
	XS933	BAC Lightning F6 <ff>	Privately owned, Farnham
	XS936	BAC Lightning F6	Castle Motors, Liskeard, Cornwall
	XT108	Agusta-Bell 47G-3 Sioux AH1 [U]	Museum of Army Flying, Middle Wallop

Serial	Type (code/other identity)	Owner/operator, location or fate	Notes
XT123	WS Sioux AH1 (XT827) [D]	AAC Middle Wallop, at main gate	
XT131	Agusta-Bell 47G-3 Sioux AH1 [B]	AAC Historic Aircraft Flight, Middle Wallop	
XT140	Agusta-Bell 47G-3 Sioux AH1	Perth Technical College	
XT141	Agusta-Bell 47G-3 Sioux AH1	Privately owned, Pontypridd	
XT150	Agusta-Bell 47G-3 Sioux AH1 (7883M) [R]	AAC Netheravon, at main gate	
XT176	WS Sioux AH1 [U]	FAA Museum, stored RNAS Yeovilton	
XT190	WS Sioux AH1	The Helicopter Museum, Weston-super-Mare	
XT200	WS Sioux AH1 [F]	Newark Air Museum, Winthorpe	
XT223	WS Sioux AH1 (G-XTUN)	Privately owned, Sherburn-in-Elmet	
XT236	WS Sioux AH1 (frame only)	North-East Aircraft Museum, stored Usworth	
XT242	WS Sioux AH1 (composite) [12]	Aeroventure, Doncaster	
XT257	WS58 Wessex HAS3 (8719M)	Privately owned, Bournemouth	
XT277	HS Buccaneer S2A (8853M) <ff>	Privately owned, Welshpool	
XT280	HS Buccaneer S2A <ff>	Dumfries & Galloway Avn Mus, Dumfries	
XT284	HS Buccaneer S2A (8855M) <ff>	Privately owned, Felixstowe	
XT288	HS Buccaneer S2B (9134M)	Royal Scottish Museum of Flight, stored E Fortune	
XT420	WS Wasp HAS1 (G-CBUI) [606]	Privately owned, Thruxton	
XT427	WS Wasp HAS1 [606]	FAA Museum, stored RNAS Yeovilton	
XT434	WS Wasp HAS1 [455]	DARA Fleetlands Apprentice School	
XT435	WS Wasp HAS1 (NZ3907/G-RIMM) [430]	Privately owned, Cranfield	
XT437	WS Wasp HAS1 [423]	Boscombe Down Aviation Collection	
XT439	WS Wasp HAS1 [605]	Privately owned, Hemel Hempstead	
XT443	WS Wasp HAS1 [422/AU]	The Helicopter Museum, Weston-super-Mare	
XT453	WS58 Wessex HU5 [A/B]	DCAE, stored *HMS Sultan*, Gosport	
XT455	WS58 Wessex HU5 [U]	DCAE AESS, *HMS Sultan*, Gosport	
XT456	WS58 Wessex HU5 (8941M) [XZ]	RAF Aldergrove, BDRT	
XT458	WS58 Wessex HU5 [622]	DCAE, stored *HMS Sultan*, Gosport	
XT463	WS58 Wessex HC5C (comp XR508) [*Clubs*]	Privately owned, Hixon, Staffs	
XT466	WS58 Wessex HU5 (8921M) [XV]	DCAE AESS, *HMS Sultan*, Gosport	
XT467	WS58 Wessex HU5 (8922M) [BF]	Privately owned, Hadleigh, Suffolk	
XT468	WS58 Wessex HU5 (comp XT460) [628]	RN, Predannack Fire School	
XT469	WS58 Wessex HU5 (8920M)	RAF No 16 MU, Stafford, ground instruction	
XT472	WS58 Wessex HU5 [XC]	The Helicopter Museum, Weston-super-Mare	
XT480	WS58 Wessex HU5 [468/RG]	East Midlands Airport Aeropark	
XT482	WS58 Wessex HU5 [ZM/VL]	FAA Museum, RNAS Yeovilton	
XT484	WS58 Wessex HU5 [H]	DCAE AESS, *HMS Sultan*, Gosport	
XT485	WS58 Wessex HU5	DCAE AESS, *HMS Sultan*, Gosport	
XT486	WS58 Wessex HU5 (8919M)	Dumfries & Galloway Avn Mus, Dumfries	
XT550	WS Sioux AH1 [D]	AAC, stored Middle Wallop	
XT575	Vickers Viscount 837 <ff>	Brooklands Museum, Weybridge	
XT581	Northrop Shelduck D1	Imperial War Museum stored, Duxford	
XT596	McD F-4K Phantom FG1	FAA Museum, RNAS Yeovilton	
XT597	McD F-4K Phantom FG1	Boscombe Down Aviation Collection	
XT601	WS58 Wessex HC2 (9277M) (composite)	RAF Odiham, BDRT	
XT604	WS58 Wessex HC2	East Midlands Airport Aeropark	
XT607	WS58 Wessex HC2 [P]	*Sunk at Chepstow, December 2007*	
XT617	WS Scout AH1	AAC Wattisham, on display	
XT621	WS Scout AH1	R. Military College of Science, Shrivenham	
XT623	WS Scout AH1	DCAE SEAE, Arborfield	
XT626	WS Scout AH1 [Q]	AAC Historic Aircraft Flt, Middle Wallop	
XT630	WS Scout AH1 (G-BXRL) [X]	Privately owned, Bruntingthorpe	
XT631	WS Scout AH1 [D]	Privately owned, Ipswich	
XT632	WS Scout AH1 (G-BZBD)	Privately owned, North Weald (spares use)	
XT633	WS Scout AH1	DCAE SEAE, Arborfield	
XT634	WS Scout AH1 (G-BYRX) [T]	Privately owned, Tollerton	
XT638	WS Scout AH1 [N]	AAC Middle Wallop, at gate	
XT640	WS Scout AH1	Privately owned, Sproughton	
XT643	WS Scout AH1 [Z]	Army, Thorpe Camp, East Wretham	
XT645	WS Scout AH1 (fuselage)	Privately owned, Ipswich	
XT671	WS58 Wessex HC2 (G-BYRC) [D]	Privately owned, Redhill	
XT672	WS58 Wessex HC2 [WE]	RAF Shawbury, on display	

Notes	*Serial*	*Type (code/other identity)*	*Owner/operator, location or fate*
	XT681	WS58 Wessex HC2 (9279M) [U]	*Scrapped, November 2007*
	XT761	WS58 Wessex HU5	DCAE AESS, *HMS Sultan*, Gosport
	XT762	WS58 Wessex HU5	Privately owned, Bristol
	XT765	WS58 Wessex HU5 [J]	RNAS Yeovilton, on display
	XT769	WS58 Wessex HU5 [823]	FAA Museum, RNAS Yeovilton
	XT770	WS58 Wessex HU5 (9055M) [P]	Privately owned, Shawell, Leics
	XT771	WS58 Wessex HU5 [620/PO]	DCAE AESS, *HMS Sultan*, Gosport
	XT773	WS58 Wessex HU5 (9123M) [822/CU]	RAF Shawbury Fire Section
	XT778	WS Wasp HAS1 [430]	FAA Museum, stored Yeovilton
	XT780	WS Wasp HAS1 [636]	Fareham Tertiary College, Hants
	XT787	WS Wasp HAS1 (NZ3905/G-KAXT)	Kennet Aviation, North Weald
	XT788	WS Wasp HAS1 (G-BMIR) [474]	Privately owned, Dunkeswell
	XT793	WS Wasp HAS1 (G-BZPP) [456]	Privately owned, Otley
	XT852	McD YF-4M Phantom FGR2	QinetiQ West Freugh Fire Section
	XT863	McD F-4K Phantom FG1 <ff>	Privately owned, Cowes, IOW
	XT864	McD F-4K Phantom FG1 (8998M/*XT684*) [BJ]	RAF Leuchars on display
	XT891	McD F-4M Phantom FGR2 (9136M) [Z]	RAF Coningsby, at main gate
	XT903	McD F-4M Phantom FGR2 <ff>	RAF Museum Restoration Centre, Cosford
	XT905	McD F-4M Phantom FGR2 (9286M) [P]	RAF North Luffenham Training Area
	XT907	McD F-4M Phantom FGR2 (9151M) [W]	DEODS, Chattenden, Kent
	XT914	McD F-4M Phantom FGR2 (9269M) [Z]	RAF Brampton, Cambs, on display
	XV101	BAC VC10 C1K [S]	RAF No 101 Sqn, Brize Norton
	XV102	BAC VC10 C1K [T]	RAF No 101 Sqn, Brize Norton
	XV104	BAC VC10 C1K [U]	RAF No 101 Sqn, Brize Norton
	XV105	BAC VC10 C1K $	RAF No 101 Sqn, Brize Norton
	XV106	BAC VC10 C1K [W]	MoD/DARA, St Athan
	XV107	BAC VC10 C1K [X]	RAF No 101 Sqn, Brize Norton
	XV108	BAC VC10 C1K [Y]	RAF No 101 Sqn, Brize Norton
	XV109	BAC VC10 C1K [Z]	RAF No 101 Sqn, Brize Norton
	XV118	WS Scout AH1 (9141M)	Privately owned, North Weald
	XV122	WS Scout AH1 [D]	R. Military College of Science, Shrivenham
	XV123	WS Scout AH1	RAF Shawbury, on display
	XV124	WS Scout AH1 [W]	DCAE SEAE, Arborfield
	XV127	WS Scout AH1	Museum of Army Flying, Middle Wallop
	XV130	WS Scout AH1 (G-BWJW) [R]	Privately owned, Thruxton
	XV131	WS Scout AH1 [Y]	AAC 70 Aircraft Workshops, Middle Wallop, BDRT
	XV134	WS Scout AH1 (G-BWLX) [P]	Privately owned, Oaksey Park
	XV136	WS Scout AH1 [X]	AAC Netheravon, on display
	XV137	WS Scout AH1 (G-CRUM)	Privately owned, Chiseldon, Wilts
	XV137	WS Scout AH1 (XV139)	AAC, Wattisham
	XV138	WS Scout AH1	Privately owned, East Dereham, Norfolk
	XV141	WS Scout AH1	REME Museum, Arborfield
	XV148	HS Nimrod MR1(mod) <ff>	Privately owned, Malmesbury
	XV161	HS Buccaneer S2B (9117M) <ff>	Dundonald Aviation Centre
	XV165	HS Buccaneer S2B <ff>	Privately owned, Bruntingthorpe
	XV168	HS Buccaneer S2B [AF]	BAE Systems Brough, on display
	XV177	Lockheed C-130K Hercules C3A	RAF Lyneham Transport Wing
	XV184	Lockheed C-130K Hercules C3	MoD/Marshalls, stored Cambridge
	XV188	Lockheed C-130K Hercules C3A	RAF Lyneham Transport Wing
	XV196	Lockheed C-130K Hercules C1	RAF Lyneham Transport Wing
	XV197	Lockheed C-130K Hercules C3	RAF Lyneham Transport Wing
	XV199	Lockheed C-130K Hercules C3	MoD/Marshalls, stored Cambridge
	XV200	Lockheed C-130K Hercules C1	RAF Lyneham Transport Wing
	XV201	Lockheed C-130K Hercules C1K <ff>	Marshalls, Cambridge
	XV202	Lockheed C-130K Hercules C3	RAF Lyneham Transport Wing
	XV205	Lockheed C-130K Hercules C1	*Crashed 24 August 2007, near Kabul, Afghanistan*
	XV208	Lockheed C-130K Hercules W2	MoD/Marshalls, Cambridge
	XV209	Lockheed C-130K Hercules C3A	RAF Lyneham Transport Wing
	XV212	Lockheed C-130K Hercules C3	RAF Lyneham Transport Wing
	XV214	Lockheed C-130K Hercules C3A	RAF Lyneham Transport Wing
	XV217	Lockheed C-130K Hercules C3	RAF Lyneham Transport Wing
	XV220	Lockheed C-130K Hercules C3	RAF Lyneham Transport Wing

Serial	Type (code/other identity)	Owner/operator, location or fate	Notes
XV221	Lockheed C-130K Hercules C3	RAF Lyneham Transport Wing	
XV226	HS Nimrod MR2	RAF Kinloss MR Wing	
XV229	HS Nimrod MR2	RAF Kinloss MR Wing	
XV231	HS Nimrod MR2	RAF Kinloss MR Wing	
XV232	HS Nimrod MR2	RAF Kinloss MR Wing	
XV235	HS Nimrod MR2	RAF Kinloss (wfu)	
XV236	HS Nimrod MR2	RAF Kinloss MR Wing	
XV238	HS Nimrod <R> (parts of G-ALYW)	*Sold to The Netherlands*	
XV240	HS Nimrod MR2	RAF Kinloss MR Wing	
XV241	HS Nimrod MR2	RAF Kinloss MR Wing	
XV244	HS Nimrod MR2	RAF Kinloss MR Wing	
XV246	HS Nimrod MR2	MoD/BAE Systems, Woodford	
XV248	HS Nimrod MR2	RAF Kinloss MR Wing	
XV249	HS Nimrod R1	RAF No 51 Sqn, Waddington	
XV250	HS Nimrod MR2	RAF Kinloss MR Wing	
XV252	HS Nimrod MR2	RAF Kinloss MR Wing	
XV253	HS Nimrod MR2 (9118M)	MoD/BAE Systems, Woodford	
XV254	HS Nimrod MR2	RAF Kinloss MR Wing	
XV255	HS Nimrod MR2	RAF Kinloss MR Wing	
XV259	BAe Nimrod AEW3 <ff>	Privately owned, Carlisle	
XV260	HS Nimrod MR2	RAF Kinloss MR Wing	
XV263	BAe Nimrod AEW3P (8967M) <ff>	BAE Systems, Brough	
XV263	BAe Nimrod AEW3P (8967M) <rf>	MoD/BAE Systems, Woodford	
XV268	DHC2 Beaver AL1 (G-BVER)	Privately owned, Cumbernauld	
XV277	HS P.1127(RAF)	Royal Scottish Mus'm of Flight, E Fortune	
XV279	HS P.1127(RAF) (8566M)	RAF Harrier Maintenance School, Wittering	
XV280	HS P.1127(RAF) <ff>	RNAS Yeovilton Fire Section	
XV290	Lockheed C-130K Hercules C3	RAF Lyneham Transport Wing	
XV294	Lockheed C-130K Hercules C3	RAF Lyneham Transport Wing	
XV295	Lockheed C-130K Hercules C1	RAF Lyneham Transport Wing	
XV299	Lockheed C-130K Hercules C3	RAF Lyneham Transport Wing	
XV301	Lockheed C-130K Hercules C3	RAF Lyneham Transport Wing	
XV302	Lockheed C-130K Hercules C3	Marshalls, Cambridge, fatigue test airframe	
XV303	Lockheed C-130K Hercules C3A	RAF Lyneham Transport Wing	
XV304	Lockheed C-130K Hercules C3A	RAF Lyneham Transport Wing	
XV305	Lockheed C-130K Hercules C3	RAF Lyneham Transport Wing	
XV307	Lockheed C-130K Hercules C3 (G-52-40)	RAF Lyneham Transport Wing	
XV328	BAC Lightning T5 <ff>	Phoenix Aviation, Bruntingthorpe	
XV333	HS Buccaneer S2B [234/H]	FAA Museum, RNAS Yeovilton	
XV337	HS Buccaneer S2C (8852M) <ff>	Privately owned, Market Drayton	
XV344	HS Buccaneer S2C	QinetiQ Farnborough, on display	
XV350	HS Buccaneer S2B	East Midlands Airport Aeropark	
XV352	HS Buccaneer S2B <ff>	RAF Manston History Museum	
XV359	HS Buccaneer S2B [035/R]	Privately owned, Topsham, Devon	
XV361	HS Buccaneer S2B	Ulster Aviation Society, stored Lisburn	
XV370	Sikorsky SH-3D [260]	DCAE AESS, *HMS Sultan*, Gosport	
XV371	WS61 Sea King HAS1(DB) [261]	SFDO, RNAS Culdrose	
XV372	WS61 Sea King HAS1	RAF HMF, St Mawgan	
XV383	Northrop Shelduck D1	Privately owned, Wimborne, Dorset	
XV401	McD F-4M Phantom FGR2 [I]	Boscombe Down Aviation Collection	
XV402	McD F-4M Phantom FGR2 <ff>	*Currently not known*	
XV406	McD F-4M Phantom FGR2 (9098M) [CK]	Solway Aviation Society, Carlisle	
XV408	McD F-4M Phantom FGR2 (9165M) [Z]	Tangmere Military Aviation Museum	
XV411	McD F-4M Phantom FGR2 (9103M) [L]	MoD FSCTE, Manston	
XV415	McD F-4M Phantom FGR2 (9163M) [E]	RAF Boulmer, on display	
XV424	McD F-4M Phantom FGR2 (9152M) [I]	RAF Museum, Hendon	
XV426	McD F-4M Phantom FGR2 <ff>	City of Norwich Aviation Museum	
XV426	McD F-4M Phantom FGR2 [P] <rf>	RAF Coningsby, BDRT	
XV460	McD F-4M Phantom FGR2 <ff>	No 2214 Sqn ATC, Usworth	
XV474	McD F-4M Phantom FGR2 [T]	The Old Flying Machine Company, Duxford	
XV490	McD F-4M Phantom FGR2 <ff>	Privately owned, Nantwich	
XV497	McD F-4M Phantom FGR2 (9295M) [D]	RAF No 23 Sqn Waddington, (preserved)	
XV498	McD F-4M Phantom FGR2 (XV500/9113M) [U]	*Scrapped at St Athan, July 2007*	
XV499	McD F-4M Phantom FGR2	RAF Leeming, WLT	

Notes	Serial	Type (code/other identity)	Owner/operator, location or fate
	XV581	McD F-4K Phantom FG1 (9070M) <ff>	No 2481 Sqn ATC, Bridge of Don
	XV582	McD F-4K Phantom FG1 (9066M) [M]	RAF Leuchars, on display
	XV586	McD F-4K Phantom FG1 (9067M) [AJ]	RAF Leuchars, on display
	XV591	McD F-4K Phantom FG1 <ff>	RAF Museum, Cosford
	XV625	WS Wasp HAS1 [471]	DCAE, stored *HMS Sultan*, Gosport
	XV631	WS Wasp HAS1 (fuselage)	QinetiQ Acoustics Dept, Farnborough
	XV642	WS61 Sea King HAS2A [259]	DCAE AESS, *HMS Sultan*, Gosport
	XV643	WS61 Sea King HAS6 [262]	DCAE, No 1 SoTT, Cosford
	XV647	WS61 Sea King HU5 [28]	RN No 771 Sqn, Culdrose
	XV648	WS61 Sea King HU5 [18]	RN No 771 Sqn, Culdrose
	XV649	WS61 Sea King ASaC7 [180]	RN No 854 Sqn, Culdrose
	XV651	WS61 Sea King HU5 [24]	MoD/QinetiQ, Boscombe Down
	XV653	WS61 Sea King HAS6 (9326M) [63/CU]	DCAE, stored *HMS Sultan*, Gosport
	XV654	WS61 Sea King HAS6 [705] (wreck)	SFDO, RNAS Culdrose
	XV655	WS61 Sea King HAS6 [270/N]	DCAE AESS, *HMS Sultan*, Gosport
	XV656	WS61 Sea King ASaC7 [185]	RN No 849 Sqn, Culdrose
	XV657	WS61 Sea King HAS5 (*ZA135*) [32/DD]	SFDO, RNAS Culdrose
	XV659	WS61 Sea King HAS6 (9324M) [62/CU]	DCAE, No 1 SoTT, Cosford
	XV660	WS61 Sea King HAS6 [69]	DCAE AESS, *HMS Sultan*, Gosport
	XV661	WS61 Sea King HU5 [26]	RN No 771 Sqn, Prestwick
	XV663	WS61 Sea King HAS6	DCAE, stored *HMS Sultan*, Gosport
	XV664	WS61 Sea King ASaC7 [190]	RN No 849 Sqn, Culdrose
	XV665	WS61 Sea King HAS6 [507/CU]	DCAE, stored *HMS Sultan*, Gosport
	XV666	WS61 Sea King HU5 [21]	RN CHFMU, Yeovilton
	XV670	WS61 Sea King HU5 [17]	RN No 771 Sqn, Culdrose
	XV671	WS61 Sea King ASaC7	RN No 854 Sqn, Culdrose
	XV672	WS61 Sea King ASaC7 [187]	RN No 857 Sqn, Culdrose
	XV673	WS61 Sea King HU5 [827/CU]	RN No 771 Sqn, Culdrose
	XV675	WS61 Sea King HAS6 [701/PW]	DCAE AESS, *HMS Sultan*, Gosport
	XV676	WS61 Sea King HAS6CR [ZE]	RN No 846 Sqn, Yeovilton
	XV677	WS61 Sea King HAS6 [269]	Aeroventure, Doncaster
	XV696	WS61 Sea King HAS6 [267/N]	DCAE, stored *HMS Sultan*, Gosport
	XV697	WS61 Sea King ASaC7 [181]	MoD/DARA, Fleetlands
	XV699	WS61 Sea King HU5 [823/CU]	RN CHFMU, Yeovilton
	XV700	WS61 Sea King HC6 [ZC]	RN No 845 Sqn, Yeovilton
	XV701	WS61 Sea King HAS6 [268/N]	DCAE, No 1 SoTT, Cosford
	XV703	WS61 Sea King HC6 [ZD]	MoD/DARA, Fleetlands
	XV705	WS61 Sea King HAR5 [29]	RN No 771 Sqn, Culdrose
	XV706	WS61 Sea King HAS6 (9344M) [017/L]	RN ETS, Culdrose
	XV707	WS61 Sea King ASaC7 [184]	RN No 849 Sqn, Culdrose
	XV708	WS61 Sea King HAS6 [501/CU]	DCAE, stored *HMS Sultan*, Gosport
	XV709	WS61 Sea King HAS6 (9303M) [263]	RAF St Mawgan, instructional use
	XV711	WS61 Sea King HAS6 [515/CT]	DCAE, stored *HMS Sultan*, Gosport
	XV712	WS61 Sea King HAS6 [269]	DCAE AESS, *HMS Sultan*, Gosport
	XV713	WS61 Sea King HAS6 [018]	DCAE AESS, *HMS Sultan*, Gosport
	XV714	WS61 Sea King ASaC7 [188]	RN No 854 Sqn, Culdrose
	XV720	WS58 Wessex HC2	DCAE, stored *HMS Sultan*, Gosport
	XV722	WS58 Wessex HC2 [WH]	Privately owned, Hixon, Staffs
	XV724	WS58 Wessex HC2	DCAE AESS, *HMS Sultan*, Gosport
	XV725	WS58 Wessex HC2 [C]	DCAE, No 1 SoTT, Cosford
	XV726	WS58 Wessex HC2 [J]	Privately owned, Hixon, Staffs
	XV728	WS58 Wessex HC2 [A]	Newark Air Museum, Winthorpe
	XV731	WS58 Wessex HC2 [Y]	Privately owned, stored Redhill
	XV732	WS58 Wessex HCC4	RAF Museum, Hendon
	XV733	WS58 Wessex HCC4	The Helicopter Museum, Weston-super-Mare
	XV741	HS Harrier GR3 [41]	SFDO, RNAS Culdrose
	XV744	HS Harrier GR3 (9167M) [3K]	R. Military College of Science, Shrivenham
	XV748	HS Harrier GR3 [3D]	Yorkshire Air Museum, Elvington
	XV751	HS Harrier GR3	Gatwick Aviation Museum, Charlwood
	XV752	HS Harrier GR3 (9075M) [B,HF]	Bletchley Park Museum, Bucks
	XV753	HS Harrier GR3 (9078M) <ff>	RNAS Culdrose, Fire Section
	XV753	HS Harrier GR3 (9078M) [53] <rf>	RN, Predannack Fire School

Serial	Type (code/other identity)	Owner/operator, location or fate	Notes
XV755	HS Harrier GR3 [M]	RNAS Yeovilton Fire Section	
XV759	HS Harrier GR3 [O] <ff>	Privately owned, Hitchin, Herts	
XV760	HS Harrier GR3 <ff>	Privately owned, Sussex	
XV779	HS Harrier GR3 (8931M)	RAF Wittering on display	
XV783	HS Harrier GR3 [83]	RN, Predannack Fire School	
XV784	HS Harrier GR3 (8909M) <ff>	Boscombe Down Aviation Collection	
XV786	HS Harrier GR3 <ff>	RNAS Culdrose	
XV786	HS Harrier GR3 [S] <rf>	RN, Predannack Fire School	
XV798	HS Harrier GR1(mod)	Bristol Aero Collection, stored Kemble	
XV804	HS Harrier GR3 (9280M) [O]	RAF North Luffenham Training Area	
XV808	HS Harrier GR3 (9076M) [08]	SFDO, RNAS Culdrose	
XV810	HS Harrier GR3 (9038M) [K]	Privately owned, Wigston, Leics	
XV814	DH106 Comet 4 (G-APDF) <ff>	Privately owned, Chipping Campden	
XV863	HS Buccaneer S2B (9115M/9139M/9145M) [S]	Privately owned, Weston, Eire	
XV864	HS Buccaneer S2B (9234M)	MoD FSCTE, Manston	
XV865	HS Buccaneer S2B (9226M)	Imperial War Museum, Duxford	
XV867	HS Buccaneer S2B <ff>	Highland Aviation Museum, Inverness	
XW175	HS Harrier T4(VAAC)	MoD/AFD/QinetiQ, Boscombe Down	
XW198	WS Puma HC1	RAF No 230 Sqn, Aldergrove	
XW199	WS Puma HC1	RAF No 1563 Flt, Basrah, Iraq	
XW200	WS Puma HC1 (wreck)	RAF, stored Shawbury	
XW201	WS Puma HC1	RAF Benson (spares use)	
XW202	WS Puma HC1	RAF, stored Shawbury	
XW204	WS Puma HC1	RAF No 230 Sqn, Aldergrove	
XW206	WS Puma HC1	RAF Benson (spares use)	
XW207	WS Puma HC1	RAF No 33 Sqn, Benson	
XW208	WS Puma HC1	RAF No 33 Sqn, Benson	
XW209	WS Puma HC1	RAF No 33 Sqn, Benson	
XW210	WS Puma HC1 (comp XW215)	RAF No 33 Sqn, Benson	
XW211	WS Puma HC1	RAF No 1563 Flt, Basrah, Iraq	
XW212	WS Puma HC1	RAF No 33 Sqn, Benson	
XW213	WS Puma HC1	RAF No 33 Sqn, Benson	
XW214	WS Puma HC1	RAF No 33 Sqn, Benson	
XW216	WS Puma HC1	RAF No 230 Sqn, Aldergrove	
XW217	WS Puma HC1	RAF No 33 Sqn, Benson	
XW218	WS Puma HC1	*Crashed 15 April 2007, Taji, Iraq*	
XW219	WS Puma HC1	RAF No 1563 Flt, Basrah, Iraq	
XW220	WS Puma HC1	RAF No 1563 Flt, Basrah, Iraq	
XW222	WS Puma HC1	Eurocopter, Marignane, France (on repair)	
XW223	WS Puma HC1	RAF No 230 Sqn, Aldergrove	
XW224	WS Puma HC1	RAF No 33 Sqn, Benson	
XW226	WS Puma HC1	RAF No 1563 Flt, Basrah, Iraq	
XW227	WS Puma HC1	Privately owned, Colsterworth, Leics	
XW229	WS Puma HC1	RAF No 33 Sqn, Benson	
XW231	WS Puma HC1	Eurocopter, Marignane, France (on repair)	
XW232	WS Puma HC1	RAF No 33 Sqn, Benson	
XW235	WS Puma HC1	RAF No 230 Sqn, Aldergrove	
XW236	WS Puma HC1	RAF No 1563 Flt, Basrah, Iraq	
XW237	WS Puma HC1	RAF No 33 Sqn, Benson	
XW241	Sud SA330E Puma	Farnborough Air Sciences Trust, Farnborough	
XW264	HS Harrier T2 <ff>	Gloucestershire Avn Coll, stored Gloucester	
XW265	HS Harrier T4A (9258M) <ff>	No 2345 Sqn ATC, RAF Leuchars	
XW265	HS Harrier T4A (9258M) <rf>	DARA, St Athan	
XW267	HS Harrier T4 (9263M) [SA]	Territorial Army, Toton, Notts	
XW269	HS Harrier T4	Boscombe Down Aviation Collection	
XW270	HS Harrier T4 (fuselage)	Coventry University, instructional use	
XW271	HS Harrier T4 [71]	RN, Predannack Fire School	
XW272	HS Harrier T4 (8783M) (fuselage) (comp XV281)	Marsh Lane Technical School, Preston	
XW276	Aérospatiale SA341 Gazelle (F-ZWRI)	Newark Air Museum, Winthorpe	
XW281	WS Scout AH1 (G-BYNZ) [T]	Privately owned, Wembury, Devon	
XW283	WS Scout AH1 [U]	RM, stored Yeovilton	
XW289	BAC Jet Provost T5A (G-BVXT/G-JPVA) [73]	Kennet Aviation, North Weald	
XW290	BAC Jet Provost T5A (9199M) [41,MA]	DCAE, No 1 SoTT, Cosford	
XW293	BAC Jet Provost T5 (G-BWCS) [Z]	Privately owned, Bournemouth	

Notes	*Serial*	*Type (code/other identity)*	*Owner/operator, location or fate*
	XW299	BAC Jet Provost T5A (9146M) [60,MB]	DCAE, No 1 SoTT, Cosford
	XW301	BAC Jet Provost T5A (9147M) [63,MC]	DCAE, No 1 SoTT, Cosford
	XW303	BAC Jet Provost T5A (9119M) [127]	RAF Halton
	XW304	BAC Jet Provost T5 (9172M) [MD]	DCAE, No 1 SoTT, Cosford
	XW309	BAC Jet Provost T5 (9179M) [V,ME]	Hartlepool College of Further Education
	XW311	BAC Jet Provost T5 (9180M) [W,MF]	Privately owned, Exeter
	XW315	BAC Jet Provost T5A <ff>	Privately owned, Wolverhampton
	XW318	BAC Jet Provost T5A (9190M) [78,MG]	DCAE, No 1 SoTT, Cosford
	XW320	BAC Jet Provost T5A (9015M) [71]	DCAE, No 1 SoTT, Cosford
	XW321	BAC Jet Provost T5A (9154M) [62,MH]	DCAE, No 1 SoTT, Cosford
	XW323	BAC Jet Provost T5A (9166M) [86]	RAF Museum, Hendon
	XW324	BAC Jet Provost T5 (G-BWSG) [K]	Privately owned, Hawarden
	XW325	BAC Jet Provost T5B (G-BWGF) [E]	Privately owned, Exeter
	XW327	BAC Jet Provost T5A (9130M) [62]	DCAE, No 1 SoTT, Cosford
	XW328	BAC Jet Provost T5A (9177M) [75,MI]	DCAE, No 1 SoTT, Cosford
	XW330	BAC Jet Provost T5A (9195M) [82,MJ]	DCAE, No 1 SoTT, Cosford
	XW333	BAC Jet Provost T5A (G-BVTC)	Global Aviation, Humberside
	XW353	BAC Jet Provost T5A (9090M) [3]	RAF Cranwell, on display
	XW354	BAC Jet Provost T5A (XW355/G-JPTV)	Privately owned, Sandtoft
	XW358	BAC Jet Provost T5A (9181M) [59,MK]	DCAE, No 1 SoTT, Cosford
	XW360	BAC Jet Provost T5A (9153M) [61,ML]	DCAE, No 1 SoTT, Cosford
	XW361	BAC Jet Provost T5A (9192M) [81,MM]	DCAE, No 1 SoTT, Cosford
	XW363	BAC Jet Provost T5A [36]	BAE Systems North West Heritage Group, Warton
	XW364	BAC Jet Provost T5A (9188M) [35,MN]	DCAE, No 1 SoTT, Cosford
	XW367	BAC Jet Provost T5A (9193M) [64,MO]	DCAE, No 1 SoTT, Cosford
	XW370	BAC Jet Provost T5A (9196M) [72,MP]	DCAE, No 1 SoTT, Cosford
	XW375	BAC Jet Provost T5A (9149M) [52]	DCAE, No 1 SoTT, Cosford
	XW404	BAC Jet Provost T5A (9049M)	Privately owned, Exeter
	XW405	BAC Jet Provost T5A (9187M) [J,MQ]	Privately owned, Ashclyst Farm, Exeter
	XW409	BAC Jet Provost T5A (9047M)	Privately owned, Bury
	XW410	BAC Jet Provost T5A (9125M) [80,MR]	DCAE, No 1 SoTT, Cosford
	XW416	BAC Jet Provost T5A (9191M) [84,MS]	DCAE, No 1 SoTT, Cosford
	XW418	BAC Jet Provost T5A (9173M) [MT]	DCAE, No 1 SoTT, Cosford
	XW419	BAC Jet Provost T5A (9120M) [125]	Privately owned, Crondall, Hants
	XW420	BAC Jet Provost T5A (9194M) [83,MU]	DCAE, No 1 SoTT, Cosford
	XW421	BAC Jet Provost T5A (9111M) [60]	Privately owned, Sproughton
	XW422	BAC Jet Provost T5A (G-BWEB) [3]	Privately owned, Kemble
	XW423	BAC Jet Provost T5A (G-BWUW) [14]	Deeside College, Connah's Quay, Clwyd
	XW425	BAC Jet Provost T5A (9200M) [H,MV]	DCAE, No 1 SoTT, Cosford
	XW430	BAC Jet Provost T5A (9176M) [77,MW]	DCAE, No 1 SoTT, Cosford
	XW432	BAC Jet Provost T5A (9127M) [76,MX]	DCAE, No 1 SoTT, Cosford
	XW433	BAC Jet Provost T5A (G-JPRO)	Air Atlantique Classic Flight, Coventry

Serial	Type (code/other identity)	Owner/operator, location or fate	Notes
XW434	BAC Jet Provost T5A (9091M) [78,MY]	DCAE, No 1 SoTT, Cosford	
XW436	BAC Jet Provost T5A (9148M) [68]	DCAE, No 1 SoTT, Cosford	
XW530	HS Buccaneer S2B	Buccaneer Service Station, Elgin	
XW541	HS Buccaneer S2B (8858M) <ff>	Privately owned, Mold	
XW544	HS Buccaneer S2B (8857M) [Y]	Privately owned, Bruntingthorpe	
XW547	HS Buccaneer S2B (9095M/9169M) [R]	RAF Museum, Hendon	
XW550	HS Buccaneer S2B <ff>	Privately owned, West Horndon, Essex	
XW560	SEPECAT Jaguar S <ff>	Boscombe Down Aviation Collection	
XW563	SEPECAT Jaguar S (*XX822*/8563M)	County Hall, Norwich, on display	
XW566	SEPECAT Jaguar B	Farnborough Air Sciences Trust, Farnborough	
XW613	WS Scout AH1 (G-BXRS)	Privately owned, New Milton, Hants	
XW616	WS Scout AH1	AAC Dishforth, instructional use	
XW630	HS Harrier GR3	RNAS Yeovilton, Fire Section	
XW635	Beagle D5/180 (G-AWSW)	Privately owned, Spanhoe	
XW664	HS Nimrod R1	RAF No 51 Sqn, Waddington	
XW665	HS Nimrod R1	RAF No 51 Sqn, Waddington	
XW666	HS Nimrod R1 <ff>	Aeroventure, Doncaster	
XW763	HS Harrier GR3 (9002M/9041M) <ff>	Privately owned, Wigston, Leics	
XW768	HS Harrier GR3 (9072M) [N]	DCAE AESS, *HMS Sultan*, Gosport	
XW784	Mitchell-Procter Kittiwake I (G-BBRN) [VL]	Privately owned, RNAS Yeovilton	
XW795	WS Scout AH1	Blessingbourne Museum, Fivemiletown, Co Tyrone, NI	
XW796	WS Scout AH1	Gunsmoke Paintball, Hadleigh, Suffolk	
XW838	WS Lynx (TAD 009)	DCAE SEAE, Arborfield	
XW839	WS Lynx	The Helicopter Museum, Weston-super-Mare	
XW844	WS Gazelle AH1	DARA Fleetlands Apprentice School	
XW846	WS Gazelle AH1	AAC No 665 Sqn/5 Regt, Aldergrove	
XW847	WS Gazelle AH1 [H]	AAC No 665 Sqn/5 Regt, Aldergrove	
XW848	WS Gazelle AH1 [D]	AAC, stored Shawbury	
XW849	WS Gazelle AH1 [G]	RM, stored Shawbury	
XW851	WS Gazelle AH1	RM, stored Shawbury	
XW852	WS Gazelle HCC4 (9331M)	DCAE, No 1 SoTT, Cosford	
XW854	WS Gazelle HT2 (G-CBSD) [46/CU]	Privately owned, Earls Colne	
XW855	WS Gazelle HCC4	RAF Museum, Hendon	
XW858	WS Gazelle HT3 (G-DMSS) [C]	Privately owned, Murton, York	
XW860	WS Gazelle HT2 (TAD021)	DCAE SEAE, Arborfield	
XW862	WS Gazelle HT3 (G-CBKC) [D]	Privately owned, Fowlmere	
XW863	WS Gazelle HT2 (TAD022) [42/CU]	DCAE SEAE, Arborfield	
XW864	WS Gazelle HT2 [54/CU]	FAA Museum, stored RNAS Yeovilton	
XW865	WS Gazelle AH1 [5C]	AAC No 29 Flt, BATUS, Suffield, Canada	
XW866	WS Gazelle HT3 (G-BXTH) [E]	Privately owned, Wigtown, D&G	
XW870	WS Gazelle HT3 (9299M) [F]	MoD FSCTE, Manston	
XW888	WS Gazelle AH1 (TAD017)	DCAE SEAE, Arborfield	
XW889	WS Gazelle AH1 (TAD018)	DCAE SEAE, Arborfield	
XW890	WS Gazelle HT2	RNAS Yeovilton, on display	
XW892	WS Gazelle AH1 (9292M) [C]	Privately owned, Sproughton	
XW893	WS Gazelle AH1 <ff>	Privately owned, East Garston, Bucks	
XW895	WS Gazelle HT2 (G-BXZD) [51/CU]	Privately owned, stored Breighton	
XW897	WS Gazelle AH1	AAC, stored Shawbury	
XW898	WS Gazelle HT3 (G-CBXT) [G]	Privately owned, Redhill	
XW899	WS Gazelle AH1 [Z]	AAC No 6(V) Flt/7 Regt, Shawbury	
XW900	WS Gazelle AH1 (TAD900)	DCAE SEAE, Arborfield	
XW902	WS Gazelle HT3 [H]	MoD/QinetiQ, Boscombe Down, spares use	
XW904	WS Gazelle AH1 [H]	AAC, stored Shawbury	
XW906	WS Gazelle HT3 [J]	QinetiQ Boscombe Down, Apprentice School	
XW908	WS Gazelle AH1 [A]	QinetiQ, Boscombe Down (spares use)	
XW909	WS Gazelle AH1	AAC, stored Shawbury	
XW912	WS Gazelle AH1 (TAD019)	DCAE SEAE, Arborfield	
XW913	WS Gazelle AH1	AAC, stored Shawbury	
XW917	HS Harrier GR3 (8975M)	RAF Cottesmore, at main gate	
XW919	HS Harrier GR3 [W]	R. Military College of Science, Shrivenham	
XW922	HS Harrier GR3 (8885M)	MoD FSCTE, Manston	
XW923	HS Harrier GR3 (8724M) <ff>	RAF Wittering, Fire Section	
XW924	HS Harrier GR3 (9073M) [G]	RAF Coningsby, preserved	

Notes	Serial	Type (code/other identity)	Owner/operator, location or fate
	XW934	HS Harrier T4 [Y]	Farnborough Air Sciences Trust, Farnborough
	XW994	Northrop Chukar D1	FAA Museum, stored RNAS Yeovilton
	XW999	Northrop Chukar D1	RNAS Culdrose, preserved
	XX105	BAC 1-11/201AC (G-ASJD)	Boscombe Down Aviation Collection
	XX108	SEPECAT Jaguar GR3	Imperial War Museum, Duxford
	XX109	SEPECAT Jaguar GR1 (8918M) [GH]	City of Norwich Aviation Museum
	XX110	SEPECAT Jaguar GR1 (8955M) [EP]	DCAE, No 1 SoTT, Cosford
	XX110	SEPECAT Jaguar GR1 <R> (BAPC 169)	DCAE, No 1 SoTT, Cosford
	XX112	SEPECAT Jaguar GR3A [EA]	DCAE, No 1 SoTT, Cosford
	XX115	SEPECAT Jaguar GR1 (8821M) (fuselage)	DCAE, No 1 SoTT, Cosford
	XX116	SEPECAT Jaguar GR3A [EO]	MoD FSCTE, Manston, Kent
	XX117	SEPECAT Jaguar GR3A [ES]	DCAE, No 1 SoTT, Cosford
	XX119	SEPECAT Jaguar GR3A (8898M) [AI]$	DCAE, No 1 SoTT, Cosford
	XX121	SEPECAT Jaguar GR1 [EQ]	Privately owned, Charlwood, Surrey
	XX139	SEPECAT Jaguar T4 [PT]	Privately owned, Sproughton
	XX140	SEPECAT Jaguar T2 (9008M) <ff>	Privately owned, Chesterfield
	XX141	SEPECAT Jaguar T2A (9297M) [T]	AMIF, RAFC Cranwell
	XX144	SEPECAT Jaguar T2A [U]	Privately owned, Sproughton
	XX145	SEPECAT Jaguar T2A	QinetiQ, Boscombe Down (spares use)
	XX146	SEPECAT Jaguar T4 [GT]	Privately owned, Sproughton
	XX150	SEPECAT Jaguar T4 [FY]	Privately owned, Bentwaters
	XX153	WS Lynx AH1 (9320M)	Museum of Army Flying, Middle Wallop
	XX154	HS Hawk T1	MoD/ETPS, Boscombe Down
	XX156	HS Hawk T1	RAF No 4 FTS, Valley
	XX157	HS Hawk T1A	RAF No 4 FTS/*208(R) Sqn*, Valley
	XX158	HS Hawk T1A	RAF No 4 FTS/*19(R) Sqn*, Valley
	XX159	HS Hawk T1A	RN FRADU, Culdrose
	XX160	HS Hawk T1	RN, stored Shawbury
	XX161	HS Hawk T1W	RN, stored Shawbury
	XX162	HS Hawk T1	RAF Centre of Aviation Medicine, Boscombe Down
	XX165	HS Hawk T1	RN FRADU, Culdrose
	XX167	HS Hawk T1W	RAF No 4 FTS/*208(R) Sqn*, Valley
	XX168	HS Hawk T1	RN FRADU, Culdrose
	XX169	HS Hawk T1	RAF No 4 FTS/*19(R) Sqn*, Valley
	XX170	HS Hawk T1	RN FRADU, Culdrose
	XX171	HS Hawk T1	RAF No 4 FTS, Valley
	XX172	HS Hawk T1	RN, stored Shawbury
	XX173	HS Hawk T1	RN, stored Shawbury
	XX174	HS Hawk T1	RAF No 4 FTS/*208(R) Sqn*, Valley
	XX175	HS Hawk T1	RN FRADU, Culdrose
	XX176	HS Hawk T1W	RAF No 4 FTS/*19(R) Sqn*, Valley
	XX177	HS Hawk T1	RAF, stored Shawbury
	XX178	HS Hawk T1W	RAF No 4 FTS/*19(R) Sqn*, Valley
	XX179	HS Hawk T1W	RAF *Red Arrows*, Scampton
	XX181	HS Hawk T1W	RAF No 4 FTS/*208(R) Sqn*, Valley
	XX184	HS Hawk T1	RN FRADU, Culdrose
	XX185	HS Hawk T1	RAF No 4 FTS/*208(R) Sqn*, Valley
	XX187	HS Hawk T1A	RAF No 4 FTS/*208(R) Sqn*, Valley
	XX188	HS Hawk T1A	RAF No 4 FTS/*19(R) Sqn*, Valley
	XX189	HS Hawk T1A	RAF No 4 FTS/*19(R) Sqn*, Valley
	XX190	HS Hawk T1A [CN]	RAF No 100 Sqn, Leeming
	XX191	HS Hawk T1A [CC]	RAF No 100 Sqn/JFACTSU, Leeming
	XX194	HS Hawk T1A [CL]	RAF No 100 Sqn, Leeming
	XX195	HS Hawk T1W	RAF No 4 FTS/*208(R) Sqn*, Valley
	XX196	HS Hawk T1A	*Crashed 20 April 2007, Mona*
	XX198	HS Hawk T1A	RN FRADU, Culdrose
	XX199	HS Hawk T1A	RAF No 4 FTS/*208(R) Sqn*, Valley
	XX200	HS Hawk T1A [CG]	RAF No 100 Sqn, Leeming
	XX201	HS Hawk T1A	RAF No 4 FTS/*208(R) Sqn*, Valley
	XX202	HS Hawk T1A [CF]	RAF No 100 Sqn, Leeming
	XX203	HS Hawk T1A	RAF No 4 FTS/*19(R) Sqn*, Valley
	XX204	HS Hawk T1A	RAF No 4 FTS/*19(R) Sqn*, Valley
	XX205	HS Hawk T1A $	RAF No 4 FTS/*208(R) Sqn*, Valley
	XX217	HS Hawk T1A	RAF No 4 FTS/*208(R) Sqn*, Valley

Serial	Type (code/other identity)	Owner/operator, location or fate	Notes
XX218	HS Hawk T1A	RAF No 4 FTS/*208(R) Sqn*, Valley	
XX219	HS Hawk T1A	RAF, stored Shawbury	
XX220	HS Hawk T1A	RAF No 4 FTS/*208(R) Sqn*, Valley	
XX221	HS Hawk T1A	RAF No 4 FTS/*19(R) Sqn*, Valley	
XX222	HS Hawk T1A [CI]	RAF No 100 Sqn, Leeming	
XX223	HS Hawk T1 <ff>	Privately owned, Charlwood, Surrey	
XX224	HS Hawk T1W	RAF No 4 FTS/*208(R) Sqn*, Valley	
XX225	HS Hawk T1	RN, stored Shawbury	
XX226	HS Hawk T1	RN, stored Shawbury	
XX227	HS Hawk T1 <R> (*XX226*/BAPC 152)	RAF M&RU, Bottesford	
XX227	HS Hawk T1A	RAF *Red Arrows*, Scampton	
XX228	HS Hawk T1A [CG]	RAF, stored Shawbury	
XX230	HS Hawk T1A [CH]	RAF No 100 Sqn, Leeming	
XX231	HS Hawk T1W	RAF No 4 FTS/*208(R) Sqn*, Valley	
XX232	HS Hawk T1	RAF, stored Shawbury	
XX233	HS Hawk T1	RAF *Red Arrows*, Scampton	
XX234	HS Hawk T1	RAF No 4 FTS, Valley	
XX235	HS Hawk T1W	RAF No 4 FTS/*208(R) Sqn*, Valley	
XX236	HS Hawk T1W	RAF No 4 FTS/*19(R) Sqn*, Valley	
XX237	HS Hawk T1	RAF *Red Arrows*, Scampton	
XX238	HS Hawk T1	RAF No 4 FTS/*208(R) Sqn*, Valley	
XX239	HS Hawk T1W	RAF, stored Shawbury	
XX240	HS Hawk T1	RAF No 4 FTS/*208(R) Sqn*, Valley	
XX242	HS Hawk T1	RAF *Red Arrows*, Scampton	
XX244	HS Hawk T1	RN FRADU, Culdrose	
XX245	HS Hawk T1	RAF No 4 FTS/*208(R) Sqn*, Valley	
XX246	HS Hawk T1A	RN FRADU, Culdrose	
XX246	HS Hawk T1A <rf>	RAF CTTS, St Athan	
XX247	HS Hawk T1A [CM]	RAF No 100 Sqn, Leeming	
XX248	HS Hawk T1A [CJ]	RAF, stored Shawbury	
XX250	HS Hawk T1	RAF No 4 FTS/*19(R) Sqn*, Valley	
XX253	HS Hawk T1A	RAF *Red Arrows*, Scampton	
XX254	HS Hawk T1A <ff>	MoD/DARA, St Athan	
XX254	HS Hawk T1A	MoD/BAE Systems, stored Scampton	
XX254	HS Hawk T1A <R>	Privately owned, Marlow, Bucks	
XX255	HS Hawk T1A	RN FRADU, Culdrose	
XX256	HS Hawk T1A	RAF No 4 FTS/*19(R) Sqn*, Valley	
XX257	HS Hawk T1A (fuselage)	Privately owned, Charlwood, Surrey	
XX258	HS Hawk T1A	RAF No 4 FTS/*19(R) Sqn*, Valley	
XX260	HS Hawk T1A	RAF *Red Arrows*, Scampton	
XX261	HS Hawk T1A	RN FRADU, Culdrose	
XX263	HS Hawk T1A	RAF No 4 FTS/*208(R) Sqn*, Valley	
XX263	HS Hawk T1 <R> (*XX253*/BAPC 171)	RAF M&RU, Bottesford	
XX264	HS Hawk T1A	RAF *Red Arrows*, Scampton	
XX265	HS Hawk T1A [CK]	RAF No 100 Sqn/JFACTSU, Leeming	
XX266	HS Hawk T1A	RAF *Red Arrows*, Scampton	
XX278	HS Hawk T1A	RAF No 4 FTS/*19(R) Sqn*, Valley	
XX280	HS Hawk T1A	RAF No 4 FTS/*19(R) Sqn*, Valley	
XX281	HS Hawk T1A [CD]	RAF No 100 Sqn, Leeming	
XX283	HS Hawk T1W	RAF No 4 FTS/*19(R) Sqn*, Valley	
XX284	HS Hawk T1A [CA]	RAF No 100 Sqn, Leeming	
XX285	HS Hawk T1A $	RAF No 100 Sqn, Leeming	
XX286	HS Hawk T1A	RAF No 4 FTS/*19(R) Sqn*, Valley	
XX287	HS Hawk T1A	RAF No 4 FTS/*19(R) Sqn*, Valley	
XX289	HS Hawk T1A [CO]	RAF No 100 Sqn, Leeming	
XX290	HS Hawk T1W [CU]	RAF, stored Shawbury	
XX292	HS Hawk T1	RAF *Red Arrows*, Scampton	
XX294	HS Hawk T1	RAF *Red Arrows*, Scampton	
XX295	HS Hawk T1W	RAF, stored Shawbury	
XX296	HS Hawk T1	RAF, stored Shawbury	
XX299	HS Hawk T1W	RAF No 4 FTS/*208(R) Sqn*, Valley	
XX301	HS Hawk T1A	RAF No 4 FTS/*208(R) Sqn*, Valley	
XX303	HS Hawk T1A	RN FRADU, Culdrose	
XX304	HS Hawk T1A <rf>	Cardiff International Airport Fire Section	
XX306	HS Hawk T1A	RAF *Red Arrows*, Scampton	
XX307	HS Hawk T1 $	RAF No 4 FTS/*208(R) Sqn*, Valley	
XX308	HS Hawk T1	RAF *Red Arrows*, Scampton	
XX309	HS Hawk T1	RAF, stored Shawbury	
XX310	HS Hawk T1W	RAF, stored Shawbury	
XX311	HS Hawk T1	RAF, stored Shawbury	

Notes	*Serial*	*Type (code/other identity)*	*Owner/operator, location or fate*
	XX312	HS Hawk T1W	MoD/BAE Systems, Warton
	XX313	HS Hawk T1W [CE]	RAF No 4 FTS/*208(R) Sqn*, Valley
	XX314	HS Hawk T1W [CN]	RAF No 4 FTS/*208(R) Sqn*, Valley
	XX315	HS Hawk T1A	RAF No 4 FTS/*19(R) Sqn*, Valley
	XX316	HS Hawk T1A	RAF No 4 FTS/*19(R) Sqn*, Valley
	XX317	HS Hawk T1A	RAF No 4 FTS/*19(R) Sqn*, Valley
	XX318	HS Hawk T1A [CQ]	RAF No 100 Sqn, Leeming
	XX319	HS Hawk T1A [CT]	RAF, stored Shawbury
	XX320	HS Hawk T1A	RAF, stored Shawbury
	XX321	HS Hawk T1A [CE]	MoD/BAE Systems, Warton
	XX322	HS Hawk T1A	RAF, stored Shawbury
	XX323	HS Hawk T1A	RAF, stored Shawbury
	XX324	HS Hawk T1A	MoD/BAE Systems, Warton
	XX325	HS Hawk T1A	RAF No 4 FTS/*208(R) Sqn*, Valley
	XX326	HS Hawk T1A <ff>	MoD/DARA, St Athan
	XX326	HS Hawk T1A	MoD/BAE Systems, Brough (on rebuild)
	XX327	HS Hawk T1	RAF Centre of Aviation Medicine, Boscombe Down
	XX329	HS Hawk T1A [CJ]	RAF No 100 Sqn, Leeming
	XX330	HS Hawk T1A	RAF No 4 FTS/*19(R) Sqn*, Valley
	XX331	HS Hawk T1A [CP]	RAF No 100 Sqn, Leeming
	XX332	HS Hawk T1A	RAF No 4 FTS/*19(R) Sqn*, Valley
	XX335	HS Hawk T1A	RAF No 100 Sqn, Leeming
	XX337	HS Hawk T1A	RAF No 4 FTS/*208(R) Sqn*, Valley
	XX338	HS Hawk T1	RAF No 4 FTS/*19(R) Sqn*, Valley
	XX339	HS Hawk T1A	RAF No 4 FTS/*208(R) Sqn*, Valley
	XX341	HS Hawk T1 ASTRA [1]	MoD/ETPS, Boscombe Down
	XX342	HS Hawk T1 [2]	MoD/ETPS, Boscombe Down
	XX343	HS Hawk T1 [3] (wreck)	Boscombe Down Aviation Collection
	XX345	HS Hawk T1A [CE]	RAF No 100 Sqn, Leeming
	XX346	HS Hawk T1A	RAF No 4 FTS/*19(R) Sqn*, Valley
	XX348	HS Hawk T1A	RAF No 4 FTS, Valley
	XX349	HS Hawk T1W	RAF No 4 FTS/*208(R) Sqn*, Valley
	XX350	HS Hawk T1A	RAF No 4 FTS/*19(R) Sqn*, Valley
	XX351	HS Hawk T1A [CQ]	RAF No 4 FTS, Valley
	XX371	WS Gazelle AH1	AAC No 12 Flt, Brüggen
	XX372	WS Gazelle AH1	MoD/QinetiQ, Boscombe Down
	XX375	WS Gazelle AH1	AAC, stored Shawbury
	XX378	WS Gazelle AH1 [Q]	AAC No 671 Sqn/2 Regt, Middle Wallop
	XX379	WS Gazelle AH1 [Y]	AAC No 658 Sqn/7 Regt, Netheravon
	XX380	WS Gazelle AH1 [A]	AAC GDSH, Middle Wallop
	XX381	WS Gazelle AH1 [C]	RM, stored Shawbury
	XX382	WS Gazelle HT3 (G-BZYB) [M]	Privately owned, Tadcaster
	XX383	WS Gazelle AH1 [D]	AAC, stored Shawbury
	XX384	WS Gazelle AH1	AAC, stored Shawbury
	XX385	WS Gazelle AH1	RAF, stored Shawbury
	XX386	WS Gazelle AH1	AAC No 12 Flt, Brüggen
	XX387	WS Gazelle AH1 (TAD 014)	DCAE SEAE, Arborfield
	XX388	WS Gazelle AH1 <ff>	Privately owned, East Garston, Bucks
	XX389	WS Gazelle AH1	AAC, stored Shawbury
	XX392	WS Gazelle AH1	AAC, Middle Wallop on display
	XX393	WS Gazelle AH1 (fuselage)	Privately owned, East Garston, Bucks
	XX394	WS Gazelle AH1 [X]	AAC, stored Shawbury
	XX396	WS Gazelle HT3 (8718M) [N]	ATF, RAFC Cranwell
	XX398	WS Gazelle AH1	AAC, stored Shawbury
	XX399	WS Gazelle AH1 [B]	AAC No 666(V) Sqn/7 Regt, Netheravon
	XX403	WS Gazelle AH1 [U]	AAC No 671 Sqn/2 Regt, Middle Wallop
	XX405	WS Gazelle AH1	AAC No 665 Sqn/5 Regt, Aldergrove
	XX406	WS Gazelle HT3 (G-CBSH) [P]	Privately owned, Hurstbourne Tarrant, Hants
	XX409	WS Gazelle AH1	AAC, stored Shawbury
	XX411	WS Gazelle AH1 [X]	Aeroventure, Doncaster
	XX411	WS Gazelle AH1 <rf>	FAA Museum, RNAS Yeovilton
	XX412	WS Gazelle AH1 [B]	RM, stored Shawbury
	XX413	WS Gazelle AH1 <ff>	Privately owned, East Garston, Bucks
	XX414	WS Gazelle AH1 [V]	DCAE, stored *HMS Sultan*, Gosport
	XX416	WS Gazelle AH1	AAC, stored Shawbury
	XX417	WS Gazelle AH1	AAC, stored Shawbury
	XX418	WS Gazelle AH1	Privately owned, East Garston, Bucks
	XX419	WS Gazelle AH1	AAC, stored Shawbury
	XX431	WS Gazelle HT2 (9300M) [43/CU]	RAF Shawbury, for display

Serial	Type (code/other identity)	Owner/operator, location or fate	Notes
XX432	WS Gazelle AH1 (G-CDNO)	Privately owned, Hurstbourne Tarrant, Hants	
XX433	WS Gazelle AH1 <ff>	Privately owned, East Garston, Bucks	
XX435	WS Gazelle AH1 [V]	QinetiQ, Boscombe Down (spares use)	
XX437	WS Gazelle AH1	AAC, stored Shawbury	
XX438	WS Gazelle AH1 [F]	AAC No 666(V) Sqn/7 Regt, Netheravon	
XX439	WS Gazelle AH1	AAC, stored Shawbury	
XX440	WS Gazelle AH1 (G-BCHN)	DARA Fleetlands Apprentice School	
XX442	WS Gazelle AH1 [E]	AAC No 666(V) Sqn/7 Regt, Netheravon	
XX443	WS Gazelle AH1 [Y]	AAC Stockwell Hall, Middle Wallop, instructional use	
XX444	WS Gazelle AH1	AAC Wattisham, instructional use	
XX445	WS Gazelle AH1 [T]	AAC No 658 Sqn/7 Regt, Netheravon	
XX447	WS Gazelle AH1 [D1]	AAC No 671 Sqn/2 Regt, Middle Wallop	
XX448	WS Gazelle AH1 [S]	AAC, stored Shawbury	
XX449	WS Gazelle AH1	MoD/QinetiQ, Boscombe Down	
XX450	WS Gazelle AH1 [D]	Privately owned, East Garston, Bucks	
XX453	WS Gazelle AH1	MoD/QinetiQ, Boscombe Down	
XX454	WS Gazelle AH1 (TAD 023) (fuselage)	DCAE SEAE, Arborfield	
XX455	WS Gazelle AH1	AAC, stored Shawbury	
XX456	WS Gazelle AH1	AAC No 3(V) Flt/7 Regt, Leuchars	
XX457	WS Gazelle AH1 <ff>	Jet Avn Preservation Grp, Long Marston	
XX460	WS Gazelle AH1 [D]	AAC No 671 Sqn/2 Regt, Middle Wallop	
XX462	WS Gazelle AH1 [W]	AAC No 658 Sqn/7 Regt, Netheravon	
XX466	HS Hunter T66B/T7	Guernsey Airport Fire Section	
XX467	HS Hunter T66B/T7 (XL605/G-TVII) [86]	Hunter Flying Ltd, Exeter	
XX476	HP137 Jetstream T2 (N1037S) [561/CU]	RN No 750 Sqn, Culdrose	
XX477	HP137 Jetstream T1 (G-AXXS/8462M) <ff>	Privately owned, Askern, Doncaster	
XX478	HP137 Jetstream T2 (G-AXXT) [564/CU]	RN No 750 Sqn, Culdrose	
XX479	HP137 Jetstream T2 (G-AXUR)	RN, Predannack Fire School	
XX481	HP137 Jetstream T2 (G-AXUP) [560/CU]	RN No 750 Sqn, Culdrose	
XX482	SA Jetstream T1 [J]	Privately owned, Hixon, Staffs	
XX483	SA Jetstream T2 [562] <ff>	Dumfries & Galloway Avn Mus, Dumfries	
XX484	SA Jetstream T2 [566/CU]	RN No 750 Sqn, Culdrose	
XX486	SA Jetstream T2 [567/CU]	RN No 750 Sqn, Culdrose	
XX487	SA Jetstream T2 [568/CU]	RN No 750 Sqn, Culdrose	
XX488	SA Jetstream T2 [562/CU]	RN No 750 Sqn, Culdrose	
XX491	SA Jetstream T1 [K]	Northbrook College, Shoreham, instructional use	
XX492	SA Jetstream T1 [A]	Newark Air Museum, Winthorpe	
XX494	SA Jetstream T1 [B]	Privately owned, Sproughton	
XX495	SA Jetstream T1 [C]	Bedford College, instructional use	
XX496	SA Jetstream T1 [D]	RAF Museum, Cosford	
XX499	SA Jetstream T1 [G]	Privately owned, Bentwaters	
XX500	SA Jetstream T1 [H]	Privately owned, Sproughton	
XX510	WS Lynx HAS2 [69/DD]	SFDO, RNAS Culdrose	
XX513	SA Bulldog T1 (G-CCMI) [10]	Privately owned, Meppershall	
XX515	SA Bulldog T1 (G-CBBC) [4]	Privately owned, Blackbushe	
XX518	SA Bulldog T1 (G-UDOG) [S]	Privately owned, North Weald	
XX520	SA Bulldog T1 (9288M) [A]	No 172 Sqn ATC, Haywards Heath	
XX521	SA Bulldog T1 (G-CBEH) [H]	Privately owned, East Dereham, Norfolk	
XX522	SA Bulldog T1 (G-DAWG) [06]	Privately owned, Barton	
XX524	SA Bulldog T1 (G-DDOG) [04]	Privately owned, North Weald	
XX525	SA Bulldog T1 (G-CBJJ) [8]	Privately owned, Norwich	
XX528	SA Bulldog T1 (G-BZON) [D]	Privately owned, Carlisle	
XX530	SA Bulldog T1 (XX637/9197M) [F]	No 2175 Sqn ATC, stored Kinloss	
XX534	SA Bulldog T1 (G-EDAV) [B]	Privately owned, Tollerton	
XX537	SA Bulldog T1 (G-CBCB) [C]	Privately owned, North Weald	
XX538	SA Bulldog T1 (G-TDOG) [O]	Privately owned, Shobdon	
XX539	SA Bulldog T1 [L]	Privately owned, Derbyshire	
XX543	SA Bulldog T1 (G-CBAB) [F]	Privately owned, Duxford	
XX546	SA Bulldog T1 (G-WINI) [03]	Privately owned, Blackbushe	
XX549	SA Bulldog T1 (G-CBID) [6]	Privately owned, Egginton	
XX550	SA Bulldog T1 (G-CBBL) [Z]	Privately owned, Fenland	
XX551	SA Bulldog T1 (G-BZDP) [E]	Privately owned, RAF Lyneham	
XX554	SA Bulldog T1 (G-BZMD) [09]	Privately owned, Wellesbourne Mountford	

Notes	Serial	Type (code/other identity)	Owner/operator, location or fate
	XX557	SA Bulldog T1	Privately owned, stored Fort Paull, Yorks
	XX561	SA Bulldog T1 (G-BZEP) [7]	Privately owned, Biggin Hill
	XX611	SA Bulldog T1 (G-CBDK) [7]	Privately owned, Coventry
	XX612	SA Bulldog T1 (G-BZXC) [A,03]	Privately owned, Dundee
	XX614	SA Bulldog T1 (G-GGRR) [V]	Privately owned, White Waltham
	XX619	SA Bulldog T1 (G-CBBW) [T]	Privately owned, Coventry
	XX621	SA Bulldog T1 (G-CBEF) [H]	Privately owned, Tollerton
	XX622	SA Bulldog T1 (G-CBGX) [B]	Privately owned, Findon, Sussex
	XX623	SA Bulldog T1 [M]	Privately owned, Hurstbourne Tarrant, Hants
	XX624	SA Bulldog T1 (G-KDOG) [E]	Privately owned, North Weald
	XX625	SA Bulldog T1 (G-CBBR) [01,N]	Privately owned, Norwich
	XX626	SA Bulldog T1 (9290M/G-CDVV) [W,02]	Privately owned, Wellesbourne Mountford
	XX628	SA Bulldog T1 (G-CBFU) [9]	Privately owned, Faversham
	XX629	SA Bulldog T1 (G-BZXZ) [V]	Privately owned, Wellesbourne Mountford
	XX630	SA Bulldog T1 (G-SIJW) [5,25]	Privately owned, Cranfield
	XX631	SA Bulldog T1 (G-BZXS) [W]	Privately owned, Sligo, Eire
	XX633	SA Bulldog T1 [X]	Privately owned, Diseworth, Leics
	XX634	SA Bulldog T1 [T]	Newark Air Museum, Winthorpe
	XX635	SA Bulldog T1 (8767M)	*Sold as N635XX, May 2007*
	XX636	SA Bulldog T1 (G-CBFP) [Y]	Privately owned, Cranfield
	XX638	SA Bulldog T1 (G-DOGG)	Privately owned, Hurstbourne Tarrant, Hants
	XX653	SA Bulldog T1 [E]	Parkway College, Stoke Gifford, Glos
	XX654	SA Bulldog T1 [3]	RAF Museum, Cosford
	XX656	SA Bulldog T1 [C]	Privately owned, Derbyshire
	XX658	SA Bulldog T1 (G-BZPS) [07]	Privately owned, Wellesbourne Mountford
	XX659	SA Bulldog T1 [E]	Privately owned, Derbyshire
	XX664	SA Bulldog T1 (F-AZTV) [04]	Privately owned, Pontoise, France
	XX665	SA Bulldog T1 (9289M)	No 2409 Sqn ATC, Halton
	XX667	SA Bulldog T1 (G-BZFN) [16]	Privately owned, Staverton
	XX668	SA Bulldog T1 (G-CBAN) [1]	Privately owned, Egginton
	XX671	SA Bulldog T1 [D]	Privately owned, Diseworth, Leics
	XX672	SA Bulldog T1 [E]	Privately owned, Spanhoe
	XX687	SA Bulldog T1 [F]	Barry Technical College, Cardiff Airport
	XX690	SA Bulldog T1 [A]	James Watt College, Greenock
	XX692	SA Bulldog T1 (G-BZMH) [A]	Privately owned, Wellesbourne Mountford
	XX694	SA Bulldog T1 (G-CBBS) [E]	Privately owned, Newcastle
	XX695	SA Bulldog T1 (G-CBBT) [3]	Privately owned, Sherburn-in-Elmet
	XX698	SA Bulldog T1 (G-BZME) [9]	Privately owned, Breighton
	XX699	SA Bulldog T1 (G-CBCV) [F]	Privately owned, Wickenby
	XX700	SA Bulldog T1 (G-CBEK) [17]	Privately owned, Blackbushe
	XX702	SA Bulldog T1 (G-CBCR) [B]	Privately owned, Egginton
	XX704	SA122 Bulldog (G-BCUV/G-112)	Privately owned, Old Sarum
	XX705	SA Bulldog T1 [5]	QinetiQ Boscombe Down, Apprentice School
	XX707	SA Bulldog T1 (G-CBDS) [4]	Privately owned, Sleap
	XX711	SA Bulldog T1 (G-CBBU) [X]	Privately owned, Egginton
	XX713	SA Bulldog T1 (G-CBJK) [2]	Privately owned, Norwich
	XX720	SEPECAT Jaguar GR3A [FL]	Privately owned, Sproughton
	XX722	SEPECAT Jaguar GR1 (9252M) <ff>	RAF St Athan, instructional use
	XX723	SEPECAT Jaguar GR3A [EU]	DCAE, No 1 SoTT, Cosford
	XX724	SEPECAT Jaguar GR3A [EC]	DCAE, No 1 SoTT, Cosford
	XX725	SEPECAT Jaguar GR3A [T]	DCAE, No 1 SoTT, Cosford
	XX726	SEPECAT Jaguar GR1 (8947M) [EB]	DCAE, No 1 SoTT, Cosford
	XX727	SEPECAT Jaguar GR1 (8951M) [ER]	DCAE, No 1 SoTT, Cosford
	XX729	SEPECAT Jaguar GR3A [EL]	DCAE, No 1 SoTT, Cosford
	XX730	SEPECAT Jaguar GR1 (8952M) [EC]	DCAE, No 1 SoTT, Cosford
	XX733	SEPECAT Jaguar GR1B [EB] (wreck)	Privately owned, Faygate
	XX734	SEPECAT Jaguar GR1 (8816M)	Gatwick Aviation Museum, Charlwood
	XX736	SEPECAT Jaguar GR1 (9110M) <ff>	Aeroventure, Doncaster
	XX737	SEPECAT Jaguar GR3A [EE]	Privately owned, Bentwaters
	XX738	SEPECAT Jaguar GR3A [ED]	DCAE, No 1 SoTT, Cosford
	XX739	SEPECAT Jaguar GR1 (8902M) [I]	RAF Syerston, instructional use
	XX741	SEPECAT Jaguar GR1A [04]	Privately owned, Sproughton

Serial	Type (code/other identity)	Owner/operator, location or fate	Notes
XX743	SEPECAT Jaguar GR1 (8949M) [EG]	DCAE, No 1 SoTT, Cosford	
XX744	SEPECAT Jaguar GR1 (9251M)	Privately owned, Sproughton	
XX745	SEPECAT Jaguar GR1A [GV]	MoD/QinetiQ, Boscombe Down	
XX746	SEPECAT Jaguar GR1 (8895M) [S]	DCAE, No 1 SoTT, Cosford	
XX747	SEPECAT Jaguar GR1 (8903M)	ATF, RAFC Cranwell	
XX748	SEPECAT Jaguar GR3A [EG]	DCAE, No 1 SoTT, Cosford	
XX751	SEPECAT Jaguar GR1 (8937M) [10]	RAF Syerston, instructional use	
XX752	SEPECAT Jaguar GR3A [EK]	DCAE, No 1 SoTT, Cosford	
XX753	SEPECAT Jaguar GR1 (9087M) <ff>	RAF M&RU, Bottesford	
XX756	SEPECAT Jaguar GR1 (8899M) [AM]	DCAE, No 1 SoTT, Cosford	
XX757	SEPECAT Jaguar GR1 (8948M) [CU]	DCAE, No 1 SoTT, Cosford	
XX761	SEPECAT Jaguar GR1 (8600M) <ff>	Boscombe Down Aviation Collection	
XX763	SEPECAT Jaguar GR1 (9009M)	Privately owned, Woodmancote, Sussex	
XX764	SEPECAT Jaguar GR1 (9010M)	Privately owned, Blackstone, Sussex	
XX765	SEPECAT Jaguar ACT	RAF Museum, Cosford	
XX766	SEPECAT Jaguar GR3A [EF]	DCAE, No 1 SoTT, Cosford	
XX767	SEPECAT Jaguar GR3A [FK]	DCAE, No 1 SoTT, Cosford	
XX818	SEPECAT Jaguar GR1 (8945M) [DE]	DCAE, No 1 SoTT, Cosford	
XX819	SEPECAT Jaguar GR1 (8923M) [CE]	DCAE, No 1 SoTT, Cosford	
XX821	SEPECAT Jaguar GR1 (8896M) [P]	AMIF, RAFC Cranwell	
XX824	SEPECAT Jaguar GR1 (9019M) [AD]	DCAE, No 1 SoTT, Cosford	
XX825	SEPECAT Jaguar GR1 (9020M) [BN]	DCAE, No 1 SoTT, Cosford	
XX826	SEPECAT Jaguar GR1 (9021M) [34,JH]	Privately owned, Sproughton	
XX829	SEPECAT Jaguar T2A [GZ]	Privately owned, Sproughton	
XX830	SEPECAT Jaguar T2 <ff>	City of Norwich Aviation Museum	
XX832	SEPECAT Jaguar T2A [EZ]	Privately owned, Bentwaters	
XX833	SEPECAT Jaguar T2B	MoD/QinetiQ, Boscombe Down (wfu)	
XX835	SEPECAT Jaguar T4 [EX]	DCAE, No 1 SoTT, Cosford	
XX836	SEPECAT Jaguar T2A [X]	Privately owned, Sproughton	
XX837	SEPECAT Jaguar T2 (8978M) [I]	DCAE, No 1 SoTT, Cosford	
XX838	SEPECAT Jaguar T4 [FZ]	Privately owned, Bentwaters	
XX840	SEPECAT Jaguar T4 [EY]	DCAE, No 1 SoTT, Cosford	
XX841	SEPECAT Jaguar T4	Privately owned, Bentwaters	
XX842	SEPECAT Jaguar T2A [FX]	Privately owned, Bentwaters	
XX845	SEPECAT Jaguar T4 [EV]	DCAE, No 1 SoTT, Cosford	
XX847	SEPECAT Jaguar T4 [EZ]	DCAE, No 1 SoTT, Cosford	
XX885	HS Buccaneer S2B (9225M/G-HHAA)	Hawker Hunter Aviation, Scampton	
XX888	HS Buccaneer S2B <ff>	Privately owned, Barnstaple	
XX889	HS Buccaneer S2B [T]	Blackburn Buccaneer Society, Kemble	
XX892	HS Buccaneer S2B <ff>	Privately owned, Perthshire	
XX893	HS Buccaneer S2B <ff>	Privately owned, Pershore	
XX894	HS Buccaneer S2B [020/R]	Buccaneer Supporters Club, Bruntingthorpe	
XX897	HS Buccaneer S2B(mod)	Blackburn Buccaneer Society, Bournemouth	
XX899	HS Buccaneer S2B <ff>	Midland Air Museum, Coventry	
XX900	HS Buccaneer S2B	Cold War Jets Collection, Bruntingthorpe	
XX901	HS Buccaneer S2B	Yorkshire Air Museum, Elvington	
XX907	WS Lynx AH1	Westland Helicopters, Yeovil, Fire Section	
XX910	WS Lynx HAS2	The Helicopter Museum, Weston-super-Mare	
XX914	BAC VC10/1103 (8777M) <rf>	RAF Defence Movements School, Brize Norton	
XX919	BAC 1-11/402AP (PI-C1121) <ff>	Boscombe Down Aviation Collection	
XX946	Panavia Tornado (P02) (8883M)	RAF Museum, Cosford	
XX947	Panavia Tornado (P03) (8797M)	Shoreham Airport, on display	
XX956	SEPECAT Jaguar GR1 (8950M) [BE]	DCAE, No 1 SoTT, Cosford	
XX958	SEPECAT Jaguar GR1 (9022M) [BK,JG]	DCAE, No 1 SoTT, Cosford	

Notes	Serial	Type (code/other identity)	Owner/operator, location or fate
	XX959	SEPECAT Jaguar GR1 (8953M) [CJ]	DCAE, No 1 SoTT, Cosford
	XX962	SEPECAT Jaguar GR1B (9257M) [E]	DCAE, No 1 SoTT, Cosford
	XX965	SEPECAT Jaguar GR1A (9254M) [C]	AMIF, RAFC Cranwell
	XX966	SEPECAT Jaguar GR1 (8904M) [EL,JJ]	DCAE, No 1 SoTT, Cosford
	XX967	SEPECAT Jaguar GR1 (9006M) [AC,JD]	DCAE, No 1 SoTT, Cosford
	XX968	SEPECAT Jaguar GR1 (9007M) [AJ,JE]	DCAE, No 1 SoTT, Cosford
	XX969	SEPECAT Jaguar GR1 (8897M) [01]	DCAE, No 1 SoTT, Cosford
	XX970	SEPECAT Jaguar GR3A [EH]	DCAE, No 1 SoTT, Cosford
	XX974	SEPECAT Jaguar GR3 [FE]	Privately owned, Sproughton
	XX975	SEPECAT Jaguar GR1 (8905M) [07]	DCAE, No 1 SoTT, Cosford
	XX976	SEPECAT Jaguar GR1 (8906M) [BD]	DCAE, No 1 SoTT, Cosford
	XX977	SEPECAT Jaguar GR1 (9132M) [DL,05] <rf>	Privately owned, Sproughton
	XX979	SEPECAT Jaguar GR1A (9306M) <rf>	*Currently not known*
	XZ101	SEPECAT Jaguar GR1A (9282M) [D]	*Scrapped at Boscombe Down, 2003*
	XZ103	SEPECAT Jaguar GR3A [EF]	DCAE, No 1 SoTT, Cosford
	XZ104	SEPECAT Jaguar GR3A [FM]	RAF St Athan (wfu)
	XZ106	SEPECAT Jaguar GR3A [FW]	Privately owned, Bentwaters
	XZ107	SEPECAT Jaguar GR3A [FH]	Privately owned, Bentwaters
	XZ109	SEPECAT Jaguar GR3A [EN]	DCAE, No 1 SoTT, Cosford
	XZ112	SEPECAT Jaguar GR3A [GW]	DCAE, No 1 SoTT, Cosford
	XZ113	SEPECAT Jaguar GR3 [FD]	Privately owned, Bentwaters
	XZ114	SEPECAT Jaguar GR3 [EO]	DCAE, No 1 SoTT, Cosford
	XZ115	SEPECAT Jaguar GR3 [ER]	DCAE, No 1 SoTT, Cosford
	XZ117	SEPECAT Jaguar GR3 [ES]	MoD/QinetiQ, Boscombe Down
	XZ118	SEPECAT Jaguar GR3 [FR]	Privately owned, Bentwaters
	XZ119	SEPECAT Jaguar GR1A (9266M) [F]	AMIF, RAFC Cranwell
	XZ130	HS Harrier GR3 (9079M) [A,HE]	No 1034 Sqn ATC, Tolworth, Surrey
	XZ131	HS Harrier GR3 (9174M) <ff>	No 2156 Sqn ATC, Brierley Hill, W Midlands
	XZ132	HS Harrier GR3 (9168M) [C]	ATF, RAFC Cranwell
	XZ133	HS Harrier GR3 [10]	Imperial War Museum, Duxford
	XZ135	HS Harrier GR3 (8848M) <ff>	RAF M&RU, Bottesford
	XZ138	HS Harrier GR3 (9040M) <ff>	RAFC Cranwell, Trenchard Hall
	XZ145	HS Harrier T4 [45]	RN, Predannack Fire School
	XZ146	HS Harrier T4 (9281M) [S]	RAF Wittering, on display
	XZ166	WS Lynx HAS2 <ff>	Farnborough Air Sciences Trust, stored Farnborough
	XZ170	WS Lynx AH9	DCAE SEAE, Arborfield
	XZ171	WS Lynx AH7	Army, Salisbury Plain
	XZ172	WS Lynx AH7	DCAE SEAE, Arborfield
	XZ173	WS Lynx AH7	AAC No 9 Regt, Dishforth
	XZ174	WS Lynx AH7 <ff>	RAF Defence Movements School, Brize Norton
	XZ176	WS Lynx AH7	RM No 847 Sqn, Yeovilton
	XZ177	WS Lynx AH7	RM No 847 Sqn, Yeovilton
	XZ178	WS Lynx AH7	MoD/DARA, Fleetlands
	XZ179	WS Lynx AH7	AAC No 9 Regt, Dishforth
	XZ180	WS Lynx AH7	RM No 847 Sqn, Yeovilton
	XZ181	WS Lynx AH1	AAC Stockwell Hall, Middle Wallop, instructional use
	XZ182	WS Lynx AH7	MoD/DARA, stored Fleetlands
	XZ183	WS Lynx AH7	MoD/DARA, stored Fleetlands
	XZ184	WS Lynx AH7	AAC No 657 Sqn, Odiham
	XZ185	WS Lynx AH7	Westland Helicopters, Yeovil
	XZ187	WS Lynx AH7	DCAE SEAE, Arborfield
	XZ188	WS Lynx AH7	DCAE SEAE, Arborfield
	XZ190	WS Lynx AH7 [F]	AAC No 671 Sqn/2 Regt, Middle Wallop
	XZ191	WS Lynx AH7	MoD/DARA, stored Fleetlands

Serial	Type (code/other identity)	Owner/operator, location or fate	Notes
XZ192	WS Lynx AH7	MoD/DARA, Fleetlands	
XZ193	WS Lynx AH7	AAC No 672 Sqn/9 Regt, Dishforth	
XZ194	WS Lynx AH7 [L]	AAC No 671 Sqn/2 Regt, Middle Wallop	
XZ195	WS Lynx AH7	AAC No 9 Regt, Dishforth	
XZ196	WS Lynx AH7 [T]	AAC No 671 Sqn/2 Regt, Middle Wallop	
XZ197	WS Lynx AH7 <ff>	MoD/DARA, stored Fleetlands	
XZ198	WS Lynx AH7	MoD/DARA, stored Fleetlands	
XZ203	WS Lynx AH7	AAC No 9 Regt, Dishforth	
XZ205	WS Lynx AH7	RM No 847 Sqn, Yeovilton	
XZ206	WS Lynx AH7 [V]	AAC No 671 Sqn/2 Regt, Middle Wallop	
XZ207	WS Lynx AH7	DCAE SEAE, Arborfield	
XZ208	WS Lynx AH7	AAC No 672 Sqn/9 Regt, Dishforth	
XZ209	WS Lynx AH7	MoD/DARA, Fleetlands	
XZ210	WS Lynx AH7	AAC No 672 Sqn/9 Regt, Dishforth	
XZ211	WS Lynx AH7	AAC No 9 Regt, Dishforth	
XZ212	WS Lynx AH7 [X]	AAC No 671 Sqn/2 Regt, Middle Wallop	
XZ213	WS Lynx AH1 (TAD 213)	DARA Fleetlands Apprentice School	
XZ214	WS Lynx AH7	MoD/DARA, Fleetlands	
XZ215	WS Lynx AH7	AAC No 9 Regt, Dishforth	
XZ216	WS Lynx AH7	AAC No 672 Sqn/9 Regt, Dishforth	
XZ217	WS Lynx AH7	AAC No 672 Sqn/9 Regt, Dishforth	
XZ218	WS Lynx AH7	Privately owned, Sproughton	
XZ219	WS Lynx AH7	AAC No 669 Sqn/9 Regt, Dishforth	
XZ220	WS Lynx AH7	MoD/DARA, Fleetlands	
XZ221	WS Lynx AH7	MoD/DARA, Fleetlands	
XZ222	WS Lynx AH7	AAC No 657 Sqn, Odiham	
XZ228	WS Lynx HAS3S [207]	RN No 815 Sqn, 207 Flt, Yeovilton	
XZ229	WS Lynx HAS3S [321]	RN No 815 Sqn, Yeovilton	
XZ230	WS Lynx HAS3S [302]	MoD/DARA, stored Fleetlands	
XZ232	WS Lynx HAS3S [219]	RN No 815 Sqn, 219 Flt, Yeovilton	
XZ233	WS Lynx HAS3S [638]	RN No 702 Sqn, Yeovilton	
XZ234	WS Lynx HAS3S [635]	RN No 702 Sqn, Yeovilton	
XZ235	WS Lynx HAS3S(ICE) [435/EE]	RN No 815 Sqn, *Endurance* Flt, Yeovilton	
XZ236	WS Lynx HMA8	RNAS Yeovilton, GI	
XZ237	WS Lynx HAS3S [313]	RN No 815 Sqn, HQ Flt, Yeovilton	
XZ238	WS Lynx HAS3S(ICE) [434/EE]	RN No 815 Sqn, *Endurance* Flt, Yeovilton	
XZ239	WS Lynx HAS3S [633]	RN No 702 Sqn, Yeovilton	
XZ245	WS Lynx HAS3S [334]	RN No 815 Sqn, *Southampton* Flt, Yeovilton	
XZ246	WS Lynx HAS3S(ICE) [435/EE]	MoD/DARA, Fleetlands	
XZ248	WS Lynx HAS3S [305]	RN No 815 Sqn, HQ Flt, Yeovilton	
XZ250	WS Lynx HAS3S [635]$	RN No 702 Sqn, Yeovilton	
XZ252	WS Lynx HAS3S	RN, Yeovilton (spares use)	
XZ254	WS Lynx HAS3S [631]	RN No 702 Sqn, Yeovilton	
XZ255	WS Lynx HMA8 [307]	RN No 815 Sqn, HQ Flt, Yeovilton	
XZ257	WS Lynx HAS3S [301]	RN No 815 Sqn, HQ Flt, Yeovilton	
XZ287	BAe Nimrod AEW3 (9140M) (fuselage)	RAF TSW, Stafford	
XZ290	WS Gazelle AH1	Army No 70 Aircraft Workshops, Middle Wallop	
XZ291	WS Gazelle AH1	AAC No 12 Flt, Brüggen	
XZ292	WS Gazelle AH1	AAC, stored Shawbury	
XZ294	WS Gazelle AH1 [X]	AAC No 658 Sqn/7 Regt, Netheravon	
XZ295	WS Gazelle AH1	AAC No 12 Flt, Brüggen	
XZ296	WS Gazelle AH1 [V]	AAC No 658 Sqn/7 Regt, Netheravon	
XZ298	WS Gazelle AH1 <ff>	AAC, Middle Wallop	
XZ299	WS Gazelle AH1 (G-CDXE)	Privately owned, Hurstbourne Tarrant, Hants	
XZ300	WS Gazelle AH1 [L] (wreck)	Army, Bramley, Hants	
XZ301	WS Gazelle AH1 [U]	AAC, stored Shawbury	
XZ303	WS Gazelle AH1	AAC No 6(V) Flt/7 Regt, Shawbury	
XZ304	WS Gazelle AH1	AAC No 6(V) Flt/7 Regt, Shawbury	
XZ305	WS Gazelle AH1 (TAD020)	AAC Middle Wallop, instructional use	
XZ307	WS Gazelle AH1	DARA Fleetlands Apprentice School	
XZ308	WS Gazelle AH1	MoD/QinetiQ, Boscombe Down	
XZ309	WS Gazelle AH1	Privately owned, Hixon, Staffs	
XZ311	WS Gazelle AH1	AAC No 6(V) Flt/7 Regt, Shawbury	
XZ312	WS Gazelle AH1	RAF Henlow, instructional use	
XZ313	WS Gazelle AH1	AAC, stored Shawbury	
XZ314	WS Gazelle AH1 [A]	AAC No 666(V) Sqn/7 Regt, Netheravon	
XZ315	WS Gazelle AH1 <ff>	Privately owned, Babcary, Somerset	
XZ316	WS Gazelle AH1 [B]	AAC, stored Shawbury	
XZ318	WS Gazelle AH1 (fuselage)	AAC, stored Shawbury	

Notes	Serial	Type (code/other identity)	Owner/operator, location or fate
	XZ320	WS Gazelle AH1	AAC No 665 Sqn/5 Regt, Aldergrove
	XZ321	WS Gazelle AH1 (G-CDNS)	Privately owned, Babcary, Somerset
	XZ322	WS Gazelle AH1 (9283M) [N]	DCAE, No 1 SoTT, Cosford
	XZ323	WS Gazelle AH1 [H]	AAC No 666(V) Sqn/7 Regt, Netheravon
	XZ324	WS Gazelle AH1	AAC, stored Shawbury
	XZ325	WS Gazelle AH1 [T]	DCAE SEAE, Arborfield
	XZ326	WS Gazelle AH1	AAC No 665 Sqn/5 Regt, Aldergrove
	XZ327	WS Gazelle AH1	AAC GDSH, Middle Wallop
	XZ328	WS Gazelle AH1 [C]	AAC No 666(V) Sqn/7 Regt, Netheravon
	XZ329	WS Gazelle AH1 (G-BZYD) [J]	Privately owned, Hurstbourne Tarrant, Hants
	XZ330	WS Gazelle AH1 [Y]	AAC Wattisham, instructional use
	XZ331	WS Gazelle AH1 [D]	AAC No 666(V) Sqn/7 Regt, Netheravon
	XZ332	WS Gazelle AH1 [O]	Army, Bramley, Hants
	XZ333	WS Gazelle AH1 [A]	DCAE SEAE, Arborfield
	XZ334	WS Gazelle AH1	AAC, Middle Wallop
	XZ335	WS Gazelle AH1	North-East Aircraft Museum, Usworth
	XZ337	WS Gazelle AH1 [Z]	AAC No 658 Sqn/7 Regt, Netheravon
	XZ338	WS Gazelle AH1 [Y]	AAC No 671 Sqn/2 Regt, Middle Wallop
	XZ340	WS Gazelle AH1 [5B]	AAC
	XZ341	WS Gazelle AH1	AAC, stored Shawbury
	XZ342	WS Gazelle AH1	AAC No 8 Flt, Credenhill
	XZ343	WS Gazelle AH1	AAC, stored Shawbury
	XZ344	WS Gazelle AH1 [Y]	AAC, stored Shawbury
	XZ345	WS Gazelle AH1	AAC No 3(V) Flt/7 Regt, Leuchars
	XZ346	WS Gazelle AH1	AAC, No 9 Regt, Dishforth
	XZ347	WS Gazelle AH1	AAC, Middle Wallop
	XZ349	WS Gazelle AH1	AAC No 3(V) Flt/7 Regt, Leuchars
	XZ355	SEPECAT Jaguar GR3A [FJ]	Privately owned, Bentwaters
	XZ356	SEPECAT Jaguar GR3A [FU]	Privately owned, Bentwaters
	XZ357	SEPECAT Jaguar GR3A	Privately owned, Sproughton
	XZ358	SEPECAT Jaguar GR1A (9262M) [L]	AMIF, RAFC Cranwell
	XZ360	SEPECAT Jaguar GR3 [FN]	Privately owned, Bentwaters
	XZ361	SEPECAT Jaguar GR3 [FT]	Privately owned, Bentwaters
	XZ363	SEPECAT Jaguar GR1A <R> (*XX824*/BAPC 151) [A]	RAF M&RU, Bottesford
	XZ364	SEPECAT Jaguar GR3A [FS]	Privately owned, Sproughton
	XZ366	SEPECAT Jaguar GR3A [FC]	Privately owned, Bentwaters
	XZ367	SEPECAT Jaguar GR3 [GP]	Privately owned, Bentwaters
	XZ368	SEPECAT Jaguar GR1 [8900M] [E]	DCAE, No 1 SoTT, Cosford
	XZ369	SEPECAT Jaguar GR3A [EU]	Privately owned, Bentwaters
	XZ370	SEPECAT Jaguar GR1 (9004M) [JB]	DCAE, No 1 SoTT, Cosford
	XZ371	SEPECAT Jaguar GR1 (8907M) [AP]	DCAE, No 1 SoTT, Cosford
	XZ372	SEPECAT Jaguar GR3 [FV]	Privately owned, Bentwaters
	XZ374	SEPECAT Jaguar GR1 (9005M) [JC]	DCAE, No 1 SoTT, Cosford
	XZ375	SEPECAT Jaguar GR1A (9255M) <ff>	City of Norwich Aviation Museum
	XZ377	SEPECAT Jaguar GR3A [EP]	DCAE, No 1 SoTT, Cosford
	XZ378	SEPECAT Jaguar GR1A [EP]	Privately owned, Topsham, Devon
	XZ382	SEPECAT Jaguar GR1 (8908M) [AE]	Cold War Jets Collection, Bruntingthorpe
	XZ383	SEPECAT Jaguar GR1 (8901M) [AF]	DCAE, No 1 SoTT, Cosford
	XZ384	SEPECAT Jaguar GR1 (8954M) [BC]	DCAE, No 1 SoTT, Cosford
	XZ385	SEPECAT Jaguar GR3A [FT]	Privately owned, Bentwaters
	XZ389	SEPECAT Jaguar GR1 (8946M) [BL]	DCAE, No 1 SoTT, Cosford
	XZ390	SEPECAT Jaguar GR1 (9003M) [35,JA]	DCAE, No 1 SoTT, Cosford
	XZ391	SEPECAT Jaguar GR3A [ET]	DCAE, No 1 SoTT, Cosford
	XZ392	SEPECAT Jaguar GR3A [EM]	DCAE, No 1 SoTT, Cosford
	XZ394	SEPECAT Jaguar GR3 [FG]	Privately owned, Bentwaters
	XZ396	SEPECAT Jaguar GR3A [EQ]	Privately owned, Bentwaters
	XZ398	SEPECAT Jaguar GR3A [EQ]	DCAE, No 1 SoTT, Cosford
	XZ399	SEPECAT Jaguar GR3A [EJ]	DCAE, No 1 SoTT, Cosford
	XZ400	SEPECAT Jaguar GR3A [FQ]	Privately owned, Bentwaters

Serial	*Type (code/other identity)*	*Owner/operator, location or fate*	*Notes*
XZ431	HS Buccaneer S2B (9233M) <ff>	Privately owned, Market Drayton, Shropshire	
XZ440	BAe Sea Harrier FA2 [40/DD]	SFDO, RNAS Culdrose	
XZ455	BAe Sea Harrier FA2 [001] (wreck)	Privately owned, Sproughton	
XZ457	BAe Sea Harrier FA2 [104]	Boscombe Down Aviation Collection	
XZ459	BAe Sea Harrier FA2 [126]	Privately owned, Shoreham	
XZ492	BAe Sea Harrier FA2 (wreck)	Privately owned, Faygate	
XZ493	BAe Sea Harrier FRS1 (comp XV760) [001/N]	FAA Museum, RNAS Yeovilton	
XZ493	BAe Sea Harrier FRS1 <ff>	RN Yeovilton, Fire Section	
XZ494	BAe Sea Harrier FA2	Privately owned, Wedmore, Somerset	
XZ497	BAe Sea Harrier FA2 [126]	Privately owned, Charlwood	
XZ499	BAe Sea Harrier FA2 [003]	FAA Museum, stored Yeovilton	
XZ559	Slingsby T61F Venture T2 (G-BUEK)	Privately owned, Tibenham	
XZ570	WS61 Sea King HAS5(mod)	DCAE, stored *HMS Sultan*, Gosport	
XZ574	WS61 Sea King HAS6 [33/CU]	DCAE, stored *HMS Sultan*, Gosport	
XZ575	WS61 Sea King HU5	MoD/AFD/QinetiQ, Boscombe Down	
XZ576	WS61 Sea King HAS6	DCAE AESS, *HMS Sultan*, Gosport	
XZ578	WS61 Sea King HU5 [708]	RN No 771 Sqn, Culdrose	
XZ579	WS61 Sea King HAS6 [707/PW]	DCAE, stored *HMS Sultan*, Gosport	
XZ580	WS61 Sea King HC6 [ZB]	MoD/DARA, Fleetlands	
XZ581	WS61 Sea King HAS6 [69/CU]	DCAE, stored *HMS Sultan*, Gosport	
XZ585	WS61 Sea King HAR3 [A]	RAF No 22 Sqn, C Flt, Valley	
XZ586	WS61 Sea King HAR3 [B]	MoD/DARA, Fleetlands	
XZ587	WS61 Sea King HAR3 [C]	RAF CHFMU, Yeovilton	
XZ588	WS61 Sea King HAR3 [D]	MoD/DARA, Fleetlands	
XZ589	WS61 Sea King HAR3 [E]	RAF No 202 Sqn, E Flt, Leconfield	
XZ590	WS61 Sea King HAR3 [F]	RAF No 22 Sqn, C Flt, Valley	
XZ591	WS61 Sea King HAR3 [G]	MoD/DARA, Fleetlands	
XZ592	WS61 Sea King HAR3	RAF No 203(R) Sqn, St Mawgan	
XZ593	WS61 Sea King HAR3 [I]	RAF No 1564 Flt, Mount Pleasant, FI	
XZ594	WS61 Sea King HAR3 [J]	RAF No 202 Sqn, D Flt, Lossiemouth	
XZ595	WS61 Sea King HAR3 [K]	RAF No 202 Sqn, E Flt, Leconfield	
XZ596	WS61 Sea King HAR3 [L]	RAF No 1564 Flt, Mount Pleasant, FI	
XZ597	WS61 Sea King HAR3 [M]	RAF No 203(R) Sqn, St Mawgan	
XZ598	WS61 Sea King HAR3	RAF No 202 Sqn, A Flt, Boulmer	
XZ599	WS61 Sea King HAR3 [P]	RAF No 203(R) Sqn, St Mawgan	
XZ605	WS Lynx AH7 [Y]	MoD/DARA, Fleetlands	
XZ606	WS Lynx AH7	AAC No 9 Regt, Dishforth	
XZ607	WS Lynx AH7	AAC No 667 Sqn/2 Regt, Middle Wallop	
XZ608	WS Lynx AH7	AAC No 657 Sqn, Odiham	
XZ609	WS Lynx AH7	MoD/DARA, stored Fleetlands	
XZ611	WS Lynx AH7	AAC No 9 Regt, Dishforth	
XZ612	WS Lynx AH7 [N]	AAC No 9 Regt, Dishforth	
XZ613	WS Lynx AH7 [F]	AAC Stockwell Hall, Middle Wallop, instructional use	
XZ615	WS Lynx AH7	AAC No 9 Regt, Dishforth	
XZ616	WS Lynx AH7	AAC No 657 Sqn, Odiham	
XZ617	WS Lynx AH7	AAC No 1 Regt, Gütersloh	
XZ630	Panavia Tornado GR1 (8976M)	RAF Halton, on display	
XZ631	Panavia Tornado GR1	Yorkshire Air Museum, Elvington	
XZ641	WS Lynx AH7	MoD/DARA, stored Fleetlands	
XZ642	WS Lynx AH7	MoD/DARA, Fleetlands	
XZ643	WS Lynx AH7	AAC No 657 Sqn, Odiham	
XZ645	WS Lynx AH7	AAC No 9 Regt, Dishforth	
XZ646	WS Lynx AH7 (really XZ649)	QinetiQ Structures Dept, Farnborough	
XZ647	WS Lynx AH7 [Z]	MoD/DARA, stored Fleetlands	
XZ648	WS Lynx AH7	RM No 847 Sqn, Yeovilton	
XZ651	WS Lynx AH7	AAC No 657 Sqn, Odiham	
XZ652	WS Lynx AH7	AAC No 9 Regt, Dishforth	
XZ653	WS Lynx AH7	AAC No 659 Sqn/9 Regt, Dishforth	
XZ654	WS Lynx AH7	RM No 847 Sqn, Yeovilton	
XZ655	WS Lynx AH7 [A]	AAC No 671 Sqn/2 Regt, Middle Wallop	
XZ661	WS Lynx AH7	MoD/DARA, Fleetlands	
XZ663	WS Lynx AH7 [I]	MoD/DARA, stored Fleetlands	
XZ666	WS Lynx AH7	DCAE SEAE, Arborfield	
XZ669	WS Lynx AH7	MoD/DARA, stored Fleetlands	
XZ670	WS Lynx AH7	AAC No 672 Sqn/9 Regt, Dishforth	
XZ671	WS Lynx AH7 <ff>	Westland Helicopters, Yeovil, instructional use	
XZ672	WS Lynx AH7	AAC No 9 Regt, Dishforth	

Notes	Serial	Type (code/other identity)	Owner/operator, location or fate
	XZ673	WS Lynx AH7	MoD/DARA, stored Fleetlands
	XZ674	WS Lynx AH7	AAC No 9 Regt, Dishforth
	XZ675	WS Lynx AH7	MoD/DARA, stored Fleetlands
	XZ676	WS Lynx AH7 [N]	AAC No 671/2 Regt, Middle Wallop
	XZ677	WS Lynx AH7	AAC No 9 Regt, Dishforth
	XZ678	WS Lynx AH7	RM No 847 Sqn, Yeovilton
	XZ679	WS Lynx AH7	AAC No 672 Sqn/9 Regt, Dishforth
	XZ680	WS Lynx AH7 [E]	AAC No 671 Sqn/2 Regt, Middle Wallop
	XZ689	WS Lynx HMA8 [338]	RN No 815 Sqn, *Campbeltown* Flt, Yeovilton
	XZ690	WS Lynx HMA8 [404/IR]	MoD/DARA, Fleetlands
	XZ691	WS Lynx HMA8 [345]	MoD/DARA, Fleetlands
	XZ692	WS Lynx HMA8DAS [426]	RN No 815 Sqn *Portland* Flt, Yeovilton
	XZ693	WS Lynx HAS3S [304]	RN No 815 Sqn, HQ Flt, Yeovilton
	XZ694	WS Lynx HAS3S [334]	MoD/DARA, Fleetlands
	XZ696	WS Lynx HAS3S [311]	RN No 815 Sqn, Yeovilton
	XZ697	WS Lynx HMA8DAS	MoD/DARA, Fleetlands
	XZ698	WS Lynx HMA8	RN No 815 Sqn OEU, Yeovilton
	XZ699	WS Lynx HAS2	FAA Museum, RNAS Yeovilton
	XZ719	WS Lynx HMA8DAS [211]	RN No 815 Sqn, 211 Flt, Yeovilton
	XZ720	WS Lynx HAS3S [407]	RN No 815 Sqn, *York* Flt, Yeovilton
	XZ721	WS Lynx HAS3S [306]	RN No 815 Sqn, HQ Flt, Yeovilton
	XZ722	WS Lynx HMA8DAS [671]$	RN No 702 Sqn, Yeovilton
	XZ723	WS Lynx HMA8 [410]	MoD/DARA, Fleetlands
	XZ725	WS Lynx HMA8 [308]	RN No 815 Sqn, HQ Flt, Yeovilton
	XZ726	WS Lynx HMA8 [202]	RN No 815 Sqn, 202 Flt, Yeovilton
	XZ727	WS Lynx HAS3S [307]	RN No 815 Sqn, HQ Flt, Yeovilton
	XZ728	WS Lynx HMA8 [326/AW]	RNAS Yeovilton, on display
	XZ729	WS Lynx HMA8 [675]	RN No 702 Sqn, Yeovilton
	XZ730	WS Lynx HAS3S [632]	RN No 702 Sqn, Yeovilton
	XZ731	WS Lynx HMA8	RN AMG, Yeovilton
	XZ732	WS Lynx HMA8DAS [673]	RN No 702 Sqn, Yeovilton
	XZ733	WS Lynx HAS3S [335]	RN No 815 Sqn, HQ Flt, Yeovilton
	XZ735	WS Lynx HAS3S [228]	RN No 815 Sqn, 228 Flt, Yeovilton
	XZ736	WS Lynx HMA8DAS [365]	RN AMG, Yeovilton
	XZ791	Northrop Shelduck D1	RNAS Culdrose, preserved
	XZ795	Northrop Shelduck D1	Museum of Army Flying, Middle Wallop
	XZ920	WS61 Sea King HU5 [707/PW]	RN No 771 Sqn, Prestwick
	XZ921	WS61 Sea King HAS6 [269/N]	DCAE, stored *HMS Sultan*, Gosport
	XZ922	WS61 Sea King HC6 [ZA]	RN No 846 Sqn, Yeovilton
	XZ930	WS Gazelle HT3 [Q]	DCAE AESS, *HMS Sultan*, Gosport
	XZ933	WS Gazelle HT3 [T]	MoD/QinetiQ, Boscombe Down, spares use
	XZ934	WS Gazelle HT3 (G-CBSI) [U]	Privately owned, Babcary, Somerset
	XZ935	WS Gazelle HCC4	DCAE, No 1 SoTT, Cosford
	XZ936	WS Gazelle HT2 [6]	MoD/ETPS, Boscombe Down
	XZ937	WS Gazelle HT2 (G-CBKA) [Y]	Privately owned, Stapleford Tawney
	XZ939	WS Gazelle HT2 [9]	MoD/ETPS, Boscombe Down
	XZ940	WS Gazelle HT2 (G-CBBV) [O]	*Sold to the Ukraine, May 2007*
	XZ941	WS Gazelle HT2 (9301M) [B]	DCAE, No 1 SoTT, Cosford
	XZ942	WS Gazelle HT2 (9305M) [42/CU]	AAC, Middle Wallop, instructional use
	XZ964	BAe Harrier GR3 [D]	Royal Engineers Museum, Chatham
	XZ966	BAe Harrier GR3 (9221M) [G]	MoD FSCTE, Manston
	XZ968	BAe Harrier GR3 (9222M) [3G]	Muckleborough Collection, Weybourne
	XZ969	BAe Harrier GR3 [69]	RN, Predannack Fire School
	XZ971	BAe Harrier GR3 (9219M)	HQ DSDA, Donnington, Shropshire, on display
	XZ987	BAe Harrier GR3 (9185M) [C]	RAF Stafford, at main gate
	XZ990	BAe Harrier GR3 <ff>	No 1220 Sqn ATC, March, Cambs
	XZ990	BAe Harrier GR3 <rf>	RAF Wittering, derelict
	XZ991	BAe Harrier GR3 (9162M) [3A]	DCAE, No 1 SoTT, Cosford
	XZ993	BAe Harrier GR3 (9240M) (fuselage)	MoD St Athan, instructional use
	XZ994	BAe Harrier GR3 (9170M) [U]	RAF Defence Movements School, Brize Norton
	XZ995	BAe Harrier GR3 (9220M/G-CBGK) [3G]	Privately owned, Oulton Broad, Suffolk
	XZ996	BAe Harrier GR3 [96]	RN, Predannack Fire School
	XZ997	BAe Harrier GR3 (9122M) [V]	RAF Museum, Hendon
	ZA101	BAe Hawk 100 (G-HAWK)	MoD/BAE Systems, Warton
	ZA105	WS61 Sea King HAR3 [Q]	MoD/DARA, Fleetlands

Serial	Type (code/other identity)	Owner/operator, location or fate	Notes
ZA110	BAe Jetstream T2 (F-BTMI) [563/CU]	RN No 750 Sqn, Culdrose	
ZA111	BAe Jetstream T2 (9Q-CTC) [565/CU]	RN No 750 Sqn, Culdrose	
ZA126	WS61 Sea King HC6 [504/CU]	MoD/Westland Helicopters, Yeovil	
ZA127	WS61 Sea King HAS6 [509/CU]	DCAE, stored *HMS Sultan*, Gosport	
ZA128	WS61 Sea King HAS6 [010]	DCAE, stored *HMS Sultan*, Gosport	
ZA129	WS61 Sea King HAS6 [502/CU]	*Scrapped at Yeovil, September 2006*	
ZA130	WS61 Sea King HU5 [19]	RN No 771 Sqn, Culdrose	
ZA131	WS61 Sea King HAS6 [271/N]	DCAE, No 1 SoTT, Cosford	
ZA133	WS61 Sea King HAS6 [831/CU]	DCAE, AESS, *HMS Sultan*, Gosport	
ZA134	WS61 Sea King HU5 [825]	MoD/DARA, stored Fleetlands	
ZA135	WS61 Sea King HAS6 [832]	DCAE, AESS, *HMS Sultan*, Gosport	
ZA136	WS61 Sea King HAS6 [018/L]	DCAE, AESS, *HMS Sultan*, Gosport (wreck)	
ZA137	WS61 Sea King HU5 [20]	RN No 771 Sqn, Culdrose	
ZA144	BAe VC10 K2 (G-ARVC) <ff>	RAF St Athan	
ZA147	BAe VC10 K3 (5H-MMT) [F]	MoD/DARA, St Athan	
ZA148	BAe VC10 K3 (5Y-ADA) [G]	RAF No 101 Sqn, Brize Norton	
ZA149	BAe VC10 K3 (5X-UVJ) [H]	RAF No 101 Sqn, Brize Norton	
ZA150	BAe VC10 K3 (5H-MOG) [J]	RAF No 101 Sqn, Brize Norton	
ZA166	WS61 Sea King HU5 [16]	RN CHFMU, Yeovilton	
ZA167	WS61 Sea King HU5 [822/CU]	RN No 771 Sqn, Culdrose	
ZA168	WS61 Sea King HAS6 [830/CU]	DCAE, AESS, *HMS Sultan*, Gosport	
ZA169	WS61 Sea King HAS6 [515/CW]	DCAE, stored *HMS Sultan*, Gosport	
ZA170	WS61 Sea King HAS5	DCAE, stored *HMS Sultan*, Gosport	
ZA175	BAe Sea Harrier FA2	Norfolk & Suffolk Avn Museum, Flixton	
ZA176	BAe Sea Harrier FA2 [126/R]	Newark Air Museum, Winthorpe	
ZA195	BAe Sea Harrier FA2	Privately owned, Farnborough	
ZA209	Short MATS-B	Museum of Army Flying, Middle Wallop	
ZA250	BAe Harrier T52 (G-VTOL)	Brooklands Museum, Weybridge	
ZA254	Panavia Tornado F2 (9253M) (fuselage)	RAF Marham, instructional use	
ZA267	Panavia Tornado F2 (9284M)	RAF Marham, instructional use	
ZA291	WS61 Sea King HC4 [N]	RN No 846 Sqn, Yeovilton	
ZA292	WS61 Sea King HC4 [WU]	RN No 848 Sqn, Yeovilton	
ZA293	WS61 Sea King HC4 [A]	RN CHFMU, Yeovilton	
ZA295	WS61 Sea King HC4 [U]	RN No 846 Sqn, Yeovilton	
ZA296	WS61 Sea King HC4	RN No 845 Sqn, Yeovilton	
ZA297	WS61 Sea King HC4 [W]	RN No 846 Sqn, Yeovilton	
ZA298	WS61 Sea King HC4	RN No 845 Sqn, Yeovilton	
ZA299	WS61 Sea King HC4 [D]	RN No 845 Sqn, Yeovilton	
ZA310	WS61 Sea King HC4 [B]	RN CHFMU, Yeovilton	
ZA312	WS61 Sea King HC4	RN CHFMU, Yeovilton	
ZA313	WS61 Sea King HC4 [M]	RN No 845 Sqn, Yeovilton	
ZA314	WS61 Sea King HC4 [WT]	RN No 848 Sqn, Yeovilton	
ZA319	Panavia Tornado GR1 (9315M)	Army, Bicester, on display	
ZA320	Panavia Tornado GR1 (9314M) [TAW]	DCAE, No 1 SoTT, Cosford	
ZA322	Panavia Tornado GR1 (9334M) [TAC]	RAF Marham, Fire Section	
ZA323	Panavia Tornado GR1 [TAZ]	DCAE, No 1 SoTT, Cosford	
ZA325	Panavia Tornado GR1 [TAX]	ARF, RAF St Athan	
ZA326	Panavia Tornado GR1P	MoD, Boscombe Down (wfu)	
ZA327	Panavia Tornado GR1	RAF, Leeming	
ZA328	Panavia Tornado GR1	BAE Systems, Warton (spares use)	
ZA353	Panavia Tornado GR1 [B-53]	MoD, Boscombe Down (wfu)	
ZA354	Panavia Tornado GR1	Yorkshire Air Museum, Elvington	
ZA355	Panavia Tornado GR1 (9310M) [TAA]	RAF Lossiemouth, WLT	
ZA356	Panavia Tornado GR1 <ff>	RAF Marham, instructional use	
ZA357	Panavia Tornado GR1 [TTV]	DCAE, No 1 SoTT, Cosford	
ZA359	Panavia Tornado GR1	BAE Systems Warton, Overseas Customer Training Centre	
ZA360	Panavia Tornado GR1 (9318M) <ff>	RAF Marham, instructional use	
ZA361	Panavia Tornado GR1 [TD]	MoD/DARA, St Athan	
ZA362	Panavia Tornado GR1 [AJ-F]	Highland Aviation Museum, Inverness	
ZA365	Panavia Tornado GR4 [001]	RAF No 15(R) Sqn, Lossiemouth	
ZA367	Panavia Tornado GR4 [002]	RAF No 617 Sqn, Lossiemouth	
ZA369	Panavia Tornado GR4A [003]	RAF No 14 Sqn, Lossiemouth	
ZA370	Panavia Tornado GR4A [004]	RAF No 31 Sqn, Marham	

Notes	Serial	Type (code/other identity)	Owner/operator, location or fate
	ZA371	Panavia Tornado GR4A [C]	RAF No 14 Sqn, Lossiemouth
	ZA372	Panavia Tornado GR4A [006]	RAF No 15(R) Sqn, Lossiemouth
	ZA373	Panavia Tornado GR4A [007]	RAF No 13 Sqn, Marham
	ZA375	Panavia Tornado GR1 (9335M) [AJ-W]	RAF Marham, Fire Section
	ZA393	Panavia Tornado GR4 [008]	RAF No 15(R) Sqn, Lossiemouth
	ZA395	Panavia Tornado GR4A [009]	RAF No 617 Sqn, Lossiemouth
	ZA398	Panavia Tornado GR4A [010]	RAF No 617 Sqn, Lossiemouth
	ZA399	Panavia Tornado GR1 (9316M) [AJ-C]	DCAE, No 1 SoTT, Cosford
	ZA400	Panavia Tornado GR4A [011]	RAF, Marham Wing
	ZA401	Panavia Tornado GR4A [XIII]	RAF No 13 Sqn, Marham
	ZA402	Panavia Tornado GR4A	MoD/BAE Systems, Warton
	ZA404	Panavia Tornado GR4A [013]	RAF No 15(R) Sqn, Lossiemouth
	ZA405	Panavia Tornado GR4A [014]	RAF No 12 Sqn, Lossiemouth
	ZA406	Panavia Tornado GR4 [015]	RAF No 12 Sqn, Lossiemouth
	ZA407	Panavia Tornado GR1 (9336M) [AJ-N]	RAF Marham, on display
	ZA409	Panavia Tornado GR1 [VII]	RAF Lossiemouth (wfu)
	ZA410	Panavia Tornado GR4 [016]	RAF No 15(R) Sqn, Lossiemouth
	ZA411	Panavia Tornado GR1 [TT]	MoD/BAE Systems, Warton
	ZA412	Panavia Tornado GR4 [017]	RAF No 15(R) Sqn, Lossiemouth
	ZA446	Panavia Tornado GR4 [AF]	RAF No 9 Sqn, Marham
	ZA447	Panavia Tornado GR4 [DE]	RAF No 31 Sqn, Marham
	ZA449	Panavia Tornado GR4 [020]	RAF No 12 Sqn, Lossiemouth
	ZA450	Panavia Tornado GR1 (9317M) [TH]	DCAE, No 1 SoTT, Cosford
	ZA452	Panavia Tornado GR4 [021]	RAF No 2 Sqn, Marham
	ZA453	Panavia Tornado GR4 [022]	RAF No 15(R) Sqn, Lossiemouth
	ZA456	Panavia Tornado GR4 [023]	RAF No 14 Sqn, Lossiemouth
	ZA457	Panavia Tornado GR1 [AJ-J]	RAF Museum, Hendon
	ZA458	Panavia Tornado GR4 [024]	RAF No 15(R) Sqn, Lossiemouth
	ZA459	Panavia Tornado GR4 [F] $	RAF No 15(R) Sqn, Lossiemouth
	ZA461	Panavia Tornado GR4 [026]	RAF No 13 Sqn, Marham
	ZA462	Panavia Tornado GR4 [027]	RAF No 14 Sqn, Lossiemouth
	ZA463	Panavia Tornado GR4 [028]	RAF, Marham Wing
	ZA465	Panavia Tornado GR1 [FF]	Imperial War Museum, Duxford
	ZA469	Panavia Tornado GR4 [029]$	RAF No 9 Sqn, Marham
	ZA470	Panavia Tornado GR4 [BQ]	RAF, stored Shawbury
	ZA472	Panavia Tornado GR4 [031]	RAF No 15(R) Sqn, Lossiemouth
	ZA473	Panavia Tornado GR4 [032]	RAF No 14 Sqn, Lossiemouth
	ZA474	Panavia Tornado GR1 (9312M)	RAF Lossiemouth (wfu)
	ZA475	Panavia Tornado GR1 (9311M)	RAF Lossiemouth, on display
	ZA492	Panavia Tornado GR4 [BO]	RAF No 14 Sqn, Lossiemouth
	ZA541	Panavia Tornado GR4 [034]	RAF No 15(R) Sqn, Lossiemouth
	ZA542	Panavia Tornado GR4 [DM]	RAF No 15(R) Sqn, Lossiemouth
	ZA543	Panavia Tornado GR4 [FF]	RAF No 12 Sqn, Lossiemouth
	ZA544	Panavia Tornado GR4 [037]	RAF No 13 Sqn, Marham
	ZA546	Panavia Tornado GR4 [AG]	RAF No 9 Sqn, Marham
	ZA547	Panavia Tornado GR4 [039]	RAF No 617 Sqn, Lossiemouth
	ZA548	Panavia Tornado GR4 [040]	RAF No 15(R) Sqn, Lossiemouth
	ZA549	Panavia Tornado GR4 [041]	RAF No 31 Sqn, Marham
	ZA550	Panavia Tornado GR4 [042]	RAF No 2 Sqn, Marham
	ZA551	Panavia Tornado GR4 [AX]	RAF No 15(R) Sqn, Lossiemouth
	ZA552	Panavia Tornado GR4 [XI]	RAF No 13 Sqn, Marham
	ZA553	Panavia Tornado GR4 [DI]	RAF No 2 Sqn, Marham
	ZA554	Panavia Tornado GR4 [BF]	RAF No 9 Sqn, Marham
	ZA556	Panavia Tornado GR4 [047]	RAF No 12 Sqn, Lossiemouth
	ZA556	Panavia Tornado GR1 <R> (*ZA368*/BAPC 155) [Z]	RAF M&RU, Bottesford
	ZA557	Panavia Tornado GR4 [048]	RAF No 617 Sqn, Lossiemouth
	ZA559	Panavia Tornado GR4 [049]	RAF Marham Wing
	ZA560	Panavia Tornado GR4 [050]	RAF No 617 Sqn, Lossiemouth
	ZA562	Panavia Tornado GR4 [TO]	RAF No 31 Sqn, Marham
	ZA563	Panavia Tornado GR4 [052]	RAF, St Athan
	ZA564	Panavia Tornado GR4 $	RAF No 31 Sqn, Marham
	ZA585	Panavia Tornado GR4 [054]	RAF No 13 Sqn, Marham
	ZA587	Panavia Tornado GR4 [055]	RAF No 15(R) Sqn, Lossiemouth
	ZA588	Panavia Tornado GR4 [056]	RAF No 12 Sqn, Lossiemouth
	ZA589	Panavia Tornado GR4 [DN]	RAF No 31 Sqn, Marham
	ZA591	Panavia Tornado GR4 [058]	RAF, Marham Wing
	ZA592	Panavia Tornado GR4 [059]	RAF No 13 Sqn, Marham

Serial	Type (code/other identity)	Owner/operator, location or fate	Notes
ZA594	Panavia Tornado GR4 [060]	RAF No 2 Sqn, Marham	
ZA595	Panavia Tornado GR4 [061]	RAF No 12 Sqn, Lossiemouth	
ZA596	Panavia Tornado GR4 [062]	RAF No 14 Sqn, Lossiemouth	
ZA597	Panavia Tornado GR4 [063]	RAF No 9 Sqn, Marham	
ZA598	Panavia Tornado GR4 [064]	MoD/AFD/QinetiQ, Boscombe Down	
ZA600	Panavia Tornado GR4 [065]	RAF Operation Telic, Qatar	
ZA601	Panavia Tornado GR4 [066, AJ-G]	RAF No 617 Sqn, Lossiemouth	
ZA602	Panavia Tornado GR4	RAF No 13 Sqn, Marham	
ZA604	Panavia Tornado GR4 [TY]	RAF No 15(R) Sqn, Lossiemouth	
ZA606	Panavia Tornado GR4 [BD]	RAF No 2 Sqn, Marham	
ZA607	Panavia Tornado GR4 [070]	RAF No 12 Sqn, Lossiemouth	
ZA608	Panavia Tornado GR4	RAF, stored St Athan	
ZA609	Panavia Tornado GR4	RAF AWC/FJWOEU/No 41(R) Sqn, Coningsby	
ZA611	Panavia Tornado GR4	RAF AWC/FJWOEU/No 41(R) Sqn, Coningsby	
ZA612	Panavia Tornado GR4 [074]	RAF No 2 Sqn, Marham	
ZA613	Panavia Tornado GR4 [075]	RAF No 12 Sqn, Lossiemouth	
ZA614	Panavia Tornado GR4 [076]	RAF No 2 Sqn, Marham	
ZA634	Slingsby T61F Venture T2 (G-BUHA) [C]	Privately owned, Saltby, Leics	
ZA652	Slingsby T61F Venture T2 (G-BUDC)	Privately owned, Enstone	
ZA670	B-V Chinook HC2 (N37010)	RAF No 27 Sqn, Odiham	
ZA671	B-V Chinook HC2 (N37011)	RAF No 7 Sqn, Odiham	
ZA673	B-V Chinook HC2 (N37016) [A]	RAF No 1310 Flt, Basrah, Iraq	
ZA674	B-V Chinook HC2 (N37019)	RAF No 27 Sqn, Odiham	
ZA675	B-V Chinook HC2 (N37020)	MoD/DARA, Fleetlands (on repair)	
ZA676	B-V Chinook HC1 (N37021/9230M) [FG] (wreck)	AAC, Wattisham	
ZA677	B-V Chinook HC2 (N37022) [AF]	RAF No 27 Sqn, Odiham	
ZA678	B-V Chinook HC1 (N37023/9229M) [EZ] (wreck)	RAF Odiham, BDRT	
ZA679	B-V Chinook HC2 (N37025)	RAF No 27 Sqn, Odiham	
ZA680	B-V Chinook HC2 (N37026)	RAF No 18 Sqn, Odiham	
ZA681	B-V Chinook HC2 (N37027) [AI]	RAF No 7 Sqn, Odiham	
ZA682	B-V Chinook HC2 (N37029)	RAF Odiham Wing	
ZA683	B-V Chinook HC2 (N37030) [AK]	RAF No 18 Sqn, Odiham	
ZA684	B-V Chinook HC2 (N37031) [AL]	RAF No 18 Sqn, Odiham	
ZA704	B-V Chinook HC2 (N37033) [AM]	RAF No 7 Sqn, Odiham	
ZA705	B-V Chinook HC2 (N37035) [AN]	RAF No 18 Sqn, Odiham	
ZA707	B-V Chinook HC2 (N37040) [AO]	RAF Odiham Wing	
ZA708	B-V Chinook HC2 (N37042)	RAF Odiham Wing	
ZA709	B-V Chinook HC2 (N37043)	RAF No 7 Sqn, Odiham	
ZA710	B-V Chinook HC2 (N37044)	RAF Odiham Wing	
ZA711	B-V Chinook HC2 (N37046)	RAF No 7 Sqn, Odiham	
ZA712	B-V Chinook HC2 (N37047) [AT]	RAF No 27 Sqn, Odiham	
ZA713	B-V Chinook HC2 (N37048) [AU]	RAF No 18 Sqn, Odiham	
ZA714	B-V Chinook HC2 (N37051) [AV]	RAF Odiham Wing	
ZA717	B-V Chinook HC1 (N37056/9238M) (wreck)	Trenchard Hall, RAF Cranwell, instructional use	
ZA718	B-V Chinook HC2 (N37058) [BN]	RAF Odiham Wing	
ZA720	B-V Chinook HC2 (N37060)	MoD/DARA, Fleetlands	
ZA726	WS Gazelle AH1 [F1]	AAC No 671 Sqn/2 Regt, Middle Wallop	
ZA728	WS Gazelle AH1 [E]	RM, stored Shawbury	
ZA729	WS Gazelle AH1	*Currently not known*	
ZA731	WS Gazelle AH1	AAC GDSH, Middle Wallop	
ZA733	WS Gazelle AH1	DARA Fleetlands Apprentice School	
ZA734	WS Gazelle AH1	Privately owned, Hixon, Staffs	
ZA735	WS Gazelle AH1	DCAE SEAE, Arborfield	
ZA736	WS Gazelle AH1	AAC No 29 Flt, BATUS, Suffield, Canada	
ZA737	WS Gazelle AH1	Museum of Army Flying, Middle Wallop	
ZA766	WS Gazelle AH1	MoD/Westland Helicopters, Yeovil	
ZA768	WS Gazelle AH1 [F] (wreck)	MoD/DARA, stored Fleetlands	
ZA769	WS Gazelle AH1 [K]	DCAE SEAE, Arborfield	
ZA771	WS Gazelle AH1	AAC, stored Shawbury	
ZA772	WS Gazelle AH1	AAC No 671 Sqn/2 Regt, Middle Wallop	
ZA773	WS Gazelle AH1 [F]	AAC, stored Shawbury	
ZA774	WS Gazelle AH1	AAC, stored Shawbury	
ZA775	WS Gazelle AH1	AAC, stored Shawbury	
ZA776	WS Gazelle AH1 [F]	RM, stored Shawbury	

Notes	Serial	Type (code/other identity)	Owner/operator, location or fate
	ZA804	WS Gazelle HT3	Privately owned, Solstice Park, Amesbury, Wilts
	ZA934	WS Puma HC1 [BZ]	*Crashed Catterick, 8 August 2007*
	ZA935	WS Puma HC1	RAF No 1563 Flt, Basrah, Iraq
	ZA936	WS Puma HC1	RAF PASF, Benson
	ZA937	WS Puma HC1	RAF PASF, Benson
	ZA938	WS Puma HC1	*Crashed Baghdad, Iraq, 21 November 2007*
	ZA939	WS Puma HC1	RAF No 230 Sqn, Aldergrove
	ZA940	WS Puma HC1	RAF No 33 Sqn, Benson
	ZA947	Douglas Dakota C3 [AI]	RAF BBMF, Coningsby
	ZB500	WS Lynx 800 (G-LYNX/ZA500)	The Helicopter Museum, Weston-super-Mare
	ZB506	WS61 Sea King Mk 4X	MoD/AFD/QinetiQ, Boscombe Down
	ZB507	WS61 Sea King HC4 [F]	RN No 845 Sqn, Yeovilton
	ZB601	BAe Harrier T4 (fuselage)	RNAS Yeovilton, Fire Section
	ZB603	BAe Harrier T8 [03/DDT]	SFDO, RNAS Culdrose
	ZB604	BAe Harrier T8 [722]	RAF Wittering
	ZB615	SEPECAT Jaguar T2A	MoD, stored Boscombe Down
	ZB625	WS Gazelle HT3 [N]	MoD/AFD/QinetiQ, Boscombe Down
	ZB627	WS Gazelle HT3 (G-CBSK) [A]	Privately owned, Battlesbridge, Essex
	ZB646	WS Gazelle HT2 (G-CBGZ) [59/CU]	Privately owned, Knebworth
	ZB665	WS Gazelle AH1	AAC, stored Shawbury
	ZB666	WS Gazelle AH1 <ff>	North-East Aircraft Museum, Usworth
	ZB667	WS Gazelle AH1	AAC No 665 Sqn/5 Regt, Aldergrove
	ZB668	WS Gazelle AH1 (TAD 015)	DCAE SEAE, Arborfield
	ZB669	WS Gazelle AH1	AAC No 665 Sqn/5 Regt, Aldergrove
	ZB670	WS Gazelle AH1	AAC Dishforth, for display
	ZB671	WS Gazelle AH1 [5A]	AAC
	ZB672	WS Gazelle AH1	Army Training Regiment, Winchester
	ZB673	WS Gazelle AH1 [P]	AAC No 671 Sqn/2 Regt, Middle Wallop
	ZB674	WS Gazelle AH1	AAC, stored Shawbury
	ZB677	WS Gazelle AH1 [5B]	AAC No 29 Flt, BATUS, Suffield, Canada
	ZB678	WS Gazelle AH1	AAC GDSH, Middle Wallop
	ZB679	WS Gazelle AH1	AAC, stored Shawbury
	ZB682	WS Gazelle AH1	MoD/DARA, stored Fleetlands
	ZB683	WS Gazelle AH1	AAC No 665 Sqn/5 Regt, Aldergrove
	ZB684	WS Gazelle AH1	RAF Defence Movements School, Brize Norton
	ZB686	WS Gazelle AH1 <ff>	AAC *Blue Eagles*, Middle Wallop (mobile display)
	ZB688	WS Gazelle AH1	AAC No 3(V) Flt/7 Regt, Leuchars
	ZB689	WS Gazelle AH1	AAC No 665 Sqn/5 Regt, Aldergrove
	ZB690	WS Gazelle AH1	MoD, stored Shawbury
	ZB691	WS Gazelle AH1	AAC No 3(V) Flt/7 Regt, Leuchars
	ZB692	WS Gazelle AH1 [S]	AAC No 671 Sqn/2 Regt, Middle Wallop
	ZB693	WS Gazelle AH1	AAC No 665 Sqn/5 Regt, Aldergrove
	ZD230	BAC Super VC10 K4 (G-ASGA) <ff>	RAF St Athan
	ZD240	BAC Super VC10 K4 (G-ASGL) <ff>	RAF St Athan
	ZD241	BAC Super VC10 K4 (G-ASGM) [N]	RAF No 101 Sqn, Mount Pleasant, FI
	ZD242	BAC Super VC10 K4 (G-ASGP) [P]	RAF St Athan
	ZD249	WS Lynx HAS3S [636]	RN No 702 Sqn, Yeovilton
	ZD250	WS Lynx HAS3S [630]	RN No 702 Sqn, Yeovilton
	ZD251	WS Lynx HAS3S [637]	RN No 702 Sqn, Yeovilton
	ZD252	WS Lynx HMA8 [697]	RN No 815 Sqn OEU, Yeovilton
	ZD253	WS Lynx HAS3S	*Broken up for spares, 2007*
	ZD254	WS Lynx HAS3S [302]	RN No 815 Sqn, HQ Flt, Yeovilton
	ZD255	WS Lynx HAS3S [350]	RN No 815 Sqn, *Cumberland* Flt, Yeovilton
	ZD257	WS Lynx HMA8 [217]	RN No 815 Sqn, 221 Flt, Yeovilton
	ZD258	WS Lynx HMA8 [672/NC]	RN No 702 Sqn, Yeovilton
	ZD259	WS Lynx HMA8DAS [425]	RN No 815 Sqn, *Kent* Flt, Yeovilton
	ZD260	WS Lynx HMA8DAS [427]	RN No 815 Sqn, *St Albans* Flt, Yeovilton
	ZD261	WS Lynx HMA8DAS [674]	RN No 702 Sqn, Yeovilton
	ZD262	WS Lynx HMA8 [312]	RN No 815 Sqn, Yeovilton
	ZD263	WS Lynx HAS3S [639]	RN No 702 Sqn, Yeovilton
	ZD264	WS Lynx HAS3S [214]	RN No 815 Sqn, 214 Flt, Yeovilton
	ZD265	WS Lynx HMA8DAS [308]	RN No 815 Sqn, HQ Flt, Yeovilton
	ZD266	WS Lynx HMA8 [699]	RN No 815 Sqn, OEU, Yeovilton
	ZD267	WS Lynx HMA8	RN ETS, Yeovilton

Serial	Type (code/other identity)	Owner/operator, location or fate	Notes
ZD268	WS Lynx HMA8 [317]	RN No 815 Sqn OEU, Yeovilton	
ZD272	WS Lynx AH7 [H]	AAC No 671 Sqn/2 Regt, Middle Wallop	
ZD273	WS Lynx AH7	AAC No 657 Sqn, Odiham	
ZD274	WS Lynx AH7	MoD/DARA, stored Fleetlands	
ZD276	WS Lynx AH7	*Broken up for spares, 2007*	
ZD277	WS Lynx AH7	MoD/DARA, stored Fleetlands	
ZD278	WS Lynx AH7	AAC No 9 Regt, Dishforth	
ZD279	WS Lynx AH7	AAC No 672 Sqn/9 Regt, Dishforth	
ZD280	WS Lynx AH7	MoD/DARA, stored Fleetlands	
ZD281	WS Lynx AH7 [K]	AAC No 671 Sqn/2 Regt, Middle Wallop	
ZD282	WS Lynx AH7 [L]	MoD/DARA, Fleetlands	
ZD283	WS Lynx AH7 [X]	MoD/DARA, Fleetlands	
ZD284	WS Lynx AH7	AAC No 9 Regt, Dishforth	
ZD285	WS Lynx AH7	MoD/AFD/QinetiQ, Boscombe Down	
ZD318	BAe Harrier GR7A	RAF Cottesmore, WLT	
ZD319	BAe Harrier GR7	MoD/QinetiQ, Boscombe Down	
ZD320	BAe Harrier GR9	MoD/BAE Systems, Warton	
ZD321	BAe Harrier GR9 [02]	RAF JUMP, Cottesmore (conversion)	
ZD322	BAe Harrier GR9A [034]	RN NSW, Cottesmore	
ZD323	BAe Harrier GR9A [04]	RAF SAM, Cottesmore	
ZD327	BAe Harrier GR9A [08A]	RAF No 4 Sqn, Cottesmore	
ZD328	BAe Harrier GR9 [09]	AWC/FJWOEU/No 41(R) Sqn, Coningsby	
ZD329	BAe Harrier GR7 [10]	RAF No 4 Sqn, Cottesmore	
ZD330	BAe Harrier GR9 [11]	RAF No 1 Sqn, Cottesmore	
ZD346	BAe Harrier GR9A [13A]	RAF No 1 Sqn, Cottesmore	
ZD347	BAe Harrier GR7A [14A]	RAF No 1 Sqn, Cottesmore	
ZD348	BAe Harrier GR9A [15A]	RAF JUMP, Cottesmore (conversion)	
ZD351	BAe Harrier GR9 [18]	RN NSW, Cottesmore	
ZD352	BAe Harrier GR9A [19]	RAF No 4 Sqn, Cottesmore	
ZD353	BAe Harrier GR5 (fuselage)	BAE Systems, Brough	
ZD354	BAe Harrier GR9 [21]	MoD/BAE Systems, Warton	
ZD375	BAe Harrier GR9 [23]	RAF HOCU/No 20(R) Sqn, Wittering	
ZD376	BAe Harrier GR7A [24A]	RAF No 1 Sqn, Cottesmore	
ZD378	BAe Harrier GR7A [26A]	RAF No 4 Sqn, Cottesmore	
ZD379	BAe Harrier GR9 [27]	RAF No 4 Sqn, Cottesmore	
ZD380	BAe Harrier GR9A [28A]	RAF No 1 Sqn, Cottesmore	
ZD401	BAe Harrier GR9 [30]	RAF HOCU/No 20(R) Sqn, Wittering	
ZD402	BAe Harrier GR9 [31]	RAF SAM, Cottesmore	
ZD403	BAe Harrier GR7 [32A]	RAF No 4 Sqn, Cottesmore	
ZD404	BAe Harrier GR7A [33A]	RAF No 1 Sqn, Cottesmore	
ZD405	BAe Harrier GR7A [34A]	RAF No 1 Sqn, Cottesmore	
ZD406	BAe Harrier GR9 [35]	RAF No 4 Sqn, Cottesmore	
ZD407	BAe Harrier GR7 [36]	RAF ARF, St Athan	
ZD408	BAe Harrier GR7A [37A]	RAF No 1 Sqn, Cottesmore	
ZD409	BAe Harrier GR9 [38]	RAF No 4 Sqn, Cottesmore	
ZD410	BAe Harrier GR9 [39] $	RAF No 4 Sqn, Cottesmore	
ZD411	BAe Harrier GR7 [40A]	RAF JUMP, Cottesmore (conversion)	
ZD412	BAe Harrier GR5 (fuselage)	Privately owned, Charlwood	
ZD431	BAe Harrier GR7A [43A]	RAF SAM, Cottesmore	
ZD433	BAe Harrier GR9A [45A]	RAF JUMP, Cottesmore (conversion)	
ZD435	BAe Harrier GR9 [47]	RAF No 1 Sqn, Cottesmore	
ZD436	BAe Harrier GR7A [48A]	RAF No 4 Sqn, Cottesmore	
ZD437	BAe Harrier GR9A [49A]	RAF JUMP, Cottesmore (conversion)	
ZD438	BAe Harrier GR9 [50]	RAF JUMP, Cottesmore (conversion)	
ZD461	BAe Harrier GR9 [51A]	RAF JUMP, Cottesmore (conversion)	
ZD462	BAe Harrier GR7 (9302M) [52]	ATTF, RAF St Athan	
ZD463	BAe Harrier GR9 [53]	RAF JUMP, Cottesmore (conversion)	
ZD465	BAe Harrier GR9A [55A]	RAF JUMP, Cottesmore (conversion)	
ZD466	BAe Harrier GR7 [56]	RAF ASF, Wittering	
ZD467	BAe Harrier GR9 [57]	RAF JUMP, Cottesmore (conversion)	
ZD468	BAe Harrier GR9 [58]	RAF HOCU/No 20(R) Sqn, Wittering	
ZD469	BAe Harrier GR7A [59A]	RAF Cottesmore (on repair)	
ZD470	BAe Harrier GR7 [60]	RAF No 1 Sqn, Cottesmore	
ZD476	WS61 Sea King HC4 [WZ]	RN No 848 Sqn, Yeovilton	
ZD477	WS61 Sea King HC4	MoD/DARA, Fleetlands	
ZD478	WS61 Sea King HC4 [J]	MoD/DARA, Fleetlands (on repair)	
ZD479	WS61 Sea King HC4 [WQ]	RN No 848 Sqn, Yeovilton	
ZD480	WS61 Sea King HC4 [E]	RN No 845 Sqn, Yeovilton	
ZD559	WS Lynx AH7	MoD/AFD/QinetiQ, Boscombe Down	
ZD560	WS Lynx AH7	MoD/ETPS, Boscombe Down	
ZD565	WS Lynx HMA8DAS [365]	RN 815 Sqn, *Argyll* Flt, Yeovilton	
ZD566	WS Lynx HMA8DAS [221]	RN No 815 Sqn, 221 Flt, Yeovilton	

Notes	*Serial*	*Type (code/other identity)*	*Owner/operator, location or fate*
	ZD574	B-V Chinook HC2 (N37077)	RAF No 18 Sqn, Odiham
	ZD575	B-V Chinook HC2 (N37078) [DC]	RAF No 18/27 Sqn, Odiham
	ZD578	BAe Sea Harrier FA2 [000,122]	RNAS Yeovilton, at main gate
	ZD579	BAe Sea Harrier FA2 [012/L]	RN, Culdrose
	ZD580	BAe Sea Harrier FA2	Privately owned, Sproughton
	ZD581	BAe Sea Harrier FA2 [124]	RN, Predannack Fire School
	ZD582	BAe Sea Harrier FA2	Privately owned, RNAS Yeovilton
	ZD607	BAe Sea Harrier FA2	DCAE AESS, *HMS Sultan*, Gosport
	ZD608	BAe Sea Harrier FA2 [731]	Privately owned, Charlwood
	ZD610	BAe Sea Harrier FA2 [006/N]	Privately owned, Dunsfold
	ZD611	BAe Sea Harrier FA2	RNAS Culdrose Fire Section
	ZD612	BAe Sea Harrier FA2	Privately owned, Topsham, Devon
	ZD613	BAe Sea Harrier FA2 [127/R]	Privately owned, Cross Green, Leeds
	ZD614	BAe Sea Harrier FA2 [122/R]	Privately owned, Sproughton
	ZD615	BAe Sea Harrier FA2	Privately owned, Charlwood
	ZD620	BAe 125 CC3	RAF No 32(The Royal) Sqn, Northolt
	ZD621	BAe 125 CC3	RAF No 32(The Royal) Sqn, Northolt
	ZD625	WS61 Sea King HC4 [P]	RN No 846 Sqn, Yeovilton
	ZD626	WS61 Sea King HC4 [S]	RN No 846 Sqn, Yeovilton
	ZD627	WS61 Sea King HC4 [WO]	RN No 848 Sqn, Yeovilton
	ZD630	WS61 Sea King HAS6 [012/L]	DCAE, stored *HMS Sultan*, Gosport
	ZD631	WS61 Sea King HAS6 [66] (fuselage)	RN, Predannack Fire School
	ZD633	WS61 Sea King HAS6 [014/L]	DCAE, stored *HMS Sultan*, Gosport
	ZD634	WS61 Sea King HAS6 [503]	DCAE, stored *HMS Sultan*, Gosport
	ZD636	WS61 Sea King ASaC7 [182]	MoD/DARA, Fleetlands
	ZD637	WS61 Sea King HAS6 [700/PW]	DCAE, AESS, *HMS Sultan*, Gosport
	ZD667	BAe Harrier GR3 (9201M) [67]	RN, Predannack Fire School
	ZD668	BAe Harrier GR3 (G-CBCU) [3E]	Privately owned, Oulton Broad, Suffolk
	ZD670	BAe Harrier GR3 [3A]	Privately owned, South Molton, Devon
	ZD703	BAe 125 CC3	RAF No 32(The Royal) Sqn, Northolt
	ZD704	BAe 125 CC3	RAF No 32(The Royal) Sqn, Northolt
	ZD707	Panavia Tornado GR4 [077]	RAF No 617 Sqn, Lossiemouth
	ZD708	Panavia Tornado GR4	MoD/BAE Systems, Warton
	ZD709	Panavia Tornado GR4 [078]	RAF No 14 Sqn, Lossiemouth
	ZD710	Panavia Tornado GR1 <ff>	Privately owned, Barnstaple
	ZD711	Panavia Tornado GR4 [079]	RAF No 12 Sqn, Lossiemouth
	ZD712	Panavia Tornado GR4 [080]	RAF No 12 Sqn, Lossiemouth
	ZD713	Panavia Tornado GR4 [F]	MoD/AFD/QinetiQ, Boscombe Down
	ZD714	Panavia Tornado GR4 [AJ-W]	RAF No 617 Sqn, Lossiemouth
	ZD715	Panavia Tornado GR4 [083]	RAF, Marham Wing
	ZD716	Panavia Tornado GR4	RAF No 9 Sqn, Marham
	ZD719	Panavia Tornado GR4 [085]	RAF No 14 Sqn, Lossiemouth
	ZD720	Panavia Tornado GR4 [086]	RAF No 617 Sqn, Lossiemouth
	ZD739	Panavia Tornado GR4	RAF AWC/FJWOEU/No 41(R) Sqn, Coningsby
	ZD740	Panavia Tornado GR4 [BG]	RAF No 14 Sqn, Lossiemouth
	ZD741	Panavia Tornado GR4 [089]	RAF No 14 Sqn, Lossiemouth
	ZD742	Panavia Tornado GR4 [FY]	RAF No 617 Sqn, Lossiemouth
	ZD743	Panavia Tornado GR4 [091]	RAF No 15(R) Sqn, Lossiemouth
	ZD744	Panavia Tornado GR4 [092]	RAF No 13 Sqn, Marham
	ZD745	Panavia Tornado GR4	RAF No 13 Sqn, Marham
	ZD746	Panavia Tornado GR4 [094]	RAF No 617 Sqn, Lossiemouth
	ZD747	Panavia Tornado GR4 [AL]	RAF No 9 Sqn, Marham
	ZD748	Panavia Tornado GR4 $	RAF No 2 Sqn, Marham
	ZD749	Panavia Tornado GR4 [AP]	MoD/AFD/QinetiQ, Boscombe Down
	ZD788	Panavia Tornado GR4 [BE]	RAF No 9 Sqn, Marham
	ZD790	Panavia Tornado GR4 [099]	RAF No 617 Sqn, Lossiemouth
	ZD792	Panavia Tornado GR4 [100]	RAF No 31 Sqn, Marham
	ZD793	Panavia Tornado GR4 [101]	RAF No 12 Sqn, Lossiemouth
	ZD810	Panavia Tornado GR4 [102]	RAF No 12 Sqn, Lossiemouth
	ZD811	Panavia Tornado GR4 [103]	RAF Lossiemouth Wing
	ZD812	Panavia Tornado GR4 [104]	RAF No 15(R) Sqn, Lossiemouth
	ZD842	Panavia Tornado GR4 [105]	RAF No 15(R) Sqn, Lossiemouth
	ZD843	Panavia Tornado GR4 [106]	RAF Lossiemouth, WLT
	ZD844	Panavia Tornado GR4 [107]	RAF TEF, Marham
	ZD847	Panavia Tornado GR4 [108]	RAF, Marham Wing
	ZD848	Panavia Tornado GR4 [109]	RAF No 9 Sqn, Marham
	ZD849	Panavia Tornado GR4 [110]	RAF No 14 Sqn, Lossiemouth
	ZD850	Panavia Tornado GR4 [111]	RAF No 9 Sqn, Marham
	ZD851	Panavia Tornado GR4 [112]	RAF No 13 Sqn, Marham
	ZD890	Panavia Tornado GR4 [113]	RAF No 2 Sqn, Marham

Serial	Type (code/other identity)	Owner/operator, location or fate	Notes
ZD892	Panavia Tornado GR4 [TG]	RAF, stored Shawbury	
ZD895	Panavia Tornado GR4 [115]	RAF, Marham Wing	
ZD899	Panavia Tornado F2	MoD, Boscombe Down, spares use	
ZD902	Panavia Tornado F2A(TIARA)	MoD/AFD/QinetiQ, Boscombe Down	
ZD906	Panavia Tornado F2 (comp ZE294) <ff>	RAF Leuchars, BDRT	
ZD932	Panavia Tornado F2 (comp ZE255) (9308M) (fuselage)	ARF, RAF St Athan	
ZD934	Panavia Tornado F2 (comp ZE786) <ff>	RAF Leeming, GI use	
ZD936	Panavia Tornado F2 (comp ZE251) <ff>	Boscombe Down Aviation Collection	
ZD938	Panavia Tornado F2 (comp ZE295) <ff>	Privately owned, Upton, Cheshire	
ZD939	Panavia Tornado F2 (comp ZE292) <ff>	DCAE Cosford, instructional use	
ZD948	Lockheed TriStar KC1 (G-BFCA)	RAF No 216 Sqn, Brize Norton	
ZD949	Lockheed TriStar K1 (G-BFCB)	RAF No 216 Sqn, Brize Norton	
ZD950	Lockheed TriStar KC1 (G-BFCC)	RAF No 216 Sqn, Brize Norton	
ZD951	Lockheed TriStar K1 (G-BFCD)	RAF No 216 Sqn, Brize Norton	
ZD952	Lockheed TriStar KC1 (G-BFCE)	RAF No 216 Sqn, Brize Norton	
ZD953	Lockheed TriStar KC1 (G-BFCF)	RAF No 216 Sqn, Brize Norton	
ZD980	B-V Chinook HC2 (N37082) [DD]	MoD/DARA, Fleetlands	
ZD981	B-V Chinook HC2 (N37083)	RAF Odiham Wing	
ZD982	B-V Chinook HC2 (N37085) [DF]	RAF No 18 Sqn, Odiham	
ZD983	B-V Chinook HC2 (N37086) [DG]	RAF No 27 Sqn, Odiham	
ZD984	B-V Chinook HC2 (N37088)	RAF No 18 Sqn, Odiham	
ZD990	BAe Harrier T8 [721]	SFDO, RNAS Culdrose	
ZD991	BAe Harrier T8 (9228M) [722/VL]	Privately owned, Sproughton	
ZD992	BAe Harrier T8 [724] (fuselage)	Privately owned, Cranfield	
ZD993	BAe Harrier T8 [723/VL]	MoD, Boscombe Down (spares use)	
ZD996	Panavia Tornado GR4A	RAF AWC/FJWOEU/No 41(R) Sqn, Coningsby	
ZE116	Panavia Tornado GR4A [116]	RAF No 13 Sqn, Marham	
ZE154	Panavia Tornado F3 (comp ZD901) [LT]	RAF Leuchars (wfu)	
ZE155	Panavia Tornado F3 [FF]	RAF No 25 Sqn, Leeming	
ZE156	Panavia Tornado F3 [WA]	RAF F3 OCU/No 56(R) Sqn, Leuchars	
ZE157	Panavia Tornado F3 [TY]	RAF AMF, Leuchars	
ZE158	Panavia Tornado F3 [HG]	RAF No 25 Sqn, Leeming	
ZE159	Panavia Tornado F3 [UV]	*Scrapped, November 2007*	
ZE160	Panavia Tornado F3 [TX]	RAF Leuchars (wfu)	
ZE161	Panavia Tornado F3 [GB]	RAF No 43 Sqn, Leuchars	
ZE162	Panavia Tornado F3 [HM]	RAF No 111 Sqn, Leuchars	
ZE163	Panavia Tornado F3 (comp ZG753) [TW]	RAF F3 OCU/No 56(R) Sqn, Leuchars	
ZE164	Panavia Tornado F3 [GD]	RAF No 111 Sqn, Leuchars	
ZE165	Panavia Tornado F3 [GE]	RAF No 43 Sqn, Leuchars	
ZE168	Panavia Tornado F3 [FA]	RAF No 25 Sqn, Leeming	
ZE199	Panavia Tornado F3 [TV]	RAF Leeming (wfu)	
ZE200	Panavia Tornado F3 [DB]	RAF No 111 Sqn, Leuchars	
ZE201	Panavia Tornado F3 [FB]	RAF No 25 Sqn, Leeming	
ZE202	Panavia Tornado F3 (MM55056)	*Scrapped, September 2007*	
ZE203	Panavia Tornado F3 [GA]	MoD/AFD/QinetiQ, Boscombe Down	
ZE204	Panavia Tornado F3 [FC]	RAF Leeming (wfu)	
ZE206	Panavia Tornado F3 [UI]	MoD/BAE Systems, Warton	
ZE207	Panavia Tornado F3 [GC]	RAF Leeming (wfu)	
ZE208	Panavia Tornado F3 (MM55060)	MoD St Athan (wfu)	
ZE209	Panavia Tornado F3 [AX]	RAF/EADS, Munich, Germany	
ZE250	Panavia Tornado F3 [TR]	RAF F3 OCU/No 56(R) Sqn, Leuchars	
ZE251	Panavia Tornado F3 (comp ZD936) [UF]	RAF St Athan (wfu)	
ZE253	Panavia Tornado F3 [AC]	RAF/EADS, Munich, Germany	
ZE254	Panavia Tornado F3 (comp ZD941) [FD]	RAF No 25 Sqn, Leeming	
ZE255	Panavia Tornado F3 (comp ZD932) [GC]	RAF No 43 Sqn, Leuchars	
ZE256	Panavia Tornado F3 [TP]	RAF Leuchars, instructional use	
ZE257	Panavia Tornado F3 [GI]	RAF No 43 Sqn, Leuchars	
ZE258	Panavia Tornado F3 (comp ZD905) [F]	MoD/DARA, St Athan	

Notes	Serial	Type (code/other identity)	Owner/operator, location or fate
	ZE287	Panavia Tornado F3 [TO]	RAF, stored Leeming
	ZE288	Panavia Tornado F3 (comp ZD940) [HA]	RAF No 111 Sqn, Leuchars
	ZE289	Panavia Tornado F3 [VX]	RAF Leeming (wfu)
	ZE292	Panavia Tornado F3 (comp ZD939) [FE]	RAF No 25 Sqn, Leeming
	ZE293	Panavia Tornado F3 [GZ]	RAF Leeming (wfu)
	ZE294	Panavia Tornado F3 (comp ZD906) [DD]	RAF Leeming (wfu)
	ZE295	Panavia Tornado F3 (comp ZD938) [DC]	RAF Leeming, WLT
	ZE338	Panavia Tornado F3 [GJ]	RAF No 43 Sqn, Leuchars
	ZE339	Panavia Tornado F3 <ff>	MoD/DARA, stored St Athan
	ZE340	Panavia Tornado F3 (*ZE758*/9298M) [GO]	DCAE, No 1 SoTT, Cosford
	ZE341	Panavia Tornado F3 [GO]	RAF No 25 Sqn, Leeming
	ZE342	Panavia Tornado F3 [FG]	RAF No 43 Sqn, Leuchars
	ZE343	Panavia Tornado F3 (comp ZD900) [DZ]	RAF F3 OCU/No 56(R) Sqn, Leuchars
	ZE350	McD F-4J(UK) Phantom (9080M) <ff>	Privately owned, Ingatestone, Essex
	ZE352	McD F-4J(UK) Phantom (9086M) <ff>	RAF Millom Museum, Haverigg
	ZE360	McD F-4J(UK) Phantom (9059M) [O]	MoD FSCTE, Manston
	ZE368	WS61 Sea King HAR3 [R]	RAF No 202 Sqn, D Flt, Lossiemouth
	ZE369	WS61 Sea King HAR3 [S]	RAF No 202 Sqn, A Flt, Boulmer
	ZE370	WS61 Sea King HAR3 [T]	MoD/DARA, Fleetlands
	ZE375	WS Lynx AH9	AAC No 1 Regt, Gütersloh
	ZE376	WS Lynx AH9	AAC No 661 Sqn/1 Regt, Gütersloh
	ZE378	WS Lynx AH7	AAC No 657 Sqn, Odiham
	ZE379	WS Lynx AH7	DCAE SEAE, Arborfield
	ZE380	WS Lynx AH9	MoD/DARA, Fleetlands
	ZE381	WS Lynx AH7 [X]	DCAE SEAE, Arborfield
	ZE395	BAe 125 CC3	RAF No 32(The Royal) Sqn, Northolt
	ZE396	BAe 125 CC3	RAF No 32(The Royal) Sqn, Northolt
	ZE410	Agusta A109A (AE-334)	AAC No 8 Flt, Credenhill
	ZE411	Agusta A109A (AE-331)	AAC No 8 Flt, Credenhill
	ZE412	Agusta A109A	AAC No 8 Flt, Credenhill
	ZE413	Agusta A109A	AAC No 8 Flt, Credenhill
	ZE416	Agusta A109E Power (G-ESLH)	MoD/ETPS, Boscombe Down
	ZE418	WS61 Sea King ASaC7 [186]	RN No 857 Sqn, Culdrose
	ZE420	WS61 Sea King ASaC7 [189]	RN No 857 Sqn, Culdrose
	ZE422	WS61 Sea King ASaC7	RN HMF, St Mawgan (conversion)
	ZE425	WS61 Sea King HC4 [WR]	RN No 848 Sqn, Yeovilton
	ZE426	WS61 Sea King HC4 [WX]	RN No 848 Sqn, Yeovilton
	ZE427	WS61 Sea King HC4 [K]	RN No 845 Sqn, Yeovilton
	ZE428	WS61 Sea King HC4	RN No 846 Sqn, Yeovilton
	ZE432	BAC 1-11/479FU (DQ-FBV)	MoD/ETPS, Boscombe Down
	ZE433	BAC 1-11/479FU (DQ-FBQ)	MoD/AFD/QinetiQ, Boscombe Down
	ZE438	BAe Jetstream T3 [76]	RN FONA/Heron Flight, Yeovilton
	ZE439	BAe Jetstream T3 [77]	RN FONA/Heron Flight, Yeovilton
	ZE440	BAe Jetstream T3 [78]	RN, stored Shawbury
	ZE441	BAe Jetstream T3 [79]	RN FONA/Heron Flight, Yeovilton
	ZE449	SA330L Puma HC1 (9017M/PA-12)	RAF No 230 Sqn, Aldergrove
	ZE477	WS Lynx 3	The Helicopter Museum, Weston-super-Mare
	ZE495	Grob G103 Viking T1 (BGA3000) [VA]	RAF CGMF, Syerston
	ZE496	Grob G103 Viking T1 (BGA3001) [VB]	RAF No 661 VGS, Kirknewton
	ZE498	Grob G103 Viking T1 (BGA3003) [VC]	RAF No 614 VGS, Wethersfield
	ZE499	Grob G103 Viking T1 (BGA3004) [VD]	RAF CGMF, Syerston
	ZE502	Grob G103 Viking T1 (BGA3007) [VF]	RAF No 622 VGS, Upavon
	ZE503	Grob G103 Viking T1 (BGA3008) [VG]	RAF No 625 VGS, Hullavington
	ZE504	Grob G103 Viking T1 (BGA3009) [VH]	RAF No 661 VGS, Kirknewton

Serial	Type (code/other identity)	Owner/operator, location or fate	Notes
ZE520	Grob G103 Viking T1 (BGA3010) [VJ]	RAF No 625 VGS, Hullavington	
ZE521	Grob G103 Viking T1 (BGA3011) [VK]	RAF No 626 VGS, Predannack	
ZE522	Grob G103 Viking T1 (BGA3012) [VL]	RAF No 621 VGS, Hullavington	
ZE524	Grob G103 Viking T1 (BGA3014) [VM]	RAF No 625 VGS, Hullavington	
ZE526	Grob G103 Viking T1 (BGA3016) [VN]	RAF No 662 VGS, Arbroath	
ZE527	Grob G103 Viking T1 (BGA3017) [VP]	RAF CGMF, Syerston	
ZE528	Grob G103 Viking T1 (BGA3018) [VQ]	RAF CGMF, Syerston	
ZE529	Grob G103 Viking T1 (BGA3019) (comp ZE655) [VR]	RAF ACCGS/No 643 VGS, Syerston	
ZE530	Grob G103 Viking T1 (BGA3020) [VS]	RAF No 611 VGS, Watton	
ZE531	Grob G103 Viking T1 (BGA3021) [VT]	RAF No 615 VGS, Kenley	
ZE532	Grob G103 Viking T1 (BGA3022) [VU]	RAF No 614 VGS, Wethersfield	
ZE533	Grob G103 Viking T1 (BGA3023) [VV]	RAF CGMF, Syerston	
ZE550	Grob G103 Viking T1 (BGA3025) [VX]	RAF CGMF, Syerston (damaged)	
ZE551	Grob G103 Viking T1 (BGA3026) [VY]	RAF No 614 VGS, Wethersfield	
ZE552	Grob G103 Viking T1 (BGA3027) [VZ]	RAF CGMF, Syerston	
ZE553	Grob G103 Viking T1 (BGA3028) [WA]	RAF No 615 VGS, Kenley	
ZE554	Grob G103 Viking T1 (BGA3029) [WB]	RAF No 611 VGS, Watton	
ZE555	Grob G103 Viking T1 (BGA3030) [WC]	RAF CGMF, Syerston	
ZE556	Grob G103 Viking T1 (BGA3031) <ff>	No 1359 Sqn ATC, Beeston, Notts	
ZE557	Grob G103 Viking T1 (BGA3032) [WE]	RAF CGMF, Syerston	
ZE558	Grob G103 Viking T1 (BGA3033) [WF]	RAF ACCGS/No 643 VGS, Syerston	
ZE559	Grob G103 Viking T1 (BGA3034) [WG]	RAF No 661 VGS, Kirknewton	
ZE560	Grob G103 Viking T1 (BGA3035) [WH]	RAF No 661 VGS, Kirknewton	
ZE561	Grob G103 Viking T1 (BGA3036) [WJ]	RAF No 614 VGS, Wethersfield	
ZE562	Grob G103 Viking T1 (BGA3037) [WK]	RAF No 626 VGS, Predannack	
ZE563	Grob G103 Viking T1 (BGA3038) [WL]	RAF No 614 VGS, Wethersfield	
ZE564	Grob G103 Viking T1 (BGA3039) [WN]	RAF No 662 VGS, Arbroath	
ZE584	Grob G103 Viking T1 (BGA3040) [WP]	RAF CGMF, Syerston	
ZE585	Grob G103 Viking T1 (BGA3041) [WQ]	RAF No 622 VGS, Upavon	
ZE586	Grob G103 Viking T1 (BGA3042) [WR]	RAF No 621 VGS, Hullavington	
ZE587	Grob G103 Viking T1 (BGA3043) [WS]	RAF No 611 VGS, Watton	
ZE590	Grob G103 Viking T1 (BGA3046) [WT]	RAF No 661 VGS, Kirknewton	
ZE591	Grob G103 Viking T1 (BGA3047) [WU]	RAF No 662 VGS, Arbroath	
ZE592	Grob G103 Viking T1 (BGA3048) <ff>	RAFGSA, Halton	
ZE593	Grob G103 Viking T1 (BGA3049) [WW]	RAF No 621 VGS, Hullavington	
ZE594	Grob G103 Viking T1 (BGA3050) [WX]	RAF ACCGS/No 643 VGS, Syerston	

Notes	Serial	Type (code/other identity)	Owner/operator, location or fate
	ZE595	Grob G103 Viking T1 (BGA3051) [WY]	RAF No 622 VGS, Upavon
	ZE600	Grob G103 Viking T1 (BGA3052) [W7]	RAF No 622 VGS, Upavon
	ZE601	Grob G103 Viking T1 (BGA3053) [XA]	RAF No 621 VGS, Hullavington
	ZE602	Grob G103 Viking T1 (BGA3054) [XB]	RAF ACCGS/No 643 VGS, Syerston
	ZE603	Grob G103 Viking T1 (BGA3055) [XC]	RAF No 615 VGS, Kenley
	ZE604	Grob G103 Viking T1 (BGA3056) [XD]	RAF No 615 VGS, Kenley
	ZE605	Grob G103 Viking T1 (BGA3057) [XE]	RAF No 626 VGS, Predannack
	ZE606	Grob G103 Viking T1 (BGA3058) [XF]	RAF No 615 VGS, Kenley
	ZE607	Grob G103 Viking T1 (BGA3059) [XG]	RAF ACCGS/No 643 VGS, Syerston
	ZE608	Grob G103 Viking T1 (BGA3060) [XH]	RAF No 625 VGS, Hullavington
	ZE609	Grob G103 Viking T1 (BGA3061) [XJ]	RAF CGMF, Syerston
	ZE610	Grob G103 Viking T1 (BGA3062) [XK]	RAF No 615 VGS, Kenley
	ZE611	Grob G103 Viking T1 (BGA3063) [XL]	RAF No 611 VGS, Watton
	ZE613	Grob G103 Viking T1 (BGA3065) [XM]	RAF No 662 VGS, Arbroath
	ZE614	Grob G103 Viking T1 (BGA3066) [XN]	RAF No 614 VGS, Wethersfield
	ZE625	Grob G103 Viking T1 (BGA3067) [XP]	RAF No 625 VGS, Hullavington
	ZE626	Grob G103 Viking T1 (BGA3068) [XQ]	RAF No 626 VGS, Predannack
	ZE627	Grob G103 Viking T1 (BGA3069) [XR]	RAF No 614 VGS, Wethersfield
	ZE628	Grob G103 Viking T1 (BGA3070) [XS]	RAF CGMF, Syerston
	ZE629	Grob G103 Viking T1 (BGA3071) [XT]	RAF No 662 VGS, Arbroath
	ZE630	Grob G103 Viking T1 (BGA3072) [XU]	RAF No 662 VGS, Arbroath
	ZE631	Grob G103 Viking T1 (BGA3073) [XV]	RAF No 661 VGS, Kirknewton
	ZE632	Grob G103 Viking T1 (BGA3074) [XW]	RAF ACCGS/No 643 VGS, Syerston
	ZE633	Grob G103 Viking T1 (BGA3075) [XX]	RAF No 611 VGS, Watton
	ZE636	Grob G103 Viking T1 (BGA3078) [XZ]	RAF ACCGS/No 643 VGS, Syerston
	ZE637	Grob G103 Viking T1 (BGA3079) [YA]	RAF No 622 VGS, Upavon
	ZE650	Grob G103 Viking T1 (BGA3080) [YB]	RAF CGMF, Syerston
	ZE651	Grob G103 Viking T1 (BGA3081) [YC]	RAF ACCGS/No 643 VGS, Syerston
	ZE652	Grob G103 Viking T1 (BGA3082) [YD]	RAF ACCGS/No 643 VGS, Syerston
	ZE653	Grob G103 Viking T1 (BGA3083) [YE]	RAF ACCGS/No 643 VGS, Syerston
	ZE656	Grob G103 Viking T1 (BGA3086) [YH]	RAF No 625 VGS, Hullavington
	ZE657	Grob G103 Viking T1 (BGA3087) [YJ]	RAF CGMF, Syerston
	ZE658	Grob G103 Viking T1 (BGA3088) [YK]	RAF No 611 VGS, Watton
	ZE677	Grob G103 Viking T1 (BGA3090) [YM]	RAF CGMF, Syerston
	ZE678	Grob G103 Viking T1 (BGA3091) [YN]	RAF No 625 VGS, Hullavington
	ZE679	Grob G103 Viking T1 (BGA3092) [YP]	RAF No 622 VGS, Upavon

Serial	Type (code/other identity)	Owner/operator, location or fate	Notes
ZE680	Grob G103 Viking T1 (BGA3093) [YQ]	RAF CGMF, Syerston	
ZE681	Grob G103 Viking T1 (BGA3094) [YR]	RAF CGMF, Syerston (damaged)	
ZE682	Grob G103 Viking T1 (BGA3095) [YS]	RAF No 662 VGS, Arbroath	
ZE683	Grob G103 Viking T1 (BGA3096) [YT]	RAF No 661 VGS, Kirknewton	
ZE684	Grob G103 Viking T1 (BGA3097) [YU]	RAF CGMF, Syerston	
ZE685	Grob G103 Viking T1 (BGA3098) [YV]	RAF CGMF, Syerston	
ZE686	Grob G103 Viking T1 (BGA3099)	RAF Museum, Hendon	
ZE690	BAe Sea Harrier FA2 [90/DD]	SFDO, RNAS Culdrose	
ZE691	BAe Sea Harrier FA2 [710]	Privately owned, Queensbury, W Yorks	
ZE692	BAe Sea Harrier FA2 [008]	SFDO, RNAS Culdrose	
ZE693	BAe Sea Harrier FA2 [717]	Privately owned, Dukinfield, Gr Manchester	
ZE694	BAe Sea Harrier FA2	Midland Air Museum, Coventry	
ZE695	BAe Sea Harrier FA2 [718]	Privately owned, Sproughton	
ZE696	BAe Sea Harrier FA2 [124/R]	*Sold to Spain, 2007*	
ZE697	BAe Sea Harrier FA2 [006]	Privately owned, Charlwood	
ZE698	BAe Sea Harrier FA2 [001]	Privately owned, Charlwood	
ZE700	BAe 146 CC2 (G-6-021)	RAF No 32(The Royal) Sqn, Northolt	
ZE701	BAe 146 CC2 (G-6-029)	RAF No 32(The Royal) Sqn, Northolt	
ZE704	Lockheed TriStar C2 (N508PA)	RAF No 216 Sqn, Brize Norton	
ZE705	Lockheed TriStar C2 (N509PA)	RAF No 216 Sqn, Brize Norton	
ZE706	Lockheed TriStar C2A (N503PA)	RAF No 216 Sqn, Brize Norton	
ZE728	Panavia Tornado F3 (comp ZD903) [FZ]	RAF No 25 Sqn, Leeming	
ZE730	Panavia Tornado F3 (MM7204)	*Scrapped, October 2007*	
ZE731	Panavia Tornado F3 [GP]	RAF No 43 Sqn, Leuchars	
ZE734	Panavia Tornado F3 [JU]$	RAF No 111 Sqn, Leuchars	
ZE735	Panavia Tornado F3 [TG]	RAF F3 OCU/No 56(R) Sqn, Leuchars	
ZE736	Panavia Tornado F3 (comp ZD937) [F]	RAF No 1435 Flt, Mount Pleasant, FI	
ZE737	Panavia Tornado F3 [GK]	MoD/BAE Systems, Warton	
ZE755	Panavia Tornado F3 [YL]	MoD/AFD/QinetiQ, Boscombe Down	
ZE756	Panavia Tornado F3	*Scrapped, October 2007*	
ZE757	Panavia Tornado F3 [FI]	RAF F3 OCU/No 56(R) Sqn, Leuchars	
ZE758	Panavia Tornado F3 [DO]	RAF No 111 Sqn, Leuchars	
ZE760	Panavia Tornado F3 (MM7206) [AP]	RAF Coningsby, on display	
ZE761	Panavia Tornado F3 (MM7203)	MoD/DARA, stored St Athan	
ZE763	Panavia Tornado F3 [FJ]	RAF No 25 Sqn, Leeming	
ZE764	Panavia Tornado F3 [FK]	RAF No 25 Sqn, Leeming	
ZE785	Panavia Tornado F3	RAF AWC/FJWOEU/No 41(R) Sqn, Coningsby	
ZE786	Panavia Tornado F3 (comp ZD934) [TF]	RAF No 43 Sqn, Leuchars	
ZE787	Panavia Tornado F3 (MM7205)	*Scrapped, September 2007*	
ZE788	Panavia Tornado F3 [GL]	MoD/BAE Systems, Warton	
ZE790	Panavia Tornado F3 [HC]	RAF No 111 Sqn, Leuchars	
ZE791	Panavia Tornado F3 [HF]	RAF No 111 Sqn, Leuchars	
ZE793	Panavia Tornado F3 (comp ZD935) [TE]	RAF ASF, Leuchers	
ZE794	Panavia Tornado F3 [FL]	RAF No 25 Sqn, Leeming	
ZE808	Panavia Tornado F3 [XV]	MoD/BAE Systems, Warton	
ZE810	Panavia Tornado F3 [GG]	RAF No 43 Sqn, Leuchars	
ZE831	Panavia Tornado F3 [FM]	RAF F3 OCU/No 56(R) Sqn, Leuchars	
ZE832	Panavia Tornado F3 (MM7202) [XP]	RAF St Athan (wfu)	
ZE834	Panavia Tornado F3 [D]	RAF No 1435 Flt, Mount Pleasant, FI	
ZE835	Panavia Tornado F3 (MM7209)	*Scrapped, September 2007*	
ZE837	Panavia Tornado F3 (MM55057) [TD]	RAF Leuchars (wfu)	
ZE838	Panavia Tornado F3 [GH]	RAF No 43 Sqn, Leuchars	
ZE839	Panavia Tornado F3 [XK]	RAF Leeming (wfu)	
ZE887	Panavia Tornado F3 [GN]	RAF No 43 Sqn, Leuchars	
ZE888	Panavia Tornado F3 [TC]	RAF Leuchars (wfu)	
ZE889	Panavia Tornado F3 [XH]	*Scrapped February 2006*	
ZE907	Panavia Tornado F3 [DA]	RAF No 111 Sqn, Leuchars	

Notes	Serial	Type (code/other identity)	Owner/operator, location or fate
	ZE908	Panavia Tornado F3 [TB]	RAF St Athan (wfu)
	ZE934	Panavia Tornado F3 [TA]	Royal Scottish Mus'm of Flight, E Fortune
	ZE936	Panavia Tornado F3 [HE]	RAF No 111 Sqn, Leuchars
	ZE941	Panavia Tornado F3 [KT]	RAF No 111 Sqn, Leuchars
	ZE942	Panavia Tornado F3 [DF]	RAF AMF, Leuchars (wfu)
	ZE961	Panavia Tornado F3 [FO]	RAF No 25 Sqn, Leeming
	ZE963	Panavia Tornado F3 [YT]	RAF F3 OCU/No 56(R) Sqn, Leuchars
	ZE964	Panavia Tornado F3 [XT]	RAF F3 OCU/No 56(R) Sqn, Leuchars
	ZE965	Panavia Tornado F3 [WT]	RAF F3 OCU/No 56(R) Sqn, Leuchars
	ZE966	Panavia Tornado F3 [VT]	Gr Manchester Museum of Science & Industry, stored
	ZE967	Panavia Tornado F3 [UT]	RAF Leuchars, at main gate
	ZE968	Panavia Tornado F3 [HB]	RAF No 111 Sqn, Leuchars
	ZE969	Panavia Tornado F3 [FH]	RAF No 25 Sqn, Leeming
	ZE982	Panavia Tornado F3 [FR]	RAF No 25 Sqn, Leeming
	ZE983	Panavia Tornado F3 [WY]	RAF No 111 Sqn, Leuchars
	ZF115	WS61 Sea King HC4 (wreck)	MoD/DARA, Fleetlands
	ZF116	WS61 Sea King HC4 [WP]	RN No 848 Sqn, Yeovilton
	ZF117	WS61 Sea King HC4 [VX]	RN No 846 Sqn, Yeovilton
	ZF118	WS61 Sea King HC4	RN No 846 Sqn, Yeovilton
	ZF119	WS61 Sea King HC4 [WY]	RN No 848 Sqn, Yeovilton
	ZF120	WS61 Sea King HC4 [VZ]	RN No 846 Sqn, Yeovilton
	ZF121	WS61 Sea King HC4 [T]	RN No 846 Sqn, Yeovilton
	ZF122	WS61 Sea King HC4 [V]	RN No 846 Sqn, Yeovilton
	ZF123	WS61 Sea King HC4 [WW]	RN No 848 Sqn, Yeovilton
	ZF124	WS61 Sea King HC4	RN CHFMU, Yeovilton (on repair)
	ZF130	BAe HS.125-600B (G-BLUW) (fuselage)	Electroworkz Nightclub, Islington
	ZF135	Shorts Tucano T1	RAF No 1 FTS, Linton-on-Ouse
	ZF136	Shorts Tucano T1	RAF, stored Shawbury
	ZF137	Shorts Tucano T1	RAF No 1 FTS, Linton-on-Ouse
	ZF138	Shorts Tucano T1	RAF, stored Shawbury
	ZF139	Shorts Tucano T1	RAF No 1 FTS/*207(R) Sqn*, Linton-on-Ouse
	ZF140	Shorts Tucano T1	RAF No 1 FTS/*207(R) Sqn*, Linton-on-Ouse
	ZF141	Shorts Tucano T1	*Sold to the USA, July 2007*
	ZF142	Shorts Tucano T1	RAF No 1 FTS, Linton-on-Ouse
	ZF143	Shorts Tucano T1	RAF No 1 FTS, Linton-on-Ouse
	ZF144	Shorts Tucano T1	RAF No 1 FTS, Linton-on-Ouse
	ZF145	Shorts Tucano T1	RAF No 1 FTS, Linton-on-Ouse
	ZF160	Shorts Tucano T1	RAF, stored Shawbury
	ZF161	Shorts Tucano T1	RAF, stored Shawbury
	ZF162	Shorts Tucano T1	RAF, stored Shawbury
	ZF163	Shorts Tucano T1	RAF, stored Shawbury
	ZF164	Shorts Tucano T1	*Sold to the USA, September 2007*
	ZF165	Shorts Tucano T1	*Sold as N8093Z, July 2007*
	ZF166	Shorts Tucano T1	RAF, stored Shawbury
	ZF167	Shorts Tucano T1 (fuselage)	Shorts, Belfast
	ZF168	Shorts Tucano T1	RAF, stored Shawbury
	ZF169	Shorts Tucano T1	RAF No 1 FTS/*72(R) Sqn*, Linton-on-Ouse
	ZF170	Shorts Tucano T1 $	RAF, stored Shawbury
	ZF171	Shorts Tucano T1	RAF No 1 FTS/*207(R) Sqn*, Linton-on-Ouse
	ZF172	Shorts Tucano T1 [MP-D]	RAF No 1 FTS/*76(R) Sqn*, Linton-on-Ouse
	ZF200	Shorts Tucano T1	Privately owned, Bentwaters
	ZF201	Shorts Tucano T1	Privately owned, Sproughton
	ZF202	Shorts Tucano T1	RAF, stored Shawbury
	ZF203	Shorts Tucano T1	RAF, stored Shawbury
	ZF204	Shorts Tucano T1	RAF No 1 FTS/*207(R) Sqn*, Linton-on-Ouse
	ZF205	Shorts Tucano T1	RAF No 1 FTS/*72(R) Sqn*, Linton-on-Ouse
	ZF206	Shorts Tucano T1	RAF, stored Shawbury
	ZF207	Shorts Tucano T1	RAF, stored Shawbury
	ZF208	Shorts Tucano T1	RAF, stored Shawbury
	ZF209	Shorts Tucano T1	RAF No 1 FTS/*72(R) Sqn*, Linton-on-Ouse
	ZF210	Shorts Tucano T1	RAF No 1 FTS/*72(R) Sqn*, Linton-on-Ouse
	ZF211	Shorts Tucano T1	RAF, stored Shawbury
	ZF212	Shorts Tucano T1	RAF, stored Shawbury
	ZF238	Shorts Tucano T1	RAF, stored Shawbury
	ZF239	Shorts Tucano T1 [MP-T]	RAF No 1 FTS/*76(R) Sqn*, Linton-on-Ouse
	ZF240	Shorts Tucano T1	RAF No 1 FTS, Linton-on-Ouse
	ZF241	Shorts Tucano T1	RAF, stored Shawbury
	ZF242	Shorts Tucano T1	RAF, stored Shawbury
	ZF243	Shorts Tucano T1	RAF No 1 FTS, Linton-on-Ouse

Serial	Type (code/other identity)	Owner/operator, location or fate	Notes
ZF244	Shorts Tucano T1	RAF No 1 FTS/*72(R) Sqn*, Linton-on-Ouse	
ZF245	Shorts Tucano T1	Privately owned, Sproughton	
ZF263	Shorts Tucano T1	RAF, stored Shawbury	
ZF264	Shorts Tucano T1	RAF No 1 FTS, Linton-on-Ouse	
ZF265	Shorts Tucano T1	*Sold to the USA, September 2007*	
ZF266	Shorts Tucano T1	RAF, stored Shawbury	
ZF267	Shorts Tucano T1	Privately owned, Market Drayton	
ZF268	Shorts Tucano T1	RAF, stored Shawbury	
ZF269	Shorts Tucano T1 [MP-O]	RAF No 1 FTS/*76(R) Sqn*, Linton-on-Ouse	
ZF284	Shorts Tucano T1	Privately owned, Shoreham	
ZF285	Shorts Tucano T1	*Sold to the USA, September 2007*	
ZF286	Shorts Tucano T1	RAF, stored Shawbury	
ZF287	Shorts Tucano T1	RAF No 1 FTS/*72(R) Sqn*, Linton-on-Ouse	
ZF288	Shorts Tucano T1	RAF, stored Shawbury	
ZF289	Shorts Tucano T1	RAF No 1 FTS, Linton-on-Ouse	
ZF290	Shorts Tucano T1	RAF No 1 FTS/*207(R) Sqn*, Linton-on-Ouse	
ZF291	Shorts Tucano T1	RAF No 1 FTS, Linton-on-Ouse	
ZF292	Shorts Tucano T1	RAF No 1 FTS/*207(R) Sqn*, Linton-on-Ouse	
ZF293	Shorts Tucano T1	RAF No 1 FTS/*72(R) Sqn*, Linton-on-Ouse	
ZF294	Shorts Tucano T1	RAF No 1 FTS/*207(R) Sqn*, Linton-on-Ouse	
ZF295	Shorts Tucano T1 $	RAF No 1 FTS, Linton-on-Ouse	
ZF315	Shorts Tucano T1	RAF, stored Shawbury	
ZF317	Shorts Tucano T1	RAF No 1 FTS, Linton-on-Ouse	
ZF318	Shorts Tucano T1	RAF, stored Shawbury	
ZF319	Shorts Tucano T1	RAF No 1 FTS, Linton-on-Ouse	
ZF320	Shorts Tucano T1	RAF, stored Shawbury	
ZF338	Shorts Tucano T1	RAF No 1 FTS, Linton-on-Ouse	
ZF339	Shorts Tucano T1	RAF No 1 FTS/*72(R) Sqn*, Linton-on-Ouse	
ZF340	Shorts Tucano T1	*Sold to the USA, July 2007*	
ZF341	Shorts Tucano T1	RAF No 1 FTS/*207(R) Sqn*, Linton-on-Ouse	
ZF342	Shorts Tucano T1	RAF No 1 FTS, Linton-on-Ouse	
ZF343	Shorts Tucano T1 [MP-S]	RAF No 1 FTS/*76(R) Sqn*, Linton-on-Ouse	
ZF344	Shorts Tucano T1	RAF No 1 FTS, Linton-on-Ouse	
ZF345	Shorts Tucano T1	RAF, stored Shawbury	
ZF346	Shorts Tucano T1	RAF, stored Shawbury	
ZF347	Shorts Tucano T1	RAF No 1 FTS, Linton-on-Ouse	
ZF348	Shorts Tucano T1	RAF, stored Shawbury	
ZF349	Shorts Tucano T1	RAF No 1 FTS/*207(R) Sqn*, Linton-on-Ouse	
ZF350	Shorts Tucano T1	RAF, stored Shawbury	
ZF372	Shorts Tucano T1	RAF, stored Shawbury	
ZF373	Shorts Tucano T1 (G-CEHJ)	Privately owned, Hawarden	
ZF374	Shorts Tucano T1	RAF No 1 FTS/*72(R) Sqn*, Linton-on-Ouse	
ZF375	Shorts Tucano T1	RAF, stored Shawbury	
ZF376	Shorts Tucano T1	RAF, stored Shawbury	
ZF377	Shorts Tucano T1	RAF No 1 FTS, Linton-on-Ouse	
ZF378	Shorts Tucano T1 [MP-W]	RAF No 1 FTS/*76(R) Sqn*, Linton-on-Ouse	
ZF379	Shorts Tucano T1	RAF No 1 FTS, Linton-on-Ouse	
ZF380	Shorts Tucano T1	RAF, stored Shawbury	
ZF405	Shorts Tucano T1	RAF, stored Shawbury	
ZF406	Shorts Tucano T1	RAF No 1 FTS, Linton-on-Ouse	
ZF407	Shorts Tucano T1	RAF No 1 FTS, Linton-on-Ouse	
ZF408	Shorts Tucano T1	RAF, stored Shawbury	
ZF409	Shorts Tucano T1	RAF No 1 FTS/*207(R) Sqn*, Linton-on-Ouse	
ZF410	Shorts Tucano T1	RAF, stored Shawbury	
ZF411	Shorts Tucano T1	*Sold to the USA, 2007*	
ZF412	Shorts Tucano T1	RAF, stored Shawbury	
ZF413	Shorts Tucano T1	RAF, stored Shawbury	
ZF414	Shorts Tucano T1	RAF, stored Shawbury	
ZF415	Shorts Tucano T1	*Sold to the USA, September 2007*	
ZF416	Shorts Tucano T1	RAF, stored Shawbury	
ZF417	Shorts Tucano T1	RAF No 1 FTS/*207(R) Sqn*, Linton-on-Ouse	
ZF418	Shorts Tucano T1	RAF, stored Shawbury	
ZF445	Shorts Tucano T1	RAF, stored Shawbury	
ZF446	Shorts Tucano T1	RAF, stored Shawbury	
ZF447	Shorts Tucano T1	RAF, stored Shawbury	
ZF448	Shorts Tucano T1 $	RAF No 1 FTS/*72(R) Sqn*, Linton-on-Ouse	
ZF449	Shorts Tucano T1	RAF, stored Shawbury	
ZF450	Shorts Tucano T1	*Sold as N8093S, July 2007*	
ZF483	Shorts Tucano T1	RAF, stored Shawbury	
ZF484	Shorts Tucano T1	RAF, stored Shawbury	
ZF485	Shorts Tucano T1 (G-BULU)	RAF No 1 FTS, Linton-on-Ouse	
ZF486	Shorts Tucano T1	RAF, stored Shawbury	

Notes	Serial	Type (code/other identity)	Owner/operator, location or fate
	ZF487	Shorts Tucano T1	RAF, stored Shawbury
	ZF488	Shorts Tucano T1	RAF, stored Shawbury
	ZF489	Shorts Tucano T1	RAF No 1 FTS/*207(R) Sqn*, Linton-on-Ouse
	ZF490	Shorts Tucano T1	RAF, stored Shawbury
	ZF491	Shorts Tucano T1	RAF No 1 FTS, Linton-on-Ouse
	ZF492	Shorts Tucano T1	RAF, stored Shawbury
	ZF510	Shorts Tucano T1	MoD/AFD/QinetiQ, Boscombe Down
	ZF511	Shorts Tucano T1	MoD/AFD/QinetiQ, Boscombe Down
	ZF512	Shorts Tucano T1	RAF No 1 FTS/*72(R) Sqn*, Linton-on-Ouse
	ZF513	Shorts Tucano T1	RAF, stored Shawbury
	ZF514	Shorts Tucano T1	RAF, stored Shawbury
	ZF515	Shorts Tucano T1	RAF No 1 FTS/*72(R) Sqn*, Linton-on-Ouse
	ZF516	Shorts Tucano T1	RAF, stored Shawbury
	ZF534	BAe EAP	Loughborough University
	ZF537	WS Lynx AH9	MoD/DARA, Fletlands
	ZF538	WS Lynx AH9	AAC No 661 Sqn/1 Regt, Gütersloh
	ZF539	WS Lynx AH9	AAC No 9 Regt, Dishforth
	ZF540	WS Lynx AH9	RM No 847 Sqn, Yeovilton
	ZF557	WS Lynx HMA8 [674]	RN No 702 Sqn, Yeovilton
	ZF558	WS Lynx HMA8	MoD/AFD/QinetiQ, Boscombe Down
	ZF560	WS Lynx HMA8 [307]	RN AMG, Yeovilton
	ZF562	WS Lynx HMA8 [670]	RN No 702 Sqn, Yeovilton
	ZF563	WS Lynx HMA8 [375]	RN No 815 Sqn, Yeovilton
	ZF573	PBN 2T Islander CC2A (G-SRAY)	RAF Northolt Station Flight
	ZF579	BAC Lightning F53	Gatwick Aviation Museum, Charlwood
	ZF580	BAC Lightning F53	BAE Systems Samlesbury, at main gate
	ZF581	BAC Lightning F53	BAE Systems, Rochester, on display
	ZF582	BAC Lightning F53 <ff>	Privatley owned, Bournemouth
	ZF583	BAC Lightning F53	Solway Aviation Society, Carlisle
	ZF584	BAC Lightning F53	Dumfries & Galloway Avn Mus, Dumfries
	ZF587	BAC Lightning F53 <ff>	Lashenden Air Warfare Museum, Headcorn
	ZF588	BAC Lightning F53 [L]	East Midlands Airport Aeropark
	ZF590	BAC Lightning F53 <rf>	Privately owned, Grainthorpe, Lincs
	ZF594	BAC Lightning F53	North-East Aircraft Museum, Usworth
	ZF595	BAC Lightning T55 (fuselage)	Privately owned, Grainthorpe, Lincs
	ZF596	BAC Lightning T55 <ff>	BAe North-West Heritage Group Warton
	ZF622	Piper PA-31 Navajo Chieftain 350 (N3548Y)	MoD/AFD/QinetiQ, Boscombe Down
	ZF641	EHI-101 [PP1]	SFDO, RNAS Culdrose
	ZF649	EHI-101 Merlin [PP5]	DCAE AESS, *HMS Sultan*, Gosport
	ZG101	EHI-101 (mock-up) [GB]	Westland Helicopters/Agusta, Yeovil
	ZG347	Northrop Chukar D2	RNAS Culdrose, preserved
	ZG471	BAe Harrier GR7A [61A]	RAF No 4 Sqn, Cottesmore
	ZG472	BAe Harrier GR7A [62A]	RAF No 1 Sqn, Cottesmore
	ZG474	BAe Harrier GR9 [64]	RAF HOCU/No 20(R) Sqn, Wittering
	ZG477	BAe Harrier GR9 [67]	MoD/AFD/QinetiQ, Boscombe Down
	ZG478	BAe Harrier GR9A [68]	RAF No 4 Sqn, Cottesmore
	ZG479	BAe Harrier GR9A [69A]	RAF No 4 Sqn, Cottesmore
	ZG480	BAe Harrier GR9 [70]	RAF No 1 Sqn, Cottesmore
	ZG500	BAe Harrier GR9A [71A]	RAF No 4 Sqn, Cottesmore
	ZG501	BAe Harrier GR9	RAF AWC/FJWOEU/No 41(R) Sqn, Coningsby
	ZG502	BAe Harrier GR9 [73]	RAF HOCU/No 20(R) Sqn, Wittering
	ZG503	BAe Harrier GR9	RAF AWC/FJWOEU/No 41(R) Sqn, Coningsby
	ZG504	BAe Harrier GR9A [75A]	RAF No 4 Sqn, Cottesmore
	ZG505	BAe Harrier GR9A [76]	RAF SAM, Cottesmore
	ZG506	BAe Harrier GR9 [77]	RAF HOCU/No 20(R) Sqn, Wittering
	ZG507	BAe Harrier GR9 [78]	RAF HOCU/No 20(R) Sqn, Wittering
	ZG508	BAe Harrier GR9	RAF SAM, Cottesmore
	ZG509	BAe Harrier GR7 [80]	RAF SAM, Cottesmore
	ZG510	BAe Harrier GR9A [81]	RN NSW, Cottesmore
	ZG511	BAe Harrier GR9 [82]	RAF HOCU/No 20(R) Sqn, Wittering
	ZG530	BAe Harrier GR9 [84]	RAF HOCU/No 20(R) Sqn, Wittering
	ZG531	BAe Harrier GR9A [85]	RAF SAM, Cottesmore (on repair)
	ZG705	Panavia Tornado GR4A [118]	RAF No 14 Sqn, Lossiemouth
	ZG706	Panavia Tornado GR1A [E]	MoD/DARA, stored St Athan
	ZG707	Panavia Tornado GR4A [119]	RAF No 12 Sqn, Lossiemouth
	ZG709	Panavia Tornado GR4A [V]	RAF No 14 Sqn, Lossiemouth
	ZG712	Panavia Tornado GR4A [F]	RAF Marham, WLT
	ZG713	Panavia Tornado GR4A [123]	RAF No 617 Sqn, Lossiemouth

Serial	Type (code/other identity)	Owner/operator, location or fate	Notes
ZG714	Panavia Tornado GR4A [124]	RAF No 13 Sqn, Marham	
ZG726	Panavia Tornado GR4A [125]	MoD/AFD/QinetiQ, Boscombe Down	
ZG727	Panavia Tornado GR4A [126]	RAF No 617 Sqn, Lossiemouth	
ZG728	Panavia Tornado F3 (MM7229)	*Scrapped, September 2007*	
ZG729	Panavia Tornado GR4A [M]	RAF No 13 Sqn, Marham	
ZG731	Panavia Tornado F3	RAF AWC/FJWOEU/No 41(R) Sqn, Coningsby	
ZG732	Panavia Tornado F3 (MM7227) [WU]	MoD St Athan (wfu)	
ZG734	Panavia Tornado F3 (MM7231)	*Scrapped, October 2007*	
ZG750	Panavia Tornado GR4 [128]	RAF No 15(R) Sqn, Lossiemouth	
ZG751	Panavia Tornado F3 [HI]	RAF No 111 Sqn, Leuchars	
ZG752	Panavia Tornado GR4 [129]	RAF No 15(R) Sqn, Lossiemouth	
ZG753	Panavia Tornado F3 [H]	RAF No 1453 Flt, Mount Pleasant, FI	
ZG754	Panavia Tornado GR4 [130]	RAF No 15(R) Sqn, Lossiemouth	
ZG755	Panavia Tornado F3 [GL]	RAF No 43 Sqn, Leuchars	
ZG756	Panavia Tornado GR4 [BX]	RAF No 12 Sqn, Lossiemouth	
ZG757	Panavia Tornado F3 [GF]	RAF No 43 Sqn, Leuchars	
ZG768	Panavia Tornado F3 (MM7233)	*Scrapped, October 2007*	
ZG769	Panavia Tornado GR4	RAF	
ZG770	Panavia Tornado F3 [WK]	RAF Leeming (wfu)	
ZG771	Panavia Tornado GR4 [133]	RAF No 13 Sqn, Marham	
ZG772	Panavia Tornado F3 [WJ]	RAF F3 OCU/No 56(R) Sqn, Leuchars	
ZG773	Panavia Tornado GR4	MoD/BAE Systems, Warton	
ZG774	Panavia Tornado F3 [WK]	RAF F3 OCU/No 56(R) Sqn, Leuchars	
ZG775	Panavia Tornado GR4 [134]	RAF No 31 Sqn, Marham	
ZG776	Panavia Tornado F3 [C]	RAF Leeming (wfu)	
ZG777	Panavia Tornado GR4 [135]	RAF No 9 Sqn, Marham	
ZG778	Panavia Tornado F3 [H]	RAF No 1435 Flt, Mount Pleasant, FI	
ZG779	Panavia Tornado GR4 [N]	RAF No 12 Sqn, Lossiemouth	
ZG780	Panavia Tornado F3 [XXV]$	RAF No 25 Sqn, Leeming	
ZG791	Panavia Tornado GR4 [137]	RAF No 13 Sqn, Marham	
ZG792	Panavia Tornado GR4 [138]	RAF No 15(R) Sqn, Lossiemouth	
ZG793	Panavia Tornado F3 [WM]	RAF Leuchars (wfu)	
ZG794	Panavia Tornado GR4 [TN]	RAF No 15(R) Sqn, Lossiemouth	
ZG795	Panavia Tornado F3 [WD]	RAF Leeming (wfu)	
ZG796	Panavia Tornado F3	RAF Leeming (wfu)	
ZG797	Panavia Tornado F3 [C]	RAF No 1435 Flt, Mount Pleasant, FI	
ZG798	Panavia Tornado F3 [WM]	RAF Leuchars, WLT	
ZG799	Panavia Tornado F3 [HJ]	RAF No 111 Sqn, Leuchars	
ZG816	WS61 Sea King HAS6 [014/L]	DCAE, stored *HMS Sultan*, Gosport	
ZG817	WS61 Sea King HAS6 [702/PW]	DCAE AESS, *HMS Sultan*, Gosport	
ZG818	WS61 Sea King HAS6 [707/PW]	DCAE, stored *HMS Sultan*, Gosport	
ZG819	WS61 Sea King HAS6 [265/N]	DCAE AESS, *HMS Sultan*, Gosport	
ZG820	WS61 Sea King HC4	RN No 845 Sqn, Yeovilton	
ZG821	WS61 Sea King HC4 [G]	RN No 845 Sqn, Yeovilton	
ZG822	WS61 Sea King HC4 [WS]	RN No 848 Sqn, Yeovilton	
ZG844	PBN 2T Islander AL1 (G-BLNE)	AAC No 1 Flt/5 Regt, Aldergrove	
ZG845	PBN 2T Islander AL1 (G-BLNT)	AAC No 1 Flt/5 Regt, Aldergrove	
ZG846	PBN 2T Islander AL1 (G-BLNU)	AAC No 1 Flt/5 Regt, Aldergrove	
ZG847	PBN 2T Islander AL1 (G-BLNV)	AAC No 1 Flt/5 Regt, Aldergrove	
ZG848	PBN 2T Islander AL1 (G-BLNY)	AAC No 1 Flt/5 Regt, Aldergrove	
ZG857	BAe Harrier GR9 [89]	MoD/BAE Systems, Warton	
ZG858	BAe Harrier GR9 [90]	RAF HOCU/No 20(R) Sqn, Wittering	
ZG859	BAe Harrier GR9A [91A]	RAF No 1 Sqn, Cottesmore	
ZG860	BAe Harrier GR9	MoD/BAE Systems, Warton	
ZG862	BAe Harrier GR9A [94A]	RN NSW, Cottesmore	
ZG875	WS61 Sea King HAS6 [013/L]	DCAE, stored *HMS Sultan*, Gosport (damaged)	
ZG879	Powerchute Raider Mk 1	*Currently not known*	
ZG884	WS Lynx AH9	AAC No 9 Regt, Dishforth	
ZG885	WS Lynx AH9	AAC No 661 Sqn/1 Regt, Gütersloh	
ZG886	WS Lynx AH9	AAC No 661 Sqn/1 Regt, Gütersloh	
ZG887	WS Lynx AH9	AAC No 661 Sqn/1 Regt, Gütersloh	
ZG888	WS Lynx AH9	AAC No 661 Sqn/1 Regt, Gütersloh	
ZG889	WS Lynx AH9	AAC No 661 Sqn/1 Regt, Gütersloh	
ZG914	WS Lynx AH9	AAC No 661 Sqn/1 Regt, Gütersloh	
ZG915	WS Lynx AH9	AAC No 661 Sqn/1 Regt, Gütersloh	
ZG916	WS Lynx AH9	AAC No 661 Sqn/1 Regt, Gütersloh	
ZG917	WS Lynx AH9	AAC No 661 Sqn/1 Regt, Gütersloh	
ZG918	WS Lynx AH9	RM No 847 Sqn, Yeovilton	
ZG919	WS Lynx AH9	RM No 847 Sqn, Yeovilton	

Notes	Serial	Type (code/other identity)	Owner/operator, location or fate
	ZG920	WS Lynx AH9	AAC No 661 Sqn/1 Regt, Gütersloh
	ZG921	WS Lynx AH9	MoD/DARA, Fleetlands
	ZG922	WS Lynx AH9	MoD/DARA, stored Fleetlands
	ZG923	WS Lynx AH9	MoD/Westland Helicopters, Yeovil
	ZG969	Pilatus PC-9 (HB-HQE)	BAE Systems Warton
	ZG989	PBN 2T Islander ASTOR (G-DLRA)	MoD/Britten-Norman, Bembridge
	ZG993	PBN 2T Islander AL1 (G-BOMD)	AAC No 1 Flight/5 Regt, Aldergrove
	ZG994	PBN 2T Islander AL1 (G-BPLN) (fuselage)	Britten-Norman, stored Bembridge
	ZG995	PBN 2T Defender AL1 (G-SURV)	AAC No 651 Sqn, Odiham
	ZG996	PBN 2T Defender AL1 (G-BWPR)	AAC No 651 Sqn, Basrah, Iraq
	ZG997	PBN 2T Defender AL2 (G-BWPV)	MoD/Britten-Norman, Bembridge
	ZG998	PBN 2T Defender AL1 (G-BWPX)	AAC No 651 Sqn, Basrah, Iraq
	ZH001	PBN 2T Defender AL2 (G-CEIO)	DE&S/Britten-Norman, for AAC
	ZH002	PBN 2T Defender AL2 (G-CEIP)	DE&S/Britten-Norman, for AAC
	ZH003	PBN 2T Defender AL2 (G-CEIR)	DE&S/Britten-Norman, for AAC
	ZH004	PBN 2T Defender AL2	DE&S/Britten-Norman, for AAC
	ZH101	Boeing E-3D Sentry AEW1	RAF No 8 Sqn/No 23 Sqn, Waddington
	ZH102	Boeing E-3D Sentry AEW1	RAF No 8 Sqn/No 23 Sqn, Waddington
	ZH103	Boeing E-3D Sentry AEW1	RAF No 8 Sqn/No 23 Sqn, Waddington
	ZH104	Boeing E-3D Sentry AEW1	RAF No 8 Sqn/No 23 Sqn, Waddington
	ZH105	Boeing E-3D Sentry AEW1	RAF No 8 Sqn/No 23 Sqn, Waddington
	ZH106	Boeing E-3D Sentry AEW1	RAF Waddington (on repair)
	ZH107	Boeing E-3D Sentry AEW1	RAF No 8 Sqn/No 23 Sqn, Waddington
	ZH115	Grob G109B Vigilant T1 [TA]	RAF No 635 VGS, Samlesbury
	ZH116	Grob G109B Vigilant T1 [TB]	RAF No 618 VGS, Odiham
	ZH117	Grob G109B Vigilant T1 [TC]	RAF No 642 VGS, Topcliffe
	ZH118	Grob G109B Vigilant T1 [TD]	RAF No 612 VGS, Abingdon
	ZH119	Grob G109B Vigilant T1 [TE]	RAF No 632 VGS, Ternhill
	ZH120	Grob G109B Vigilant T1 [TF]	RAF No 632 VGS, Ternhill
	ZH121	Grob G109B Vigilant T1 [TG]	RAF No 612 VGS, Abingdon
	ZH122	Grob G109B Vigilant T1 [TH]	RAF No 616 VGS, Henlow
	ZH123	Grob G109B Vigilant T1 [TJ]	RAF No 637 VGS, Little Rissington
	ZH124	Grob G109B Vigilant T1 [TK]	RAF No 642 VGS, Topcliffe
	ZH125	Grob G109B Vigilant T1 [TL]	RAF No 613 VGS, Halton
	ZH126	Grob G109B Vigilant T1 (D-KGRA) [TM]	RAF No 632 VGS, Ternhill
	ZH127	Grob G109B Vigilant T1 (D-KEEC) [TN]	RAF No 616 VGS, Henlow
	ZH128	Grob G109B Vigilant T1 [TP]	RAF No 624 VGS, Chivenor RMB
	ZH129	Grob G109B Vigilant T1 [TQ]	RAF No 635 VGS, Samlesbury
	ZH139	BAe Harrier GR7 <R> (BAPC 191/*ZD472*)	RAF M&RU, Bottesford
	ZH144	Grob G109B Vigilant T1 [TR]	RAF No 631 VGS, Woodvale
	ZH145	Grob G109B Vigilant T1 [TS]	RAF ACCGS/No 644 VGS, Syerston
	ZH146	Grob G109B Vigilant T1 [TT]	RAF No 664 VGS, Newtownards
	ZH147	Grob G109B Vigilant T1 [TU]	RAF No 631 VGS, Woodvale
	ZH148	Grob G109B Vigilant T1 [TV]	RAF No 664 VGS, Newtownards
	ZH184	Grob G109B Vigilant T1 [TW]	RAF No 632 VGS, Ternhill
	ZH185	Grob G109B Vigilant T1 [TX]	RAF No 636 VGS, Swansea
	ZH186	Grob G109B Vigilant T1 [TY]	RAF No 613 VGS, Halton
	ZH187	Grob G109B Vigilant T1 [TZ]	RAF No 633 VGS, Cosford
	ZH188	Grob G109B Vigilant T1 [UA]	RAF No 633 VGS, Cosford
	ZH189	Grob G109B Vigilant T1 [UB]	RAF No 636 VGS, Swansea
	ZH190	Grob G109B Vigilant T1 [UC]	RAF No 624 VGS, Chivenor RMB
	ZH191	Grob G109B Vigilant T1 [UD]	RAF No 645 VGS, Topcliffe
	ZH192	Grob G109B Vigilant T1 [UE]	RAF No 635 VGS, Samlesbury
	ZH193	Grob G109B Vigilant T1 [UF]	RAF No 633 VGS, Cosford
	ZH194	Grob G109B Vigilant T1 [UG]	RAF No 624 VGS, Chivenor RMB
	ZH195	Grob G109B Vigilant T1 [UH]	RAF No 642 VGS, Topcliffe
	ZH196	Grob G109B Vigilant T1 [UJ]	RAF ACCGS/No 644 VGS, Syerston
	ZH197	Grob G109B Vigilant T1 [UK]	RAF ACCGS/No 644 VGS, Syerston
	ZH200	BAe Hawk 200	BAE Systems Warton, Overseas Customer Training Centre
	ZH205	Grob G109B Vigilant T1 [UL]	RAF No 635 VGS, Samlesbury
	ZH206	Grob G109B Vigilant T1 [UM]	RAF No 631 VGS, Woodvale
	ZH207	Grob G109B Vigilant T1 [UN]	RAF No 632 VGS, Ternhill
	ZH208	Grob G109B Vigilant T1 [UP]	RAF No 645 VGS, Topcliffe
	ZH209	Grob G109B Vigilant T1 [UQ]	RAF No 634 VGS, St Athan
	ZH211	Grob G109B Vigilant T1 [UR]	RAF CGMF, Syerston
	ZH247	Grob G109B Vigilant T1 [US]	RAF No 618 VGS, Odiham

Serial	Type (code/other identity)	Owner/operator, location or fate	Notes
ZH248	Grob G109B Vigilant T1 [UT]	RAF No 645 VGS, Topcliffe	
ZH249	Grob G109B Vigilant T1 [UU]	RAF No 633 VGS, Cosford	
ZH263	Grob G109B Vigilant T1 [UV]	RAF No 637 VGS, Little Rissington	
ZH264	Grob G109B Vigilant T1 [UW]	RAF No 613 VGS, Halton	
ZH265	Grob G109B Vigilant T1 [UX]	RAF No 612 VGS, Abingdon	
ZH266	Grob G109B Vigilant T1 [UY]	RAF No 635 VGS, Samlesbury	
ZH267	Grob G109B Vigilant T1 [UZ]	RAF No 645 VGS, Topcliffe	
ZH268	Grob G109B Vigilant T1 [SA]	RAF No 612 VGS, Abingdon	
ZH269	Grob G109B Vigilant T1 [SB]	RAF CGMF, Syerston	
ZH270	Grob G109B Vigilant T1 [SC]	RAF CGMF, Syerston	
ZH271	Grob G109B Vigilant T1 [SD]	RAF No 637 VGS, Little Rissington	
ZH278	Grob G109B Vigilant T1 (D-KAIS) [SF]	RAF No 616 VGS, Henlow	
ZH279	Grob G109B Vigilant T1 (D-KNPS) [SG]	RAF No 634 VGS, St Athan	
ZH536	PBN 2T Islander CC2 (G-BSAH)	RAF Northolt Station Flight	
ZH537	PBN 2T Islander CC2 (G-SELX)	RAF Northolt Station Flight	
ZH540	WS61 Sea King HAR3A [U]	RAF No 22 Sqn, A Flt, Chivenor RMB	
ZH541	WS61 Sea King HAR3A [V]	RAF No 22 Sqn, A Flt, Chivenor RMB	
ZH542	WS61 Sea King HAR3A [W]	RAF No 22 Sqn, B Flt, Wattisham	
ZH543	WS61 Sea King HAR3A [X]	RAF No 22 Sqn, B Flt, Wattisham	
ZH544	WS61 Sea King HAR3A	RAF No 22 Sqn, B Flt, Wattisham	
ZH545	WS61 Sea King HAR3A [Z]	RAF CHFMU, RNAS Yeovilton	
ZH552	Panavia Tornado F3 [ST]	RAF F3 OCU/No 56(R) Sqn, Leuchars	
ZH553	Panavia Tornado F3 [RT]	RAF F3 OCU/No 56(R) Sqn, Leuchars	
ZH554	Panavia Tornado F3 [QT]	RAF F3 OCU/No 56(R) Sqn, Leuchars	
ZH555	Panavia Tornado F3 [PT]	RAF No 43 Sqn, Leuchars	
ZH556	Panavia Tornado F3 [HT]	MoD/AFD/QinetiQ, Boscombe Down	
ZH557	Panavia Tornado F3 [NT]	RAF No 43 Sqn, Leuchars	
ZH559	Panavia Tornado F3 [GT]	RAF F3 OCU/No 56(R) Sqn, Leuchars	
ZH588	Eurofighter Typhoon (DA2)	MoD/DARA, St Athan	
ZH590	Eurofighter Typhoon (DA4)	RAF Coningsby, GI use	
ZH653	BAe Harrier T10	MoD/BAE Systems, Warton	
ZH654	BAe Harrier T10 <ff>	RAF, Cottesmore	
ZH655	BAe Harrier T10 (fuselage)	RAF, Cottesmore	
ZH656	BAe Harrier T12 [104]	RAF JUMP, Cottesmore (conversion)	
ZH657	BAe Harrier T10 [105]	RAF No 4 Sqn, Cottesmore	
ZH658	BAe Harrier T10 [106]	RAF, stored Cottesmore	
ZH659	BAe Harrier T10 [107]	RAF No 4 Sqn, Cottesmore	
ZH660	BAe Harrier T12 [108]	RAF HOCU/No 20(R) Sqn, Wittering	
ZH661	BAe Harrier T12 [109]	RAF HOCU/No 20(R) Sqn, Wittering	
ZH662	BAe Harrier T10 [110]	RAF No 1 Sqn, Cottesmore	
ZH663	BAe Harrier T12 [111]	RAF HOCU/No 20(R) Sqn, Wittering	
ZH664	BAe Harrier T10 [112]	RAF No 1 Sqn, Cottesmore	
ZH665	BAe Harrier T12 [113]	RAF HOCU/No 20(R) Sqn, Wittering	
ZH763	BAC 1-11/539GL (G-BGKE)	MoD/AFD/QinetiQ, Boscombe Down	
ZH775	B-V Chinook HC2 (N7424J) [HB]	RAF No 18 Sqn, Odiham	
ZH776	B-V Chinook HC2 (N7424L)	RAF No 27 Sqn, Odiham	
ZH777	B-V Chinook HC2 (N7424M)	MoD/AFD/QinetiQ, Boscombe Down	
ZH796	BAe Sea Harrier FA2 [001/L]	RN, stored Shawbury	
ZH797	BAe Sea Harrier FA2 [97/DD]	SFDO, RNAS Culdrose	
ZH798	BAe Sea Harrier FA2 [002/L]	SFDO, RNAS Culdrose	
ZH799	BAe Sea Harrier FA2 [98/DD]	Privately owned, Bentwaters	
ZH800	BAe Sea Harrier FA2 (ZH801) [123]	RAF Cottesmore, preserved	
ZH801	BAe Sea Harrier FA2 (ZH800) [001]	RAF Cottesmore, preserved	
ZH802	BAe Sea Harrier FA2 [711]	SFDO, RNAS Culdrose	
ZH803	BAe Sea Harrier FA2 [03/DD]	SFDO, RNAS Culdrose	
ZH804	BAe Sea Harrier FA2 [003/L]	RN, stored Shawbury	
ZH806	BAe Sea Harrier FA2 [007]	Privately owned, Bentwaters	
ZH807	BAe Sea Harrier FA2 <ff>	Privately owned, Newport, Isle of Wight	
ZH809	BAe Sea Harrier FA2	SFDO, RNAS Culdrose	
ZH810	BAe Sea Harrier FA2 [125]	Privately owned, Sproughton	
ZH811	BAe Sea Harrier FA2 [002/L]	RN, stored Shawbury	
ZH812	BAe Sea Harrier FA2 [005/L]	RN, stored Shawbury	
ZH813	BAe Sea Harrier FA2 [010/L]	RN, stored Shawbury	
ZH814	Bell 212HP AH1 (G-BGMH)	AAC No 7 Flt, Brunei	
ZH815	Bell 212HP AH1 (G-BGCZ)	AAC No 7 Flt, Brunei	
ZH816	Bell 212HP AH1 (G-BGMG)	AAC No 7 Flt, Brunei	
ZH821	EHI-101 Merlin HM1	MoD/Westland Helicopters, Yeovil	
ZH822	EHI-101 Merlin HM1	RN MDMF, Culdrose	
ZH823	EHI-101 Merlin HM1	RN MDMF, Culdrose	
ZH824	EHI-101 Merlin HM1	RN No 829 Sqn, Culdrose	

Notes	Serial	Type (code/other identity)	Owner/operator, location or fate
	ZH825	EHI-101 Merlin HM1 [583]	RN MDMF, Culdrose
	ZH826	EHI-101 Merlin HM2	MoD/Westland Helicopters, Yeovil (conversion)
	ZH827	EHI-101 Merlin HM1	MoD/DARA, stored Fleetlands
	ZH828	EHI-101 Merlin HM1 [74]	RN No 829 Sqn, Culdrose
	ZH829	EHI-101 Merlin HM1	RN No 814 Sqn, Culdrose
	ZH830	EHI-101 Merlin HM1	MoD/AFD/QinetiQ, Boscombe Down
	ZH831	EHI-101 Merlin HM1 [14]	RN No 820 Sqn, Culdrose
	ZH832	EHI-101 Merlin HM1	MoD/AFD/QinetiQ, Boscombe Down
	ZH833	EHI-101 Merlin HM1 [585]	RN No 824 Sqn, Culdrose
	ZH834	EHI-101 Merlin HM1 [538/CU]	RN No 700M OEU, Culdrose
	ZH835	EHI-101 Merlin HM1	RN No 820 Sqn, Culdrose
	ZH836	EHI-101 Merlin HM1	RN No 824 Sqn, Culdrose
	ZH837	EHI-101 Merlin HM1 [501]	RN No 829 Sqn, Culdrose
	ZH838	EHI-101 Merlin HM1 [586/CU]	RN No 824 Sqn, Culdrose
	ZH839	EHI-101 Merlin HM1 [581/CU]	RN MDMF, Culdrose
	ZH840	EHI-101 Merlin HM1 [415/MM]	RN No 829 Sqn, *Monmouth* Flt, Culdrose
	ZH841	EHI-101 Merlin HM1 [264]	RN No 814 Sqn, Culdrose
	ZH842	EHI-101 Merlin HM1 [537/CU]	RN No 700M OEU, Culdrose
	ZH843	EHI-101 Merlin HM1	RN No 820 Sqn, Culdrose
	ZH844	EHI-101 Merlin HM1	RN FSAIC, Yeovilton (damaged)
	ZH845	EHI-101 Merlin HM1 [265]	RN No 814 Sqn, Culdrose
	ZH846	EHI-101 Merlin HM1 [800]	RN No 829 Sqn, Culdrose
	ZH847	EHI-101 Merlin HM1 [013/CU]	RN No 820 Sqn, Culdrose
	ZH848	EHI-101 Merlin HM1 [82]	RN MDMF, Culdrose
	ZH849	EHI-101 Merlin HM1 [69]	RN MDMF, Culdrose
	ZH850	EHI-101 Merlin HM1 [462/CU]	RN No 700M OEU, Culdrose
	ZH851	EHI-101 Merlin HM1 [01]	RN No 829 Sqn, Culdrose
	ZH852	EHI-101 Merlin HM1 [372/NL]	RN MDMF, Culdrose
	ZH853	EHI-101 Merlin HM1	RN MDMF, Culdrose
	ZH854	EHI-101 Merlin HM1	RN No 820 Sqn, Culdrose
	ZH855	EHI-101 Merlin HM1 [267/CU]	RN No 814 Sqn, Culdrose
	ZH856	EHI-101 Merlin HM1 [266]	RN No 814 Sqn, Culdrose
	ZH857	EHI-101 Merlin HM1 [415/WM]	RN No 829 Sqn, *Monmouth* Flt, Culdrose
	ZH858	EHI-101 Merlin HM1 [84]	RN No 824 Sqn, Culdrose
	ZH860	EHI-101 Merlin HM1 [269]	RN No 820 Sqn, Culdrose
	ZH861	EHI-101 Merlin HM1 [85]	RN No 824 Sqn, Culdrose
	ZH862	EHI-101 Merlin HM1 [81]	RN No 824 Sqn, Culdrose
	ZH863	EHI-101 Merlin HM1 [011]	RN MDMF, Culdrose
	ZH864	EHI-101 Merlin HM1 [268]	RN No 814 Sqn, Culdrose
	ZH865	Lockheed C-130J-30 Hercules C4 (N130JA)	RAF Lyneham Transport Wing
	ZH866	Lockheed C-130J-30 Hercules C4 (N130JE)	RAF Lyneham Transport Wing
	ZH867	Lockheed C-130J-30 Hercules C4 (N130JJ)	RAF Lyneham Transport Wing
	ZH868	Lockheed C-130J-30 Hercules C4 (N130JN)	RAF Lyneham Transport Wing
	ZH869	Lockheed C-130J-30 Hercules C4 (N130JV)	RAF Lyneham Transport Wing
	ZH870	Lockheed C-130J-30 Hercules C4 (*N73235*/N78235)	RAF Lyneham Transport Wing
	ZH871	Lockheed C-130J-30 Hercules C4 (N73238)	RAF Lyneham Transport Wing
	ZH872	Lockheed C-130J-30 Hercules C4 (N4249Y)	RAF Lyneham Transport Wing
	ZH873	Lockheed C-130J-30 Hercules C4 (N4242N)	RAF Lyneham Transport Wing
	ZH874	Lockheed C-130J-30 Hercules C4 (N41030)	RAF Lyneham Transport Wing
	ZH875	Lockheed C-130J-30 Hercules C4 (N4099R)	RAF Lyneham Transport Wing
	ZH876	Lockheed C-130J-30 Hercules C4 (N4080M)	*Crashed Al-Asmarah, Iraq, 12 February 2007*
	ZH877	Lockheed C-130J-30 Hercules C4 (N4081M)	RAF Lyneham Transport Wing
	ZH878	Lockheed C-130J-30 Hercules C4 (N73232)	RAF Lyneham Transport Wing
	ZH879	Lockheed C-130J-30 Hercules C4 (N4080M)	RAF Lyneham Transport Wing
	ZH880	Lockheed C-130J Hercules C5 (N73238)	RAF Lyneham Transport Wing

Serial	Type (code/other identity)	Owner/operator, location or fate	Notes
ZH881	Lockheed C-130J Hercules C5 (N4081M)	RAF Lyneham Transport Wing	
ZH882	Lockheed C-130J Hercules C5 (N4099R)	RAF Lyneham Transport Wing	
ZH883	Lockheed C-130J Hercules C5 (N4242N)	RAF Lyneham Transport Wing	
ZH884	Lockheed C-130J Hercules C5 (N4249Y)	RAF Lyneham Transport Wing	
ZH885	Lockheed C-130J Hercules C5 (N41030)	RAF Lyneham Transport Wing	
ZH886	Lockheed C-130J Hercules C5 (N73235)	RAF Lyneham Transport Wing	
ZH887	Lockheed C-130J Hercules C5 (N4187W)	RAF Lyneham Transport Wing	
ZH888	Lockheed C-130J Hercules C5 (N4187)	RAF Lyneham Transport Wing	
ZH889	Lockheed C-130J Hercules C5 (N4099R)	RAF Lyneham Transport Wing	
ZH890	Grob G109B Vigilant T1 [SE]	RAF No 663 VGS, Kinloss	
ZH891	B-V Chinook HC2A (N20075)	RAF No 18 Sqn, Odiham	
ZH892	B-V Chinook HC2A (N2019V) [HG]	RAF No 18 Sqn, Odiham	
ZH893	B-V Chinook HC2A (N2025L) [BM]	RAF No 27 Sqn, Odiham	
ZH894	B-V Chinook HC2A (N2026E)	RAF No 18 Sqn, Odiham	
ZH895	B-V Chinook HC2A (N2034K)	RAF No 18 Sqn, Odiham	
ZH896	B-V Chinook HC2A (N2038G)	MoD/AFD/QinetiQ, Boscombe Down	
ZH897	B-V Chinook HC3 (N2045G)	MoD/AFD/QinetiQ, Boscombe Down	
ZH898	B-V Chinook HC3 (N2057Q)	DE&S, stored Boscombe Down	
ZH899	B-V Chinook HC3 (N2057R)	DE&S, stored Boscombe Down	
ZH900	B-V Chinook HC3 (N2060H)	DE&S, stored Boscombe Down	
ZH901	B-V Chinook HC3 (N2060M)	DE&S, stored Boscombe Down	
ZH902	B-V Chinook HC3 (N2064W)	DE&S, stored Boscombe Down	
ZH903	B-V Chinook HC3 (N20671)	DE&S, stored Boscombe Down	
ZH904	B-V Chinook HC3 (N2083K)	DE&S, stored Boscombe Down	
ZH907	Panavia Tornado IDS (RSAF 7503)	MoD/BAE Systems, Warton	
ZH917	Panavia Tornado IDS (RSAF 6631)	MoD/BAE Systems, Warton	
ZJ100	BAe Hawk 102D	BAE Systems Warton	
ZJ117	EHI-101 Merlin HC3	MoD/AFD/QinetiQ, Boscombe Down	
ZJ118	EHI-101 Merlin HC3 [B]	RAF MDMF, RNAS Culdrose	
ZJ119	EHI-101 Merlin HC3 [C]	RAF No 28 Sqn, Benson	
ZJ120	EHI-101 Merlin HC3 [D]	RAF No 28 Sqn, Benson	
ZJ121	EHI-101 Merlin HC3 [E]	MoD/Westland Helicopters, Yeovil	
ZJ122	EHI-101 Merlin HC3 [F]	RAF MDMF, RNAS Culdrose	
ZJ123	EHI-101 Merlin HC3 [G]	RAF MDMF, RNAS Culdrose	
ZJ124	EHI-101 Merlin HC3 [H]	RAF No 1419 Flt, Basrah, Iraq	
ZJ125	EHI-101 Merlin HC3 [J]	RAF No 1419 Flt, Basrah, Iraq	
ZJ126	EHI-101 Merlin HC3 [K]	RAF No 28 Sqn, Benson	
ZJ127	EHI-101 Merlin HC3 [L]	MoD/Westland Helicopters, Yeovil	
ZJ128	EHI-101 Merlin HC3 [M]	RAF No 28 Sqn, Benson	
ZJ129	EHI-101 Merlin HC3 [N]	RAF No 28 Sqn, Benson	
ZJ130	EHI-101 Merlin HC3 [O]	RAF No 28 Sqn, Benson	
ZJ131	EHI-101 Merlin HC3 [P]	RAF MDMF, RNAS Culdrose	
ZJ132	EHI-101 Merlin HC3 [Q]	RAF MDMF, RNAS Culdrose	
ZJ133	EHI-101 Merlin HC3 [R]	RAF No 28 Sqn, Benson	
ZJ134	EHI-101 Merlin HC3 [S]	RAF MDMF, RNAS Culdrose	
ZJ135	EHI-101 Merlin HC3 [T]	RAF No 28 Sqn, Benson	
ZJ136	EHI-101 Merlin HC3 [U]	RAF No 28 Sqn, Benson	
ZJ137	EHI-101 Merlin HC3 [W]	RAF No 1419 Flt, Basrah, Iraq	
ZJ138	EHI-101 Merlin HC3 [X]	RAF No 1419 Flt, Basrah, Iraq	
ZJ164	AS365N-2 Dauphin 2 (G-BTLC)	RN/Bond Helicopters, Plymouth	
ZJ165	AS365N-2 Dauphin 2 (G-NTOO)	RN/Bond Helicopters, Plymouth	
ZJ166	WAH-64 Apache AH1 (N9219G)	AAC No 673 Sqn/2 Regt, Middle Wallop	
ZJ167	WAH-64 Apache AH1 (N3266B)	AAC No 662 Sqn/3 Regt, Wattisham	
ZJ168	WAH-64 Apache AH1 (N3123T)	AAC No 4 Regt, Wattisham	
ZJ169	WAH-64 Apache AH1 (N3114H)	AAC No 673 Sqn/2 Regt, Middle Wallop	
ZJ170	WAH-64 Apache AH1 (N3065U)	AAC No 4 Regt, Wattisham	
ZJ171	WAH-64 Apache AH1 (N3266T)	AAC No 662 Sqn/3 Regt, Wattisham	
ZJ172	WAH-64 Apache AH1	AAC No 664 Sqn/4 Regt, Wattisham	
ZJ173	WAH-64 Apache AH1 (N3266W)	AAC No 4 Regt, Wattisham	
ZJ174	WAH-64 Apache AH1	AAC No 663 Sqn/3 Regt, Wattisham	
ZJ175	WAH-64 Apache AH1 (N3218V)	AAC No 4 Regt, Wattisham	
ZJ176	WAH-64 Apache AH1	AAC No 663 Sqn/3 Regt, Wattisham	

Notes	Serial	Type (code/other identity)	Owner/operator, location or fate
	ZJ177	WAH-64 Apache AH1	AAC No 4 Regt, Wattisham
	ZJ178	WAH-64 Apache AH1	AAC No 663 Sqn/3 Regt, Wattisham
	ZJ179	WAH-64 Apache AH1	AAC No 659 Sqn/4 Regt, Wattisham
	ZJ180	WAH-64 Apache AH1	AAC No 662 Sqn/3 Regt, Wattisham
	ZJ181	WAH-64 Apache AH1	AAC No 4 Regt, Wattisham
	ZJ182	WAH-64 Apache AH1	AAC No 662 Sqn/3 Regt, Wattisham
	ZJ183	WAH-64 Apache AH1	AAC No 662 Sqn/3 Regt, Wattisham
	ZJ184	WAH-64 Apache AH1	AAC No 4 Regt, Wattisham
	ZJ185	WAH-64 Apache AH1	AAC No 654 Sqn/4 Regt, Wattisham
	ZJ186	WAH-64 Apache AH1	AAC, Wattisham
	ZJ187	WAH-64 Apache AH1	AAC No 663 Sqn/3 Regt, Wattisham
	ZJ188	WAH-64 Apache AH1	MoD/Westland Helicopters, Yeovil
	ZJ189	WAH-64 Apache AH1	AAC No 4 Regt, Wattisham
	ZJ190	WAH-64 Apache AH1	AAC No 663 Sqn/3 Regt, Wattisham
	ZJ191	WAH-64 Apache AH1	AAC No 663 Sqn/3 Regt, Wattisham
	ZJ192	WAH-64 Apache AH1	AAC No 663 Sqn/3 Regt, Wattisham
	ZJ193	WAH-64 Apache AH1	AAC No 4 Regt, Wattisham
	ZJ194	WAH-64 Apache AH1	AAC No 662 Sqn/3 Regt, Wattisham
	ZJ195	WAH-64 Apache AH1	AAC No 654 Sqn/4 Regt, Wattisham
	ZJ196	WAH-64 Apache AH1	AAC No 664 Sqn/4 Regt, Wattisham
	ZJ197	WAH-64 Apache AH1	AAC, Wattisham
	ZJ198	WAH-64 Apache AH1	AAC, Wattisham
	ZJ199	WAH-64 Apache AH1	AAC No 673 Sqn/2 Regt, Middle Wallop
	ZJ200	WAH-64 Apache AH1	MoD/AFD/QinetiQ, Boscombe Down
	ZJ202	WAH-64 Apache AH1	AAC, Wattisham
	ZJ203	WAH-64 Apache AH1	AAC No 654 Sqn/4 Regt, Wattisham
	ZJ204	WAH-64 Apache AH1	AAC No 664 Sqn/4 Regt, Wattisham
	ZJ205	WAH-64 Apache AH1	AAC No 662 Sqn/3 Regt, Wattisham
	ZJ206	WAH-64 Apache AH1	AAC No 673 Sqn/2 Regt, Middle Wallop
	ZJ207	WAH-64 Apache AH1	AAC No 673 Sqn/2 Regt, Middle Wallop
	ZJ208	WAH-64 Apache AH1	AAC No 663 Sqn/3 Regt, Wattisham
	ZJ209	WAH-64 Apache AH1	AAC No 663 Sqn/3 Regt, Wattisham
	ZJ210	WAH-64 Apache AH1	AAC No 664 Sqn/4 Regt, Wattisham
	ZJ211	WAH-64 Apache AH1	AAC No 673 Sqn/2 Regt, Middle Wallop
	ZJ212	WAH-64 Apache AH1	AAC No 673 Sqn/2 Regt, Middle Wallop
	ZJ213	WAH-64 Apache AH1	AAC No 673 Sqn/2 Regt, Middle Wallop
	ZJ214	WAH-64 Apache AH1	AAC No 673 Sqn/2 Regt, Middle Wallop
	ZJ215	WAH-64 Apache AH1	AAC No 673 Sqn/2 Regt, Middle Wallop
	ZJ216	WAH-64 Apache AH1	AAC No 673 Sqn/2 Regt, Middle Wallop
	ZJ217	WAH-64 Apache AH1	AAC No 673 Sqn/2 Regt, Middle Wallop
	ZJ218	WAH-64 Apache AH1	AAC No 656 Sqn/4 Regt, Wattisham
	ZJ219	WAH-64 Apache AH1	AAC No 673 Sqn/2 Regt, Middle Wallop
	ZJ220	WAH-64 Apache AH1	AAC No 673 Sqn/2 Regt, Middle Wallop
	ZJ221	WAH-64 Apache AH1	AAC No 673 Sqn/2 Regt, Middle Wallop
	ZJ222	WAH-64 Apache AH1	AAC, Wattisham
	ZJ223	WAH-64 Apache AH1	AAC No 662 Sqn/3 Regt, Wattisham
	ZJ224	WAH-64 Apache AH1	AAC No 656 Sqn/4 Regt, Wattisham
	ZJ225	WAH-64 Apache AH1	AAC No 656 Sqn/4 Regt, Wattisham
	ZJ226	WAH-64 Apache AH1	AAC No 663 Sqn/3 Regt, Wattisham
	ZJ227	WAH-64 Apache AH1	AAC No 656 Sqn/4 Regt, Wattisham
	ZJ228	WAH-64 Apache AH1	AAC No 656 Sqn/4 Regt, Wattisham
	ZJ229	WAH-64 Apache AH1	AAC No 656 Sqn/4 Regt, Wattisham
	ZJ230	WAH-64 Apache AH1	AAC No 663 Sqn/3 Regt, Wattisham
	ZJ231	WAH-64 Apache AH1	AAC No 663 Sqn/3 Regt, Wattisham
	ZJ232	WAH-64 Apache AH1	AAC No 663 Sqn/3 Regt, Wattisham
	ZJ233	WAH-64 Apache AH1	AAC No 656 Sqn/4 Regt, Wattisham
	ZJ234	Bell 412EP Griffin HT1 (G-BWZR) [S]	DHFS No 60(R) Sqn, RAF Shawbury
	ZJ235	Bell 412EP Griffin HT1 (G-BXBF) [I]	DHFS No 60(R) Sqn, RAF Shawbury
	ZJ236	Bell 412EP Griffin HT1 (G-BXBE) [X]	DHFS No 60(R) Sqn, RAF Shawbury
	ZJ237	Bell 412EP Griffin HT1 (G-BXFF) [T}	DHFS No 60(R) Sqn, RAF Shawbury
	ZJ238	Bell 412EP Griffin HT1 (G-BXHC) [Y]	DHFS No 60(R) Sqn, RAF Shawbury
	ZJ239	Bell 412EP Griffin HT1 (G-BXFH) [R]	DHFS No 60(R) Sqn, RAF Shawbury
	ZJ240	Bell 412EP Griffin HT1 (G-BXIR) [U]	DHFS No 60(R) Sqn/SARTU, RAF Valley
	ZJ241	Bell 412EP Griffin HT1 (G-BXIS) [L]	DHFS No 60(R) Sqn, RAF Shawbury
	ZJ242	Bell 412EP Griffin HT1 (G-BXDK) [E]	DHFS No 60(R) Sqn/SARTU, RAF Valley
	ZJ243	AS350BA Squirrel HT2 (G-BWZS)	DHFS, RAF Shawbury

Serial	Type (code/other identity)	Owner/operator, location or fate	Notes
ZJ244	AS350BA Squirrel HT2 (G-BXMD)	School of Army Aviation/No 670 Sqn, Middle Wallop	
ZJ245	AS350BA Squirrel HT2 (G-BXME)	School of Army Aviation/No 670 Sqn, Middle Wallop	
ZJ246	AS350BA Squirrel HT2 (G-BXMJ)	School of Army Aviation/No 670 Sqn, Middle Wallop	
ZJ247	AS350BA Squirrel HT2 (G-BXNB)	School of Army Aviation/No 670 Sqn, Middle Wallop	
ZJ248	AS350BA Squirrel HT2 (G-BXNE)	School of Army Aviation/No 670 Sqn, Middle Wallop	
ZJ249	AS350BA Squirrel HT2 (G-BXNJ)	School of Army Aviation/No 670 Sqn, Middle Wallop	
ZJ250	AS350BA Squirrel HT2 (G-BXNY)	School of Army Aviation/No 670 Sqn, Middle Wallop	
ZJ251	AS350BA Squirrel HT2 (G-BXOG)	DHFS, RAF Shawbury	
ZJ252	AS350BA Squirrel HT2 (G-BXOK)	School of Army Aviation/No 670 Sqn, Middle Wallop	
ZJ253	AS350BA Squirrel HT2 (G-BXPG)	School of Army Aviation/No 670 Sqn, Middle Wallop	
ZJ254	AS350BA Squirrel HT2 (G-BXPJ)	DHFS, RAF Shawbury	
ZJ255	AS350BB Squirrel HT1 (G-BXAG)	DHFS, RAF Shawbury	
ZJ256	AS350BB Squirrel HT1 (G-BXCE)	DHFS, RAF Shawbury	
ZJ257	AS350BB Squirrel HT1 (G-BXDJ)	DHFS, RAF Shawbury	
ZJ258	AS350BB Squirrel HT1 (G-BXEO)	RAF Shawbury (wreck)	
ZJ260	AS350BB Squirrel HT1 (G-BXGB)	DHFS, RAF Shawbury	
ZJ261	AS350BB Squirrel HT1 (G-BXGJ)	DHFS, RAF Shawbury	
ZJ262	AS350BB Squirrel HT1 (G-BXHB)	DHFS, RAF Shawbury	
ZJ264	AS350BB Squirrel HT1 (G-BXHW)	DHFS, RAF Shawbury	
ZJ265	AS350BB Squirrel HT1 (G-BXHX)	DHFS, RAF Shawbury	
ZJ266	AS350BB Squirrel HT1 (G-BXIL)	DHFS, RAF Shawbury	
ZJ267	AS350BB Squirrel HT1 (G-BXIP)	DHFS, RAF Shawbury	
ZJ268	AS350BB Squirrel HT1 (G-BXJE)	DHFS, RAF Shawbury	
ZJ269	AS350BB Squirrel HT1 (G-BXJN)	DHFS, RAF Shawbury	
ZJ270	AS350BB Squirrel HT1 (G-BXJR)	DHFS, RAF Shawbury	
ZJ271	AS350BB Squirrel HT1 (G-BXKE)	DHFS, RAF Shawbury	
ZJ272	AS350BB Squirrel HT1 (G-BXKN)	DHFS, RAF Shawbury	
ZJ273	AS350BB Squirrel HT1 (G-BXKP)	DHFS, RAF Shawbury	
ZJ274	AS350BB Squirrel HT1 (G-BXKR)	DHFS, RAF Shawbury	
ZJ275	AS350BB Squirrel HT1 (G-BXLB)	DHFS, RAF Shawbury	
ZJ276	AS350BB Squirrel HT1 (G-BXLE)	DHFS, RAF Shawbury	
ZJ277	AS350BB Squirrel HT1 (G-BXLH)	DHFS, RAF Shawbury	
ZJ278	AS350BB Squirrel HT1 (G-BXMB)	DHFS, RAF Shawbury	
ZJ279	AS350BB Squirrel HT1 (G-BXMC)	DHFS, RAF Shawbury	
ZJ280	AS350BB Squirrel HT1 (G-BXMI)	DHFS, RAF Shawbury	
ZJ488	GAF Jindivik 800 (A92-808)	Caernarfon Museum	
ZJ496	GAF Jindivik 900 (A92-901)	Farnborough Air Sciences Trust, Farnborough	
ZJ514	BAE Systems Nimrod MRA4 (XV251) [PA-4]	DE&S/BAE Systems, Woodford (conversion)	
ZJ515	BAE Systems Nimrod MRA4 (XV258) [PA-5]	DE&S/BAE Systems, Woodford (conversion)	
ZJ516	BAE Systems Nimrod MRA4 (XV247) [PA-1]	MoD/AFD/QinetiQ, Boscombe Down	
ZJ517	BAE Systems Nimrod MRA4 (XV242) [PA-3]	MoD/BAE Systems, Warton	
ZJ518	BAE Systems Nimrod MRA4 (XV234) [PA-2]	MoD/BAE Systems, Woodford	
ZJ519	BAE Systems Nimrod MRA4 (XZ284) [PA-6]	DE&S/BAE Systems, Woodford (conversion)	
ZJ520	BAE Systems Nimrod MRA4 (XV233) [PA-7]	DE&S/BAE Systems, Woodford (conversion)	
ZJ521	BAE Systems Nimrod MRA4 (XV227) [PA-8]	BAE Systems, for RAF	
ZJ522	BAE Systems Nimrod MRA4 (XV245) [PA-9]	BAE Systems, for RAF	
ZJ523	BAE Systems Nimrod MRA4 (XV228) [PA-10]	BAE Systems, for RAF	
ZJ524	BAE Systems Nimrod MRA4 (XV243) [PA-11]	BAE Systems, for RAF	
ZJ525	BAE Systems Nimrod MRA4 (XV253) [PA-12]	BAE Systems, for RAF	

Notes	Serial	Type (code/other identity)	Owner/operator, location or fate
	ZJ526	BAE Systems Nimrod MRA4 [PA-13]	*Cancelled*
	ZJ527	BAE Systems Nimrod MRA4 [PA-14]	*Cancelled*
	ZJ528	BAE Systems Nimrod MRA4 [PA-15]	*Cancelled*
	ZJ529	BAE Systems Nimrod MRA4 [PA-16]	*Cancelled*
	ZJ530	BAE Systems Nimrod MRA4 [PA-17]	*Cancelled*
	ZJ531	BAE Systems Nimrod MRA4 [PA-18]	*Cancelled*
	ZJ635	AS355F-1 Twin Squirrel (G-NEXT)	*Sold as G-WDKR, March 2007*
	ZJ645	D-BD Alpha Jet (98+62)	MoD/AFD/QinetiQ, Boscombe Down
	ZJ646	D-BD Alpha Jet (98+55)	MoD/AFD/QinetiQ, Boscombe Down
	ZJ647	D-BD Alpha Jet (98+71)	MoD/AFD/QinetiQ, Boscombe Down
	ZJ648	D-BD Alpha Jet (98+09)	MoD/AFD/QinetiQ, Boscombe Down
	ZJ649	D-BD Alpha Jet (98+73)	MoD/ETPS, Boscombe Down
	ZJ650	D-BD Alpha Jet (98+35)	MoD/QinetiQ, stored Boscombe Down
	ZJ651	D-BD Alpha Jet (41+42)	MoD/ETPS, Boscombe Down
	ZJ652	D-BD Alpha Jet (41+09)	MoD/QinetiQ Boscombe Down, spares use
	ZJ653	D-BD Alpha Jet (40+22)	MoD/QinetiQ Boscombe Down, spares use
	ZJ654	D-BD Alpha Jet (41+02)	MoD/QinetiQ Boscombe Down, spares use
	ZJ655	D-BD Alpha Jet (41+19)	MoD/QinetiQ Boscombe Down, spares use
	ZJ656	D-BD Alpha Jet (41+40)	MoD/QinetiQ Boscombe Down, spares use
	ZJ690	Bombardier Sentinel R1 (C-GJRG)	RAF No 5 Sqn, Waddington
	ZJ691	Bombardier Sentinel R1 (C-FZVM)	DE&S/Raytheon, Chester
	ZJ692	Bombardier Sentinel R1 (C-FZWW)	DE&S/Raytheon, Chester
	ZJ693	Bombardier Sentinel R1 (C-FZXC)	RAF No 5 Sqn, Waddington
	ZJ694	Bombardier Sentinel R1 (C-FZYL)	DE&S/Raytheon, Chester
	ZJ699	Eurofighter Typhoon (PT001)	MoD/BAE Systems, Warton
	ZJ700	Eurofighter Typhoon (PS002)	MoD/BAE Systems, Warton
	ZJ703	Bell 412EP Griffin HAR2 (G-CBST) [*Spades*,3]	RAF No 84 Sqn, Akrotiri
	ZJ704	Bell 412EP Griffin HAR2 (G-CBWT) [*Clubs*,4]	RAF No 84 Sqn, Akrotiri
	ZJ705	Bell 412EP Griffin HAR2 (G-CBXL) [*Hearts*, 5]	RAF No 84 Sqn, Akrotiri
	ZJ706	Bell 412EP Griffin HAR2 (G-CBYR) [*Diamonds*, 6]	RAF No 84 Sqn, Akrotiri
	ZJ707	Bell 412EP Griffin HT1 (G-CBUB) [O]	DHFS No 60(R) Sqn, RAF Shawbury
	ZJ708	Bell 412EP Griffin HT1 (G-CBVP) [K]	DHFS No 60(R) Sqn, RAF Shawbury
	ZJ780	AS.365N-3 Dauphin II	For AAC
	ZJ781	AS.365N-3 Dauphin II	For AAC
	ZJ782	AS.365N-3 Dauphin II	For AAC
	ZJ783	AS.365N-3 Dauphin II	For AAC
	ZJ800	Eurofighter Typhoon T1 [BC]	RAF No 29(R) Sqn, Coningsby
	ZJ801	Eurofighter Typhoon T1 [BJ]	RAF No 29(R) Sqn, Coningsby
	ZJ802	Eurofighter Typhoon T1 [BB]	RAF No 29(R) Sqn, Coningsby
	ZJ803	Eurofighter Typhoon T1 [BA]	RAF No 29(R) Sqn, Coningsby
	ZJ804	Eurofighter Typhoon T1	MoD/BAE Systems, Warton
	ZJ805	Eurofighter Typhoon T1 [BD]	RAF No 29(R) Sqn, Coningsby
	ZJ806	Eurofighter Typhoon T1A [BE]	RAF No 29(R) Sqn, Coningsby
	ZJ807	Eurofighter Typhoon T1A [BF]	RAF No 29(R) Sqn, Coningsby
	ZJ808	Eurofighter Typhoon T1A [BG]	RAF No 29(R) Sqn, Coningsby
	ZJ809	Eurofighter Typhoon T1A [BH]	MoD/BAE Systems, Warton
	ZJ810	Eurofighter Typhoon T1A [BI]	RAF, stored Coningsby (damaged)
	ZJ811	Eurofighter Typhoon T1A [DZ]	RAF No 11 Sqn, Coningsby
	ZJ812	Eurofighter Typhoon T1A [BK]	RAF No 29(R) Sqn, Coningsby
	ZJ813	Eurofighter Typhoon T1A [BL]	RAF No 29(R) Sqn, Coningsby
	ZJ814	Eurofighter Typhoon T1A [QO-Z]	RAF No 3 Sqn, Coningsby
	ZJ815	Eurofighter Typhoon T3 [AY]	RAF No 17(R) Sqn, Coningsby
	ZJ910	Eurofighter Typhoon F2 [BV]	RAF No 29(R) Sqn, Coningsby
	ZJ911	Eurofighter Typhoon F2 [BZ]	RAF No 29(R) Sqn, Coningsby
	ZJ912	Eurofighter Typhoon F2 [AB]	MoD/BAE Systems, Warton
	ZJ913	Eurofighter Typhoon F2 [AA]	MoD/BAE Systems, Warton
	ZJ914	Eurofighter Typhoon F2 [DE]	RAF No 11 Sqn, Coningsby
	ZJ915	Eurofighter Typhoon F2 [BY]	RAF No 29(R) Sqn, Coningsby
	ZJ916	Eurofighter Typhoon F2 [QO-U]	MoD/BAE Systems, Warton
	ZJ917	Eurofighter Typhoon F2 [QO-G]	MoD/BAE Systems, Warton

Serial	Type (code/other identity)	Owner/operator, location or fate	Notes
ZJ918	Eurofighter Typhoon F2 [QO-L]	RAF No 3 Sqn, Coningsby	
ZJ919	Eurofighter Typhoon F2 [DC]	RAF No 11 Sqn, Coningsby	
ZJ920	Eurofighter Typhoon F2 [BX]	MoD/BAE Systems, Warton	
ZJ921	Eurofighter Typhoon F2 [BW]	MoD/BAE Systems, Warton	
ZJ922	Eurofighter Typhoon F2 [QO-C]	RAF No 3 Sqn, Coningsby	
ZJ923	Eurofighter Typhoon F2 [QO-E]	RAF No 3 Sqn, Coningsby	
ZJ924	Eurofighter Typhoon F2 [DD]	MoD/BAE Systems, Warton	
ZJ925	Eurofighter Typhoon F2 [QO-R]	RAF No 3 Sqn, Coningsby	
ZJ926	Eurofighter Typhoon F2 [QO-Y]	RAF No 3 Sqn, Coningsby	
ZJ927	Eurofighter Typhoon F2 [AG]	RAF No 17(R) Sqn, Coningsby	
ZJ928	Eurofighter Typhoon F2 [AF]	RAF No 17(R) Sqn, Coningsby	
ZJ929	Eurofighter Typhoon F2 [QO-A]	RAF No 3 Sqn, Coningsby	
ZJ930	Eurofighter Typhoon FGR4 [AA]	RAF No 17(R) Sqn, Coningsby	
ZJ931	Eurofighter Typhoon F2 [DA]	RAF No 11 Sqn, Coningsby	
ZJ932	Eurofighter Typhoon F2 [DB]	RAF No 11 Sqn, Coningsby	
ZJ933	Eurofighter Typhoon FGR4 [DF]	RAF No 11 Sqn, Coningsby	
ZJ934	Eurofighter Typhoon F2 [QO-T]	RAF No 3 Sqn, Coningsby	
ZJ935	Eurofighter Typhoon FGR4	RAF No 11 Sqn, Coningsby	
ZJ936	Eurofighter Typhoon F2 [QO-S]	RAF No 3 Sqn, Coningsby	
ZJ937	Eurofighter Typhoon F2 [QO-W]	RAF No 3 Sqn, Coningsby	
ZJ938	Eurofighter Typhoon FGR4	MoD/BAE Systems, Warton	
ZJ939	Eurofighter Typhoon FGR4 [DXI]	RAF No 11 Sqn, Coningsby	
ZJ940	Eurofighter Typhoon FGR4	RAF, Coningsby	
ZJ941	Eurofighter Typhoon FGR4 [DG]	RAF No 11 Sqn, Coningsby	
ZJ942	Eurofighter Typhoon FGR4 [DH]	RAF No 11 Sqn, Coningsby	
ZJ943	Eurofighter Typhoon FGR4	MoD/BAE Systems, Warton	
ZJ944	Eurofighter Typhoon FGR4	DE&S/BAE Systems, for RAF	
ZJ945	Eurofighter Typhoon FGR4	DE&S/BAE Systems, for RAF	
ZJ946	Eurofighter Typhoon FGR4	DE&S/BAE Systems, for RAF	
ZJ947	Eurofighter Typhoon FGR4	DE&S/BAE Systems, for RAF	
ZJ948	Eurofighter Typhoon FGR4	DE&S/BAE Systems, for RAF	
ZJ949	Eurofighter Typhoon FGR4	DE&S/BAE Systems, for RAF	
ZJ950	Eurofighter Typhoon FGR4	DE&S/BAE Systems, for RAF	
ZJ951	BAE Systems Hawk 120D	BAE Systems, Warton	
ZJ954	SA330H Puma HC1 (SAAF 144)	RAF No 33 Sqn, Benson	
ZJ955	SA330H Puma HC1 (SAAF 148)	RAF PASF, Benson (damaged)	
ZJ956	SA330H Puma HC1 (SAAF 172)	RAF No 230 Sqn, Aldergrove	
ZJ957	SA330H Puma HC1 (SAAF 169)	Westland Helicopters, for RAF	
ZJ958	SA330H Puma (SAAF 173)	DE&S, stored DSDC Llangennech	
ZJ959	SA330H Puma (SAAF 184)	DE&S, stored DSDC Llangennech	
ZJ960	Grob G109B Vigilant T1 (D-KSMU) [SH]	RAF No 618 VGS, Odiham	
ZJ961	Grob G109B Vigilant T1 (D-KLCW) [SJ]	RAF ACCGS/No 644 VGS, Syerston	
ZJ962	Grob G109B Vigilant T1 (D-KBEU) [SK]	RAF No 613 VGS, Halton	
ZJ963	Grob G109B Vigilant T1 (D-KMSN) [SL]	RAF No 642 VGS, Topcliffe	
ZJ964	Bell 212HP AH1 (G-BJGV) [A]	AAC No 25 Flt, Belize	
ZJ965	Bell 212HP AH1 (G-BJGU) [B]	*Crashed 5 September 2007, Belize*	
ZJ966	Bell 212HP AH1 (G-BJJO) [C]	AAC No 25 Flt, Belize	
ZJ967	Grob G109B Vigilant T1 (G-DEWS) [SM]	RAF CGMF, Syerston	
ZJ968	Grob G109B Vigilant T1 (N109BT) [SN]	RAF CGMF, Syerston	
ZJ969	Bell 212HP AH1 (G-BGLJ) [D]	AAC No 25 Flt, Belize	
ZJ990	EHI-101 Merlin HC3A (M-501) [AA]	Westland Helicopters, for RAF	
ZJ992	EHI-101 Merlin HC3A (M-503) [AB]	RAF No 78 Sqn, Benson	
ZJ994	EHI-101 Merlin HC3A (M-505) [AC]	RAF No 78 Sqn, Benson	
ZJ995	EHI-101 Merlin HC3A (M-506) [AD]	Westland Helicopters, for RAF	
ZJ998	EHI-101 Merlin HC3A (M-509) [AE]	Westland Helicopters, for RAF	
ZJ999	EHI-101 Merlin Mk512	*To Denmark as M-510, 2006*	
ZK001	EHI-101 Merlin HC3A (M-511) [AF]	Westland Helicopters, for RAF	
ZK002	EHI-101 Merlin Mk512	*To Denmark as M-512, 2006*	
ZK003	EHI-101 Merlin Mk512	*To Denmark as M-513, 19 January 2007*	
ZK004	EHI-101 Merlin Mk512	*To Denmark as M-514, 2 February 2007*	
ZK005	Grob G109B Vigilant T1 (OH-797) [SP]	RAF ACCGS/No 644 VGS, Syerston	
ZK010	BAE Systems Hawk T2	MoD/BAE Systems, Warton	
ZK011	BAE Systems Hawk T2	MoD/BAE Systems, Warton	
ZK012	BAE Systems Hawk T2	Reservation for RAF	

Notes	Serial	Type (code/other identity)	Owner/operator, location or fate
	ZK013	BAE Systems Hawk T2	Reservation for RAF
	ZK014	BAE Systems Hawk T2	Reservation for RAF
	ZK015	BAE Systems Hawk T2	Reservation for RAF
	ZK016	BAE Systems Hawk T2	Reservation for RAF
	ZK017	BAE Systems Hawk T2	Reservation for RAF
	ZK018	BAE Systems Hawk T2	Reservation for RAF
	ZK019	BAE Systems Hawk T2	Reservation for RAF
	ZK020	BAE Systems Hawk T2	Reservation for RAF
	ZK021	BAE Systems Hawk T2	Reservation for RAF
	ZK022	BAE Systems Hawk T2	Reservation for RAF
	ZK023	BAE Systems Hawk T2	Reservation for RAF
	ZK024	BAE Systems Hawk T2	Reservation for RAF
	ZK025	BAE Systems Hawk T2	Reservation for RAF
	ZK026	BAE Systems Hawk T2	Reservation for RAF
	ZK027	BAE Systems Hawk T2	Reservation for RAF
	ZK028	BAE Systems Hawk T2	Reservation for RAF
	ZK029	BAE Systems Hawk T2	Reservation for RAF
	ZK030	BAE Systems Hawk T2	Reservation for RAF
	ZK031	BAE Systems Hawk T2	Reservation for RAF
	ZK032	BAE Systems Hawk T2	Reservation for RAF
	ZK033	BAE Systems Hawk T2	Reservation for RAF
	ZK034	BAE Systems Hawk T2	Reservation for RAF
	ZK035	BAE Systems Hawk T2	Reservation for RAF
	ZK036	BAE Systems Hawk T2	Reservation for RAF
	ZK037	BAE Systems Hawk T2	Reservation for RAF
	ZK045	BAE Systems Hawk T2	Reservation for RAF
	ZK046	BAE Systems Hawk T2	Reservation for RAF
	ZK047	BAE Systems Hawk T2	Reservation for RAF
	ZK048	BAE Systems Hawk T2	Reservation for RAF
	ZK049	BAE Systems Hawk T2	Reservation for RAF
	ZK050	BAE Systems Hawk T2	Reservation for RAF
	ZK051	BAE Systems Hawk T2	Reservation for RAF
	ZK052	BAE Systems Hawk T2	Reservation for RAF
	ZK053	BAE Systems Hawk T2	Reservation for RAF
	ZK054	BAE Systems Hawk T2	Reservation for RAF
	ZK055	BAE Systems Hawk T2	Reservation for RAF
	ZK056	BAE Systems Hawk T2	Reservation for RAF
	ZK057	BAE Systems Hawk T2	Reservation for RAF
	ZK058	BAE Systems Hawk T2	Reservation for RAF
	ZK059	BAE Systems Hawk T2	Reservation for RAF
	ZK060	Eurofighter EF.2000A Typhoon	BAE Systems, for R Saudi AF
	ZK061	Eurofighter EF.2000A Typhoon	BAE Systems, for R Saudi AF
	ZK062	Eurofighter EF.2000A Typhoon	BAE Systems, for R Saudi AF
	ZK063	Eurofighter EF.2000A Typhoon	BAE Systems, for R Saudi AF
	ZK064	Eurofighter EF.2000A Typhoon	BAE Systems, for R Saudi AF
	ZK065	Eurofighter EF.2000A Typhoon	BAE Systems, for R Saudi AF
	ZK066	Eurofighter EF.2000A Typhoon	BAE Systems, for R Saudi AF
	ZK067	Eurofighter EF.2000A Typhoon	BAE Systems, for R Saudi AF
	ZK068	Eurofighter EF.2000B Typhoon	BAE Systems, for R Saudi AF
	ZK069	Eurofighter EF.2000B Typhoon	BAE Systems, for R Saudi AF
	ZK070	Eurofighter EF.2000B Typhoon	BAE Systems, for R Saudi AF
	ZK071	Eurofighter EF.2000B Typhoon	BAE Systems, for R Saudi AF
	ZK072	Eurofighter EF.2000B Typhoon	BAE Systems, for R Saudi AF
	ZK073	Eurofighter EF.2000B Typhoon	BAE Systems, for R Saudi AF
	ZK074	Eurofighter EF.2000A Typhoon	BAE Systems, for R Saudi AF
	ZK075	Eurofighter EF.2000A Typhoon	BAE Systems, for R Saudi AF
	ZK076	Eurofighter EF.2000A Typhoon	BAE Systems, for R Saudi AF
	ZK077	Eurofighter EF.2000A Typhoon	BAE Systems, for R Saudi AF
	ZK078	Eurofighter EF.2000A Typhoon	BAE Systems, for R Saudi AF
	ZK079	Eurofighter EF.2000A Typhoon	BAE Systems, for R Saudi AF
	ZK080	Eurofighter EF.2000A Typhoon	BAE Systems, for R Saudi AF
	ZK081	Eurofighter EF.2000A Typhoon	BAE Systems, for R Saudi AF
	ZK082	Eurofighter EF.2000A Typhoon	BAE Systems, for R Saudi AF
	ZK083	Eurofighter EF.2000A Typhoon	BAE Systems, for R Saudi AF
	ZK113	Panavia Tornado IDS (RSAF 6606)	MoD/BAE Systems, Warton
	ZK114	M2370 UAV	For QinetiQ
	ZK115	WS Super Lynx 64	*To South Africa as 191, 26 July 2007*
	ZK116	WS Super Lynx 64	*To South Africa as 192, 26 July 2007*
	ZK117	WS Super Lynx 64	*To South Africa as 193, 11 July 2007*
	ZK118	WS Super Lynx 64	*To South Africa as 194, 11 July 2007*
	ZK119	Pilatus PC-9 (HB-HQU/RSAF 2204)	MoD/BAE Systems, Warton

Serial	Type (code/other identity)	Owner/operator, location or fate	Notes
ZK120*	Lockheed Martin Desert Hawk DH1+ UAV	For Army	
ZK121	BAE Systems Hawk 132	BAE Systems, for India as A3480	
ZK122	BAE Systems Hawk 132	BAE Systems, for India as A3481	
ZK123	BAE Systems Hawk 132	BAE Systems, for India as A3482	
ZK124	BAE Systems Hawk 132	BAE Systems, for India as A3483	
ZK125	BAE Systems Hawk 132	*To India as A3484, 13 December 2007*	
ZK126	BAE Systems Hawk 132	BAE Systems, for India as A3485	
ZK127	BAE Systems Hawk 132	BAE Systems, for India as A3486	
ZK128	BAE Systems Hawk 132	*To India as A3487, 8 November 2007*	
ZK129	BAE Systems Hawk 132	*To India as A3488, 8 November 2007*	
ZK130	BAE Systems Hawk 132	*To India as A3489, 13 December 2007*	
ZK131	BAE Systems Hawk 132	BAE Systems, for India as A3490	
ZK132	BAE Systems Hawk 132	BAE Systems, for India as A3491	
ZK133	BAE Systems Hawk 132	BAE Systems, for India as A3492	
ZK134	BAE Systems Hawk 132	BAE Systems, for India as A3493	
ZK135	BAE Systems Hawk 132	BAE Systems, for India as A3494	
ZK136	BAE Systems Hawk 132	BAE Systems, for India as A3495	
ZK137	BAE Systems Hawk 132	BAE Systems, for India as A3496	
ZK138	BAE Systems Hawk 132	BAE Systems, for India as A3497	
ZK139	BAE Systems Hawk 132	BAE Systems, for India as A3498	
ZK140	BAE Systems Hawk 132	BAE Systems, for India as A3499	
ZK141	BAE Systems Hawk 132	BAE Systems, for India as A3500	
ZK142	BAE Systems Hawk 132	BAE Systems, for India as A3501	
ZK143	BAE Systems Hawk 132	BAE Systems, for India as A3502	
ZK144	BAE Systems Hawk 132	BAE Systems, for India as A3503	
ZK450	Beech Super King Air B200 (G-RAFJ) [J]	SERCO/RAF No 3 FTS/45(R) Sqn, Cranwell	
ZK451	Beech Super King Air B200 (G-RAFK) [K]	SERCO/RAF No 3 FTS/45(R) Sqn, Cranwell	
ZK452	Beech Super King Air B200 (G-RAFL) [L]	SERCO/RAF No 3 FTS/45(R) Sqn, Cranwell	
ZK453	Beech Super King Air B200 (G-RAFM) $	SERCO/RAF No 3 FTS/45(R) Sqn, Cranwell	
ZK454	Beech Super King Air B200 (G-RAFN) [N]	SERCO/RAF No 3 FTS/45(R) Sqn, Cranwell	
ZK455	Beech Super King Air B200 (G-RAFO)	Reservation for SERCO/RAF	
ZK456	Beech Super King Air B200 (G-RAFP)	Reservation for SERCO/RAF	
ZK457	Beech Super King Air 200 (G-ROWN)	MoD	
ZK501	Elbit Hermes 450 UAV	Army 32 Regt Royal Artillery, Afghanistan	
ZK502	Elbit Hermes 450 UAV	Army 32 Regt Royal Artillery, Afghanistan	
ZK503	Elbit Hermes 450 UAV	Army 32 Regt Royal Artillery, Afghanistan	
ZK504	Elbit Hermes 450 UAV	Army 32 Regt Royal Artillery, Afghanistan	
ZK505	Elbit Hermes 450 UAV	Army 32 Regt Royal Artillery, Afghanistan	
ZK506	Elbit Hermes 450 UAV	Army 32 Regt Royal Artillery, Afghanistan	
ZK507	Elbit Hermes 450 UAV	Army 32 Regt Royal Artillery, Afghanistan	
ZK508	Elbit Hermes 450 UAV	Army 32 Regt Royal Artillery, Afghanistan	
ZK509	Elbit Hermes 450 UAV	Army 32 Regt Royal Artillery, Afghanistan	
ZK510	Elbit Hermes 450 UAV	Army 32 Regt Royal Artillery, Afghanistan	
ZK511	Elbit Hermes 450 UAV	Army 32 Regt Royal Artillery, Afghanistan	
ZK512	Elbit Hermes 450 UAV	Army 32 Regt Royal Artillery, Afghanistan	
ZK513	Elbit Hermes 450 UAV	Army 32 Regt Royal Artillery, Afghanistan	
ZK514	Elbit Hermes 450 UAV	Army 32 Regt Royal Artillery, Afghanistan	
ZK515	Elbit Hermes 450 UAV	Army 32 Regt Royal Artillery, Afghanistan	
ZK516	Elbit Hermes 450 UAV	Army 32 Regt Royal Artillery, Afghanistan	
ZK517	Elbit Hermes 450 UAV	Army 32 Regt Royal Artillery, Afghanistan	
ZK518	Elbit Hermes 450 UAV	Army 32 Regt Royal Artillery, Afghanistan	
ZK519	Elbit Hermes 450 UAV	Army 32 Regt Royal Artillery, Afghanistan	
ZK520	Elbit Hermes 450 UAV	Army 32 Regt Royal Artillery, Afghanistan	
ZK531	BAe Hawk T53 (LL-5306)	MoD/BAE Systems, Warton	
ZK532	BAe Hawk T53 (LL-5315)	MoD/BAE Systems, Warton	
ZK533	BAe Hawk T53 (LL-5317)	MoD/BAE Systems, Warton	
ZK534	BAe Hawk T53 (LL-5319)	BAE Systems, Brough	
ZK535	BAe Hawk T53 (LL-5320)	MoD/BAE Systems, Warton	
ZM400	Airbus A400M	Reservation for RAF	
ZM401	Airbus A400M	Reservation for RAF	
ZM402	Airbus A400M	Reservation for RAF	
ZM403	Airbus A400M	Reservation for RAF	

Notes	Serial	Type (code/other identity)	Owner/operator, location or fate
	ZM404	Airbus A400M	Reservation for RAF
	ZM405	Airbus A400M	Reservation for RAF
	ZM406	Airbus A400M	Reservation for RAF
	ZM407	Airbus A400M	Reservation for RAF
	ZM408	Airbus A400M	Reservation for RAF
	ZM409	Airbus A400M	Reservation for RAF
	ZM410	Airbus A400M	Reservation for RAF
	ZM411	Airbus A400M	Reservation for RAF
	ZM412	Airbus A400M	Reservation for RAF
	ZM413	Airbus A400M	Reservation for RAF
	ZM414	Airbus A400M	Reservation for RAF
	ZM415	Airbus A400M	Reservation for RAF
	ZM416	Airbus A400M	Reservation for RAF
	ZM417	Airbus A400M	Reservation for RAF
	ZM418	Airbus A400M	Reservation for RAF
	ZM419	Airbus A400M	Reservation for RAF
	ZM420	Airbus A400M	Reservation for RAF
	ZM421	Airbus A400M	Reservation for RAF
	ZM422	Airbus A400M	Reservation for RAF
	ZM423	Airbus A400M	Reservation for RAF
	ZM424	Airbus A400M	Reservation for RAF
	ZR321	Agusta A.109E Power Elite (G-CDVB)	RAF No 32(The Royal) Sqn, Northolt
	ZR322	Agusta A.109E Power Elite (G-CDVC)	RAF No 32(The Royal) Sqn, Northolt
	ZR323	Agusta A.109E Power Elite (G-CDVE)	RAF No 32(The Royal) Sqn, Northolt
	ZT800	WS Super Lynx Mk 300	MoD/Westland Helicopters, Yeovil
	ZZ171	Boeing C-17A Globemaster III (00-201/N171UK)	RAF No 99 Sqn, Brize Norton
	ZZ172	Boeing C-17A Globemaster III (00-202/N172UK)	RAF No 99 Sqn, Brize Norton
	ZZ173	Boeing C-17A Globemaster III (00-203/N173UK)	RAF No 99 Sqn, Brize Norton
	ZZ174	Boeing C-17A Globemaster III (00-204/N174UK)	RAF No 99 Sqn, Brize Norton
	ZZ175	Boeing C-17A Globemaster III (07-0205)	Boeing, for RAF
	ZZ176	Boeing C-17A Globemaster III	Boeing, for RAF
	ZZ190	Hawker Hunter F58 (J-4066/G-HHAE)	Hawker Hunter Aviation/FR Aviation, Bournemouth
	ZZ191	Hawker Hunter F58 (J-4058/G-HHAD)	Hawker Hunter Aviation/FR Aviation, Bournemouth
	ZZ192	Grob G109B Vigilant T1 (D-KLVI) [SQ]	RAF ACCGS/No 644 VGS, Syerston
	ZZ193	Grob G109B Vigilant T1 (D-KBLO) [SR]	For RAF
	ZZ200	General Atomics Reaper UAV	RAF No 39 Sqn, Creech AFB, Nevada, USA
	ZZ201	General Atomics Reaper UAV	RAF No 39 Sqn, Creech AFB, Nevada, USA
	ZZ202	General Atomics Reaper UAV	General Atomics, for RAF
	ZZ203	General Atomics Reaper UAV	General Atomics, for RAF
	ZZ204	General Atomics Reaper UAV	General Atomics, for RAF
	ZZ205	General Atomics Reaper UAV	General Atomics, for RAF
	ZZ206	General Atomics Reaper UAV	General Atomics, for RAF
	ZZ207	General Atomics Reaper UAV	General Atomics, for RAF
	ZZ208	General Atomics Reaper UAV	General Atomics, for RAF
	ZZ209	General Atomics Reaper UAV	General Atomics, for RAF
	ZZ210	General Atomics Reaper UAV	General Atomics, for RAF
	ZZ211	General Atomics Reaper UAV	General Atomics, for RAF
	ZZ212	General Atomics Reaper UAV	General Atomics, for RAF
	ZZ213	General Atomics Reaper UAV	General Atomics, for RAF
	ZZ250	BAE Systems Taranis UAV	BAE Systems, Warton
	ZZ251	BAE Systems Herti UAV	BAE Systems, Warton
	ZZ330	Airbus A330 FSTA	Reservation for RAF
	ZZ331	Airbus A330 FSTA	Reservation for RAF
	ZZ332	Airbus A330 FSTA	Reservation for RAF
	ZZ333	Airbus A330 FSTA	Reservation for RAF
	ZZ334	Airbus A330 FSTA	Reservation for RAF
	ZZ335	Airbus A330 FSTA	Reservation for RAF

Serial	Type (code/other identity)	Owner/operator, location or fate	Notes
ZZ336	Airbus A330 FSTA	Reservation for RAF	
ZZ337	Airbus A330 FSTA	Reservation for RAF	
ZZ338	Airbus A330 FSTA	Reservation for RAF	
ZZ339	Airbus A330 FSTA	Reservation for RAF	
ZZ340	Airbus A330 FSTA	Reservation for RAF	
ZZ341	Airbus A330 FSTA	Reservation for RAF	
ZZ342	Airbus A330 FSTA	Reservation for RAF	
ZZ343	Airbus A330 FSTA	Reservation for RAF	
ZZ400	AgustaWestland Super Lynx	For RN	
ZZ401	AgustaWestland Super Lynx	For RN	
ZZ402	AgustaWestland Super Lynx	For RN	
ZZ403	AgustaWestland Super Lynx	For RN	
ZZ404	AgustaWestland Super Lynx	For RN	
ZZ405	AgustaWestland Super Lynx	For RN	
ZZ406	AgustaWestland Super Lynx	For RN	
ZZ407	AgustaWestland Super Lynx	For RN	
ZZ408	AgustaWestland Super Lynx	For RN	
ZZ409	AgustaWestland Super Lynx	For RN	
ZZ410	AgustaWestland Super Lynx	For RN	
ZZ411	AgustaWestland Super Lynx	For RN	
ZZ412	AgustaWestland Super Lynx	For RN	
ZZ413	AgustaWestland Super Lynx	For RN	
ZZ414	AgustaWestland Super Lynx	For RN	
ZZ415	AgustaWestland Super Lynx	For RN	
ZZ416	Hawker Beechcraft Super King Air 350C (G-JENC)	DE&S/Raytheon, Chester	
ZZ417	Hawker Beechcraft Super King Air 350C (G-NICY)	DE&S/Raytheon, Chester	
ZZ418	Hawker Beechcraft Super King Air 350C (G-JIMG)	For Army	
ZZ419	Hawker Beechcraft Super King Air 350C (G-OTCS)	For Army	
ZZ420*	Meggitt BTT-3 Banshee	For Army	

SE5a Replica F8010 is actually G-BDWJ and it lives on a private airstrip in Somerset.

Tiger Moth II G-ANMY still wears its former military serial DE470 as well as its current UK civil registration. It is based at RAF Cosford.

Beagle A61 Terrier II G-ASMZ wears its former marks VF516. It is based at Eggesford in Devon.

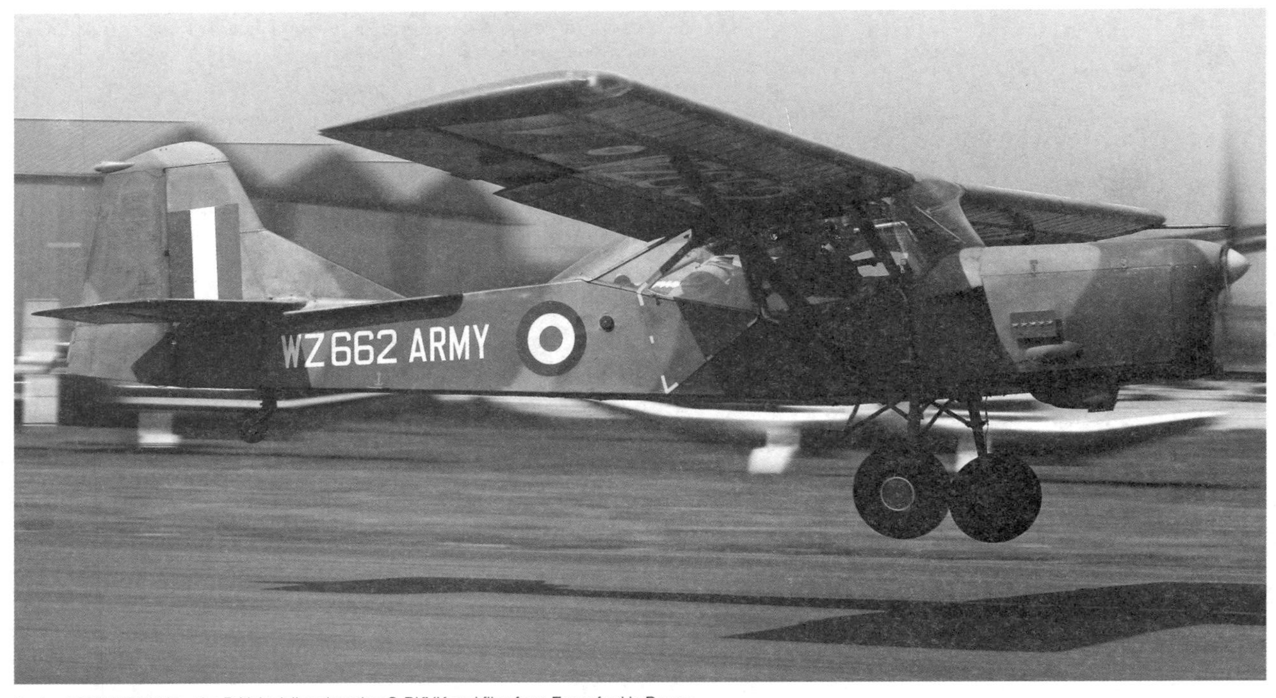

Auster AOP9 WZ662 has the British civil registration G-BKVK and flies from Eggesford in Devon.

Hawk T1 XX175 is one of a handful operated by the Royal Navy with FRADU at Culdrose.

Despite wearing markings suggesting that it was once XX704 with the RAF, Bulldog G-BCUV actually flew with the Ghanaian Air Force. The real XX704 was sold in the US in 2002.

Lynx AH.7 XZ663, coded I, is operated from the School of Army Aviation at Middle Wallop by 671 Squadron.

RAF Coningsby is now home to only a handful of Tornado F3s as the Eurofighter Typhoon takes their place. ZE785 is in the brightly coloured markings of 41(R) Squadron.

ZF119, coded WY, is a Sea King HC4 operated by 848 Naval Air Squadron at Yeovilton.

Much of the RAF Tucano fleet now wears brightly coloured squadron markings. Those on ZF515 are the markings of 72(R) Squadron.

Alpha Jet ZJ646 belongs to QinetiQ and is based at Boscombe Down. Rarely seen away from its home base, its former Luftwaffe colour scheme is still very much in evidence.

Two-seat Typhoon ZJ801 is coded BJ and wears the distinctive, if slightly misleading, markings of 29(R) Squadron, based at RAF Coningsby.

Typhoon F2 ZJ910, coded BV, is operated by 29(R) Squadron, based at RAF Coningsby.

Indian Air Force Hawk 132 A3483 is one of several on order. Flown in UK skies as ZK124, the UK military serial can just be made out on the lower fuselage just behind the wing.

Belgian Air Component SF.260D ST-48 is operated by 1 Wing at Bevekom. It helpfully has the type painted on the tail!

HN-452 is a Finnish Air Force F-18C Hornet, operated by HavLLv 11 at Rovaniemi.

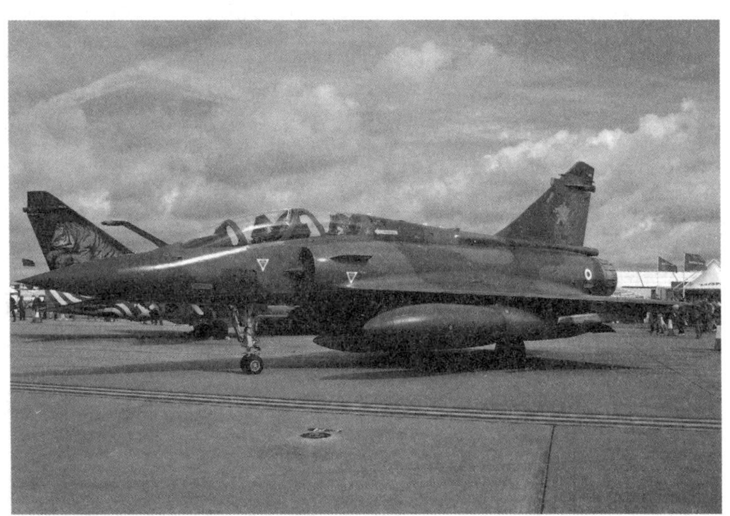

Mirage 2000D 605/3-XD of the French Air Force is operated by Escadron de Chasse 03/003 'Ardennes' at Nancy. Notice the boar's head markings of EC 03.003 on the tail.

Falcon 20DC G-FRAP flies from Bournemouth with FR Aviation.

The Falcon 10 is an increasingly rare type but Falcon 10(MER) 101 continues to be operated by ES 57 from Landivisiau in Northern Brittany.

Aircraft in UK Military Service with Civil Registrations

Serial	Type (code/other identity)	Owner/operator, location or fate	Notes
EC-EVM	AS.350B-2 Ecureuil	SERCO, RAF Shawbury, for RAF	
G-BFER	Bell 212	Bristow Helicopters, Shawbury, for AAC	
G-BONT	Slingsby T.67M Firefly 2	HCS/DEFTS, Middle Wallop	
G-BUUA	Slingsby T.67M Firefly 2	HCS/DEFTS, Middle Wallop	
G-BUUB	Slingsby T.67M Firefly 2	HCS/DEFTS, Middle Wallop	
G-BUUC	Slingsby T.67M Firefly 2	HCS/DEFTS, Middle Wallop	
G-BUUK	Slingsby T.67M Firefly 2	HCS/DEFTS, Middle Wallop	
G-BWXA	Slingsby T.67M Firefly 260	HCS/DEFTS, Barkston Heath	
G-BWXB	Slingsby T.67M Firefly 260	HCS/DEFTS, Barkston Heath	
G-BWXC	Slingsby T.67M Firefly 260	HCS/DEFTS, Barkston Heath	
G-BWXD	Slingsby T.67M Firefly 260	HCS/DEFTS, Barkston Heath	
G-BWXE	Slingsby T.67M Firefly 260	HCS/DEFTS, Barkston Heath	
G-BWXF	Slingsby T.67M Firefly 260	HCS/DEFTS, Barkston Heath	
G-BWXG	Slingsby T.67M Firefly 260	HCS/DEFTS, Barkston Heath	
G-BWXH	Slingsby T.67M Firefly 260	HCS/DEFTS, Barkston Heath	
G-BWXI	Slingsby T.67M Firefly 260	HCS/DEFTS, Barkston Heath	
G-BWXJ	Slingsby T.67M Firefly 260	HCS/DEFTS, Barkston Heath	
G-BWXK	Slingsby T.67M Firefly 260	HCS/DEFTS, Barkston Heath	
G-BWXL	Slingsby T.67M Firefly 260	HCS/DEFTS, Barkston Heath	
G-BWXM	Slingsby T.67M Firefly 260	HCS/DEFTS, Barkston Heath	
G-BWXN	Slingsby T.67M Firefly 260	HCS/DEFTS, Barkston Heath	
G-BWXO	Slingsby T.67M Firefly 260	HCS/DEFTS, Barkston Heath	
G-BWXR	Slingsby T.67M Firefly 260	HCS/DEFTS, Barkston Heath	
G-BWXS	Slingsby T.67M Firefly 260	HCS/DEFTS, Barkston Heath	
G-BWXT	Slingsby T.67M Firefly 260	HCS/DEFTS, Barkston Heath	
G-BWXU	Slingsby T.67M Firefly 260	HCS/DEFTS, Barkston Heath	
G-BWXV	Slingsby T.67M Firefly 260	HCS/DEFTS, Barkston Heath	
G-BWXW	Slingsby T.67M Firefly 260	HCS/DEFTS, Barkston Heath	
G-BWXX	Slingsby T.67M Firefly 260	HCS/DEFTS, Barkston Heath	
G-BWXY	Slingsby T.67M Firefly 260	HCS/DEFTS, Barkston Heath	
G-BWXZ	Slingsby T.67M Firefly 260	HCS/DEFTS, Barkston Heath	
G-BYUA	Grob G.115E Tutor	Bombardier/Cambridge UAS/University of London AS/No 1 EFTS (2 Sqn), Wyton	
G-BYUB	Grob G.115E Tutor	Bombardier/CFS Tutor Sqn/East Midlands Universities AS/No 1 EFTS (1 Sqn), Cranwell	
G-BYUC	Grob G.115E Tutor	Bombardier/CFS Tutor Sqn/East Midlands Universities AS/No 1 EFTS (1 Sqn), Cranwell	
G-BYUD	Grob G.115E Tutor	Bombardier/Universities of Glasgow & Strathclyde AS, Glasgow	
G-BYUE	Grob G.115E Tutor	Bombardier/CFS Tutor Sqn/East Midlands Universities AS/No 1 EFTS (1 Sqn), Cranwell	
G-BYUF	Grob G.115E Tutor	Bombardier/University of Birmingham AS, Cosford	
G-BYUG	Grob G.115E Tutor	Bombardier/Cambridge UAS/University of London AS/No 1 EFTS (2 Sqn), Wyton	
G-BYUH	Grob G.115E Tutor	Bombardier/Southampton UAS, Boscombe Down	
G-BYUI	Grob G.115E Tutor	Bombardier/Liverpool UAS/Manchester and Salford Universities AS, Woodvale	
G-BYUJ	Grob G.115E Tutor	Bombardier/Southampton UAS, Boscombe Down	
G-BYUK	Grob G.115E Tutor	Bombardier/University of Birmingham AS, Cosford	
G-BYUL	Grob G.115E Tutor	Bombardier/Southampton UAS, Boscombe Down	
G-BYUM	Grob G.115E Tutor	Bombardier/East of Scotland UAS, Leuchars	
G-BYUN	Grob G.115E Tutor	Bombardier/University of Wales AS, St Athan	
G-BYUO	Grob G.115E Tutor	Bombardier/Cambridge UAS/University of London AS/No 1 EFTS (2 Sqn), Wyton	
G-BYUP	Grob G.115E Tutor	Bombardier/East of Scotland UAS, Leuchars	

Civil-Registered Aircraft in UK Military Service

Notes	Serial	Type (code/other identity)	Owner/operator, location or fate
	G-BYUR	Grob G.115E Tutor	Bombardier/East of Scotland UAS, Leuchars
	G-BYUS	Grob G.115E Tutor	Bombardier/Cambridge UAS/University of London AS/No 1 EFTS (2 Sqn), Wyton
	G-BYUT	Grob G.115E Tutor	Bombardier/University of Wales AS, St Athan
	G-BYUU	Grob G.115E Tutor	Bombardier/East of Scotland UAS, Leuchars
	G-BYUV	Grob G.115E Tutor	Bombardier/Bristol UAS, Colerne
	G-BYUW	Grob G.115E Tutor	Bombardier/East of Scotland UAS, Leuchars
	G-BYUX	Grob G.115E Tutor	Bombardier/East of Scotland UAS, Leuchars
	G-BYUY	Grob G.115E Tutor	Bombardier/East of Scotland UAS, Leuchars
	G-BYUZ	Grob G.115E Tutor	Bombardier/Liverpool UAS/Manchester and Salford Universities AS, Woodvale
	G-BYVA	Grob G.115E Tutor	Bombardier/CFS Tutor Sqn/East Midlands Universities AS/No 1 EFTS (1 Sqn), Cranwell
	G-BYVB	Grob G.115E Tutor	Bombardier/Oxford UAS, Benson
	G-BYVC	Grob G.115E Tutor	Bombardier/Cambridge UAS/University of London AS/No 1 EFTS (2 Sqn), Wyton
	G-BYVD	Grob G.115E Tutor	Bombardier/Cambridge UAS/University of London AS/No 1 EFTS (2 Sqn), Wyton
	G-BYVE	Grob G.115E Tutor	Bombardier/Cambridge UAS/University of London AS/No 1 EFTS (2 Sqn), Wyton
	G-BYVF	Grob G.115E Tutor	Bombardier/RN No 727 Sqn, Yeovilton
	G-BYVG	Grob G.115E Tutor	Bombardier/Yorkshire Universities AS/ No 1 EFTS (3 Sqn), Church Fenton
	G-BYVH	Grob G.115E Tutor	Bombardier/CFS Tutor Sqn/East Midlands Universities AS/No 1 EFTS (1 Sqn), Cranwell
	G-BYVI	Grob G.115E Tutor	Bombardier/Yorkshire Universities AS/ No 1 EFTS (3 Sqn), Church Fenton
	G-BYVJ	Grob G.115E Tutor	Bombardier/Yorkshire Universities AS/ No 1 EFTS (3 Sqn), Church Fenton
	G-BYVK	Grob G.115E Tutor	Bombardier/RN No 727 Sqn, Yeovilton
	G-BYVL	Grob G.115E Tutor	Bombardier/Oxford UAS, Benson
	G-BYVM	Grob G.115E Tutor	Bombardier/East of Scotland UAS, Leuchars
	G-BYVN	Grob G.115E Tutor	Bombardier/RN No 727 Sqn, Yeovilton
	G-BYVO	Grob G.115E Tutor	Bombardier/CFS Tutor Sqn/East Midlands Universities AS/No 1 EFTS (1 Sqn), Cranwell
	G-BYVP	Grob G.115E Tutor	Bombardier/CFS Tutor Sqn/East Midlands Universities AS/No 1 EFTS (1 Sqn), Cranwell
	G-BYVR	Grob G.115E Tutor	Bombardier/CFS Tutor Sqn/East Midlands Universities AS/No 1 EFTS (1 Sqn), Cranwell
	G-BYVS	Grob G.115E Tutor	Bombardier/CFS Tutor Sqn/East Midlands Universities AS/No 1 EFTS (1 Sqn), Cranwell
	G-BYVT	Grob G.115E Tutor	Bombardier/Cambridge UAS/University of London AS/No 1 EFTS (2 Sqn), Wyton
	G-BYVU	Grob G.115E Tutor	Bombardier/Oxford UAS, Benson
	G-BYVV	Grob G.115E Tutor	Bombardier/Northumbrian Universities AS, Leeming
	G-BYVW	Grob G.115E Tutor	Bombardier/University of Wales AS, St Athan
	G-BYVX	Grob G.115E Tutor	Bombardier/Yorkshire Universities AS/ No 1 EFTS (3 Sqn), Church Fenton
	G-BYVY	Grob G.115E Tutor	Bombardier/University of Birmingham AS, Cosford
	G-BYVZ	Grob G.115E Tutor	Bombardier/Yorkshire Universities AS/ No 1 EFTS (3 Sqn), Church Fenton
	G-BYWA	Grob G.115E Tutor	Bombardier/Oxford UAS, Benson
	G-BYWB	Grob G.115E Tutor	Bombardier/CFS Tutor Sqn/East Midlands Universities AS/No 1 EFTS (1 Sqn), Cranwell
	G-BYWC	Grob G.115E Tutor	Bombardier/Oxford UAS, Benson

Serial	Type (code/other identity)	Owner/operator, location or fate	Notes
G-BYWD	Grob G.115E Tutor	Bombardier/Cambridge UAS/University of London AS/No 1 EFTS (2 Sqn), Wyton	
G-BYWE	Grob G.115E Tutor	Bombardier/Oxford UAS, Benson	
G-BYWF	Grob G.115E Tutor	Bombardier/CFS Tutor Sqn/East Midlands Universities AS/No 1 EFTS (1 Sqn), Cranwell	
G-BYWG	Grob G.115E Tutor	Bombardier/CFS Tutor Sqn/East Midlands Universities AS/No 1 EFTS (1 Sqn), Cranwell	
G-BYWH	Grob G.115E Tutor	Bombardier/Northumbrian Universities AS, Leeming	
G-BYWI	Grob G.115E Tutor	Bombardier/Liverpool UAS/Manchester and Salford Universities AS, Woodvale	
G-BYWJ	Grob G.115E Tutor	Bombardier/Liverpool UAS/Manchester and Salford Universities AS, Woodvale	
G-BYWK	Grob G.115E Tutor	Bombardier/Southampton UAS, Boscombe Down	
G-BYWL	Grob G.115E Tutor	Bombardier/CFS Tutor Sqn/East Midlands Universities AS/No 1 EFTS (1 Sqn), Cranwell	
G-BYWM	Grob G.115E Tutor	Bombardier/RN No 727 Sqn, Yeovilton	
G-BYWN	Grob G.115E Tutor	Bombardier/Liverpool UAS/Manchester and Salford Universities AS, Woodvale	
G-BYWO	Grob G.115E Tutor	Bombardier/Yorkshire Universities AS/ No 1 EFTS (3 Sqn), Church Fenton	
G-BYWP	Grob G.115E Tutor	Bombardier/Yorkshire Universities AS/ No 1 EFTS (3 Sqn), Church Fenton	
G-BYWR	Grob G.115E Tutor	Bombardier/Cambridge UAS/University of London AS/No 1 EFTS (2 Sqn), Wyton	
G-BYWS	Grob G.115E Tutor	Bombardier/Yorkshire Universities AS/ No 1 EFTS (3 Sqn), Church Fenton	
G-BYWT	Grob G.115E Tutor	Bombardier/Northumbrian Universities AS, Leeming	
G-BYWU	Grob G.115E Tutor	Bombardier/Cambridge UAS/University of London AS/No 1 EFTS (2 Sqn), Wyton	
G-BYWV	Grob G.115E Tutor	Bombardier/Yorkshire Universities AS/ No 1 EFTS (3 Sqn), Church Fenton	
G-BYWW	Grob G.115E Tutor	Bombardier/Southampton UAS, Boscombe Down	
G-BYWX	Grob G.115E Tutor	Bombardier/Bristol UAS, Colerne	
G-BYWY	Grob G.115E Tutor	Bombardier/CFS Tutor Sqn/East Midlands Universities AS/No 1 EFTS (1 Sqn), Cranwell	
G-BYWZ	Grob G.115E Tutor	Bombardier/CFS Tutor Sqn/East Midlands Universities AS/No 1 EFTS (1 Sqn), Cranwell	
G-BYXA	Grob G.115E Tutor	Bombardier/Liverpool UAS/Manchester and Salford Universities AS, Woodvale	
G-BYXB	Grob G.115E Tutor	Bombardier/Southampton UAS, Boscombe Down	
G-BYXC	Grob G.115E Tutor	Bombardier/Oxford UAS, Benson	
G-BYXD	Grob G.115E Tutor	Bombardier/Southampton UAS, Boscombe Down	
G-BYXE	Grob G.115E Tutor	Bombardier/Yorkshire Universities AS/ No 1 EFTS (3 Sqn), Church Fenton	
G-BYXF	Grob G.115E Tutor	Bombardier/Cambridge UAS/University of London AS/No 1 EFTS (2 Sqn), Wyton	
G-BYXG	Grob G.115E Tutor	Bombardier/Cambridge UAS/University of London AS/No 1 EFTS (2 Sqn), Wyton	
G-BYXH	Grob G.115E Tutor	Bombardier/Bristol UAS, Colerne	
G-BYXI	Grob G.115E Tutor	Bombardier/Liverpool UAS/Manchester and Salford Universities AS, Woodvale	
G-BYXJ	Grob G.115E Tutor	Bombardier/Southampton UAS, Boscombe Down	
G-BYXK	Grob G.115E Tutor	Bombardier/RN No 727 Sqn, Yeovilton	
G-BYXL	Grob G.115E Tutor	Bombardier/University of Birmingham AS, Cosford	
G-BYXM	Grob G.115E Tutor	Bombardier/CFS Tutor Sqn/East Midlands Universities AS/No 1 EFTS (1 Sqn), Cranwell	

Notes	Serial	Type (code/other identity)	Owner/operator, location or fate
	G-BYXN	Grob G.115E Tutor	Bombardier/CFS Tutor Sqn/East Midlands Universities AS/No 1 EFTS (1 Sqn), Cranwell
	G-BYXO	Grob G.115E Tutor	Bombardier/University of Birmingham AS, Cosford
	G-BYXP	Grob G.115E Tutor	Bombardier/Cambridge UAS/University of London AS/No 1 EFTS (2 Sqn), Wyton
	G-BYXR	Grob G.115E Tutor	Bombardier/Oxford UAS, Benson
	G-BYXS	Grob G.115E Tutor	Bombardier/RN No 727 Sqn, Yeovilton
	G-BYXT	Grob G.115E Tutor	Bombardier/Cambridge UAS/University of London AS/No 1 EFTS (2 Sqn), Wyton
	G-BYXX	Grob G.115E Tutor	Bombardier/Liverpool UAS/Manchester and Salford Universities AS, Woodvale
	G-BYXY	Grob G.115E Tutor	Bombardier/Cambridge UAS/University of London AS/No 1 EFTS (2 Sqn), Wyton
	G-BYXZ	Grob G.115E Tutor	Bombardier/CFS Tutor Sqn/East Midlands Universities AS/No 1 EFTS (1 Sqn), Cranwell
	G-BYYA	Grob G.115E Tutor	Bombardier/Northumbrian Universities AS, Leeming
	G-BYYB	Grob G.115E Tutor	Bombardier/University of Birmingham AS, Cosford
	G-DOIT	AS.350B-2 Ecureuil	SERCO/DHFS, RAF Shawbury
	G-FFRA	Dassault Falcon 20DC (N902FR)	FR Aviation, Bournemouth
	G-FRAD	Dassault Falcon 20E	FR Aviation, Bournemouth
	G-FRAF	Dassault Falcon 20E (N911FR)	FR Aviation, Bournemouth
	G-FRAH	Dassault Falcon 20DC (N900FR)	FR Aviation, Bournemouth
	G-FRAI	Dassault Falcon 20E (N901FR)	FR Aviation, Durham/Tees Valley
	G-FRAJ	Dassault Falcon 20E (N903FR)	FR Aviation, Durham/Tees Valley
	G-FRAK	Dassault Falcon 20DC (N905FR)	FR Aviation, Bournemouth
	G-FRAL	Dassault Falcon 20DC (N904FR)	FR Aviation, Bournemouth
	G-FRAO	Dassault Falcon 20DC (N906FR)	FR Aviation, Bournemouth
	G-FRAP	Dassault Falcon 20DC (N908FR)	FR Aviation, Bournemouth
	G-FRAR	Dassault Falcon 20DC (N909FR)	FR Aviation, Durham/Tees Valley
	G-FRAS	Dassault Falcon 20C (117501)	FR Aviation, Durham/Tees Valley
	G-FRAT	Dassault Falcon 20C (117502)	FR Aviation, Durham/Tees Valley
	G-FRAU	Dassault Falcon 20C (117504)	FR Aviation, Durham/Tees Valley
	G-FRAW	Dassault Falcon 20ECM (117507)	FR Aviation, Durham/Tees Valley
	G-FRBA	Dassault Falcon 20C	FR Aviation, Bournemouth
	G-RAFO	Beech Super King Air B200	SERCO/RAF No 3 FTS/45 (R) Sqn, Cranwell
	G-RAFP	Beech Super King Air B200	SERCO/RAF No 3 FTS/45 (R) Sqn, Cranwell

Tutor G-BYWL is operated from RAF Cranwell by 1 Squadron, No 1 EFTS.

RAF Maintenance Command/Support Command/Logistics Command 'M' number cross-reference

1764M/K4972
2015M/K5600
2292M/K8203
2361M/K6035
3118M/H5199/(BK892)
3858M/X7688
4354M/BL614
4552M/T5298
5377M/EP120
5405M/LF738
5466M/*BN230*/(LF751)
5690M/MK356
5718M/BM597
5758M/DG202
6457M/ML427
6490M/LA255
6640M/RM694
6850M/TE184
6946M/RW388
6948M/DE673
6960M/MT847
7008M/EE549
7014M/N6720
7015M/NL985
7035M/*K2567*/(DE306)
7060M/VF301
7090M/EE531
7118M/LA198
7119M/LA226
7150M/PK683
7154M/WB188
7174M/VX272
7175M/VV106
7200M/VT812
7241M/TE311/(*MK178*)
7243M/TE462
7245M/RW382
7246M/TD248
7256M/TB752
7257M/TB252
7279M/TB752
7281M/TB252
7288M/PK724
7293M/*TB675*/(RW393)
7323M/VV217
7325M/R5868
7326M/VN485
7362M/475081/(VP546)
7416M/WN907
7421M/WT660
7422M/WT684
7428M/WK198
7432M/WZ724
7438M/*18671*/(WP905)
7443M/WX853
7458M/WX905
7464M/XA564
7470M/XA553
7473M/XE946
7491M/WT569
7496M/WT612
7499M/WT555
7510M/WT694
7525M/WT619
7530M/WT648
7532M/WT651
7533M/WT680
7544M/WN904
7548M/PS915
7556M/WK584
7564M/XE982
7570M/XD674
7582M/WP190
7583M/WP185
7602M/WE600
7605M/WS692
7606M/WV562
7607M/TJ138
7615M/WV679
7616M/WW388
7618M/WW442
7622M/WV606
7631M/VX185
7641M/XA634
7645M/WD293
7648M/XF785
7673M/WV332
7689M/*WW421*/(WW450)
7694M/WV486
7696M/WV493
7698M/WV499
7704M/TW536
7705M/WL505
7706M/WB584
7709M/WT933
7711M/PS915
7712M/WK281
7715M/XK724
7716M/WS776
7718M/WA577
7719M/WK277
7737M/XD602
7741M/VZ477
7750M/*WK864*/(WL168)
7751M/WL131
7755M/WG760
7758M/PM651
7759M/PK664
7761M/XH318
7762M/XE670
7764M/XH318
7770M/*XF506*/(WT746)
7793M/XG523
7796M/WJ676
7798M/XH783
7806M/TA639
7809M/XA699
7816M/WG763
7817M/TX214
7825M/WK991
7827M/XA917
7829M/XH992
7839M/WV781
7841M/WV783
7851M/WZ706
7854M/XM191
7855M/XK416
7859M/XP283
7860M/XL738
7862M/XR246
7863M/*XP248*
7864M/XP244
7865M/TX226
7866M/XH278
7868M/WZ736
7869M/WK935
7872M/*WZ826*/(XD826)
7881M/WD413
7883M/XT150
7891M/XM693
7894M/XD818
7895M/WF784
7898M/XP854
7900M/WA576
7906M/WH132
7917M/WA591
7928M/XE849
7930M/WH301
7931M/RD253
7932M/WZ744
7933M/XR220
7937M/WS843
7938M/XH903
7939M/XD596
7940M/XL764
7955M/XH767
7957M/XF545
7960M/WS726
7961M/WS739
7964M/WS760
7965M/WS792
7967M/WS788
7971M/XK699
7973M/WS807
7976M/XK418
7979M/XM529
7980M/XM561
7982M/XH892
7983M/XD506
7984M/XN597
7986M/WG777
7988M/XL149
7990M/XD452
7997M/XG452
7998M/*XM515*/(XD515)
8005M/WG768
8009M/XG518
8010M/XG547
8012M/VS562
8017M/XL762
8018M/XN344
8019M/WZ869
8021M/XL824
8022M/XN341
8027M/XM555
8032M/XH837
8033M/XD382
8034M/XL703
8041M/XF690
8043M/XF836
8046M/XL770
8049M/WE168
8050M/XG329
8052M/WH166
8054AM/XM410
8054BM/XM417
8055AM/XM402
8055BM/XM404
8056M/XG337
8057M/XR243
8063M/WT536
8070M/EP120
8072M/PK624
8073M/TB252
8075M/RW382
8078M/XM351
8080M/XM480
8081M/XM468
8082M/XM409
8084M/XM369
8086M/TB752
8092M/WK654
8094M/WT520
8097M/XN492
8101M/WH984
8102M/WT486
8103M/WR985
8106M/WR982
8114M/WL798
8117M/WR974
8118M/WZ549
8119M/WR971
8121M/XM474
8124M/WZ572
8128M/WH775
8131M/WT507
8140M/XJ571
8142M/XJ560
8147M/XR526
8151M/WV795
8153M/WV903
8154M/WV908
8155M/WV797
8156M/XE339
8158M/XE369
8160M/XD622
8161M/XE993
8162M/WM913
8164M/*WN105*/(WF299)
8165M/WH791
8169M/WH364
8173M/XN685
8176M/WH791
8177M/*WM311*/(WM224)
8179M/XN928
8183M/*XN972*/(XN962)
8184M/WT520
8186M/WR977
8187M/WH791
8189M/*WD615* (WD646)
8190M/XJ918
8192M/XR658
8198M/WT339
8203M/XD377
8205M/XN819
8206M/WG419
8209M/WG418
8210M/WG471
8211M/WK570
8213M/WK626

RAF Maintenance Command Cross-reference

8215M/WP869
8216M/WP927
8229M/XM355
8230M/XM362
8234M/XN458
8235M/XN549
8236M/XP573
8237M/XS179
8238M/XS180
8344M/WH960
8350M/WH840
8352M/XN632
8355M/KN645
8357M/WK576
8359M/WF825
8361M/WB670
8362M/WG477
8364M/WG464
8365M/XK421
8366M/XG454
8367M/XG474
8368M/XF926
8369M/WE139
8370M/N1671
8371M/XA847
8372M/K8042
8373M/P2617
8375M/NX611
8376M/RF398
8377M/R9125
8378M/*T9707*
8379M/DG590
8380M/Z7197
8382M/VR930
8383M/K9942
8384M/X4590
8385M/N5912
8386M/NV778
8387M/T6296
8388M/XL993
8389M/VX573
8392M/SL674
8394M/WG422
8395M/WF408
8396M/XK740
8399M/WR539
8401M/XP686
8406M/XP831
8407M/XP585
8408M/XS186
8409M/XS209
8410M/XR662
8413M/XM192
8414M/XM173
8417M/XM144
8422M/XM169
8427M/XM172
8429M/XH592
8434M/XM411
8436M/XN554
8437M/WG362
8439M/WZ846
8440M/WD935
8442M/XP411
8453M/XP745
8458M/XP672
8459M/XR650
8460M/XP680
8462M/XX477
8463M/XP355
8464M/XJ758
8465M/W1048
8466M/L-866
8467M/WP912
8468M/MM5701/(BT474)
8470M/584219
8471M/701152
8472M/120227/(VN679)
8473M/WP190
8474M/494083
8475M/360043/(PJ876)
8476M/24
8477M/4101/(DG200)
8478M/10639
8479M/730301
8481M/191614
8482M/112372/(VK893)
8483M/420430
8484M/5439
8485M/997
8486M/BAPC 99
8487M/J-1172
8488M/WL627
8491M/WJ880
8493M/XR571
8494M/XP557
8495M/XR672
8501M/XP640
8502M/XP686
8508M/XS218
8509M/XT141
8514M/XS176
8535M/XN776
8538M/XN781
8545M/XN726
8546M/XN728
8548M/WT507
8549M/WT534
8554M/TG511
8561M/XS100
8563M/*XX822*/(XW563)
8565M/*WT720*/(E-408)
8566M/XV279
8570M/XR954
8573M/XM708
8575M/XP542
8576M/XP502
8578M/XR534
8582M/XE874
8583M/BAPC 94
8585M/XE670
8586M/XE643
8588M/XR681
8589M/XR700
8590M/XM191
8591M/XA813
8595M/XH278
8598M/WP270
8600M/XX761
8602M/*PF179*/(XR541)
8604M/XS104
8606M/XP530
8608M/XP540
8610M/XL502
8611M/WF128
8618M/*XS111*/(XP504)
8620M/XP534
8621M/XR538
8624M/*XR991*/(XS102)
8627M/XP558
8628M/XJ380
8630M/WG362
8631M/XR574
8633M/3W-17/MK732
8634M/WP314
8640M/XR977
8642M/XR537
8645M/XD163
8648M/XK526
8653M/XS120
8655M/XN126
8656M/XP405
8657M/VZ634
8661M/XJ727
8662M/XR458
8666M/XE793
8668M/WJ821
8671M/XJ435
8672M/XP351
8673M/XD165
8676M/XL577
8679M/XF526
8680M/XF527
8681M/XG164
8682M/XP404
8693M/WH863
8696M/WH773
8702M/XG196
8703M/VW453
8706M/XF383
8708M/XF509
8709M/XG209
8710M/XG274
8711M/XG290
8713M/XG225
8718M/XX396
8719M/XT257
8722M/WJ640
8724M/XW923
8726M/XP299
8727M/XR486
8728M/WT532
8729M/WJ815
8733M/XL318
8736M/XF375
8739M/XH170
8740M/WE173
8741M/XW329
8743M/WD790
8746M/XH171
8749M/XH537
8751M/XT255
8753M/WL795
8762M/WH740
8764M/XP344
8768M/A-522
8769M/A-528
8770M/XL623
8771M/XM602
8772M/WR960
8777M/XX914
8778M/XM598
8779M/XM607
8780M/WK102
8781M/WE982
8782M/XH136
8783M/XW272
8785M/XS642
8789M/XK970
8792M/XP345
8793M/XP346
8794M/XP398
8796M/XK943
8797M/XX947
8799M/WV787
8800M/XG226
8807M/XL587
8810M/XJ825
8816M/XX734
8818M/XK527
8820M/VP952
8821M/XX115
8822M/VP957
8828M/XS587
8830M/XF515
8831M/XG160
8832M/*XG168*/(XG172)
8833M/XL569
8834M/*XL571*
8836M/XL592
8838M/*34037*/(429356)
8839M/*69*/(XG194)
8840M/XG252
8841M/XE606
8848M/XZ135
8852M/XV337
8853M/XT277
8855M/XT284
8857M/XW544
8858M/XW541
8863M/XG154
8867M/XK532
8868M/WH775
8869M/WH957
8870M/WH964
8871M/WJ565
8873M/XR453
8874M/XE597
8875M/XE624
8876M/*VM791*/(XA312)
8880M/XF435
8881M/XG254
8883M/XX946
8884M/VX275
8885M/XW922
8886M/XA243
8888M/XA231
8889M/XN239
8890M/WT532
8892M/XL618
8895M/XX746
8896M/XX821
8897M/XX969
8898M/XX119
8899M/XX756
8900M/XZ368
8901M/XZ383
8902M/XX739
8903M/XX747
8904M/XX966
8905M/XX975
8906M/XX976
8907M/XZ371
8908M/XZ382
8909M/XV784
8910M/XL160
8911M/XH673
8918M/XX109
8919M/XT486
8920M/XT469
8921M/XT466
8922M/XT467
8923M/XX819
8924M/XP701
8925M/XP706
8931M/XV779
8932M/XR718
8934M/XR749
8935M/XR713
8937M/XX751
8938M/WV746
8941M/XT456

8942M/XN185
8943M/XE799
8944M/WZ791
8945M/XX818
8946M/XZ389
8947M/XX726
8948M/XX757
8949M/XX743
8950M/XX956
8951M/XX727
8952M/XX730
8953M/XX959
8954M/XZ384
8955M/XX110
8957M/XN582
8961M/XS925
8967M/XV263
8969M/XR753
8972M/XR754
8973M/XS922
8974M/XM473
8975M/XW917
8976M/XZ630
8978M/XX837
8983M/XM478
8984M/XN551
8985M/WK127
8986M/XV261
8987M/XM358
8990M/XM419
8995M/XM425
8996M/XM414
8998M/XT864
9002M/XW763
9003M/XZ390
9004M/XZ370
9005M/XZ374
9006M/XX967
9007M/XX968
9008M/XX140
9009M/XX763
9010M/XX764
9011M/XM412
9012M/XN494
9014M/XN584
9015M/XW320
9017M/ZE449
9019M/XX824
9020M/XX825
9021M/XX826
9022M/XX958
9026M/XP629
9027M/XP556
9028M/XP563
9032M/XR673
9033M/XS181
9036M/XM350
9038M/XV810
9039M/XN586
9040M/XZ138
9041M/XW763
9042M/XL954
9044M/XS177
9046M/XM349
9047M/XW409
9048M/XM403
9049M/XW404
9052M/WJ717
9055M/XT770
9056M/XS488
9059M/ZE360
9066M/XV582
9067M/XV586
9070M/XV581
9072M/XW768
9073M/XW924
9075M/XV752
9076M/XV808
9078M/XV753
9079M/XZ130
9080M/ZE350
9086M/ZE352
9087M/XX753
9090M/XW353
9091M/XW434
9092M/XH669
9093M/WK124
9095M/XW547
9096M/WV322
9098M/XV406
9103M/XV411
9110M/XX736
9111M/XW421
9115M/XV863
9117M/XV161
9118M/XV253
9119M/XW303
9120M/XW419
9122M/XZ997
9123M/XT773
9125M/XW410
9127M/XW432
9130M/XW327
9131M/*DD931*
9132M/XX977
9133M/*413573*
9134M/XT288
9136M/XT891
9137M/XN579
9139M/XV863
9140M/XZ287
9141M/XV118
9143M/XN589
9145M/XV863
9146M/XW299
9147M/XW301
9148M/XW436
9149M/XW375
9150M/*FX760*
9151M/XT907
9152M/XV424
9153M/XW360
9154M/XW321
9155M/WL679
9162M/XZ991
9163M/XV415
9166M/XW323
9167M/XV744
9168M/XZ132
9169M/XW547
9170M/XZ994
9172M/XW304
9173M/XW418
9174M/XZ131
9175M/P1344
9176M/XW430
9177M/XW328
9179M/XW309
9180M/XW311
9181M/XW358
9185M/XZ987
9187M/XW405
9188M/XW364
9190M/XW318
9191M/XW416
9192M/XW361
9193M/XW367
9194M/XW420
9195M/XW330
9196M/XW370
9197M/*XX530*/(XX637)
9199M/XW290
9200M/XW425
9201M/ZD667
9203M/*3066*
9205M/*E449*
9206M/F6314
9207M/8417/18
9208M/F938
9210M/MF628
9211M/733682
9212M/*KL216*/
(45-49295)
9213M/N5182
9215M/XL164
9216M/XL190
9218M/XL563
9219M/XZ971
9220M/XZ995
9221M/XZ966
9222M/XZ968
9224M/XL568
9225M/XX885
9226M/XV865
9227M/XB812
9229M/ZA678
9230M/ZA676
9233M/XZ431
9234M/XV864
9236M/WV318
9237M/XF445
9238M/ZA717
9239M/7198/18
9241M/XS639
9242M/XH672
9246M/XS714
9248M/WB627
9249M/WV396
9251M/XX744
9252M/XX722
9253M/ZA254
9254M/XX965
9255M/XZ375
9257M/XX962
9258M/XW265
9259M/XS710
9260M/XS734
9261M/*W2068*
9262M/XZ358
9263M/XW267
9264M/XS735
9265M/WK585
9266M/XZ119
9267M/XW269
9268M/XR529
9269M/XT914
9270M/XZ145
9272M/XS486
9273M/XS726
9274M/XS738
9275M/XS729
9276M/XS733
9277M/XT601
9278M/XS643
9279M/XT681
9280M/XV804
9281M/XZ146
9282M/XZ101
9283M/XZ322
9284M/ZA267
9285M/XR806
9286M/XT905
9287M/WP962
9288M/XX520
9289M/XX665
9290M/XX626
9292M/XW892
9293M/XX830
9295M/XV497
9297M/XX141
9298M/ZE340
9299M/XW870
9300M/XX431
9301M/XZ941
9302M/ZD462
9303M/XV709
9305M/XZ942
9306M/XX979
9308M/ZD932
9310M/ZA355
9311M/ZA475
9312M/ZA474
9314M/ZA320
9315M/ZA319
9316M/ZA399
9317M/ZA450
9318M/ZA360
9319M/XR516
9320M/XX153
9321M/XZ367
9322M/ZB686
9323M/XV643
9324M/XV659
9326M/XV653
9328M/ZD607
9329M/ZD578
9330M/ZB684
9331M/XW852
9332M/XZ935
9334M/ZA322
9335M/ZA375
9336M/ZA407
9337M/ZA774
9338M/ZA325
9339M/ZA323
9340M/XX745
9341M/ZA357
9342M/XR498
9343M/XR506
9344M/XV706

RN Landing Platform and Shore Station Code-letters

Code	Deck Letters	Vessel Name & Pennant No	Vessel Type & Unit
—	AB	HMS *Albion* (L14)	Assault
—	AS	RFA *Argus* (A135)	Aviation Training ship
365/6	AY	HMS *Argyll* (F231)	Type 23 (815 Sqn)
—	BD	RFA *Sir Bedivere* (L3004)	Landing ship
—	BV	RFA *Black Rover* (A273)	Fleet tanker
350/1	CL	HMS *Cumberland* (F85)	Type 22 (815 Sqn)
348	CM	HMS *Chatham* (F87)	Type 22 (815 Sqn)
338	CT	HMS *Campbeltown* (F86)	Type 22 (815 Sqn)
—	CU	RNAS Culdrose (HMS *Seahawk*)	
412/3	CW	HMS *Cornwall* (F99)	Type 22 (815 Sqn)
—	DC	HMS *Dumbarton Castle* (P265)	Fishery protection
—	DG	RFA *Diligence* (A132)	Maintenance
411	EB	HMS *Edinburgh* (D97)	Type 42 (815 Sqn)
434/5	EE	HMS *Endurance* (A171)	Ice Patrol (815 Sqn)
420	EX	HMS *Exeter* (D89)	Type 42 (815 Sqn)
—	FA	RFA *Fort Austin* (A386)	Support ship
—	FE	RFA *Fort Rosalie* (A385)	Support ship
—	FL	DARA Fleetlands	
410	GC	HMS *Gloucester* (D96)	Type 42 (815 Sqn)
—	GD	RFA *Sir Galahad* (L3005)	Landing ship
—	GV	RFA *Gold Rover* (A271)	Fleet tanker
404	IR	HMS *Iron Duke* (F234)	Type 23 (815 Sqn)
425	KT	HMS *Kent* (F78)	Type 23 (815 Sqn)
—	L	HMS *Illustrious* (R06)	Carrier
457	LA	HMS *Lancaster* (F229)	Type 23 (829 Sqn)
—	LC	HMS *Leeds Castle* (P258)	Fishery protection
332	LP	HMS *Liverpool* (D92)	Type 42 (815 Sqn)
360	MC	HMS *Manchester* (D95)	Type 42 (815 Sqn)
415	MM	HMS *Monmouth* (F235)	Type 23 (829 Sqn)
444	MR	HMS *Montrose* (F236)	Type 23 (815 Sqn)
—	N	HMS *Invincible* (R05)	Carrier
372	NL	HMS *Northumberland* (F238)	Type 23 (829 Sqn)
417	NM	HMS *Nottingham* (D91)	Type 42 (815 Sqn)
—	O	HMS *Ocean* (L12)	Helicopter carrier
426	PD	HMS *Portland* (F79)	Type 23 (815 Sqn)
—	PV	RFA *Sir Percivale* (L3036)	Landing ship
—	R	HMS *Ark Royal* (R07)	Carrier
474	RM	HMS *Richmond* (F239)	Type 23 (815 Sqn)
427	SB	HMS *St Albans* (F83)	Type 23 (815 Sqn)
375	SM	HMS *Somerset* (F82)	Type 23 (815 Sqn)
334	SN	HMS *Southampton* (D90)	Type 42 (815 Sqn)
422	SU	HMS *Sutherland* (F81)	Type 23 (815 Sqn)
—	TM	RFA *Sir Tristram* (L3505)	Landing ship
—	VL	RNAS Yeovilton (HMS *Heron*)	
462	WM	HMS *Westminster* (F237)	Type 23 (829 Sqn)
407	YK	HMS *York* (D98)	Type 42 (815 Sqn)
—	—	HMS *Bulwark* (L15)	Assault
	—	HMS *Daring*	Type 45
	—	HMS *Dauntless*	Type 45
	—	HMS *Diamond*	Type 45
	—	RFA *Cardigan Bay* (L3009)	Landing ship
—	—	RFA *Fort Victoria* (A387)	Auxiliary Oiler
—	—	RFA *Fort George* (A388)	Auxiliary Oiler
	—	RFA *Largs Bay* (L3006)	Landing ship
	—	RFA *Lyme Bay* (L3007)	Landing ship
	—	RFA *Mounts Bay* (L3008)	Landing ship
	—	RFA *Wave Knight* (A389)	Fleet tanker
—	—	RFA *Wave Ruler* (A390)	Fleet tanker

Ships' Numeric Code – Deck Letters Analysis

	0	1	2	3	4	5	6	7	8	9
33			LP		SN				CT	
34									CM	
35	CL	CL								
36	MC					AY	AY			
37			NL			SM				
38										
40					IR			YK		
41	GC	EB	CW	CW		MM		NM		
42	EX	SU			KT	PD	SB			
43					EE	EE				
44					MR					
45								LA		
46			WM							
47					RM					

Note that some of these codes are no longer being worn as Lynx acquire markings of the Flight that operates them instead.

RN Code – Squadron – Base – Aircraft Cross-check

Deck/Base Code Numbers	*Letters*	*Unit*	*Location*	*Aircraft Type(s)*
010 — 020	CU	820 Sqn	Culdrose	Merlin HM1
180 — 190	CU	849 Sqn	Culdrose	Sea King ASaC7
180 — 190	CU	854 Sqn	Culdrose	Sea King ASaC7
180 — 190	CU	857 Sqn	Culdrose	Sea King ASaC7
200 — 228	*	815 Sqn	Yeovilton	Lynx HAS3/HMA8
264 — 274	R	814 Sqn	Culdrose	Merlin HM1
300 — 308	VL	815 Sqn	Yeovilton	Lynx HAS3/HMA8
318 — 319	VL	815 Sqn OEU	Yeovilton	Lynx HMA8
332 — 479	*	815 Sqn	Yeovilton	Lynx HAS3/HMA8
500 — 515	CU	829 Sqn	Culdrose	Merlin HM1
535 — 541	CU	700M OEU	Culdrose	Merlin HM1
560 — 573	CU	750 Sqn	Culdrose	Jetstream T2
576 — 579	-	FONA	Yeovilton	Jetstream T3
580 — 585	CU	824 Sqn	Culdrose	Merlin HM1
630 — 648	VL	702 Sqn	Yeovilton	Lynx HAS3
670 — 676	VL	702 Sqn	Yeovilton	Lynx HMA8
820 — 831	CU	771 Sqn	Culdrose	Sea King HU5/HAS6

*See foregoing separate ships' Deck Letters Analysis
Note that only the 'last two' digits of the Code are worn by some aircraft types, especially helicopters.

Royal Air Force Squadron Markings

This table gives brief details of the markings worn by aircraft of RAF squadrons at the beginning of 2008. While this may help to identify the operator of a particular machine, it may not always give the true picture. For example, from time to time aircraft are loaned to other units while others (such as those with No 4 FTS at Valley) wear squadron marks but are actually operated on a pool basis. Squadron badges are usually located on the front fuselage.

Squadron	*Type(s) operated*	*Base(s)*	*Distinguishing marks & other comments*
No 1 Sqn	Harrier GR7A/GR9/GR9A/T10	RAF Cottesmore	Badge: A red & white winged number 1 on a white diamond. Tail fin has a red stripe with the badge repeated on it.
No 2 Sqn	Tornado GR4/GR4A	RAF Marham	Badge: A wake knot on a white circular background flanked on either side by black and white triangles. Tail fin has a black stripe with white triangles and the badge repeated on it.
No 3 Sqn	Typhoon T1A/F2	RAF Coningsby	Badge: A blue cockatrice on a white circular background flanked by two green bars edged with yellow. Tail fin has a green stripe edged with yellow. Aircraft are coded QO-*
No 4 Sqn	Harrier GR7A/GR9/T10	RAF Cottesmore	Badge: A yellow lightning flash inside a red and black circle flanked by bars on either side repeating this design. Tail fin has a yellow lightning flash on a red and black stripe.
No 5 Sqn	Sentinel R1	RAF Waddington	Badge (on tail): A green maple leaf on a white circle over a red horizontal band.
No 7 Sqn	Chinook HC2/ Gazelle AH1	RAF Odiham	Badge (on tail): A blue badge containing the seven stars of Ursa Major ('The Plough') in yellow. Aircraft pooled with No 18 Sqn and No 27 Sqn.
No 8 Sqn	Sentry AEW1	RAF Waddington	Badge (on tail): A grey, sheathed, Arabian dagger. Aircraft pooled with No 23 Sqn and No 54(R) Sqn.
No 9 Sqn	Tornado GR4	RAF Marham	Badge: A green bat on a black circular background, flanked by yellow and green horizontal stripes. The green bat also appears on the tail, edged in yellow.
No 11 Sqn	Typhoon T1A/F2/T3/FGR4	RAF Coningsby	Badge (on tail): Two eagles in flight on a white shield. The roundel is flanked by yellow and black triangles. Aircraft are coded D*
No 12 Sqn	Tornado GR4	RAF Lossiemouth	Roundel is superimposed on a green chevron. Tail fin has a black & white horizontal stripe with the squadron badge, a fox's head on a white circle, in the middle.
No 13 Sqn	Tornado GR4/GR4A	RAF Marham	A yellow lightning flash on a green and blue background on the nose. Badge (on tail): A lynx's head over a dagger on a white shield.
No 14 Sqn	Tornado GR4	RAF Lossiemouth	Badge: A red cross on a white circle, with wings either side, flanked by blue diamonds on a white background. The blue diamonds are repeated horizontally across the tail.

Squadron	*Type(s) operated*	*Base(s)*	*Distinguishing marks & other comments*
No 15(R) Sqn [NTOCU]	Tornado GR4	RAF Lossiemouth	Roman numerals XV appear in white on the tail.
No 17(R) Sqn	Typhoon T1A/F2/T3/FGR4	Coningsby	Badge (on tail): A gauntlet on a black and white shield. Roundel is flanked by two white bars which have a pair of jagged black lines running along them horizontally. Aircraft are coded A*.
No 18 Sqn	Chinook HC2	RAF Odiham	Badge (on tail): A red winged horse on a black circle. Aircraft pooled with No 7 Sqn and No 27 Sqn.
No 19(R) Sqn	Hawk T1/T1A/T1W	RAF Valley	Badge (on tail): A fish flanked by two wings on a yellow circle. Aircraft also carry black and white checks either side of the roundel on the fuselage. Aircraft pooled with No 208(R) Sqn; part of No 4 FTS.
No 20(R) Sqn [HOCU]	Harrier GR7A/GR9/T10	RAF Wittering	Badge: An eagle in a white circle flanked by a white stripe on a blue background. On the tail is a stripe made up of black, yellow, green and red triangles.
No 22 Sqn	Sea King HAR3/HAR3A	A Flt: RMB Chivenor B Flt: Wattisham C Flt: RAF Valley	Badge: A black pi symbol in front of a white Maltese cross on a red circle.
No 23 Sqn	Sentry AEW1	RAF Waddington	Badge (on tail): A red eagle preying on a yellow falcon. Aircraft pooled with No 8 Sqn and No 54(R) Sqn.
No 24 Sqn	Hercules C1/C3/C4/C5	RAF Lyneham	No squadron markings carried. Aircraft pooled with No 30 Sqn, No 47 Sqn and No 70 Sqn.
No 25 Sqn	Tornado F3	RAF Leeming	Badge (on tail): A hawk on a gauntlet. Aircraft are coded F*.
No 27 Sqn	Chinook HC2	RAF Odiham	Badge (on tail): An dark green elephant on a green circle, flanked by green and dark green stripes. Aircraft pooled with No 7 Sqn and No 18 Sqn.
No 28 Sqn	Merlin HC3/HC3A	RAF Benson	Badge: A winged horse above two white crosses on a red shield.
No 29(R) Sqn [TOCU]	Typhoon T1A/F2	Coningsby	Badge (on tail): An eagle in flight, preying on a buzzard, with three red Xs across the top. The roundel is flanked by two white bars outlined by a red line, each containing three red Xs. Aircraft are coded B*.
No 30 Sqn	Hercules C1/C3/C4/C5	RAF Lyneham	No squadron markings carried. Aircraft pooled with No 24 Sqn, No 47 Sqn, No 57(R) Sqn and No 70 Sqn.
No 31 Sqn	Tornado GR4	RAF Marham	Badge: A gold, five-pointed star on a yellow circle flanked by yellow and green checks. The star is repeated on the tail.
No 32 (The Royal) Sqn	BAe 125 CC3/146 CC2/ Agusta 109	RAF Northolt	No squadron markings carried but aircraft carry a distinctive livery with a blue flash along the middle of the fuselage and a red tail.
No 33 Sqn	Puma HC1	RAF Benson	Badge: A stag's head.

RAF Squadron Markings

Squadron	*Type(s) operated*	*Base(s)*	*Distinguishing marks & other comments*
No 39 Sqn	Predator/ Reaper	Nellis AFB Creech AFB	No markings worn
No 41(R) Sqn [FJWOEU]	Harrier GR7/GR7A/GR9/ Tornado F3/GR4	RAF Coningsby	Badge: A red, double armed cross, flanked by red and white horizontal stripes. Stripes repeated on tail.
No 42(R) Sqn [NOCU]	Nimrod MR2	RAF Kinloss	No squadron markings usually carried. Aircraft pooled with No 120 Sqn, No 201 Sqn and No 206 Sqn.
No 43 Sqn	Tornado F3	RAF Leuchars	Badge (on tail): A black and red gamecock in a band of black and white squares.
No 45(R) Sqn	Raytheon Beech Super King Air 200	RAF Cranwell	Aircraft carry a dark blue stripe on the tail superimposed with red diamonds. Part of No 3 FTS.
No 47 Sqn	Hercules C1/C3/C4/C5	RAF Lyneham	No squadron markings usually carried. Aircraft pooled with No 24 Sqn, 30 Sqn and No 70 Sqn.
No 51 Sqn	Nimrod R1	RAF Waddington	Badge (on tail): A red goose in flight.
No 54(R) Sqn [ISTAR OCU]	Sentry AEW1/Nimrod R1	RAF Waddington	Based aircraft as required.
No 55(R) Sqn	Dominie T1	RAF Cranwell	Badge (on tail): A blue fist holding an arrow on a white circle. Part of No 3 FTS.
No 56(R) Sqn [F3OCU]	Tornado F3	RAF Leuchars	Badge (on tail): A gold phoenix rising from red flames. The tail fin has a stripe made up of red and white checks.
No 60(R) Sqn	Griffin HT1	RAF Shawbury [DHFS] & RAF Valley [SARTU]	No squadron markings usually carried.
No 70 Sqn	Hercules C1/C3/C4/C5	RAF Lyneham	No squadron markings usually carried. Aircraft pooled with No 24 Sqn, No 30 Sqn and No 47 Sqn.
No 72(R) Sqn	Tucano T1	RAF Linton-on-Ouse	Badge: A black swift in flight on a red disk, flanked by blue bars edged with red. The blue bars edged with red also flank the roundel on the fuselage; part of No 1 FTS.
No 76(R) Sqn	Tucano T1	RAF Linton-on-Ouse	Badge (on tail): A black lion on a white square. Aircraft are coded MP-*; part of No 1 FTS.
No 78 Sqn	Merlin HC3A	RAF Benson	Badge: A yellow, heraldic tiger with two tails, on a black circle.
No 84 Sqn	Griffin HAR2	RAF Akrotiri	Badge (on tail): A scorpion on a playing card symbol (diamonds, clubs etc). Aircraft carry a vertical light blue stripe through the roundel on the fuselage.
No 99 Sqn	Globemaster III	RAF Brize Norton	Badge (on tail): A black puma leaping.
No 100 Sqn	Hawk T1/T1A	RAF Leeming	Badge (on tail): A skull in front of two bones crossed. Aircraft are usually coded C*. Incorporates the Joint Forward Air Control Training and Standards Unit (JFACTSU)
No 101 Sqn	VC10 C1K/K3/K4	RAF Brize Norton	Badge (on tail): A lion behind a castle turret.

Squadron	*Type(s) operated*	*Base(s)*	*Distinguishing marks & other comments*
No 111 Sqn	Tornado F3	RAF Leuchars	Badge (on tail): A cross in front of crossed swords on a light grey circle, flanked by a stripe of darker grey.
No 120 Sqn	Nimrod MR2	RAF Kinloss	No squadron markings usually carried. Aircraft pooled with No 42(R) Sqn, No 201 Sqn and No 206 Sqn.
No 201 Sqn	Nimrod MR2	RAF Kinloss	No squadron markings usually carried. Aircraft pooled with No 42(R) Sqn, No 120 Sqn and No 206 Sqn.
No 202 Sqn	Sea King HAR3	A Flt: RAF Boulmer D Flt: RAF Lossiemouth E Flt: RAF Leconfield	Badge: A mallard alighting on a white circle.
No 203(R) Sqn	Sea King HAR3	RAF St Mawgan	Badge: A green sea horse on a white circle.
No 207(R) Sqn	Tucano T1	RAF Linton-on-Ouse	Badge: A red winged lion on a white disk. The roundel on the fuselage is flanked by red bars edged with yellow; part of No 1 FTS
No 208(R) Sqn	Hawk T1/T1A/T1W	RAF Valley	Badge (on tail): A Sphinx inside a white circle, flanked by flashes of yellow. Aircraft also carry blue and yellow bars either side of the roundel on the fuselage and a blue and yellow chevron on the nose. Aircraft pooled with No 19(R) Sqn; part of No 4 FTS.
No 216 Sqn	TriStar K1/KC1/C2/C2A	RAF Brize Norton	Badge (on tail): An eagle in flight with a bomb in its claws.
No 230 Sqn	Puma HC1	RAF Aldergrove	Badge: A tiger in front of a palm tree on a black pentagon.
No 617 Sqn	Tornado GR4	RAF Lossiemouth	Badge: Dam breached, flanked on either side by red lightning flashes on a black background. Tail fin is black with a red lightning flash.
No 1310 Flt	Chinook HC2	Basrah, Iraq	No markings carried. Part of Joint Helicopter Force (Iraq).
No 1312 Flt	VC10 K3/K4 (101 Sqn) Hercules (LTW)	RAF Mount Pleasant	Badge (on tail): A red Maltese cross on a white circle, flanked by red and white horizontal bars.
No 1419 Flt	Merlin HC3	Basrah, Iraq	No markings carried. Part of Joint Helicopter Force (Iraq).
No 1435 Flt	Tornado F3	RAF Mount Pleasant	Badge (on tail): A red Maltese cross on a white circle, flanked by red and white horizontal bars.
No 1563 Flt	Puma HC1	Basrah, Iraq	No markings carried. Part of Joint Helicopter Force (Iraq).
No 1564 Flt	Chinook HC2/ Sea King HAR3	RAF Mount Pleasant	No markings known.

University Air Squadrons/ Air Experience Flights*

All 14 UASs and their embedded AEFs are now part of No 1 Elementary Flying School and carry its crest on the tail. The No 1 EFTS crest consists of a Tiger Moth above a chrysalis, surrounded by a blue circle, topped with a red crown with the motto 'Ab Initio' beneath. Changes in April 2006 led to the creation of three new elementary flying training squadrons as part of No 1 EFTS and these share aircraft in a pool with other units at the same location.

UAS aircraft carry squadron badges and markings, usually on the tail. Squadron crests all consist of a white circle surrounded by a blue circle, topped with a red crown and having a yellow scroll beneath. Each differs by the motto on the scroll, the UAS name running around the blue circle & by the contents at the centre and it is the latter which are described below. All AEFs come under the administration of local UASs and these are listed here.

UAS	*Base*	*Marks*
Bristol UAS/ No 3 AEF	Colerne	A sailing ship on water.
Cambridge UAS/ No 5 AEF	RAF Wyton	A heraldic lion in front of a red badge. Aircraft pooled with University of London AS and No 1 EFTS (2 Sqn)
East Midlands Universities AS/ No 7 AEF	RAF Cranwell	A yellow quiver, full of arrows. Aircraft pooled with CFS Tutor Sqn and No 1 EFTS (1 Sqn)
East of Scotland UAS/ No 12 AEF	RAF Leuchars	An open book in front of a white diagonal cross edged in blue.
Liverpool UAS	RAF Woodvale	A bird atop an open book, holding a branch in its beak. Aircraft pooled with Manchester and Salford Universities AS
Manchester and Salford Universities AS/ No 10 AEF	RAF Woodvale	A bird of prey with a green snake in its beak. Aircraft pooled with Liverpool UAS
Northumbrian Universities AS/ No 11 AEF	RAF Leeming	A white cross on a blue background.
Oxford UAS/ No 6 AEF	RAF Benson	An open book in front of crossed swords.
Southampton UAS/ No 2 AEF	Boscombe Down	A red stag in front of a stone pillar.
Universities of Glasgow and Strathclyde AS/No 4 AEF	Glasgow	A bird of prey in flight, holding a branch in its beak, in front of an upright sword.
University of Birmingham AS/ No 8 AEF	DCAE Cosford	A blue griffon with two heads.
University of London AS	RAF Wyton	A globe superimposed over an open book. Aircraft pooled with Cambridge UAS and No 1 EFTS (2 Sqn)
University of Wales AS/ No 1 AEF	MoD St Athan	A red Welsh dragon in front of an open book,clasping a sword. Some aircraft have the dragon in front of white and green squares.
Yorkshire Universities AS/ No 9 AEF	RAF Church Fenton	An open book in front of a Yorkshire rose with leaves. Aircraft pooled with No 1 EFTS (3 Sqn)

Fleet Air Arm Squadron Markings

This table gives brief details of the markings worn by aircraft of FAA squadrons. Squadron badges, when worn, are usually located on the front fuselage. All FAA squadron badges comprise a crown atop a circle edged in gold braid and so the badge details below list only what appears in the circular part.

Squadron	*Type(s) operated*	*Base(s)*	*Distinguishing marks & other comments*
No 700M OEU	Merlin HM1	RNAS Culdrose	Badge: A pair of gold scales on a background of blue and white waves, flanked by two bees.
No 702 Sqn	Lynx HAS3/HMA8	RNAS Yeovilton	Badge: A Lynx rearing up in front of a circle comprising alternate dark blue and white sectors.
No 727 Sqn	Heron	RNAS Yeovilton	Badge: The head of Britannia wearing a gold helmet on a background of blue and white waves.
No 750 Sqn	Jetstream T2	RNAS Culdrose	Badge: A Greek runner bearing a torch & sword on a background of blue and white waves.
No 771 Sqn	Sea King HU5/HAS6	RNAS Culdrose & Prestwick	Badge: Three bees on a background of blue and white waves.
No 792 Sqn	Mirach	RNAS Culdrose	Badge: (Not worn) A panther's head on a gold background.
No 800 Sqn	Harrier GR7A/GR9/T10	RAF Cottesmore	Badge (on engine intakes): A trident and crossed swords on a red circle, flanked by red triangles. Aircraft carry a red triangle on the tail.
No 814 Sqn	Merlin HM1	RNAS Culdrose	Badge: A winged tiger mask on a background of dark blue and white waves.
No 815 Sqn	Lynx HAS3/HMA8	RNAS Yeovilton	Badge: A winged, gold harpoon on a background of blue and white waves.
No 820 Sqn	Merlin HM1	RNAS Culdrose	Badge: A flying fish on a background of blue and white waves.
No 824 Sqn	Merlin HM1	RNAS Culdrose	Badge: A heron on a background of blue and white waves.
No 829 Sqn	Merlin HM1	RNAS Culdrose	Badge: A kingfisher hovering on a background of blue and white waves.
No 845 Sqn	Sea King HC4	RNAS Yeovilton	Badge: A dragonfly on a background of blue and white waves.
No 846 Sqn	Sea King HC4	RNAS Yeovilton	Badge: A swordsman riding a winged horse whilst attacking a serpent on a background of blue and white waves. Aircraft are usually coded V*.
No 847 Sqn	Gazelle AH1 & Lynx AH7	RNAS Yeovilton	Badge: A gold sea lion on a blue background.
No 848 Sqn	Sea King HC4	RNAS Yeovilton	Badge: Inside a red circle, a hawk in flight with a torpedo in its claws above white and blue waves. Aircraft are usually coded W*.
No 849 Sqn	Sea King ASaC7	RNAS Culdrose	Badge: A winged streak of lightning with an eye in front on a background of blue and white waves.
No 854 Sqn	Sea King ASaC7	RNAS Culdrose	Badge: A winged lion in front of a sword.
No 857 Sqn	Sea King ASaC7	RNAS Culdrose	Badge: A hand emerging from the waves, clutching a sword aloft.

Historic Aircraft in Overseas Markings

Some *historic, classic and warbird* aircraft carry the markings of overseas air arms and can be seen in the UK, mainly preserved in museums and collections or taking part in air shows.

Notes	*Serial*	*Type (code/other identity)*	*Owner/operator, location or fate*
	ARGENTINA		
	-	Bell UH-1H Iroquois (AE-406/*998-8888*) [Z]	RAF Valley, instructional use
	0729	Beech T-34C Turbo Mentor	FAA Museum, stored RNAS Yeovilton
	0767	Aermacchi MB339AA	Rolls-Royce Heritage Trust, stored Derby
	A-515	FMA IA58 Pucara (ZD485)	RAF Museum, Cosford
	A-517	FMA IA58 Pucara (G-BLRP)	Privately owned, Channel Islands
	A-522	FMA IA58 Pucara (8768M)	FAA Museum, at NE Aircraft Museum, Usworth
	A-528	FMA IA58 Pucara (8769M)	Norfolk & Suffolk Avn Museum, Flixton
	A-533	FMA IA58 Pucara (ZD486) <ff>	Privately owned, Cheltenham
	A-549	FMA IA58 Pucara (ZD487)	Imperial War Museum, Duxford
	AE-409	Bell UH-1H Iroquois [656]	Museum of Army Flying, Middle Wallop
	AE-422	Bell UH-1H Iroquois	FAA Museum, stored RNAS Yeovilton
	AUSTRALIA		
	A2-4	Supermarine Seagull V (VH-ALB)	RAF Museum, Hendon
	A16-199	Lockheed Hudson IIIA (G-BEOX) [SF-R]	RAF Museum, Hendon
	A17-48	DH82A Tiger Moth (G-BPHR)	Privately owned, Wanborough, Wilts
	A19-144	Bristol 156 Beaufighter XIc (JM135/A8-324)	The Fighter Collection, Duxford
	A79-808	DH115 Vampire T33	De Havilland Aviation, Swansea
	A92-255	GAF Jindivik 102	DPA/QinetiQ, Boscombe Down, apprentice use
	A92-664	GAF Jindivik 4A	Boscombe Down Aviation Collection
	A92-708	GAF Jindivik 4A	Bristol Aero Collection, stored Kemble
	A92-908	GAF Jindivik 900 (ZJ503)	No 2445 Sqn ATC, Llanbedr
	BELGIUM		
	FT-36	Lockheed T-33A	Dumfries & Galloway Avn Mus, Dumfries
	H-50	Noorduyn AT-16 Harvard IIB (OO-DAF)	Privately owned, Braaschaat, Belgium
	HD-75	Hanriot HD1 (G-AFDX)	RAF Museum, Hendon
	IF-68	Hawker Hunter F6 <ff>	Norfolk & Suffolk Avn Museum, Flixton
	L-44	Piper L-18C Super Cub (OO-SPQ)	Royal Aéro Para Club de Spa, Belgium
	L-47	Piper L-18C Super Cub (OO-SPG)	Aeroclub Braaschaat VZW, Braaschaat, Belgium
	L-156	Piper L-18C Super Cub (OO-LGB)	Aeroclub Braaschaat VZW, Braaschaat, Belgium
	V-18	SNCAN Stampe SV-4B (OO-GWD)	Antwerp Stampe Centre, Antwerp-Deurne, Belgium
	V-29	SNCAN Stampe SV-4B (OO-GWB)	Antwerp Stampe Centre, Antwerp-Deurne, Belgium
	BOLIVIA		
	FAB184	SIAI-Marchetti SF.260W (G-SIAI)	Privately owned, Booker
	BOTSWANA		
	OJ1	BAC Strikemaster 83 (ZG805/G-BXFU)	Global Aviation, Humberside
	BRAZIL		
	1317	Embraer T-27 Tucano	Shorts, Belfast (engine test bed)
	BURKINA FASO		
	BF-8431	SIAI-Marchetti SF.260 (G-NRRA) [31]	Privately owned, Oaksey Park
	CANADA		
	622	Piasecki HUP-3 Retriever (51-16622/N6699D)	The Helicopter Museum, Weston-super-Mare
	920	VS Stranraer (CF-BXO) [Q-N]	RAF Museum, Hendon
	3349	NA64 Yale (G-BYNF)	Privately owned, Duxford
	5403	Hawker Hurricane X (G-HHII)	Hangar 11 Collection, Milden

Serial	Type (code/other identity)	Owner/operator, location or fate	Notes
5429	Hawker Hurricane XIIA (BW881/G-KAMM) [Z]	*Sold to the USA, 2007*	
5450	Hawker Hurricane XII (G-TDTW)	Hawker Restorations Ltd, Milden	
5487	Hawker Hurricane II (G-CBOE)	Privately owned, Thruxton	
9048	Bristol 149 Bolingbroke IV <ff>	Bristol Aero Collection, Kemble	
9048	Bristol 149 Bolingbroke IV <rf>	Bristol Aero Collection, stored Filton	
9754	Consolidated PBY-5A Catalina (VP-BPS) [P]	Privately owned, Lee-on-Solent	
9893	Bristol 149 Bolingbroke IVT	Imperial War Museum store, Duxford	
9940	Bristol 149 Bolingbroke IVT	Royal Scottish Mus'm of Flight, E Fortune	
15195	Fairchild PT-19A Cornell	RAF Museum Reserve Collection, Stafford	
16693	Auster J/1N Alpha (G-BLPG) [693]	Privately owned, Clacton	
18393	Avro Canada CF-100 Canuck 4B (G-BCYK)	Imperial War Museum, Duxford	
18671	DHC1 Chipmunk 22 (WP905/7438M/G-BNZC) [671]	The Shuttleworth Collection, Old Warden	
20249	Noorduyn AT-16 Harvard IIB (PH-KLU) [XS-249]	Privately owned, Texel, The Netherlands	
20310	CCF T-6J Harvard IV (G-BSBG) [310]	Privately owned, Tatenhill	
21417	Canadair CT-133 Silver Star	Yorkshire Air Museum, Elvington	
23140	Canadair CL-13 Sabre [AX] <rf>	Midland Air Museum, Coventry	
23380	Canadair CL-13 Sabre <rf>	RAF Millom Museum, Haverigg	
FH153	Noorduyn AT-16 Harvard IIB (G-BBHK) [58]	Privately owned, Booker	
FJ777	Boeing-Stearman PT-17D Kaydet (41-8689/G-BIXN)	Privately owned, Rendcomb	

CHINA

Serial	Type (code/other identity)	Owner/operator, location or fate	Notes
2632016	Nanchang CJ-6A Chujiao (G-BXZB) (also wears *2632019*)	Privately owned, Hibaldstow	
2751219	Nanchang CJ-6A Chujiao (G-BVVG) [68]	Privately owned, Fishburn	

CROATIA

Serial	Type (code/other identity)	Owner/operator, location or fate	Notes
8110	Avia FL3 (G-AGFT)	Privately owned, Sandtoft	

CZECH REPUBLIC

Serial	Type (code/other identity)	Owner/operator, location or fate	Notes
0219	Mil Mi-24D (340219)	Privately owned, March, Cambs	
3677	Letov S-102 (MiG-15) (613677)	Royal Scottish Mus'm of Flight, E Fortune	
3794	Letov S-102 (MiG-15) (623794)	Norfolk & Suffolk Avn Museum, Flixton	
9147	Mil Mi-4	The Helicopter Museum, Weston-super-Mare	

DENMARK

Serial	Type (code/other identity)	Owner/operator, location or fate	Notes
A-011	SAAB A-35XD Draken	Privately owned, Grainthorpe, Lincs	
AR-107	SAAB S-35XD Draken	Newark Air Museum, Winthorpe	
E-419	Hawker Hunter F51 (G-9-441)	North-East Aircraft Museum, Usworth	
E-420	Hawker Hunter F51 (G-9-442)	Privately owned, Walton-on-Thames	
E-421	Hawker Hunter F51 (G-9-443)	Brooklands Museum, Weybridge	
E-423	Hawker Hunter F51 (G-9-444)	SWWAPS, Lasham	
E-424	Hawker Hunter F51 (G-9-445)	Aeroventure, Doncaster	
ET-272	Hawker Hunter T7 <ff>	Boulton Paul Association, Wolverhampton	
ET-273	Hawker Hunter T7 <ff>	Aeroventure, Doncaster	
K-682	Douglas C-47A Skytrain (OY-BPB)	Foreningen For Flyvende Mus, Vaerløse, Denmark	
L-866	Consolidated PBY-6A Catalina (8466M)	RAF Museum, Cosford	
R-756	Lockheed F-104G Starfighter	Midland Air Museum, Coventry	
S-881	Sikorsky S-55C	The Helicopter Museum, Weston-super-Mare	
S-882	Sikorsky S-55C	Paintball Adventure West, Lulsgate	
S-886	Sikorsky S-55C	Hamburger Hill Paintball, Marksbury, Somerset	
S-887	Sikorsky S-55C	The Helicopter Museum, Weston-super-Mare	

EGYPT

Serial	Type (code/other identity)	Owner/operator, location or fate	Notes
764	Mikoyan MiG-21SPS <ff>	Privately owned, Northampton	
771	WS61 Sea King 47 (WA.826)	DCAE AESS, *HMS Sultan*, Gosport	
773	WS61 Sea King 47 (WA.823)	RNAS Yeovilton Fire Section	
774	WS61 Sea King 47 (WA.822)	DCAE AESS, *HMS Sultan*, Gosport	

Notes	*Serial*	*Type (code/other identity)*	*Owner/operator, location or fate*
	775	WS61 Sea King 47 (WA.824)	DCAE AESS, *HMS Sultan*, Gosport
	776	WS61 Sea King 47 (WA.825)	DCAE AESS, *HMS Sultan*, Gosport
	0446	Mikoyan MiG-21UM <ff>	Thameside Aviation Museum, Tilbury
	7907	Sukhoi Su-7 <ff>	Robertsbridge Aviation Society, Mayfield
	FINLAND		
	GN-101	Folland Gnat F1 (XK741)	Midland Air Museum, Coventry
	VI-3	Valtion Viima 2 (OO-EBL)	Privately owned, Braaschaat, Belgium
	FRANCE		
	1/4513	Spad XIII <R> (G-BFYO/*S3398*)	American Air Museum, Duxford
	20	MH1521C1 Broussard (G-BWGG) [315-SQ]	Privately owned, Rednal
	37	Nord 3400 (G-ZARA) [MAB]	Privately owned, Boston
	67	SNCAN 1101 Noralpha (F-GMCY) [CY]	Privately owned, la Ferté-Alais, France
	70	Dassault Mystère IVA	Midland Air Museum, Coventry
	78	Nord 3202B-1 (G-BIZK)	Privately owned, Little Snoring
	79	Dassault Mystère IVA [2-EG]	Norfolk & Suffolk Avn Museum, Flixton
	82	Curtiss Hawk 75 (G-CCVH)	The Fighter Collection, Duxford
	82	NA T-28D Fennec (F-AZKG)	Privately owned, Strasbourg, France
	83	Dassault Mystère IVA [8-MS]	Newark Air Museum, Winthorpe
	83	Morane-Saulnier MS.733 Alcyon (F-AZKS)	Privately owned, Montlucon, France
	84	Dassault Mystère IVA [8-NF]	Lashenden Air Warfare Museum, Headcorn
	85	Dassault Mystère IVA [8-MV]	Cold War Jets Collection, Bruntingthorpe
	101	Dassault Mystère IVA [8-MN]	*Scrapped at RAF Molesworth, July 2007*
	104	MH1521M Broussard (F-GHFG) [307-FG]	Privately owned, Montceau-les-Mines,France
	105	Nord N2501F Noratlas (F-AZVM) [62-SI]	Le Noratlas de Provence, Marseilles, France
	121	Dassault Mystère IVA [8-MY]	City of Norwich Aviation Museum
	128	Morane-Saulnier MS.733 Alcyon (F-BMMY)	Privately owned, St Cyr, France
	143	Morane-Saulnier MS.733 Alcyon (G-MSAL)	Privately owned, Spanhoe
	146	Dassault Mystère IVA [8-MC]	North-East Aircraft Museum, Usworth
	156	SNCAN Stampe SV-4B (G-NIFE)	Privately owned, Gloucester
	157	Morane-Saulnier MS.230 Et2 (G-AVEB) [M-573,01]	Privately owned, Didcot
	185	MH1521M Broussard (G-BWLR)	Privately owned, Staverton
	208	MH1521C1 Broussard (G-YYYY) [IR]	Privately owned, Eggesford
	282	Dassault MD311 Flamant (F-AZFX) [316-KY]	Memorial Flt Association, la Ferté-Alais, France
	290	Dewoitine D27 (F-AZJD)	Amicale J-B Salis, la Ferté-Alais, France
	316	MH1521M Broussard (F-GGKR) [315-SN]	Privately owned, Lognes, France
	318	Dassault Mystère IVA [8-NY]	Dumfries & Galloway Avn Mus, Dumfries
	319	Dassault Mystère IVA [8-ND]	Rebel Air Museum, Andrewsfield
	354	Morane-Saulnier MS315E-D2 (G-BZNK)	Privately owned, Hemswell
	394	SNCAN Stampe SV-4C (G-BIMO)	Privately owned, Dunsfold
	538	Dassault Mirage IIIE [3-QH]	Yorkshire Air Museum, Elvington
	1058	SO1221 Djinn (FR108) [CDL]	The Helicopter Museum, Weston-super-Mare
	17473	Lockheed T-33A	Midland Air Museum, Coventry
	42157	NA F-100D Super Sabre [11-ML]	North-East Aircraft Museum, Usworth
	54439	Lockheed T-33A (55-4439) [WI]	North-East Aircraft Museum, Usworth
	63938	NA F-100F Super Sabre [11-MU]	Lashenden Air Warfare Museum, Headcorn
	121748	Grumman F8F-2P Bearcat (F-AZRJ) [5834/P]	Privately owned, Anemasse, France
	125716	Douglas AD-4N Skyraider (F-AZFN) [22-DG]	Privately owned, Mélun, France
	127002	Douglas AD-4NA Skyraider (F-AZHK) [20-LN]	Privately owned, Avignon, France
	133704	CV F4U-5NL Corsair (124541/F-AZYS) [14.F.6]	Privately owned, Avignon, France
	517692	NA T-28S Fennec (G-TROY) [142]	Privately owned, Duxford

Serial	*Type (code/other identity)*	*Owner/operator, location or fate*	*Notes*
18-5395	Piper L-18C Super Cub (52-2436/G-CUBJ) [CDG]	Privately owned, Old Warden	
51-7545	NA T-28S Fennec (N14113)	Privately owned, Duxford	
C850	Salmson 2A2 <R>	Barton Aviation Heritage Society, Barton	
MS824	Morane-Saulnier Type N <R> (G-AWBU)	Privately owned, Compton Abbas	
N1977	Nieuport Scout 17/23 <R> (*N1723*/G-BWMJ) [8]	Privately owned, Popham	
TE184	VS361 Spitfire LFXVIE (6850M/G-MXVI) [D]	Privately owned, Booker	
GERMANY			
-	Fieseler Fi103R-IV (V-1) (BAPC 91)	Lashenden Air Warfare Museum, Headcorn	
-	Focke-Achgelis Fa330A-1 (8469M)	RAF Museum, Cosford	
-	Fokker Dr1 Dreidekker <R> (BAPC 88)	FAA Museum, RNAS Yeovilton	
-	Messerschmitt Bf109 <R> (*6357*/BAPC 74) [6]	Kent Battle of Britain Museum, Hawkinge	
1	Hispano HA 1.112M1L Buchon (C4K-102/G-BWUE)	Spitfire Ltd, Duxford	
2	Messerschmitt Bf109G-10 (151591/D-FDME)	Messerschmitt Stiftung, Manching, Germany	
3	SNCAN 1101 Noralpha (G-BAYV)	Barton Aviation Heritage Society, Barton	
6	Messerschmitt Bf109G-2/Trop (10639/8478M/G-USTV)	RAF Museum, Hendon	
7	Messerschmitt Bf109G-4 (D-FWME)	Messerschmitt Aircraft Co, Albstadt, Germany	
8	Focke Wulf Fw190 <R> (G-WULF)	Privately owned, Halfpenny Green	
9	Focke Wulf Fw190 <R> (G-CCFW)	Privately owned, Kemble	
14	Messerschmitt Bf109 <R> (BAPC 67)	Kent Battle of Britain Museum, Hawkinge	
14	Nord 1002 (G-ETME)	Privately owned, White Waltham	
14	SNCAN 1101 Noralpha (G-BSMD)	Privately owned, Prestwick	
152/17	Fokker Dr1 Dreidekker <R> (G-ATJM)	Privately owned, East Garston, Bucks	
157/18	Fokker D.VIII <R> (BAPC 239)	Norfolk & Suffolk Air Museum, Flixton	
210/16	Fokker EIII (BAPC 56)	Science Museum, South Kensington	
403/17	Fokker EIII <R> (G-CDXR)	Privately owned, Popham	
422/15	Fokker EIII <R> (G-AVJO)	Privately owned, Compton Abbas	
425/17	Fokker Dr1 Dreidekker <R> (BAPC 133)	Kent Battle of Britain Museum, Hawkinge	
450/17	Fokker Dr1 Dreidekker <R> (G-BVGZ)	Privately owned, Breighton	
477/17	Fokker Dr1 Dreidekker <R> (G-FOKK)	Privately owned, Sywell	
626/8	Fokker DVII <R> (N6268)	Privately owned, Booker	
764	Mikoyan MiG-21SPS <ff>	Privately owned, Booker	
959	Mikoyan MiG-21SPS	Midland Air Museum, Coventry	
1190	Messerschmitt Bf109E-3 [4]	Imperial War Museum, Duxford	
1342	Messerschmitt Bf109E-3 (N342FH)	*Exported to the USA, 2006*	
1480	Messerschmitt Bf109 <R> (BAPC 66) [6]	Kent Battle of Britain Museum, Hawkinge	
1801/18	Bowers Fly Baby 1A (G-BNPV)	Privately owned, Chessington	
1803/18	Bowers Fly Baby 1A (G-BUYU)	Privately owned, Chessington	
1983	Messerschmitt Bf109E-3 (G-EMIL)	Privately owned, Surrey	
2088	Fieseler Fi156A Storch (G-STCH)	*Repainted as GM+A1, 2007*	
2100	Focke-Wulf Fw189A-1 (G-BZKY) [V7+1H]	Privately owned, Sandown	
3523	Messerschmitt Bf109E-7	Privately owned, Lancing	
3523	Messerschmitt Bf109E-7	Privately owned, Lancing	
4034	Messerschmitt Bf109E (G-CDTI)	Privately owned,	
4101	Messerschmitt Bf109E-3 (DG200/8477M) [12]	RAF Museum, Hendon	
4477	CASA 1.131E Jungmann (G-RETA) [GD+EG]	The Shuttleworth Collection, Old Warden	
6234	Junkers Ju87R-4 (G-STUK)	Privately owned, Surrey	
7198/18	LVG CVI (G-AANJ/9239M)	RAF Museum, Hendon	
7485	Messerschmitt Bf109F-4	Charleston Aviation Services, Colchester	
8147	Messerschmitt Bf109F-4	Charleston Aviation Services, Colchester	
8417/18	Fokker DVII (9207M)	RAF Museum, Hendon	

Notes	*Serial*	*Type (code/other identity)*	*Owner/operator, location or fate*
	12802	Antonov An-2T (D-FOFM)	Historische Flugzeuge, Grossenhain, Germany
	15458	Messerschmitt Bf109F-4	Charleston Aviation Services, Colchester
	100143	Focke-Achgelis Fa330A-1	Imperial War Museum, Duxford
	100502	Focke-Achgelis Fa330A-1	The Real Aeroplane Company, Breighton
	100509	Focke-Achgelis Fa330A-1	Science Museum, stored Wroughton
	100545	Focke-Achgelis Fa330A-1	Fleet Air Arm Museum, stored RNAS Yeovilton
	100549	Focke-Achgelis Fa330A-1	Lashenden Air Warfare Museum, Headcorn
	110451	Fieseler Fi156D Storch (G-STOR)	Privately owned, Surrey
	112372	Messerschmitt Me262A-2a (AM.51/VK893/8482M) [4]	RAF Museum, Hendon
	120076	Heinkel He162A-2 Salamander (VH523/AM.59) [4]	Aero Vintage, Westfield, Sussex
	120227	Heinkel He162A-2 Salamander (VN679/AM.65/8472M) [2]	RAF Museum, Hendon
	120235	Heinkel He162A-1 Salamander (AM.68)	Imperial War Museum, Lambeth
	191316	Messerschmitt Me163B Komet	Science Museum, South Kensington
	191454	Messerschmitt Me163B Komet <R> (BAPC 271)	The Shuttleworth Collection, Old Warden
	191614	Messerschmitt Me163B Komet (8481M)	RAF Museum, Cosford
	191659	Messerschmitt Me163B Komet (8480M) [15]	Royal Scottish Mus'm of Flight, E Fortune
	211028	Focke Wulf Fw190D-9 (G-DORA)	Privately owned, Surrey
	280020	Flettner Fl282/B-V20 Kolibri (frame only)	Midland Air Museum, Coventry
	360043	Junkers Ju88R-1 (PJ876/8475M) [D5+EV]	RAF Museum, Hendon
	420430	Messerschmitt Me410A-1/U2 (AM.72/8483M) [3U+CC]	RAF Museum, Cosford
	475081	Fieseler Fi156C-7 Storch (VP546/ AM.101/7362M)[GM+AK]	RAF Museum, Cosford
	494083	Junkers Ju87D-3 (8474M) [RI+JK]	RAF Museum, Hendon
	500453	Messerschmitt Me262-1a (N94503)	Privately owned, Martham, Norfolk
	584219	Focke Wulf Fw190F-8/U1 (AM.29/8470M) [38]	RAF Museum, Hendon
	701152	Heinkel He111H-23 (8471M) [NT+SL]	RAF Museum, Hendon
	730301	Messerschmitt Bf110G-4 (AM.34/8479M) [D5+RL]	RAF Museum, Hendon
	733682	Focke Wulf Fw190A-8/R7 (AM.75/9211M)	Imperial War Museum, Lambeth
	980554	Flugwerk Fw190A-8/N	Privately owned, Duxford
	2+1	Focke Wulf Fw190 <R> (G-SYFW) [7334]	Privately owned, Wickenby
	17+TF	CASA 1.133C Jungmeister (G-BZTJ)	Privately owned, Turweston
	22+35	Lockheed F-104G Starfighter	SWWAPS, Lasham
	22+57	Lockheed F-104G Starfighter	Privately owned, Grainthorpe, Lincs
	23.02	Albatros B.II <R> (D-EKGH)	Historischer Flugzeugbau, Fürstenwalde, Germany
	28+08	Aero L-39ZO Albatros (142/28+04)	Privately owned, Long Stratton, Norfolk
	2E+RA	Fieseler Fi-156C-3 Storch (F-AZRA)	Amicale J-B Salis, la Ferté-Alais, France
	4+1	Focke Wulf Fw190 <R> (G-BSLX)	Privately owned, Norwich
	4V+BG	Amiot AAC1/Ju52 (Port.AF 6316) [9]	Imperial War Museum, Duxford
	6G+ED	Slepcev Storch (G-BZOB) [5447]	Privately owned, Croydon, Cambs
	58+89	Dornier Do28D-2 Skyservant (D-ICDY)	Privately owned, Uetersen, Germany
	80+39	MBB Bo.105M	Privately owned, Coney Park, Leeds
	80+40	MBB Bo.105M	Privately owned, Coney Park, Leeds
	81+00	MBB Bo.105M	The Helicopter Museum, Weston-super-Mare
	96+21	Mil Mi-24D (406)	Imperial War Museum, Duxford
	96+26	Mil Mi-24D (429)	The Helicopter Museum, Weston-super-Mare
	97+04	Putzer Elster B (G-APVF)	Privately owned, Breighton

Serial	Type (code/other identity)	Owner/operator, location or fate	Notes
98+14	Sukhoi Su-22M-4	Hawker Hunter Aviation Ltd, stored Scampton	
99+24	NA OV-10B Bronco (F-AZKM)	Privately owned, Montelimar, France	
99+32	NA OV-10B Bronco (G-BZGK)	Privately owned, Duxford	
AZ+JU	CASA 3.52L (F-AZJU)	Amicale J-B Salis, la Ferté-Alais, France	
BU+CC	CASA 1.131E Jungmann (G-BUCC)	Privately owned, Sandown	
BU+CK	CASA 1.131E Jungmann (G-BUCK)	Privately owned, White Waltham	
CC+43	Pilatus P-2 (G-CJCI)	Privately owned, Norwich	
CF+HF	Morane-Saulnier MS502 (EI-AUY)	Imperial War Museum, Duxford	
D5397/17	Albatros DVA <R> (G-BFXL)	FAA Museum, RNAS Yeovilton	
DM+BK	Morane-Saulnier MS505 (G-BPHZ)	Historic Aircraft Collection, Duxford	
ES+BH	Messerschmitt Bf108B-2 (D-ESBH)	Messerschmitt Stiftung, Manching, Germany	
FI+S	Morane-Saulnier MS505 (G-BIRW)	Royal Scottish Mus'm of Flight, E Fortune	
FM+BB	Messerschmitt Bf109G-6 (D-FMBB)	Messerschmitt Stiftung, Manching, Germany	
FW+WC	Flug Werk FW190A-8/N (D-FWWC)	Flug Werk, Manching, Germany	
GL+SU	Bücker Bü1181B-1 Bestmann (G-GLSU)	Privately owned, Old Warden	
GM+A1	Fieseler Fi156A Storch (G-STCH)	Privately owned, Old Warden	
LG+03	Bücker Bü133C Jungmeister (G-AEZX)		
NJ+C11	Nord 1002 (G-ATBG)	Privately owned, Booker	
NQ+NR	Klemm Kl35D (D-EQXD)	Privately owned, Old Warden	
S4+A07	CASA 1.131E Jungmann (G-BWHP)	Privately owned, Yarcombe, Devon	
S5+B06	CASA 1.131E Jungmann 2000 (G-BSFB)	Privately owned, Old Buckenham	

GHANA

Serial	Type (code/other identity)	Owner/operator, location or fate	Notes
G-102	SA122 Bulldog	Privately owned, stored Salisbury	
G-108	SA122 Bulldog (G-BCUP)	Privately owned, stored Salisbury	

GREECE

Serial	Type (code/other identity)	Owner/operator, location or fate	Notes
51-6171	NA F-86D Sabre	North-East Aircraft Museum, Usworth	
52-6541	Republic F-84F Thunderflash [541]	North-East Aircraft Museum, Usworth	
63-8418	Northrop F-5A	Martin-Baker Ltd, Chalgrove, Fire Section	

HONG KONG

Serial	Type (code/other identity)	Owner/operator, location or fate	Notes
HKG-5	SA128 Bulldog (G-BULL)	Privately owned, Old Sarum	
HKG-6	SA128 Bulldog (G-BPCL)	Privately owned, North Weald	
HKG-11	Slingsby T.67M Firefly 200 (G-BYRY)	Privately owned, Tibenham	
HKG-13	Slingsby T.67M Firefly 200 (G-BXKW)	Privately owned, Tibenham	

HUNGARY

Serial	Type (code/other identity)	Owner/operator, location or fate	Notes
501	Mikoyan MiG-21PF	Imperial War Museum, Duxford	
503	Mikoyan MiG-21SMT (G-BRAM)	RAF Museum, Cosford	

INDIA

Serial	Type (code/other identity)	Owner/operator, location or fate	Notes
Q497	EE Canberra T4 (WE191) (fuselage)	Dumfries & Galloway Avn Mus, Dumfries	

INDONESIA

Serial	Type (code/other identity)	Owner/operator, location or fate	Notes
LL-5313	BAe Hawk T53	BAE Systems, Brough	

IRAQ

Serial	Type (code/other identity)	Owner/operator, location or fate	Notes
333	DH115 Vampire T55 <ff>	Aeroventure, Doncaster	

ITALY

Serial	Type (code/other identity)	Owner/operator, location or fate	Notes
MM5701	Fiat CR42 (BT474/8468M) [13-95]	RAF Museum, Hendon	
MM52801	Fiat G46-3B (G-BBII) [4-97]	Privately owned, Sandown	
MM53692	CCF T-6G Texan	RAeS Medway Branch, Rochester	
MM53774	Fiat G59-4B (I-MRSV) [181]	Privately owned, Parma, Italy	
MM54099	NA T-6G Texan (G-BRBC) [RR-56]	Privately owned, Chigwell	
MM54-2372	Piper L-21B Super Cub	Privately owned, Kesgrave, Suffolk	
W7	Avia FL3 (G-AGFT)	*Repainted in Croatian marks as 8110, 2005*	

Notes	*Serial*	*Type (code/other identity)*	*Owner/operator, location or fate*
	JAPAN		
	-	Yokosuka MXY 7 Ohka II (BAPC 159)	Defence School, Chattenden
	24	Kawasaki Ki100-1B (8476M/BAPC 83)	RAF Museum, Hendon
	997	Yokosuka MXY 7 Ohka II (8485M/BAPC 98)	Gr Manchester Mus of Science & Industry
	5439	Mitsubishi Ki46-III (8484M/BAPC 84)	RAF Museum, Cosford
	15-1585	Yokosuka MXY 7 Ohka II (BAPC 58)	Science Museum, at FAA Museum, RNAS Yeovilton
	I-13	Yokosuka MXY 7 Ohka II (8486M/BAPC 99)	RAF Museum, Cosford
	Y2-176	Mitsubishi A6M3-2 Zero (3685) [76]	Imperial War Museum, Duxford
	JORDAN		
	408	SA125 Bulldog (G-BDIN)	Privately owned, Lasham
	MEXICO		
	EPC-152	Mudry/CAARP CAP-10B (G-CCXC) [52]	Privately owned, Hatch
	MYANMAR		
	UB424	VS361 Spitfire IX (SL633/UB425/G-CZAF)	Historic Flying Ltd, Duxford
	UB441	VS361 Spitfire IX (ML119/N94149)	Privately owned, Sandown
	NETHERLANDS		
	16-218	Consolidated PBY-5A Catalina (2459/PH-PBY)	Neptune Association, Lelystad, The Netherlands
	174	Fokker S-11 Instructor (E-31/G-BEPV)	Privately owned, Spanhoe
	204	Lockheed SP-2H Neptune [V]	RAF Museum, Cosford
	A-12	DH82A Tiger Moth (PH-TYG)	Privately owned, Gilze-Rijen, The Netherlands
	B-64	Noorduyn AT-16 Harvard IIB (PH-LSK)	KLu Historic Flt, Gilze-Rijen, The Netherlands
	B-71	Noorduyn AT-16 Harvard IIB (PH-MLM)	KLu Historic Flt, Gilze-Rijen, The Netherlands
	B-118	Noorduyn AT-16 Harvard IIB (PH-IIB)	KLu Historic Flt, Gilze-Rijen, The Netherlands
	E-14	Fokker S-11 Instructor (PH-AFS)	Privately owned, Lelystad, The Netherlands
	E-15	Fokker S-11 Instructor (G-BIYU)	Privately owned, Bagby
	E-18	Fokker S-11 Instructor (PH-HTC)	Duke of Brabant AF, Eindhoven, The Netherlands
	E-20	Fokker S-11 Instructor (PH-GRB)	Privately owned, Gilze-Rijen, The Netherlands
	E-27	Fokker S-11 Instructor (PH-HOL)	Privately owned, Lelystad, The Netherlands
	E-32	Fokker S-11 Instructor (PH-HOI)	Privately owned, Gilze-Rijen, The Netherlands
	E-36	Fokker S-11 Instructor (PH-ACG)	Privately owned, Lelystad, The Netherlands
	E-39	Fokker S-11 Instructor (PH-HOG)	Privately owned, Lelystad, The Netherlands
	G-29	Beech D18S (PH-KHV)	KLu Historic Flt, Gilze-Rijen, The Netherlands
	H-98	VS509 Spitfire T9 (G-CCCA)	Historic Flying Ltd, Duxford
	MH424	VS361 Spitfire LFIXC (MJ271/H-53)	Privately owned, Duxford
	MK732	VS361 Spitfire LFIXC (8633M/PH-OUQ) [3W-17]	KLu Historic Flt, Gilze-Rijen, The Netherlands
	N-202	Hawker Hunter F6 [10] <ff>	Privately owned, Eaglescott
	N-250	Hawker Hunter F6 (G-9-185) <ff>	Imperial War Museum, Duxford
	N-268	Hawker Hunter FGA78 (Qatar QA-10)	Yorkshire Air Museum, Elvington
	N-315	Hawker Hunter T7 (XM121)	Jet Avn Preservation Grp, Long Marston
	N-321	Hawker Hunter T8C (G-BWGL)	Stichting Hawker Hunter Foundation, Leeuwarden, The Netherlands

Serial	Type (code/other identity)	Owner/operator, location or fate	Notes
N5-149	NA B-25J Mitchell (44-29507/ *HD346*/N320SQ) [232511]	Duke of Brabant AF, Gilze-Rijen, The Netherlands	
R-55	Piper L-18C Super Cub (52-2466/G-BLMI)	Privately owned, White Waltham	
R-109	Piper L-21B Super Cub (54-2337/PH-GAZ)	KLu Historic Flt, Gilze-Rijen, The Netherlands	
R-122	Piper L-21B Super Cub (54-2412/PH-PPW)	KLu Historic Flt, Gilze-Rijen, The Netherlands	
R-137	Piper L-21B Super Cub (54-2427/PH-PSC)	Privately owned, Gilze-Rijen, The Netherlands	
R-151	Piper L-21B Super Cub (54-2441/G-BIYR)	Privately owned, Dunkeswell	
R-156	Piper L-21B Super Cub (54-2446/G-ROVE)	Privately owned, Headcorn	
R-163	Piper L-21B Super Cub (54-2453/G-BIRH)	Privately owned, Hinton-in-the-Hedges	
R-167	Piper L-21B Super Cub (54-2457/G-LION)	Privately owned, Turweston, Bucks	
R-177	Piper L-21B Super Cub (54-2467/PH-KNR)	KLu Historic Flt, Gilze-Rijen, The Netherlands	
R-181	Piper L-21B Super Cub (54-2471/PH-GAU)	Privately owned, Gilze-Rijen, The Netherlands	
R-345	Piper J-3C Cub (PH-UCS)	Privately owned, The Netherlands	
S-9	DHC2 L-20A Beaver (55-4585/PH-DHC)	KLu Historic Flt, Gilze-Rijen, The Netherlands	
NEW ZEALAND			
NZ3909	WS Wasp HAS1 (XT782)	Kennet Aviation, North Weald	
NZ6361	BAC Strikemaster 87 (OJ5/G-BXFP)	Privately owned, Chalgrove	
NORTH KOREA			
-	WSK Lim-2 (MiG-15) (01420/G-BMZF)	FAA Museum, RNAS Yeovilton	
NORTH VIETNAM			
1211	WSK Lim-5 (MiG-17F) (G-MIGG)	Privately owned, Bournemouth	
NORWAY			
848	Piper L-18C Super Cub (LN-ACL) [FA-N]	Privately owned, Norway	
56321	SAAB S91B Safir (G-BKPY) [U-AB]	Newark Air Museum, Winthorpe	
OMAN			
425	BAC Strikemaster 82A (G-SOAF)	Privately owned, Hawarden	
801	Hawker Hunter T66B <ff>	Privately owned, Exeter	
801	Hawker Hunter T66B <rf>	Privately owned, Hawarden	
853	Hawker Hunter FR10 (XF426)	RAF Museum, Hendon	
POLAND			
05	WSK SM-2 (Mi-2) (1005)	The Helicopter Museum, Weston-super-Mare	
309	WSK SBLim-2A (MiG-15UTI) <ff>	R Scottish Mus'm of Flight, stored E Fortune	
408	WSK-PZL Mielec TS-11 Iskra (1H-0408)	Midland Air Museum, Coventry	
1018	WSK-PZL Mielec TS-11 Iskra (1H-1018/G-ISKA)	Cold War Jets Collection, Bruntingthorpe	
1120	WSK Lim-2 (MiG-15bis)	RAF Museum, Cosford	
PORTUGAL			
85	Isaacs Fury II (G-BTPZ)	Privately owned, Ormskirk	
1360	OGMA/DHC1 Chipmunk T20 (G-BYYU) (fuselage)	Privately owned, Little Staughton	
1365	OGMA/DHC1 Chipmunk T20 (G-DHPM)	Privately owned, Sywell	
1372	OGMA/DHC1 Chipmunk T20 (HB-TUM)	Privately owned, Switzerland	
1373	OGMA/DHC1 Chipmunk T20 (G-CBJG)	Privately owned, Spanhoe	
1377	DHC1 Chipmunk 22 (G-BARS)	Privately owned, Yeovilton	

Notes	Serial	Type (code/other identity)	Owner/operator, location or fate
	1741	CCF Harvard IV (G-HRVD)	Privately owned, Bruntingthorpe
	1747	CCF T-6J Harvard IV (20385/G-BGPB)	The Aircraft Restoration Co, Duxford
	QATAR		
	QA12	Hawker Hunter FGA78 <ff>	Privately owned, Cwmbran
	QP30	WS Lynx Mk 28 (G-BFDV/TD 013)	DCAE SEAE, Arborfield
	QP31	WS Lynx Mk 28	DARA Fleetlands Apprentice School
	QP32	WS Lynx Mk 28 (TAD 016)	DCAE, SEAE, Arborfield
	ROMANIA		
	29	LET L-29 Delfin <ff>	Privately owned, Shropshire
	47	LET L-29 Delfin	Privately owned, Ashton-under-Lyne
	RUSSIA (& FORMER SOVIET UNION)		
	-	LET L-29S Delfin (491273/YL-PAG)	Privately owned, Breighton
	-	Mil Mi-24D (3532461715415)	Privately owned, North Weald
	-	Mil Mi-24D (3532464505029)	Midland Air Museum, Coventry
	-	Yakovlev Yak-52 (811202/YL-CBI)	Privately owned, Hawarden
	1 w	SPP Yak C-11 (G-BZMY)	Privately owned, North Weald
	01 y	Yakovlev Yak-52 (9311709/G-YKSZ)	Privately owned, White Waltham
	03 w	Yakovlev Yak-52 (899803/G-YAKR)	Privately owned, North Weald
	04 r	Mikoyan MiG-23ML (024003607)	Newark Air Museum, Winthorpe
	05 r	Yakovlev Yak-50 (832507/YL-CBH)	Privately owned, Hawarden
	5 w	Yakovlev Yak-3UA (0470204/D-FYGJ)	Privately owned, Sleap
	07 y	WSK SM-1 (Mi-1) (Polish AF 2007)	The Helicopter Museum, Weston-super-Mare
	07 y	Yakovlev Yak-18M (G-BMJY)	Privately owned, East Garston, Bucks
	09 y	Yakovlev Yak-52 (9411809/G-BVMU)	Privately owned, Shipdham
	9 w	SPP Yak C-11 (1701139/G-OYAK)	Privately owned, Little Gransden
	9 y	Polikarpov Po-2 (0094/N588NB)	The Shuttleworth Collection, Old Warden
	10 y	Yakovlev Yak-50 (801810/G-BTZB)	Privately owned, Lee-on-Solent
	10 y	Yakovlev Yak-52 (822710/G-CBMD)	Privately owned, Headcorn
	11 y	SPP Yak C-11 (G-YCII)	Privately owned, Woodchurch, Kent
	12 r	LET L-29 Delfin (194555/ES-YLM/G-DELF)	Privately owned, Manston
	12 w	Yakovlev Yak-3M (0470107/D-FJAK)	MDM Aviation, Freiburg, Germany
	15 w	SPP Yak C-11 (170103/D-FYAK)	Classic Aviation Company, Hannover, Germany
	18 r	LET L-29S Delfin (591771/YL-PAF)	Privately owned, Hawarden
	19 w	Polikarpov I-15bis <R> (4439/FLARF-02089)	Privately owned, Duxford
	20 w	Lavochkin La-11	The Fighter Collection, Duxford
	20 bl	Yakovlev Yak-52 (790404/YL-CBJ)	Privately owned, Hawarden
	21 w	Yakovlev Yak-3UA (0470203/G-CDBJ)	Privately owned, Headcorn
	21 w	Yakovlev Yak-9UM (0470403/D-FENK)	Privately owned, Magdeburg, Germany
	23 y	Bell P-39Q Airacobra (44-2911)	Privately owned, Sussex
	23 r	Mikoyan MiG-27D (83712515040)	Privately owned, Hawarden
	26 bl	Yakovlev Yak-52 (9111306/G-BVXK)	Privately owned, White Waltham
	27 w	Yakovlev Yak-3UTI-PW (9/04623/F-AZIM)	Capel Aviation, la Ferté-Alais, France
	27 r	Yakovlev Yak-52 (9111307/G-YAKX)	Privately owned, Popham
	31 bl	Yakovlev Yak-52 (9111311/G-YAKV)	Privately owned, Rendcomb
	33 r	Yakovlev Yak-50 (853206/G-YAKZ)	Privately owned, Compton Abbas
	33 w	Yakovlev Yak-52 (899915/G-YAKH)	Privately owned, White Waltham
	35 r	Sukhoi Su-17M-3 (25102)	Privately owned, Hawarden
	36 w	LET/Yak C-11 (171101/G-KYAK)	Privately owned, North Weald
	36 w	SPP Yak C-11 (171103/G-IYAK)	*Sold to Germany, November 2007*

Serial	Type (code/other identity)	Owner/operator, location or fate	Notes
42 w	Yakovlev Yak-52 (888911/G-CBRU)	Privately owned, Rochester	
43 bl	Yakovlev Yak-52 (877601/G-BWSV)	Privately owned, North Weald	
48 bl	Yakovlev Yak-52 (9111413/G-CBSN)	Privately owned, Manston	
49 r	Yakovlev Yak-50 (822305/G-YAKU)	Privately owned, Compton Abbas	
50 bk	Yakovlev Yak-50 (812101/G-CBPM)	Privately owned, High Cross	
50 bl	Yakovlev Yak-52 (9111415/G-CBRW)	Privately owned, White Waltham	
51 r	LET L-29 Delfin (893019/G-BZNT)	Privately owned, Caernarfon	
51 y	Yakovlev Yak-50 (812004/G-BWYK)	Privately owned, West Meon, Hants	
52 r	Yakovlev Yak-52 (800708/G-CBPY)	Privately owned, Sherburn-in-Elmet	
52 y	Yakovlev Yak-52 (878202/G-BWVR)	Privately owned, Barton	
54 r	Sukhoi Su-17M (69004)	Privately owned, Hawarden	
55 bl	Yakovlev Yak-52 (9111505/G-BVOK)	Intrepid Aviation, North Weald	
56 r	Yakovlev Yak-52 (811504)	Privately owned, Hawarden	
61 r	Yakovlev Yak-50 (842710/G-YAKM)	Privately owned, Compton Abbas	
66 r	Yakovlev Yak-52 (855905/G-YAKN)	Privately owned, Compton Abbas	
67 r	Yakovlev Yak-52 (822013/G-CBSL)	Privately owned, Leicester	
69 r	Hawker Hunter FGA9 (8839M/XG194)	RAF North Luffenham Training Area	
69 bl	Yakovlev Yak-52 (899413/G-XYAK)	Privately owned, Old Buckenham	
69 y	Yakovlev Yak-52 (888712/G-CCSU)	Privately owned, Germany	
71 r	Mikoyan MiG-27M (61912507006)	Newark Air Museum, Winthorpe	
74 w	Yakovlev Yak-52 (877404/G-LAOK) [JA-74, IV-62]	Privately owned, Tollerton	
93 w	Yakovlev Yak-50 (853001/G-JYAK) [R]	Privately owned, North Weald	
100 bl	Yakovlev Yak-52 (866904/G-YAKI)	Privately owned, Popham	
139 y	Yakovlev Yak-52 (833810/G-BWOD)	Privately owned, Sywell	
1342	Yakovlev Yak-1 (G-BTZD)	Privately owned, Westfield, Sussex	
1870710	Ilyushin Il-2 (G-BZVW)	Privately owned, Wickenby	
1878576	Ilyushin Il-2 (G-BZVX)	Privately owned, Wickenby	
1-12	Yakovlev Yak-52 (9011013/RA-02293)	Privately owned, Halfpenny Green	
(RK858)	VS361 Spitfire LFIX	The Fighter Collection, Duxford	
(SM639)	VS361 Spitfire LFIX	Privately owned, Catfield	

SAUDI ARABIA

Serial	Type (code/other identity)	Owner/operator, location or fate	Notes
1104	BAC Strikemaster 80 (G-SMAS)	Privately owned, Hawarden	
1107	BAC Strikemaster 80	*Currently not known*	
1112	BAC Strikemaster 80 (G-FLYY)	Privately owned, Hawarden	
1120	BAC Strikemaster 80A (G-RSAF)	Privately owned, Hawarden	
1125	BAC Strikemaster 80A	Privately owned, Bentwaters	
1130	BAC Strikemaster 80A (G-CDHB)	Privately owned, Humberside	
1133	BAC Strikemaster 80A (G-BESY)	Imperial War Museum, Duxford	
53-686	BAC Lightning F53 (ZF592)	City of Norwich Aviation Museum	
55-713	BAC Lightning T55 (ZF598)	Midland Air Museum, Coventry	

SINGAPORE

Serial	Type (code/other identity)	Owner/operator, location or fate	Notes
311	BAC Strikemaster 84 (G-MXPH)	Privately owned, North Weald	
323	BAC Strikemaster 81 (N21419)	Privately owned, stored Hawarden	

SOUTH AFRICA

Serial	Type (code/other identity)	Owner/operator, location or fate	Notes
91	Westland Wasp HAS1 (pod)	Privately owned, Oaksey Park	
92	Westland Wasp HAS1 (G-BYCX)	Privately owned, Chiseldon	
221	DH115 Vampire T55 <ff>	Privately owned, Hemel Hempstead	
6130	Lockheed Ventura II (AJ469)	RAF Museum, stored Cosford	
7429	NA AT-6D Harvard III (D-FASS)	Privately owned, Aachen, Germany	

SOUTH VIETNAM

Serial	Type (code/other identity)	Owner/operator, location or fate	Notes
24550	Cessna L-19E Bird Dog (G-PDOG) [GP]	Privately owned, Lincs	

SPAIN

Serial	Type (code/other identity)	Owner/operator, location or fate	Notes
B.2I-27	CASA 2.111B (He111H-16) (B.2I-103)	Imperial War Museum, stored Duxford	
C.4E-88	Messerschmitt Bf109E	Privately owned, East Garston, Bucks	
E.3B-114	CASA 1.131E Jungmann (G-BJAL)	Privately owned, Breighton	
E.3B-143	CASA 1.131E Jungmann (G-JUNG)	Privately owned, White Waltham	

Notes	Serial	Type (code/other identity)	Owner/operator, location or fate
	E.3B-153	CASA 1.131E Jungmann (G-BPTS) [781-75]	Privately owned, Duxford
	E.3B-350	CASA 1.131E Jungmann (G-BHPL) [05-97]	Privately owned, Compton Abbas
	(E.3B-369)	CASA 1.131E Jungmann (G-BPDM) [781-32]	Privately owned, Heighington
	E.3B-494	CASA 1.131E Jungmann (G-CDLC) [81-47]	Privately owned, Kemble
	E.3B-521	CASA 1.131E Jungmann [781-3]	RAF Museum, Hendon
	E.18-2	Piper PA-31P Navajo 425	Bentwaters Cold War Museum
	EM-01	DH60G Moth (G-AAOR)	Privately owned, Rendcomb
	ES.1-4	Bücker Bü133C Jungmeister (G-BUTX)	Privately owned, Breighton
	ES.1-16	CASA 1.133L Jungmeister	Privately owned, Stretton, Cheshire
	SWEDEN		
	-	Thulin A/Bleriot XI (SE-XMC)	Privately owned, Loberod, Sweden
	081	CFM 01 Tummelisa <R> (SE-XIL)	Privately owned, Loberod, Sweden
	2542	Fiat CR42 (G-CBLS)	The Fighter Collection, Duxford
	05108	DH60 Moth	Privately owned, Langham
	17239	SAAB B-17A (SE-BYH) [7-J]	Flygvapenmuseum, Linköping, Sweden
	28693	DH100 Vampire FB6 (J-1184/SE-DXY) [9-G]	Scandinavian Historic Flight, Oslo, Norway
	29640	SAAB J-29F [20-08]	Midland Air Museum, Coventry
	29670	SAAB J-29F (SE-DXB) [10-R]	Flygvapenmuseum/F10 Wing, Angelholm, Sweden
	32028	SAAB 32A Lansen (G-BMSG)	Privately owned, Cranfield
	34066	Hawker Hunter F58 (J-4089/LN-HNT) [9-G]	Scandinavian Historic Flight, Oslo, Norway
	35075	SAAB J-35J Draken [40]	Dumfries & Galloway Aviation Museum
	35515	SAAB J-35F Draken [49]	Irvin-GQ, Llangeinor
	37918	SAAB AJSH-37 Viggen [57]	Newark Air Museum, Winthorpe
	SWITZERLAND		
	-	DH112 Venom FB54 (J-1758/N203DM)	Grove Technology Park, Wantage, Oxon
	A-10	CASA 1.131E Jungmann (G-BECW)	Privately owned, Rochester
	A-12	Bücker Bu131B Jungmann (G-CCHY)	Privately owned, Booker
	A-52	CASA 1.131E Jungmann 2000 (G-BZVS)	*Sold to Switzerland, April 2007*
	A-57	CASA 1.131E Jungmann (G-BECT)	Privately owned, Goodwood
	A-125	Pilatus P-2 (G-BLKZ)	Privately owned, Duxford
	A-701	Junkers Ju52/3m (HB-HOS)	Ju-Air, Dubendorf, Switzerland
	A-702	Junkers Ju52/3m (HB-HOT)	Ju-Air, Dubendorf, Switzerland
	A-703	Junkers Ju52/3m (HB-HOP)	Ju-Air, Dubendorf, Switzerland
	A-806	Pilatus P3-03 (G-BTLL)	Privately owned, stored Headcorn
	C-552	EKW C-3605 (G-DORN)	Privately owned, Bournemouth
	C-558	EKW C-3605 (G-CCYZ)	Privately owned, Wickenby
	J-1008	DH100 Vampire FB6	Mosquito Aircraft Museum, London Colney
	J-1172	DH100 Vampire FB6 (8487M)	RAF Museum Reserve Collection, Stafford
	J-1573	DH112 Venom FB50 (G-VICI)	Privately owned, Bournemouth
	J-1605	DH112 Venom FB50 (G-BLID)	Gatwick Aviation Museum, Charlwood, Surrey
	J-1629	DH112 Venom FB50	Air Atlantique Classic Flight, Coventry
	J-1649	DH112 Venom FB50	Air Atlantique Classic Flight, Coventry
	J-1704	DH112 Venom FB54	RAF Museum, Cosford
	J-1712	DH112 Venom FB54 <ff>	Privately owned, Deeside, Wales
	J-1790	DH112 Venom FB50 (J-1632/G-VNOM)	Mosquito Aircraft Museum, London Colney
	J-4015	Hawker Hunter F58 (J-4040/HB-RVS)	Privately owned, St Stephan, Switzerland
	J-4021	Hawker Hunter F58 (G-HHAC)	Hawker Hunter Aviation Ltd, Scampton
	J-4031	Hawker Hunter F58 (G-BWFR)	Privately owned, Exeter
	J-4064	Hawker Hunter F58 (HB-RVQ)	Fliegermuseum Altenrhein, Switzerland
	J-4072	Hawker Hunter F58 (G-HHAB)	Hawker Hunter Aviation Ltd, Scampton
	J-4081	Hawker Hunter F58 (G-HHAF)	Hawker Hunter Aviation Ltd, Scampton
	J-4083	Hawker Hunter F58 (G-EGHH)	Privately owned, Exeter
	J-4086	Hawker Hunter F58 (HB-RVU)	Privately owned, Altenrhein, Switzerland

Serial	*Type (code/other identity)*	*Owner/operator, location or fate*	*Notes*
J-4090	Hawker Hunter F58 (G-SIAL)	Privately owned, Exeter	
J-4091	Hawker Hunter F58	British Aviation Heritage, Bruntingthorpe	
J-4201	Hawker Hunter T68 (HB-RVR)	Amici dell'Hunter, Sion, Switzerland	
J-4205	Hawker Hunter T68 (HB-RVP)	Fliegermuseum Altenrhein, Switzerland	
U-80	Bücker Bü133D Jungmeister (G-BUKK)	Privately owned, Kirdford, W Sussex	
U-95	Bücker Bü133C Jungmeister (G-BVGP)	Privately owned, Booker	
U-99	Bücker Bü133C Jungmeister (G-AXMT)	Privately owned, Breighton	
U-110	Pilatus P-2 (G-PTWO)	Privately owned, Earls Colne	
V-54	SE3130 Alouette II (G-BVSD)	Privately owned, Glos	
USA			
-	Noorduyn AT-16 Harvard IIB (KLu B-168)	American Air Museum, Duxford	
001	Ryan ST-3KR Recruit (G-BYPY)	Privately owned, Old Warden	
14	Boeing-Stearman A75N-1 Kaydet (G-ISDN)	Privately owned, Kemble	
23	Fairchild PT-23 (N49272)	Privately owned, Sleap	
26	Boeing-Stearman A75N-1 Kaydet (G-BAVO)	Privately owned, Tibenham	
27	NA SNJ-7 Texan (90678/G-BRVG)	Privately owned, Goodwood	
43	Noorduyn AT-16 Harvard IIB (43-13064/G-AZSC) [SC]	Privately owned, North Weald	
44	Boeing-Stearman D75N-1 Kaydet (42-15852/G-RJAH)	Privately owned, Rendcomb	
49	Curtiss P-40M Kittyhawk (43-5802/G-KITT/*P8196*)	Hangar 11 Collection, North Weald	
85	WAR P-47 Thunderbolt <R> (G-BTBI)	Privately owned, Perth	
112	Boeing-Stearman PT-13D Kaydet (42-17397/G-BSWC)	Privately owned, Staverton	
284	Curtiss P-40B Warhawk (41-13297/G-CDWH) [18P]	The Fighter Collection, Duxford	
379	Boeing-Stearman PT-13D Kaydet (42-14865/G-ILLE)	Privately owned, Tibenham	
399	Boeing-Stearman N2S-5 Kaydet (38495/N67193)	Privately owned, Gelnhausen, Germany	
441	Boeing-Stearman N2S-4 Kaydet (30010/G-BTFG)	Privately owned, Manston	
540	Piper L-4H Grasshopper (43-29877/G-BCNX)	Privately owned, Monewden	
560	Bell UH-1H Iroquois (73-22077/G-HUEY)	Privately owned, North Weald	
578	Boeing-Stearman N2S-5 Kaydet (N1364V)	Privately owned, North Weald	
628	Beech D17S (44-67761/N18V)	Privately owned, stored East Garston, Bucks	
669	Boeing-Stearman A75N-1 Kaydet (37869/G-CCXA)	Privately owned, Old Buckenham	
699	Boeing-Stearman N2S-3 Kaydet (38233/G-CCXB)	Privately owned, Old Buckenham	
718	Boeing-Stearman PT-13D Kaydet (42-17555/N5345N)	Privately owned, Tibenham	
744	Boeing-Stearman A75N-1 Kaydet (42-16532/OO-USN)	Privately owned, Wevelgem, Belgium	
854	Ryan PT-22 Recruit (42-17378/G-BTBH)	Privately owned, Old Warden	
855	Ryan PT-22 Recruit (41-15510/N56421)	Privately owned, Sleap	
897	Aeronca 11AC Chief (G-BJEV) [E]	Privately owned, English Bicknor, Glos	
1102	Boeing-Stearman N2S-5 Kaydet (G-AZLE) [102]	Privately owned, Tongham	
1164	Beech D18S (G-BKGL)	The Aircraft Restoration Co, Duxford	
1180	Boeing-Stearman N2S-3 Kaydet (3403/G-BRSK)	Privately owned, Morley	
3072	NA T-6G Texan (49-3072/G-TEXN)	Privately owned, Shoreham	
3397	Boeing-Stearman N2S-3 Kaydet (G-OBEE) [174]	Privately owned, Old Buckenham	
4406	Naval Aircraft Factory N3N-3 (G-ONAF) [12]	Privately owned, Sandown	

Notes	*Serial*	*Type (code/other identity)*	*Owner/operator, location or fate*
	6136	Boeing-Stearman A75N-1 Kaydet (42-16136/G-BRUJ) [205]	Privately owned, Liverpool
	6771	Republic F-84F Thunderstreak (BAF FU-6)	RAF Museum, stored Cosford
	7797	Aeronca L-16A (47-0797/G-BFAF)	Privately owned, Finmere
	8084	NA AT-6D Harvard III (42-85068/LN-AMY)	The Old Flying Machine Company, Duxford
	8178	NA F-86A Sabre (48-0178/G-SABR) [FU-178]	Golden Apple Operations/ARC, Duxford
	8242	NA F-86A Sabre (48-0242) [FU-242]	Midland Air Museum, Coventry
	01532	Northrop F-5E Tiger II <R>	RAF Alconbury on display
	02538	Fairchild PT-19B (N33870)	Privately owned, Greenham Common
	07539	Boeing-Stearman N2S-3 Kaydet (N63590) [143]	Privately owned, Billericay
	14286	Lockheed T-33A (51-4286)	American Air Museum, Duxford
	O-14419	Lockheed T-33A (51-4419)	Midland Air Museum, Coventry
	14863	NA AT-6D Harvard III (41-33908/G-BGOR)	Privately owned, Rednal
	15154	Bell OH-58A Kiowa (70-15154)	R. Military College of Science, Shrivenham
	15990	Bell AH-1F Hueycobra (67-19590)	Museum of Army Flying, stored Middle Wallop
	16445	Bell AH-1F Hueycobra (69-16445)	R. Military College of Science, Shrivenham
	16506	Hughes OH-6A Cayuse (67-16506)	The Helicopter Museum, Weston-super-Mare
	16579	Bell UH-1H Iroquois (66-16579)	The Helicopter Museum, Weston-super-Mare
	16718	Lockheed T-33A (51-6718)	City of Norwich Aviation Museum
	17962	Lockheed SR-71A (61-7962)	American Air Museum, Duxford
	18263	Boeing-Stearman PT-17 Kaydet (41-8263/N38940) [822]	Privately owned, Tibenham
	19252	Lockheed T-33A (51-9252)	Tangmere Military Aviation Museum
	21509	Bell UH-1H Iroquois (72-21509/G-UHIH)	Privately owned, Blackpool
	21605	Bell UH-1H Iroquois (72-21605)	American Air Museum, Duxford
	21714	Grumman F8F-2P Bearcat (121714/G-RUMM) [201-B]	The Fighter Collection, Duxford
	24538	Kaman HH-43F Huskie (62-4535)	Midland Air Museum, Coventry
	24541	Cessna L-19E Bird Dog (N134TT)	Privately owned, Yarcombe, Devon
	24568	Cessna L-19E Bird Dog (LN-WNO)	Army Aviation Norway, Kjeller, Norway
	28521	CCF Harvard IV (G-TVIJ) [TA-521]	Privately owned, Woodchurch, Kent
	30861	NA TB-25J Mitchell (44-30861/N9089Z)	Privately owned, Booker
	31145	Piper L-4B Grasshopper (43-1145/G-BBLH) [26-G]	Privately owned, Biggin Hill
	31171	NA B-25J Mitchell (44-31171/N7614C)	American Air Museum, Duxford
	31430	Piper L-4B Grasshopper (43-1430/G-BHVV)	Privately owned, Rochester
	31952	Aeronca O-58B Defender (G-BRPR)	Privately owned, Earls Colne
	34037	NA TB-25N Mitchell (44-29366/N9115Z/8838M)	RAF Museum, Hendon
	37414	McD F-4C Phantom (63-7414)	Midland Air Museum, Coventry
	39624	Wag Aero Sport Trainer (G-BVMH) [39-D]	Privately owned, Temple Bruer
	40467	Grumman F6F-5K Hellcat (80141/G-BTCC) [19]	The Fighter Collection, Duxford
	41386	Thomas-Morse S4 Scout <R> (G-MJTD)	Privately owned, Lutterworth
	42165	NA F-100D Super Sabre (54-2165) [VM]	American Air Museum, Duxford
	42174	NA F-100D Super Sabre (54-2174) [UH]	Midland Air Museum, Coventry
	42196	NA F-100D Super Sabre (54-2196)	Norfolk & Suffolk Avn Museum, Flixton
	46214	Grumman TBM-3E Avenger (69327/CF-KCG) [X-3]	American Air Museum, Duxford
	48846	Boeing B-17G Flying Fortress (44-8846/F-AZDX) [DS-M]	Assoc Fortresse Toujours Volant, Paris, France
	53319	Grumman TBM-3R Avenger (HB-RDG) [319-RB]	Privately owned, Lausanne, Switzerland
	54433	Lockheed T-33A (55-4433)	Norfolk & Suffolk Avn Museum, Flixton

Serial	*Type (code/other identity)*	*Owner/operator, location or fate*	*Notes*
54884	Piper L-4J Grasshopper (45-4884/N61787) [57-D]	Privately owned, Chiseldon	
56498	Douglas C-54Q Skymaster (N44914)	Privately owned, stored North Weald	
60312	McD F-101F Voodoo (56-0312)	Midland Air Museum, Coventry	
60689	Boeing B-52D Stratofortress (56-0689)	American Air Museum, Duxford	
63000	NA F-100D Super Sabre (54-2212) [FW-000]	USAF Croughton, Oxon, at gate	
63319	NA F-100D Super Sabre (54-2269) [FW-319]	RAF Lakenheath, on display	
63428	Republic F-105G Thunderchief (62-4428) [WW]	USAF Croughton, Oxon, at gate	
66692	Lockheed U-2CT (56-6692)	American Air Museum, Duxford	
70270	McD F-101B Voodoo (57-270) (fuselage)	Midland Air Museum, Coventry	
80105	Replica SE5a <R> (PH-WWI/G-CCBN) [19]	Privately owned, Thruxton	
80995	Cessna 337D Super Skymaster (F-BRPQ)	Privately owned, Strasbourg, France	
82062	DHC U-6A Beaver (58-2062)	Midland Air Museum, Coventry	
91822	Republic F-105D Thunderchief (59-1822)	Imperial War Museum, Duxford	
93542	CCF Harvard IV (G-BRLV) [LTA-542]	Privately owned, North Weald	
96995	CV F4U-4 Corsair (OE-EAS) [BR-37]	Flying Bulls, Salzburg, Austria	
97264	CV F4U-4 Corsair (F-AZVJ) [403]	*Sold to the US, October 2007*	
111836	NA AT-6C Harvard IIA (41-33262/G-TSIX) [JZ-6]	Privately owned, Tatenhill	
111989	Cessna L-19A Bird Dog (51-11989/N33600)	Museum of Army Flying, Middle Wallop	
114700	NA T-6G Texan (51-14700/G-TOMC)	Privately owned, Netherthorpe	
115042	NA T-6G Texan (51-15042/G-BGHU) [TA-042]	Privately owned, Headcorn	
115227	NA T-6G Texan (51-15227/G-BKRA)	Privately owned, Staverton	
115302	Piper L-18C Super Cub (51-15302/G-BJTP) [TP]	Privately owned, Defford	
115684	Piper L-21A Super Cub (51-15684/G-BKVM) [DC]	Privately owned, Strubby	
124143	Douglas AD-4NA Skyraider (F-AZDP) [205-RM]	Amicale J-B Salis, la Ferté-Alais, France	
124485	Boeing B-17G Flying Fortress (44-85784/G-BEDF)[DF-A]	B-17 Preservation Ltd, Duxford	
124724	CV F4U-5NL Corsair (F-AZEG) [22]	Amicale J-B Salis, la Ferté-Alais, France	
126922	Douglas AD-4NA Skyraider (G-RADR) [402-AK]	Kennet Aviation, North Weald	
126956	Douglas AD-4NA Skyraider (F-AZDQ) [3-RM]	Aéro Retro, St Rambert d'Albon, France	
134076	NA AT-6D Harvard III (41-34671/F-AZSC) [TA076]	Privately owned, Yvetot, France	
138179	NA T-28A Trojan (OE-ESA) [BA]	The Flying Bulls, Salzburg, Austria	
138266	NA T-28B Trojan (HB-RCT) [266-CT]	Jet Alpine Fighter, Sion, Switzerland	
140547	NA T-28C Trojan (F-AZHN) [IF-28]	Privately owned, Toussus le Noble, France	
140566	NA T-28C Trojan (N556EB) [252]	Privately owned, la Ferté-Alais, France	
146289	NA T-28C Trojan (N99153) [2W]	Norfolk & Suffolk Avn Museum, Flixton	
150225	WS58 Wessex 60 (G-AWOX) [123]	Privately owned, Lulsgate	
155529	McD F-4J(UK) Phantom (ZE359) [AJ-114]	American Air Museum, Duxford	
155848	McD F-4S Phantom [WT-11]	Royal Scottish Mus'm of Flight, E Fortune	
159233	HS AV-8A Harrier [CG-33]	Imperial War Museum North, Salford Quays	
160608	Lockheed EC-130Q Hercules (N14781)	Marshalls, Cambridge (for KLu)	
162068	McD AV-8B Harrier II <ff>	Aeroventure, Doncaster	
162071	McD AV-8B Harrier II (fuselage)	Rolls-Royce, Filton	
162313	Lockheed EC-130Q Hercules (N9239G)	Marshalls, Cambridge (for KLu)	
162737	McD AV-8B Harrier II (fuselage) [38]	MoD/DARA, St Athan	
162958	McD AV-8B Harrier II (fuselage)	QinetiQ, Boscombe Down	
162964	McD AV-8B Harrier II <ff>	RAF Wittering	

Notes	Serial	Type (code/other identity)	Owner/operator, location or fate
	162964	McD AV-8B Harrier II <rf>	BAE Systems, Brough
	163177	McD AV-8B Harrier II (fuselage)	BAE Systems, Warton
	163205	McD AV-8B Harrier II (fuselage)	MoD/DARA, St Athan
	212540	Noorduyn AT-16 Harvard IIB (42-12540/G-BBHK) [RD-40]	*Repainted as FH153, 2007*
	217786	Boeing-Stearman PT-17 Kaydet (41-8169/CF-EQS) [25]	American Air Museum, Duxford
	219993	Bell P-39Q Airacobra (42-19993/G-CEJU)	The Fighter Collection, Duxford
	224319	Douglas C-47B Skytrain (44-77047/G-AMSN) <ff>	Privately owned, Sussex
	226413	Republic P-47D Thunderbolt (45-49192/N47DD) [ZU-N]	American Air Museum, Duxford
	231983	Boeing B-17G Flying Fortress (44-83735/F-BDRS)[IY-G]	American Air Museum, Duxford
	234539	Fairchild PT-19B Cornell (42-34539/N50429) [63]	Privately owned, Dunkeswell
	236657	Piper L-4A Grasshopper (42-36657/G-BGSJ) [72-D]	Privately owned, Langport
	237123	Waco CG-4A Hadrian (BAPC 157) (fuselage)	Yorkshire Air Museum, Elvington
	238410	Piper L-4A Grasshopper (42-38410/G-BHPK) [44-A]	Privately owned, Tibenham
	241079	Waco CG-4A Hadrian <R>	Assault Glider Association, Shawbury
	243809	Waco CG-4A Hadrian (BAPC 185)	Museum of Army Flying, Middle Wallop
	252983	Schweizer TG-3A (42-52983/N66630)	Imperial War Museum, stored Duxford
	298177	Stinson L-5A Sentinel (42-98177/N6438C) [8-R]	Privately owned, Tibenham
	314887	Fairchild Argus III (43-14887/G-AJPI)	Privately owned, Eelde, The Netherlands
	315211	Douglas C-47A (43-15211/N1944A) [J8-Z]	Privately owned, Kemble
	315509	Douglas C-47A (43-15509/G-BHUB) [W7-S]	American Air Museum, Duxford
	329405	Piper L-4H Grasshopper (43-29405/G-BCOB) [23-A]	Privately owned, South Walsham, Norfolk
	329417	Piper L-4A Grasshopper (42-38400/G-BDHK)	Privately owned, English Bicknor, Glos
	329471	Piper L-4H Grasshopper (43-29471/G-BGXA) [44-F]	Privately owned, Martley, Worcs
	329601	Piper L-4H Grasshopper (43-29601/G-AXHR) [44-D]	Privately owned, Nayland
	329854	Piper L-4H Grasshopper (43-29854/G-BMKC) [44-R]	Privately owned, Newtownards
	329934	Piper L-4H Grasshopper (43-29934/G-BCPH) [72-B]	Privately owned, Thatcham
	330238	Piper L-4H Grasshopper (43-30238/G-LIVH) [24-A]	Privately owned, Barton
	330485	Piper L-4H Grasshopper (43-30485/G-AJES) [44-C]	Privately owned, Shifnal
	343251	Boeing-Stearman N2S-5 Kaydet (43517/G-NZSS) [27]	Privately owned, Kidlington
	411622	NA P-51D Mustang (44-74427/F-AZSB) [G4-C]	Amicale J-B Salis, la Ferté-Alais, France
	413317	NA P-51D Mustang (44-74409/N51RT) [VF-B]	RAF Museum, Hendon
	413521	NA P-51D Mustang (44-13521/G-MRLL) [5Q-B]	Privately owned, Hardwick, Norfolk
	413573	NA P-51D Mustang (44-73415/ 9133M/N6526D) [B6-V]	RAF Museum, Cosford
	413704	NA P-51D Mustang (44-73149/G-BTCD) [B7-H]	The Old Flying Machine Company, Duxford
	414151	NA P-51D Mustang (44-73140/NL314BG) [HO-M]	Privately owned, Greenham Common
	414419	NA P-51D Mustang (45-15118/G-MSTG) [LH-F]	Privately owned, Hardwick, Norfolk
	414450	NA P-51D Mustang (44-73877/N167F) [B6-S]	Scandinavian Historic Flight, Oslo, Norway
	433915	Consolidated PBY-5A Catalina (G-PBYA)	Privately owned, Duxford

Serial	*Type (code/other identity)*	*Owner/operator, location or fate*	*Notes*
434602	Douglas A-26B Invader (44-34602/N167B) [B]	Scandinavian Historic Flight, Oslo, Norway	
436021	Piper J/3C Cub 65 (G-BWEZ)	Privately owned, Strathaven, Strathclyde	
442268	Noorduyn AT-16 Harvard IIB (KF568/LN-TEX) [TA-268]	Scandinavian Historic Flight, Oslo, Norway	
454467	Piper L-4J Grasshopper (45-4467/G-BILI) [44-J]	Privately owned, White Waltham	
454537	Piper L-4J Grasshopper (45-4537/G-BFDL) [04-J]	Privately owned, Shempston Farm, Lossiemouth	
458811	NA B-25J Mitchell (45-8811/HB-RDE) [SB]	Jet Alpine Fighter, Sion, Switzerland	
461748	Boeing B-29A Superfortress (44-61748/G-BHDK) [Y]	American Air Museum, Duxford	
463209	NA P-51D Mustang <R> (BAPC 255) [WZ-S]	American Air Museum, Duxford	
463864	NA P-51D Mustang (44-63864/G-CBNM) [HL-W]	The Fighter Collection, Duxford	
472035	NA P-51D Mustang (44-72035/G-SIJJ)	Hangar 11 Collection, North Weald	
472216	NA P-51D Mustang (44-72216/G-BIXL) [HO-M]	Privately owned, East Garston, Bucks	
472218	CAC-18 Mustang 22 (A68-192/G-HAEC) [WZ-I]	Privately owned, Woodchurch, Kent	
472218	NA P-51D Mustang (44-73979) [WZ-I]	Imperial War Museum, Lambeth	
472773	NA P-51D Mustang (44-72773/D-FPSI) [QP-M]	Privately owned, Freiburg, Germany	
474425	NA P-51D Mustang (44-74425/PH-PSI) [OC-G]	Privately owned, Lelystad, The Netherlands	
474923	NA P-51D Mustang (44-74923/N6395)	Privately owned, Lelystad, The Netherlands	
479744	Piper L-4H Grasshopper (44-79744/G-BGPD) [49-M]	Privately owned, Marsh, Bucks	
479766	Piper L-4H Grasshopper (44-79766/G-BKHG) [63-D]	Privately owned, Frogland Cross	
480015	Piper L-4H Grasshopper (44-80015/G-AKIB) [44-M]	Privately owned, Bodmin	
480133	Piper L-4J Grasshopper (44-80133/G-BDCD) [44-B]	Privately owned, Slinfold	
480173	Piper J-3C Cub 65 (G-RRSR) [57-H]	Privately owned, Wellesbourne Mountford	
480321	Piper L-4J Grasshopper (44-80321/G-FRAN) [44-H]	Privately owned, Rayne, Essex	
480480	Piper L-4J Grasshopper (44-80480/G-BECN) [44-E]	Privately owned, Rayne, Essex	
480551	Piper L-4J Grasshopper (44-80551/LN-KLT) [43-S]	Scandinavian Historic Flight, Oslo, Norway	
480636	Piper L-4J Grasshopper (44-80636/G-AXHP) [58-A]	Privately owned, Spanhoe	
480723	Piper L-4J Grasshopper (44-80723/G-BFZB) [E5-J]	Privately owned, Egginton	
480752	Piper L-4J Grasshopper (44-80752/G-BCXJ) [39-E]	Privately owned, Old Sarum	
483868	Boeing B-17G Flying Fortress (44-83868/N5237V) [A-N]	RAF Museum, Hendon	
493209	NA T-6G Texan (49-3209/G-DDMV/*41*)	Privately owned, Rochester	
511701A	Beech C-45H (51-11701/G-BSZC) [AF258]	Privately owned, Bryngwyn Bach	
2100882	Douglas C-47A (42-100882/N473DC) [3X-P]	Privately owned, Liverpool	
2100884	Douglas C-47A (42-100884/N147DC) [L4-D]	Privately owned, Dunsfold	
00195700	Cessna F.150G (G-OIDW)	Privately owned, Halfpenny Green	
3-1923	Aeronca O-58B Defender (43-1923/G-BRHP)	Privately owned, Chiseldon	
18-2001	Piper L-18C Super Cub (52-2401/G-BIZV)	Privately owned, Croydon, Cambs	
39-139	Beech YC-43 Traveler (N295BS)	Duke of Brabant AF, Eindhoven, The Netherlands	
40-2538	Farichild PT-19A (N33870)	Privately owned, Martham, Norfolk	
41-33275	NA AT-6C Texan (G-BICE) [CE]	Privately owned, Monewden	

Notes	Serial	Type (code/other identity)	Owner/operator, location or fate
	42-12417	Noorduyn AT-16 Harvard IIB (Klu. B-163)	Privately owned, Earls Colne
	42-17553	Boeing-Stearman PT-13D Kaydet (N1731B) [716]	Privately owned, Bidford-on-Avon, Warks
	42-35870	Talyorcraft DCO-65 (G-BWLJ) [129]	Privately owned, Nayland
	42-58678	Taylorcraft DF-65 (G-BRIY) [IY]	Privately owned, Carlisle
	42-78044	Aeronca 11AC Chief (G-BRXL)	Privately owned, Thurrock
	42-84555	NA AT-6D Harvard III (FAP.1662/G-ELMH) [EP-H]	Privately owned, Hardwick, Norfolk
	42-93510	Douglas C-47A Skytrain [CM] <ff>	Privately owned, Kew
	43-9628	Douglas A-20G Havoc <ff>	Privately owned, Hinckley, Leics
	44-4315	Bell P-63C Kingcobra	Privately owned, Redhill
	44-4368	Bell P-63C Kingcobra	Privately owned, Redhill
	44-13954	NA P-51D Mustang (G-UAKE)	Mustang Restoration Co Ltd, Coventry
	44-14574	NA P-51D Mustang (fuselage)	East Essex Aviation Museum, Clacton
	44-42914	Douglas DC-4 (N31356)	Privately owned, stored North Weald
	44-51228	Consolidated B-24M Liberator [RE-N]	American Air Museum, Duxford
	44-79609	Piper L-4H Grasshopper (G-BHXY) [PR]	Privately owned, Bodmin
	44-80594	Piper L-4J Grasshopper (G-BEDJ)	Privately owned, White Waltham
	44-80647	Piper L-4J Grasshopper (D-EGAF)	The Vintage Aircraft Co, Fürstenwalde, Germany
	44-83184	Fairchild UC-61K Argus III (G-RGUS)	Privately owned, Snitterby
	46-11042	Wolf WII <R> (G-BMZX) [7]	Privately owned, Kilrush, Eire
	51-9036	Lockheed T-33A	Newark Air Museum, Winthorpe
	51-15319	Piper L-18C Super Cub (G-FUZZ) [A-319]	Privately owned, Elvington
	51-15555	Piper L-18C Super Cub (G-OSPS)	Privately owned, Weston, Eire
	52-8543	CCF T-6J Harvard IV (G-BUKY) [66]	Privately owned, Breighton
	54-005	NA F-100D Super Sabre (54-2163)	Dumfries & Galloway Avn Mus, Dumfries
	54-223	NA F-100D Super Sabre (54-2223)	Newark Air Museum, Winthorpe
	54-2445	Piper L-21B Super Cub (G-OTAN) [A-445]	Privately owned, Andrewsfield
	54-2447	Piper L-21B Super Cub (G-SCUB)	Privately owned, Anwick
	63-699	McD F-4C Phantom (63-7699) [CG]	Midland Air Museum, Coventry
	64-17657	Douglas A-26A Invader (N99218) <ff>	Privately owned, Catfield
	65-777	McD F-4C Phantom (63-7419) [LN]	RAF Lakenheath, on display
	67-120	GD F-111E Aardvark (67-0120) [UH]	American Air Museum, Duxford
	68-0060	GD F-111E Aardvark <ff>	Dumfries & Galloway Avn Mus, Dumfries
	72-1447	GD F-111F Aardvark <ff>	American Air Museum, Duxford
	72-448	GD F-111E Aardvark (68-0011) [LN]	RAF Lakenheath, on display
	74-0177	GD F-111F Aardvark [CC]	RAF Museum, Cosford
	76-020	McD F-15A Eagle (76-0020) [BT]	American Air Museum, Duxford
	76-124	McD F-15B Eagle (76-0124) [LN]	RAF Lakenheath, instructional use
	77-259	Fairchild A-10A Thunderbolt (77-0259) [AR]	American Air Museum, Duxford
	80-219	Fairchild GA-10A Thunderbolt (80-0219) [AR]	RAF Alconbury, on display
	82-23762	B-V CH-47D Chinook <ff>	RAF Odiham, instructional use
	83-24104	B-V CH-47D Chinook [BN] <ff>	RAF Museum, Hendon
	92-048	McD F-15A Eagle (74-0131) [LN]	RAF Lakenheath, on display
	146-11083	Wolf WII <R> (G-BNAI) [5]	Privately owned, Haverfordwest
	G-57	Piper L-4A Grasshopper (42-36375/G-AKAZ)	Privately owned, Duxford
	H-57	Piper L-4A Grasshopper (42-36375/G-AKAZ)	*Repainted as G-57, 2007*

YEMEN

Notes	Serial	Type (code/other identity)	Owner/operator, location or fate
	104	BAC Jet Provost T.52A (G-PROV)	Privately owned, North Weald

YUGOSLAVIA

Notes	Serial	Type (code/other identity)	Owner/operator, location or fate
	30139	Soko P-2 Kraguj [139]	Privately owned, Biggin Hill
	30140	Soko P-2 Kraguj (G-RADA) [140]	Privately owned, Biggin Hill

Serial	Type (code/other identity)	Owner/operator, location or fate	Notes
30146	Soko P-2 Kraguj (G-BSXD) [146]	Privately owned, Morpeth, Northumberland	
30149	Soko P-2 Kraguj (G-SOKO) [149]	Privately owned, Wickenby	
30151	Soko P-2 Kraguj [151]	Privately owned, Sopley, Hants	

Focke-Wulf 190 Replica G-CCFW is based at Kemble.

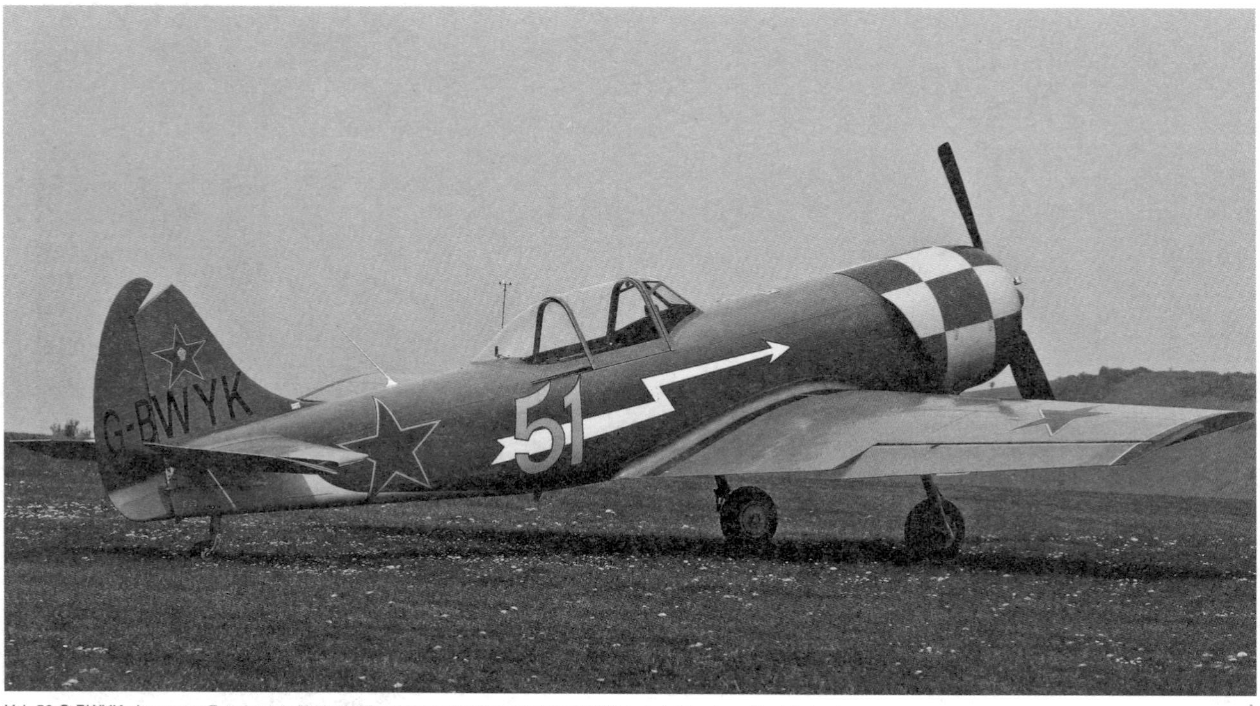

Yak-50 G-BWYK also wears Russian markings. Notice the construction number 812004 just visible above the tailwheel.

CASA 1.131E Jungmann G-CDLC flies in its former Spanish Air Force markings as E.3B-494, coded 81-47. It is based at Kemble.

Tornado ECR 46+44 is based at Lechfeld in Germany with Jagdbombergeschwader 32 (JbG-32).

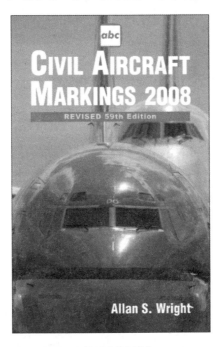

Irish Military Aircraft Markings

Notes	Serial	Type (cther identity)	Owner/operator, location
	C7	Avro 631 Cadet (EI-AGO)	IAC, Baldonnel
	34	Miles M14A Magister (N5392)	National Museum of Ireland, Dublin
	141	Avro 652A Anson C19	IAC Museum, Baldonnel
	161	VS509 Spitfire T9 (G-CCCA)	*Repainted in Dutch marks as H-98, April 2007*
	164	DHC1 Chipmunk T20	IAC Museum, Baldonnel
	168	DHC1 Chipmunk T20	IAC Museum, Baldonnel
	172	DHC1 Chipmunk T20	IAC, stored Baldonnel
	173	DHC1 Chipmunk T20	South East Aviation Enthusiasts, Dromod
	176	DH104 Dove 4 (VP-YKF)	South East Aviation Enthusiasts, Waterford
	177	Percival P56 Provost T51 (G-BLIW)	Privately owned, Shoreham
	181	Percival P56 Provost T51	Privately owned, Thatcham
	183	Percival P56 Provost T51	IAC Museum, Baldonnel
	184	Percival P56 Provost T51	South East Aviation Enthusiasts, Dromod
	187	DH115 Vampire T55	South East Aviation Enthusiasts, Dromod
	191	DH115 Vampire T55	IAC Museum, Baldonnel
	192	DH115 Vampire T55	South East Aviation Enthusiasts, Dromod
	195	Sud SA316 Alouette III (F-WJDH)	IAC, stored Baldonnel
	196	Sud SA316 Alouette III (F-WKQB)	IAC, stored Baldonnel
	197	Sud SA316 Alouette III	IAC, stored Baldonnel
	198	DH115 Vampire T11 (XE977)	National Museum of Ireland, Dublin
	199	DHC1 Chipmunk T22	IAC, stored Baldonnel
	202	Sud SA316 Alouette III	IAC Museum, Baldonnel
	203	Reims-Cessna FR172H	IAC No 104 Sqn/1 Operations Wing, Baldonnel
	205	Reims-Cessna FR172H	IAC No 104 Sqn/1 Operations Wing, Baldonnel
	206	Reims-Cessna FR172H	IAC No 104 Sqn/1 Operations Wing, Baldonnel
	207	Reims-Cessna FR172H	IAC, stored Waterford
	208	Reims-Cessna FR172H	IAC No 104 Sqn/1 Operations Wing, Baldonnel
	210	Reims-Cessna FR172H	IAC No 104 Sqn/1 Operations Wing, Baldonnel
	211	Sud SA316 Alouette III	IAC, stored Baldonnel
	212	Sud SA316 Alouette III	IAC, stored Baldonnel
	213	Sud SA316 Alouette III	IAC, stored Baldonnel
	214	Sud SA316 Alouette III	IAC, stored Baldonnel
	215	Fouga CM170 Super Magister	Dublin Institute of Technology
	216	Fouga CM170 Super Magister	National Museum of Ireland, Dublin
	218	Fouga CM170 Super Magister	Shannon Aerospace
	219	Fouga CM170 Super Magister	IAC Museum, Baldonnel
	220	Fouga CM170 Super Magister	Cork University, instructional use
	231	SIAI SF-260WE Warrior	IAC Museum, stored Baldonnel
	240	Beech Super King Air 200MR	IAC No 102 Sqn/1 Operations Wing, Baldonnel
	251	Grumman G1159C Gulfstream IV (N17584)	IAC No 102 Sqn/1 Operations Wing, Baldonnel
	252	Airtech CN.235 MPA Persuader	IAC No 101 Sqn/1 Operations Wing, Baldonnel
	253	Airtech CN.235 MPA Persuader	IAC No 101 Sqn/1 Operations Wing, Baldonnel
	254	PBN-2T Defender 4000 (G-BWPN)	IAC No 106 Sqn/1 Operations Wing, Baldonnel
	255	AS355N Twin Squirrel (G-BXEV)	IAC No 106 Sqn/1 Operations Wing, Baldonnel
	256	Eurocopter EC135T-1 (G-BZRM)	IAC No 106 Sqn/1 Operations Wing, Baldonnel
	258	Gates Learjet 45 (N5009T)	IAC No 102 Sqn/1 Operations Wing, Baldonnel
	260	Pilatus PC-9M (HB-HQS)	IAC Flying Training School, Baldonnel
	261	Pilatus PC-9M (HB-HQT)	IAC Flying Training School, Baldonnel
	262	Pilatus PC-9M (HB-HQU)	IAC Flying Training School, Baldonnel
	263	Pilatus PC-9M (HB-HQV)	IAC Flying Training School, Baldonnel
	264	Pilatus PC-9M (HB-HQW)	IAC Flying Training School, Baldonnel
	265	Pilatus PC-9M (HB-HQX)	IAC Flying Training School, Baldonnel
	266	Pilatus PC-9M (HB-HQY)	IAC Flying Training School, Baldonnel
	267	Pilatus PC-9M (HB-HQZ)	IAC Flying Training School, Baldonnel

Serial	Type (other identity)	Owner/operator, location	Notes
268	Pilatus PC-9M	IAC (option)	
269	Pilatus PC-9M	IAC (option)	
270	Eurocopter EC135P-2	IAC No 302 Sqn/3 Operations Wing, Baldonnel	
271	Eurocopter EC135P-2	IAC No 302 Sqn/3 Operations Wing, Baldonnel	
272	Eurocopter EC135T-2 (G-CECT)	IAC No 106 Sqn/1 Operations Wing, Baldonnel	
273	Eurocopter EC135P-2	IAC, on order	
274	AgustaWestland AW.139	IAC No 301 Sqn/3 Operations Wing, Baldonnel	
275	AgustaWestland AW.139	IAC No 301 Sqn/3 Operations Wing, Baldonnel	
276	AgustaWestland AW.139	IAC No 301 Sqn/3 Operations Wing, Baldonnel	
277	AgustaWestland AW.139	IAC No 301 Sqn/3 Operations Wing, Baldonnel	
278	AgustaWestland AW.139	IAC, on order	
279	AgustaWestland AW.139	IAC, on order	

The red 'R' on the intake of this German Air Force F-4F Phantom II denotes JG-71 'Richthofen' although in fact it was being flown by a JG-74 crew at the time when this photo was taken. The Phantom is slowly disappearing from European skies.

Overseas Military Aircraft Markings

Aircraft included in this section include those likely to be seen visiting UK civil and military airfields on transport flights, exchange visits, exercises and for air shows. It is not a comprehensive list of *all* aircraft operated by the air arms concerned.

ALGERIA
Force Aérienne Algérienne/ Al Quwwat al Jawwiya al Jaza'eriya

Lockheed C-130H Hercules

7T-WHE (4935)
7T-WHF (4934)
7T-WHI (4930)
7T-WHJ (4928)
7T-WHQ (4926)
7T-WHR (4924)
7T-WHS (4912)
7T-WHT (4911)
7T-WHY (4913)
7T-WHZ (4914)

Lockheed C-130H-30 Hercules

7T-WHA (4997)
7T-WHB (5224)
7T-WHD (4987)
7T-WHL (4989)
7T-WHM (4919)
7T-WHN (4894)
7T-WHO (4897)
7T-WHP (4921)

Grumman G.1159C Gulfstream IVSP

Ministry of Defence, Boufarik
7T-VPC (1418)
7T-VPM (1421)
7T-VPR (1288)
7T-VPS (1291)

Gulfstream Aerospace Gulfstream V

Ministry of Defence, Boufarik
7T-VPG (617)

AUSTRALIA
Royal Australian Air Force

Airbus KC-30B (A.330-203 MRTT)

33 Sqn, Amberley
A39-001 (on order)
A39-002 (on order)
A39-003 (on order)
A39-004 (on order)

Boeing 707-338C

33 Sqn, Amberley
A20-624

Boeing 737-7DF/-7DT/-7ES AEW&C

34 Sqn, Canberra
A30-001 737-7ES
A30-002 737-7ES
A30-003 737-7ES
A30-004 737-7ES
A30-005 737-7ES
A30-006 737-7ES
A36-001 737-7DT
A36-002 737-7DF

Boeing C-17A Globemaster III

36 Sqn, Amberley
A41-206
A41-207
A41-208
A41-209

Canadair CL.604 Challenger

34 Sqn, Canberra
A37-001
A37-002
A37-003

Lockheed C-130H Hercules/ C-130J-30 Hercules II

37 Sqn, Richmond, NSW

C-130H

A97-001
A97-002
A97-003
A97-004
A97-005
A97-006
A97-007
A97-008
A97-009
A97-010
A97-011
A97-012

C-130J-30

A97-440
A97-441
A97-442
A97-447
A97-448
A97-449
A97-450
A97-464
A97-465
A97-466
A97-467
A97-468

Lockheed AP-3C Orion

10/11 Sqns, Maritime Patrol Group, Edinburgh, NSW
A9-656 11 Sqn
A9-657 11 Sqn
A9-658 10 Sqn
A9-659 11 Sqn
A9-660 10 Sqn
A9-661 10 Sqn
A9-662 11 Sqn
A9-663 11 Sqn
A9-664 11 Sqn
A9-665 10 Sqn
A9-751 11 Sqn
A9-752 10 Sqn
A9-753 10 Sqn
A9-755 10 Sqn
A9-756 11 Sqn
A9-757 10 Sqn
A9-758 10 Sqn
A9-759 10 Sqn
A9-760 10 Sqn

AUSTRIA
Öesterreichische Luftstreitkräfte

Agusta-Bell AB.206A JetRanger

Fliegerregiment I
2 Hubschrauberstaffel, Tulln
3C-JA
3C-JB
3C-JC
3C-JD
3C-JE
3C-JF
3C-JG
3C-JH
3C-JI
3C-JJ
3C-JM

Agusta-Bell AB.212/Bell 212*

Fliegerregiment III
1 & 2 Hubschrauberstaffel, Linz
5D-HB
5D-HC
5D-HD
5D-HF
5D-HG
5D-HH
5D-HI
5D-HJ
5D-HK
5D-HL
5D-HN
5D-HO
5D-HP
5D-HQ
5D-HR
5D-HS
5D-HT
5D-HU
5D-HV
5D-HW
5D-HX
5D-HY*
5D-HZ

Bell OH-58B Kiowa

Fliegerregiment I
3 Hubschrauberstaffel, Tulln
3C-OA
3C-OB
3C-OC
3C-OD
3C-OE
3C-OG
3C-OH
3C-OI
3C-OJ
3C-OK

3C-OL

Eurofighter EF.2000
7L-WA
7L-WB
7L-WC
7L-WD
7L-WE
7L-WF
7L-WG
7L-WH
7L-WI
7L-WJ
7L-WK
7L-WL
7L-WM
7L-WN
7L-WO

Lockheed C-130K Hercules
Fliegerregiment III
Transportstaffel, Linz
8T-CA
8T-CB
8T-CC

Northrop F-5E Tiger II
Fliegerregiment II
2 Staffel/Uberwg, Graz
J-3004
J-3005
J-3014
J-3030
J-3033
J-3036
J-3038
J-3041
J-3052
J-3056
J-3057
J-3065

Pilatus PC-6B/B2-H2 Turbo Porter/ PC-6B/B2-H4 Turbo Porter*
Fliegerregiment I
Flachenstaffel, Tulln
3G-EA
3G-EB
3G-EC
3G-ED
3G-EE
3G-EF
3G-EG
3G-EH
3G-EJ
3G-EK
3G-EL
3G-EM
3G-EN*

Pilatus PC-7 Turbo Trainer
Fliegerschule, Zeltweg
3H-FA
3H-FB
3H-FC
3H-FD
3H-FE
3H-FF
3H-FG
3H-FH
3H-FI
3H-FJ
3H-FK
3H-FL
3H-FM
3H-FN
3H-FO
3H-FP

SAAB 105ÖE
Fliegerregiment III
Dusenstaffel, Linz
(yellow)
B (105402)
D (105404)
E (105405)
G (105407)
I (105409)
J (105410)
(green)
B (105412)
D (105414)
GF-16 (105416)
GG-17 (105417)
(red)
B (105422)
C (105423)
D (105424)
E (105425)
F (105426)
G (105427)
H (105428)
I (105429)
J (105430)
(blue)
A (105431)
B (105432)
C (105433)
D (105434)
E (105435)
F (105436)
G (105437)
I (105439)
J (105440)

Short SC7 Skyvan 3M
Fliegerregiment I
Flachenstaffel, Tulln
5S-TA
5S-TB

Sikorsky S-70A
Fliegerregiment I
1 Hubschrauberstaffel, Tulln
6M-BA
6M-BB
6M-BC
6M-BD
6M-BE
6M-BF
6M-BG
6M-BH
6M-BI

BAHRAIN

BAE RJ.85/RJ.100*
Bahrain Defence Force
A9C-BDF*
A9C-HWR

Boeing 747SP-21
Bahrain Amiri Flt
A9C-HMH

Boeing 747-4P8
Bahrain Amiri Flt
A9C-HMK

Grumman G.1159 Gulfstream IITT/ G.1159C Gulfstream IV-SP
Govt of Bahrain
A9C-BAH Gulfstream IV-SP
A9C-BG Gulfstream IITT

BELGIUM

Composante Aérienne Belge/ Belgische Luchtcomponent

D-BD Alpha Jet E
11 Smaldeel (1 Wg),
Cazaux, France (ET 02.008)
AT-01
AT-02
AT-03
AT-05
AT-06
AT-08
AT-10
AT-11
AT-12
AT-13
AT-14
AT-15
AT-17
AT-18
AT-19
AT-20
AT-21
AT-22
AT-23
AT-24
AT-25
AT-26
AT-27
AT-28
AT-29
AT-30
AT-31
AT-32
AT-33

Airbus A.310-322
21 Smaldeel (15 Wg),
Melsbroek
CA-01
CA-02

Dassault Falcon 900B
21 Smaldeel (15 Wg),
Melsbroek
CD-01

Embraer ERJ.135LR/ERJ.145LR*
21 Smaldeel (15 Wg),
Melsbroek
CE-01
CE-02
CE-03*
CE-04*

Lockheed C-130H Hercules
20 Smaldeel (15 Wg), Melsbroek
CH-01
CH-03
CH-04
CH-05
CH-07
CH-08
CH-09
CH-10
CH-11
CH-12
CH-14

Dassault Falcon 20E
21 Smaldeel (15 Wg), Melsbroek
CM-01
CM-02

General Dynamics F-16 MLU
1,350 Smaldeel (2 Wg), Florennes [FS];
31,349 Smaldeel, OCU (10 Wg), Kleine-Brogel [BL]

FA-56	F-16A	2 Wg
FA-57	F-16A	2 Wg
FA-67	F-16A	2 Wg
FA-68	F-16A	2 Wg
FA-69	F-16A	10 Wg
FA-70	F-16A	10 Wg
FA-71	F-16A	10 Wg
FA-72	F-16A	2 Wg
FA-77	F-16A	10 Wg
FA-81	F-16A	2 Wg
FA-82	F-16A	10 Wg
FA-83	F-16A	2 Wg
FA-84	F-16A	2 Wg
FA-86	F-16A	10 Wg
FA-87	F-16A	10 Wg
FA-89	F-16A	10 Wg
FA-91	F-16A	2 Wg
FA-92	F-16A	2 Wg
FA-94	F-16A	10 Wg$
FA-95	F-16A	10 Wg
FA-97	F-16A	10 Wg
FA-98	F-16A	10 Wg
FA-99	F-16A	10 Wg
FA-100	F-16A	2 Wg
FA-101	F-16A	2 Wg$
FA-102	F-16A	10 Wg
FA-103	F-16A	10 Wg
FA-104	F-16A	10 Wg
FA-106	F-16A	10 Wg
FA-107	F-16A	2 Wg
FA-108	F-16A	2 Wg
FA-109	F-16A	2 Wg
FA-110	F-16A	10 Wg
FA-111	F-16A	10 Wg
FA-114	F-16A	2 Wg
FA-115	F-16A	2 Wg
FA-116	F-16A	2 Wg
FA-117	F-16A	2 Wg
FA-118	F-16A	10 Wg
FA-119	F-16A	10 Wg
FA-120	F-16A	2 Wg
FA-121	F-16A	2 Wg
FA-123	F-16A	10 Wg
FA-124	F-16A	10 Wg
FA-125	F-16A	10 Wg
FA-126	F-16A	2 Wg
FA-127	F-16A	2 Wg
FA-128	F-16A	2 Wg
FA-129	F-16A	10 Wg
FA-130	F-16A	2 Wg
FA-131	F-16A	2 Wg$
FA-132	F-16A	10 Wg
FA-133	F-16A	2 Wg
FA-134	F-16A	10 Wg
FA-135	F-16A	2 Wg
FA-136	F-16A	2 Wg
FB-02	F-16B	2 Wg
FB-04	F-16B	10 Wg
FB-05	F-16B	2 Wg
FB-09	F-16B	2 Wg
FB-10	F-16B	2 Wg
FB-12	F-16B	2 Wg
FB-14	F-16B	10 Wg
FB-15	F-16B	OCU
FB-17	F-16B	2 Wg
FB-18	F-16B	10 Wg$
FB-20	F-16B	10 Wg
FB-21	F-16B	2 Wg
FB-22	F-16B	2 Wg
FB-23	F-16B	10 Wg
FB-24	F-16B	OCU

Westland Sea King Mk48/48A*
40 Smaldeel, Koksijde
RS-01
RS-02
RS-03*
RS-04
RS-05$

SIAI Marchetti SF260D*/SF260M/SF260M+
Ecole de Pilotage Elementaire (5 Sm/1 Wg), Bevekom
ST-02
ST-03
ST-04
ST-06
ST-12
ST-15+
ST-16+
ST-17+
ST-18
ST-19
ST-20
ST-22
ST-23
ST-24+
ST-25
ST-26+
ST-27
ST-30
ST-31
ST-32
ST-34
ST-35
ST-36
ST-40*
ST-41*
ST-42*
ST-43*
ST-44*
ST-45*
ST-46*
ST-47*
ST-48*

Composante Terrestre Belge/ Belgische Landcomponent
Sud SA318C/SE3130* Alouette II
Liaison Flight & SLV, Bierset
A-22* Liaison Flt

A-44	SLV
A-47	Liaison Flt
A-49	Liaison Flt
A-50	SLV
A-53	Liaison Flt
A-55	SLV
A-57	Liaison Flt
A-59	Liaison Flt
A-61	SLV
A-64	Liaison Flt
A-65	SLV
A-66	SLV
A-68	Liaison Flt
A-69	Liaison Flt
A-70	SLV
A-74	Liaison Flt
A-77	SLV
A-78	SLV
A-79	SLV
A-80	SLV

Agusta A109HA/HO*
16 Smaldeel MRH, Bierset;
17 Smaldeel MRH, Bierset;
18 Smaldeel MRH, Bierset;
SLV, Bierset

H-01*	SLV
H-02*	18 Sm MRH
H-05*	18 Sm MRH
H-06*	17 Sm MRH
H-07*	17 Sm MRH
H-21	18 Sm MRH
H-22	17 Sm MRH
H-24	17 Sm MRH
H-25	18 Sm MRH
H-26	18 Sm MRH
H-27	18 Sm MRH
H-28	17 Sm MRH
H-29	18 Sm MRH
H-30	18 Sm MRH
H-31	18 Sm MRH
H-33	18 Sm MRH
H-35	18 Sm MRH
H-36	17 Sm MRH
H-37	18 Sm MRH
H-38	17 Sm MRH
H-40	18 Sm MRH
H-41	SLV
H-42	SLV
H-43	17 Sm MRH
H-46	17 Sm MRH

Composante Marine Belge/ Belgische Marinecomponent
Sud SA316B Alouette III
Koksijde Heli Flight

M-1	(OT-ZPA)
M-2	(OT-ZPB)
M-3	(OT-ZPC)

Police Fédérale/Federal Politie
Cessna 182 Skylane
Luchsteundetachment, Melsbroek

G-01	C.182Q

G-04 C.182R

MDH
MD.520N
Luchsteundetachment, Melsbroek
G-14
G-15

MDH
MD.900 Explorer
Luchsteundetachment, Melsbroek
G-10
G-11
G-12

Cadets de l'Air/Luchtcadetten
Piper L-21B Super Cub
Bases: Florennes, Goetsenhoeven & Zoersel
LB-01
LB-02
LB-03
LB-05
LB-06

BOTSWANA
Botswana Defence Force
Grumman
G.1159C Gulfstream IV
VIP Sqn, Sir Seretse Kharma IAP
OK1

Lockheed
C-130B Hercules
Z10 Sqn, Thebephatshwa
OM-1
OM-2
OM-3

BRAZIL
Força Aérea Brasileira
Boeing KC-137
2° GT 2° Esq, Galeão
2401
2402
2403
2404

Lockheed
C-130 Hercules
1° GT, 1° Esq, Galeão;
1° GTT, 1° Esq, Afonsos

2451	C-130E	1° GTT
2453	C-130E	1° GTT
2454	C-130E	1° GTT
2456	C-130E	1° GTT
2458	SC-130E	1° GT
2459	C-130E	1° GTT
2461	KC-130H	1° GT
2462	KC-130H	1° GT
2463	C-130H	1° GT
2464	C-130H	1° GT
2465	C-130H	1° GT
2466	C-130H	1° GT
2467	C-130H	1° GT
2470	C-130H	1° GT
2471	C-130H	1° GT
2472	C-130H	1° GT
2473	C-130H	1° GT
2474	C-130H	1° GT
2475	C-130H	1° GT
2476	C-130H	1° GT
2477	C-130H	1° GT
2478	C-130H	1° GT
2479	C-130H	1° GT

BRUNEI
Airbus A.340
Brunei Govt, Bandar Seri Begawan
V8-BKH A.340-212

Boeing 747-430
Brunei Govt, Bandar Seri Begawan
V8-ALI

Boeing 767-27GER
Brunei Govt, Bandar Seri Bergawan
V8-MHB

Gulfstream Aerospace
Gulfstream V
Brunei Govt, Bandar Seri Bergawan
V8-001

BULGARIA
Bulgarsky Voenno-Vazdushni Sily
Aeritalia C-27J
16 TAB, Sofia/Vrazh de bna
071
074

Antonov An-30
16 TAP, Sofia/Dobroslavtzi
055

Pilatus PC.XII/45
16 TAP, Sofia/Dobroslavtzi
020

Bulgarian Govt
Boeing 737-548
Bulgarian Govt, Sofia
LZ-BOR

Dassault Falcon 2000
Bulgarian Govt, Sofia
LZ-OOI

Tupolev Tu-134A-3
Bulgarian Govt, Sofia
LZ-TUG

Tupolev Tu-154M
Bulgarian Govt, Sofia
LZ-BTZ

BURKINA FASO
Boeing 727-14/727-282*
Govt of Burkina Faso, Ouagadougou
XT-BBE
XT-BFA*

CAMEROON
Grumman
G.1159A Gulfstream III
Govt of Cameroon, Yaounde
TJ-AAW

CANADA
Canadian Forces
Lockheed
CC-130 Hercules
CC-130E/CC-130E(SAR)*
413 Sqn, Greenwood (SAR) (14 Wing);
424 Sqn, Trenton (SAR) (8 Wing);
426 Sqn, Trenton (8 Wing);
435 Sqn, Winnipeg (17 Wing);
436 Sqn, Trenton (8 Wing)

130305*	8 Wing
130306*	14 Wing
130307	8 Wing
130308*	8 Wing
130310*	8 Wing
130313	8 Wing
130316	8 Wing
130319	8 Wing
130320	8 Wing
130323	8 Wing
130324*	8 Wing
130325	8 Wing
130326	8 Wing
130327	8 Wing
130328	8 Wing

CC-130H/CC-130H(T)*

130332	8 Wing
130333	17 Wing
130334	8 Wing
130335	8 Wing
130336	17 Wing
130337	8 Wing
130338*	17 Wing
130339*	17 Wing
130340*	17 Wing
130341*	17 Wing
130342*	17 Wing

CC-130H-30

130343	8 Wing
130344	8 Wing

Lockheed
CP-140 Aurora/
CP-140A Arcturus*
404 Sqn, Greenwood (14 Wing);
405 Sqn, Greenwood (14 Wing);
407 Sqn, Comox (19 Wing)

140101	407 Sqn
140102	14 Wing
140103	407 Sqn
140104	14 Wing
140105	407 Sqn
140106	14 Wing
140107	14 Wing
140108	14 Wing
140109	14 Wing
140110	407 Sqn
140111	14 Wing
140112	407 Sqn
140113	407 Sqn
140114	407 Sqn
140115	14 Wing
140116	14 Wing
140117	14 Wing
140118	407 Sqn
140120*	14 Wing
140121*	14 Wing

De Havilland Canada
CT-142
402 Sqn, Winnipeg (17 Wing)
142803 CT-142

142804 CT-142
142805 CT-142
142806 CT-142

Canadair
CC-144 Challenger
412 Sqn, Ottawa (8 Wing)
144601 CC-144A
144614 CC-144B
144615 CC-144B
144616 CC-144B
144617 CC-144C
144618 CC-144C

Airbus
CC-150 Polaris
(A310-304/A310-304F*)
437 Sqn, Trenton (8 Wing)
15001 [991]
15002* [992]
15003* [993]
15004* [994]
15005* [995]

Boeing
CC-177
(C-17A Globemaster III)
429 Sqn, Trenton (8 Wing)
177701
177702
177703
177704

CHILE
Fuerza Aérea de Chile
Boeing 707
Grupo 10, Santiago
902 707-351C
903 707-330B
904 707-358C

Boeing 737
Grupo 10, Santiago
921 737-58N
922 737-330

Extra EA-300L
Los Halcones
132 [6]
145 [2]
146 [3]
147 [4]
149 [1]

Grumman
G.1159C Gulfstream IV
Grupo 10, Santiago
911

Lockheed
C-130B/H Hercules
Grupo 10, Santiago
995 C-130H
996 C-130H
997 C-130B

CROATIA
Hrvatske Zračne Snage
Pilatus PC-9*/PC-9M
92 ZB, Pula;
93 ZB, Zadar
051* 93 ZB
052* 93 ZB
053* 93 ZB
054 93 ZB
055 93 ZB
056 93 ZB
057 93 ZB
058 93 ZB
059 93 ZB
060 93 ZB
061 93 ZB
062 93 ZB
063 93 ZB
064 93 ZB
065 93 ZB
066 93 ZB
067 92 ZB
068 93 ZB
069 93 ZB
070 93 ZB

Canadair
CL.601 Challenger
Croatian Govt, Zagreb
9A-CRO
9A-CRT

CZECH REPUBLIC
Ceske Vojenske Letectvo
Aero L-39/L-59 Albatros
221.TL/22.zL, Náměšt;
CLV, Pardubice
0103 L-39C CLV
0106 L-39C CLV
0107 L-39C CLV
0108 L-39C CLV
0113 L-39C CLV
0115 L-39C CLV
0440 L-39C CLV
0441 L-39C CLV
0444 L-39C CLV
0445 L-39C CLV
0448 L-39C CLV
2341 L-39ZA 221.TL/22.zL
2344 L-39ZA 221.TL/22.zL
2347 L-39ZA 221.TL/22.zL
2350 L-39ZA 221.TL/22.zL
2415 L-39ZA 221.TL/22.zL
2418 L-39ZA 221.TL/22.zL
2421 L-39ZA 221.TL/22.zL
2424 L-39ZA 221.TL/22.zL
2427 L-39ZA 221.TL/22.zL
2430 L-39ZA 221.TL/22.zL
2433 L-39ZA 221.TL/22.zL
2436 L-39ZA 221.TL/22.zL
3903 L-39ZA 221.TL/22.zL
5013 L-39ZA 221.TL/22.zL
5015 L-39ZA 221.TL/22.zL
5017 L-39ZA 221.TL/22.zL
5019 L-39ZA 221.TL/22.zL

Aero
L-159A ALCA/L-159B/L-159T-1
212.TL/21.zTL, Cáslav;
LZO, Praha/Kbely
L-159A
6048 212.TL/21.zTL
6049 212.TL/21.zTL
6050 212.TL/21.zTL
6051 212.TL/21.zTL
6052 212.TL/21.zTL
6053 212.TL/21.zTL
6054 212.TL/21.zTL
6055 212.TL/21.zTL
6057 212.TL/21.zTL
6058 212.TL/21.zTL
6059 212.TL/21.zTL
6060 212.TL/21.zTL
6061 212.TL/21.zTL
6062 212.TL/21.zTL
6063 212.TL/21.zTL
6064 212.TL/21.zTL
6065 212.TL/21.zTL
6066 212.TL/21.zTL$
6068 212.TL/21.zTL
6070 212.TL/21.zTL
L-159B
5831 LZO
5832 LZO
6073
L-159T-1
6067 212.TL/21.zTL
6071 212.TL/21.zTL
6072 212.TL/21.zTL
6075 212.TL/21.zTL

Airbus A.319CJ-115X
241.dlt/24.zDL, Praha/Kbely
2801
2802

Antonov An-26/An-26Z-1M*
241.dlt/24.zDL, Praha/Kbely
2408
2409
2507
3209*
4201

Antonov An-30FG
241.dlt/24.zDL, Praha/Kbely
1107

Canadair
CL.601-3A Challenger
241.dlt/24.zDL, Praha/Kbely
5105

LET 410 Turbolet
241.dlt/24.zDL, Praha/Kbely;
CLV, Pardubice
0503 L-410MA 241.dlt
0712 L-410UVP-S 241.dlt
0731 L-410UVP-E CLV
0926 L-410UVP-T 241.dlt
0928 L-410UVP-T 241.dlt
0929 L-410UVP-T 241.dlt
1132 L-410UVP-T 241.dlt
1134 L-410UVP-T 241.dlt
1504 L-410UVP 241.dlt
1525 L-410FG 241.dlt
1526 L-410FG 241.dlt
2312 L-410UVP-E 241.dlt
2601 L-410UVP-E 241.dlt
2602 L-410UVP-E 241.dlt
2710 L-410UVP-E 241.dlt

Mil Mi-17/
Mi-171Sh*
232.vrl/23.zVrL, Přerov;
CLV, Pardubice
0803 232.vrl/23.zVrL
0805 232.vrl/23.zVrL
0811 232.vrl/23.zVrL
0825 232.vrl/23.zVrL
0828 232.vrl/23.zVrL
0831 232.vrl/23.zVrL
0832 232.vrl/23.zVrL

0834	232.vrl/23.zVrL
0835	232.vrl/23.zVrL
0837	CLV
0839	232.vrl/23.zVrL
0840	232.vrl/23.zVrL
0848	232.vrl/23.zVrL
0849	232.vrl/23.zVrL
0850	232.vrl/23.zVrL
9767*	232.vrl/23.zVrL
9774*	232.vrl/23.zVrL
9781*	232.vrl/23.zVrL
9799*	232.vrl/23.zVrL
9806*	232.vrl/23.zVrL
9813*	232.vrl/23.zVrL
9825*	232.vrl/23.zVrL
9826*	232.vrl/23.zVrL
9837*	232.vrl/23.zVrL
9844*	232.vrl/23.zVrL
9868*	232.vrl/23.zVrL
9873*	232.vrl/23.zVrL
9887*	232.vrl/23.zVrL
9892*	232.vrl/23.zVrL
9904*	232.vrl/23.zVrL
9915*	232.vrl/23.zVrL
9926*	232.vrl/23.zVrL

Mil Mi-24/Mi-35
231.lbvr/23.zVrL, Přerov

0702	Mi-24V1
0705	Mi-24V1
0710	Mi-24V1
0788	Mi-24V1
0790	Mi-24V1
0815	Mi-24V1
0835	Mi-24V2
0837	Mi-24V2
0981	Mi-24V2
3361	Mi-35
3362	Mi-35
3365	Mi-35
3366	Mi-35
3367	Mi-35
3368	Mi-35
3369	Mi-35
3370	Mi-35
3371	Mi-35
7353	Mi-35$
7354	Mi-35
7355	Mi-35
7356	Mi-35
7357	Mi-35
7358	Mi-35
7360	Mi-35

SAAB Gripen
211.TL/21.zTL, Cáslav
JAS 39C
9234
9235
9236
9237
9238
9239
9240
9241
9242
9243
9244
9245
JAS 39D
9819
9820

Yakovlev Yak-40
241.dlt/24.zDL, Praha/Kbely

0260	Yak-40
1257	Yak-40K

DENMARK
Flyvevåbnet
Lockheed
C-130J-30 Hercules II
Eskadrille 721, Aalborg
B-536
B-537
B-538
B-583

Canadair
CL.604 Challenger
Eskadrille 721, Aalborg
C-080
C-168
C-172

General Dynamics
F-16 MLU
Eskadrille 727, Skrydstrup;
Eskadrille 730, Skrydstrup

E-004	F-16A	Esk 730
E-005	F-16A	
E-006	F-16A	Esk 730
E-007	F-16A	Esk 727
E-008	F-16A	Esk 730
E-011	F-16A	Esk 727
E-016	F-16A	Esk 730
E-017	F-16A	Esk 730
E-018	F-16A	Esk 730
E-024	F-16A	Esk 730
E-070	F-16A	Esk 730
E-074	F-16A	Esk 730
E-075	F-16A	Esk 727
E-107	F-16A	Esk 730
E-180	F-16A	Esk 727
E-182	F-16A	Esk 730
E-184	F-16A	Esk 727
E-187	F-16A	Esk 730
E-188	F-16A	Esk 727
E-189	F-16A	Esk 730
E-190	F-16A	Esk 727
E-191	F-16A	Esk 727
E-192	F-16A	Esk 727
E-193	F-16A	Esk 727
E-194	F-16A	Esk 730
E-195	F-16A	Esk 727
E-196	F-16A	Esk 730
E-197	F-16A	Esk 730
E-198	F-16A	Esk 727
E-199	F-16A	Esk 730
E-200	F-16A	Esk 727
E-202	F-16A	Esk 730
E-203	F-16A	Esk 727
E-596	F-16A	Esk 730
E-597	F-16A	Esk 730
E-598	F-16A	Esk 727
E-599	F-16A	Esk 727
E-600	F-16A	Esk 727
E-601	F-16A	Esk 730
E-602	F-16A	Esk 730
E-603	F-16A	Esk 730
E-604	F-16A	Esk 730
E-605	F-16A	Esk 727
E-606	F-16A	Esk 727
E-607	F-16A	Esk 727
E-608	F-16A	Esk 727
E-609	F-16A	
E-610	F-16A	Esk 730
E-611	F-16A	Esk 727
ET-022	F-16B	Esk 727
ET-197	F-16B	Esk 727
ET-198	F-16B	Esk 727
ET-199	F-16B	Esk 730
ET-204	F-16B	Esk 727
ET-206	F-16B	Esk 730
ET-207	F-16B	Esk 730
ET-208	F-16B	Esk 727
ET-210	F-16B	Esk 727
ET-612	F-16B	Esk 727
ET-613	F-16B	Esk 727
ET-614	F-16B	Esk 727
ET-615	F-16B	Esk 727

AgustaWestland
EH.101 Mk.512
Eskadrille 722, Vaerløse
M-502
M-504
M-507
M-508
M-510
M-512
M-513
M-514

Aérospatiale
AS.550C-2 Fennec
Eskadrille 724, Vandel
P-090
P-234
P-254
P-275
P-276
P-287
P-288
P-319
P-320
P-339
P-352
P-369

SAAB
T-17 Supporter
Eskadrille 721, Aalborg;
Flyveskolen, Karup (FLSK)

T-401	FLSK
T-402	Esk 721
T-403	FLSK
T-404	FLSK
T-405	FLSK
T-407	Esk 721
T-408	FLSK
T-409	FLSK
T-410	FLSK
T-411	FLSK
T-412	FLSK
T-413	FLSK
T-414	Esk 721
T-415	FLSK
T-417	FLSK
T-418	Esk 721
T-419	FLSK
T-420	FLSK
T-421	FLSK
T-423	FLSK
T-425	FLSK
T-426	FLSK
T-427	FLSK
T-428	FLSK
T-429	FLSK

T-430 FLSK
T-431 Esk 721
T-432 FLSK

Sikorsky S-61A Sea King
Eskadrille 722, Vaerløse
Detachments at:
Aalborg, Ronne, Skrydstrup
U-275
U-276
U-277
U-278
U-279
U-280
U-481

Søvaernets Flyvetjaeneste (Navy)
Westland Lynx Mk 80/90B
Eskadrille 728, Karup
S-134 Mk 90B
S-142 Mk 90B
S-170 Mk 90B
S-175 Mk 80
S-181 Mk 90B
S-191 Mk 90B
S-249 Mk 90B
S-256 Mk 90B

EGYPT
Al Quwwat al-Jawwiya il Misriya
Lockheed C-130H/C-130H-30* Hercules
16 Sqn, Cairo West
1271/SU-BAB
1272/SU-BAC
1273/SU-BAD
1274/SU-BAE
1275/SU-BAF
1277/SU-BAI
1278/SU-BAJ
1279/SU-BAK
1280/SU-BAL
1281/SU-BAM
1282/SU-BAN
1283/SU-BAP
1284/SU-BAQ
1285/SU-BAR
1286/SU-BAS
1287/SU-BAT
1288/SU-BAU
1289/SU-BAV
1290/SU-BEW
1291/SU-BEX
1292/SU-BEY
1293/SU-BKS*
1294/SU-BKT*
1295/SU-BKU*
1296
1297
1298

Egyptian Govt
Airbus A.340-211
Egyptian Govt, Cairo
SU-GGG

Grumman G.1159A Gulfstream III/ G.1159C Gulfstream IV/ G.1159C Gulftream IV-SP/ Gulfstream 400
Egyptian Air Force/Govt, Cairo
SU-BGM Gulfstream IV
SU-BGU Gulfstream III
SU-BGV Gulfstream III
SU-BNC Gulfstream IV
SU-BND Gulfstream IV
SU-BNO Gulfstream IV-SP
SU-BNP Gulfstream IV-SP
SU-BPE Gulfstream 400
SU-BPF Gulfstream 400

FINLAND
Suomen Ilmavoimat
CASA 295M
Tukilentolaivue,
Jyväskylä/Tikkakoski
CC-1
CC-2

Fokker F.27 Friendship
Tukilentolaivue, Jyväskylä/Tikkakoski
FF-1 F.27-100
FF-3 F.27-400M

McDonnell Douglas F-18 Hornet
Hävittäjälentolaivue 11, Roveniemi;
Hävittäjälentolaivue 21, Tampere/Pirkkala;
Hävittäjälentolaivue 31, Kuopio/Rissala;
Koelentokeskus, Halli
F-18C Hornet
HN-401 HavLLv 31
HN-402 HavLLv 11
HN-403 HavLLv 31
HN-404 HavLLv 31
HN-405 HavLLv 31
HN-406 HavLLv 21
HN-407 HavLLv 11
HN-408 HavLLv 31
HN-409 HavLLv 21
HN-410 HavLLv 31
HN-411 HavLLv 11
HN-412 HavLLv 31
HN-413 HavLLv 21
HN-414 KoelntK
HN-415 HavLLv 31
HN-416 HavLLv 21
HN-417 HavLLv 21
HN-418 HavLLv 31
HN-419 HavLLv 31
HN-420 HavLLv 31
HN-421 HavLLv 21
HN-422 HavLLv 31
HN-423 HavLLv 11
HN-424 HavLLv 31
HN-425 HavLLv 31
HN-426 HavLLv 11
HN-427 HavLLv 21
HN-428 HavLLv 11
HN-429 HavLLv 21
HN-431 HavLLv 31
HN-432 HavLLv 31
HN-433 HavLLv 21
HN-434 HavLLv 11
HN-435 HavLLv 31
HN-436 HavLLv 11
HN-437 HavLLv 11
HN-438 HavLLv 31
HN-439 HavLLv 21
HN-440 HavLLv 31
HN-441 HavLLv 31
HN-442 HavLLv 11
HN-443 HavLLv 31
HN-444 HavLLv 21
HN-445 HavLLv 11
HN-446 HavLLv 31
HN-447 HavLLv 11
HN-448 HavLLv 21
HN-449 HavLLv 21
HN-450 HavLLv 31
HN-451 HavLLv 31
HN-452 HavLLv 11
HN-453 HavLLv 31
HN-454 HavLLv 21
HN-455 HavLLv 31
HN-456 HavLLv 31
HN-457 HavLLv 21
F-18D Hornet
HN-461 HavLLv 21
HN-462 KoelntK
HN-463 HavLLv 21
HN-464 HavLLv 11
HN-465 HavLLv 31
HN-466 HavLLv 11
HN-467 HavLLv 31
HN-468 (on order)

BAe Hawk 51/51A*
Hävittäjälentolaivue 41, Kauhava
HW-301
HW-303
HW-304
HW-306
HW-307
HW-308
HW-309
HW-310
HW-311
HW-312
HW-314
HW-315
HW-316
HW-318
HW-319
HW-320
HW-321
HW-322
HW-326
HW-327
HW-328
HW-329
HW-330
HW-331
HW-332
HW-333
HW-334
HW-337
HW-338
HW-339
HW-340
HW-341
HW-342
HW-343
HW-344
HW-345
HW-346
HW-347
HW-348
HW-349

HW-350
HW-351*
HW-352*
HW-353*
HW-354*
HW-355*
HW-356*
HW-357*

Gates
Learjet 35A
Tukilentolaivue, Jyväskylä/Tikkakoski;
Tukilentolaivue (Det.), Kuopio/Rissala*
LJ-1*
LJ-2
LJ-3

FRANCE
Armée de l'Air
Aérospatiale
TB-30 Epsilon
Cartouche Dorée,
(EPAA 00.315) Cognac;
EPAA 00.315, Cognac;
SOCATA, Tarbes
Please note: A large number of these machines are kept in temporary storage at Chateaudun

1	315-UA
3	FZ SOCATA
4	315-UC
5	315-UD
6	315-UE
7	315-UF
8	315-UG
9	315-UH
10	315-UI
12	315-UK
13	315-UL
14	315-UM
16	315-UO
20	315-US
21	315-UT
26	315-UY
27	315-UZ
28	315-VA
30	315-VC
32	315-VE
34	315-VG
35	315-VH
36	315-VI
39	315-VL
40	315-VM
41	315-VN
43	315-VP
44	315-VQ
46	315-VS
47	315-VT
50	315-VW
56	315-WA
57	F-ZVLB
61	315-WD
62	315-WE
63	315-WF
64	315-WG
65	315-WH
66	315-WI
67	315-WJ
68	315-WK
69	315-WL
70	315-WM
73	315-WP
74	315-WQ
77	315-WT
78	315-WU
79	315-WV
80	315-WW
82	315-WY
83	315-WZ
84	315-XA
85	315-XB
87	315-XD
90	F-SEXG [0]*
91	315-XH
92	315-XI
93	315-XJ
95	315-XL
96	315-XM
97	315-XN
99	315-XP
100	315-XQ
101	F-SEXR [1]*
102	F-SEXS [2]*
103	315-XT
104	F-SEXU [3]*
105	315-XV
106	315-XW
108	315-XY
110	315-YA
111	315-YB
112	315-YC
113	315-YD
114	315-YE
115	315-YF
116	315-YG
117	315-YH
118	315-YI
120	315-YK
121	315-YL
122	315-YM
125	315-YP
126	315-YQ
127	315-YR
129	315-YT
130	315-YU
131	315-YV
132	315-YW
133	315-YX
134	315-YY
136	315-ZA
138	315-ZC
139	315-ZD
140	315-ZE
141	F-SEZF [4]*
142	315-ZG
143	315-ZH
144	315-ZI
146	315-ZK
149	315-ZM
150	315-ZN
152	315-ZO
153	315-ZP
154	315-ZQ
155	315-ZR
158	315-ZS
159	315-ZT

Airbus A.310-304
ET 03.060 *Esterel*,
Paris/Charles de Gaulle

418	F-RADC
421	F-RADA
422	F-RADB

Airbus A.319CJ-115
ETEC 00.065, Villacoublay

1485	F-RBFA
1556	F-RBFB

Airbus A.340-212
ET 03.060 *Esterel*,
Paris/Charles de Gaulle

075	F-RAJA
081	F-RAJB

Airtech CN-235M-200
ETL 01.062 *Vercours*, Creil;
ET 03.062 *Ventoux*, Mont-de-Marsan;
ETOM 00.052 *La Tontouta*, Noumea;
ETOM 00.058 *Antilles*, Fort de France;
ETOM 00.082 *Maine*, Faaa-Tahiti

045	62-IB	03.062
065	82-IC	00.082
066	52-ID	00.052
071	62-IE	03.062
072	82-IF	00.082
105	52-IG	00.052
107	52-IH	00.052
111	62-II	01.062
114	62-IJ	01.062
123	62-IM	03.062
128	62-IK	03.062
129	62-IL	01.062
137	62-IN	00.058
141	62-IO	00.058
152	62-IP	01.062
156	62-IQ	01.062
158	62-IR	01.062
160	62-IS	01.062
165	62-IT	01.062

Boeing C-135 Stratotanker
GRV 00.093 *Bretagne*, Istres

470	C-135FR	93-CA
471	C-135FR	93-CB
472	C-135FR	93-CC
474	C-135FR	93-CE
475	C-135FR	93-CF
497	KC-135R	93-CM
525	KC-135R	93-CN
574	KC-135R	93-CP
735	C-135FR	93-CG
736	C-135FR	93-CH
737	C-135FR	93-CI
738	C-135FR	93-CJ
739	C-135FR	93-CK
740	C-135FR	93-CL

Boeing E-3F Sentry
EDCA 00.036, Avord

201	36-CA
202	36-CB
203	36-CC
204	36-CD

CASA 212-300 Aviocar
CEV, Cazaux & Istres

377	MO
378	MP
386	MQ

Cessna 310
CEV, Cazaux & Istres

190 310N BL
193 310N BG
194 310N BH
513 310N BE
569 310R CS
693 310N BI
820 310Q CL
981 310Q BF

D-BD Alpha Jet
AMD-BA, Istres;
CEAM (EC 02.330), Mont-de-Marsan;
CEV, Cazaux & Istres;
CITac 00.339 *Aquitaine*, Luxeuil;
EAC 00.314, Tours;
EE 05.002 *Côte d'Or*, Dijon & St Dizier;
EPNER, Istres;
ERS 01.091 *Gascogne*, Mont-de-Marsan;
ETO 01.008 *Saintonge*, Cazaux;
GE 00.312, Salon de Provence;
Patrouille de France (PDF) (EPAA 20.300), Salon de Provence

01	F-ZJTS	CEV
E1		CEV
E3		
E4		CEV
E5	314-LV	00.314
E7	2-PF	05.002
E8		CEV
E9	314-LF	00.314
E10	314-UL	00.314
E11	2-FB	05.002
E12		CEV
E13		
E14	314-TP	00.314
E15		
E17	314-LW	00.314
E18	330-AK	CEAM
E19	314-UJ	00.314
E20	8-MS	01.008
E21		
E22	314-LS	00.314
E23		
E24	8-MP	01.008
E25	314-TJ	00.314
E26	312-RU	00.312
E28	330-AJ	CEAM
E29		
E30	8-MD	01.008
E31		
E32	2-PV	05.002
E33	2-PE	05.002
E34		
E35	2-PX	05.002
E36	314-UF	00.314
E37		
E38	314-LH	00.314
E41	F-TERA	*PDF* [4]
E42	314-TA	00.314
E43	314-LI	00.314
E44	8-MJ	01.008
E45	314-TF	00.314
E46	F-TERN	*PDF*
E47	314-TR	00.314
E48	8-MH	01.008
E49	314-LB	00.314
E51	2-PR	05.002
E52		
E53		
E55	314-UC	00.314
E58	314-TK	00.314
E59	314-LY	00.314
E60		EPNER
E61	314-LQ	00.314
E63		
E64	314-TL	00.314
E65		
E66	8-ME	01.008
E67	314-TB	00.314
E68	339-DK	00.339
E69	314-TO	00.314
E72	314-LA	00.314
E73	312-RV	00.312
E74	8-MI	01.008
E75	F-TERW	*PDF* [3]
E76		
E79		
E80		CEV
E81		
E82	314-TW	00.314
E83	314-TZ	00.314
E84	314-UK	00.314
E85	8-MT	01.008
E86		
E87	314-LC	00.314
E88	314-LL	00.314
E89	314-LX	00.314
E90	330-AI	CEAM
E91	8-ML	01.008
E92	8-MK	01.008
E93	314-LG	00.314
E94	F-TERH	*PDF*
E95		
E96	314-TC	00.314
E97	2-PY	05.002
E98	8-MF	01.008
E99	330-AH	CEAM
E100		EPNER
E101	314-TT	00.314
E102	314-LM	00.314
E103	314-UA	00.314
E104	314-TG	00.314
E105		
E106		
E107	314-UD	00.314
E108	8-MU	01.008
E109	314-UN	00.314
E110		
E112	314-TS	00.314
E113	314-TD	00.314
E114		
E115	8-MR	01.008
E116	2-PW	05.002
E117	F-TERI	*PDF* [5]
E118	339-DN	00.339
E119		
E120	314-LG	00.314
E121		
E122	F-TERD	*PDF* [0]
E123		
E124	314-TE	00.314
E125	314-LK	00.314
E126	314-TU	00.314
E127	314-TV	00.314
E128	314-TM	00.314
E129	314-UB	00.314
E130	F-TERP	*PDF*
E131		
E132	314-LZ	00.314
E133	8-MN	01.008
E134	F-TERM	*PDF*
E135	F-TERX	*PDF* [1]
E136		
E137	314-LJ	00.314
E138		
E139	2-FC	05.002
E140	2-FA	05.002
E141	314-TN	00.314
E142	314-LO	00.314
E143	312-RS	00.312
E144	2-PJ	05.002
E145		
E146		
E147		
E148	314-LU	00.314
E149	8-MO	01.008
E150		
E151	8-MC	01.008
E152		
E153		
E154		
E155		
E156	314-TI	00.314
E157		
E158	F-TERF	*PDF* [2]
E159		
E160	F-TERC	*PDF* [6]
E161		
E162	F-TERJ	*PDF* [9]
E163	F-TERB	*PDF* [8]
E164	8-MB	01.008
E165	F-TERE	*PDF* [7]
E166	314-LT	00.314
E167	314-UH	00.314
E168	2-PP	05.002
E169	314-LE	00.314
E170	314-UN	00.314
E171	314-LR	00.314
E173	314-LH	00.314
E176	8-MA	01.008

Dassault Falcon 20
CEV, Cazaux & Istres
Falcon 20C
79 CT
86 CG
96 CB
104 CW
124 CC
131 CD
138 CR
188 CX
Falcon 20E
252 CA
263 CY
288 CV
Falcon 20F
375 CZ

Dassault Falcon 50
ETEC 00.065, Villacoublay
5 F-RAFI
27 (F-RAFK)
34 (F-RAFL)
78 F-RAFJ

Dassault Falcon 900
ETEC 00.065, Villacoublay
02 (F-RAFP)
004 (F-RAFQ)

Dassault
Mirage F.1
CEAM (EC 02.330), Mont-de-Marsan;
CEV, Cazaux & Istres;
ER 01.033 *Belfort*, & ER 02.033 *Savoie*, Reims;
GC 01.030 *Alsace* & GC 02.030 *Normandie Niemen*, Colmar

Mirage F.1CT

219	30-SP	01.030
220		
223	30-QX	02.030
225		
226	30-SY	01.030
227	330-AP	CEAM
228	30-QT	02.030
229	30-QW	02.030
230		
231	30-QK	02.030
232	33-FK	02.033
233	30-QT	02.030
234		
235		
236	30-SB	01.030
238		
241		
242	30-QA	02.030
243	30-SN	01.030
244	30-QH	02.030
245	30-SX	01.030
246		
248		
251		
252		
253	30-QU	02.030
255		
256	30-SH	01.030
257	30-SF	01.030
258	33-FO	03.033
260	30-QB	02.030
261	30-QY	02.030
262	30-QO	02.030
264		
265		
267	30-QC	02.030
268	30-SM	01.030
271	30-QQ	02.030
272	30-QZ	02.030
273	30-QF	02.030
274	30-QJ	02.030
275	30-QN	02.030
278	30-SG	01.030
279	30-QL	02.030
280	30-QD	02.030
281	30-QV	02.030
283	30-QI	02.030

Mirage F.1B

502	30-SW	01.030
504	30-ST	01.030
507	30-SE	01.030
509	30-SD	01.030
510	30-SL	01.030
511	30-SQ	01.030
512	30-SU	01.030
513	30-SV	01.030
514	30-SA	01.030
516	30-SI	01.030
517	30-SC	01.030
518	30-SR	01.030
519	30-SK	01.030
520	30-SO	01.030

Mirage F.1CR

602		CEV
603	33-NU	02.033
604	33-CF	01.033
605	33-CO	01.033
606	33-CU	01.033
607	33-NV	02.033
608		
610	33-CI	01.033
611	33-NM	02.033
612	33-NJ	02.033
613	33-CC	01.033
614	33-NR	02.033
615	33-CR	01.033
616	33-CX	01.033
617	33-CD	01.033
620	33-CT	01.033
622	33-NH	02.033
623	33-CM	01.033
624	33-NY	02.033
627	33-NT	02.033
628	33-NB	02.033
630	33-CN	01.033
631	330-AA	CEAM
632	33-CQ	01.033
634	33-CK	01.033
635	33-NP	02.033
636	33-NL	02.033
637	33-CP	01.033
638	33-NX	02.033
640	33-NV	02.033
641	33-NI	02.033
642	33-CG	02.033
643	33-CE	01.033
645	33-CH	01.033
646	33-NW	02.033
647		
648		
649	330-AB	CEAM
650	33-NZ	02.033
651	33-NB	02.033
653	33-CV	01.033
654	33-NC	02.033
655	33-NG	02.033
656	33-CS	01.033
657	33-NA	02.033
658	33-CW	01.033
659	33-CA	01.033
660	33-CY	01.033
661	33-NK	02.033
662	33-NF	01.033

Dassault
Mirage 2000B
AMD-BA, Istres;
CEAM (EC 02.330), Mont-de-Marsan;
CEV, Cazaux & Istres;
EC 02.005 *Ile de France*, Orange;
EC 01.012 *Cambrésis* &
EC 02.012 *Picardie*, Cambrai

501	(BX1)	CEV
504		CEV
505	5-OY	02.005
506	5-OD	02.005
508	5-OP	02.005
509	5-OK	02.005
510	5-OQ	02.005
512	5-OU	02.005
514	5-OE	02.005
515	5-OG	02.005
516		
518	5-OM	02.005
519	5-OW	02.005
520	5-OS	02.005
521	5-ON	02.005
522	5-OV	02.005
523	12-YT	01.012
524	330-AM	CEAM
525		
526	12-YP	01.012
527		
528	12-KS	02.012
529	12-KJ	02.012
530	5-OL	02.005

Dassault
Mirage 2000C/2000-5F*
CEAM (EC 02.330), Mont-de-Marsan;
CEV, Istres;
EC 01.002 *Cigognes*, Dijon;
EC 02.005 *Ile de France*, Orange;
EC 01.012 *Cambrésis* &
EC 02.012 *Picardie*, Cambrai;
EC 04.033 *Vexin*, Djibouti

	01*	CEV
1	5-OJ	02.005
2		CEV
11	5-OF	02.005
13		
17	5-OZ	02.005
20		
21	5-OI	02.005
36	5-OC	02.005
38*		
40*	2-EX	01.002
42*	2-EY	01.002
43*		
44*	2-EQ	01.002
45*	2-EF	01.002
46*	2-EN	01.002
47*	2-EP	01.002
48*	2-EW	01.002
49*	2-EA	01.002
51*	330-AS	CEAM
52*	2-EH	01.002
53*		
54*		
55*	2-EU	01.002
56*	2-EG	01.002
57*	2-ET	01.002
58*		
59*	2-EV	01.002
61*	$	01.002
62*	2-ED	01.002
63*	2-EM	01.002
64	330-AQ	CEAM
65*	2-EK	01.002
66*	2-EO	01.002
67*		
68*		
70*	330-AD	CEAM
71*		
73*	2-ES	01.002
74*	2-EU	01.002
76*	2-EB	01.002
77*	330-AX	CEAM
78*	2-EC	01.002
79		
80	12-YJ	01.012
81		
82	12-YL	01.012
83	12-YC	01.012

85 12-YE 01.012
86
87 12-KN 02.012
88 12-KP 02.012
89 12-KA 02.012
90 12-YS 01.012
91 12-KL 02.012
92 330-AW CEAM
93 12-YA 01.012
94 12-YI 01.012
95 12-KM 02.012
96 12-KI 02.012
97
98 12-YU 01.012
99 12-YB$ 01.012
100 12-YG 01.012
101 12-KE 02.012
102 12-KR 02.012
103 12-YN 01.012
104 12-KG 02.012
105 12-YF$ 01.012
106
107 12-YD 01.012
108 12-KV 02.012
109 12-YH 01.012
111 12-KF 02.012
112
113 12-YO 01.012
114 12-KU 02.012
115 12-YM 01.012
117 12-KQ 02.012
118 12-YE 01.012
119 12-KO 02.012
120 12-KC 02.012
121 12-KN 02.012
122 12-YA 01.012
123
124 12-YT 01.012
X7 CEV

Dassault
Mirage 2000D
AMD-BA, Istres;
CEAM (EC 02.330), Mont-de-Marsan;
CEV, Istres;
EC 01.003 *Navarre*, EC 02.003 *Champagne* & EC 03.003 *Ardennes*, Nancy;
EC 04.033 *Vexin*, Djibouti

601
602 3-XJ 03.003
603
604 3-IN 01.003
605 3-XD 03.003
606 3-JC 02.003
607 CEV
609 3-IF 01.003
610 3-XX 03.003
611 3-JG 02.003
612 3-JK 02.003
613 3-XG 03.003
614 3-JU 02.003
615 3-JY 02.003
616 3-XH 03.003
617 3-IS 01.003
618 3-XC 03.003
619 3-IM 01.003
620
622 3-IL 01.003
623 3-XW 03.003
624 3-IH 01.003
625
626
627 3-JP 02.003
628
629 3-XO 03.003
630 3-XU 03.003
631 3-JO 02.003
632 3-XE 03.003
634 3-IC 01.003
635 3-XP 03.003
636 3-JQ 02.003
637
638 3-IJ 01.003
639 3-JJ 02.003
640 3-IR 01.003
641 3-JW 02.003
642
643 3-IC 01.003
644 3-IU 01.003
645
646 3-IC 01.003
647 3-IO 01.003
648 3-XT 03.003
649
650 3-IA 01.003
651 3-JV 02.003
652 3-XN 03.003
653 3-ID 01.003
654 3-IT 01.003
655 3-IK 01.003
657
658 3-JN 02.003
659 3-XR 03.003
660 3-JF 02.003
661 3-XI 03.003
662 3-XA 03.003
664 3-JU 02.003
665 330-AE CEAM
666 330-AR CEAM
667 3-JX 02.003
668 3-IG 01.003
669 3-XV 03.003
670 3-IQ 01.003
671 3-XK 03.003
672
673 CEV
674 3-IR 01.003
675 3-JI 02.003
676 CEV
677 3-JT 01.003
678 3-JA 02.003
679 3-JX 01.003
680 3-XM 03.003
681 330-AG CEAM
682 3-JR 02.003
683 3-IV 01.003
684 3-IW 01.003
685 3-XZ 03.003
686 3-JH 02.003
D02 CEV

Dassault
Mirage 2000N
CEAM (EC 02.330), Mont-de-Marsan;
CEV, Istres;
EC 01.004 *Dauphiné* & EC 02.004 *Lafayette*, Luxeuil;
EC 03.004 *Limousin*, Istres

301 CEV
303 CEV
304 4-CA 03.004
305 4-CS 03.004
306 4-BL 02.004
307 4-CH 03.004
309 4-AO 01.004
310 4-CE 03.004
311 4-AF 01.004
312 4-CN 03.004
313 4-CR 03.004
314 4-AX 01.004
315 4-BF 02.004
316
317 4-BP 02.004
319 4-AC 01.004
320 4-CD 03.004
322 4-CP 03.004
323 4-AN 01.004
324 4-CX 03.004
325 4-CC 03.004
326 4-AS 01.004
327 4-CJ 03.004
329 4-BH 02.004
330 4-AT 01.004
331 4-BO 02.004
332 4-BN 02.004
333 4-AB 01.004
334 330-AV CEAM
335 4-AE 01.004
336 4-BI 02.004
337 4-AK 01.004
338 4-CG 03.004
339 4-AD 01.004
340
341
342 4-BA 02.004
343 4-AH 01.004
344 4-BV 02.004
345 4-BU 02.004
348 4-AL 01.004
349 4-AA 01.004
350 330-AN CEAM
351 4-AQ 01.004
353 4-AM 01.004
354 4-BJ 02.004
355 4-AE 01.004
356 4-BX 02.004
357 4-CO 03.004
358 4-BQ 02.004
359 4-BG 02.004
360 4-CB 03.004
361 4-CA 03.004
362 4-CU 03.004
363 4-BK 02.004
364 4-BB 02.004
365 4-AI 01.004
366 4-BC 02.004
367 4-AS 01.004
368 4-AR 01.004
369 4-AG 01.004
370 4-CQ 03.004
371 4-BD 02.004
372 4-CM 03.004
373 4-CF 03.004
374 4-BS 02.004
375 4-CL 03.004

Dassault
Rafale-B
AMD-BA, Istres;
CEAM (EC 02.330), Mont-de-Marsan; CEV, Istres;
EC 01.007 *Provence*, St Dizier

301 CEV
302 330-AC CEAM
303 330-EA CEAM

304	330-EB	CEAM
305	330-EC$	CEAM
306	330-ED	CEAM
307	7-IA	01.007
308	7-HA	01.007
309	7-HB	01.007
310	7-HC	01.007
311	7-HD	01.007
312	7-HF	01.007
313	7-HI	01.007
314	7-HP	01.007
315	7-HK	01.007
317	7-HO	01.007
318	7-HM	01.007
319	7-HN	01.007
320	7-HV	01.007
321	7-HQ	01.007
322	7-HU	01.007
323	7-HT	01.007
324	7-HW	01.007
325	7-HX	01.007
326		
327		
328		
329		
330		
331		
332		
333		
334		
335		
B01		CEV

Dassault
Rafale-C
AMD-BA, Istres;
CEAM (EC 02.330), Mont-de-Marsan;
CEV, Istres;
EC 01.007 *Provence*,St Dizier

101		CEV
102	330-EF	CEAM
103	7-HR	01.007
104	7-HH	01.007
105	7-HE	01.007
106	7-HG	01.007
107	7-HJ	01.007
108	7-HS	01.007
109		
110		
111		
112		
C01		CEV

DHC-6 Twin Otter 200/300*
ET 00.042 *Ventoux*, Mont-de-Marsan;
GAM 00.056 *Vaucluse*, Evreux

292	CC	00.056
298	CD	00.056
300	CE	00.056
730*	CA	00.042
745*	CV	00.042
790*	CW	00.042

Embraer
EMB.121AA/AN* Xingu
EAT 00.319, Avord

054	YX
055*	YZ
064	YY
066*	ZA
69*	
070*	ZC
072	YA
073	YB
075	YC
076	YD
77*	ZD
078	YE
080	YF
082	YG
083*	ZE
084	YH
086	YI
089	YJ
090*	ZF
091	YK
092	YL
095	YM
096	YN
098	YO
099	YP
101	YR
102	YS
103	YT
105	YU
107	YV
108	YW
111	YQ

Embraer
EMB.312F Tucano
GE 00.312, Salon de Provence

438	312-UW
439	312-UY
456	312-JA
457	312-JB
458	312-JC
459	312-JD
460	312-JE
461	312-JF
462	312-JG
463	312-JH
464	312-JI
466	312-JK
467	312-JL
468	312-JM
469	312-JN
470	312-JO
471	312-JP
472	312-JQ
473	312-JR
474	312-JS
475	312-JT
477	312-JU
478	312-JV
479	312-JX
480	312-JY
481	312-JZ
483	312-UB
484	312-UC
485	312-UD
486	312-UE
487	312-UF
488	312-UG
489	312-UH
490	312-UI
491	312-UJ
492	312-UK
493	312-UL
494	312-UM
495	312-UN
496	312-UO
497	312-UP
498	312-UQ
499	312-UR
500	312-US
501	312-UT
503	312-UV
504	312-UX

Eurocopter
AS.332 Super Puma/
AS.532 Cougar/
EC.725AP Cougar
EH 01.067 *Pyrénées*, Cazaux;
EH 03.067 *Parisis*, Villacoublay;
EH 05.067 *Alpilles*, Aix-en-Provence;
ETOM 00.082 *Maine*, Faaa-Tahiti;
GAM 00.056 *Vaucluse*, Evreux;
CEAM, Mont-de-Marsan

2014	AS.332C	PN	05.067
2057	AS.332C	PO	00.082
2093	AS.332L	PP	05.067
2233	AS.332L-1	FY	00.056
2235	AS.332L-1	67-FZ	03.067
2244	AS.332C	PM	00.082
2342	AS.532UL	FX	00.056
2369	AS.532UL	FW	00.056
2375	AS.532UL	FV	00.056
2377	AS.332L-1	67-FU	03.067
2461	EC.725AP	SA	01.067
2549	EC.725AP	SB	01.067
2552	EC.725AP	SE	01.067
2555	EC.725AP	SF	01.067
2619	EC.725AP	SC	05.067
2626	EC.725AP	SD	01.067

Lockheed
C-130H/C-130H-30*
Hercules
ET 02.061 *Franche-Comté*, Orléans

4588	61-PM
4589	61-PN
5114	61-PA
5116	61-PB
5119	61-PC
5140	61-PD
5142*	61-PE
5144*	61-PF $
5150*	61-PG $
5151*	61-PH
5152*	61-PI
5153*	61-PJ
5226*	61-PK
5227*	61-PL

SOCATA TBM 700A
CEV, Cazaux & Istres;
ETM 01.040 *Moselle*, Metz;
ETM 02.040 *Médoc*, Bordeaux;
ETEC 00.065, Villacoublay;
EdC 00.070, Chateaudun

33	XA	02.040
77	XD	01.040
78	XE	00.065
93	XL	00.065
95	XH	02.040
103	XI	00.065
104	XJ	00.070
105	XK	00.065
106	MN	CEV
110	XP	01.040
111	XM	01.040

117	XN	01.040
125	XO	00.065
131	XQ	00.065
146	XR	00.065
147	XS	00.065

Transall
C-160F/C-160NG GABRIEL*/ C-160R
CEAM (EET 06.330), Mont-de-Marsan;
CEV, Cazaux & Istres;
EEA 01.054 *Dunkerque*, Metz;
ET 01.061 *Touraine* & ET 03.061 *Poitou*, Orléans;
ET 01.064 *Bearn* & ET 02.064 *Anjou*, Evreux;
ETOM 00.050 *Réunion*, St Denis;
ETOM 00.055 *Ouessant*, Dakar;
ETOM 00.058 *Guadeloupe*, Pointe-à-Pitre;
ETOM 00.088 *Larzac*, Djibouti

RA02	C-160R	61-MI	01.061
R1	C-160R	61-MA	01.061
R2	C-160R	61-MB	01.061
R3	C-160R	61-MC	00.058
R4	C-160R	61-MD	01.061
R11	C-160R	61-MF	01.061
R15	C-160R	61-MJ	01.061
R18	C-160R	61-MM	01.061
R42	C-160R	61-MN	01.061
R43	C-160R	61-MO	01.061
R48	C-160R	61-MT	01.061
F49	C-160F	59-MU	CEV
R51	C-160R	61-MW	01.061
R54	C-160R	61-MZ	01.061
R55	C-160R	61-ZC	03.061
R86	C-160R	61-ZD	03.061
R87	C-160R	61-ZE	00.050
R88	C-160R	61-ZF	00.050
R89	C-160R	61-ZG	03.061
R90	C-160R	61-ZH	03.061
R91	C-160R	61-ZI	03.061
R92	C-160R	61-ZJ	03.061
R93	C-160R	61-ZK	03.061
R94	C-160R	61-ZL	03.061
R95	C-160R	61-ZM	03.061
R96	C-160R	61-ZN	03.061
R97	C-160R	61-ZA	03.061
R98	C-160R	61-ZP	00.050
R99	C-160R	61-ZQ	03.061
R153	C-160R	61-ZS	03.061
R154	C-160R	61-ZT	03.061
R157	C-160R	61-ZW	03.061
R158	C-160R	61-ZX	03.061
R159	C-160R	61-ZY	03.061
R160	C-160R	61-ZZ	03.061
R201	C-160R	64-GA	01.064
R202	C-160R	64-GB	02.064
R203	C-160R	64-GC	01.064
R204	C-160R	64-GD	02.064
R205	C-160R	64-GE	01.064
R206	C-160R	64-GF	02.064
R207	C-160R	64-GG	01.064
R208	C-160R	64-GH	02.064
R210	C-160R	64-GJ	02.064
R211	C-160R	64-GK	01.064
R212	C-160R	64-GL	02.064
R213	C-160R	64-GM	01.064
R214	C-160R	64-GN	02.064
R215	C-160R	64-GO	01.064
F216	C-160NG*	54-GT	01.054
R217	C-160R	64-GQ	01.064
R218	C-160R	64-GR	02.064
F221	C-160NG*	GS	01.054
R223	C-160R	64-GW	01.064
R224	C-160R	64-GX	02.064
R225	C-160R	64-GY	01.064
R226	C-160R	64-GZ	02.064

Aéronavale/Marine
Aérospatiale
SA.321G Super Frelon
32 Flottille, Hyères & Lanvéoc/Poulmic
118
134
137
144
148
160
162
163
165

Dassault-Breguet
Atlantique 2
21 Flottille, Nimes/Garons;
23 Flottille, Lorient/Lann Bihoué

1	21F
2	21F
3	21F
4	23F
5	21F
6	23F
7	21F
8	23F
9	21F
10	21F
11	23F
12	23F
13	21F
14	23F
15	21F
16	21F
17	21F
18	21F
19	23F
20	23F
21	21F
22	23F
23	21F
24	21F
25	23F
26	21F
27	23F
28	21F

Dassault
Falcon 10(MER)
ES 57, Landivisiau
32
101
129
133
143
185

Dassault
Falcon 20G Guardian
25 Flottille, Papeete & Tontouta
48
65
72
77
80

Dassault
Falcon 50 SURMAR
24 Flottille, Lorient/Lann Bihoué
7
30
36
132

Dassault
Rafale-M
12 Flottille, Landivisiau;
AMD-BA, Istres;
CEV, Istres

M01	CEV
M02	CEV
1	CEV
2	12F
3	12F
4	12F
5	12F
6	12F
7	12F
8	12F
9	12F
10	12F
11	12F
12	12F
13	12F
14	
15	
16	
17	
18	

Dassault
Super Etendard
11 Flottille, Landivisiau;
17 Flottille, Landivisiau;
CEV, Cazaux & Istres

1	17F
2	11F
3	11F
4	17F
6	11F
8	11F
10	17F
11	11F
12	17F
13	11F
14	CEV
15	17F
16	17F
17	17F
18	17F
19	11F
23	17F
24	11F
25	11F
28	11F
30	11F
31	17F
32	17F
33	11F
35	11F
37	17F
38	11F
39	11F

41 17F
43 11F
44 17F
45 17F
46 11F
47 11F
48 17F
49 11F$
50 11F
51 17F
52 17F
55 11F
57 17F
59 17F
61 17F
62 11F$
64 11F
65 17F
66 11F
68 CEV
69 11F
71 17F

Embraer
EMB.121AN Xingu
24 Flottille, Lorient/Lann Bihoué;
28 Flottille, Nimes/Garons
30 24F
47 24F
65 28F
67 24F
68 24F
71 28F
74 24F
79 28F
81 24F
85 24F
87 24F

Eurocopter
AS.365/AS.565 Panther
35 Flottille, Hyères, (with detachments at Cherbourg, La Rochelle & Le Touquet)
36 Flottille, Hyères
17 AS.365N 35F
19 AS.365N 35F
24 AS.365N 35F
57 AS.365N 35F
81 AS.365N 35F
91 AS.365N 35F
157 AS.365N 35F
313 AS.365F1 35F
318 AS.365F1 35F
322 AS.365F1 35F
355 AS.565MA 36F
362 AS.565MA 35F
436 AS.565MA 36F
452 AS.565MA 36F
453 AS.565MA 35F
466 AS.565MA 36F
482 AS.565MA 36F
486 AS.565MA 36F
488 AS.565MA 36F
503 AS.565MA 35F
505 AS.565MA 36F
506 AS.565MA 35F
507 AS.565MA 36F
511 AS.565MA 36F
519 AS.565MA 36F
522 AS.565MA 36F
524 AS.565MA 36F
542 AS.565MA 36F

NH Industries
NH.90-NFH
1018

Nord 262E Frégate
24 Flottille, Lorient/Lann Bihoué;
28 Flottille, Nimes/Garons;
ERCE, Hyères;
ES 10, Hyères;
ES 55, Aspretto
45 28F
46 28F
51 28F
53 28F
60 28F
63 28F
69 28F
70 28F
71 28F
72 28F
73 28F
75 28F
79 28F
100 28F

Northrop Grumman
E-2C Hawkeye
4 Flottille, Lorient/Lann Bihoué
1 (165455)
2 (165456)
3 (166417)

Sud
SA.316B/SA.319B/SE.3160
Alouette III
ES 22/ESHE, Lanvéoc/Poulmic;
13 SE.3160
14 SE.3160
18 SE.3160
41 SE.3160
100 SA.319B
114 SA.319B
161 SA.319B
237 SA.319B
244 SE.3160
245 SE.3160
268 SA.319B
279 SE.3160
302 SA.319B
303 SA.319B
309 SA.319B
314 SA.319B
347 SA.319B
358 SA.319B
731 SA.316B
806 SA.316B
809 SA.316B
997 SA.319B

Westland
Lynx HAS2(FN)/HAS4(FN)*
31 Flottille, Hyères;
34 Flottille, Lanvéoc/Poulmic;
CEPA, Hyères;
260 34F
263 34F
264 31F
265 31F
266 31F
267 31F
269 31F
270 31F
271 34F
272 34F
273 34F
274 31F
275 31F
276 31F
621 34F
622 34F
623 34F
624 34F
625 34F
627 34F
801* 34F
802* 34F
804* 31F
806* 34F
807* 34F
808* 34F
810* 34F
811* 34F
812* 31F
813* 34F
814* 34F

Aviation Legére de l'Armée de Terre (ALAT)
Pilatus
PC-6B/B2-H4 Turbo Porter
1 GSALAT, Montauban
887 MCA
888 MCB
889 MCC
890 MCD
891 MCE

SOCATA
TBM 700A/TBM/700B*
EAAT, Rennes
35 ABW
70 ABX
80 ABY
94 ABZ
99 ABO
100 ABP
115 ABQ
136 ABR
139 ABS
156* ABT
159* ABU
160* ABV

French Govt
Aérospatiale
AS.350B Ecureuil
Douanes Francaises;
Sécurité Civile*
F-ZBBN AS.350B*
F-ZBDV AS.350BA
F-ZBFC AS.350B-1*
F-ZBFD AS.350B-1*
F-ZBFH AS.350BA
F-ZBFT AS.350B-2*

Aérospatiale
AS.355F-1 Twin Ecureuil
Douanes Francaises
F-ZBAC (5026)
F-ZBEF (5236)
F-ZBEJ (5003)
F-ZBEK (5298)

F-ZBEL (5299)

Beech
Super King Air B200
Sécurité Civile
F-ZBFJ 98
F-ZBFK 96
F-ZBMB 97

Canadair CL-415
Sécurité Civile
F-ZBEG 39
F-ZBEU 42
F-ZBFN 33
F-ZBFP 31
F-ZBFS 32
F-ZBFV 37
F-ZBFW 38
F-ZBFX 34
F-ZBFY 35
F-ZBME 44
F-ZBMF 45
F-ZBMG 48

Cessna F.406 Caravan II
Douanes Francaises
F-ZBAB (0025)
F-ZBBB (0039)
F-ZBCE (0042)
F-ZBCF (0077)
F-ZBCG (0066)
F-ZBCH (0075)
F-ZBCI (0070)
F-ZBCJ (0074)
F-ZBEP (0006)
F-ZBES (0017)
F-ZBFA (0001)
F-ZBGA (0086)
F-ZBGD (0090)
F-ZBGE (0061)

Conair
Turbo Firecat
Sécurité Civile
F-ZBAA 22
F-ZBAP 12
F-ZBAZ 01
F-ZBCZ 23
F-ZBEH 20
F-ZBET 15
F-ZBEW 11
F-ZBEY 07
F-ZBMA 24

Dassault Falcon 20
AVDEF, Nimes/Garons
F-GPAA Falcon 20ECM
F-GPAB Falcon 20E
F-GPAD Falcon 20E

De Havilland Canada
DHC-8Q-402MR
Sécurité Civile
F-ZBMC 73
F-ZBMD 74

Eurocopter
EC.135T-2
Douanes Francaises
F-ZBGF
F-ZBGG
F-ZBGH
F-ZBGI
F-ZBGJ

Eurocopter
EC.145
Sécurité Civile
F-ZBPA
F-ZBPD
F-ZBPE
F-ZBPF
F-ZBPG
F-ZBPH
F-ZBPI
F-ZBPJ
F-ZBPK
F-ZBPL
F-ZBPM
F-ZBPN
F-ZBPO
F-ZBPP
F-ZBPQ
F-ZBPR
F-ZBPS
F-ZBPT
F-ZBPU
F-ZBPV
F-ZBPW
F-ZBPX
F-ZBPY
F-ZBPZ
F-ZBQA
F-ZBQB
F-ZBQC
F-ZBQD
F-ZBQE
F-ZBQF

Civil operated aircraft in military use
Grob G120A-F
EADS/EPAA 00.315, Cognac
F-GUKA
F-GUKB
F-GUKC
F-GUKD
F-GUKE
F-GUKF
F-GUKG
F-GUKH
F-GUKI
F-GUKJ
F-GUKK
F-GUKL
F-GUKM
F-GUKN
F-GUKO
F-GUKP
F-GUKR
F-GUKS

GERMANY

Luftwaffe, Marineflieger
Airbus A.310-304/MRTT*
1/FBS, Köln-Bonn
10+21
10+22
10+23
10+24*
10+25*
10+26*
10+27*

Canadair
CL601-1A Challenger
3/FBS, Köln-Bonn
12+02
12+03
12+04
12+05
12+06
12+07

Eurofighter
EF.2000A/EF.2000B*
EADS, Manching;
JG-73 *Steinhoff*, Laage;
JG-74 *Molders*, Neuburg/Donau;
TsLw-1, Kaufbeuren;
WTD-61, Ingolstadt
30+02* JG-73
30+03* JG-73
30+04* JG-73
30+05* JG-74
30+06 JG-73
30+07 TsLw-1
30+09 JG-73
30+10* JG-73
30+11 JG-73
30+12 JG-73
30+13 JG-73
30+14* JG-73
30+15 JG-73
30+16 JG-73
30+17* JG-73
30+18 JG-73
30+19 JG-74
30+20* JG-73
30+21 JG-73
30+22 TsLw-1
30+23 JG-74
30+24* JG-74
30+25 JG-74
30+26 JG-74
30+27* JG-74
30+28 JG-74
30+29 JG-74
30+30 JG-74
30+31* JG-73
30+32 JG-74
30+33 JG-74
30+35* JG-74
30+38* JG-74
30+39 JG-74
30+40 JG-74
30+42*
98+03* EADS
98+04 EADS
98+30 WTD-61
98+31* EADS

McD F-4F Phantom
JG-71 *Richthoven*, Wittmundhaven;
JG-74 *Molders*, Neuburg/Donau;
TsLw-1, Kaufbeuren;
WTD-61, Ingolstadt
37+01 JG-71
37+03 JG-71
37+04 TsLw-1
37+13 JG-71
37+14 TsLw-1
37+15 WTD-61
37+16 WTD-61$

37+17	JG-71
37+22	JG-71
37+26	JG-71
37+48	JG-71
37+63	JG-71
37+65	JG-71
37+75	JG-71
37+77	JG-71
37+79	JG-71
37+81	JG-74
37+84	JG-71
37+85	JG-71
37+88	JG-71
37+89	JG-71
37+92	JG-71
37+96	JG-71
38+00	JG-74
38+01	JG-71
38+02	JG-74
38+03	JG-74
38+06	JG-71
38+10	JG-74
38+12	JG-71
38+13	WTD-61
38+16	JG-74
38+20	JG-74
38+26	JG-71
38+29	JG-74
38+31	JG-74
38+33	JG-74
38+36	JG-71
38+37	JG-71
38+39	JG-74
38+40	WTD-61
38+42	JG-71
38+43	JG-71
38+44	JG-71
38+45	JG-71
38+46	JG-71
38+48	JG-71
38+50	JG-74
38+54	JG-71
38+55	JG-71
38+56	JG-71
38+57	JG-71
38+58	JG-71
38+60	JG-71
38+61	JG-71
38+62	JG-74
38+67	JG-71
38+68	JG-74
38+69	JG-71
38+70	JG-74
38+73	JG-71
38+74	JG-71
38+75	JG-71
99+91	WTD-61

Panavia Tornado Strike/ Trainer[1]/ECR[2]

AkG-51 *Immelmann*, Schleswig/Jagel;
EADS, Manching;
GAFTTC, Holloman AFB, USA;
JbG-31 *Boelcke*, Nörvenich;
JbG-32, Lechfeld;
JbG-33, Büchel;
TsLw-1, Kaufbeuren;
WTD-61, Ingolstadt

43+01[1]	JbG-31
43+02[1]	AkG-51
43+07[1]	AkG-51
43+08[1]	JbG-32
43+10[1]	JbG-33
43+18	JbG-31
43+20	JbG-31
43+23[1]	JbG-33
43+25	JbG-31
43+29[1]	JbG-31
43+31[1]	JbG-31
43+32	JbG-31
43+34	TsLw-1
43+35[1]	AkG-51
43+37[1]	JbG-32
43+38	JbG-31
43+41	JbG-31
43+42[1]	
43+43[1]	JbG-32
43+45[1]	JbG-32
43+46	AkG-51
43+48	AkG-51
43+52	JbG-31
43+54	TsLw-1
43+57	GAFTTC
43+58	JbG-33
43+59	TsLw-1
43+60	
43+62	JbG-33
43+65	JbG-31
43+71	JbG-32
43+72	JbG-33
43+73	AkG-51
43+75	JbG-31
43+78	TsLw-1
43+79	AkG-51
43+81	AkG-51
43+87	AkG-51
43+92[1]	JbG-31
43+94[1]	GAFTTC
43+97[1]	AkG-51
43+98	AkG-51
44+00	JbG-33
44+02	JbG-32
44+06	AkG-51
44+07	JbG-31
44+13	TsLw-1
44+16[1]	JbG-31
44+17	AkG-51
44+21	JbG-31
44+23	JbG-33
44+26	JbG-33
44+27	WTD-61
44+29	JbG-31
44+30	JbG-31
44+32	JbG-31
44+33	JbG-33
44+34	AkG-51
44+38[1]	GAFTTC
44+39[1]	GAFTTC
44+46	JbG-33
44+52	JbG-31
44+55	JbG-32
44+58	JbG-31
44+61	AkG-51
44+62	JbG-32
44+64	AkG-51
44+65	AkG-51
44+66	JbG-31
44+68	AkG-51
44+69	AkG-51
44+70	JbG-31
44+72[1]	AkG-51
44+73[1]	
44+75[1]	JbG-31
44+77	JbG-31
44+78	JbG-31
44+79	JbG-33
44+80	JbG-31
44+83	JbG-33
44+87	AkG-51
44+90	AkG-51
44+92	JbG-33
44+94	JbG-33
44+95	JbG-33
44+96	AkG-51
44+97	AkG-51
45+00	JbG-33
45+01	JbG-31
45+02	JbG-31
45+03	WTD-61$
45+04	JbG-33
45+06	AkG-51
45+07	JbG-33
45+08	JbG-33
45+09	JbG-33
45+10	JbG-32
45+11	JbG-31
45+12[1]	JbG-32
45+13[1]	AkG-51
45+14[1]	JbG-31
45+15[1]	GAFTTC
45+16[1]	JbG-33
45+17	GAFTTC
45+19	JbG-33
45+20	AkG-51
45+21	JbG-33
45+22	JbG-31
45+23	JbG-31
45+24	JbG-33
45+25	AkG-51
45+28	JbG-31
45+31	JbG-33
45+33	JbG-33
45+34	JbG-33
45+35	JbG-32
45+36	JbG-31
45+37	JbG-33
45+38	JbG-32
45+39	JbG-31
45+40	AkG-51
45+41	JbG-32
45+42	JbG-31
45+43	JbG-32
45+44	JbG-33
45+45	JbG-31
45+46	JbG-33
45+47	TsLw-1
45+49	JbG-33
45+50	AkG-51
45+51	AkG-51
45+52	JbG-33
45+53	JbG-33
45+54	GAFTTC
45+55	GAFTTC
45+56	JbG-31
45+57	AkG-51
45+59	JbG-31
45+61[1]	AkG-51
45+60[1]	AkG-51
45+64	JbG-31
45+66	AkG-51
45+67	AkG-51
45+68	JbG-31
45+69	JbG-33
45+70[1]	JbG-31
45+71	JbG-32
45+72	JbG-32
45+73[1]	GAFTTC

45+74	TsLw-1
45+76	AkG-51
45+77[1]	JbG-33
45+78	JbG-33
45+79	JbG-31
45+81	JbG-31
45+82	JbG-31
45+84	JbG-31
45+85	AkG-51
45+86	JbG-33
45+87	JbG-33
45+88	JbG-31
45+89	AkG-51
45+90	JbG-33
45+91	AkG-51
45+92	JbG-31
45+93	AkG-51
45+94	JbG-33
45+95	JbG-31
45+98	GAFTTC
45+99[1]	GAFTTC
46+00[1]	GAFTTC
46+01	GAFTTC
46+02	JbG-33
46+04[1]	GAFTTC
46+05[1]	AkG-51
46+07[1]	GAFTTC
46+08[1]	JbG-32
46+09[1]	GAFTTC
46+10	WTD-61
46+11	JbG-33
46+12	JbG-33
46+13	AkG-51
46+14	AkG-51
46+15	AkG-51
46+18	AkG-51
46+19	JbG-33
46+20	AkG-51
46+21	AkG-51
46+22	AkG-51
46+23[2]	JbG-32
46+24[2]	JbG-32
46+25[2]	JbG-32
46+26[2]	JbG-32
46+27[2]	JbG-32
46+28[2]	JbG-32
46+29[2]	JbG-32
46+30[2]	JbG-32
46+31[2]	JbG-32
46+32[2]	JbG-32
46+33[2]	JbG-32
46+34[2]	JbG-32
46+35[2]	JbG-32
46+36[2]	JbG-32
46+37[2]	JbG-32
46+38[2]	JbG-32
46+39[2]	JbG-32
46+40[2]	JbG-32
46+41[2]	JbG-32
46+43[2]	JbG-32
46+44[2]	JbG-32
46+45[2]	JbG-32
46+46[2]	JbG-32
46+48[2]	JbG-32$
46+49[2]	JbG-32
46+50[2]	JbG-32
46+51[2]	JbG-32
46+52[2]	JbG-32
46+53[2]	JbG-32
46+54[2]	JbG-32
46+55[2]	JbG-32
46+56[2]	JbG-32
46+57[2]	JbG-32
98+59	WTD-61
98+60	WTD-61
98+77	WTD-61
98+79[2]	WTD-61

Transall C-160D
LTG-61, Landsberg;
LTG-62, Wunstorf;
LTG-63, Hohn;
WTD-61, Ingolstadt

50+06	LTG-61
50+07	LTG-61
50+08	LTG-61
50+09	LTG-61
50+10	LTG-61
50+17	LTG-62
50+29	LTG-62
50+33	LTG-61
50+34	LTG-63
50+35	LTG-62
50+36	LTG-62
50+37	LTG-62
50+38	LTG-62
50+40	LTG-61
50+41	LTG-62
50+42	LTG-63
50+44	LTG-61
50+45	LTG-63
50+46	LTG-62
50+47	LTG-61
50+48	LTG-61$
50+49	LTG-63
50+50	LTG-62
50+51	LTG-61
50+52	LTG-62
50+53	LTG-61
50+54	LTG-62
50+55	LTG-62
50+56	LTG-63
50+57	LTG-62
50+58	LTG-62
50+59	LTG-63
50+60	LTG-62
50+61	LTG-62
50+62	LTG-62
50+64	LTG-61
50+65	LTG-62
50+66	LTG-61
50+67	LTG-63
50+68	LTG-61
50+69	LTG-61
50+70	LTG-62
50+71	LTG-63
50+72	LTG-63
50+73	LTG-62
50+74	LTG-61
50+75	LTG-63
50+76	LTG-63
50+77	LTG-63
50+78	LTG-62
50+79	LTG-62
50+81	LTG-62
50+82	LTG-63
50+83	LTG-62
50+84	LTG-61
50+85	LTG-63
50+86	LTG-61
50+87	LTG-63
50+88	LTG-61
50+89	LTG-62
50+90	LTG-62
50+91	LTG-62
50+92	LTG-61
50+93	LTG-62
50+94	LTG-63
50+95	LTG-63
50+96	LTG-61
50+97	LTG-62
50+98	LTG-61
50+99	LTG-61
51+00	LTG-62
51+01	LTG-62
51+02	LTG-63$
51+03	LTG-62
51+04	LTG-61
51+05	LTG-62
51+06	LTG-63
51+07	LTG-62
51+08	WTD-61
51+09	LTG-63
51+10	LTG-61
51+11	LTG-62
51+12	LTG-63
51+13	LTG-63
51+14	LTG-62
51+15	LTG-61

Dornier Do.228LM
MFG-3, Nordholz
57+01
57+04

Lockheed P-3C Orion
MFG-3, Nordholz
60+01
60+02
60+03
60+04
60+05
60+06
60+07
60+08

Breguet Br.1150 Atlantic *Elint
MFG-3, Nordholz
61+03*
61+06*

Eurocopter AS.532U-2 Cougar
3/FBS, Berlin-Tegel
82+01
82+02
82+03

Westland Super Lynx Mk88A
MFG-3, Nordholz
83+02
83+03
83+04
83+05
83+06
83+07
83+09
83+10
83+11
83+12
83+13
83+15
83+17
83+18
83+19
83+20

83+21
83+22
83+23
83+24
83+25

Westland Sea King HAS41
MFG-5, Kiel-Holtenau
89+50
89+51
89+52
89+53
89+54
89+55
89+56
89+57
89+58
89+60
89+61
89+62
89+63
89+64
89+65
89+66
89+67
89+68
89+69
89+70
89+71

Heeresfliegertruppe Eurocopter AS.665 Tiger
Ecole Franco-Allemande, Le Luc, France;
WTD-61, Ingolstadt

74+03	WTD-61
74+04	Eurocopter
74+05	EFA
74+06	EFA
74+07	EFA
74+08	EFA
74+09	EFA
74+10	
74+11	
74+13	
74+15	
74+16	
74+17	
74+18	
74+19	
74+20	
74+21	
74+22	
74+24	
74+28	
74+29	
74+30	
74+31	
74+32	
98+12	WTD-61
98+14	
98+23	
98+25	
98+26	
98+27	

NH Industries NH.90-TTH
HFWS, Bückeburg;
WTD-61, Ingolstadt

78+01	
78+02	HFWS
78+03	HFWS
78+04	HFWS
78+05	
78+06	
78+07	
98+90	

Eurocopter EC.135P-1
HFWS, Bückeburg
82+51
82+52
82+53
82+54
82+55
82+56
82+57
82+59
82+60
82+61
82+62
82+63
82+64
82+65

Sikorsky/VFW CH-53G/CH-53GS*
HFWS, Bückeburg;
MTHR-15, Rheine-Bentlage;
MTHR-25, Laupheim;
TsLw-3, Fassberg;
WTD-61, Ingolstadt

84+01*	WTD-61
84+02	WTD-61$
84+05	HFWS
84+06	MTHR-15
84+09	TsLw-3
84+10	HFWS
84+11	HFWS
84+12	MTHR-15
84+13	HFWS
84+14	HFWS
84+15*	MTHR-25
84+16	HFWS
84+17	MTHR-25
84+18	HFWS
84+19	TsLw-3
84+21	HFWS
84+22	MTHR-15
84+23	
84+24	MTHR-15
84+25*	
84+26	MTHR-15
84+27	HFWS
84+28	MTHR-25
84+29	MTHR-15
84+30*	MTHR-15
84+31	MTHR-15
84+32	MTHR-25
84+33	
84+34	MTHR-15
84+35	HFWS
84+36	MTHR-15
84+37	HFWS
84+38	MTHR-25
84+39	MTHR-15
84+40	MTHR-25
84+41	HFWS
84+42*	MTHR-25
84+43	MTHR-25
84+44	MTHR-25
84+45*	MTHR-25
84+46	MTHR-15
84+47	MTHR-25
84+48	HFWS
84+49	HFWS
84+50	HFWS
84+51*	MTHR-25
84+52*	MTHR-25
84+53	MTHR-25
84+54	MTHR-25
84+55	WTD-61
84+57	HFWS
84+58	MTHR-25
84+59	MTHR-25
84+60	MTHR-25
84+62*	MTHR-25
84+63	MTHR-25
84+64*	MTHR-25
84+65	MTHR-25
84+66*	MTHR-25
84+67*	MTHR-15
84+68	MTHR-15
84+69	HFWS
84+70	MTHR-15
84+71	MTHR-15
84+72	MTHR-15
84+73*	MTHR-15
84+74	MTHR-15
84+75	MTHR-15
84+76	HFWS
84+78	HFWS
84+79*	MTHR-15
84+80	MTHR-15
84+82	MTHR-15
84+83	MTHR-15
84+84	MTHR-15
84+85*	MTHR-15
84+86	MTHR-15
84+87	MTHR-15
84+88	MTHR-15
84+89	HFWS
84+90	MTHR-15
84+91*	MTHR-25
84+92	MTHR-25
84+94	
84+95	MTHR-25
84+96	MTHR-25
84+97	MTHR-25
84+98*	MTHR-15
84+99	MTHR-15
85+00*	HFWS
85+01	MTHR-25
85+02	MTHR-15
85+03	MTHR-15
85+04	MTHR-15
85+05	MTHR-25
85+06	MTHR-25
85+07*	MTHR-25
85+08	MTHR-15
85+10*	MTHR-25
85+11	MTHR-25
85+12*	MTHR-15

MBB Bo.105P
HFUS-1, Holzdorf;
HFUS-7, Mendig;
HFVAS-100, Celle;
HFVS-910, Bückeburg;
HFWS, Bückeburg;
KHR-26, Roth;
KHR-36, Fritzlar;
TsLw-3, Fassberg;
WTD-61, Ingolstadt

86+01	
86+02	KHR-36

86+03 HFWS
86+04 KHR-36
86+05 HFWS
86+06 HFWS
86+07 HFWS
86+08 HFWS
86+09 HFWS
86+10 HFVAS-100
86+11
86+12 HFWS
86+13 HFWS
86+14 KHR-36
86+15 KHR-26
86+16 HFWS
86+17 HFVS-910
86+18 HFWS
86+19 HFWS
86+20 HFWS
86+21 HFVAS-100
86+22 HFVAS-100
86+23 TsLw-3
86+24 HFVS-910
86+25 HFVAS-100
86+26 HFVS-910
86+27 KHR-26
86+28 HFWS
86+29 HFVS-910
86+30 KHR-26
86+31 HFUS-1
86+32 KHR-26
86+33 KHR-26
86+34 HFUS-1
86+35 KHR-26
86+36 HFVAS-100
86+37
86+38 KHR-36
86+39 HFWS
86+41 HFVAS-100
86+42 KHR-26
86+43
86+44 HFWS
86+45 KHR-36
86+46 HFWS
86+47 HFVAS-100
86+48 HFVAS-100
86+49 KHR-36
86+50
86+51 HFVS-910
86+52 HFUS-1
86+53 HFVAS-100
86+54 HFUS-1
86+55
86+56 HFWS
86+57
86+58 KHR-36
86+59 HFVAS-100
86+60 HFWS
86+61 KHR-26
86+62 HFVS-910
86+63 KHR-26
86+64 KHR-26
86+65 KHR-26
86+66 KHR-26
86+67 HFVAS-100
86+68 KHR-36
86+69 KHR-26
86+70 HFVAS-100
86+71 KHR-36
86+72
86+73 HFWS
86+74 KHR-36
86+76 KHR-26
86+77 HFWS
86+78
86+79
86+80
86+83 TsLw-3
86+84 KHR-26
86+85 HFUS-1
86+86 HFVAS-100
86+87
86+88 HFUS-1
86+89 HFUS-1
86+90 KHR-26
86+92 KHR-36
86+93 HFVS-910
86+95 HFUS-1
86+96 KHR-26
86+97 KHR-36
86+98
86+99 TsLw-3
87+01 KHR-26
87+02 KHR-26
87+03 TsLw-3
87+04
87+06 KHR-36
87+07 KHR-26
87+08 KHR-26
87+09 HFWS
87+10 KHR-26
87+11 KHR-36
87+12 KHR-36
87+13 KHR-36
87+15 KHR-36
87+16 HFVAS-100
87+17 KHR-36
87+18 HFVAS-100
87+19 KHR-36
87+20 KHR-26
87+22
87+23 HFVAS-100
87+24 HFUS-7
87+25 KHR-26
87+26 HFUS-1
87+27 HFVAS-100
87+28 HFVAS-100
87+29 HFVS-910
87+30
87+31 HFVS-910
87+34 KHR-26
87+35 KHR-26
87+37 KHR-26
87+38 KHR-36$
87+39 KHR-26
87+41 HFWS
87+43 KHR-36
87+44 HFUS-1
87+45 HFUS-1
87+46 KHR-36
87+47 HFWS
87+48 HFVAS-100
87+49 HFVAS-100
87+50 KHR-36
87+51 HFVAS-100
87+52 HFUS-1
87+53 KHR-26
87+55 HFVS-910
87+56 TsLw-3
87+58 HFWS
87+59 HFWS
87+60 KHR-36
87+61 KHR-36
87+62 HFWS
87+63 HFWS
87+64 KHR-36
87+65 KHR-36
87+66 KHR-36
87+67 HFVAS-100
87+68 HFWS
87+70
87+71 HFWS
87+72
87+73 HFWS
87+75 KHR-26
87+76
87+77
87+78 HFUS-1
87+79
87+80 HFUS-1
87+81 TsLw-3
87+82
87+83 KHR-36
87+85
87+86 KHR-26
87+87
87+88 KHR-26
87+89 KHR-36
87+90 HFWS
87+91
87+92 KHR-26
87+94 KHR-26
87+96 KHR-26
87+97 KHR-26
87+98 HFWS
87+99 KHR-36
88+01 KHR-36
88+02 KHR-36
88+04 KHR-36
88+05 HFVS-910
88+06 KHR-36
88+07 HFVAS-100
88+08 HFWS
88+09
88+10 HFVS-910
88+11 KHR-36
88+12 HFVAS-100

GHANA

Ghana Air Force

Fokker

F-28 Fellowship 3000

VIP Flight, Accra

G-530

GREECE

Ellinikí Polemikí Aeroporía

Aeritalia C-27J

354 Mira, Elefsis

4117
4118
4120
4121
4122
4123
4124
4125
4128

Dassault Mirage 2000

331 MAPK/114 PM, Tanagra;
332 MAPK/114 PM, Tanagra

Mirage 2000BG

201 332 MAPK
202 332 MAPK
204 332 MAPK

Mirage 2000EG

210 332 MAPK
212 332 MAPK
213 332 MAPK

215 332 MAPK
216 332 MAPK
217 332 MAPK
218 332 MAPK
219 332 MAPK
220 332 MAPK
221 332 MAPK
226 332 MAPK
228 332 MAPK
230 332 MAPK
231 332 MAPK
232 332 MAPK
233 332 MAPK
234 332 MAPK
235 332 MAPK
236 332 MAPK
237 332 MAPK
239 332 MAPK
240 332 MAPK
241 332 MAPK
242 332 MAPK
243 332 MAPK
245 332 MAPK

Mirage 2000-5BG

505 331 MAPK
506 331 MAPK
507 331 MAPK
508 331 MAPK
509 331 MAPK

Mirage 2000-5EG

511 331 MAPK
514 331 MAPK
511 331 MAPK
527 331 MAPK
546 331 MAPK
547 331 MAPK
548 331 MAPK
549 331 MAPK
550 331 MAPK
551 331 MAPK
552 331 MAPK
553 331 MAPK
554 331 MAPK
555 331 MAPK

Embraer ERJ-135BJ Legacy/ ERJ.145H/ERJ.135LR

356 MTM/112 PM, Elefsís;
380 Mira/112 PM, Elefsís

135L-484 ERJ-135BJ 356 MTM
145-209 ERJ-135LR 356 MTM
145-374 ERJ-145H 380 Mira
145-671 ERJ-145H 380 Mira
145-729 ERJ-145H 380 Mira
145-757 ERJ-145H 380 Mira

Gulfstream Aerospace Gulfstream V

356 MTM/112 PM, Elefsís

678

Lockheed C-130H Hercules

356 MTM/112 PM, Elefsís

**ECM*

741*
742
743
744
745
746
747*
749
751
752

Lockheed F-16C/F-16D* Fighting Falcon

330 Mira/111 PM, Nea Ankhialos;
337 Mira/110 PM, Larissa;
340 Mira/115PM, Souda;
341 Mira/111 PM, Nea Ankhialos;
343 Mira/115PM, Souda;
346 MAPK/110 PM, Larissa;
347 Mira/111 PM, Nea Ankhialos

046 341 Mira
047 347 Mira
048 341 Mira
049 347 Mira
050 341 Mira
051 347 Mira
052 341 Mira
053 347 Mira
054 341 Mira
055 347 Mira
056 341 Mira
057 347 Mira
058 341 Mira
059 347 Mira
060 341 Mira
061 347 Mira
062 341 Mira
063 347 Mira
064 341 Mira
065 347 Mira
066 341 Mira
067 347 Mira
068 341 Mira
069 347 Mira
070 341 Mira
071 347 Mira
072 341 Mira
073 347 Mira
074 341 Mira
075 347 Mira
076 341 Mira
077* 341 Mira
078* 347 Mira
079* 347 Mira
080* 347 Mira
081* 347 Mira
082* 341 Mira
083* 347 Mira
084* 341 Mira
110 330 Mira
111 330 Mira
112 346 MAPK
113 330 Mira
114 346 MAPK
115 330 Mira
116 330 Mira
117 330 Mira
118 346 MAPK
119 330 Mira
120 346 MAPK
121 330 Mira
122 346 MAPK
124 346 MAPK
125 330 Mira
126 346 MAPK
127 330 Mira
128 346 MAPK
129 330 Mira
130 346 MAPK
132 346 MAPK
133 330 Mira
134 346 MAPK
136 346 MAPK
138 346 MAPK
139 330 Mira
140 346 MAPK
141 330 Mira
143 330 Mira
144* 330 Mira
145* 330 Mira
146* 346 MAPK
147* 330 Mira
148* 346 MAPK
149* 346 MAPK
500 337 Mira
501 337 Mira
502 337 Mira
503 343 Mira
504 340 Mira
505 343 Mira
506 340 Mira
507 337 Mira
508 337 Mira
509 343 Mira
510 340/343 Mira
511 340/343 Mira
512 340/343 Mira
513 343 Mira
515 340/343 Mira
517 340/343 Mira
518 340/343 Mira
519 340 Mira
520 340/343 Mira
521 340 Mira
522 340/343 Mira
523 340 Mira
524 337 Mira
525 340/343 Mira
526 340 Mira
527 340/343 Mira
528 337 Mira
529 340 Mira
530 337 Mira
531 340/343 Mira
532 337 Mira
533 340 Mira
534 340 Mira
535 340/343 Mira
536 340 Mira
537 340 Mira
538 340/343 Mira
539 340/343 Mira
600* 340/343 Mira
601* 343 Mira
602* 340 Mira
603* 340 Mira
604* 340 Mira
605* 340 Mira
606* 337 Mira
607* 340/343 Mira
608* 340 Mira
609* 337 Mira
610* 340 Mira
611* 337 Mira
612* 337 Mira
613* 340/343 Mira
614* 340/343 Mira
615* 343 Mira
616* 340/343 Mira

617*	343 Mira
618*	343 Mira
619*	337 Mira

LTV A-7 Corsair II
335 Mira/116 PM, Áraxos;
336 Mira/116 PM, Áraxos

155404	TA-7C	
155424	TA-7C	
155477	TA-7C	
155489	TA-7C	
155507	TA-7C	
155774	TA-7C	(156774)
156738	TA-7C	
156747	TA-7C	
156750	TA-7C	
156753	TA-7C	
156767	TA-7C	
156768	TA-7C	
156790	TA-7C	
156795	TA-7C	
157502	A-7E	
158021	A-7E	
158824	A-7E	
158825	A-7E	
159263	A-7E	
159274	A-7E	
159285	A-7E	
159639	A-7E	
159640	A-7E	
159645	A-7E	
159648	A-7E	
159658	A-7E	
159967	A-7E	
159975	A-7E	
159980	A-7E	
159999	A-7E	
160002	A-7E	
160537	A-7E	
160541	A-7E	
160543	A-7E	
160552	A-7E	
160556	A-7E	
160557	A-7E	
160560	A-7E	
160566	A-7E	
160616	A-7E	
160617	A-7E	
160710	A-7E	
160716	A-7E$	
160717	A-7E	
160728	A-7E	
160736	A-7E	
160857	A-7E	
160862	A-7E	
160864	A-7E	
160865	A-7E	
160866	A-7E	
160873	A-7E	

HUNGARY
Hungarian Defence Forces
Antonov An-26
89 VSD, Szolnok
110
405
406
407
603

Mikoyan MiG-29/29UB*
59 HRO, Kecskemét
04
06
09
10
14
15
16
18
21
23
25*
26*
27*
28*
29*

SAAB 39C/39D* Gripen
59 HRO, Kecskemét
30
31
32
33
34
35
36
37
38
39
40
41
42*
43*

ISRAEL
Heyl ha'Avir
Boeing 707
120 Sqn, Tel Aviv

120	RC-707
128	RC-707
137	RC-707
140	KC-707
242	VC-707
248	KC-707
250	KC-707
255	EC-707
260	KC-707
264	RC-707
272	VC-707
275	KC-707
290	KC-707

Lockheed C-130 Hercules
103 Sqn & 131 Sqn, Tel Aviv

102	C-130H
106	C-130H
208	C-130E
305	C-130E
309	C-130E
310	C-130E
313	C-130E
314	C-130E
316	C-130E
420	KC-130H
427	C-130H
428	C-130H
435	C-130H
436	C-130H
522	KC-130H
545	KC-130H

ITALY
Aeronautica Militare Italiana
Aeritalia G222/C-27J
9ª Brigata Aerea, Pratica di Mare: 14° Stormo/8° Gruppo;
46ª Brigata Aerea, Pisa: 98° Gruppo;
RSV, Pratica di Mare

G222RM

MM62139	14-20	8

G222TCM

MM62146		8

C-27J

CSX62127		Alenia
MM62215	46-80	98
MM62217	46-81	98
MM62218	46-82	98
MM62220	46-83	98

Aeritalia-EMB AMX/AMX-T*
32° Stormo, Amendola: 13° Gruppo & 101° Gruppo;
51° Stormo, Istrana: 103° Gruppo & 132° Gruppo;
RSV, Pratica di Mare

MMX596		Alenia
MMX597		Alenia
MM7101		
MM7115		
MM7116	32-11	13
MM7120		
MM7125		
MM7126		
MM7131	51-11	103
MM7132	51-01	103
MM7133	51-32	132
MM7139	51-24	103
MM7141		
MM7143	51-21	103
MM7144	51-03	103
MM7145		
MM7146	51-25	103
MM7147	32-01$	13
MM7148	51-50	132
MM7149		
MM7151	51-27	103
MM7152		
MM7155		
MM7156		
MM7157	$	
CSX7158	RS-12	RSV
MM7159	51-10$	103
MM7160	32-14	13
MM7161	51-31	132
MM7162		
MM7163	51-26	103
MM7164		
MM7165	51-45	132
MM7166		
MM7167	51-37	132
MM7168	51-50	132
MM7169	32-26	13
MM7170	32-05	13
MM7171	RS-11	RSV
MM7172	51-42	132
MM7173		
MM7174	32-01	13
MM7175		
MM7176	51-46	132
MM7178	32-24	13
MM7179	51-47	132
MM7180	32-20	13

MM7182	51-52	132
MM7183	32-03	13
MM7184	51-54	132
MM7185	51-55	132
MM7186	32-30	101
MM7189		
MM7190	51-60	132
MM7191	51-61	132
MM7192	32-02	13
MM7193	51-63	132
MM7194	51-64	132
MM7195		
MM7196	32-13	13
MM7197	32-21	13
MM7198		
MM55029*	32-50	101
MM55030*	32-41	101
MM55031*	32-40	101
MM55034*	RS-18	RSV
MM55035*		
MM55036*	32-52	101
MM55037*	32-64	101
MM55038*		
MM55040*	32-52	101
MM55041*	32-55	101
MM55042*	32-56	101
MM55043*	32-65	101
MM55044*	32-57	101
MM55046*	32-47	101
MM55047*	32-53	101
MM55049*	32-46	101
MM55050*	32-63	101
MM55051*	32-42	101

Aermacchi MB339A/MB339CD*
36° Stormo, Gioia del Colle:
12° Gruppo;
51° Stormo, Istrana:
651ª SC;
61° Stormo, Lecce:
212° Gruppo & 213° Gruppo;
Aermacchi, Venegono;
Frecce Tricolori [FT]
(313° Gruppo), Rivolto
(MB339A/PAN);
RSV, Pratica di Mare

MM54440	61-00	
MM54441	61-71	
MM54442	61-112	
MM54443	61-50	
MM54445	61-25	
MM54446	61-01	
MM54447	61-02	
MM54451	61-116	
MM54452		
CSX54453	RS-11	RSV
MM54456	61-10	
MM54458	61-12	
MM54459	61-13	
MM54462	61-16	
MM54463	61-17	
MM54465	51-77	
MM54467	61-23	
MM54468	61-24	
MM54471	61-27	
MM54472	61-30	
MM54473	5	[FT]
MM54475	3	[FT]
MM54477		[FT]
MM54479		[FT]
MM54480		[FT]
MM54482	10	[FT]
MM54484	61-101	
MM54485		[FT]
MM54486		[FT]
MM54487	4	[FT]
MM54488	61-32	
MM54489	61-33	
MM54490	61-34	
MM54492	61-36	
MM54493	61-37	
MM54494	51-75	
MM54496	61-42	
MM54499	61-45	
MM54500	1	[FT]
MM54503	61-51	
MM54504	61-52	
MM54505	7	[FT]
MM54506	51-74	
MM54507	61-55	
MM54509	61-57	
MM54510	61-60	
MM54511	61-61	
MM54512	61-62	
MM54514	61-64	
MM54515	61-76	
MM54516	51-75	
MM54517		[FT]
MM54518	61-70	
MM54532		
MM54533	61-72	
MM54534	2	[FT]
MM54535	61-74	
MM54536		[FT]
MM54537		
MM54539		[FT]
MM54542		[FT]
MM54543	8	[FT]
CSX54544*	RS-30	
MM54546	51-67	
MM54547		[FT]
MM54548	61-106	
MM54549	61-107	
MM54550	61-110	
MM54551	0	[FT]
MM55052	6	[FT]
MM55053	61-114	
MM55054	61-15	
MM55055	61-20	
MM55058	61-41	
MM55059	61-26	
MM55062*	36-14	
MM55063*	RS-27	RSV
MM55064*	36-10	
MM55065*	36-02	
MM55066*	36-03	
MM55067*	36-07	
MM55068*	RS-27	RSV
MM55069*	36-01	
MM55070*	36-12$	
MM55072*	36-05	
MM55073*	RS-26	RSV
MM55074*	36-06	
MM55075*	36-15	
MM55076*	36-04	
MM55077*	RS-28	RSV
MM55078*	RS-29	RSV
MM55079*		
MM55080*	61-150	
MM55081*	61-151	
MM55082*	61-152	
MM55084*	61-154	
MM55085*	61-155	
MM55086*	61-156	
MM55087*	61-167	
MM55088*	61-160	
MM55089*	61-161	
MM55090*	61-162	
MM55091*	61-163	

Aermacchi M346
Aermacchi, Venegono
CMX615
CMX616

Agusta-Sikorsky HH-3F Pelican
15° Stormo,
Pratica di Mare:
85° Gruppo SAR

MM80974	15-01
MM80975	15-02$
MM80976	15-03
MM80977	15-04
MM80978	15-05
MM80979	15-06
MM80980	15-07
MM80981	15-10
MM80982	15-11
MM80983	15-12
MM80984	15-13
MM80985	15-14
MM80986	15-15
MM80988	15-19
MM80989	15-20
MM80990	15-21
MM80991	15-22
MM80992	15-23
MM81337	15-25
MM81339	15-27
MM81340	15-28
MM81341	15-29
MM81342	15-30
MM81343	15-31
MM81344	15-32
MM81345	15-33
MM81346	15-34
MM81347	15-35
MM81348	15-36
MM81349	15-37
MM81350	15-38

Airbus A.319CJ-115X
31° Stormo,
Roma-Ciampino:
306° Gruppo
MM62174
MM62209
MM62243

Boeing 707-3F5C
9ª Brigata Aerea,
Pratica di Mare:
8° Gruppo

MM62151	14-04

Boeing 767T/T (767-2EYER)
9ª Brigata Aerea,
Pratica di Mare:
8° Gruppo

MM62226	14-01
MM62227	14-02
MM62228	14-03
MM62229	14-04

Breguet Br.1150 Atlantic
41° Stormo, Catania:
88° Gruppo

MM40108	41-70
MM40109	41-71
MM40110	41-72
MM40111	41-73
MM40113	41-74
MM40114	41-76
MM40115	41-77
MM40116	41-01
MM40117	41-02
MM40118	41-03
MM40119	41-04
MM40120	41-05
MM40121	41-06
MM40122	41-07
MM40123	41-10
MM40124	41-11
MM40125	41-12

Dassault Falcon 50
31° Stormo,
Roma-Ciampino:
93° Gruppo
MM62026
MM62029

Dassault
Falcon 900EX/900EX EASy*
31° Stormo,
Roma-Ciampino:
93° Gruppo
MM62171
MM62172
MM62210
MM62244*
MM62245*

Eurofighter
EF.2000A/EF.2000B*
4° Stormo, Grosseto:
9° Gruppo & 20° Gruppo;
36° Stormo, Gioia del Colle:
12° Gruppo;
Alenia, Torino/Caselle;
RSV, Pratica di Mare

MMX602	RS-01	RSV
MMX603	Alenia	
MMX614*	Alenia	
MM7235	4-69	
MM7270	4-20	20
MM7271	36-12	12
MM7272	36-03	12
MM7273	36-02	12
MM7274	4-10	9
MM7275	4-11	9
MM7276	36-01	12
MM7277	4-19	
MM7278	4-12	9
MM7279	4-49	
MM7280	4-13	9
MM7281	4-14	9
MM7282	4-15	9
MM7284		
MM7285	4-16	9
MM7286	4-29	
MM7287		
MM7288		
MM7289		
MM7290		
MM7291		
MM7292		
MM7293		
MM7294		
MM7295		
MM7296		
MM7297		
MM7298		
MM7299		
CSX55092*	4-25	20
MM55093*	4-31	20
MM55094*	4-27	20
MM55095*	4-23	20
MM55096*	4-30	20
MM55097*	4-24	20
MM55128*	4-26	20
MM55129*	4-32	20
MM55130*		

Lockheed
C-130J/C-130J-30/KC-130J*
Hercules II
46ª Brigata Aerea, Pisa:
2° Gruppo & 50° Gruppo

C-130J

MM62175	46-40	2
MM62176*	46-41	2
MM62177	46-42	2
MM62178	46-43	2
MM62179	46-44	2
MM62180	46-45	2
MM62181	46-46	50
MM62182	46-47	50
MM62183	46-48	50
MM62184	46-49	50
MM62185	46-50	50
MM62186	46-51	50

C-130J-30

MM62187	46-53	50
MM62188	46-54	50
MM62189	46-55	50
MM62190	46-56	50
MM62191	46-57	50
MM62192	46-58	50
MM62193	46-59	50
MM62194	46-60	50
MM62195	46-61	50
MM62196	46-62	50

Lockheed (GD)
F-16A-ADF/F-16B*
5° Stormo, Cervia:
23° Gruppo
37° Stormo, Trapani:
18° Gruppo

MM7236	23
MM7238	23
MM7239	23
MM7240	18
MM7241	18
MM7242	18
MM7243	23
MM7244	23
MM7245	23
MM7246	18
MM7247	18
MM7248	18
MM7249	18
MM7250	18
MM7251	23
MM7252	23
MM7253	18
MM7254	18
MM7255	18
MM7256	18
MM7257	18
MM7258	23
MM7259	23
MM7260	18
MM7261	18
MM7262	23
MM7263	18
MM7264	23
MM7265	18
MM7266*	18
MM7267*	18
MM7268*	23
MM7269*	23

Panavia
Tornado Strike/
Trainer[1]/ECR[2]
6° Stormo, Ghedi:
102° Gruppo &
154° Gruppo;
50° Stormo, Piacenza:
155° Gruppo;
156° Gruppo Autonomo,
Gioia del Colle;
RSV, Pratica di Mare

MM7002		
MM7003		
MM7004	6-53	102
MM7005[2]	$	156
MM7006	6-31$	102
MM7007	6-01	154
MM7008	36-51	156
MM7009	36-46	156
MM7011	6-13	154
MM7013	36-156	156
MM7014		Alenia
MM7015		RSV
MM7016	6-20	154
MM7018	6-46	102
MM7019[2]	50-05	155
MM7020[2]	50-21	155
MM7021[2]	50-01	155
MM7022	6-23	154
MM7023	36-31	156
MM7024	36-41	156
MM7025	6-05	154
MM7026	6-35	102
MM7027[2]		
MM7028		
MM7029		
MM7030[2]	50-04	155
MM7031	36-37	156
MM7033	36-47	156
MM7034[2]	50-53	155
MM7035	6-27	154
MM7036[2]	50-..	155
MM7037	6-16	154
MM7038	6-37	102
MM7039	6-02	154
MM7040		
CSX7041	RS-06	RSV
MM7042	36-57	156
MM7043	6-25	154
MM7044	50-53	155
MM7046[2]	6-06	154
MM7047[2]	50-43	155
MM7048		
MM7049	36-42	156
MM7050	36-44	156
MM7051[2]	50-45	155
MM7052[2]	50-02	155
MM7053[2]	50-07	155
MM7054[2]	50-40	155

MM7055	50-42	155
MM7056	36-50	156
MM7057	36-54	156
MM7058	6-11	154
MM7059	50-47	155
MM7061	6-14	154
MM7062[2]	50-44	155
MM7063	6-26	154
MM7064	6-24	154
MM7065	6-25	154
MM7066		
MM7067		
MM7068[2]	50-46	155
MM7070[2]		
MM7071	6-12	154
MM7072	6-30	102
MM7073[2]	6-34	102
MM7075	36-53	156
MM7078	36-30	156
CMX7079[2]		Alenia
MM7080	6-33	102
MM7081		
MM7082[2]		
MM7083	36-36	156
MM7084		
CMX7085	36-50	Alenia
MM7086	36-35	156
MM7087	6-36	102
MM7088	6-10	154
MM55000[1]	6-51	102
MM55002[1]	6-52	102
MM55003[1]		
MM55004[1]		
MM55005[1]	6-40	102
MM55006[1]	6-03	154
MM55007[1]	36-55	156
MM55008[1]	6-45	102
MM55009[1]	36-56	156
MM55010[1]	6-42	102
MM55011[1]	6-54	102

Piaggio
P-180AM Avanti
9ª Brigata Aerea,
Pratica di Mare:
71° Gruppo;
36° Stormo, Gioia del Colle:
636ª SC;
RSV, Pratica di Mare

MM62159		71
MM62160	54	RSV
MM62161		71
MM62162		71
MM62163		71
CSX62164		RSV
MM62199		636
MM62200	9-01	71
MM62201		71
MM62202		71
MM62203		71
MM62204	9-02	71
MM62205		71
MM62206		71
MM62207		71

Aviazione dell'Esercito
Dornier Do.228-212
28° Gruppo Squadrone
Cavalleria dell'Aria, Viterbo

MM62156	E.I.101
MM62157	E.I.101
MM62158	E.I.101

Piaggio
P-180AM Avanti
28° Gruppo Squadrone Det,
Cavalleria dell'Aria,
Roma/Ciampino
MM62167
MM62168
MM62169

Guardia Costiera
Aérospatiale
ATR.42-400MP
3° Nucleo, Pescara

MM62170	10-01
MM62208	10-02

Guardia di Finanza
Aérospatiale
ATR.42-400MP
Gruppo Esplorazione
Aeromarittima,
Pratica di Mare

MM62165	GF-13
MM62166	GF-14
MM62230	GF-15

Piaggio
P-180AM Avanti
Gruppo Esplorazione
Aeromarittima,
Pratica di Mare

MM62248	GF-18
MM62249	GF-19

Marina Militare Italiana
Augusta Westland
EH.101 Mk.110/
Mk410*
1° Grupelicot, La Spezia/Luni

MM81480	2-01
MM81481	2-02
CSX81482	2-03
MM81483	2-04
MM81485	2-06
MM81486	2-07
MM81487	2-08
MM81488	2-09
MM81489	2-10
MM81490	2-11
MM81491	2-12
MM81492*	2-13
MM81493*	2-14
MM81494*	2-15
MM81633*	2-18
MM81634*	2-19
MM81635*	2-20
MM81636*	2-21

McDonnell Douglas
AV-8B/TAV-8B Harrier II+
Gruppo Aerei Imbarcarti,
Taranto/Grottaglie
AV-8B

MM7199	1-03
MM7200	1-04
MM7201	1-05
MM7212	1-06
MM7213	1-07
MM7214	1-08
MM7215	1-09
MM7217	1-11
MM7218	1-12
MM7219	1-13
MM7220	1-14
MM7221	1-15
MM7222	1-16
MM7223	1-18
MM7224	1-19

TAV-8B

MM55032	1-01
MM55033	1-02

Italian Govt
Dassault Falcon 900
Italian Govt/Soc. CAI,
Roma/Ciampino
I-CAEX
I-DIES
I-NUMI

IVORY COAST
Grumman
G.1159C Gulfstream IV
Ivory Coast Govt, Abidjan
TU-VAD

JAPAN
Japan Air Self Defence Force
Boeing 747-47C
701st Flight Sqn, Chitose
20-1101
20-1102

JORDAN
Al Quwwat al Jawwiya
al Malakiya al Urduniya
Extra EA-300LP
Royal Jordanian Falcons,
Amman
JY-RFA
JY-RFB
JY-RFC
JY-RFD
JY-RFE

Extra EA-300S
Royal Jordanian Falcons,
Amman
JY-RNA
JY-RNC
JY-RND
JY-RNE
JY-RNG
JY-RNL

Lockheed C-130H Hercules
3 Sqn, Amman/Marka
344
345
346
347

Jordanian Govt
Airbus A.340-211
Jordanian Govt, Amman
JY-ABH

Boeing 737-7BC
Jordanian Govt, Amman
VP-BFA

Canadair
CL.604 Challenger
Jordanian Govt, Amman
JY-ONE
JY-TWO

Lockheed L.1011 TriStar 500
Jordanian Govt, Amman
JY-HKJ

KAZAKHSTAN
Boeing 767-2DKER
Govt of Kazakhstan, Almaty
UN-B6701

Tupolev Tu-154B-2
Govt of Kazakhstan, Almaty
UN-85464

KENYA
Kenyan Air Force
Fokker 70ER
308

KUWAIT
Al Quwwat al Jawwiya al Kuwaitiya
Lockheed L100-30 Hercules
41 Sqn, Kuwait International
KAF 323
KAF 324
KAF 325

Kuwaiti Govt
Airbus A.300C4-620
Kuwaiti Govt, Safat
9K-AHI

Airbus A.310-308
Kuwaiti Govt, Safat
9K-ALD

Airbus A.320-212
Kuwaiti Govt, Safat
9K-AKD

Boeing 747-469
Kuwaiti Govt, Safat
9K-ADE

Gulfstream Aerospace Gulfstream V
Kuwaiti Govt/Kuwait Airways, Safat
9K-AJD
9K-AJE
9K-AJF

KYRGYZSTAN
Tupolev Tu-134A-3
Govt of Kyrgyzstan, Bishkek
EX-65119

Tupolev Tu-154B/Tu-154M
Govt of Kyrgyzstan, Bishkek

EX-85294	Tu-154B
EX-85718	Tu-154M
EX-85762	Tu-154M

LITHUANIA
Karines Oro Pajegos
Aeritalia C-27J
Transporto Eskadrile, Siauliai-Zokniai
06

Antonov An-26RV
Transporto Eskadrile, Siauliai-Zokniai
03
04
05

LET 410UVP Turbolet
Transporto Eskadrile, Siauliai-Zokniai
01
02

Mil Mi-8
Sraigtasparniu Eskadrile, Panevezys/Pajuostis

02	Mi-8T
09	Mi-8T
10	Mi-8T
11	Mi-8PS
14	Mi-8T
20	Mi-8T
21	Mi-8MTV-1
22	Mi-8MTV-1
23	Mi-8T

LUXEMBOURG
NATO
Boeing 707TCA (CT-49A)
NAEW&CF, Geilenkirchen
LX-N19997
LX-N20000
LX-N20199

Boeing E-3A
NAEW&CF, Geilenkirchen
LX-N90442
LX-N90443$
LX-N90444
LX-N90445
LX-N90446
LX-N90447
LX-N90448
LX-N90449
LX-N90450
LX-N90451
LX-N90452
LX-N90453
LX-N90454
LX-N90455
LX-N90456
LX-N90458
LX-N90459

MACEDONIA
Macedonian Govt
Bombardier Lear 60
Macedonian Govt, Skopje
Z3-MKD

MALAYSIA
Royal Malaysian Air Force/ Tentera Udara Diraja Malaysia
Boeing 737-7H6
2 Sqn, Simpang
M53–01

Bombardier BD.700-1A10 Global Express
2 Sqn, Simpang
M48-02

Dassault Falcon 900
2 Sqn, Simpang
M37-01

Lockheed C-130 Hercules
14 Sqn, Labuan;
20 Sqn, Subang

M30-01	C-130H(MP)	20 Sqn
M30-02	C-130H	20 Sqn
M30-03	C-130H	14 Sqn
M30-04	C-130H-30	20 Sqn
M30-05	C-130H	14 Sqn
M30-06	C-130H	14 Sqn
M30-07	C-130T	20 Sqn
M30-08	C-130H(MP)	20 Sqn
M30-09	C-130H(MP)	20 Sqn
M30-10	C-130H-30	20 Sqn
M30-11	C-130H-30	20 Sqn
M30-12	C-130H-30	20 Sqn
M30-14	C-130H-30	20 Sqn
M30-15	C-130H-30	20 Sqn
M30-16	C-130H-30	20 Sqn

Malaysian Govt
Airbus A.319CJ-115X
9M-NAA

MALTA
Bombardier Learjet 60
Govt of Malta, Luqa
9H-AEE

MEXICO
Fuerza Aérea Mexicana
Boeing 757-225
8° Grupo Aéreo, Mexico City
TP-01 (XC-UJM)

MOROCCO
Force Aérienne Royaume Marocaine/ Al Quwwat al Jawwiya al Malakiya Marakishiya
Airtech CN.235M-100
Escadrille de Transport, Rabat

023	CNA-MA
024	CNA-MB
025	CNA-MC
026	CNA-MD
027	CNA-ME
028	CNA-MF
031	CNA-MG

CAP-232
Marche Verte

28	CNA-BP [7]
29	CN-ABQ [6]
31	CN-ABR [5]
36	CNA-BS [4]
37	CNA-BT [3]
41	CN-ABU [2]
42	CN-ABV [1]
43	CN-ABW
44	CN-ABX

Lockheed C-130H Hercules
Escadrille de Transport, Rabat

4535	CN-AOA

4551	CN-AOC
4581	CN-AOE
4583	CN-AOF
4713	CN-AOG
4717	CN-AOH
4733	CN-AOI
4738	CN-AOJ
4739	CN-AOK
4742	CN-AOL
4875	CN-AOM
4876	CN-AON
4877	CN-AOO
4888	CN-AOP
4892	CN-AOQ
4907	CN-AOR
4909	CN-AOS
4940	CN-AOT

Govt of Morocco

Cessna 560 Citation V

Govt of Morocco, Rabat

CNA-NW

Dassault Falcon 50

Govt of Morocco, Rabat

CN-ANO

Grumman G.1159 Gulfstream IITT/ G.1159A Gulfstream III

Govt of Morocco, Rabat

CNA-NL	Gulfstream IITT
CNA-NU	Gulfstream III
CNA-NV	Gulfstream III

NAMIBIA

Dassault Falcon 900B

Namibian Govt, Windhoek

V5-NAM

NETHERLANDS

Koninklijke Luchtmacht

Agusta-Bell AB.412SP

303 Sqn, Leeuwarden

R-01
R-02
R-03

Boeing-Vertol CH-47 Chinook

298 Sqn, Soesterberg

CH-47D Chinook

D-101
D-102
D-103
D-106
D-661
D-662
D-663
D-664
D-665
D-666
D-667

CH-47F Chinook

D-890	(on order)
D-891	(on order)
D-892	(on order)
D-893	(on order)
D-894	(on order)
D-895	(on order)

Eurocopter AS.532U-2 Cougar

300 Sqn, Gilze-Rijen

S-400
S-419
S-433
S-438
S-440
S-441
S-442
S-444
S-445
S-447
S-450
S-453
S-454
S-456
S-457
S-458
S-459

Fokker 50

334 Sqn, Eindhoven

U-05
U-06

General Dynamics F-16

TGp/311/312/313 Sqns, Volkel;
322/323 Sqns, Leeuwarden;
306 Sqn/178th FW, Springfield Beckley Municipal Airport, Ohio, USA

J-001	F-16AM	312 Sqn
J-002	F-16AM	313 Sqn
J-003	F-16AM	311 Sqn
J-004	F-16AM	311 Sqn
J-005	F-16AM	311 Sqn
J-006	F-16AM	311 Sqn
J-008	F-16AM	313 Sqn
J-009	F-16AM	313 Sqn
J-010	F-16AM	306 Sqn
J-011	F-16AM	312 Sqn
J-013	F-16AM	322 Sqn
J-014	F-16AM	313 Sqn
J-015	F-16AM	313 Sqn
J-016	F-16AM	312 Sqn
J-017	F-16AM	311 Sqn
J-018	F-16AM	313 Sqn
J-019	F-16AM	313 Sqn
J-020	F-16AM	313 Sqn
J-021	F-16AM	312 Sqn
J-055	F-16AM	313 Sqn
J-057	F-16AM	322 Sqn
J-058	F-16AM	312 Sqn
J-060	F-16AM	313 Sqn
J-061	F-16AM	313 Sqn
J-062	F-16AM	313 Sqn
J-063	F-16AM	313 Sqn
J-064	F-16BM	312 Sqn
J-065	F-16BM	306 Sqn
J-066	F-16BM	323 Sqn
J-067	F-16BM	306 Sqn
J-135	F-16AM	322 Sqn
J-136	F-16AM	311 Sqn
J-138	F-16AM	322 Sqn
J-142	F-16AM	312 Sqn
J-144	F-16AM	323 Sqn
J-145	F-16AM	306 Sqn
J-146	F-16AM	312 Sqn
J-192	F-16AM	311 Sqn
J-193	F-16AM	312 Sqn
J-196	F-16AM	313 Sqn
J-197	F-16AM	311 Sqn
J-198	F-16AM	322 Sqn
J-199	F-16AM	313 Sqn
J-201	F-16AM	322 Sqn
J-202	F-16AM	323 Sqn
J-203	F-16AM	323 Sqn
J-204	F-16AM	323 Sqn
J-207	F-16AM	322 Sqn
J-208	F-16BM	306 Sqn
J-209	F-16BM	306 Sqn
J-210	F-16BM	323 Sqn
J-254	F-16AM	311 Sqn
J-255	F-16AM	312 Sqn
J-362	F-16AM	323 Sqn
J-365	F-16AM	312 Sqn
J-366	F-16AM	322 Sqn
J-367	F-16AM	306 Sqn
J-368	F-16BM	312 Sqn
J-369	F-16BM	306 Sqn
J-508	F-16AM	313 Sqn
J-509	F-16AM	313 Sqn
J-510	F-16AM	306 Sqn
J-511	F-16AM	311 Sqn
J-512	F-16AM	313 Sqn
J-513	F-16AM	311 Sqn
J-514	F-16AM	313 Sqn
J-515	F-16AM	311 Sqn
J-516	F-16AM	322 Sqn
J-616	F-16AM	323 Sqn
J-617	F-16AM	313 Sqn
J-620	F-16AM	306 Sqn
J-623	F-16AM	306 Sqn
J-624	F-16AM	322 Sqn
J-627	F-16AM	323 Sqn
J-628	F-16AM	322 Sqn
J-630	F-16AM	311 Sqn
J-631	F-16AM	323 Sqn
J-632	F-16AM	322 Sqn
J-635	F-16AM	313 Sqn
J-636	F-16AM	312 Sqn
J-637	F-16AM	311 Sqn
J-638	F-16AM	311 Sqn
J-640	F-16AM	312 Sqn
J-641	F-16AM	312 Sqn
J-642	F-16AM	311 Sqn
J-643	F-16AM	313 Sqn
J-644	F-16AM	313 Sqn
J-646	F-16AM	311 Sqn
J-647	F-16AM	306 Sqn
J-648	F-16AM	322 Sqn
J-653	F-16BM	306 Sqn
J-864	F-16AM	313 Sqn
J-866	F-16AM	311 Sqn
J-867	F-16AM	311 Sqn
J-868	F-16AM	322 Sqn
J-869	F-16AM	322 Sqn
J-870	F-16AM	306 Sqn
J-871	F-16AM	323 Sqn
J-872	F-16AM	323 Sqn
J-873	F-16AM	323 Sqn
J-874	F-16AM	312 Sqn
J-875	F-16AM	323 Sqn
J-876	F-16AM	322 Sqn
J-877	F-16AM	322 Sqn
J-879	F-16AM	322 Sqn
J-881	F-16AM	323 Sqn
J-882	F-16BM	306 Sqn
J-884	F-16BM	312 Sqn

Grumman
G-1159C Gulfstream IV
334 Sqn, Eindhoven
V-11

Lockheed
C-130H-30 Hercules
336 Sqn, Eindhoven
G-273
G-275

MDH
AH-64D Apache Longbow
301 Sqn, Gilze-Rijen
Q-01
Q-02
Q-03
Q-04
Q-05
Q-06
Q-07
Q-08
Q-09
Q-10
Q-11
Q-12
Q-13
Q-14
Q-15
Q-16
Q-17
Q-18
Q-19
Q-21
Q-22
Q-23
Q-24
Q-25
Q-26
Q-27
Q-28
Q-29
Q-30

NH Industries
NH.90-NFH
N-088 (on order)

McDonnell Douglas
DC-10*/KDC-10
334 Sqn, Eindhoven
T-235
T-255*
T-264

Pilatus
PC-7 Turbo Trainer
131 EMVO Sqn,
Woensdrecht
L-01
L-02
L-03
L-04
L-05
L-06
L-07
L-08
L-09
L-10
L-11
L-12
L-13

Sud Alouette III
300 Sqn, Soesterberg
A-247
A-275
A-292
A-301

Marine Luchtvaart Dienst
Westland SH-14D Lynx
MARHELI (7 Sqn & 860 Sqn), De Kooij (7 Sqn operates 860 Sqn aircraft on loan)
260
261
262
264
265
266
267
268
272
273
274
277
278
279
280
281
283

Netherlands Govt
Fokker 70
Dutch Royal Flight, Schiphol
PH-KBX

NEW ZEALAND
Royal New Zealand Air Force
Boeing 757-2K2
40 Sqn, Whenuapai
NZ7571
NZ7572

Lockheed
C-130H Hercules
40 Sqn, Whenuapai
NZ7001
NZ7002
NZ7003
NZ7004
NZ7005

Lockheed
P-3K Orion
5 Sqn, Whenuapai
NZ4201
NZ4202
NZ4203
NZ4204
NZ4205
NZ4206

NIGERIA
Federal Nigerian Air Force
Lockheed
C-130H/C-130H-30* Hercules
88 MAG, Lagos
NAF-910
NAF-912
NAF-913
NAF-917*
NAF-918*

Nigerian Govt
Boeing 737-7N6
Federal Govt of Nigeria, Lagos
5N-FGT [001]

Dassault Falcon 900
Federal Govt of Nigeria, Lagos
5N-FGE
5N-FGO

Grumman
G.1159C Gulfstream V
Federal Govt of Nigeria, Lagos
5N-FGP

Gulfstream Aerospace
Gulfstream V
Federal Govt of Nigeria, Lagos
5N-FGS

NORWAY
Luftforsvaret
Bell 412SP
339 Skv, Bardufoss;
720 Skv, Rygge

139	339 Skv
140	720 Skv
141	720 Skv
142	720 Skv
143	339 Skv
144	339 Skv
145	720 Skv
146	339 Skv
147	720 Skv
148	339 Skv
149	339 Skv
161	339 Skv
162	339 Skv
163	720 Skv
164	720 Skv
165	720 Skv
166	720 Skv
167	720 Skv
194	720 Skv

Dassault
Falcon 20 ECM
717 Skv, Rygge
041
053
0125

General Dynamics
F-16 MLU
331 Skv, Bodø;
332 Skv, Rygge;
338 Skv, Ørland

272	F-16A	332 Skv
273	F-16A	332 Skv
275	F-16A	331 Skv
276	F-16A	338 Skv
277	F-16A	332 Skv
279	F-16A	338 Skv
281	F-16A	332 Skv
282	F-16A	338 Skv
284	F-16A	338 Skv
285	F-16A	338 Skv
286	F-16A	338 Skv
288	F-16A	338 Skv
289	F-16A	332 Skv

291	F-16A	338 Skv
292	F-16A	338 Skv
293	F-16A	338 Skv
295	F-16A	338 Skv
297	F-16A	338 Skv
298	F-16A	338 Skv
299	F-16A	331 Skv
302	F-16B	332 Skv
304	F-16B	338 Skv
305	F-16B	338 Skv
306	F-16B	332 Skv
658	F-16A	338 Skv
659	F-16A	338 Skv
660	F-16A	331 Skv
661	F-16A	338 Skv
662	F-16A	332 Skv
663	F-16A	331 Skv
664	F-16A	331 Skv
665	F-16A	332 Skv
666	F-16A	331 Skv
667	F-16A	331 Skv
668	F-16A	331 Skv
669	F-16A	331 Skv
670	F-16A	331 Skv
671	F-16A	331 Skv
672	F-16A	331 Skv
673	F-16A	331 Skv
674	F-16A	331 Skv
675	F-16A	331 Skv
677	F-16A	331 Skv
678	F-16A	331 Skv
680	F-16A	331 Skv
681	F-16A	338 Skv
682	F-16A	331 Skv
683	F-16A	331 Skv
686	F-16A	331 Skv
687	F-16A	331 Skv
688	F-16A	331 Skv
689	F-16B	331 Skv
690	F-16B	338 Skv
691	F-16B	338 Skv
692	F-16B	332 Skv$
693	F-16B	338 Skv
711	F-16B	338 Skv

Lockheed
C-130H Hercules
335 Skv, Gardermoen
952
954
955
956

Lockheed P-3C Orion
333 Skv, Andøya
3296
3297
3298
3299

Lockheed P-3N Orion
333 Skv, Andøya
4576
6603

NH Industries
NH.90-NFH
013

Northrop F-5
Eye of the Tiger
Project, Rygge
F-5A
131
134
902
F-5B
136
243
244
906

Westland
Sea King Mk 43/
Mk 43A/Mk 43B
330 Skv:
A Flt, Bodø;
B Flt, Banak;
C Flt, Ørland;
D Flt, Sola

060	Mk 43
062	Mk 43
066	Mk 43
069	Mk 43
070	Mk 43
071	Mk 43B
072	Mk 43
073	Mk 43
074	Mk 43
189	Mk 43A
322	Mk 43B
329	Mk 43B
330	Mk 43B

Kystvakt (Coast Guard)
Westland Lynx Mk86
337 Skv, Bardufoss
207
216
228
232
235
237

OMAN
Royal Air Force of Oman
BAC 1-11/485GD
4 Sqn, Seeb
551
552
553

Lockheed
C-130H Hercules
16 Sqn, Seeb
501
502
503

Omani Govt
Airbus A320-233
Govt of Oman, Seeb
A4O-AA

Boeing 747-430
Govt of Oman, Seeb
A4O-OMN

Boeing 747SP-27
Govt of Oman, Seeb
A4O-SO

Grumman
G.1159C Gulfstream IV
Govt of Oman, Seeb
A4O-AB
A4O-AC

PAKISTAN
Pakistan Fiza'ya
Boeing 707-340C
12 Sqn, Islemabad
68-19866 12 Sqn

Pakistani Govt
Boeing 737-33A
Govt of Pakistan, Karachi
AP-BEH

Gulfstream Aerospace
G.1159C Gulfstream IV-SP
Govt of Pakistan, Karachi
J-755

Gulfstream Aerospace
G.450
Govt of Pakistan, Karachi
J-756

PERU
Fuerza Aérea Peruana
Douglas DC-8-62AF
370 (OB-1372)

POLAND
Sily Powietrzne RP
Antonov An-26
13 ELTR, Powidz
1406
1508
1509
1602
1603

CASA 295M
13 ELTR, Powidz
011
012
013
014
015
016
017
018
019
020

Lockheed Martin (GD)
F-16C/F-16D*
Fighting Falcon
3 ELT, Poznan/Krzesiny
6 ELT, Powidz;
10 ELT, Lask

4040	
4041	6 ELT
4042	3 ELT
4043	3 ELT
4044	3 ELT
4045	3 ELT
4046	3 ELT
4047	3 ELT
4048	3 ELT
4049	3 ELT
4050	3 ELT
4051	3 ELT

4052 6 ELT
4053 6 ELT
4054 6 ELT
4055 6 ELT
4056 6 ELT
4057 6 ELT
4058 6 ELT
4059 6 ELT
4060 6 ELT
4061 6 ELT
4062 6 ELT
4063 6 ELT
4064 10 ELT
4065 10 ELT
4066
4067
4068
4069
4070
4071
4072
4073
4074
4075
4076* 6 ELT
4077* 3 ELT
4078* 3 ELT
4079* 3 ELT
4080* 3 ELT
4081* 3 ELT
4082* 6 ELT
4083* 6 ELT
4084* 6 ELT
4085* 10 ELT
4086* 10 ELT
4087*

Mikoyan MiG-29A/UB*
1 ELT, Minsk/Mazowiecki;
41 ELT, Malbork
15* 1 ELT
28* 1 ELT
38 1 ELT
40 1 ELT
42* 1 ELT
54 1 ELT
56 1 ELT
59 1 ELT
64* 41 ELT
65 1 ELT
66 1 ELT
67 1 ELT
70 41 ELT
77 1 ELT
83 1 ELT
89 1 ELT
92 1 ELT
105 1 ELT
108 1 ELT
111 1 ELT
114 1 ELT
115 1 ELT
4101 41 ELT
4103 41 ELT
4104 41 ELT
4105* 41 ELT
4110* 41 ELT
4111 41 ELT
4113 41 ELT
4115* 41 ELT
4116 41 ELT
4118 41 ELT
4120 41 ELT
4121 41 ELT
4122 41 ELT
4123* 41 ELT

PZL M28 Bryza
2 ELTL, Bydgoszcz;
13 ELTR, Powidz;
1 OSL, Deblin;
36 SPLT, Warszawa
0203 M28TD 1 OSL
0204 M28TD 1 OSL
0205 M28TD 36 SPLT
0206 M28TD 36 SPLT
0207 M28TD 13 ELTR
0208 M28TD 13 ELTR
0209 M28TD 13 ELTR
0210 M28TD 13 ELTR
0212 M28TD 13 ELTR
0213 M28PT 13 ELTR
0214 M28PT 13 ELTR
0215 M28PT 13 ELTR
0216 M28PT 13 ELTR
0217 M28PT 13 ELTR
0723 M28RL 2 ELTL
1003 M28TD 13 ELTR

Sukhoi Su-22UM-3K*/ Su-22M-4
8 ELT, Miroslawiec;
40 ELT, Swidwin
001* 8 ELT
203* 40 ELT
307* 40 ELT
310* 40 ELT
508* 8 ELT
509* 40 ELT
605* 40 ELT
706* 40 ELT
707* 40 ELT$
3201 8 ELT
3203 8 ELT
3215 8 ELT
3304 40 ELT
3305 40 ELT
3306 40 ELT
3407
3508 8 ELT$
3509 8 ELT
3612 40 ELT
3710 40 ELT
3713 40 ELT$
3715 40 ELT
3816 40 ELT
3817 40 ELT
3819 40 ELT
3920 40 ELT
4604 8 ELT
7308 40 ELT
7309 40 ELT
7410 40 ELT
7411 40 ELT
7412 40 ELT
7820 40 ELT
8101 40 ELT
8102 8 ELT
8103 8 ELT
8205 40 ELT
8206 40 ELT
8308 8 ELT
8309 8 ELT
8310 40 ELT
8511 40 ELT
8613 8 ELT
8715 40 ELT
8816 40 ELT
8818 8 ELT$
8919 8 ELT$
9101 40 ELT
9102 40 ELT$
9103 40 ELT
9204 40 ELT
9306 40 ELT
9409 40 ELT$
9410 40 ELT
9513 40 ELT
9615 8 ELT
9616 40 ELT

Tupolev Tu-154M
36 SPLT, Warszawa
101
102

Yakovlev Yak-40
36 SPLT, Warszawa
044
045
047
048

Lotnictwo Marynarki Wojennej
PZL M28 Bryza
28 EL, Gdynia/Babie Doly;
30 EL, Cewice/Siemirowice
0404 M28B-E 28 EL
0405 M28B-E 28 EL
0810 M28B-1R PZL
1006 M28B-1R 30 EL
1007 M28B-1 28 EL
1008 M28B-1R 30 EL
1017 M28B-1R 30 EL
1022 M28B-1R 30 EL
1114 M28B-1R 28 EL
1115 M28B-1R 30 EL
1116 M28B-1R 28 EL
1117 M28B-1 28 EL
1118 M28B-1 28 EL

PORTUGAL
Força Aérea Portuguesa
Aérospatiale TB-30 Epsilon
Esq 101, Beja
11401
11402
11403
11404
11405
11406
11407
11409
11410
11411
11413
11414
11415
11416
11417
11418

CASA 212A/212ECM* Aviocar
Esq 401, Sintra;
Esq 502, Sintra;
Esq 711, Lajes
16504 Esq 502

16505 Esq 502
16507 Esq 502
16508 Esq 502
16509 Esq 502
16510 Esq 401
16512 Esq 401
16513 Esq 711
16514 Esq 711
16517 Esq 711
16524* Esq 401

CASA 212-300MP Aviocar
Esq 401, Sintra
17201
17202

D-BD Alpha Jet
Esq 103, Beja;
Asas de Portugal, Beja*
15201
15202*
15204
15205
15206*
15208*
15209
15210
15211
15213
15214
15215
15216
15217
15218
15219
15220*
15221
15222
15223
15224
15225
15226
15227
15228
15229
15230
15231
15232
15233
15235
15236
15237
15238
15239
15240
15242
15243
15244
15246
15247
15250*

Dassault Falcon 50
Esq 504, Lisbon/Montijo
17401
17402
17403

EHI EH-101 Mk514/Mk515/Mk516
Esq 751, Montijo
(with a detachment at Lajes*)

Mk514
19601
19602*
19603
19604
19605
19606
Mk515
19607
19608
Mk516
19609*
19610
19611*
19612

Lockheed C-130H/C-130H-30* Hercules
Esq 501, Lisbon/Montijo
16801*
16802*
16803
16804
16805
16806*

Lockheed Martin (GD) F-16 Fighting Falcon
(MLU aircraft are marked with a *)
Esq 201, Monte Real;
Esq 301, Monte Real

15101	F-16A	Esq 201
15102	F-16A	Esq 201
15103	F-16A	Esq 201
15104	F-16A*	Esq 201
15105	F-16A	Esq 201
15106	F-16A	Esq 201
15107	F-16A	Esq 201
15108	F-16A	Esq 201
15109	F-16A	Esq 201
15110	F-16A	Esq 201
15112	F-16A	Esq 201
15113	F-16A	Esq 201
15114	F-16A	Esq 201
15115	F-16A	Esq 201
15116	F-16A	Esq 201
15117	F-16A	Esq 201
15118	F-16B	Esq 201
15119	F-16B	Esq 201
15120	F-16B	Esq 201
15121	F-16A*	Esq 301
15122	F-16A	
15123	F-16A	Esq 301
15124	F-16A	Esq 301
15125	F-16A	
15126	F-16A	
15127	F-16A	
15128	F-16A	
15129	F-16A	
15130	F-16A	
15131	F-16A	Esq 301
15132	F-16A	
15133	F-16A*	Esq 301
15134	F-16A	
15135	F-16A	
15136	F-16A	
15137	F-16B*	Esq 301
15138	F-16A*	Esq 301
15139	F-16B*	Esq 301
15140	F-16B	
15141	F-16A	

Lockheed P-3C/P-3P Orion
Esq 601, Lisbon/Montijo
14803 P-3P
14805 P-3P
14807 P-3C
14808 P-3C
14809 P-3C
14810 P-3C
14811 P-3C

Marinha
Westland Super Lynx Mk 95
Esq de Helicopteros, Lisbon/Montijo
19201
19202
19203
19204
19205

QATAR

Airbus A.310-304
Qatari Govt, Doha
A7-AAF

Airbus A.319CJ-133
Qatari Govt, Doha
A7-HHJ

Airbus A.320-232
Qatari Govt, Doha
A7-AAG

Airbus A.330-202
Qatari Govt, Doha
A7-HJJ

Airbus A.340-211/-541*
Qatari Govt, Doha
A7-HHH*
A7-HHK

ROMANIA

Fortele Aeriene Romania
Antonov An-26
Escadrilla 902, Bucharest/Otopeni
801
808
809
810

Lockheed C-130B/C-130H* Hercules
Escadrilla 901, Bucharest/Otopeni
5927
5930
6150
6166*
6191*

Romanian Govt
Boeing 707-3K1C
Romanian Govt, Bucharest/Otopeni
YR-ABB

RUSSIA
Voenno-Vozdushniye Sily Rossioki Federatsii (Russian Air Force)

Sukhoi Su-27
TsAGI, Gromov Flight Institute, Zhukhovsky
595 Su-27P
597 Su-30
598 Su-27P

Russian Govt
Ilyushin Il-62M
Russian Govt, Moscow
RA-86466
RA-86467
RA-86468
RA-86536
RA-86537
RA-86539
RA-86540
RA-86553
RA-86554
RA-86559
RA-86561
RA-86710
RA-86711
RA-86712

Ilyushin Il-96-300
Russian Govt, Moscow
RA-96012
RA-96016

Tupolev Tu-134A
Russian Govt, Moscow
RA-65904

Tupolev Tu-154M
Russian Govt, Moscow;
Open Skies*
RA-85629
RA-85631
RA-85645
RA-85655*
RA-85659
RA-85666
RA-85843

SAUDI ARABIA
Al Quwwat al Jawwiya as Sa'udiya

BAe 125-800/-800B*
1 Sqn, Riyadh
HZ-105
HZ-109*
HZ-110*

Boeing 737-7DP/-8DP*
1 Sqn, Riyadh
HZ-101
HZ-102*

Boeing E-3A/KE-3A/RE-3A Sentry
18 Sqn, Riyadh;
19 Sqn, Riyadh

1801	E-3A	18 Sqn
1802	E-3A	18 Sqn
1803	E-3A	18 Sqn
1804	E-3A	18 Sqn
1805	E-3A	18 Sqn
1811	KE-3A	18 Sqn
1812	KE-3A	18 Sqn
1813	KE-3A	18 Sqn
1814	KE-3A	18 Sqn
1815	KE-3A	18 Sqn
1816	KE-3A	18 Sqn
1818	KE-3A	18 Sqn
1901	RE-3A	19 Sqn

Cessna 550 Citation II
1 Sqn, Riyadh
HZ-133
HZ-134
HZ-135
HZ-136

Grumman G.1159C Gulfstream IV
1 Sqn, Riyadh
HZ-103

Lockheed C-130/L.100 Hercules
1 Sqn, Prince Sultan AB;
4 Sqn, Jeddah;
16 Sqn, Prince Sultan AB;
32 Sqn, Prince Sultan AB

111	VC-130H	1 Sqn
112	VC-130H	1 Sqn
451	C-130E	4 Sqn
452	C-130E	4 Sqn
455	C-130E	4 Sqn
461	C-130H	4 Sqn
462	C-130H	4 Sqn
463	C-130H	4 Sqn
464	C-130H	4 Sqn
465	C-130H	4 Sqn
466	C-130H	4 Sqn
467	C-130H	4 Sqn
468	C-130H	4 Sqn
472	C-130H	4 Sqn
473	C-130H	4 Sqn
474	C-130H	4 Sqn
475	C-130H	4 Sqn
483	C-130E	4 Sqn
1601	C-130H	16 Sqn
1602	C-130H	16 Sqn
1603	C-130H	16 Sqn
1604	C-130H	16 Sqn
1605	C-130H	16 Sqn
1606	C-130E	16 Sqn
1607	C-130E	16 Sqn
1608	C-130E	16 Sqn
1609	C-130E	16 Sqn
1611	C-130E	16 Sqn
1614	C-130H	16 Sqn
1615	C-130H	16 Sqn
1618	C-130H	16 Sqn
1619	C-130H	16 Sqn
1622	C-130H-30	16 Sqn
1623	C-130H-30	16 Sqn
1624	C-130H	16 Sqn
1625	C-130H	16 Sqn
1626	C-130H	16 Sqn
1630	C-130H-30	16 Sqn
1631	L.100-30	16 Sqn
1632	L.100-30	16 Sqn
3201	KC-130H	32 Sqn
3202	KC-130H	32 Sqn
3203	KC-130H	32 Sqn
3204	KC-130H	32 Sqn
3205	KC-130H	32 Sqn
3206	KC-130H	32 Sqn
3207	KC-130H	32 Sqn
HZ-114	VC-130H	1 Sqn
HZ-115	VC-130H	1 Sqn
HZ-116	VC-130H	1 Sqn
HZ-117	L.100-30	1 Sqn
HZ-128	L.100-30	1 Sqn
HZ-129	L.100-30	1 Sqn

Saudi Govt
Airbus A.340-211
Royal Embassy of Saudi Arabia, Riyadh
HZ-124

Boeing 747-3G1/468*
Saudi Royal Flight, Jeddah
HZ-HM1A
HZ-HM1

Boeing 747SP-68
Saudi Govt, Jeddah;
Saudi Royal Flight, Jeddah

HZ-AIF	Govt
HZ-AIJ	Royal Flight
HZ-HM1B	Royal Flight

Boeing 757-23A
Saudi Govt, Jeddah
HZ-HMED

Boeing MD-11
Saudi Royal Flight, Jeddah
HZ-AFA1
HZ-HM7

Canadair CL.604 Challenger
Saudi Royal Flight, Jeddah
HZ-AFA2

Dassault Falcon 900
Saudi Govt, Jeddah
HZ-AFT
HZ-AFZ

Grumman G.1159A Gulfstream III
Armed Forces Medical Services, Riyadh;
Saudi Govt, Jeddah

HZ-AFN	Govt
HZ-AFR	Govt
HZ-MS3	AFMS

Grumman G.1159C Gulfstream IV
Armed Forces Medical Services, Riyadh;
Saudi Govt, Jeddah

HZ-AFU	Govt
HZ-AFV	Govt
HZ-AFW	Govt
HZ-AFX	Govt
HZ-AFY	Govt
HZ-MS4	AFMS

Gulfstream Aerospace Gulfstream V
Armed Forces Medical Services, Riyadh
HZ-MS5A
HZ-MS5B

Lockheed
C-130H/L.100 Hercules
Armed Forces Medical Services, Riyadh
HZ-MS6 L.100-30
HZ-MS7 C-130H
HZ-MS09 L.100-30

SINGAPORE
Republic of Singapore Air Force
Boeing
KC-135R Stratotanker
112 Sqn, Changi
750
751
752
753

Lockheed
C-130 Hercules
122 Sqn, Paya Lebar
720 KC-130B
721 KC-130B
724 KC-130B
725 KC-130B
730 C-130H
731 C-130H
732 C-130H
733 C-130H
734 KC-130H
735 C-130H

SLOVAKIA
Slovenské Vojenske Letectvo
Aero L-39 Albatros
1 SLK/2 Letka, Sliač [SL]
0745 L-39V
1701 L-39ZA
1725 L-39ZA
1730 L-39ZA
4701 L-39ZA
4703 L-39ZA
4707 L-39ZA
4711 L-39ZA
5251 L-39CM
5252 L-39CM
5253 L-39CM
5254 L-39CM
5301 L-39CM
5302 L-39CM

Antonov An-24V
SDoLt/1 Dopravná Roj, Malacky
2903

Antonov An-26
SDoLt/1 Dopravná Roj, Malacky
2506

LET 410 Turbolet
1 SLK/3 Letka, Sliač [SL];
SDoLt/2 Dopravná Roj, Malacky
0730 L-410UVP SDoLt
0927 L-410T 1 SLK
1133 L-410T SDoLt
1521 L-410FG SDoLt
2311 L-410UVP SDoLt
2421 L-410UVP SDoLt

Mikoyan MiG-29AS/UBS*
1 SLK/1 Letka, Sliač [SL]
0619
0820
0921
1303*
2123
3709
3911
4401*
5113
5304*
5515
5817
6124
6425
6526
6627
6728
7501
8003
8605
9308

Mil M-17
3 Vrtulnikové Letcecké Kridlo/2 Letka, Prešov
0807
0808
0812
0820
0821
0823
0824
0826
0827
0841
0842
0844
0845
0846
0847

Mil Mi-24
3 Vrtulnikové Letcecké Kridlo/1 Letka, Prešov
0100 Mi-24D
0101 Mi-24D
0149 Mi-24D
0150 Mi-24D
0215 Mi-24D
0222 Mi-24D
0223 Mi-24D
0704 Mi-24V
0707 Mi-24V
0708 Mi-24V
0786 Mi-24V
0787 Mi-24V
0813 Mi-24V
0814 Mi-24V
0832 Mi-24V
0833 Mi-24V
0927 Mi-24V
4009 Mi-24D
6040 Mi-24DU

Slovak Govt
Tupolev Tu-154M
Slovak Govt, Bratislava/Ivanka
OM-BYO
OM-BYR

Yakovlev Yak-40
Slovak Govt, Bratislava/Ivanka
OM-BYE
OM-BYL

SLOVENIA
Slovene Army
LET 410UVP-E
LTO, Brnik
L4-01

Pilatus PC-9M
1/2/3 OSBL, Cerklje
L9-51
L9-53
L9-61
L9-62
L9-63
L9-64
L9-65
L9-66
L9-67
L9-68
L9-69

SOUTH AFRICA
South African Air Force/
Suid Afrikaanse Lugmag
Boeing 737-7ED
21 Sqn, Waterkloof
ZS-RSA

Dassault Falcon 900
21 Sqn, Waterkloof
ZS-NAN

Lockheed
C-130B/C-130BZ* Hercules
28 Sqn, Waterkloof
401
402*
403
404
405*
406*
407*
408*
409*

SPAIN
Ejército del Aire
Airbus A.310-304
Grupo 45, Torrejón
T.22-1 45-50
T.22-2 45-51

Airtech
CN.235M-10 (T.19A)/
CN.235M-100 (T.19B)/
CN.235M-100 (MPA) (D.4)
Ala 35, Getafe
T.19A-01 35-60
T.19A-02 35-61
T.19B-03 35-21
T.19B-04 35-22
T.19B-05 35-23
T.19B-06 35-24
T.19B-07 35-25
T.19B-08 35-26
T.19B-09 35-27
T.19B-10 35-28
T.19B-11 35-29

T.19B-13 35-31
T.19B-14 35-32
T.19B-15 35-33
T.19B-16 35-34
T.19B-17 35-35
T.19B-18 35-36
T.19B-19 35-37
T.19B-20 35-38
D.4-01

Boeing 707
47 Grupo Mixto, Torrejón
TK.17-1 331B 47-01
T.17-2 331B 47-02
T.17-3 368C 47-03
TM.17-4 351C 47-04

CASA 101EB Aviojet
Grupo 54, Torrejón;
Grupo de Escuelas de Matacán (74);
AGA, San Javier (79);
Patrulla Aguila, San Javier*
E.25-01 79-01 [8]*
E.25-05 79-05
E.25-06 79-06
E.25-07 79-07 [3]*
E.25-08 79-08
E.25-09 79-09
E.25-10 79-10
E.25-11 79-11
E.25-12 79-12
E.25-13 79-13
E.25-14 79-14 [4]*
E.25-15 79-15
E.25-16 79-16
E.25-17 74-40
E.25-18 74-42
E.25-19 79-19
E.25-20 79-20
E.25-21 79-21 [6]*
E.25-22 79-22 [7]*
E.25-23 79-23
E.25-24 79-24
E.25-25 79-25
E.25-26 79-26
E.25-27 79-27 [2]*
E.25-28 79-28 [1]*
E.25-29 74-45
E.25-31 79-31
E.25-33 74-02
E.25-34 79-34
E.25-35 54-20
E.25-37 79-37
E.25-38 79-38
E.25-40 79-40
E.25-41 74-41
E.25-43 74-43
E.25-44 79-44
E.25-45 79-45
E.25-46 79-46
E.25-47 79-47
E.25-48 79-48
E.25-49 79-49
E.25-50 79-33
E.25-51 74-07
E.25-52 79-34
E.25-53 74-09
E.25-54 79-35
E.25-55 54-21
E.25-56 74-11
E.25-57 74-12
E.25-59 74-13
E.25-61 54-22
E.25-62 79-17
E.25-63 74-17
E.25-65 79-95
E.25-66 74-20
E.25-67 74-21
E.25-68 74-22
E.25-69 79-97
E.25-71 74-25
E.25-72 74-26
E.25-73 79-98
E.25-74 74-28
E.25-75 74-29
E.25-76 74-30
E.25-78 79-02
E.25-79 79-39
E.25-80 79-03
E.25-81 74-34
E.25-83 74-35
E.25-84 79-04
E.25-86 79-32 [5]*
E.25-87 79-29
E.25-88 74-39

CASA 212 Aviocar
212A (T.12B)/
212B (TR.12A)/
212D (TE.12B)/
212DE (TM.12D)/
212S (D.3A)/
212S1 (D.3B)/
212-200 (T.12D)/
212-200 (TR.12D)
Ala 37, Villanubla;
47 Grupo Mixto, Torrejón;
CLAEX, Torrejón (54);
Ala 72, Alcantarilla;
Grupo Esc, Matacán (74);
AGA (Ala 79), San Javier;
403 Esc, Getafe;
801 Esc, Palma/ Son San Juan;
803 Esc, Cuatro Vientos;
INTA, Torrejón
D.3A-1 (801 Esc)
D.3A-2 (803 Esc)
D.3B-3 (803 Esc)
D.3B-4 (801 Esc)
D.3B-5 (801 Esc)
D.3B-6 (801 Esc)
D.3B-7 (803 Esc)
D.3B-8 (801 Esc)
TR.12A-4 403-02
TR.12A-5 403-03
TR.12A-6 403-04
TR.12A-8 403-06
T.12B-9 74-83
T.12B-12 74-82
T.12B-15 37-02
T.12B-21 72-03
T.12B-22 72-02
T.12B-25 74-72
T.12B-33 72-04
T.12B-34 74-74
T.12B-36 37-10
T.12B-37 72-05
TE.12B-40 74-84
T.12B-47 72-06
T.12B-49 72-07
T.12B-55 72-08
T.12B-58 74-86
T.12B-61 47-11
T.12B-63 72-14
T.12B-65 74-80
T.12B-66 72-09
T.12B-67 74-81
T.12B-70 37-17
TM.12D-72 47-12
TM.12D-74 54-11
T.12D-75 403-07
TR.12D-76 37-60
TR.12D-77 37-61
TR.12D-78 37-62
TR.12D-79 37-63
TR.12D-80 37-64
TR.12D-81 37-65

CASA 295
Ala 35, Getafe;
T.21-01 35-39
T.21-02 35-40
T.21-03 35-41
T.21-04 35-42
T.21-05 35-43
T.21-06 35-44
T.21-07 35-45
T.21-08 35-46
T.21-09 35-47
T.21-10 35-48
T.21-11 35-49
T.21-12 35-50
T.21-13 (on order)

Cessna 560 Citation VI
403 Esc, Getafe
TR.20-01 403-11
TR.20-02 403-12

Dassault Falcon 20D/E
47 Grupo Mixto, Torrejón
TM.11-1 20E 47-21
TM.11-2 20D 47-22
TM.11-3 20D 47-23
TM.11-4 20E 47-24

Dassault Falcon 900/900B*
Grupo 45, Torrejón
T.18-1 45-40
T.18-2 45-41
T.18-3* 45-42
T.18-4* 45-43
T.18-5* 45-44

Dassault Mirage F.1BM*/F.1M
Ala 14, Albacete
C.14-04 14-02
C.14-06 14-03
C.14-10 14-05
C.14-11 14-06
C.14-13 14-07
C.14-15 14-09
C.14-17 14-11
C.14-18 14-12
C.14-20 14-13
C.14-21 14-14
C.14-22 14-15
CE.14-27* 14-70
CE.14-30* 14-71
CE.14-31* 14-72
C.14-36 14-18
C.14-37 14-19
C.14-38 14-20
C.14-40 14-21
C.14-41 14-22
C.14-42 14-23

C.14-43 14-24
C.14-44 14-25
C.14-45 14-26
C.14-52 14-29
C.14-54 14-30
C.14-56 14-31
C.14-57 14-32
C.14-58 14-33
C.14-60 14-34
C.14-63 14-36
C.14-64 14-37$
C.14-66 14-38
C.14-67 14-39
C.14-68 14-40
C.14-69 14-41
C.14-70 14-42
C.14-72 14-44
C.14-73 14-45
CE.14-87* 14-73
C.14-88 14-46
C.14-89 14-47
C.14-90 14-48
C.14-91 14-49

Eurofighter
EF.2000A/EF.2000B* Tifon
Ala 11, Morón;
CASA, Getafe
CE.16-01* 11-70
CE.16-02* 11-71
CE.16-03* 11-72
CE.16-04* 11-73
CE.16-05* 11-74
CE.16-06* 11-75
CE.16-07* 11-76
CE.16-08* 11-77
C.16-20 11-91
C.16-21 11-01
C.16-22 11-02
C.16-23 11-03
C.16-24 11-04
C.16-25 11-05
C.16-26 11-06
C.16-27 11-07
C.16-28 11-08
C.16-29 11-09
C.16-30 11-10
C.16-31

Fokker
F.27M Friendship 400MPA
802 Esc, Gando, Las Palmas
D.2-01
D.2-02 802-11
D.2-03

Lockheed
C-130H/C-130H-30/
KC-130H Hercules
311 Esc/312 Esc (Ala 31), Zaragoza
TL.10-01 C-130H-30 31-01
T.10-02 C-130H 31-02
T.10-03 C-130H 31-03
T.10-04 C-130H 31-04
TK.10-5 KC-130H 31-50
TK.10-6 KC-130H 31-51
TK.10-07 KC-130H 31-52
T.10-8 C-130H 31-05
T.10-9 C-130H 31-06
T.10-10 C-130H 31-07
TK.10-11 KC-130H 31-53
TK.10-12 KC-130H 31-54

Lockheed
P-3A/P-3B/P-3M Orion
Grupo 22, Morón
P.3-01 P-3A 22-21
P.3B-08 P-3M 22-31
P.3B-09 P-3M 22-32
P.3B-10 P-3M 22-33
P.3-11 P-3B 22-34
P.3-12 P-3B 22-35

McDonnell Douglas
F-18 Hornet
Ala 12, Torrejón;
Ala 15, Zaragoza;
Esc 462, Gran Canaria
EF-18B+ Hornet
CE.15-1 15-70
CE.15-2 15-71
CE.15-3 15-72
CE.15-4 15-73
CE.15-5 15-74
CE.15-6 15-75
CE.15-7 15-76
CE.15-8 12-71
CE.15-9 15-77
CE.15-10 12-73
CE.15-11 12-74
CE.15-12 12-75
EF-18A+/EF-18M* Hornet
C.15-13 12-01
C.15-14 15-01
C.15-15 15-02$
C.15-16 15-03
C.15-18 15-05
C.15-20 15-07
C.15-21 15-08
C.15-22 15-09
C.15-23 15-10
C.15-24 15-11
C.15-25 15-12
C.15-26 15-13$
C.15-27 15-14
C.15-28 15-15
C.15-29 15-16
C.15-30 15-17
C.15-31 15-18
C.15-32 15-19
C.15-33 15-20
C.15-34 15-21
C.15-35 15-22
C.15-36 15-23
C.15-37 15-24
C.15-38 15-25
C.15-39 15-26
C.15-40 15-27
C.15-41 15-28
C.15-43 15-30
C.15-44* 12-02
C.15-45 12-03
C.15-46 12-04
C.15-47 15-31
C.15-48 12-06
C.15-49 12-07
C.15-50 12-08
C.15-51 12-09
C.15-52 12-10
C.15-53 12-11
C.15-54* 12-12
C.15-55 12-13
C.15-56 12-14
C.15-57* 12-15
C.15-58* 12-16
C.15-59 12-17
C.15-60 12-18
C.15-61 12-19
C.15-62 12-20
C.15-64 12-22
C.15-65 12-23
C.15-66 12-24
C.15-67 15-33
C.15-68 12-26
C.15-69* 12-27
C.15-70* 12-28
C.15-72 12-30
F/A-18A/EF-18M* Hornet
C.15-73 46-01
C.15-74 46-02
C.15-75 46-03
C.15-77 46-05
C.15-78 46-06
C.15-79 46-07
C.15-80 21-08
C.15-81 11-09
C.15-82 46-10
C.15-83 46-11
C.15-84 46-12
C.15-85 46-13
C.15-86* 46-14
C.15-87 46-15
C.15-88 46-16
C.15-89 46-17
C.15-90 46-18
C.15-92 46-20
C.15-93 46-21
C.15-94 46-22
C.15-95 46-23
C.15-96 46-24

Arma Aérea de l'Armada Española
BAe/McDonnell Douglas
EAV-8B/EAV-8B+/
TAV-8B Harrier II
Esc 009, Rota
EAV-8B
VA.1A-15 01-903
VA.1A-19 01-907
VA.1A-21 01-909
VA.1A-22 01-910
VA.1A-23 01-911
VA.1A-24 01-914
EAV-8B+
VA.1B-25 01-915
VA.1B-26 01-916
VA.1B-27 01-917
VA.1B-28 01-918
VA.1B-29 01-919
VA.1B-30 01-920
VA.1B-35 01-924
VA.1B-36 01-923
VA.1B-37 01-925
VA.1B-38 01-926
VA.1B-39 01-927
TAV-8B
VA.1B-33 01-922

Cessna 550 Citation II
Esc 004, Rota
U.20-1 01-405
U.20-2 01-406
U.20-3 01-407

Cessna 650 Citation VII
Esc 004, Rota
U.21-01 01-408

SUDAN
Dassault Falcon 50
Sudanese Govt, Khartoum
ST-PSR

Dassault Falcon 900B
Sudanese Govt, Khartoum
ST-PSA

SWEDEN
Svenska Flygvapnet
Grumman
G.1159C Gulfstream 4 (Tp.102A/S.102B Korpen/ Tp.102C)
Flottiljer 17M, Stockholm/ Bromma & Malmslätt
Tp.102A
102001 021
S.102B Korpen
102002 022
102003 023
Tp.102C
102004 024

Lockheed
C-130H Hercules (Tp.84)
Flottiljer 7, Såtenäs
84001 841
84002 842
84003 843
84004 844
84005 845
84006 846
84007 847
84008 848

Rockwell
Sabreliner-40 (Tp.86)
FMV, Malmslätt
86001 861

SAAB JAS 39 Gripen
Flottiljer 4, Östersund/Frösön;
Flottiljer 7, Såtenäs [G];
Flottiljer 17, Ronneby/Kallinge;
Flottiljer 21, Luleå/Kallax
FMV, Malmslätt
JAS 39
39-5 55 FMV
JAS 39A
39101 51 FMV
39103 103 FMV
39104 04 F7
39106 106
39107 107 F7
39109 09 F7
39110 10 F7
39112 112 F7
39114 14 F7
39115 15 F7
39116 16 SAAB
39117 17 F7
39118 18 SAAB
39119 19 F7
39120 120 F21
39121 121 F21
39122 122 F7
39123 123 F7
39124 124 F7
39125 125 F21
39126 126 F21
39127 127 F21
39128 128 F7
39129 129 F7
39131 131 F7
39132 132 F7
39133 133 FMV
39134 134 F7
39135 135 F21
39136 136 F7
39137 137 F17
39138 138 F7
39139 139 F21
39140 140 F21
39141 141 F17
39142 142 F7
39143 143 F7
39144 44 SAAB
39145 145 F7
39146 146 F7
39147 147 F7
39148 148 F7
39149 149 F7
39150 150 F7
39151 151 F7
39152 152 F17
39153 153 F7
39154 154 F7
39155 155 F17
39157 157 F21
39158 158 F17
39159 159 F7
39160 160 F7
39161 161 F17
39162 162 F7
39163 163 F17
39164 164 F17
39166 166 F17
39167 167 F7
39168 168 F7
39169 169 F17
39170 170 F17
39171 171 F17
39172 172 F7
39173 173 F7
39174 174 F7
39175 175 F17
39176 176 F7
39177 177 F17
39178 178 F17
39179 179 F7
39180 180 F17
39181 181 F7
39182 182 F7
39183 183 F7
39185 185 F7
39186 186 F17
39187 187 F17
39188 188 F7
39189 189 F7
39190 190 F17
39191 191 F7
39192 192 F7
39193 193 F21
39194 194 F21
39195 195 F21
39196 196 F21
39197 197 F21
39198 198 F21
39199 199 F21
39200 200 F21
39201 201 F21
39202 202 F21
39203 203 F21
39204 204 F21
39205 205 F21
39206 206 F21
JAS 39B
39800 58 FMV
39801 801 F21
39802 802 SAAB
39803 803 F7
39804 804 F7
39805 805 F7
39806 806 F7
39807 807 F7
39808 808 F7
39809 809 F7
39810 810 F7
39811 811 F7
39812 812 F7
39813 813 F7
39814 814 F7
JAS 39C
39-6 6 FMV
39208 208 SAAB
39209 209 FMV
39210 210 FMV
39211 211 FMV
39212 212 F17
39213 213 F17
39214 214 FMV
39215 215 FMV
39216 216 F17
39217 217 F17
39218
39219 219 F17
39220 220 F17
39221 221 F17
39222
39223 223 F17
39224 224 F17
39225 225 F17
39226 226 F17
39227 227 SAAB
39228 228 FMV
39229 229 FMV
39230 230 F17
39231 231 FMV
39232 232 FMV
39233 233 FMV
39246 246 F17
39247 247 F17
39248 248 SAAB
39249 249 FMV
39250
39251 251 FMV
39252 252 F21
39253 253 F17
39254 254 FMV
39255 255 FMV
39256 256 F17
39257
39258 258 F17
39260 260 F17
39261 261 SAAB
39262 262 F21
39263 263 F21
39264 264 F17
39265 265 F21
39266
39267
39268
39269
39270
39271
39272
39273

39274		
39275		
39276		

JAS 39D

39815	815	F21
39816		
39817	817	F17
39818		
39821	821	F17
39822	822	SAAB
39823	823	F7
39824	824	FMV
39825	825	F21
39826	826	FMV
39827	827	F17
39828	828	F21

SAAB
SF.340 (OS.100 & Tp.100C)/
SF.340AEW&C
(S.100B & S.100D)
Argus
Flottiljer 17, Ronneby/Kallinge;
Flottiljer 17M, Malmslätt;
Flottiljer 21, Luleå/Kallax

OS.100

100001	001	F17M

S.100B

100002	002	F17M
100005	005	F17M
100006	006	F17M
100007	007	F17M

Tp.100C

100008	008	F17
100009	009	F21

S.100D

100003	003	F17M
100004	004	F17M

Förvarsmaktens
Helikopterflottilj
Aérospatiale
AS.332M-1 Super Puma
(Hkp.10/Hkp.10B*)
1. HkpSkv, Lycksele & Östersund/Frösön;
3. HkpSkv, Berga, Goteborg/ Säve, & Ronneby/Kallinge;
Helikopterflottiljen (Hkpflj), Malmslätt

10401	91	3.HkpSkv
10402	92	Hkpflj
10403*	93	Hkpflj
10405	95	Hkpflj
10406*	96	Hkpflj
10407	97	Hkpflj
10408	98	Hkpflj
10410*	90	3.HkpSkv
10411	88	Hkpflj
10412	89	1.HkpSkv

Agusta
A109LUH Power (Hkp.15)
FMV, Malmslätt;
Helikopterflottiljen (Hkpflj), Malmslätt

Hkp.15A

15021	21	
15022	22	Hkpflj
15023	23	Hkpflj
15024	24	Hkpflj
15025	25	Hkpflj
15026	26	Hkpflj
15027	27	Hkpflj
15028	28	Hkpflj
15029	29	Hkpflj
15030	30	
15031	31	Hkpflj
15032	32	Hkpflj

Hkp.15B

15033	33
15034	34
15035	35
15036	36
15037	37
15038	38
15039	39
15040	40

MBB Bo.105CBS (Hkp.9A)
3. HkpSkv, Berga, Goteborg/ Säve, & Ronneby/Kallinge;
Helikopterflottiljen (Hkpflj), Malmslätt

09201	01	Hkpflj
09202	02	3.HkpSkv
09203	03	Hkpflj
09205	05	3.HkpSkv
09206	06	Hkpflj
09207	07	Hkpflj
09208	08	Hkpflj
09209	09	Hkpflj
09211	11	Hkpflj
09212	12	Hkpflj
09215	15	Hkpflj
09216	16	3.HkpSkv
09217	17	3.HkpSkv
09218	18	Hkpflj
09219	19	Hkpflj
09220	20	Hkpflj
09221	90	Hkpflj

NH Industries
NH.90-HCV (Hkp.14A)
FMV, Malmslätt

141042	42	FMV
141043	43	FMV
141044	44	FMV

Vertol/Kawasaki-Vertol 107
2. HkpSkv, Berga, Goteborg/ Säve, & Ronneby/Kallinge;
3. HkpSkv, Berga, Goteborg/ Säve, & Ronneby/Kallinge;
FMV (Flygvapnet), Malmslätt;
Helikopterflottiljen (Hkpflj), Malmslätt

Vertol 107-II-15 (Hkp.4B)

04061	61	3.HkpSkv
04063	63	2.HkpSkv
04064	64	2.HkpSkv

Kawasaki-Vertol
KV.107-II-16 (Hkp.4C)

04065	65	3.HkpSkv
04067	67	3.HkpSkv
04068	68	Hkpflj
04069	69	2.HkpSkv
04070	70	Hkpflj
04071	71	Hkpflj
04072	72	FMV

Vertol 107-II-15 (Hkp.4D)

04073	73	2.HkpSkv
04074	74	3.HkpSkv
04075	75	3.HkpSkv
04076	76	3.HkpSkv

SWITZERLAND
Schweizerische Flugwaffe
(Most aircraft are pooled centrally. Some carry unit badges but these rarely indicate actual operators.)

Aérospatiale
AS.332M-1/AS.532UL
Super Puma
Lufttransport Staffel 3 (LtSt 3), Dübendorf;
Lufttransport Staffel 4 (LtSt 4), Dübendorf;
Lufttransport Staffel 5 (LtSt 5), Payerne;
Lufttransport Staffel 6 (LtSt 6), Alpnach;
Lufttransport Staffel 8 (LtSt 8), Alpnach
Detachments at Emmen, Meiringen & Sion

AS.332M-1
T-311
T-312
T-313
T-314
T-315
T-316
T-317
T-318
T-319
T-320
T-321
T-322
T-323
T-324
T-325

AS.532UL
T-331
T-332
T-333
T-334
T-335
T-336
T-337
T-338
T-339
T-340
T-341
T-342

Aérospatiale
SA.365N Dauphin
Gruppe Transport Flugzeuge, Dübendorf
T-771

Cessna
560XL Citation Excel
Gruppe Transport Flugzeuge, Dübendorf
T-784

Dassault Falcon 50
Gruppe Transport Flugzeuge, Dübendorf
T-783

Eurocopter
EC.635
Gruppe Transport Flugzeuge, Dübendorf
T-353

McDonnell Douglas F/A-18 Hornet
Flieger Staffel 11 (FlSt 11), Meiringen;
Escadrille d'Aviation 17 (EdAv 17), Payerne;
Flieger Staffel 18 (FlSt 18), Payerne
F/A-18C
J-5001
J-5002
J-5003
J-5004
J-5005
J-5006
J-5007
J-5008
J-5009
J-5010
J-5011$
J-5012
J-5013
J-5014
J-5015
J-5016
J-5017
J-5018
J-5019
J-5020
J-5021
J-5022
J-5023
J-5024
J-5025
J-5026
F/A-18D
J-5232
J-5233
J-5234
J-5235
J-5236
J-5237
J-5238

Northrop F-5 Tiger II
Armasuisse, Emmen;
Escadrille d'Aviation 6 (EdAv 6), Sion;
Flieger Staffel 8 (FlSt 8), Meiringen;
Flieger Staffel 11 (FlSt 11), Meiringen;
Flieger Staffel 19 (FlSt 19), Sion;
Instrumentation Flieger Staffel 14 (InstruFlSt 14), Dübendorf;
Patrouille Suisse, Emmen (*P. Suisse*)
F-5E
J-3001
J-3015
J-3043
J-3044
J-3054
J-3055
J-3060
J-3062
J-3063
J-3067
J-3068
J-3069
J-3070
J-3072
J-3073
J-3074
J-3075
J-3076
J-3077
J-3079
J-3080 *P. Suisse*
J-3081 *P. Suisse*
J-3082 *P. Suisse*
J-3083 *P. Suisse*
J-3084 *P. Suisse*
J-3085 *P. Suisse*
J-3086 *P. Suisse*
J-3087 *P. Suisse*
J-3088 *P. Suisse*
J-3089 *P. Suisse*
J-3090 *P. Suisse*
J-3091 *P. Suisse*
J-3092
J-3093
J-3094
J-3095 *P. Suisse*
J-3096
J-3097
J-3098
F-5F
J-3201
J-3202
J-3203
J-3204
J-3205
J-3206
J-3207
J-3208
J-3209
J-3210
J-3211
J-3212

Pilatus PC.6B/B2-H2 Turbo Porter
Lufttransport Staffel 5 (LtSt 5), Emmen
V-612
V-613
V-614
V-616
V-617
V-618
V-619
V-620
V-622$
V-623
V-631
V-632
V-633
V-634
V-635

Pilatus PC-7 Turbo Trainer
Pilotenschule, Emmen
A-902
A-903
A-904
A-906
A-907
A-908
A-909
A-910
A-911
A-912
A-913
A-914
A-915
A-916
A-917
A-918
A-919
A-922
A-923
A-924
A-925
A-926
A-927
A-928
A-929
A-930
A-931
A-932
A-933
A-934
A-935
A-936
A-937
A-938
A-939
A-940
A-941

Pilatus PC-9
Zielfligerstaffel 12, Sion
C-401
C-402
C-405
C-406
C-407
C-408
C-409
C-410
C-411
C-412

Pilatus PC-21
A-101
A-102
A-103
A-104
A-105
A-106

Beechcraft 1900D
Gruppe Transport Flugzeuge, Dübendorf
D-CBIG

Pilatus PC-12/45
Swiss Govt, Emmen
HB-FOG

SYRIA

Dassault Falcon 900
Govt of Syria, Damascus
YK-ASC

TANZANIA

Gulfstream G.550

Tanzanian Govt, Dar-es-Salaam
5H-ONE

THAILAND

Airbus A.310-324

Royal Flight, Bangkok
L.13-1/34 (HS-TYQ) [44-444]

Boeing 737-448/-8Z6*

Royal Flight, Bangkok
HS-HRH [99-999]
HS-TYS* [55-555]

TUNISIA

Boeing 737-7HJ

Govt of Tunisia, Tunis
TS-IOO

TURKEY

Türk Hava Kuvvetleri

Boeing 737-7FS AEW&C

06-001 (on order)

Boeing KC-135R Stratotanker

101 Filo, Incirlik
00325
00326
23539
23563
23567
57-2609
80110

Cessna 650 Citation VII

212 Filo, Ankara/Etimesğut
004
005

Grumman G.1159C Gulfstream IV

211 Filo, Ankara/Etimesğut
003
TC-ATA
TC-GAP/001

Lockheed C-130B Hercules

222 Filo, Erkilet
3496 (23496)
10960
10963
70527
80736

Lockheed C-130E Hercules

222 Filo, Erkilet
01468 12-468
01947
13187
63-186
63-3188 188
63-3189
73-991 12-991

Transall C-160D

221 Filo, Erkilet
68-020
68-023
69-019
69-021
69-024
69-026
69-027
69-028 12-028
69-029
69-031
69-032
69-033
69-034
69-035 12-035
69-036
69-038
69-040

TUSAS-GD F-16C/F-16D*
Fighting Falcon

3 AJEÜ, Konya:
132 Filo;
4 AJÜ, Akinci:
141 Filo, 142 Filo &
143/Öncel Filo;
5 AJÜ, Merzifon:
151 Filo & 152 Filo;
6 AJÜ, Bandirma:
161 Filo & 162 Filo;
8 AJÜ, Diyarbakir:
181 Filo & 182 Filo;
9 AJÜ, Balikesir:
191 Filo & 192 Filo

86-0066 Öncel Filo
86-0068 Öncel Filo
86-0069 Öncel Filo
86-0070 Öncel Filo
86-0071 Öncel Filo
86-0072 Öncel Filo
86-0192* Öncel Filo
86-0193* Öncel Filo
86-0194* Öncel Filo
86-0195* Öncel Filo
86-0196* Öncel Filo
87-0002* Öncel Filo
87-0003* Öncel Filo
87-0009 Öncel Filo
87-0010 Öncel Filo
87-0011 Öncel Filo
87-0013 Öncel Filo
87-0014 Öncel Filo
87-0015 Öncel Filo
87-0016 Öncel Filo
87-0017 Öncel Filo
87-0018 Öncel Filo
87-0019 Öncel Filo
87-0020 Öncel Filo
87-0021 Öncel Filo
88-0013* Öncel Filo
88-0014* 141 Filo
88-0015* 141 Filo
88-0019 Öncel Filo
88-0020 Öncel Filo
88-0021 Öncel Filo
88-0024 142 Filo
88-0025 141 Filo
88-0026 142 Filo
88-0027 Öncel Filo
88-0028 191 Filo
88-0029 142 Filo
88-0030 191 Filo
88-0031 Öncel Filo
88-0032 Öncel Filo
88-0033 141 Filo
88-0034 141 Filo
88-0035 141 Filo
88-0036 141 Filo
88-0037 141 Filo
89-0022 141 Filo
89-0023 141 Filo
89-0024 141 Filo
89-0025 141 Filo
89-0026 141 Filo
89-0027 141 Filo
89-0028 141 Filo
89-0030 141 Filo
89-0031 Öncel Filo
89-0032 141 Filo
89-0034 162 Filo
89-0035 162 Filo
89-0036 162 Filo
89-0037 162 Filo
89-0038 162 Filo
89-0039 162 Filo
89-0040 162 Filo
89-0041 162 Filo
89-0042* Öncel Filo
89-0043* 162 Filo
89-0044* 162 Filo
89-0045* 182 Filo
90-0001 162 Filo
90-0004 162 Filo
90-0005 162 Filo
90-0006 162 Filo
90-0007 162 Filo
90-0008 162 Filo
90-0009 162 Filo
90-0010 162 Filo
90-0011 162 Filo
90-0012 161 Filo
90-0013 161 Filo
90-0014 162 Filo
90-0016 161 Filo
90-0017 161 Filo
90-0018 161 Filo
90-0019 161 Filo
90-0020 162 Filo
90-0021 161 Filo
90-0022* 161 Filo
90-0023* 161 Filo
90-0024* 161 Filo
91-0001 161 Filo
91-0002 161 Filo
91-0003 161 Filo
91-0004 161 Filo
91-0005 161 Filo
91-0006 161 Filo
91-0007 161 Filo
91-0008 141 Filo
91-0010 141 Filo
91-0011 141 Filo
91-0012 141 Filo
91-0013 192 Filo
91-0014 141 Filo
91-0015 182 Filo
91-0016 182 Filo
91-0017 182 Filo
91-0018 182 Filo
91-0019 182 Filo
91-0020 182 Filo
91-0022* 141 Filo
91-0024* 141 Filo
92-0001 182 Filo
92-0002 182 Filo
92-0003 162 Filo
92-0004 182 Filo
92-0005 191 Filo
92-0006 182 Filo
92-0007 182 Filo

92-0008 191 Filo
92-0009 191 Filo
92-0010 182 Filo
92-0011 182 Filo
92-0012 182 Filo
92-0013 182 Filo
92-0014 182 Filo
92-0015 182 Filo
92-0016 182 Filo
92-0017 182 Filo
92-0018 182 Filo
92-0019 181 Filo
92-0020 181 Filo
92-0021 181 Filo
92-0022* 181 Filo
92-0023* 181 Filo
92-0024* 182 Filo
93-0001 181 Filo
93-0003 181 Filo
93-0004 181 Filo
93-0005 181 Filo
93-0006 181 Filo
93-0007 181 Filo
93-0008 181 Filo
93-0009 181 Filo
93-0010 181 Filo
93-0011 181 Filo
93-0012 181 Filo
93-0013 181 Filo
93-0014 181 Filo
93-0658 151 Filo
93-0659 151 Filo
93-0660 152 Filo
93-0661 151 Filo
93-0663 151 Filo
93-0664 151 Filo
93-0665 152 Filo
93-0667 151 Filo
93-0668
93-0669 151 Filo
93-0670 151 Filo
93-0671 152 Filo
93-0672 152 Filo
93-0673 152 Filo
93-0674 152 Filo
93-0675 192 Filo
93-0676 192 Filo
93-0677 192 Filo$
93-0678 192 Filo
93-0679 192 Filo
93-0680 192 Filo$
93-0681 192 Filo
93-0682 192 Filo
93-0683 192 Filo
93-0684 192 Filo
93-0685 192 Filo
93-0686 192 Filo
93-0687 192 Filo
93-0688 192 Filo
93-0689 192 Filo
93-0690 192 Filo
93-0691*
93-0692* 151 Filo
93-0693* 152 Filo
93-0694*
93-0695* 192 Filo
93-0696* 192 Filo
94-0071 192 Filo
94-0072 191 Filo
94-0073 191 Filo
94-0074 191 Filo
94-0075 191 Filo
94-0076 191 Filo
94-0077 191 Filo
94-0078 191 Filo
94-0079 191 Filo
94-0080 191 Filo
94-0082 191 Filo
94-0083 191 Filo
94-0084 191 Filo
94-0085 191 Filo
94-0086 191 Filo
94-0088
94-0089 152 Filo
94-0090 152 Filo
94-0091 152 Filo
94-0092
94-0093
94-0094 152 Filo
94-0095 152 Filo
94-0096 152 Filo
94-0105* 191 Filo
94-0106* 191 Filo
94-0108* 152 Filo
94-0109* 151 Filo
94-0110* 152 Filo
94-1557* 152 Filo
94-1558* Öncel Filo
94-1559* 152 Filo
94-1560* 151 Filo
94-1561* 191 Filo
94-1562* 192 Filo
94-1563* 192 Filo
94-1564* 191 Filo

Turkish Govt
Airbus A.319CJ-115X
Turkish Govt, Ankara
TC-ANA

TURKMENISTAN
BAe 1000B
Govt of Turkmenistan, Ashkhabad
EZ-B021

Boeing 757-23A
Govt of Turkmenistan, Ashkhabad
EZ-A010

UGANDA
Grumman G.1159C Gulfstream IV
Govt of Uganda, Entebbe
5X-UEF

UKRAINE
Ukrainian Air Force
Ilyushin Il-76MD/Il-76T
321 TAP, Uzin
76413 Il-76MD
76520 Il-76T
76531 Il-76MD
76536 Il-76MD
76559 Il-76MD
76564 Il-76MD
76565 Il-76MD
76566 Il-76MD
76580 Il-76MD
76585 Il-76MD
76596 Il-76MD
76598 Il-76MD
76601 Il-76MD
76633 Il-76MD
76645 Il-76MD
76647 Il-76MD
76657 Il-76MD
76661 Il-76MD
76665 Il-76MD
76683 Il-76MD
76697 Il-76MD
76698 Il-76MD
76699 Il-76MD
76767 Il-76MD
86915 Il-76MD
86922 Il-76MD
86923 Il-76MD
UR-76537 Il-76MD
UR-76677 Il-76MD
UR-76697 Il-76MD

Ilyushin Il-62M
Govt of Ukraine, Kiev
UR-86527
UR-86528

UNITED ARAB EMIRATES
United Arab Emirates Air Force
AgustaWestland AW.139
Dubai Air Wing
DU-139
DU-140

Lockheed C-130H/L.100-30* Hercules
Abu Dhabi
1211
1212
1213
1214
Dubai
311* [A6-QFY]
312*

United Arab Emirates Air Navy
Gates LearJet 35A
Abu Dhabi
801

UAE Govt
Airbus A.319CJ-113X
Dubai Air Wing
A6-ESH

Antonov AN-124
UAE Govt
UR-ZYD

Boeing 737-7BC/7F0/7Z5/8AJ/8EC/8EO/8EX
Govt of Abu Dhabi;
Govt of Dubai
A6-AIN 7Z5 Abu Dhabi
A6-AUH 8EX Dubai
A6-DAS 7Z5 Abu Dhabi
A6-DFR 7Z5 Abu Dhabi
A6-HEH 8AJ Dubai
A6-HRS 7F0 Dubai
A6-LIW 7Z5 Dubai
A6-MRM 8EC Dubai
A6-MRS 8EO Dubai

Boeing 747-2B4BF/422/48E/4F6
Dubai Air Wing;
Govt of Abu Dhabi

A6-GDP	2B4BF	Dubai
A6-HRM	422	Dubai
A6-MMM	422	Dubai
A6-UAE	48E	Dubai
A6-YAS	4F6	Abu Dhabi

Boeing 747SP-31/ 747SP-Z5*
Govt of Dubai
A6-SMR
A6-ZSN*

Boeing 767-341ER
Govt of Abu Dhabi
A6-SUL

Grumman G.1159C Gulfstream IV
Dubai Air Wing
A6-HHH

VENEZUELA

Fuerza Aérea Venezolana
Airbus A319CJ-133X
Esc 41, Caracas
0001

YEMEN

Boeing 747SP-27
Govt of Yemen, Sana'a
7O-YMN

YUGOSLAVIA

Dassault Falcon 50
Govt of Yugoslavia, Belgrade
YU-BNA

The badge on the tail indicates that this Dutch Air Force F-16AM is operated by 322 Squadron, based at Leeuwarden. The Dutch F-16 fleet is currently being reduced with sales to Chile and Jordan.

With the retirement of the Greek Air Force's A-7H Corsairs in 2007, even fewer of these machines are now active. TA-7C 156747 is flown by 335 Mira, based at Araxos.

With replacement Airbuses on order, the days of the BAC 1-11 in service with the Royal Air Force of Oman are numbered. Here is 552, operated by 4 Squadron, based at Seeb.

Brightly coloured Swiss Air Force F-5E Tiger II J-3090 is one of several that fly with its Patrouille Suisse aerobatic team.

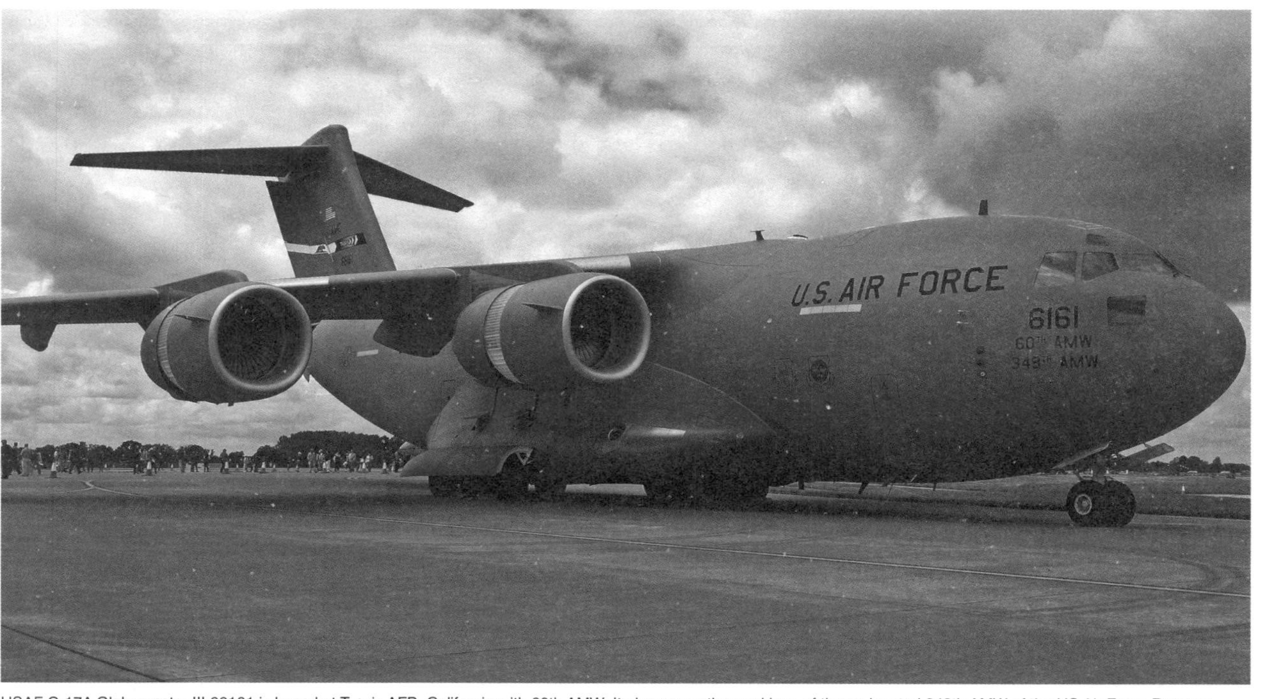

USAF C-17A Globemaster III 66161 is based at Travis AFB, California with 60th AMW. It also wears the markings of the co-located 349th AMW of the US Air Force Reserve.

10017 is a B-52H Stratofortress operated by the 93rd Bomb Squadron, 917th Wing US Air Force Reserve Command, based at Barksdale AFB, Louisiana.

The Lockheed F-117A Nighthawk is now being phased out of USAF service. Depicted is 80-788 of the 8th Fighter Squadron, 49th Fighter Wing, Holloman AFB, New Mexico.

US Military Aircraft Markings

All USAF aircraft have been allocated a fiscal year (FY) number since 1921. Individual aircraft are given a serial according to the fiscal year in which they are ordered. The numbers commence at 0001 and are prefixed with the year of allocation. For example F-15C Eagle 84-001 (84-0001) was the first aircraft ordered in 1984. The fiscal year (FY) serial is carried on the technical data block which is usually stencilled on the left-hand side of the aircraft just below the cockpit. The number displayed on the fin is a corruption of the FY serial. Most tactical aircraft carry the fiscal year in small figures followed by the last three or four digits of the serial in large figures. Large transport and tanker aircraft such as C-130s and KC-135s sometimes display a five-figure number commencing with the last digit of the appropriate fiscal year and four figures of the production number. An example of this is KC-135R 58-0128 which displays 80128 on its fin.

US Army serials have been allocated in a similar way to USAF serials although in recent years an additional zero has been added so that all US Army serials now have the two-figure fiscal year part followed by five digits. This means that, for example C-20E 70140 is officially 87-00140 although as yet this has not led to any alterations to serials painted on aircraft.

USN and USMC serials follow a straightforward numerical sequence which commenced, for the present series, with the allocation of 00001 to an SB2C Helldiver by the Bureau of Aeronautics in 1940. Numbers in the 167000 series are presently being issued. They are usually carried in full on the rear fuselage of the aircraft.

US Coast Guard serials began with the allocation of the serial 1 to a Loening OL-5 in 1927.

UK-based USAF Aircraft

The following aircraft are normally based in the UK. They are listed in numerical order of type with individual aircraft in serial number order, as depicted on the aircraft. The number in brackets is either the alternative presentation of the five-figure number commencing with the last digit of the fiscal year, or the fiscal year where a five-figure serial is presented on the aircraft. Where it is possible to identify the allocation of aircraft to individual squadrons by means of colours carried on fin or cockpit edge, this is also provided.

McDonnell Douglas
F-15C Eagle/F-15D Eagle/
F-15E Strike Eagle
LN: 48th FW, RAF Lakenheath:
492nd FS *bl*ue/white
493rd FS black/*y*ellow
494th FS *r*ed/white

Type				Notes
00-3000	F-15E	*bl*		
00-3001	F-15E	*r*		
00-3002	F-15E	*r*	[494th FS]	
00-3003	F-15E	*r*		
00-3004	F-15E	*r*		
01-2000	F-15E	*r*		
01-2001	F-15E	*m*	[48th OG]	
01-2002	F-15E	*r*	[494th FS]	
01-2003	F-15E	*r*		
01-2004	F-15E	*m*	[48th FW]	
83-0018	F-15C	*y*		
84-0001	F-15C	*y*		
84-0004	F-15C	*y*		
84-0009	F-15C	*y*		
84-0010	F-15C	*y*		
84-0014	F-15C	*y*		
84-0015	F-15C	*y*		
84-0019	F-15C	*y*		
84-0027	F-15C	*y*	[493rd FS]	
84-0044	F-15D	*y*		
86-0147	F-15C	*y*		
86-0154	F-15C	*y*		
86-0156	F-15C	*y*		
86-0159	F-15C	*y*		
86-0160	F-15C	*y*		
86-0163	F-15C	*y*		
86-0164	F-15C	*y*		
86-0165	F-15C	*y*		
86-0166	F-15C	*y*		
86-0167	F-15C	*y*		
86-0171	F-15C	*y*		
86-0172	F-15C	*y*		
86-0174	F-15C	*y*		
86-0175	F-15C	*y*		
86-0176	F-15C	*y*		
86-0178	F-15C	*y*		
86-0182	F-15D	*y*		
91-0301	F-15E	*bl*		
91-0302	F-15E	*bl*		
91-0303	F-15E	*bl*		
91-0304	F-15E	*bl*		
91-0306	F-15E	*bl*		
91-0307	F-15E	*bl*		
91-0308	F-15E	*bl*		
91-0309	F-15E	*bl*		
91-0310	F-15E	*r*		
91-0311	F-15E	*bl*		
91-0312	F-15E	*bl*		
91-0313	F-15E	*r*		
91-0314	F-15E	*r*		
91-0315	F-15E	*r*		
91-0316	F-15E	*r*		
91-0317	F-15E	*r*		
91-0318	F-15E	*r*		
91-0320	F-15E	*r*		
91-0321	F-15E	*bl*		
91-0324	F-15E	*r*		
91-0326	F-15E	*r*		
91-0329	F-15E	*bl*		
91-0331	F-15E	*r*		
91-0332	F-15E	*bl*		

Type				Notes
91-0334	F-15E	*r*		
91-0335	F-15E	*r*		
91-0602	F-15E	*r*		
91-0603	F-15E	*r*		
91-0604	F-15E	*r*		
91-0605	F-15E	*bl*		
92-0364	F-15E	*bl*		
96-0201	F-15E	*bl*		
96-0202	F-15E	*bl*		
96-0204	F-15E	*bl*		
96-0205	F-15E	*bl*		
97-0217	F-15E	*bl*		
97-0218	F-15E	*m*	[48th FW]	
97-0219	F-15E	*bl*		
97-0220	F-15E	*bl*		
97-0221	F-15E	*bl*	[492nd FS]	
97-0222	F-15E	*r*		
98-0131	F-15E	*bl*		
98-0132	F-15E	*bl*		
98-0133	F-15E	*bl*		
98-0134	F-15E	*bl*		
98-0135	F-15E	*bl*		

Sikorsky HH-60G Blackhawk

56th RQS/48th FW,
RAF Lakenheath

26109 (FY88)
26205 (FY89)
26206 (FY89)
26208 (FY89)
26212 (FY89)

Lockheed C-130 Hercules

352nd SOG, RAF Mildenhall:
7th SOS* & 67th SOS,

Type		Notes
14859 (FY64)	C-130E	
40476 (FY84)	MC-130H*	
70023 (FY87)	MC-130H*	
70024 (FY87)	MC-130H*	
70126 (FY87)	MC-130H*	
80192 (FY88)	MC-130H*	
90280 (FY89)	MC-130H*	
95825 (FY69)	MC-130P	
95826 (FY69)	MC-130P	
95828 (FY69)	MC-130P	
95831 (FY69)	MC-130P	
95832 (FY69)	MC-130P	

Boeing KC-135R Stratotanker

351st ARS/100th ARW,
RAF Mildenhall [D] (*r/w/bl*)

00328 (FY60)
00331 (FY60)
00350 (FY60)
00355 (FY60)
23519 (FY62)
37987 (FY63)
38045 (FY63)
80036 (FY58)
80086 (FY58)
80093 (FY58)
80100 (FY58)

USAF F-16C 88-0413 wears special marks for the 510th Fighter Squadron 'Buzzards' and is based at Aviano in Italy.

European-based USAF Aircraft

These aircraft are normally based in Western Europe with the USAFE. They are shown in numerical order of type designation, with individual aircraft in serial number order as carried on the aircraft. Fiscal year (FY) details are also provided if necessary. The unit allocation and operating bases are given for most aircraft.

Fairchild
A-10A Thunderbolt II
SP: 52nd FW, Spangdahlem, Germany:
81st FS *y*ellow

Type		Notes
78-0701	*y*	
79-0207	*y*	
80-0217	*y*	
80-0281	*y*	[81st FS]
81-0945	*y*	
81-0948	*y*	
81-0951	*y*	
81-0952	*y*	[81st FS]
81-0954	*y*	
81-0956	*y*	
81-0962	*y*	
81-0963	*y*	
81-0966	*y*	
81-0976	*y*	
81-0978	*y*	
81-0980	*y*	
81-0983	*y*	
81-0984	*y*	
81-0985	*y*	
81-0988	*y*	
81-0991	*y*	
81-0992	*m*	[52nd OG]
82-0649	*y*	
82-0650	*y*	
82-0654	*y*	
82-0656	*y*	

Beech
C-12 Super King Air
US Embassy Flight, Budapest, Hungary

FY83
30495 C-12D
FY76
60168 C-12C

Lockheed (GD)
F-16C/F-16D*
AV: 31st FW, Aviano, Italy:
510th FS *pur*ple/white
555th FS *g*ree*n*/yellow
SP: 52nd FW, Spangdahlem, Germany:
22nd FS *r*ed/white
23rd FS *bl*ue/white

Type			Notes
87-0350	AV	*gn*	
87-0351	AV	*m*	[31st OSS]
87-0355	AV	*pr*	
87-0359	AV	*gn*	
88-0413	AV	*pr*	[510th FS]
88-0425	AV	*gn*	
88-0435	AV	*gn*	
88-0443	AV	*pr*	
88-0444	AV	*pr*	
88-0446	AV	*gn*	
88-0491	AV	*pr*	
88-0525	AV	*pr*	
88-0526	AV	*gn*	
88-0532	AV	*gn*	
88-0535	AV	*gn*	
88-0541	AV	*pr*	
89-2001	AV	*m*	[31st FW]
89-2009	AV	*gn*	
89-2011	AV	*pr*	
89-2016	AV	*gn*	[16th AF]
89-2018	AV	*gn*	
89-2023	AV	*gn*	
89-2024	AV	*gn*	
89-2026	AV	*gn*	
89-2029	AV	*pr*	
89-2030	AV	*pr*	
89-2035	AV	*gn*	[555th FS]
89-2038	AV	*gn*	
89-2039	AV	*gn*	
89-2041	AV	*gn*	
89-2044	AV	*gn*	
89-2046	AV	*pr*	
89-2047	AV	*pr*	
89-2049	AV	*pr*	[USAFE]
89-2057	AV	*gn*	
89-2068	AV	*gn*	
89-2102	AV	*gn*	
89-2118	AV	*pr*	
89-2137	AV	*pr*	[31st OG]
89-2178*	AV	*pr*	
90-0709	AV	*pr*	
90-0772	AV	*gn*	
90-0773	AV	*gn*	
90-0777*	AV	*pr*	
90-0795*	AV	*gn*	
90-0796*	AV	*pr*	
90-0800*	AV	*gn*	
90-0813	SP	*r*	
90-0818	SP	*r*	
90-0827	SP	*r*	
90-0828	SP	*r*	
90-0829	SP	*r*	[22nd FS]
90-0831	SP	*r*	
90-0833	SP	*r*	
90-0843*	SP	*r*	
90-0846*	SP	*bl*	
91-0336	SP	*r*	
91-0338	SP	*r*	
91-0339	SP	*r*	
91-0340	SP	*r*	
91-0341	SP	*r*	
91-0342	SP	*r*	
91-0343	SP	*r*	
91-0344	SP	*r*	
91-0351	SP	*r*	
91-0352	SP	*m*	[52nd FW]
91-0391	SP	*r*	
91-0402	SP	*bl*	
91-0403	SP	*bl*	
91-0405	SP	*bl*	
91-0406	SP	*r*	
91-0407	SP	*bl*	
91-0408	SP	*r*	
91-0409	SP	*bl*	
91-0410	SP	*bl*	
91-0412	SP	*bl*	
91-0414	SP	*bl*	

Type			
91-0416	SP	*bl*	[52nd OG]
91-0417	SP	*bl*	
91-0418	SP	*bl*	
91-0419	SP	*bl*	
91-0420	SP	*bl*	
91-0421	SP	*bl*	
91-0464*	SP	*r*	
91-0472*	SP	*bl*	
91-0474*	SP	*bl*	
91-0481*	SP	*bl*	
92-3915	SP	*bl*	
92-3918	SP	*bl*	
96-0080	SP	*bl*	[23rd FS]
96-0081	SP	*bl*	
96-0082	SP	*bl*	
96-0083	SP	*bl*	

Grumman
C-20H Gulfstream IV
76th AS/86th AW, Ramstein, Germany
FY90
00300
FY92
20375

Gates C-21A
Learjet
76th AS/86th AW, Ramstein, Germany
FY84
40081
40082
40083
40084
40085
40087
40109
40110
40111
40112

Gulfstream Aerospace
C-37A Gulfstream V
309th AS/86th AW, Chievres, Belgium
FY01
10076

Boeing C-40B
76th AS/86th AW, Ramstein, Germany
FY02
20042

Lockheed C-130E
Hercules
37th AS/86th AW, Ramstein,
Germany [RS] (*bl/w*)

01260	(FY70)
01264	(FY70)
01271	(FY70)
10935	(FY68)
17681	(FY64)
18240	(FY64)
21299	(FY72)
21835	(FY62)
37792	(FY63)
37825	(FY63)
37840	(FY63)
37879	(FY63)
37885	(FY63)
37897	(FY63)
40502	(FY64)
40527	(FY64)

European-based US Navy Aircraft

Fairchild C-26D
NAF Naples, Italy;
NAF Sigonella, Italy

Type	
900528	Naples
900530	Sigonella
900531	Naples
910502	Sigonella

European-based US Army Aircraft

Beech
C-12 Huron
'F' Co, 6th Btn, 52nd Avn Reg't, Wiesbaden;
Det. 'G' Co, 6th Btn, 52nd Avn Reg't, Aviano, Italy;
'A' Co, 2nd Btn, 228th Avn Reg't, Heidelberg;
1st Military Intelligence Btn, Wiesbaden;
SHAPE Flight Det, Chievres

Type		
FY84		
40156	C-12U	F/6-52nd Avn
40157	C-12U	Det. G/6-52nd Avn
40158	C-12U	F/6-52nd Avn
40160	C-12U	Det. G/6-52nd Avn
40161	C-12U	F/6-52nd Avn
40162	C-12U	F/6-52nd Avn
40163	C-12U	F/6-52nd Avn
40165	C-12U	F/6-52nd Avn
FY94		
40315	C-12R	A/2-228th Avn
40316	C-12R	A/2-228th Avn
40318	C-12R	A/2-228th Avn
40319	C-12R	A/2-228th Avn
FY95		
50091	C-12R	A/2-228th Avn
FY85		
50147	RC-12K	1st MIB
50148	RC-12K	1st MIB
50149	RC-12K	1st MIB
50150	RC-12K	1st MIB
50152	RC-12K	1st MIB
50153	RC-12K	1st MIB

Notes Type

50155 RC-12K 1st MIB
FY86
60079 C-12J SHAPE Flt Det

Cessna UC-35A Citation V
'E' Co, 6th Btn, 52nd Avn Reg't, Wiesbaden
FY95
50123
50124
FY97
70101
70102
70105
FY99
90102

Boeing-Vertol CH-47D Chinook
'B' Co, 5th Btn, 158th Avn Reg't, Ansbach
FY87
70072
70073
FY88
80099
80100
80101
80102
80103
80104
80106
FY89
90138
90139
90140
90141
90142
90143
90144
90145

Sikorsky H-60 Black Hawk
'A' Co, 3rd Btn, 158th Avn Reg't, Ansbach;
'B' Co, 3rd Btn, 158th Avn Reg't, Ansbach;
'A' Co, 5th Btn, 158th Avn Reg't, Ansbach;
'C' Co, 5th Btn, 158th Avn Reg't, Ansbach;
'G' Co, 6th Btn, 52nd Avn Reg't, Aviano;
'A' Co, 127th Divisional Avn Support Btn, Bad Kreuznach;
SHAPE Flight Det, Chievres;
'B' Co, 70th Transportation Reg't, Coleman Barracks;
'B' Co, 7th Btn, 159th AVIM, Illesheim;
'C' Co, 1st Btn, 214th Avn Reg't, Landstuhl;
6th Avn Co, Vicenza, Italy
FY82
23675 UH-60A C/5-158th Avn
23735 UH-60A C/1-214th Avn
23745 UH-60A C/1-214th Avn
23750 UH-60A C/1-214th Avn
23752 UH-60A C/1-214th Avn
23754 UH-60A C/1-214th Avn
23755 UH-60A C/1-214th Avn
23756 UH-60A C/1-214th Avn

Notes Type

23757 UH-60A C/1-214th Avn
FY83
23855 UH-60A C/1-214th Avn
23868 UH-60A C/1-214th Avn
23869 UH-60A C/1-214th Avn
FY84
23951 UH-60A C/5-158th Avn
23975
FY86
24531 UH-60A C/5-158th Avn
24532 UH-60A C/1-214th Avn
24538 UH-60A C/1-214th Avn
24551 UH-60A C/1-214th Avn
FY87
24583 UH-60A SHAPE Flt Det
24584 UH-60A SHAPE Flt Det
24589 UH-60A C/1-214th Avn
24621 UH-60A C/1-214th Avn
24642 UH-60A C/1-214th Avn
24643 UH-60A C/1-214th Avn
24644 UH-60A C/5-158th Avn
24645 UH-60A C/5-158th Avn
24647 UH-60A C/1-214th Avn
26001 UH-60A C/5-158th Avn
26003 UH-60A G/6-52nd Avn
26004 UH-60A C/5-158th Avn
FY88
26019 UH-60A C/1-214th Avn
26020 UH-60A C/1-214th Avn
26021 UH-60A G/6-52nd Avn
26023 UH-60A C/1-214th Avn
26025 UH-60A C/1-214th Avn
26026 UH-60A G/6-52nd Avn
26027 UH-60A C/1-214th Avn
26031 UH-60A C/1-214th Avn
26037 UH-60A B/7-159th AVIM
26039 UH-60A C/5-158th Avn
26040 UH-60A A/5-158th Avn
26045 UH-60A C/5-158th Avn
26052 UH-60A G/6-52nd Avn
26054 UH-60A C/1-214th Avn
26055 UH-60A C/1-214th Avn
26063 UH-60A G/6-52nd Avn
26067 UH-60A G/6-52nd Avn
26072 UH-60A C/1-214th Avn
26080 UH-60A C/1-214th Avn
26085 UH-60A C/1-214th Avn
26086 UH-60A C/1-214th Avn
FY89
26145 UH-60A G/6-52nd Avn
26153 UH-60A C/1-214th Avn
26165 UH-60A C/1-214th Avn
FY94
26551 UH-60L G/6-52nd Avn
FY95
26621 UH-60L A/5-158th Avn
26628 UH-60L A/5-158th Avn
26629 UH-60L A/5-158th Avn
26630 UH-60L A/5-158th Avn
26631 UH-60L A/5-158th Avn
26632 UH-60L A/5-158th Avn
26633 UH-60L A/5-158th Avn
26635 UH-60L A/5-158th Avn
26636 UH-60L A/5-158th Avn
26637 UH-60L A/5-158th Avn
26638 UH-60L A/5-158th Avn
26639 UH-60L A/5-158th Avn
26640 UH-60L A/5-158th Avn
26641 UH-60L 3-158th Avn
26642 UH-60L 3-158th Avn
26643 UH-60L 3-158th Avn
26644 UH-60L A/5-158th Avn

Type			Notes
26646	UH-60L	A/5-158th Avn	
26647	UH-60L	A/5-158th Avn	
26648	UH-60L	A/5-158th Avn	
26651	UH-60L	3-158th Avn	
26652	UH-60L	3-158th Avn	
FY96			
26674	UH-60L	3-158th Avn	
26675	UH-60L	3-158th Avn	
26676	UH-60L	3-158th Avn	
26677	UH-60L	3-158th Avn	
26678	UH-60L	3-158th Avn	
26680	UH-60L	3-158th Avn	
26683	UH-60L	3-158th Avn	
26684	UH-60L	3-158th Avn	
26687	UH-60L	3-158th Avn	
26690	UH-60L	3-158th Avn	
26691	UH-60L	3-158th Avn	

MDH AH-64D Apache
2nd Btn, 159th Avn Reg't, Illesheim;
3rd Btn, 159th Avn Reg't, Illesheim

Type		Notes
FY96		
05007	3-159th Avn	
05009	3-159th Avn	
05011	3-159th Avn	
05015	3-159th Avn	
05018	3-159th Avn	
05020	3-159th Avn	
05021	3-159th Avn	
05022	3-159th Avn	
FY99		
05109	3-159th Avn	
05114	3-159th Avn	
05126	3-159th Avn	
05139	3-159th Avn	
05143	3-159th Avn	
FY00		
05175	2-159th Avn	
05178	3-159th Avn	
05190	3-159th Avn	
05199	2-159th Avn	
05200	2-159th Avn	
05205	2-159th Avn	
05206	2-159th Avn	
05207	2-159th Avn	
05208	2-159th Avn	
05209	2-159th Avn	
05210	2-159th Avn	
05212	2-159th Avn	
05213	2-159th Avn	
05214	2-159th Avn	
05215	2-159th Avn	
05216	3-159th Avn	
05217	2-159th Avn	
05218	2-159th Avn	
05220	2-159th Avn	
05225	2-159th Avn	
05226	2-159th Avn	
05230	3-159th Avn	
05231	2-159th Avn	
05232	2-159th Avn	
FY01		
05233	3-159th Avn	
05243	3-159th Avn	
05250	3-159th Avn	
05253	3-159th Avn	
05273	3-159th Avn	
05274	3-159th Avn	
05284	3-159th Avn	

US-based USAF Aircraft

The following aircraft are normally based in the USA but are likely to be seen visiting the UK from time to time. The presentation is in numerical order of the type, commencing with the B-**1B** and concluding with the C-**135**. The aircraft are listed in numerical progression by the serial actually carried externally. Fiscal year information is provided, together with details of mark variations and in some cases operating units. Where base-code letter information is carried on the aircrafts' tails, this is detailed with the squadron/ base data; for example the 7th Wing's B-1B 60105 carries the letters DY on its tail, thus identifying the Wing's home base as Dyess AFB, Texas.

Rockwell B-1B Lancer
7th BW, Dyess AFB, Texas [DY]:
9th BS (*bk/w*), 13th BS (*r*) & 28th BS (*bl/w*);
28th BW, Ellsworth AFB, South Dakota [EL]:
34th BS (*bk/r*) & 37th BS (*bk/y*);
419th FLTS/412th TW, Edwards AFB, California [ED]

Type		Notes
FY84		
40049	412th TW	
FY85		
50059	7th BW *bl/w*	
50060	28th BW *bk/r*	
50061	7th BW *bl/w*	
50064	7th BW *bl/w*	
50065	7th BW *bl/w*	
50066	28th BW	
50068	412th TW	
50069	7th BW	
50072	7th BW *y/bk*	
50073	7th BW *bl/w*	
50074	7th BW *r*	
50075	412th TW	
50077	28th BW	
50079	28th BW *bk/r*	
50080	7th BW *bl/w*	
50081	28th BW *bk/y*	
50083	28th BW *bk/r*	
50084	28th BW *bk/r*	
50085	28th BW *bk/y*	
50087	28th BW *bk/y*	
50088	7th BW *y/bk*	
50089	7th BW *bl/w*	
50090	7th BW *bl/w*	
50091	28th BW *bk/y*	
FY86		
60093	28th BW *bk/y*	
60094	28th BW *bk/y*	
60095	28th BW	
60097	7th BW	
60098	7th BW *bl/w*	

Notes	Type			
	60099	28th BW *bk/y*		
	60100	7th BW *bl/w*		
	60101	7th BW *bl/w*		
	60102	28th BW *bk/y*		
	60103	7th BW *bl/w*		
	60104	28th BW *bk/y*		
	60105	7th BW *bl/w*		
	60107	7th BW *bl/w*		
	60108	7th BW *bl/w*		
	60109	7th BW		
	60110	7th BW *y/bk*		
	60111	28th BW *bk/r*		
	60112	7th BW *y/bk*		
	60113	28th BW *bk/y*		
	60115	28th BW		
	60116	28th BW		
	60118	28th BW *bk/y*		
	60119	7th BW *bl/w*		
	60120	7th BW *y/bk*		
	60121	28th BW *bk/y*		
	60122	7th BW *r*		
	60123	7th BW *y/bk*		
	60124	7th BW *bl/w*		
	60125	28th BW *bk/r*		
	60126	7th BW *bl/w*		
	60127	28th BW *bk/y*		
	60129	28th BW		
	60130	28th BW *bk/y*		
	60132	7th BW *bl/w*		
	60133	7th BW *bk/w*		
	60134	28th BW *bk/r*		
	60135	7th BW *bl/w*		
	60136	7th BW *bl/w*		
	60137	7th BW *bl/w*		
	60138	7th BW		
	60139	28th BW *bl/y*		
	60140	7th BW *y/bk*		

Northrop B-2 Spirit
419th FLTS/412th TW, Edwards AFB, California [ED];
509th BW, Whiteman AFB, Missouri [WM]:
13th BS, 393rd BS & 715th BS
(Names are given where known. Each begins *Spirit of ...*)

FY90		
00040	509th BW	*Alaska*
00041	509th BW	*Hawaii*
FY92		
20700	509th BW	*Florida*
FY82		
21066	509th BW	*America*
21067	509th BW	*Arizona*
21068	412th TW	*New York*
21069	509th BW	*Indiana*
21070	509th BW	*Ohio*
21071	509th BW	*Mississippi*
FY93		
31085	509th BW	*Oklahoma*
31086	509th BW	*Kitty Hawk*
31087	509th BW	*Pennsylvania*
31088	509th BW	*Louisiana*
FY88		
80328	509th BW	*Texas*
80329	509th BW	*Missouri*
80330	509th BW	*California*
80331	509th BW	*South Carolina*
80332	509th BW	*Washington*
FY89		
90127	509th BW	*Kansas*
90128	509th BW	*Nebraska*
90129	509th BW	*Georgia*

Lockheed U-2
9th RW, Beale AFB, California [BB]:
1st RS, 5th RS & 99th RS (*bk/r*);
Lockheed, Palmdale;
Warner Robins Air Logistics Centre [WR]

FY68		
68-10329	U-2S	9th RW
68-10331	U-2S	9th RW
68-10336	U-2S	WR ALC
68-10337	U-2S	9th RW
FY80		
80-1064	TU-2S	9th RW
80-1065	TU-2S	9th RW
80-1066	U-2S	9th RW
80-1067	U-2S	Lockheed
80-1068	U-2S	9th RW
80-1069	U-2S	9th RW
80-1070	U-2S	9th RW
80-1071	U-2S	9th RW
80-1073	U-2S	9th RW
80-1074	U-2S	9th RW
80-1076	U-2S	9th RW
80-1077	U-2S	9th RW
80-1078	TU-2S	9th RW
80-1079	U-2S	9th RW
80-1080	U-2S	9th RW
80-1081	U-2S	9th RW
80-1083	U-2S	9th RW
80-1084	U-2S	9th RW
80-1085	U-2S	9th RW
80-1086	U-2S	9th RW
80-1087	U-2S	9th RW
80-1089	U-2S	9th RW
80-1090	U-2S	9th RW
80-1091	TU-2S	9th RW
80-1092	U-2S	9th RW
80-1093	U-2S	9th RW
80-1094	U-2S	9th RW
80-1096	U-2S	9th RW
80-1099	U-2S	9th RW

Boeing E-3 Sentry
552nd ACW, Tinker AFB, Oklahoma [OK]:
960th AACS (*w*), 963rd AACS (*bk*), 964th AACS (*r*), 965th AACS (*y*) & 966th AACS (*bl*);
961st AACS/18th Wg, Kadena AB, Japan [ZZ] (*or*);
962nd AACS/3rd Wg, Elmendorf AFB, Alaska [AK] (*gn*);

FY80		
00137	E-3C	*r*
00138	E-3C	*gn*
00139	E-3C	*gn*
FY81		
10004	E-3C	*m*
10005	E-3C	*w*
FY71		
11407	E-3B	*w*
11408	E-3B	*r*
FY82		
20006	E-3C	*r*
20007	E-3C	*w*
FY83		
30008	E-3C	*w*
30009	E-3C	*w*
FY73		
31674	JE-3C	Boeing

Type			Notes
31675	E-3B	*gn*	
FY75			
50556	E-3B	*bl*	
50557	E-3B	*r*	
50558	E-3B	*r*	
50559	E-3B	*r*	
50560	E-3B	*w*	
FY76			
61604	E-3B	*bl*	
61605	E-3B	*w*	
61606	E-3B	*r*	
61607	E-3B	*r*	
FY77			
70351	E-3B	*w*	
70352	E-3B	*r*	
70353	E-3B	*r*	
70355	E-3B	*r*	
70356	E-3B	*w*	
FY78			
80576	E-3B	*r*	
80577	E-3B	*or*	
80578	E-3B	*w*	
FY79			
90001	E-3B	*bl*	
90002	E-3B	*r*	
90003	E-3B	*m*	

Boeing E-4B

1st ACCS/55th Wg, Offutt AFB, Nebraska [OF]

31676	(FY73)
31677	(FY73)
40787	(FY74)
50125	(FY75)

Lockheed C-5 Galaxy

60th AMW, Travis AFB, California: 21st AS (*bk/gd*) & 22nd AS (*bk/bl*);
137th AS/105th AW, Stewart AFB, New York (*bl*);
155th AS/164th AW, Memphis, Tennessee ANG (*r*);
167th AS/167th AW, Martinsburg, West Virginia ANG [WV] (*r*);
68th AS/433rd AW AFRC, Kelly AFB, Texas;
436th AW, Dover AFB, Delaware: 9th AS (*y/bl*);
337th AS/439th AW AFRC, Westover ARB, Massachusetts (*bl/r*);
445th AW AFRC, Wright-Patterson AFB, Ohio (*si*): 89th AS & 356th AS

Type				Notes
FY70				
00445	C-5A	433rd AW		
00446	C-5A	433rd AW		
00447	C-5A	445th AW	*si*	
00448	C-5A	445th AW	*si*	
00449	C-5A	164th AW	*r*	
00451	C-5A	433rd AW		
00452	C-5A	167th AW	*r*	
00453	C-5A	433rd AW		
00454	C-5A	164th AW	*r*	
00455	C-5A	445th AW	*si*	
00456	C-5A	433rd AW		
00457	C-5A	445th AW	*si*	
00459	C-5A	164th AW	*r*	
00460	C-5A	105th AW	*bl*	
00461	C-5A	445th AW	*si*	
00462	C-5A	167th AW	*r*	
00463	C-5A	167th AW	*r*	
00464	C-5A	105th AW	*bl*	
00465	C-5A	164th AW	*r*	
00466	C-5A	433rd AW		
00467	C-5A	167th AW	*r*	
FY83				
31285	C-5B	436th AW	*y/bl*	
FY84				
40060	C-5B	60th AMW	*bk/bl*	
40061	C-5M	436th AW	*y*	
40062	C-5M	60th AMW	*bk/gd*	
FY85				
50001	C-5M	436th AW	*m*	
50002	C-5M	436th AW	*y*	
50003	C-5M	436th AW	*y*	
50004	C-5M	60th AMW		
50005	C-5M	436th AW	*y*	
50006	C-5B	439th AW	*bl/r*	
50007	C-5B	436th AW	*y/bl*	
50008	C-5B	60th AMW	*bk/gd*	
50009	C-5B	439th AW	*bl/r*	
50010	C-5B	60th AMW	*bk/gd*	
FY86				
60011	C-5B	60th AMW		
60012	C-5B	439th AW	*bl/r*	
60013	C-5M	436th AW	*y/bl*	
60014	C-5B	439th AW	*bl/r*	
60015	C-5B	436th AW	*y/bl*	
60016	C-5B	60th AMW	*bk/bl*	
60017	C-5B	436th AW	*y/bl*	
60018	C-5B	439th AW	*bl/r*	
60019	C-5B	436th AW	*y/bl*	
60020	C-5B	436th AW	*y/bl*	
60021	C-5B	439th AW	*bl/r*	
60022	C-5B	60th AMW	*bk/bl*	
60023	C-5B	439th AW	*bl/r*	
60024	C-5B	60th AMW	*bk/bl*	
60025	C-5M	436th AW	*y/bl*	
60026	C-5B	60th AMW	*bk/gd*	
FY87				
70027	C-5B	436th AW	*y/bl*	
70028	C-5B	60th AMW	*bk/bl*	
70029	C-5B	436th AW	*y/bl*	
70030	C-5B	60th AMW	*bk/bl*	
70031	C-5B	436th AW	*y/bl*	
70032	C-5B	60th AMW	*bk/bl*	
70033	C-5B	439th AW	*bl/r*	
70034	C-5B	60th AMW	*bk/bl*	
70035	C-5B	436th AW	*y/bl*	
70036	C-5B	60th AMW	*bk/gd*	
70037	C-5B	439th AW	*bl/r*	
70038	C-5B	439th AW	*bl/r*	
70039	C-5B	436th AW	*y/bl*	
70040	C-5B	60th AMW	*bk/gd*	
70041	C-5B	439th AW	*bl/r*	
70042	C-5B	60th AMW	*bk/bl*	
70043	C-5B	436th AW	*y/bl*	
70044	C-5B	60th AMW	*bk/bl*	
70045	C-5M	436th AW	*y/bl*	
FY68				
80211	C-5A	167th AW	*r*	
80212	C-5A	105th AW	*bl*	
80213	C-5C	60th AMW	*bk/gd*	
80214	C-5A	433rd AW		
80215	C-5A	445th AW	*si*	
80216	C-5C	60th AMW	*bk/gd*	
80217	C-5A	167th AW	*r*	
80219	C-5A	445th AW	*si*	
80220	C-5A	433rd AW		
80221	C-5A	433rd AW		
80222	C-5A	439th AW	*bl/r*	
80223	C-5A	433rd AW		
80224	C-5A	105th AW	*bl*	
80225	C-5A	105th AW	*bl*	

Notes	Type			
	80226	C-5A	105th AW	*bl*
	FY69			
	90001	C-5A	105th AW	*bl*
	90002	C-5A	433rd AW	
	90003	C-5M	445th AW	*si*
	90005	C-5A	445th AW	*si*
	90006	C-5A	433rd AW	
	90007	C-5A	433rd AW	
	90008	C-5A	105th AW	*bl*
	90009	C-5A	105th AW	*bl*
	90010	C-5A	164th AW	*r*
	90011	C-5A	439th AW	*bl/r*
	90012	C-5A	105th AW	*bl*
	90013	C-5A	445th AW	*si*
	90014	C-5A	433rd AW	
	90015	C-5A	105th AW	*bl*
	90016	C-5A	433rd AW	
	90017	C-5A	164th AW	*r*
	90018	C-5A	164th AW	*r*
	90019	C-5A	164th AW	*r*
	90020	C-5A	445th AW	*si*
	90021	C-5A	105th AW	*bl*
	90022	C-5A	167th AW	*r*
	90023	C-5A	105th AW	*bl*
	90024	C-5M	436th AW	*y/bl*
	90025	C-5A	164th AW	*r*
	90026	C-5A	433rd AW	
	90027	C-5A	439th AW	*bl/r*

Boeing E-8 J-STARS

116th ACW, Robins AFB, Georgia [WR]:
12th ACCS (*gn*), 16th ACCS (*bk*), 128th ACS/Georgia ANG (*r*) & 330th CTS (*y*);
Grumman, Melbourne, Florida

FY00			
02000	E-8C	116th ACW	
FY90			
00175	E-8A	Grumman	
FY01			
12005	E-8C	116th ACW	
FY02			
29111	E-8C	116th ACW	
FY92			
23289	E-8C	116th ACW	*m*
23290	E-8C	116th ACW	*bk*
FY93			
30597	E-8C	116th ACW	*gn*
31097	E-8C	116th ACW	*r*
FY94			
40284	E-8C	116th ACW	*r*
40285	E-8C	116th ACW	*bk*
FY95			
50121	E-8C	116th ACW	*r*
50122	E-8C	116th ACW	*r*
FY96			
60042	E-8C	116th ACW	*bk*
60043	E-8C	116th ACW	
FY86			
60416	TE-8A	116th ACW	*y*
60417	TE-8A	116th ACW	*y*
FY97			
70100	E-8C	116th ACW	*r*
70200	E-8C	116th ACW	*bk*
70201	E-8C	116th ACW	*r*
FY99			
90006	E-8C	116th ACW	*gn*

McDonnell Douglas KC-10A Extender

60th AMW, Travis AFB, California:
6th ARS (*bk/bl*) & 9th ARS (*bk/r*);
305th AMW, McGuire AFB, New Jersey:
2nd ARS (*bl/r*) & 32nd ARS (*bl*)

FY82		
20191	60th AMW	*bk/bl*
20192	60th AMW	*bk/r*
20193	60th AMW	*bk/bl*
FY83		
30075	60th AMW	*bk/r*
30076	60th AMW	*bk/bl*
30077	60th AMW	*bk/r*
30078	60th AMW	*bk/bl*
30079	305th AMW	*bl/r*
30080	60th AMW	*bk/bl*
30081	305th AMW	*bl*
30082	305th AMW	*bl*
FY84		
40185	60th AMW	*bk/bl*
40186	305th AMW	*bl/r*
40187	60th AMW	*bk/bl*
40188	305th AMW	*bl/r*
40189	60th AMW	*bk/bl*
40190	305th AMW	*bl/r*
40191	60th AMW	*bk/bl*
40192	305th AMW	*bl/y*
FY85		
50027	305th AMW	*bl/r*
50028	305th AMW	*bl/r*
50029	60th AMW	*bk/r*
50030	305th AMW	*bl/r*
50031	305th AMW	*bl/r*
50032	305th AMW	*bl/y*
50033	305th AMW	*bl*
50034	305th AMW	*bl/r*
FY86		
60027	305th AMW	*bl*
60028	305th AMW	*bl/r*
60029	60th AMW	*bk/r*
60030	305th AMW	*bl/r*
60031	60th AMW	*bk/r*
60032	60th AMW	*bk/r*
60033	60th AMW	*bk/r*
60034	60th AMW	*bk/r*
60035	305th AMW	*bl*
60036	305th AMW	*bl*
60037	60th AMW	*bk/r*
60038	60th AMW	*bk/r*
FY87		
70117	60th AMW	*bk/r*
70118	60th AMW	*bk/bl*
70119	60th AMW	*bk/r*
70120	305th AMW	*bl*
70121	305th AMW	*bl*
70122	305th AMW	*bl/r*
70123	305th AMW	*bl*
70124	305th AMW	*bl/y*
FY79		
90433	305th AMW	*bl*
90434	305th AMW	*bl/r*
91710	305th AMW	*bl/r*
91711	305th AMW	*bl*
91712	305th AMW	*bl/r*
91713	305th AMW	*bl*
91946	60th AMW	*bk/bl*
91947	305th AMW	*bl*
91948	60th AMW	*bk/bl*
91949	305th AMW	*bl/r*
91950	60th AMW	*bk/bl*

Type				Notes
91951		60th AMW	*bk/bl*	

Boeing
C-17 Globemaster III

3rd Wg, Elmendorf AFB, Alaska: 535th AS (*w/bk*);
15th AW, Hickam AFB, Hawaii: 535th AS (*r/y*);
60th AMW, Travis AFB, California: 21st AS (*bk/gd*);
62nd AW, McChord AFB, Washington (*gn*): 4th AS, 7th AS,8th AS & 10th AS;
58th AS/97th AMW, Altus AFB, Oklahoma (*r/y*);
172nd AW, Jackson Int'l Airport, Mississippi ANG: 183rd AS (*bl/gd*);
305th AMW, McGuire AFB, New Jersey (*bl*): 6th AS & 13th AS;
417th FLTS/412th TW, Edwards AFB, California [ED];
436th AW, Dover AFB, Delaware: 3rd AS (*y/r*);
437th AW, Charleston AFB, South Carolina (*y/bl*): 14th AS, 15th AS, 16th AS & 17th AS;
452nd AMW AFRC, March ARB, California (*or/y*): 729th AS

Type				Notes
FY00				
00171	C-17A	3rd Wg	*w/bk*	
00172	C-17A	3rd Wg	*w/bk*	
00173	C-17A	3rd Wg	*w/bk*	
00174	C-17A	3rd Wg	*w/bk*	
00175	C-17A	62nd AW	*gn*	
00176	C-17A	62nd AW	*gn*	
00177	C-17A	62nd AW	*gn*	
00178	C-17A	62nd AW	*gn*	
00179	C-17A	62nd AW	*gn*	
00180	C-17A	62nd AW	*gn*	
00181	C-17A	62nd AW	*gn*	
00182	C-17A	62nd AW	*gn*	
00183	C-17A	62nd AW	*gn*	
00184	C-17A	62nd AW	*gn*	
00185	C-17A	62nd AW	*gn*	
FY90				
00532	C-17A	97th AMW	*r/y*	
00533	C-17A	62nd AW	*gn*	
00534	C-17A	437th AW	*y/bl*	
00535	C-17A	62nd AW	*gn*	
FY01				
10186	C-17A	62nd AW	*gn*	
10187	C-17A	62nd AW	*gn*	
10188	C-17A	437th AW	*y/bl*	
10189	C-17A	437th AW	*y/bl*	
10190	C-17A	437th AW	*y/bl*	
10191	C-17A	437th AW	*y/bl*	
10192	C-17A	437th AW	*y/bl*	
10193	C-17A	437th AW	*y/bl*	
10194	C-17A	437th AW	*y/bl*	
10195	C-17A	437th AW	*y/bl*	
10196	C-17A	437th AW	*y/bl*	
10197	C-17A	437th AW	*y/bl*	
FY02				
21098	C-17A	437th AW	*y/bl*	
21099	C-17A	437th AW	*y/bl*	
21100	C-17A	437th AW	*y/bl*	
21101	C-17A	437th AW	*y/bl*	
21102	C-17A	62nd AW	*gn*	
21103	C-17A	62nd AW	*gn*	
21104	C-17A	62nd AW	*gn*	
21105	C-17A	62nd AW	*gn*	
21106	C-17A	62nd AW	*gn*	
21107	C-17A	62nd AW	*gn*	
21108	C-17A	62nd AW	*gn*	
21109	C-17A	62nd AW	*gn*	
21110	C-17A	62nd AW	*gn*	
21111	C-17A	62nd AW	*gn*	
21112	C-17A	172nd AW	*bl/gd*	
FY92				
23291	C-17A	62nd AW	*gn*	
23292	C-17A	437th AW	*y/bl*	
23293	C-17A	437th AW	*y/bl*	
23294	C-17A	97th AMW	*r/y*	
FY93				
30599	C-17A	97th AMW	*r/y*	
30600	C-17A	62nd AW	*gn*	
30601	C-17A	97th AMW	*r/y*	
30602	C-17A	97th AMW	*r/y*	
30603	C-17A	437th AW	*y/bl*	
30604	C-17A	437th AW	*y/bl*	
FY03				
33113	C-17A	172nd AW	*bl/gd*	
33114	C-17A	172nd AW	*bl/gd*	
33115	C-17A	172nd AW	*bl/gd*	
33116	C-17A	172nd AW	*bl/gd*	
33117	C-17A	172nd AW	*bl/gd*	
33118	C-17A	172nd AW	*bl/gd*	
33119	C-17A	172nd AW	*bl/gd*	
33120	C-17A	62nd AW	*gn*	
33121	C-17A	412th TW		
33122	C-17A	437th AW	*y/bl*	
33123	C-17A	437th AW	*y/bl*	
33124	C-17A	437th AW	*y/bl*	
33125	C-17A	305th AMW	*bl*	
33126	C-17A	305th AMW	*bl*	
33127	C-17A	305th AMW	*bl*	
FY94				
40065	C-17A	97th AMW	*r/y*	
40066	C-17A	437th AW	*y/bl*	
40067	C-17A	437th AW	*y/bl*	
40068	C-17A	437th AW	*y/bl*	
40069	C-17A	437th AW	*y/bl*	
40070	C-17A	437th AW	*y/bl*	
FY04				
44128	C-17A	305th AMW	*bl*	
44129	C-17A	305th AMW	*bl*	
44130	C-17A	305th AMW	*bl*	
44131	C-17A	305th AMW	*bl*	
44132	C-17A	305th AMW	*bl*	
44133	C-17A	305th AMW	*bl*	
44134	C-17A	305th AMW	*bl*	
44135	C-17A	305th AMW	*bl*	
44136	C-17A	305th AMW	*bl*	
44137	C-17A	305th AMW	*bl*	
44138	C-17A	452nd AMW	*or/y*	
FY95				
50102	C-17A	437th AW	*y/bl*	
50103	C-17A	437th AW	*y/bl*	
50104	C-17A	437th AW	*y/bl*	
50105	C-17A	437th AW	*y/bl*	
50106	C-17A	437th AW	*y/bl*	
50107	C-17A	437th AW	*y/bl*	
FY05				
55139	C-17A	452nd AMW	*or/y*	
55140	C-17A	452nd AMW	*or/y*	
55141	C-17A	452nd AMW	*or/y*	
55142	C-17A	452nd AMW	*or/y*	
55143	C-17A	452nd AMW	*or/y*	
55144	C-17A	452nd AMW	*or/y*	
55145	C-17A	452nd AMW	*or/y*	
55146	C-17A	15th AW	*r/y*	
55147	C-17A	15th AW	*r/y*	

Notes	Type			
	55148	C-17A	15th AW	*r/y*
	55149	C-17A	15th AW	*r/y*
	55150	C-17A	15th AW	*r/y*
	55151	C-17A	15th AW	*r/y*
	55152	C-17A	15th AW	*r/y*
	55153	C-17A	15th AW	*r/y*
	FY96			
	60001	C-17A	97th AMW	*r/y*
	60002	C-17A	437th AW	*y/bl*
	60003	C-17A	62nd AW	*gn*
	60004	C-17A	437th AW	*y/bl*
	60005	C-17A	437th AW	*y/bl*
	60006	C-17A	437th AW	*y/bl*
	60007	C-17A	437th AW	*y/bl*
	60008	C-17A	437th AW	*y/bl*
	FY06			
	66154	C-17A	60th AMW	*bk/gd*
	66155	C-17A	60th AMW	*bk/gd*
	66156	C-17A	60th AMW	*bk/gd*
	66157	C-17A	60th AMW	*bk/gd*
	66158	C-17A	60th AMW	*bk/gd*
	66159	C-17A	60th AMW	*bk/gd*
	66160	C-17A	60th AMW	*bk/gd*
	66161	C-17A	60th AMW	*bk/gd*
	66162	C-17A	60th AMW	*bk/gd*
	66163	C-17A	60th AMW	*bk/gd*
	66164	C-17A	60th AMW	*bk/gd*
	66165	C-17A	436th AW	*y/r*
	66166	C-17A	436th AW	*y/r*
	66167	C-17A	436th AW	*y/r*
	66168	C-17A	436th AW	*y/r*
	FY87			
	70025	C-17A	412th TW	
	FY97			
	70041	C-17A	437th AW	*y/bl*
	70042	C-17A	437th AW	*y/bl*
	70043	C-17A	437th AW	*y/bl*
	70044	C-17A	437th AW	*y/bl*
	70045	C-17A	437th AW	*y/bl*
	70046	C-17A	437th AW	*y/bl*
	70047	C-17A	437th AW	*y/bl*
	70048	C-17A	437th AW	*y/bl*
	FY07			
	77169	C-17A	436th AW	*y/r*
	77170	C-17A	436th AW	*y/r*
	77171	C-17A	436th AW	*y/r*
	77172	C-17A		
	77173	C-17A		
	77174	C-17A		
	77175	C-17A		
	77176	C-17A		
	77177	C-17A		
	77178	C-17A		
	77179	C-17A		
	77180	C-17A		
	FY98			
	80049	C-17A	62nd AW	*gn*
	80050	C-17A	62nd AW	*gn*
	80051	C-17A	97th AMW	*r/y*
	80052	C-17A	62nd AW	*gn*
	80053	C-17A	97th AMW	*r/y*
	80054	C-17A	437th AW	*y/bl*
	80055	C-17A	62nd AW	*gn*
	80056	C-17A	62nd AW	*gn*
	80057	C-17A	62nd AW	*y/bl*
	FY88			
	80265	C-17A	62nd AW	*gn*
	80266	C-17A	437th AW	*y/bl*
	FY08			
	88181	C-17A		
	88182	C-17A		
	88183	C-17A		
	88184	C-17A		
	88185	C-17A		
	88186	C-17A		
	88187	C-17A		
	88188	C-17A		
	88189	C-17A		
	88190	C-17A		
	FY99			
	90058	C-17A	62nd AW	*gn*
	90059	C-17A	97th AMW	*r/y*
	90060	C-17A	62nd AW	*gn*
	90061	C-17A	62nd AW	*gn*
	90062	C-17A	62nd AW	*gn*
	90063	C-17A	62nd AW	*gn*
	90064	C-17A	62nd AW	*gn*
	90165	C-17A	62nd AW	*gn*
	90166	C-17A	62nd AW	*gn*
	90167	C-17A	3rd Wg	*w/bk*
	90168	C-17A	3rd Wg	*w/bk*
	90169	C-17A	3rd Wg	*w/bk*
	90170	C-17A	3rd Wg	*w/bk*
	FY89			
	91189	C-17A	97th AMW	*r/y*
	91190	C-17A	437th AW	*y/bl*
	91191	C-17A	437th AW	*y/bl*
	91192	C-17A	437th AW	*y/bl*

Grumman

C-20 Gulfstream III/IV

89th AW, Andrews AFB, Maryland:
99th AS;
OSAC/PAT, US Army, Andrews AFB, Maryland;
Pacific Flight Detachment, Hickam AFB, Hawaii

C-20B Gulfstream III

Notes	Type	
	FY86	
	60201	89th AW
	60202	89th AW
	60203	89th AW
	60204	89th AW
	60206	89th AW
	60403	89th AW

C-20C Gulfstream III

Notes	Type	
	FY85	
	50049	89th AW
	50050	89th AW

C-20E Gulfstream III

Notes	Type	
	FY87	
	70139	Pacific Flt Det
	70140	OSAC/PAT

C-20F Gulfstream IV

Notes	Type	
	FY91	
	10108	OSAC/PAT

Boeing VC-25A

89th AW, Andrews AFB, Maryland

FY82
28000
FY92
29000

Pilatus U-28A

319th SOS/1st SOW, Hurlburt Field, Florida

FY05
50409
50419
50424
50447
50482
50573

Type | Notes

Boeing C-32
1st AS/89th AW, Andrews AFB, Maryland;
227th SOF/108th ARW, McGuire AFB, New Jersey
FY00
09001 C-32B 227th SOF
FY02
24452 C-32B 227th SOF
25001 C-32B 227th SOF
FY98
80001 C-32A 89th AW
80002 C-32A 89th AW
FY99
90003 C-32A 89th AW
90004 C-32A 89th AW

Gulfstream Aerospace C-37A Gulfstream V
6th AMW, MacDill AFB, Florida: 310th AS;
15th ABW, Hickam AFB, Hawaii: 65th AS;
89th AW, Andrews AFB, Maryland: 99th AS;
OSAC/PAT, US Army, Andrews AFB, Maryland
FY01
10028 6th AMW
10029 6th AMW
10030 6th AMW
10065 15th ABW
FY02
21863 OSAC/PAT
FY04
41778 OSAC/PAT
FY97
71944 OSAC/PAT
70400 89th AW
70401 89th AW
FY99
90402 89th AW
90404 89th AW

IAI C-38A Astra
201st AS/113th FW, DC ANG, Andrews AFB, Maryland
FY94
41569
41570

Boeing C-40
15th ABW, Hickam AFB, Hawaii: 65th AS;
86th AW, Ramstein, Germany: 76th AS;
89th AW, Andrews AFB, Maryland: 1st AS;
201st AS/113th FW, DC ANG, Andrews AFB, Maryland;
73rd AS/932nd AW AFRC, Scott AFB, Illinois
FY01
10005 C-40B 89th AW
10015 C-40B 15th ABW
10040 C-40B 89th AW
10041 C-40B 89th AW
FY02
20042 C-40B 86th AW
20201 C-40C 201st AS
20202 C-40C 201st AS
20203 C-40C 201st AS
20204 C-40C 201st AS
FY05
50730 C-40C 932nd AW
50932 C-40C 932nd AW

Boeing T-43A
562nd FTS/12th FTW, Randolph AFB, Texas [RA] (*bk/y*)
FY71
11404
FY72
20288
FY73
31150
31151
31152
31153$
31154
31156

Boeing B-52H Stratofortress
2nd BW, Barksdale AFB, Louisiana [LA]: 11th BS (*gd*), 20th BS (*bl*) & 96th BS (*r*);
23rd BS/5th BW, Minot AFB, North Dakota [MT] (*r/y*);
49th TES/53rd TEG, Barksdale AFB, Louisiana [OT];
93rd BS/917th Wg AFRC, Barksdale AFB, Louisiana [BD] (*y/bl*);
419th FLTS/412th TW Edwards AFB, California [ED]
FY60
00001 2nd BW *r*
00002 2nd BW *gd*
00003 93rd BS *y/bl*
00004 5th BW *r/y*
00005 5th BW *r/y*
00007 5th BW *r/y*
00008 2nd BW *r*
00009 5th BW *r/y*
00010 2nd BW *r*
00011 2nd BW *gd*
00012 2nd BW *r*
00013 2nd BW *r*
00014 2nd BW *bl*
00015 5th BW *r/y*
00016 2nd BW *r*
00017 2nd BW *gd*
00018 5th BW *r/y*
00019 2nd BW *r*
00020 2nd BW *bl*
00022 2nd BW *r*
00023 5th BW *r/y*
00024 5th BW *r/y*
00025 2nd BW *bl*
00026 5th BW *r/y*
00028 2nd BW *r*
00029 5th BW *r/y*
00030 2nd BW *bl*
00031 53rd TEG
00032 2nd BW *gd*
00033 5th BW *r/y*
00034 5th BW *r/y*
00035 2nd BW *gd*
00036 419th FLTS
00037 2nd BW *r*
00038 2nd BW *r*
00041 93rd BS *y/bl*
00042 93rd BS *y/bl*
00043 2nd BW *bl*
00044 5th BW *r/y*
00045 93rd BS *y/bl*

Notes	Type		
	00046	2nd BW	*bl*
	00047	2nd BW	
	00048	2nd BW	*bl*
	00049	53rd TEG	
	00050	412th TW	
	00051	5th BW	*r/y*
	00052	2nd BW	*r*
	00053	2nd BW	*bl*
	00054	2nd BW	*gd*
	00055	5th BW	*r/y*
	00056	5th BW	*r/y*
	00057	2nd BW	*gd*
	00058	2nd BW	*gd*
	00059	2nd BW	*r*
	00060	5th BW	*r/y*
	00061	2nd BW	*gd*
	00062	2nd BW	*bl*
	FY61		
	10001	5th BW	*r/y*
	10002	2nd BW	*bl*
	10003	2nd BW	*bl*
	10004	2nd BW	*bl*
	10005	5th BW	*r/y*
	10006	2nd BW	*bl*
	10007	5th BW	*r/y*
	10008	93rd BS	*y/bl*
	10009	2nd BW	*r*
	10010	2nd BW	*bl*
	10011	2nd BW	*gd*
	10012	2nd BW	*r*
	10013	2nd BW	*r*
	10014	5th BW	*r/y*
	10015	2nd BW	*gd*
	10016	2nd BW	*gd*
	10017	93rd BS	*y/bl*
	10018	5th BW	*r/y*
	10019	2nd BW	*gd*
	10020	2nd BW	*gd*
	10021	93rd BS	*y/bl*
	10022	93rd BS	*y/bl*
	10023	2nd BW	*bl*
	10024	2nd BW	*r*
	10027	5th BW	*r/y*
	10028	2nd BW	*bl*
	10029	93rd BS	*y/bl*
	10031	2nd BW	*r*
	10032	5th BW	*r/yl*
	10034	5th BW	*r/y*
	10035	5th BW	*r/y*
	10036	2nd BW	*bl*
	10038	2nd BW	*gd*
	10039	2nd BW	*gd*
	10040	5th BW	*r/y*

Lockheed F-117A Nighthawk

49th FW, Holloman AFB, New Mexico [HO]: 8th FS (*y*) & 9th FS (*r*)
445th FLTS/412th TW, Edwards AFB, California [ED]

Type				
79-783	(79-10783)	ED		
79-784	(79-10784)	ED		
80-786	(80-0786)	HO	*r*	
80-787	(80-0787)	HO	*y*	
80-788	(80-0788)	HO	*y*	
80-791	(80-0791)	HO	*y*	
81-794	(81-10794)	HO	*r*	
81-796	(81-10796)	HO	*r*	[49th OG]
81-797	(81-10797)	HO	*r*	
81-798	(81-10798)	HO	*r*	[49th FW]
82-799	(82-0799)	HO	*r*	
82-800	(82-0800)	HO	*y*	[8th FS]
82-801	(82-0801)	HO		
82-802	(82-0802)	HO	*y*	
82-804	(82-0804)	HO	*y*	
82-805	(82-0805)	HO	*r*	
83-807	(83-0807)	HO	*r*	
83-808	(83-0808)	HO	*r*	
84-809	(84-0809)	HO	*r*	[9th FS]
84-810	(84-0810)	HO	*r*	
84-811	(84-0811)	ED		
84-812	(84-0812)	HO		
84-824	(84-0824)	HO	*r*	
84-825	(84-0825)	HO	*y*	
84-826	(84-0826)	HO	*r*	
84-827	(84-0827)	HO	*y*	
84-828	(84-0828)	HO	*r*	
85-813	(85-0813)	HO	*r*	
85-814	(85-0814)	HO	*r*	
85-816	(85-0816)	HO	*y*	[49th FW]
85-818	(85-0818)	HO	*y*	
85-819	(85-0819)	HO	*y*	[49th FW]
85-829	(85-0829)	HO	*r*	
85-830	(85-0830)	HO	*r*	
85-831	(85-0831)	ED		
85-833	(85-0833)	HO	*r*	
85-834	(85-0834)	HO	*y*	
85-836	(85-0836)	HO	*r*	
86-821	(86-0821)	HO	*r*	
86-822	(86-0822)	HO		
86-823	(86-0823)	HO	*y*	
86-837	(86-0837)	HO	*y*	
86-838	(86-0838)	HO	*y*	
86-839	(86-0839)	HO	*y*	
86-840	(86-0840)	HO	*y*	
88-841	(88-0841)	HO	*r*	[9th FS]
88-842	(88-0842)	HO	*y*	
88-843	(88-0843)	HO	*y*	

Lockheed C-130 Hercules

1st SOS/353rd SOG, Kadena AB, Japan;
4th SOS/1st SOW, Hurlburt Field, Florida;
7th SOS/352nd SOG, RAF Mildenhall, UK;
8th SOS/1st SOW, Duke Field, Florida;
9th SOS/1st OG, Eglin AFB, Florida;
15th SOS/1st SOW, Hurlburt Field, Florida;
16th SOS/1st SOW, Hurlburt Field, Florida;
17th SOS/353rd SOG, Kadena AB, Japan;
37th AS/86th AW, Ramstein AB, Germany [RS] (*bl/w*);
39th RQS/920th RQW AFRC, Patrick AFB, Florida [FL];
41st ECS/55th Wg, Davis-Monthan AFB, Arizona [DM] (*bl*);
41st RQS/23rd Wg, Moody AFB, Georgia [FT] (*bl*);
43rd AW, Pope AFB, North Carolina [FT]:
2nd AS (*gn/bl*);
43rd ECS/55th Wg, Davis-Monthan AFB, Arizona [DM] (*r*);
53rd WRS/403rd AW AFRC, Keesler AFB, Missouri;
58th SOW, Kirtland AFB, New Mexico:
550th SOS;
67th SOS/352nd SOG, RAF Mildenhall, UK;
71st RQS/23rd Wg, Moody AFB, Georgia [FT] (*bl*);

Type | Notes

73rd SOS/27th SOW, Cannon AFB, New Mexico;
79th RQS/563rd RQG, Davis-Monthan AFB, Arizona [DM];
95th AS/440th AW AFRC, Pope AFB, North Carolina (*w/r*);
96th AS/934th AW AFRC, Minneapolis/St Paul, Minnesota (*pr*);
102nd RQS/106th RQW, Suffolk Field, New York ANG [LI];
105th AS/118th AW, Nashville, Tennessee ANG (*r*);
109th AS/133rd AW, Minneapolis/St Paul, Minnesota ANG [MN] (*pr/bk*);
115th AS/146th AW, Channel Island ANGS, California ANG [CI] (*gn*);
122nd FS/159th FW, NAS New Orleans, Louisiana ANG [JZ];
130th AS/130th AW, Yeager Int'l Airport, Charleston West Virginia ANG [WV] (*pr/y*);
130th RQS/129th RQW, Moffet Field, California ANG [CA] (*bl*);
135th AS/135th AW, Martin State Airport, Maryland ANG [MD] (*bk/y*);
139th AS/109th AW, Schenectady, New York ANG [NY];
142nd AS/166th AW, New Castle County Airport, Delaware ANG [DE] (*bl*);
143rd AS/143rd AW, Quonset, Rhode Island ANG [RI] (*r*);
144th AS/176th CW, Kulis ANGB, Alaska ANG (*bk/y*);
154th TS/189th AW, Little Rock, Arkansas ANG (*r*);
156th AS/145th AW, Charlotte, North Carolina ANG [NC] (*bl*);
157th FS/169th FW, McEntire ANGS, South Carolina ANG [SC];
158th AS/165th AW, Savannah, Georgia ANG (*r*);
159th FS/125th FW, Jacksonville, Florida ANG;
164th AS/179th AW, Mansfield, Ohio ANG [OH] (*bl*);
165th AS/123rd AW, Standiford Field, Kentucky ANG [KY];
167th AS/167th AW, Martinsburg, West Virginia ANG [WV] (*r*);
169th AS/182nd AW, Peoria, Illinois ANG [IL];
180th AS/139th AW, Rosecrans Memorial Airport, Missouri ANG [XP] (*y*);
181st AS/136th AW, NAS Dallas, Texas ANG (*bl/w*);
187th AS/153rd AW, Cheyenne, Wyoming ANG [WY];
189th AS/124th Wg, Boise, Idaho ANG [ID];
192nd AS/152nd AW, Reno, Nevada ANG [NV] (*w*);
193rd SOS/193rd SOW, Harrisburg, Pennsylvania ANG [PA];
198th AS/156th AW, San Juan, Puerto Rico ANG;
204th AS/154th Wg, Hickam AFB, Hawaii ANG [HH];
210th RQS/176th CW, Kulis ANGB, Alaska ANG [AK];
314th AW, Little Rock AFB, Arkansas: 48th AS (*y*) & 62nd AS (*bl*);
317th AG, Dyess AFB, Texas: 39th AS (*r*) & 40th AS (*bl*);
327th AS/913th AW AFRC, NAS Willow Grove, Pennsylvania (*bk*);
328th AS/914th AW AFRC, Niagara Falls, New York [NF] (*bl*);
357th AS/908th AW AFRC, Maxwell AFB, Alabama (*bl*);
374th AW, Yokota AB, Japan [YJ]: 36th AS (*r*);
412th TW Edwards AFB, California: 452nd FLTS [ED];
463rd AG Little Rock AFB, Arkansas [LK]: 41st AS (*w*), 50th AS (*r*) & 61st AS (*gn*);
645th Materiel Sqn, Palmdale, California [D4];
700th AS/94th AW AFRC, Dobbins ARB, Georgia [DB] (*bl*);
711th SOS/919th SOW AFRC, Duke Field, Florida;
731st AS/302nd AW AFRC, Peterson AFB, Colorado (*pr/w*);
757th AS/910th AW AFRC, Youngstown ARS, Ohio [YO] (*bl*);
758th AS/911th AW AFRC, Pittsburgh ARS, Pennsylvania (*bk/y*);
773rd AS/910th AW AFRC, Youngstown ARS, Ohio [YO] (*r*);
815th AS/403rd AW AFRC, Keesler AFB, Missouri [KT] (*r*);
LMTAS, Marietta, Georgia

FY90			
00162	MC-130H	15th SOS	
00163	AC-130U	4th SOS	
00164	AC-130U	4th SOS	
00165	AC-130U	4th SOS	
00166	AC-130U	4th SOS	
00167	AC-130U	4th SOS	
FY80			
00320	C-130H	158th AS	*r*
00321	C-130H	158th AS	*r*
00322	C-130H	158th AS	*r*
00323	C-130H	158th AS	*r*
00324	C-130H	158th AS	*r*
00325	C-130H	158th AS	*r*
00326	C-130H	158th AS	*r*
00332	C-130H	158th AS	*r*
FY90			
01057	C-130H	142nd AS	*bl*
01058	C-130H	189th AS	
FY70			
01260	C-130E	37th AS	*bl/w*
01264	C-130E	37th AS	*bl/w*
01271	C-130E	37th AS	*bl/w*
FY90			
01791	C-130H	164th AS	*bl*
01792	C-130H	164th AS	*bl*
01793	C-130H	164th AS	*bl*
01794	C-130H	164th AS	*bl*
01795	C-130H	164th AS	*bl*
01796	C-130H	164th AS	*bl*
01797	C-130H	164th AS	*bl*
01798	C-130H	164th AS	*bl*
FY00			
01934	EC-130J	193rd SOS	
FY90			
02103	HC-130N	210th RQS	
09107	C-130H	757th AS	*bl*
09108	C-130H	757th AS	*bl*

Notes	Type			
	FY81			
	10626	C-130H	700th AS	*bl*
	10627	C-130H	700th AS	*bl*
	10628	C-130H	700th AS	*bl*
	10629	C-130H	700th AS	*bl*
	10630	C-130H	700th AS	*bl*
	10631	C-130H	700th AS	*bl*
	FY68			
	10935	C-130E	37th AS	*bl/w*
	10941	C-130E	43rd AW	*gn/bl*
	10948	C-130E	463rd AG	*gn*
	FY91			
	11231	C-130H	165th AS	
	11232	C-130H	165th AS	
	11233	C-130H	165th AS	
	11234	C-130H	165th AS	
	11235	C-130H	165th AS	
	11236	C-130H	165th AS	
	11237	C-130H	165th AS	
	11238	C-130H	165th AS	
	11239	C-130H	165th AS	
	FY01			
	11461	C-130J	115th AS	*gn*
	11462	C-130J	115th AS	*gn*
	FY91			
	11651	C-130H	189th AS	
	11652	C-130H	189th AS	
	11653	C-130H	189th AS	
	FY01			
	11935	EC-130J	193rd SOS	
	FY61			
	12358	C-130E	154th TS	*r*
	12367	C-130E	314th AW	*bl*
	12369	C-130E	198th AS	
	12370	C-130E	463rd AG	*gn*
	12372	C-130E	115th AS	*gn*
	FY64			
	14852	HC-130P	71st RQS	*bl*
	14853	HC-130P	71st RQS	*bl*
	14854	MC-130P	9th SOS	
	14855	HC-130P	39th RQS	
	14858	MC-130P	58th SOW	
	14859	C-130E	67th SOS	
	14860	HC-130P	79th RQS	
	14861	C-130H	105th AS	*r*
	14862	EC-130H	55th Wg	
	14863	HC-130P	71st RQS	*bl*
	14864	HC-130P	39th RQS	
	14865	HC-130P	71st RQS	*bl*
	14866	C-130H	159th FS	
	17681	C-130E	37th AS	*bl/w*
	18240	C-130E	37th AS	*bl/w*
	FY91			
	19141	C-130H	96th AS	*pr*
	19142	C-130H	96th AS	*pr*
	19143	C-130H	96th AS	*pr*
	19144	C-130H	96th AS	*pr*
	FY82			
	20054	C-130H	144th AS	*bk/y*
	20055	C-130H	144th AS	*bk/y*
	20056	C-130H	144th AS	*bk/y*
	20057	C-130H	144th AS	*bk/y*
	20058	C-130H	144th AS	*bk/y*
	20059	C-130H	144th AS	*bk/y*
	20060	C-130H	144th AS	*bk/y*
	20061	C-130H	144th AS	*bk/y*
	FY02			
	20314	C-130J	314th AW	*y*
	FY92			
	20253	AC-130U	4th SOS	
	20547	C-130H	463rd AG	*r*
	20548	C-130H	463rd AG	*r*

Notes	Type			
	20549	C-130H	463rd AG	*r*
	20550	C-130H	463rd AG	*r*
	20551	C-130H	463rd AG	*r*
	20552	C-130H	463rd AG	*r*
	20553	C-130H	463rd AG	*r*
	20554	C-130H	463rd AG	*r*
	21094	LC-130H	139th AS	
	21095	LC-130H	139th AS	
	FY72			
	21289	C-130E	463rd AG	*gn*
	21290	C-130E	463rd AG	*gn*
	21292	C-130E	463rd AG	*gn*
	21299	C-130E	37th AS	*bl/w*
	FY02			
	21434	C-130J	143rd AS	*r*
	FY92			
	21451	C-130H	169th AS	
	21452	C-130H	169th AS	
	21453	C-130H	156th AS	*bl*
	21454	C-130H	156th AS	*bl*
	FY02			
	21463	C-130J	115th AS	*gn*
	21464	C-130J	115th AS	*gn*
	FY92			
	21531	C-130H	187th AS	
	21532	C-130H	187th AS	
	21533	C-130H	187th AS	
	21534	C-130H	187th AS	
	21535	C-130H	187th AS	
	21536	C-130H	187th AS	
	21537	C-130H	187th AS	
	21538	C-130H	187th AS	
	FY62			
	21784	C-130E	154th TS	*r*
	21786	C-130E	314th AW	
	21787	C-130E	154th TS	*r*
	21788	C-130E	154th TS	*r*
	21789	C-130E	314th AW	*bk*
	21791	MC-130E	17th SOS	
	21792	C-130E	463rd AG	*gn*
	21798	C-130E	314th AW	*bk*
	21799	C-130E	317th AG	
	21801	C-130E	154th TS	*r*
	21804	C-130E	314th AW	*bl*
	21806	C-130E	317th AG	
	21808	C-130E	314th AW	*bk*
	21810	C-130E	314th AW	*bl*
	21811	C-130E	43rd AG	
	21817	C-130E	189th AS	
	21820	C-130E	198th AS	
	21823	C-130E	43rd AW	
	21824	C-130E	154th TS	*r*
	21829	C-130E		
	21833	C-130E	43rd AW	
	21834	C-130E	463rd AG	*gn*
	21835	C-130E	37th AS	*bl/w*
	21836	HC-130P	71st RQS	*bl*
	21837	C-130E	43rd AW	*gn/bl*
	21842	C-130E	154th TS	*r*
	21843	MC-130E	711th SOS	
	21844	C-130E	314th AW	
	21846	C-130E	189th AS	
	21847	C-130E	43rd AW	
	21848	C-130E	314th AW	*bk*
	21850	C-130E	314th AW	*bk*
	21851	C-130E	43rd AW	
	21852	C-130E	327th AS	*bk*
	21855	C-130E	43rd AW	
	21856	C-130E	463rd AG	*gn*
	21857	C-130E	16th SOS	
	21858	C-130E	198th AS	

Type				Notes
21859	C-130E	122nd FS		
21862	C-130E	463rd AG		
21863	EC-130E			
21864	C-130E	43rd AW	gn/bl	
FY92				
23021	C-130H	773rd AS	*r*	
23022	C-130H	328th AS	*bl*	
23023	C-130H	773rd AS	*r*	
23024	C-130H	328th AS	*bl*	
23281	C-130H	328th AS	*bl*	
23282	C-130H	328th AS	*bl*	
23283	C-130H	328th AS	*bl*	
23284	C-130H	328th AS	*bl*	
23285	C-130H	328th AS	*bl*	
23286	C-130H	328th AS	*bl*	
23287	C-130H	328th AS	*bl*	
23288	C-130H	328th AS	*bl*	
FY02				
28155	C-130J	815th AS	*r*	
FY83				
30486	C-130H	139th AS		
30487	C-130H	139th AS		
30488	C-130H	139th AS		
30489	C-130H	139th AS		
30490	LC-130H	139th AS		
30491	LC-130H	139th AS		
30492	LC-130H	139th AS		
30493	LC-130H	139th AS		
FY93				
31036	C-130H	463rd AG	*r*	
31037	C-130H	463rd AG	*r*	
31038	C-130H	463rd AG	*r*	
31039	C-130H	463rd AG	*r*	
31040	C-130H	463rd AG	*r*	
31041	C-130H	463rd AG	*r*	
31096	LC-130H	139th AS		
FY83				
31212	MC-130H	15th SOS		
FY93				
31455	C-130H	156th AS	*bl*	
31456	C-130H	156th AS	*bl*	
31457	C-130H	156th AS	*bl*	
31458	C-130H	156th AS	*bl*	
31459	C-130H	156th AS	*bl*	
31561	C-130H	156th AS	*bl*	
31562	C-130H	156th AS	*bl*	
31563	C-130H	156th AS	*bl*	
FY73				
31580	EC-130H	43rd ECS	*r*	
31581	EC-130H	43rd ECS	*r*	
31582	C-130H	317th AG	*r*	
31583	EC-130H	43rd ECS	*r*	
31584	EC-130H	43rd ECS	*r*	
31585	EC-130H	41st ECS	*bl*	
31586	EC-130H	41st ECS	*bl*	
31587	EC-130H	55th Wg		
31588	EC-130H	41st ECS	*bl*	
31590	EC-130H	43rd ECS	*r*	
31592	EC-130H	41st ECS	*bl*	
31594	EC-130H	41st ECS	*bl*	
31595	EC-130H	43rd ECS	*r*	
31597	C-130H	317th AG	*r*	
31598	C-130H	317th AG	*r*	
FY93				
32041	C-130H	169th AS		
32042	C-130H	167th AS	*r*	
32104	HC-130N	210th RQS		
32105	HC-130N	210th RQS		
32106	HC-130N	210th RQS		
37311	C-130H	187th AS		
37312	C-130H	169th AS		
37313	C-130H	187th AS		

Type				Notes
37314	C-130H	187th AS		
FY63				
37764	C-130E	463rd AG	*gn*	
37769	C-130E	463rd AG	*gn*	
37770	C-130E	43rd AW	*gn/bl*	
37782	C-130E	43rd AW	*gn/or*	
37784	C-130E	314th AW	*bl*	
37786	C-130E	198th AS		
37791	C-130E	314th AW	*bl*	
37792	C-130E	37th AS	*bl/w*	
37796	C-130E	314th AW	*bk*	
37800	C-130E	154th TS	*r*	
37811	C-130E	143rd AS	*r*	
37812	C-130E	154th TS	*r*	
37814	C-130E	71st RQS	*bl*	
37815	C-130E	193rd SOS		
37816	EC-130E	16th SOW		
37817	C-130E	463rd AW	*gn*	
37818	C-130E	169th AS		
37823	C-130E	43rd AW		
37824	C-130E	143rd AS	*r*	
37825	C-130E	37th AS	*bl/w*	
37828	EC-130E	193rd SOS		
37829	C-130E	314th AW	*bk*	
37831	C-130E	463rd AG	*gn*	
37832	C-130E	314th AW	*bk*	
37833	C-130E	327th AS	*bk*	
37834	C-130E	43rd AW	*gn/bl*	
37837	C-130E	43rd AW		
37840	C-130E	37th AS	*bl/w*	
37845	C-130E	463rd AG		
37847	C-130E	314th AW		
37848	C-130E	43rd AW		
37851	C-130E	198th AS		
37852	C-130E	463rd AG	*gn*	
37853	C-130E	43rd AW		
37856	C-130E	463rd AG	*gn*	
37859	C-130E	143rd AS	*r*	
37864	C-130E	314th AW	*bl*	
37867	C-130E	327th AS	*bk*	
37868	C-130E	317th AG		
37872	C-130E	463rd AG	*gn*	
37877	C-130E	314th AW		
37879	C-130E	37th AS	*bl/w*	
37883	C-130E	43rd AW		
37884	C-130E	463rd AG	*gn*	
37885	C-130E	37th AS	*bl/w*	
37889	C-130E	143rd AS	*r*	
37890	C-130E	314th AW	*bl*	
37894	C-130E	463rd AG	*gn*	
37895	C-130E	198th AS		
37896	C-130E	314th AW	*bk*	
37897	C-130E	37th AS	*bl/w*	
FY03				
38154	C-130J	815th AS	*r*	
FY63				
39810	C-130E	71st RQS	*bl*	
39812	C-130E	314th AW	*bk*	
39813	C-130E	314th AW		
39815	C-130E	198th AS		
FY84				
40204	C-130H	700th AS	*bl*	
40205	C-130H	700th AS	*bl*	
40206	C-130H	142nd AS	*bl*	
40207	C-130H	142nd AS	*bl*	
40208	C-130H	142nd AS	*bl*	
40209	C-130H	142nd AS	*bl*	
40210	C-130H	142nd AS	*bl*	
40212	C-130H	142nd AS	*bl*	
40213	C-130H	142nd AS	*bl*	
40476	MC-130H	7th SOS		

Notes	Type			
	FY64			
	40502	C-130E	37th AS	*bl/w*
	40510	C-130E	198th AS	
	40512	C-130E	314th AW	
	40515	C-130E	198th AS	
	40519	C-130E	314th AW	*bl*
	40520	C-130E	157th FS	
	40521	C-130E	159th FS	
	40523	MC-130E	8th SOS	
	40526	C-130E	154th TS	*r*
	40527	C-130E	37th AS	*bl/w*
	40544	C-130E	198th AS	
	40551	MC-130E	711th SOS	
	40561	MC-130E	711th SOS	
	40562	MC-130E	711th SOS	
	40566	MC-130E	711th SOS	
	40567	MC-130E	8th SOS	
	40568	MC-130E	711th SOS	
	40571	MC-130E	711th SOS	
	40572	MC-130E	412th TW	
	FY74			
	41658	C-130H	374th AW	*r*
	41659	C-130H	374th AW	*r*
	41660	C-130H	374th AW	*r*
	41661	C-130H	317th AG	
	41663	C-130H	317th AG	*bl*
	41664	C-130H	317th AG	*bl*
	41665	C-130H	317th AG	*bl*
	41666	C-130H	317th AG	*bl*
	41667	C-130H	317th AG	*bl*
	41668	C-130H	374th AW	*r*
	41669	C-130H	317th AG	*bl*
	41670	C-130H	317th AG	*r*
	41671	C-130H	317th AG	*bl*
	41673	C-130H	317th AG	*bl*
	41674	C-130H	317th AG	*r*
	41675	C-130H	317th AG	*r*
	41676	C-130H	317th AG	
	41677	C-130H	317th AG	
	41679	C-130H	317th AG	*bl*
	41680	C-130H	317th AG	*r*
	41682	C-130H	317th AG	
	41684	C-130H	374th AW	*r*
	41685	C-130H	374th AW	*r*
	41687	C-130H	317th AG	*r*
	41688	C-130H	317th AG	*bl*
	41689	C-130H	317th AG	*bl*
	41690	C-130H	374th AW	*r*
	41691	C-130H	317th AG	*r*
	41692	C-130H	374th AW	*r*
	42061	C-130H	317th AG	*r*
	42062	C-130H	374th AW	*r*
	42063	C-130H	317th AG	*bl*
	42065	C-130H	317th AG	*bl*
	42066	C-130H	374th AW	*r*
	42067	C-130H	317th AG	*r*
	42069	C-130H	317th AG	*r*
	42070	C-130H	374th AW	*r*
	42071	C-130H	374th AW	*r*
	42072	C-130H	317th AG	*bl*
	42130	C-130H	317th AG	*r*
	42131	C-130H	374th AW	*r*
	42132	C-130H	317th AG	*r*
	42133	C-130H	374th AW	*r*
	42134	C-130H	317th AG	*r*
	FY04			
	43142	C-130J	314th AW	*y*
	43143	C-130J	314th AW	*y*
	43144	C-130J	314th AW	*y*
	FY94			
	46701	C-130H	169th AS	
	46702	C-130H	167th AS	*r*

Notes	Type			
	46703	C-130H	169th AS	
	46704	C-130H	167th AS	*r*
	46705	C-130H	167th AS	*r*
	46706	C-130H	167th AS	*r*
	46707	C-130H	130th AS	*pr/y*
	46708	C-130H	130th AS	*pr/y*
	47310	C-130H	731st AS	*pr/w*
	47315	C-130H	731st AS	*pr/w*
	47316	C-130H	731st AS	*pr/w*
	47317	C-130H	731st AS	*pr/w*
	47318	C-130H	731st AS	*pr/w*
	47319	C-130H	731st AS	*pr/w*
	47320	C-130H	731st AS	*pr/w*
	47321	C-130H	731st AS	*pr/w*
	FY04			
	48151	C-130J	115th AS	*gn*
	48152	C-130J	115th AS	*gn*
	48153	C-130J	815th AS	*r*
	FY85			
	50011	MC-130H	15th SOS	
	50035	C-130H	357th AS	*bl*
	50036	C-130H	357th AS	*bl*
	50037	C-130H	357th AS	*bl*
	50038	C-130H	357th AS	*bl*
	50039	C-130H	357th AS	*bl*
	50040	C-130H	357th AS	*bl*
	50041	C-130H	773rd AS	*r*
	50042	C-130H	357th AS	*bl*
	FY65			
	50962	TC-130H	43rd ECS	*r*
	50963	C-130H	105th AS	*r*
	50964	HC-130P	79th RQS	
	50966	C-130H	105th AS	*r*
	50967	HC-130H	122nd FS	
	50968	C-130H	105th AS	*r*
	50970	HC-130P	39th RQS	
	50971	MC-130P	58th SOW	
	50973	HC-130P	71st RQS	*bl*
	50974	HC-130P	102nd RQS	
	50975	MC-130P	58th SOW	
	50976	HC-130P	39th RQS	
	50977	HC-130H	39th RQS	
	50978	HC-130P	102nd RQS	
	50979	NC-130H	46th TW	
	50981	HC-130P	71st RQS	*bl*
	50982	HC-130P	41st RQS	*bl*
	50983	MC-130P	71st RQS	*bl*
	50984	C-130H	105th AS	*r*
	50985	C-130H	327th AS	*bk*
	50986	HC-130P	71st RQS	*bl*
	50987	HC-130P	71st RQS	*bl*
	50988	HC-130P	71st RQS	*bl*
	50989	EC-130H	41st ECS	*bl*
	50991	MC-130P	9th SOS	
	50992	MC-130P	17th SOS	
	50993	MC-130P	17th SOS	
	50994	MC-130P	17th SOS	
	FY95			
	51001	C-130H	109th AS	*pr/bk*
	51002	C-130H	109th AS	*pr/bk*
	FY85			
	51361	C-130H	181st AS	*bl/w*
	51362	C-130H	181st AS	*bl/w*
	51363	C-130H	181st AS	*bl/w*
	51364	C-130H	181st AS	*bl/w*
	51365	C-130H	181st AS	*bl/w*
	51366	C-130H	181st AS	*bl/w*
	51367	C-130H	181st AS	*bl/w*
	51368	C-130H	181st AS	*bl/w*
	FY05			
	51435	C-130J	143rd AS	*r*
	51436	C-130J	143rd AS	*r*

Type				Notes
51465	C-130J	115th AS	*gn*	
51466	C-130J	115th AS	*gn*	
53145	C-130J	463rd AG	*w*	
53146	C-130J	314th AW	*y*	
53147	C-130J	314th AW	*y*	
FY95				
56709	C-130H	156th AS	*bl*	
56710	C-130H	156th AS	*bl*	
56711	C-130H	156th AS	*bl*	
56712	C-130H	156th AS	*bl*	
FY05				
58152	C-130J	815th AS	*r*	
58156	C-130J	815th AS	*r*	
58157	C-130J	815th AS	*r*	
58158	C-130J	815th AS	*r*	
FY66				
60212	HC-130P	130th RQS	*bl*	
60215	MC-130P	17th SOS		
60216	HC-130P	130th RQS	*bl*	
60217	MC-130P	9th SOS		
60219	HC-130P	130th RQS	*bl*	
60220	MC-130P	102nd RQS		
60221	HC-130P	58th SOW		
60222	HC-130P	102nd RQS		
60223	MC-130P	9th SOS		
60224	HC-130P	79th RQS		
60225	MC-130P	9th SOS		
FY86				
60410	C-130H	95th AS	*w/r*	
60411	C-130H	95th AS	*w/r*	
60412	C-130H	95th AS	*w/r*	
60413	C-130H	95th AS	*w/r*	
60414	C-130H	95th AS	*w/r*	
60415	C-130H	95th AS	*w/r*	
60418	C-130H	95th AS	*w/r*	
60419	C-130H	95th AS	*w/r*	
FY96				
61003	C-130H	109th AS	*pr/bk*	
61004	C-130H	109th AS	*pr/bk*	
61005	C-130H	109th AS	*pr/bk*	
61006	C-130H	109th AS	*pr/bk*	
61007	C-130H	109th AS	*pr/bk*	
61008	C-130H	109th AS	*pr/bk*	
FY86				
61391	C-130H	180th AS	*y*	
61392	C-130H	180th AS	*y*	
61393	C-130H	180th AS	*y*	
61394	C-130H	180th AS	*y*	
61395	C-130H	180th AS	*y*	
61396	C-130H	180th AS	*y*	
61397	C-130H	180th AS	*y*	
61398	C-130H	180th AS	*y*	
FY06				
61437	C-130J	143rd AS	*r*	
61438	C-130J	143rd AS	*r*	
61467	C-130J	115th AS	*gn*	
FY86				
61699	MC-130H			
FY76				
63300	LC-130R	139th AS		
63302	LC-130R	139th AS		
FY06				
64631	C-130J	463rd AG	*w*	
64632	C-130J	463rd AG	*w*	
64633	C-130J	463rd AG	*w*	
64634	C-130J	463rd AG	*w*	
FY96				
65300	WC-130J	53rd WRS		
65301	WC-130J	53rd WRS		
65302	WC-130J	53rd WRS		
67322	C-130H	731st AS	*pr/w*	
67323	C-130H	731st AS	*pr/w*	
67324	C-130H	731st AS	*pr/w*	
67325	C-130H	731st AS	*pr/w*	
68153	EC-130J	193rd SOS		
68154	EC-130J	193rd SOS		
FY06				
68159	C-130J	815th AS	*r*	
FY87				
70023	MC-130H	7th SOS		
70024	MC-130H	7th SOS		
70125	MC-130H	15th SOS		
70126	MC-130H	7th SOS		
70128	AC-130U	4th SOS		
FY97				
71351	C-130J	135th AS	*bk/y*	
71352	C-130J	135th AS	*bk/y*	
71353	C-130J	135th AS	*bk/y*	
71354	C-130J	135th AS	*bk/y*	
71931	EC-130J	193rd SOS		
75303	WC-130J	53rd WRS		
75304	WC-130J	53rd WRS		
75305	WC-130J	53rd WRS		
75306	WC-130J	53rd WRS		
FY87				
79281	C-130H	96th AS	*pr*	
79282	C-130H	95th AS	*w/r*	
79283	C-130H	96th AS	*pr*	
79284	MC-130W			
79285	C-130H	96th AS	*pr*	
79286	MC-130W	8th SOS		
79287	C-130H	96th AS	*pr*	
79288	MC-130W			
FY88				
80191	MC-130H	1st SOS		
80192	MC-130H	7th SOS		
80193	MC-130H	16th SOS		
80194	MC-130H	58th SOW		
80195	MC-130H	1st SOS		
80264	MC-130H	1st SOS		
FY78				
80806	C-130H	758th AS	*bk/y*	
80807	C-130H	758th AS	*bk/y*	
80808	C-130H	758th AS	*bk/y*	
80809	C-130H	758th AS	*bk/y*	
80810	C-130H	758th AS	*bk/y*	
80811	C-130H	758th AS	*bk/y*	
80812	C-130H	758th AS	*bk/y*	
80813	C-130H	758th AS	*bk/y*	
FY88				
81301	MC-130W			
81302	MC-130W			
81303	MC-130W			
81304	MC-130W			
81305	MC-130W			
81306	MC-130W			
81307	MC-130W	58th SOW		
81308	MC-130W	73rd SOS		
FY98				
81355	C-130J	135th AS	*bk/y*	
81356	C-130J	135th AS	*bk/y*	
81357	C-130J	135th AS	*bk/y*	
81358	C-130J	135th AS	*bk/y*	
FY88				
81803	MC-130H	1st SOS		
FY98				
81932	EC-130J	193rd SOS		
FY88				
82101	HC-130N	102nd RQS		
82102	HC-130N	71st RQS	*bl*	
84401	C-130H	95th AS	*w/r*	
84402	C-130H	95th AS	*w/r*	
84403	C-130H	95th AS	*w/r*	
84404	C-130H	95th AS	*w/r*	

Notes	Type			
	84405	C-130H	95th AS	*w/r*
	84406	C-130H	95th AS	*w/r*
	84407	C-130H	95th AS	*w/r*
	FY98			
	85307	WC-130J	53rd WRS	
	85308	WC-130J	53rd WRS	
	FY89			
	90280	MC-130H		
	90281	MC-130H	15th SOS	
	90282	MC-130H	7th SOS	
	90283	MC-130H	15th SOS	
	FY79			
	90473	C-130H	192nd AS	*w*
	90474	C-130H	192nd AS	*w*
	90475	C-130H	192nd AS	*w*
	90476	C-130H	192nd AS	*w*
	90477	C-130H	192nd AS	*w*
	90478	C-130H	192nd AS	*w*
	90479	C-130H	192nd AS	*w*
	90480	C-130H	192nd AS	*w*
	FY89			
	90509	AC-130U	4th SOS	
	90510	AC-130U	4th SOS	
	90511	AC-130U	4th SOS	
	90512	AC-130U	4th SOS	
	90513	AC-130U	4th SOS	
	90514	AC-130U	4th SOS	
	91051	C-130H	105th AS	*r*
	91052	AC-130U		
	91053	AC-130U		
	91054	AC-130U		
	91055	C-130H	105th AS	*r*
	91056	AC-130U	LMTAS	
	91181	C-130H	105th AS	*r*
	91182	C-130H	105th AS	*r*
	91183	C-130H	105th AS	*r*
	91184	C-130H	105th AS	*r*
	91185	C-130H	105th AS	*r*
	91186	C-130H	105th AS	*r*
	91187	C-130H	105th AS	*r*
	91188	C-130H	105th AS	*r*
	FY99			
	91431	C-130J	143rd AS	*r*
	91432	C-130J	143rd AS	*r*
	91433	C-130J	143rd AS	*r*
	91933	EC-130J	193rd SOS	
	95309	WC-130J	53rd WRS	
	FY69			
	95819	MC-130P	9th SOS	
	95820	MC-130P	9th SOS	
	95821	MC-130P	58th SOW	
	95822	MC-130P	9th SOS	
	95823	MC-130P	9th SOS	
	95825	MC-130P	67th SOS	
	95826	MC-130P	67th SOS	
	95827	MC-130P	9th SOS	
	95828	MC-130P	67th SOS	
	95829	HC-130N	58th SOW	
	95830	HC-130N	39th RQS	
	95831	MC-130P	67th SOS	
	95832	MC-130P	67th SOS	
	95833	HC-130N	58th SOW	
	96568	AC-130H	16th SOS	
	96569	AC-130H	16th SOS	
	96570	AC-130H	16th SOS	
	96572	AC-130H	16th SOS	
	96573	AC-130H	16th SOS	
	96574	AC-130H	16th SOS	
	96575	AC-130H	16th SOS	
	96577	AC-130H	16th SOS	
	FY89			
	99101	C-130H	357th AS	*bl*

Notes	Type			
	99102	C-130H	757th AS	*bl*
	99103	C-130H	757th AS	*bl*
	99104	C-130H	757th AS	*bl*
	99105	C-130H	757th AS	*bl*
	99106	C-130H	757th AS	*bl*

Boeing C-135

6th AMW, MacDill AFB, Florida: 91st ARS (*y/bl*);
15th ABW, Hickam AFB, Hawaii: 65th AS;
18th Wg, Kadena AB, Japan [ZZ]: 909th ARS (*w*);
19th ARG, Robins AFB, Georgia: 99th ARS (*y/bl*);
22nd ARW, McConnell AFB, Kansas: 344th ARS (*y/bk*), 349th ARS (*y/bl*) 350th ARS (*y/r*) & 384th ARS (*y/pr*);
55th Wg, Offutt AFB, Nebraska [OF]: 38th RS (*gn*), 45th RS (*bk*) & 343rd RS;
88th ABW, Wright-Patterson AFB, Ohio;
92nd ARW, Fairchild AFB, Washington: 92nd ARS (*bk*), 93rd ARS (*bl*), & 97th ARS (*y*);
97th AMW, Altus AFB, Oklahoma: 54th ARS & 55th ARS (*y/r*);
100th ARW, RAF Mildenhall, UK [D]: 351st ARS (*r/w/bl*);
106th ARS/117th ARW, Birmingham, Alabama ANG (*w/r*);
108th ARS/126th ARW, Scott AFB, Illinois ANG (*w/bl*);
108th ARW, McGuire AFB, New Jersey ANG: 141st ARS (*bk/y*) & 150th ARS (*bl*);
117th ARS/190th ARW, Forbes Field, Kansas ANG (*bl/y*);
121st ARW, Rickenbacker ANGB, Ohio ANG: 145th ARS & 166th ARS (*bl*);
126th ARS/128th ARW, Mitchell Field, Wisconsin ANG (*w/bl*);
132nd ARS/101st ARW, Bangor, Maine ANG (*w/gn*);
133rd ARS/157th ARW, Pease ANGB, New Hampshire ANG (*bl*);
136th ARS/107th ARW, Niagara Falls, New York ANG (*bl*);
151st ARS/134th ARW, Knoxville, Tennessee ANG (*w/or*);
153rd ARS/186th ARW, Meridian, Mississippi ANG (*bk/gd*);
168th ARS/168th ARW, Eielson AFB, Alaska ANG (*bl/y*);
171st ARS/127th Wg, Selfridge ANGB, Michigan ANG;
171st ARW, Greater Pittsburgh, Pennsylvania ANG: 146th ARS (*y/bk*) & 147th ARS (*bk/y*);
173rd ARS/155th ARW, Lincoln, Nebraska ANG (*r/w*);
174th ARS/185th ARW, Sioux City, Iowa ANG (*y/bk*);
191st ARS/151st ARW, Salt Lake City, Utah ANG (*bl/bk*);
196th ARS/163rd ARW, March ARB, California ANG (*bl/w*);
197th ARS/161st ARW, Phoenix, Arizona ANG;
203rd ARS/154th Wg, Hickam AFB, Hawaii ANG [HH] (*y/bk*);

319th ARW, Grand Forks AFB, North Dakota: 905th ARS (*bl*), 906th ARS (*y*), & 912th ARS (*w*);
366th Wg, Mountain Home AFB, Idaho [MO]: 22nd ARS (*y/gn*);
412th TW, Edwards AFB, California [ED]: 452nd FLTS (*bl*);
434th ARW AFRC, Grissom AFB, Indiana: 72nd ARS (*bl*) & 74th ARS (*r/w*);
452nd AMW AFRC, March ARB, California: 336th ARS (*y*);
459th ARW AFRC, Andrews AFB, Maryland: 756th ARS (*y/bk*);
507th ARW AFRC, Tinker AFB, Oklahoma: 465th ARS (*bl/y*);
645th Materiel Sqn, Greenville, Texas;
916th ARW AFRC, Seymour Johnson AFB, North Carolina: 77th ARS (*gn*);
927th ARW AFRC, Selfridge ANGB, Michigan: 63rd ARS (*pr/w*);
940th ARW AFRC, Beale AFB, California: 314th ARS (*r/bk*)

FY60

	Type			Notes
00313	KC-135R	6th AMW	*y/bl*	
00314	KC-135R	434th ARW	*r*	
00315	KC-135R	126th ARS	*w/bl*	
00316	KC-135R			
00318	KC-135R	203rd ARS	*y/bk*	
00319	KC-135R	22nd ARW		
00320	KC-135R	319th ARW	*y/r*	
00321	KC-135R	97th AMW	*y/r*	
00322	KC-135R	434th ARW	*bl*	
00323	KC-135R	203rd ARS	*y/bk*	
00324	KC-135R	319th ARW	*w*	
00327	KC-135E	191st ARS	*bl/bk*	
00328	KC-135R	100th ARW	*r/w/bl*	
00329	KC-135R	203rd ARS	*y/bk*	
00331	KC-135R	100th ARW	*r/w/bl*	
00332	KC-135R	319th ARW	*w*	
00333	KC-135R	92nd ARW	*bk*	
00334	KC-135R	168th ARS	*bl/y*	
00335	KC-135T	22nd ARW	*y/bk*	
00336	KC-135T	92nd ARW		
00337	KC-135T	92nd ARW	*m*	
00339	KC-135T	18th Wg	*w*	
00341	KC-135R	121st ARW	*bl*	
00342	KC-135T	319th ARW		
00343	KC-135T	19th ARG	*y/bl*	
00344	KC-135T	18th Wg	*w*	
00345	KC-135T	940th ARW	*r/bk*	
00346	KC-135T	940th ARW	*r/bk*	
00347	KC-135R	121st ARW	*bl*	
00348	KC-135R	22nd ARW		
00349	KC-135R	916th ARW	*gn*	
00350	KC-135R	100th ARW	*r/w/bl*	
00351	KC-135R	319th ARW		
00353	KC-135R	6th AMW	*y/bl*	
00355	KC-135R	100th ARW	*r/w/bl*	
00356	KC-135R	22nd ARW		
00357	KC-135R	22nd ARW		
00358	KC-135R	136th ARS	*bl*	
00359	KC-135R	434th ARW	*r/w*	
00360	KC-135R	97th AMW	*y/r*	
00362	KC-135R	22nd ARW	*y/r*	
00363	KC-135R	434th ARW	*bl*	
00364	KC-135R	434th ARW	*r/w*	
00365	KC-135R			
00366	KC-135R	19th ARG	*y/bl*	
00367	KC-135R	121st ARW	*bl*	

FY61

	Type			Notes
10264	KC-135R	121st ARW	*bl*	
10266	KC-135R	173rd ARS	*r/w*	
10267	KC-135R	92nd ARW	*y*	
10268	KC-135E	940th ARW	*r/bk*	
10270	KC-135E	927th ARW	*pr/w*	
10272	KC-135R	434th ARW	*r/w*	
10275	KC-135R	191st ARS	*bl/bk*	
10276	KC-135R	173rd ARS	*r/w*	
10277	KC-135R			
10280	KC-135R	452nd AMW	*y*	
10281	KC-135E	117th ARS	*bl/y*	
10284	KC-135R	319th ARW	*bl*	
10288	KC-135R	92nd ARW	*bk*	
10290	KC-135R	203rd ARS	*y/bk*	
10292	KC-135R	319th ARW		
10293	KC-135R	22nd ARW	*y/r*	
10294	KC-135R	940th ARW	*r/bk*	
10295	KC-135R	6th AMW	*y/bl*	
10298	KC-135R	126th ARS	*w/bl*	
10299	KC-135R			
10300	KC-135R	6th AMW	*y/bl*	
10302	KC-135R	97th AMW	*y/r*	
10303	KC-135R	916th ARW	*gn*	
10304	KC-135R	97th AMW	*y/r*	
10305	KC-135R	6th AMW	*y/bl*	
10306	KC-135R	18th Wg	*w*	
10307	KC-135R	459th ARW	*y/bk*	
10308	KC-135R	97th AMW	*y/r*	
10309	KC-135R	126th ARS	*w/bl*	
10310	KC-135R	133rd ARS	*bl*	
10311	KC-135R	22nd ARW	*y*	
10312	KC-135R	452nd AMW	*y*	
10313	KC-135R	916th ARW	*gn*	
10314	KC-135R	319th ARW		
10315	KC-135R	22nd ARW		
10317	KC-135R	22nd ARW	*y*	
10318	KC-135R	22nd ARW		
10320	KC-135R	412th TW	*bl*	
10321	KC-135R	18th Wg	*w*	
10323	KC-135R	319th ARW		
10324	KC-135R	452nd AMW	*y*	
10327	EC-135N	412th TW	*bl*	
10330	EC-135E	412th TW	*bl*	
12662	RC-135S	55th Wg	*bk*	
12663	RC-135S	55th Wg	*bk*	
12666	NC-135W	645th MS		
12667	WC-135W	55th Wg	*bk*	
12670	OC-135B	55th Wg		
12672	OC-135B	55th Wg		

FY64

	Type			Notes
14828	KC-135R	191st ARS	*bl/bk*	
14829	KC-135R	319th ARW		
14830	KC-135R	6th AMW	*y/bl*	
14831	KC-135R	197th ARS		
14832	KC-135R	203rd ARS	*y/bk*	
14833	KC-135R	92nd ARW	*bk*	
14834	KC-135R	434th ARW	*r/w*	
14835	KC-135R	452nd AMW	*y*	
14836	KC-135R	197th ARS		
14837	KC-135R	92nd ARW		
14838	KC-135R	92nd ARW		
14839	KC-135R	136th ARS	*bl*	
14840	KC-135R	121st ARW	*bl*	
14841	RC-135V	55th Wg	*bl*	
14842	RC-135V	55th Wg	*gn*	
14843	RC-135V	55th Wg	*gn*	
14844	RC-135V	55th Wg	*gn*	
14845	RC-135V	55th Wg	*bl*	
14846	RC-135V	55th Wg	*gn*	
14847	RC-135U	55th Wg	*bk*	
14848	RC-135V	55th Wg	*gn*	
14849	RC-135U	55th Wg	*bk*	

Notes	Type			
	FY62			
	23498	KC-135R	18th Wg	*w*
	23499	KC-135R	22nd ARW	*y*
	23500	KC-135R	126th ARS	*w/bl*
	23502	KC-135R	6th AMW	*y/bl*
	23503	KC-135R		
	23504	KC-135R	191st ARS	*bl/bk*
	23505	KC-135R	97th AMW	*y/r*
	23506	KC-135R	133rd ARS	*bl*
	23507	KC-135R	18th Wg	*w*
	23508	KC-135R	19th ARG	*y/bl*
	23509	KC-135R	916th ARW	*gn*
	23510	KC-135R	434th ARW	*r/w*
	23511	KC-135R	121st ARW	*bl*
	23512	KC-135R	126th ARS	*w/bl*
	23513	KC-135R		
	23514	KC-135R	203rd ARS	*y/bk*
	23515	KC-135R	133rd ARS	*bl*
	23516	KC-135R	197th ARS	
	23517	KC-135R	22nd ARW	
	23518	KC-135R	434th ARW	*bl*
	23519	KC-135R	100th ARW	*r/w/bl*
	23520	KC-135R	6th AMW	*y/bl*
	23521	KC-135R	434th ARW	*r/w*
	23523	KC-135R	19th ARG	*y/bl*
	23524	KC-135R	106th ARS	*w/r*
	23526	KC-135R	173rd ARS	*r/w*
	23527	KC-135E	927th ARW	*pr/w*
	23528	KC-135R	927th ARW	*pr/w*
	23529	KC-135R	319th ARW	
	23530	KC-135R	434th ARW	*bl*
	23531	KC-135R	121st ARW	*bl*
	23533	KC-135R	319th ARW	*w*
	23534	KC-135R	19th ARG	*y/bl*
	23537	KC-135R	22nd ARW	
	23538	KC-135R	22nd ARW	
	23540	KC-135R	92nd ARW	*bk*
	23541	KC-135R	319th ARW	
	23542	KC-135R	916th ARW	*gn*
	23543	KC-135R	459th ARW	*y/bk*
	23544	KC-135R	19th ARG	*y/bl*
	23545	KC-135R	22nd ARW	
	23546	KC-135R	319th ARW	
	23547	KC-135R	133rd ARS	*bl*
	23548	KC-135R	22nd ARW	
	23549	KC-135R	6th AMW	*y/bl*
	23550	KC-135R	197th ARS	
	23551	KC-135R	22nd ARW	
	23552	KC-135R	97th AMW	*y/r*
	23553	KC-135R	319th ARW	
	23554	KC-135R	19th ARG	*y/bl*
	23556	KC-135R	459th ARW	*y/bk*
	23557	KC-135R	940th ARW	*r/bk*
	23558	KC-135R	940th ARW	*r/bk*
	23559	KC-135R	22nd ARW	*gy/si*
	23561	KC-135R	319th ARW	
	23562	KC-135R	319th ARW	
	23564	KC-135R	97th AMW	*y/r*
	23565	KC-135R	92nd ARW	
	23566	KC-135E		
	23568	KC-135R	97th AMW	*y/r*
	23569	KC-135R	19th ARG	*y/bl*
	23571	KC-135R	168th ARS	*bl/y*
	23572	KC-135R		
	23573	KC-135R	319th ARW	
	23575	KC-135R	92nd ARW	*bk*
	23576	KC-135R	133rd ARS	*bl*
	23577	KC-135R	916th ARW	*gn*
	23578	KC-135R	22nd ARW	
	23580	KC-135R	927th ARW	*pr/w*
	23582	WC-135C	55th Wg	*bk*
	24125	RC-135W	55th Wg	*bk*
	24126	RC-135W	55th Wg	*bl*
	24127	TC-135W	55th Wg	
	24128	RC-135S	55th Wg	
	24129	TC-135W	55th Wg	*gn*
	24130	RC-135W	55th Wg	*gn*
	24131	RC-135W	55th Wg	*gn*
	24132	RC-135W	55th Wg	*gn*
	24133	TC-135S	55th Wg	*bk*
	24134	RC-135W	55th Wg	*gn*
	24135	RC-135W	55th Wg	*bk*
	24138	RC-135W	55th Wg	*gn*
	24139	RC-135W	55th Wg	*gn*
	FY63			
	37976	KC-135R	319th ARW	
	37977	KC-135R	22nd ARW	
	37978	KC-135R	97th AMW	*y/r*
	37979	KC-135R	92nd ARW	
	37980	KC-135R	412th TW	
	37981	KC-135R	136th ARS	*bl*
	37982	KC-135R	22nd ARW	*gy/si*
	37984	KC-135R	106th ARS	*w/r*
	37985	KC-135R	507th ARW	*bl/y*
	37987	KC-135R	100th ARW	*r/w/bl*
	37988	KC-135R	173rd ARS	*r/w*
	37991	KC-135R	173rd ARS	*r/w*
	37992	KC-135R	121st ARW	*bl*
	37993	KC-135R	121st ARW	*m*
	37995	KC-135R	22nd ARW	*gy*
	37996	KC-135R	434th ARW	*bl*
	37997	KC-135R	319th ARW	*bl*
	37999	KC-135R	18th Wg	*w*
	38000	KC-135R	22nd ARW	*gy/si*
	38002	KC-135R	22nd ARW	*gy/si*
	38003	KC-135R	22nd ARW	
	38004	KC-135R	117th ARS	*bl/y*
	38006	KC-135R	97th AMW	*y/r*
	38007	KC-135R	106th ARS	*w/r*
	38008	KC-135R	100th ARW	*r/w/bl*
	38011	KC-135R	18th Wg	*w*
	38012	KC-135R	319th ARW	
	38013	KC-135R	121st ARW	*bl*
	38014	KC-135R	927th ARW	*pr/w*
	38015	KC-135R	168th ARS	*bl/y*
	38017	KC-135R	97th AMW	*y/r*
	38018	KC-135R	173rd ARS	*r/w*
	38019	KC-135R	97th AMW	*y/r*
	38020	KC-135R		
	38021	KC-135R	319th ARW	*w*
	38022	KC-135R	22nd ARW	*m*
	38023	KC-135R	197th ARS	
	38024	KC-135R	452nd AMW	*y*
	38025	KC-135R	100th ARW	*r/w/bl*
	38026	KC-135R	191st ARS	*bl/bk*
	38027	KC-135R	97th AMW	*y/r*
	38028	KC-135R	117th ARS	*bl/y*
	38029	KC-135R	126th ARS	*w/bl*
	38030	KC-135R	203rd ARS	*y/bk*
	38031	KC-135R	92nd ARW	*y/bl*
	38032	KC-135R	434th ARW	*bl*
	38033	KC-135R	100th ARW	*r/w/bl*
	38034	KC-135R	97th AMW	*y/r*
	38035	KC-135R	106th ARS	*w/r*
	38036	KC-135R	136th ARS	*bl*
	38037	KC-135R	319th ARW	
	38038	KC-135R	6th AMW	*y/bl*
	38039	KC-135R	507th ARW	*bl/y*
	38040	KC-135R	19th ARG	*y/bl*
	38041	KC-135R	434th ARW	*bl*
	38043	KC-135R	168th ARS	*bl/y*
	38044	KC-135R	927th ARW	*pr/w*
	38045	KC-135R	100th ARW	*r/w/bl*
	38050	NKC-135E	412th TW	*bl*

US-based USN/USMC Aircraft

Type | *Notes*

Lockheed P-3 Orion
CinCLANT/VP-30, NAS Jacksonville, Florida;
CNO/VP-30, NAS Jacksonville, Florida;
NASC-FS, Point Mugu, California;
USNTPS, NAS Point Mugu, California;
VP-1, NAS Whidbey Island, Washington [YB];
VP-4, MCBH Kaneohe Bay, Hawaii [YD];
VP-5, NAS Jacksonville, Florida [LA];
VP-8, NAS Jacksonville, Florida [LC];
VP-9, MCBH Kaneohe Bay, Hawaii [PD];
VP-10, NAS Jacksonville, Florida [LD];
VP-16, NAS Jacksonville, Florida [LF];
VP-26, NAS Jacksonville, Florida [LK];
VP-30, NAS Jacksonville, Florida [LL];
VP-40, NAS Whidbey Island, Washington [QE];
VP-45, NAS Jacksonville, Florida [LN];
VP-46, NAS Whidbey Island, Washington [RC];
VP-47, MCBH Kaneohe Bay, Hawaii [RD];
VP-62, NAS Jacksonville, Florida [LT];
VP-69, NAS Whidbey Island, Washington [PJ];
VPU-1, NAS Jacksonville, Florida;
VPU-2, MCBH Kaneohe Bay, Hawaii;
VQ-1, NAS Whidbey Island, Washington [PR];
VQ-2, NAS Whidbey Island, Washington;
VX-1, NAS Patuxent River, Maryland;
VX-20, Patuxent River, Maryland;
VX-30, NAS Point Mugu, California;
VXS-1, Patuxent River, Maryland

				Notes
148889		UP-3A	USNTPS	
150521	[341]	NP-3D	VX-30	
150522	[340]	NP-3D	VX-30	
152141	[408]	P-3A	VP-1	
152150	[303]	NP-3D	VX-30	
152165	[404]	P-3A	VP-1	
153443	[443]	NP-3D	USNTPS	
154587	[587]	NP-3D	VXS-1	
154589	[589]	NP-3D	VXS-1	
156507	[PR-31]	EP-3E	VQ-1	
156509	[LL-509]	P-3C	VP-30	
156510	[LL-510]	P-3C	VP-30	
156511	[PR-32]	EP-3E	VQ-1	
156514	[PR-33]	EP-3E	VQ-1	
156515	[515]	P-3C	VP-9	
156517	[PR-34]	EP-3E	VQ-1	
156519	[519]	EP-3E	VQ-2	
156521	[LD-521]	P-3C	VP-10	
156527	[527]	P-3C	VP-47	
156528	[PR-36]	EP-3E	VQ-1	
156529	[24]	EP-3E	VQ-2	
157316	[316]	EP-3E	VQ-2	
157318	[PR-318]	EP-3E	VQ-1	
157319	[LL-319]	P-3C	VP-30	
157322	[LL-322]	P-3C	VP-30	
157325	[25]	EP-3E	VQ-2	
157326	[326]	EP-3E	VQ-2	
157327	[LL-327]	P-3C	VP-30	
157329	[LT-329]	P-3C	VP-62	
157330	[330]	P-3C	VP-5	
157331	[LA-331]	P-3C	VP-9	
158204	[204]	NP-3C	VX-20	
158206	[LL-206]	P-3C	VP-30	
158210	[210]	P-3C	VP-45	
158214	[LL-214]	P-3C	VP-30	
158215	[LL-215]	P-3C	VP-30	
158222	[LL-51]	P-3C	VP-30	
158224	[224]	P-3C	VP-16	
158225	[LD-225]	P-3C	VP-10	
158227	[BH-300]	NP-3D	VX-30	
158563	[YD-563]	P-3C	VP-4	
158564	[LK-564]	P-3C	VP-26	
158567	[LA-567]	P-3C	VP-5	
158568	[301]	NP-3C	VX-30	
158570	[570]	P-3C	VX-1	
158571	[LL-571]	P-3C	VP-30	
158573	[RD-573]	P-3C	VP-47	
158574		P-3C	NASC-FS	
158912	[912]	P-3C	VX-20	
158914	[914]	P-3C	VP-40	
158915	[915]	P-3C	VP-4	
158916	[LF-916]	P-3C	VP-16	
158917	[917]	P-3C	VP-8	
158918	[918]	P-3C	VP-1	
158919	[919]	P-3C	VP-45	
158921	[YD-921]	P-3C	VP-4	
158922	[922]	P-3C	VP-30	
158923	[923]	P-3C	VP-47	
158924	[924]	P-3C	VP-45	
158925	[925]	P-3C	VP-4	
158926	[926]	P-3C	VP-46	
158927	[927]	P-3C	VP-4	
158928		P-3C	VPU-2	
158929	[929]	P-3C	VP-45	
158934	[934]	P-3C	VP-40	
158935	[LL-935]	P-3C	VP-30	
159318	[LD-318]	P-3C	VP-10	
159320	[320]	P-3C	VP-40	
159322	[LL-322]	P-3C	VP-30	
159323	[323]	P-3C	VP-47	
159326	[326]	P-3C	VP-4	
159329	[329]	P-3C	VP-45	
159503	[503]	P-3C	VP-46	
159504		P-3C	VPU-2	
159506	[506]	P-3C	VP-47	
159507	[RD-507]	P-3C	VP-47	
159512	[LT-512]	P-3C	VP-62	
159513	[LL-513]	P-3C	VP-30	
159514	[LL-514]	P-3C	VP-30	
159884	[PR-884]	P-3C	VQ-1	
159885	[885]	P-3C	VP-40	
159887		EP-3E	VQ-2	
159889	[YD-889]	P-3C	VP-4	
159893	[26]	EP-3E	VQ-2	
159894	[LL-894]	P-3C	VP-30	
160283	[283]	P-3C	VP-47	
160285		P-3C	VPU-1	
160287	[LL-287]	P-3C	VP-30	
160290	[290]	P-3C	VX-20	
160291		EP-3E	VQ-1	
160292	[292]	P-3C	VPU-2	
160293		P-3C	NASC-FS	
160610	[YD-610]	P-3C	VP-4	
160612	[PR-52]	P-3C	VQ-1	
160761		P-3C	VP-9	
160762		P-3C	VPU-2	
160763	[763]	P-3C	VQ-2	
160764	[764]	EP-3E	VQ-1	
160765	[LL-765]	P-3C	VP-30	
160766	[766]	P-3C	VPU-2	

Notes	Type			
	160767	[LF-767]	P-3C	VP-16
	160770	[770]	P-3C	VP-5
	160999	[LL-999]	P-3C	VP-30
	161001	[PJ-001]	P-3C	VP-69
	161002	[LD-002]	P-3C	VP-10
	161005	[JA-07]	P-3C	VX-1
	161006	[LK-006]	P-3C	VP-26
	161007	[007]	P-3C	VQ-2
	161008	[008]	P-3C	VP-4
	161009	[LA-009]	P-3C	VP-5
	161010	[LL-010]	P-3C	VP-30
	161011	[011]	P-3C	VP-45
	161012	[PD-012]	P-3C	VP-9
	161013	[LL-013]	P-3C	VP-30
	161014	[LT-014]	P-3C	VP-62
	161121		P-3C	NASC-FS
	161122	[226]	P-3C	VPU-1
	161124	[LA-124]	P-3C	VP-5
	161125	[125]	P-3C	VP-30
	161126	[126]	P-3C	VP-26
	161127	[127]	P-3C	VP-8
	161129	[LT-129]	P-3C	VP-62
	161132	[132]	P-3C	VP-26
	161329	[LT-329]	P-3C	VP-62
	161331	[331]	P-3C	VQ-2
	161332	[LF-332]	P-3C	VP-16
	161333	[333]	P-3C	VP-8
	161334	[LL-334]	P-3C	VP-30
	161335	[PD-335]	P-3C	VP-9
	161336	[336]	P-3C	VP-8
	161337	[337]	P-3C	VP-47
	161338	[338]	P-3C	VP-8
	161339	[339]	P-3C	VP-26
	161404	[404]	P-3C	VP-26
	161405	[405]	P-3C	VP-8
	161406	[PR-406]	P-3C	VQ-1
	161407	[407]	P-3C	VP-10
	161408	[PJ-408]	P-3C	VP-69
	161409	[LT-409]	P-3C	VP-62
	161410		EP-3E	VQ-1
	161411		P-3C	NASC-FS
	161412	[412]	P-3C	VP-69
	161413	[413]	P-3C	VX-1
	161414	[414]	P-3C	VP-26
	161415	[LK-415]	P-3C	VP-26
	161585		P-3C	VPU-1
	161586	[586]	P-3C	VP-10
	161587	[587]	P-3C	VP-46
	161588	[588]	P-3C	VP-1
	161589	[589]	P-3C	VP-46
	161590	[590]	P-3C	VP-46
	161591	[LT-591]	P-3C	VP-62
	161592	[PJ-592]	P-3C	VP-69
	161593	[593]	P-3C	VP-1
	161594	[LL-594]	P-3C	VP-30
	161595	[595]	P-3C	VP-46
	161596	[596]	P-3C	VP-26
	161763	[YD-763]	P-3C	VP-4
	161764	[YD-764]	P-3C	VP-4
	161765	[765]	P-3C	VP-30
	161766	[YD-766]	P-3C	VP-4
	161767	[767]	P-3C	VP-26
	162314	[RC-314]	P-3C	VP-46
	162315	[315]	P-3C	VP-40
	162316	[LK-316]	P-3C	VP-26
	162317	[317]	P-3C	VP-8
	162318	[318]	P-3C	VP-45
	162770	[770]	P-3C	VP-40
	162771	[771]	P-3C	VP-40
	162772	[QE-772]	P-3C	VP-40
	162773	[773]	P-3C	VP-8
	162774	[774]	P-3C	VX-20

Notes	Type			
	162775	[775]	P-3C	VP-4
	162776	[LD-776]	P-3C	VP-10
	162777	[LV-777]	P-3C	VP-66
	162778	[RD-778]	P-3C	VP-47
	162998	[YD-998]	P-3C	VP-4
	162999	[999]	P-3C	VP-16
	163000	[000]	P-3C	VP-40
	163001	[001]	P-3C	VP-26
	163002	[PJ-002]	P-3C	VP-69
	163003	[LT-003]	P-3C	VP-62
	163004	[PJ-004]	P-3C	VP-69
	163006	[LA-006]	P-3C	VP-5
	163289	[289]	P-3C	VP-40
	163290	[LL-290]	P-3C	VP-30
	163291	[LT-291]	P-3C	VP-62
	163292	[LA-292]	P-3C	VP-5
	163293	[293]	P-3C	VP-40
	163294	[LF-294]	P-3C	VP-16
	163295	[PJ-295]	P-3C	VP-69

Boeing E-6B Mercury

Boeing, McConnell AFB, Kansas;
VQ-3 & VQ-4, SCW-1,
Tinker AFB, Oklahoma

162782	VQ-4
162783	VQ-3
162784	VQ-4
163918	VQ-3
163919	VQ-3
163920	VQ-3
164386	VQ-4
164387	VQ-3
164388	VQ-4
164404	VQ-4
164405	VQ-4
164406	VQ-3
164407	VQ-4
164408	VQ-4
164409	VQ-4
164410	VQ-4

McDonnell Douglas C-9B Skytrain II/DC-9-32*

VMR-1, Cherry Point MCAS, North Carolina;
VR-46, Atlanta, Georgia [JS];
VR-52, Willow Grove NAS, Pennsylvania [JT];
VR-56, Norfolk NAS, Virginia [JU];
VR-61, Whidbey Island NAS, Washington [RS];

159113	[RS]	VR-61
159114	[RS]	VR-61
159115		VR-61
159116		VR-61
159117	[JU]	VR-56
159118	[JU]	VR-56
159119	[JU]	VR-56
159120	[JU]	VR-56
160046		VMR-1
160047		VMR-1
160048	[JT]	VR-52
160049	[JT]	VR-52
160050	[JT]	VR-52
160051	[JT]	VR-52
161266	[JS]	VR-46
161529	[JS]	VR-46
161530	[JS]	VR-46
164606*	[RS]	VR-61
164608*	[RS]	VR-61

Grumman C-20A/C-20D Gulfstream III/C-20G Gulfstream IV*
MASD, NAF Washington, Maryland;
VR-1, NAF Washington, Maryland;
VR-48, NAF Washington, Maryland [JR];
VR-51, MCBH Kaneohe Bay, Hawaii [RG]

Type			Notes
C-20A			
830500		VR-1	
C-20D			
163691		VR-1	
163692		VR-1	
C-20G			
165093	[JR]	VR-48	
165094		VR-51	
165151	[JR]	VR-48	
165152	[RG]	VR-51	
165153		MASD	

Gulfstream Aerospace C-37B Gulfstream V
VR-1, NAF Washington, Maryland;

Type		Notes
166375	VR-1	
166376	VR-1	
166377	VR-1	
166378	VR-1	
166379		

Boeing C-40A Clipper
VR-57, NAS North Island, California [RX];
VR-58, NAS Jacksonville, Florida [JV];
VR-59, NAS Fort Worth JRB, Texas [RY]

Type			Notes
165829	[JV]	VR-58	
165830	[RY]	VR-59	
165831	[RY]	VR-59	
165832	[JV]	VR-58	
165833	[RY]	VR-59	
165834	[JV]	VR-58	
165835	[RX]	VR-57	
165836	[RX]	VR-57	
166693	[RX]	VR-57	

Lockheed C-130 Hercules
VR-53, NAF Washington, Maryland [AX];
VR-54, NAS New Orleans, Louisiana [CW];
VR-55, NAS Point Mugu, California [RU];
VR-62, NAS Jacksonville, Florida [JW];
VR-64, NAS Willow Grove, Pennsylvania [BD];
VMGR-152, Futenma MCAS, Japan [QD];
VMGR-234, NAS Fort Worth, Texas [QH];
VMGR-252, Cherry Point MCAS, North Carolina [BH];
VMGRT-253, Cherry Point MCAS, North Carolina [GR];
VMGR-352, MCAS Miramar, California [QB];
VMGR-452, Stewart Field, New York [NY];
VX-20, Patuxent River, Maryland;
VX-30, NAS Point Mugu, California

Type				Notes
147573	[QD]	KC-130F	VMGR-152	
148891	[QD]	KC-130F	VMGR-152	
148893	[401]	KC-130F	VX-30	
148894		KC-130F	VX-20	
148897	[400]	KC-130F	VX-30	
149803	[GR]	KC-130F	VMGRT-253	
149807	[QD]	KC-130F	VMGR-152	
149808		KC-130F	VX-20	
149815		KC-130F	VX-20	
150686	[BH]	KC-130F	VMGR-252	
160013	[QD]	KC-130R	VMGR-152	
160016	[QD]	KC-130R	VMGR-152	
160625	[QD]	KC-130R	VMGR-152	
160626	[QD]	KC-130R	VMGR-152	
160627	[QD]	KC-130R	VMGR-152	
160628	[QD]	KC-130R	VMGR-152	
162308	[QH]	KC-130T	VMGR-234	
162309	[QH]	KC-130T	VMGR-234	
162310	[QH]	KC-130T	VMGR-234	
162311	[QH]	KC-130T	VMGR-234	
162785	[QH]	KC-130T	VMGR-234	
162786	[QH]	KC-130T	VMGR-234	
163022	[QH]	KC-130T	VMGR-234	
163023	[QH]	KC-130T	VMGR-234	
163310	[QH]	KC-130T	VMGR-234	
163311	[NY]	KC-130T	VMGR-452	
163591	[NY]	KC-130T	VMGR-452	
163592	[NY]	KC-130T	VMGR-452	
164105	[NY]	KC-130T	VMGR-452	
164106	[NY]	KC-130T	VMGR-452	
164180	[NY]	KC-130T	VMGR-452	
164181	[NY]	KC-130T	VMGR-452	
164441	[NY]	KC-130T	VMGR-452	
164442	[NY]	KC-130T	VMGR-452	
164597	[NY]	KC-130T-30	VMGR-452	
164598	[QH]	KC-130T-30	VMGR-234	
164762	[CW]	C-130T	VR-54	
164763		C-130T	*Blue Angels*	
164993	[BD]	C-130T	VR-64	
164994	[BD]	C-130T	VR-64	
164995	[AX]	C-130T	VR-53	
164996	[BD]	C-130T	VR-64	
164997	[AX]	C-130T	VR-53	
164998	[AX]	C-130T	VR-53	
164999	[AX]	KC-130T	VR-53	
165000	[NY]	KC-130T	VMGR-452	
165158	[CW]	C-130T	VR-54	
165159	[CW]	C-130T	VR-54	
165160	[CW]	C-130T	VR-54	
165161	[BD]	C-130T	VR-64	
165162	[QH]	KC-130T	VMGR-234	
165163	[QH]	KC-130T	VMGR-234	
165313	[JW]	C-130T	VR-62	
165314	[JW]	C-130T	VR-62	
165315	[NY]	KC-130T	VMGR-452	
165316	[NY]	KC-130T	VMGR-452	
165348	[JW]	C-130T	VR-62	
165349	[BD]	C-130T	VR-64	
165350	[RU]	C-130T	VR-55	
165351	[RU]	C-130T	VR-55	
165352	[NY]	KC-130T	VMGR-452	
165353	[NY]	KC-130T	VMGR-452	
165378	[RU]	C-130T	VR-55	
165379	[RU]	C-130T	VR-55	
165735	[BH]	KC-130J	VMGR-252	
165736	[QB]	KC-130J	VMGR-352	
165737	[BH]	KC-130J	VMGR-252	
165738	[BH]	KC-130J	VMGR-252	
165739	[BH]	KC-130J	VMGR-252	
165809	[BH]	KC-130J	VMGR-252	
165810	[BH]	KC-130J	VMGR-252	
165957	[BH]	KC-130J	VMGR-252	
166380	[BH]	KC-130J	VMGR-252	
166381	[BH]	KC-130J	VMGR-252	
166382	[BH]	KC-130J	VMGR-252	
166472	[BH]	KC-130J	VMGR-252	
166473		KC-130J	VX-20	

Notes	Type			
	166511	[BH]	KC-130J	VMGR-252
	166512	[QB]	KC-130J	VMGR-352
	166513	[QB]	KC-130J	VMGR-352
	166514	[QB]	KC-130J	VMGR-352
	166762	[QB]	KC-130J	VMGR-352
	166763	[QB]	KC-130J	VMGR-352
	166764	[QB]	KC-130J	VMGR-352
	166765	[QB]	KC-130J	VMGR-352
	167108	[QB]	KC-130J	VMGR-352
	167109	[QD]	KC-130J	VMGR-152
	167110	[QB]	KC-130J	VMGR-352
	167111	[QB]	KC-130J	VMGR-352
	167112		KC-130J	
	167923	[QD]	KC-130J	VMGR-152
	167924	[QB]	KC-130J	VMGR-352
	167925	[QD]	KC-130J	VMGR-152
	167926	[QD]	KC-130J	VMGR-152

US-based US Coast Guard Aircraft

Notes *Type*

Canadair C-43A Challenger
USCG, Washington DC
02

Gulfstream Aerospace C-37A Gulfstream V
USCG, Washington DC
01

Lockheed C-130 Hercules
USCGS Barbers Point, Hawaii;
USCGS Clearwater, Florida;
USCGS Elizabeth City, North Carolina;
USCGS Kodiak, Alaska;
USCGS Sacramento, California

Notes	Type		
	1500	HC-130H	Elizabeth City
	1501	HC-130H	Clearwater
	1502	HC-130H	Elizabeth City
	1503	HC-130H	Elizabeth City
	1504	HC-130H	Clearwater
	1700	HC-130H	Kodiak
	1701	HC-130H	Barbers Point
	1702	HC-130H	Barbers Point
	1703	HC-130H	Sacramento
	1704	HC-130H	Sacramento
	1705	HC-130H	Kodiak
	1706	HC-130H	Barbers Point
	1707	HC-130H	Clearwater
	1708	HC-130H	Clearwater
	1709	HC-130H	Sacramento
	1711	HC-130H	Elizabeth City
	1712	HC-130H	Clearwater
	1713	HC-130H	Barbers Point
	1714	HC-130H	Barbers Point
	1715	HC-130H	Sacramento
	1716	HC-130H	Sacramento
	1717	HC-130H	Barbers Point
	1718	HC-130H	Sacramento
	1719	HC-130H	Clearwater
	1720	HC-130H	Clearwater
	1790	HC-130H	Kodiak
	2001	HC-130J	Elizabeth City
	2002	HC-130J	Elizabeth City
	2003	HC-130J	Elizabeth City
	2004	HC-130J	Elizabeth City
	2005	HC-130J	Elizabeth City
	2006	HC-130J	Elizabeth City

Aircraft in US Government or Military Service with Civil Registrations

Notes *Type*

BAe 125-800A (C-29A)
Federal Aviation Administration, Oklahoma

Notes	Type	
	N94	(88-0269)
	N95	(88-0270)
	N96	(88-0271)
	N97	(88-0272)
	N98	(88-0273)
	N99	(88-0274)

Canadair CL.601/CL.604* Challenger
Federal Aviation Administration, Oklahoma
N85
N86
N87
N88*

Military Aviation Sites on the Internet

The list below is not intended to be a complete list of military aviation sites on the Internet. The sites listed cover Museums, Locations, Air Forces, Companies and Organisations that are mentioned elsewhere in 'Military Aircraft Markings'. Sites listed are in English or contain sufficient English to be reasonably easily understood. Each site address is believed to be correct at the time of going to press. Additions are welcome, via the usual address found at the front of the book, or via e-mail to admin@aviation-links.co.uk. An up to date copy of this list is to be found at http://www.aviation-links.co.uk/.

Name of site	*Internet dial (all prefixed 'http://')*
MILITARY SITES-UK	
No 1 Regiment Army Air Corps	www.army.mod.uk/aac/units/1_regiment_aac/
No 1 Sqn	www.raf.mod.uk/structure/1squadron.cfm
No 2 Sqn	www.rafmarham.co.uk/organisation/2squadron/2squadron.htm
No 3 Flt	www.leuchars.raf.mod.uk/lodg3aac.htm
No 3 Regiment Army Air Corps	www.army.mod.uk/aac/units/3_regiment_aac/
No 3 Sqn	www.raf.mod.uk/structure/3squadron.cfm
No 4 Regiment Army Air Corps	www.army.mod.uk/aac/units/4_regiment_aac/
No 4 Sqn	www.raf.mod.uk/structure/4squadron.cfm
No 5 Regiment Army Air Corps	www.army.mod.uk/aac/units/5_regiment_aac/
No 5 Sqn	www.raf.mod.uk/structure/5squadron.cfm
No 6 Sqn	www.raf.mod.uk/structure/6squadron.cfm
No 7 Regiment Army Air Corps	www.army.mod.uk/aac/units/7_regiment_aac_v_/
No 7 Sqn	www.raf.mod.uk/structure/7squadron.cfm
No 8 Sqn	8squadron.co.uk/
No 9 Regiment Army Air Corps	www.army.mod.uk/aac/units/9_regiment_aac/
No 9 Sqn	www.raf.mod.uk/structure/9squadron.cfm
No 12 Sqn	www.raf.mod.uk/structure/12squadron.cfm
No 13 Sqn	www.rafmarham.co.uk/organisation/13squadron/13squadron.htm
No 14 Sqn	www.raf.mod.uk/structure/14squadron.cfm
No 15(R) Sqn	www.raf.mod.uk/structure/15squadron.cfm
No 17(R) Sqn	www.raf.mod.uk/structure/17squadron.cfm
No 18 Sqn	www.raf.mod.uk/structure/18squadron.cfm
No 19(R) Sqn	www.rafvalley.org/19sqn/home.htm
No 20(R) Sqn	www.raf.mod.uk/structure/20squadron.cfm
No 22 Sqn	www.raf.mod.uk/structure/22squadron.cfm
No 23 Sqn	23-squadron.co.uk/
No 24 Sqn	www.raf.mod.uk/structure/24squadron.cfm
No 25 Sqn	www.raf.mod.uk/structure/25squadron.cfm
No 27 Sqn	www.raf.mod.uk/structure/27squadron.cfm
No 28 Sqn	www.raf.mod.uk/structure/28squadron.cfm
No 29(R) Sqn	www.raf.mod.uk/structure/29squadron.cfm
No 31 Sqn	www.rafmarham.co.uk/organisation/31squadron/31sqn.htm
No 32(The Royal) Sqn	www.raf.mod.uk/structure/32squadron.cfm
No 33 Sqn	www.raf.mod.uk/structure/33squadron.cfm
No 41(R) Sqn	www.raf.mod.uk/structure/41squadron.cfm
No 42(R) Sqn	www.raf.mod.uk/squadrons/h42.html
No 43 Sqn	www.leuchars.raf.mod.uk/sqn43.htm
No 45(R) Sqn	www.raf.mod.uk/rafcranwell/aboutus/45sqn.cfm
No 51 Sqn	website.lineone.net/~redgoose/
No 55(R) Sqn	www.raf.mod.uk/rafcranwell/aboutus/55sqn.cfm
No 56(R) Sqn	www.leuchars.raf.mod.uk/sqn56.htm
No 60(R) Sqn	www.raf.mod.uk/structure/60squadron.cfm
No 70 Sqn	www.raf.mod.uk/structure/70squadron.cfm
No 72(R) Sqn	www.raf.mod.uk/structure/72squadron.cfm
No 76(R) Sqn	www.raf.mod.uk/raflintononouse/aboutus/76rsqn.cfm
No 78 Sqn	www.raf.mod.uk/structure/78squadron.cfm
No 84 Sqn	www.raf.mod.uk/structure/84squadron.cfm
No 99 Sqn	www.raf.mod.uk/structure/99squadron.cfm
No 100 Sqn	www.raf.mod.uk/structure/100squadron.cfm
No 101 Sqn	www.raf.mod.uk/structure/101squadron.cfm
No 111 Sqn	www.leuchars.raf.mod.uk/sqn111.htm
No 120 Sqn	www.raf.mod.uk/structure/120squadron.cfm
No 201 Sqn	www.raf.mod.uk/structure/201squadron.cfm
No 202 Sqn	www.raf.mod.uk/structure/202squadron.cfm
No 207(R) Sqn	www.raf.mod.uk/structure/207squadron.cfm
No 208(R) Sqn	www.rafvalley.org/208sqn/index.html
No 216 Sqn	www.raf.mod.uk/structure/216squadron.cfm
No 230 Sqn	www.raf.mod.uk/structure/230squadron.cfm

Name of site	*Internet URL (all prefixed 'http://')*
No 617 Sqn	www.raf.mod.uk/structure/617squadron.cfm
No 700M NAS	www.royal-navy.mod.uk/server/show/nav.2237
No 702 NAS	www.royal-navy.mod.uk/server/show/nav.2243
No 727 NAS	www.royal-navy.mod.uk/server/show/nav.2252
No 750 NAS	www.royal-navy.mod.uk/server/show/nav.2256
No 771 NAS	www.royal-navy.mod.uk/server/show/nav.2258
No 800 NAS	www.royal-navy.mod.uk/server/show/nav.5618
No 801 NAS	www.royal-navy.mod.uk/server/show/nav.2291
No 814 NAS	www.royal-navy.mod.uk/server/show/nav.2298
No 815 NAS	www.royal-navy.mod.uk/server/show/nav.2303
No 820 NAS	www.royal-navy.mod.uk/server/show/nav.2308
No 824 NAS	www.royal-navy.mod.uk/server/show/nav.2311
No 829 NAS	www.royal-navy.mod.uk/server/show/nav.2320
No 845 NAS	www.royal-navy.mod.uk/server/show/nav.2333
No 846 NAS	www.royal-navy.mod.uk/server/show/nav.2340
No 847 NAS	www.royal-navy.mod.uk/server/show/nav.2355
No 848 NAS	www.royal-navy.mod.uk/server/show/nav.2360
No 849 NAS	www.royal-navy.mod.uk/server/show/nav.2362
Aberdeen, Dundee and St Andrews UAS	dialspace.dial.pipex.com/town/way/gba87/adstauas/
The Army Air Corps	www.army.mod.uk/aac/
Blue Eagles Home Page	www.deltaweb.co.uk/eagles/
Cambridge University Air Squadron	www.srcf.ucam.org/cuas/
East Midlands UAS	www.emuas.dial.pipex.com/
Fleet Air Arm	www.royal-navy.mod.uk/server/show/nav.2232
Liverpool University Air Squadron	www.sn63.dial.pipex.com/
Manchester & Salford Universities Air Sqn	www.masuas.co.uk/
Ministry of Defence	www.mod.uk/
Oxford University Air Sqn	users.ox.ac.uk/~ouairsqn/
QinetiQ	www.qinetiq.com/
RAF Benson	www.raf.mod.uk/rafbenson/
RAF Brize Norton	www.raf.mod.uk/rafbrizenorton/
RAF Church Fenton (unofficial)	www.rafchurchfenton.org.uk/
RAF College Cranwell	www.cranwell.raf.mod.uk/
RAF Coningsby	www.raf.mod.uk/rafconingsby/
RAF Cosford	www.raf.mod.uk/dcaecosford/
RAF Cottesmore	www.raf.mod.uk/rafcottesmore/
RAF Leuchars	www.leuchars.raf.mod.uk/
RAF Linton-on-Ouse	www.raf.mod.uk/raflintononouse/
RAF Lossiemouth	www.raf.mod.uk/raflossiemouth/
RAF Lyneham	www.raf.mod.uk/raflyneham/
RAF Marham	www.rafmarham.co.uk/
RAF Northolt	www.raf.mod.uk/rafnortholt/
RAF Northolt (unofficial)	www.fly.to/Northolt/
RAF Odiham	www.raf.mod.uk/rafodiham/
RAF Shawbury	www.raf.mod.uk/rafshawbury/
RAF Valley	www.raf.mod.uk/rafvalley/
RAF Waddington	www.raf.mod.uk/rafwaddington/
RAF Wittering	www.raf.mod.uk/rafwittering/
Red Arrows	www.raf.mod.uk/reds/
Royal Air Force	www.raf.mod.uk/
Royal Auxiliary Air Force	www.rauxaf.mod.uk/
University of London Air Sqn	www.ulasonline.org.uk/
Yorkshire UAS	www.yuas.dial.pipex.com/
MILITARY SITES-US	
Air Combat Command	www.acc.af.mil/
Air Force Reserve Command	www.afrc.af.mil/
Air National Guard	www.ang.af.mil/
Aviano Air Base	www.aviano.af.mil/
Liberty Wing Home Page (48th FW)	www.lakenheath.af.mil/
NASA	www.nasa.gov/
Mildenhall	www.mildenhall.af.mil/
Ramstein Air Base	www.ramstein.af.mil/
Spangdahlem Air Base	www.spangdahlem.af.mil/
USAF	www.af.mil/
USAF Europe	www.usafe.af.mil/
USAF World Wide Web Sites	www.af.mil/sites/
US Army	www.army.mil/
US Marine Corps	www.usmc.mil/
US Navy	www.navy.mil/
US Navy Patrol Squadrons (unofficial)	www.vpnavy.com/
MILITARY SITES-ELSEWHERE	

Name of site	*Internet URL (all prefixed 'http://')*
Armée de l'Air	www.defense.gouv.fr/air/
Aeronautica Militare	www.aeronautica.difesa.it
Austrian Armed Forces (in German)	www.bmlv.gv.at/
Belgian Air Force	www.mil.be/aircomp/index.asp?LAN=E
Canadian Forces	www.forces.ca/
Finnish Defence Force	www.mil.fi/english/
Forca Aerea Portuguesa	www.emfa.pt/
Frecce Tricolori	users.iol.it/gromeo/
German Marine	www.deutschemarine.de/
Greek Air Force	www.haf.gr/en/
Irish Air Corps	www.military.ie/aircorps/
Israeli Defence Force/Air Force	www.idf.il/
Luftforsvaret	www.mil.no/
Luftwaffe	www.luftwaffe.de/
NATO	www.nato.int/
Royal Australian Air Force	www.defence.gov.au/RAAF/
Royal Danish Air Force (in Danish)	www.ftk.dk/
Royal Netherlands AF	www.luchtmacht.nl/
Royal New Zealand AF	www.airforce.mil.nz/
Singapore Air Force	www.mindef.gov.sg/rsaf/
South African AF Site (unofficial)	www.saairforce.co.za/
Swedish Air Force	www.flygvapnet.mil.se/
Swedish Military Aviation (unofficial)	www.canit.se/%7Egriffon/aviation/
Turkish General Staff (Armed Forces)	www.tsk.mil.tr/
AIRCRAFT & AERO ENGINE MANUFACTURERS	
AgustaWestland	www.agustawestland.com/
BAE Systems	www.baesystems.com/
Bell Helicopter Textron	www.bellhelicopter.textron.com/
Boeing	www.boeing.com/
Bombardier	www.bombardier.com/
Britten-Norman	www.britten-norman.com/
CFM International	www.cfm56.com/
Dassault	www.dassault-aviation.com/
EADS	www.eads.net/
Embraer	www.embraer.com/
General Electric	www.ge.com/
Gulfstream Aerospace	www.gulfstream.com/
Hawker Beechcraft	www.hawkerbeechcraft.com/
Kaman Aerospace	www.kaman.com/
Lockheed Martin	www.lockheedmartin.com/
Rolls-Royce	www.rolls-royce.com/
SAAB	www.saab.se/
Sikorsky	www.sikorsky.com/
UK AVIATION MUSEUMS	
Aeroventure	www.aeroventure.org.uk/
Bournemouth Aviation Museum	www.aviation-museum.co.uk/
Brooklands Museum	www.brooklandsmuseum.com/
City of Norwich Aviation Museum	www.cnam.co.uk/
de Havilland Aircraft Heritage Centre	www.hertsmuseums.org.uk/dehavilland/index.htm
Dumfries & Galloway Aviation Museum	www.dumfriesaviationmuseum.com/
Fleet Air Arm Museum	www.fleetairarm.com/
Gatwick Aviation Museum	www.gatwick-aviation-museum.co.uk/
The Helicopter Museum	www.helicoptermuseum.co.uk/
Imperial War Museum, Duxford	www.iwm.org.uk/duxford/
Imperial War Museum, Duxford (unofficial)	dspace.dial.pipex.com/town/square/rcy85/
The Jet Age Museum	www.jetagemuseum.org/
Lincs Aviation Heritage Centre	freespace.virgin.net/nick.tasker/ekirkby.htm
Midland Air Museum	www.midlandairmuseum.co.uk/
Museum of Army Flying	www.flying-museum.org.uk/
Museum of Berkshire Aviation	www.museumofberkshireaviation.co.uk/
Museum of Flight, East Fortune	www.nms.ac.uk/flight/index.asp
Museum of Science & Industry, Manchester	www.msim.org.uk/
Newark Air Museum	www.newarkairmuseum.org/
North East Aircraft Museum	www.neam.co.uk/
RAF Museum, Hendon	www.rafmuseum.org.uk/
Science Museum, South Kensington	www.sciencemuseum.org.uk/
Yorkshire Air Museum, Elvington	www.yorkshireairmuseum.co.uk
AVIATION SOCIETIES	
Air Britain	www.air-britain.com/
British Aircraft Preservation Council	www.bapc.org.uk/
Cleveland Aviation Society	homepage.ntlworld.com/phillip.charlton/

Name of site	*Internet URL (all prefixed 'http://')*
Cottesmore Aviation Group	www.cottesmore-ag.com/
East London Aviation Society	www.westrowops.co.uk/newsletter/elas.htm
Gilze-Rijen Aviation Society	www.gras-spotters.nl/
LAAS International	www.laasdata.com/
Lowestoft Aviation Society	www.lowestoftaviationsociety.org/
Royal Aeronautical Society	www.raes.org.uk/
Scottish Air News	www.scottishairnews.co.uk/
Scramble (Dutch Aviation Society)	www.scramble.nl/
Solent Aviation Society	www.solent-aviation-society.co.uk/
Spitfire Society	www.spitfiresociety.demon.co.uk/
The Aviation Society Manchester	www.tasmanchester.com/
Ulster Aviation Society	www.d-n-a.net/users/dnetrAzQ/
Wolverhampton Aviation Group	www.wolverhamptonaviationgroup.co.uk/
OPERATORS OF HISTORIC AIRCRAFT	
The Aircraft Restoration Company	www.arc-duxford.co.uk/
Battle of Britain Memorial Flight	www.bbmf.co.uk/
Catalina Online	www.catalina.org.uk/
De Havilland Aviation	www.dehavilland.net/
Delta Jets	www.deltajets.com/
Hangar 11 Collection	www.hangar11.co.uk/
Hunter Flying	www.hunterflyingclub.co.uk/
Old Flying Machine Company	www.ofmc.co.uk/
Royal Navy Historic Flight	www.royalnavyhistoricflight.org.uk/
The Fighter Collection	www.fighter-collection.com/
The Real Aeroplane Company	www.realaero.com/
The Shuttleworth Collection	www.shuttleworth.org/
The Vulcan Operating Company	www.tvoc.co.uk/
SITES RELATING TO SPECIFIC TYPES OF MILITARY AIRCRAFT	
The 655 Maintenance & Preservation Society	www.xm655.com/
The Avro Shackleton Page	users.bigpond.net.au/Shackleton/
B-24 Liberator	www.b24bestweb.com/
EE Canberra	www.bywat.co.uk/
English Electric Lightning - Vertical Reality	www.aviation-picture-hangar.co.uk/Lightning.html
The Eurofighter site	www.eurofighter-typhoon.co.uk/
The ex FRADU Canberra Site	www.fradu-hunters.co.uk/canberra/
The ex FRADU Hunter Site	www.fradu-hunters.co.uk/
F-4 Phantom II Society	www.f4phantom.com/
F-16: The Complete Reference	www.f-16.net/
F-86 Web Page	f-86.tripod.com/
F-105 Thunderchief	www.geocities.com/Pentagon/7002/
The Gripen	www.gripen.com/
Jet Provost Heaven	www.jetprovosts.com
K5083 - Home Page (Hawker Hurricane)	www3.mistral.co.uk/k5083/
Lockheed C-130 Hercules	hometown.aol.com/SamC130/
Lockheed SR-71 Blackbird	www.wvi.com/~lelandh/sr-71~1.htm
The MiG-21 Page	www.topedge.com/panels/aircraft/sites/kraft/mig.htm
P-3 Orion Research Group	home.wxs.nl/~p3orin/
Scramble on the Web - SAAB Viggen Database	www.scramble.nl/viggen.htm
Thunder & Lightnings (Postwar British Aircraft)	www.thunder-and-lightnings.co.uk/
UK Apache Resource Centre	www.ukapache.com/
MISCELLANEOUS	
Aerodata	www.aerodata.biz/
The AirNet Web Site	www.aviation-links.co.uk/
Demobbed - Out of Service British Military Aircraft	demobbed.org.uk/
Euro Demobbed	www.eurodemobbed.org.uk/
Fighter Control	fightercontrol.co.uk/
Joseph F. Baugher's US Military Serials Site	home.att.net/%7Ejbaugher/
Military Aviation	www.crakehal.demon.co.uk/aviation/aviation.htm
Military Aviation Review/MAP	www.mar.co.uk/
Pacific Aviation Database Organisation	www.gfiapac.com/
Plane Talk	forum.planetalk.net/
Polish Aviation Site	aviation.pol.pl/
Scramble on the Web - Air Show Reports	www.scramble.nl/airshows.htm
Target Lock Military Aviation E-zine	www.targetlock.org.uk/
UKAR Message Board	www.ukar.co.uk/
UK Military Aircraft Serials Resource Centre	www.ukserials.com/
UK Military Spotting	www.thunder-and-lightnings.co.uk/spotting/